THE PRESOCRATIC PHILOSOPHERS

THE PRESOCRATIC PHILOSOPHERS

A CRITICAL HISTORY WITH A SELECTION OF TEXTS

BY

G. S. KIRK

Professor of Classics in Yale University and Fellow of Trinity Hall, Cambridge

&

J. E. RAVEN

Fellow of King's College and Lecturer in Classics in the University of Cambridge

CAMBRIDGE

AT THE UNIVERSITY PRESS

PUBLISHED BY
THE SYNDICS OF THE CAMBRIDGE UNIVERSITY PRESS
Bentley House, 200 Euston Road, London, N.W. 1
American Branch: 32 East 57th Street, New York, N.Y. 10022

Standard Book Numbers
521 05891 0 clothbound
521 09169 1 paperback

First published	*1957*
Reprinted with corrections	*1960, 1962, 1963*
Reprinted	*1964, 1966, 1969, 1971, 1973*

First printed in Great Britain at the University Press, Cambridge
Reprinted by offset-litho in the United States of America

To

F. H. SANDBACH

PREFACE

This book is designed primarily for those who have more than a casual interest in the history of early Greek thought; but by translating all Greek passages, and confining some of the more detailed discussion to small-type notes at the end of paragraphs, we have also aimed to make the book useful for those students of the history of philosophy or science who have no previous acquaintance with this important and fascinating field.

Two points should be emphasized. First, we have limited our scope to the chief Presocratic 'physicists' and their forerunners, whose main preoccupation was with the nature (*physis*) and coherence of things as a whole. More specialized scientific interests were simultaneously developing throughout the sixth and fifth centuries B.C., especially in mathematics, astronomy, geography, medicine and biology; but for lack of space, and to some extent of evidence, we have not pursued these topics beyond the interests of the chief physicists. We have also excluded the Sophists, whose positive philosophical contribution, often exaggerated, lay mainly in the fields of epistemology and semantics. Secondly, we have not set out to produce a necessarily orthodox exposition (if, indeed, such a thing is conceivable in a field where opinion is changing so rapidly), but have preferred in many places to put forward our own interpretations. At the same time we have usually mentioned other interpretations of disputed points, and have always tried to present the reader with the main materials for the formation of his own judgement.

The part of the book dealing with the Ionian tradition, including its forerunners and also the atomists and Diogenes (i.e. chapters I–VI, XVII and XVIII), with the note on the sources, is by G. S. Kirk, while the part dealing with the Italian tradition, and also the chapters on Anaxagoras and Archelaus (i.e. chapters VII–XVI), are by J. E. Raven. The contributions of each author were of course subjected to detailed criticism by the other, and the planning of the book as a whole is by both.

The scale of different sections of the book is admittedly rather variable. Where the evidence is fuller and clearer—particularly where considerable fragments survive, as for example in the case of Parmenides—the commentary can naturally be shorter; where the evidence is sparser and more confusing, as for example in the case of Anaximander or the Pythagoreans, our own explanations must be longer and more involved. Chapter I in particular, which deals with a part of the subject which is often neglected, is perhaps more detailed in parts than its ultimate importance demands, and non-specialists are advised to leave it until last.

Only the most important texts have been quoted, and those in an inevitably personal selection. For a nearly complete collection of fragments and testimonies the reader should turn to H. Diels, *Die Fragmente der Vorsokratiker* (5th and later editions, Berlin, 1934–54, edited by W. Kranz). This fundamental work is referred to by the abbreviation DK. Where a DK number (e.g. DK 28 A 12) is appended to the reference of a passage quoted in the present work, this means that DK, in the section referred to, quotes more of the passage in question than we do. DK references are omitted where less, or no more, of the text is given, and also in the case of fragments (where the fragment-number, always in Diels' numeration, is the same as the number in the relevant B-section in DK). Where supplements occur in texts quoted, without further information, they are usually by Diels, and reference may be made to the textual notes in DK.

We are obviously indebted to many friends for suggestions and help; and also, as goes without saying, to previous writers like Zeller, Burnet, Cornford, Ross and Cherniss. Many of these debts are recorded in the text. For typographical advice and assistance we are indebted to the printing staff of the Cambridge University Press. H. Lloyd-Jones and I. R. D. Mathewson read the proofs and made many valuable suggestions. Another outstanding contribution was made by F. H. Sandbach, whose numerous acute and learned comments on the final draft were of the utmost value, and to whom, as an unworthy offering, we should like to dedicate this book.

G.S.K.
J.E.R.

CAMBRIDGE
May 1957

CONTENTS

ABBREVIATIONS

The following abbreviations may be mentioned; others should be self-evident:

AJP *American Journal of Philology.*

ANET *Ancient Near Eastern Texts relating to the Old Testament*, ed. J. B. Pritchard (Princeton, 2nd edition, 1955).

CP *Classical Philology.*

CQ *Classical Quarterly.*

DK *Die Fragmente der Vorsokratiker*, 5th to 7th editions, by H. Diels, edited with additions by W. Kranz. (The 6th and 7th editions are photographic reprints, 1951–2 and 1954, of the 5th, with Nachträge by Kranz.)

EGP John Burnet, *Early Greek Philosophy*, 4th edition, 1930 (a reprint with corrections of 3rd edition, 1920).

GGN *Nachrichten v. d. Gesellschaft zu Göttingen* (Phil.-hist. Klasse).

JHS *Journal of Hellenic Studies.*

J. Phil. *Journal of Philology.*

LSJ Liddell and Scott, *A Greek-English Lexicon*, 9th edition, 1925–40, revised by H. Stuart Jones and R. McKenzie.

Rh. M. *Rheinisches Museum.*

Σ Scholium or scholiast.

SB Ber. *Sitzungsberichte d. preussischen Akademie d. Wissenschaft.*

SVF *Stoicorum Veterum Fragmenta*, ed. H. von Arnim (Leipzig, 1903–5).

References to the commentators on Aristotle (e.g. Simplicius and Alexander) are by page-number and line-number in the appropriate volume of the Berlin Academy *Commentaria in Aristotelem Graeca.*

NOTE ON THE SECOND IMPRESSION

Since this is a second impression rather than a second edition, we have been able to make only relatively slight improvements. Some new material appears on pp. 94, 142, 285, 306, 426; otherwise the main alterations, apart from the correction of a number of minor mistakes, misprints and defects of emphasis, occur on pp. 58, 116, 156, 267 f., 365, 423. There are a few additions to the short bibliography on pp. 446 ff.

G. S. K.
J. E. R.

December 1959

NOTE ON THE THIRD IMPRESSION

Part of the account of Zeno, pp. 287–92, has been substantially altered; otherwise there are minor corrections or re-wordings on pp. 36, 39, 47, 88, 110, 143, 145, 323. Two items are added to the short bibliography.

G. S. K.
J. E. R.

November 1961

NOTE ON THE FOURTH IMPRESSION

The most considerable of a small number of minor corrections or alterations of emphasis occur on pp. 131, 137, 170, 212 and 214, 275, 302, 335. Four additions are made to the short bibliography.

G. S. K.
J. E. R.

November 1962

INTRODUCTORY NOTE

THE SOURCES FOR PRESOCRATIC PHILOSOPHY

A. DIRECT QUOTATIONS

The actual fragments of the Presocratic thinkers are preserved as quotations in subsequent ancient authors, from Plato in the fourth century B.C. to Simplicius in the sixth century A.D., and even, in rare cases, to late Byzantine writers like John Tzetzes. The date of the source in which a quotation occurs is not, of course, a reliable guide to its accuracy. Thus Plato is notoriously lax in his quotations from all sources; he often mixes quotation with paraphrase, and his attitude to his predecessors is frequently not objective but humorous or ironical. The Neoplatonist Simplicius, on the other hand, who lived a whole millennium after the Presocratics, made long and evidently accurate quotations, in particular from Parmenides, Empedocles, Anaxagoras and Diogenes of Apollonia; not for the sake of literary embellishment, but because in his commentaries on the *Physics* and *de caelo* of Aristotle he found it necessary to expound Aristotle's views on his predecessors by setting down their actual words. At times Simplicius did this at greater length than was essential because, as he tells us, a particular ancient work had become so rare.

Aristotle, like Plato, gave comparatively few direct quotations, and his main value is as a summarizer and critic of earlier thinkers. Apart from Plato, Aristotle, and Simplicius, the following notable sources of *verbatim* extracts may be singled out for special mention:

(i) Plutarch, the Academic philosopher, historian and essayist of the second century A.D., in his extensive *Moral Essays* made hundreds of quotations (often expanded, interpolated or partly reworded by himself) from the Presocratic thinkers.

(ii) Sextus 'Empiricus', the Sceptic philosopher and physician of the late second century A.D., expounded the theories of Aenesidemus, who lived some two centuries earlier and himself relied to a great extent on Hellenistic sources. Sextus quotes many early passages bearing on cognition and the reliability of the senses.

(iii) Clement of Alexandria, the learned head of the Catechetical school, lived in the second half of the second century A.D. and the early years of the third. A convert to Christianity, Clement nevertheless maintained his interest in Greek literature of all kinds, and used a wide knowledge and a remarkable memory to point his comparisons between paganism and Christianity with frequent quotations from the Greek poets and philosophers (chiefly in his *Protrepticus* and the eight books of *Stromateis* or *Miscellanies*).

(iv) Hippolytus, a theologian in Rome in the 3rd century A.D., wrote a *Refutation of all Heresies* in nine books, which attacked Christian heresies by claiming them to be revivals of pagan philosophy. For example, the Noetian heresy was a revival of Heraclitus' theory of the coincidence of opposites—a contention which Hippolytus attempted to substantiate by the quotation of no less than seventeen sayings of Heraclitus, many of them otherwise unknown.

(v) Diogenes Laertius compiled, probably in the third century A.D., a trivial but from our point of view important *Lives of Famous Philosophers* in ten books. In his biographical and doxographical notices, derived mainly from Hellenistic sources, he included occasional short quotations.

(vi) John Stobaeus, the fifth-century A.D. anthologist, assembled in his *Anthologium* educative extracts from the whole range of Greek literature, but with special emphasis on ethical sayings. Many Presocratic fragments (notably of Democritus) are preserved by him, often in a somewhat impure form. Stobaeus' main sources were the handbooks and compendia which proliferated in the Alexandrian period.

In addition to the main sources noted above, quotations from the Presocratics occur sporadically elsewhere: in the Epicurean Philodemus; in Stoics like Marcus Aurelius and eclectics like Maximus of Tyre; in Christian writers other than Clement and Hippolytus, for example in Origen; occasionally in Aetius (see B, 4, *b*; direct quotations in Aetius are rare); in technical authors like Galen the doctor, Strabo the geographer and Athenaeus the anthologist of food and drink; and, not least important, in Neoplatonic writers from Numenius, Plotinus, Porphyry and Iamblichus (the last two of whom wrote on Pythagoras) down to Proclus and, of course, the invaluable Simplicius.

To conclude these notes on the sources of direct quotations, it must be emphasized that the author of a direct quotation need not have seen the original work, since summaries, anthologies and compendia of every kind, known as early as Hippias (p. 94 n. 2) and produced in large numbers in the three centuries following the foundation of Alexandria, were regarded as an adequate substitute for most prose originals of a technical nature.

B. TESTIMONIA

(1) PLATO is the earliest commentator on the Presocratics (though there were occasional references in Euripides and Aristophanes). His comments, however, are for the most part only casual ones, inspired, like many of his quotations, by irony or amusement. Thus his references to Heraclitus, Parmenides and Empedocles are more often than not light-hearted *obiter dicta*, and one-sided or exaggerated ones at that, rather than sober and objective historical judgements. Provided this is recognized, Plato has much of value to tell us. One passage, *Phaedo* 96 ff., gives a useful but brief survey of fifth-century physical preoccupations.

(2) ARISTOTLE gave more serious attention to his philosophical predecessors than Plato had done, and prefaced some of his treatises with formal surveys of their opinions, notably in *Metaphysics* A. However, his judgements are often distorted by his view of earlier philosophy as a stumbling progress towards the truth that Aristotle himself revealed in his physical doctrines, especially those concerning causation. There are also, of course, many acute and valuable criticisms, and a store of factual information.

(3) THEOPHRASTUS undertook the history of previous philosophy, from Thales to Plato, as part of his contribution to the encyclopaedic activity organized by his master Aristotle—just as Eudemus undertook the history of theology, astronomy and mathematics and Menon that of medicine. According to Diogenes Laertius' list of his works, Theophrastus wrote sixteen (or eighteen) books of *Physical Opinions* (or *Opinions of the Physicists*; the Greek genitive is Φυσικῶν δοξῶν); these were later epitomized in two volumes. Only the last book, *On sensation*, is extant in its greater part; but important extracts from the first book, *On material principles*, were copied down by Simplicius in his commentary on Aristotle's *Physics*. (Some of these extracts Simplicius derived from lost commentaries by the important Peripatetic commentator Alexander

of Aphrodisias.) In this first book Theophrastus treated the different thinkers in roughly chronological order, adding their city, patronymic, and sometimes date or mutual relationship. In the remaining books the order was chronological only within the main logical divisions. In addition to the general history Theophrastus wrote special works on Anaximenes, Empedocles, Anaxagoras, Archelaus, and (in several volumes) Democritus. These have unfortunately perished; presumably Theophrastus went to greater pains to consult the original sources for these thinkers. From the available evidence, however, his judgements even on them were often derived directly from Aristotle, without much attempt to apply a new and objective criticism.

(4) THE DOXOGRAPHICAL TRADITION. (*a*) *Its general nature.* Theophrastus' great work became the standard authority for the ancient world on Presocratic philosophy, and is the source of most subsequent collections of 'opinions' (δόξαι, ἀρέσκοντα or *placita*). These collections took different forms. (i) In close reproductions of Theophrastus' arrangement each major topic was considered in a separate section, the different thinkers being treated successively within each section. This was the method of Aetius and his source, the '*Vetusta Placita*' (see p. 5). (ii) Biographical doxographers considered all the opinions of each philosopher together, in company with details of his life—supplied, to a large extent, by the febrile imaginations of Hellenistic biographers and historians like Hermippus of Smyrna, Hieronymus of Rhodes and Neanthes of Cyzicus. The result is exemplified in the biographical medley of Diogenes Laertius. (iii) Another type of doxographical work is seen in the Διαδοχαί, or accounts of philosophical successions. Its originator was the Peripatetic Sotion of Alexandria, who around 200 B.C. wrote a survey of previous philosophers arranged by schools. The known thinkers were related to each other in a descending line of master and pupil (here Sotion was extending and formalizing a process begun by Theophrastus); in addition, the Ionian school was clearly distinguished from the Italian. Many of the patristic doxographical summaries (notably those in Eusebius, Irenaeus, Arnobius, Theodoretus—who, however, also made direct use of Aetius—and St Augustine) were based on the brief accounts in the Succession-writers. (iv) The chronographer Apollodorus of Alexandria composed, in the middle of the second century B.C., a metrical account of the

dates and opinions of the philosophers. This rested partly on Sotion's division into schools and masters, partly on the chronology of Eratosthenes, who had sensibly assigned dates to artists, philosophers and writers as well as to political events. Apollodorus filled in the gaps left by Eratosthenes, on very arbitrary principles: a philosopher's *acme* or period of chief activity was assumed to be at the age of forty, and was made to coincide with the nearest of a number of major chronological epochs, for example the capture of Sardis in 546/5 B.C. or the foundation of Thurii in 444/3. Further, a supposed pupil was always made forty years younger than his supposed master.

(*b*) *Aetius and the 'Vetusta Placita'*. Two extant doxographical summaries, closely resembling each other, were independently derived from a lost original—the collection of *Opinions* made by Aetius, an otherwise unknown compilator, probably of the second century A.D., whose name is known from a reference in Theodoretus. These extant summaries are the *Epitome of physical opinions*, in five books, which falsely claims to be by Plutarch; and the *Physical extracts* which appear in book I (for the most part) of Stobaeus' *Anthologium*. (From the former, which was widely read, are derived notices in pseudo-Galen, Athenagoras, Achilles and Cyril.) Diels in his great *Doxographi Graeci* arranged these two sources in parallel columns as the *Placita* of Aetius. This forms our most extensive, if not always our most accurate, doxographical authority.

Aetius' work was based, not directly on Theophrastus' history, but upon an intermediate summary of it produced, probably, in the Posidonian school in the first century B.C. This lost work was named by Diels the *Vetusta Placita*. In it Stoic, Epicurean and Peripatetic opinions were added to those recorded by Theophrastus, and much that was derived from Theophrastus was subjected to Stoic re-formulation. Aetius himself added further Stoic and Epicurean opinions, as well as a few definitions and introductory comments. A direct use of the *Vetusta Placita* was made by Varro (in Censorinus' *de die natali*), and is seen also in the brief doxography in Cicero, *Academica priora* II, 37, 118.

(*c*) *Other important doxographical sources*. (i) *Hippolytus*. The first book of his *Refutation of all Heresies*, the so-called *Philosophoumena* once attributed to Origen, is a biographical doxography containing separate accounts of the main philosophers. The sections on

Thales, Pythagoras, Empedocles, Heraclitus, the Eleatics and the Atomists come from a trifling biographical summary and are of small value, unlike those on Anaximander, Anaximenes, Anaxagoras, Archelaus and Xenophanes, which come from a fuller and much more valuable biographical source. At many points the comments of the second group are more detailed, and less inaccurate, than the corresponding ones in Aetius. (ii) *The pseudo-Plutarchean Stromateis*. These short 'Miscellanies' (which must be distinguished from the *Epitome*, from Aetius, also ascribed to Plutarch) are preserved by Eusebius; they come from a source similar to that of the second group in Hippolytus. They differ in that they concentrate on the subject-matter of the earlier books in Theophrastus, those that dealt with the material principle, cosmogony, and the heavenly bodies; and they contain much verbiage and pretentious interpretation. However, some important details are preserved which do not occur elsewhere. (iii) *Diogenes Laertius*. Apart from biographical details culled from many sources, some useful chronological data from Apollodorus, and deplorable epigrams from the pen of Diogenes himself, the opinions of each thinker are usually set out in two distinct doxographical notes: the first (what Diogenes called the κεφαλαιώδης or summary account) from a worthless biographical source like that used by Hippolytus in the first group, and the second (the ἐπὶ μέρους or detailed account) from a fuller and more reliable epitome like that used by Hippolytus for his second group.

(5) CONCLUSION. It must be remembered that many writers who were independent of the direct Theophrastean tradition are known to have devoted special works to the early philosophers. For example the fourth-century-B.C. Academic, Heraclides of Pontus, wrote four books on Heraclitus, and so did the Stoic Cleanthes; while Aristotle's pupil Aristoxenus wrote biographies which included one of Pythagoras. Allowance must be made, therefore, for the possibility of isolated non-Theophrastean judgements appearing in later eclectic sources like Plutarch or Clement; though most such judgements that we can recognize show signs, nevertheless, of Aristotelian, or of Stoic, Epicurean, or Sceptic, influence. Theophrastus remains the main source of information, and his work is known to us through the doxographers, through the quotations by Simplicius, and through the extant *de sensu*. From these it is evident that Theophrastus was strongly influenced

by Aristotle—who, as has been stated, did not aim, as Theophrastus should have done, at extreme historical objectivity. Theophrastus was no more successful than is to be expected in understanding the motives of an earlier period and a different world of thought; a further defect was that, once having extracted a general pattern of explanations, particularly for cosmological events, he tended to impose it, perhaps too boldly, in cases where he lacked full evidence—cases which seem to have been not infrequent. Thus it is legitimate to feel complete confidence in our understanding of a Presocratic thinker only when the Aristotelian or Theophrastean interpretation, even if it can be accurately reconstructed, is confirmed by relevant and well-authenticated extracts from the philosopher himself.

CHAPTER I

THE FORERUNNERS OF PHILOSOPHICAL COSMOGONY

In this long preliminary chapter certain ideas are examined which are not truly 'philosophical'; they are mythological rather than rationalistic in context, but may nevertheless appear as significant preludes to the truly rational attempts to explain the world, attempts which began with Thales.

We are not concerned here with pure mythology, but with concepts which, although expressed in the language and through the personages of myth, are not mythopoeic in kind but are the result of a direct, empirical, non-symbolical way of thinking. These quasi-rationalistic views of the world are most frequently concerned with its earliest history, starting from its actual birth or creation; for this way of thinking was incidental to the attempt (made most notably by Hesiod in the *Theogony*) to systematize the manifold deities of legend by deriving them from a common ancestor or pair of ancestors at the beginning of the world. Yet the active investigation of the world's ancestry, whether mainly mythical as in Hesiod or mainly rational as in the Milesian philosophers, must have been carried on only by the few. The general structure of the present world, the common environment of experience, was of wider interest; and here a common, naïve, extroverted but nevertheless partly mythical outlook seems to have been widely accepted. It appears from time to time in Homer and is briefly described in §1. In §§2 and 3 two concepts are examined which were later credited with cosmogonical importance by the Greeks themselves, those of Okeanos and of Nyx (Night). §§4, 5 and 6 are concerned with three special accounts, all of primarily non-philosophical character but all treating of cosmogonical topics: first the Hesiodic *Theogony*, then the various cosmogonical ideas associated with Orpheus, finally (at greater and indeed somewhat disproportionate length) the intriguing but fragmentary views of Pherecydes of Syros. In the case of Night, and of Orphic cosmogony, the conclusions will be largely negative: little of direct significance for the development of Presocratic thought is revealed, although in view of constant assertions to the contrary it is as well to subject the evidence to a careful scrutiny. Pherecydes may have written his book no earlier than Anaximander, but its matter is likely to be in part traditional, and therefore not irrelevant to the state of cosmogonical speculation even before Thales. On some points reference will be made to the comparative mythology of earlier near-eastern cultures, especially Babylonian, Egyptian, and Hittite. There are strong similarities between some of the Greek theogonical and cosmogonical stories and the theogonical myths of the great river-civilizations and their neighbours; these similarities help to explain some details of Greek accounts down to and including Thales. Translations of the main non-Greek texts are most conveniently to be found in *Ancient Near Eastern Texts relating to the Old Testament*, ed. J. B. Pritchard (Princeton, 2nd ed. 1955), which will be referred to as Pritchard *ANET*. Useful summaries, both in the Pelican series, are H. Frankfort and others, *Before Philosophy*,[1] and O. R. Gurney, *The Hittites*.

Nothing will be said in this chapter about the development of the concept of the soul. The Homeric idea of the *psyche* or breath-soul as an insubstantial image of the body, giving it life and surviving it in a wretched, bloodless existence in Hades, is too familiar to need description here. Rohde's *Psyche*, E. R. Dodds' *The Greeks and the Irrational* (Berkeley, 1951), or chapter 5 of Jaeger's *Theology of the Early Greek Philosophers* (Oxford, 1947), give a good account of the popular, pre-philosophical idea of the soul. Pythagoras was possibly the first Greek explicitly to treat the soul as something of moral importance, and Heraclitus first clearly indicated that knowledge of the soul was relevant to knowledge of the structure of the cosmos. Yet the conception that the substance of the soul was related to *aither*, or to the substance of the stars, seems from fifth-century B.C. poetical contexts to have existed for some time already as part of the complex body of popular beliefs, alongside the distinct Homeric concept of a breath-soul. These antecedents will be summarized in the chapters on Thales, Anaximenes, Heraclitus and Empedocles (see pp. 95 ff., 159 ff., 200, 205 ff., 360). The main object of the earliest deliberate efforts to explain the world remained the description of its *growth* from a simple, and therefore fully comprehensible, beginning. Matters concerned with human life seemed to belong to a different type of enquiry, in which the old inherited assumptions, though sometimes

[1] American title: *The Intellectual Adventure of Ancient Man.*

inconsistent, were still valid. It is with the derivation of the world as a whole, then, regarded as external to its human centre, that the rest of this chapter will be mainly concerned. It will nevertheless be seen that the world's original state, and the method by which it diversified itself, were imagined anthropomorphically, in terms of a parent or pair of parents. This genealogical approach persisted even after the eventual abandonment by the Milesian philosophers of the traditional mythological framework.

1. THE NAÏVE VIEW OF THE WORLD

A popular conception of the nature of the world, which can be traced mainly in scattered references in Homer, is roughly as follows. The sky is a solid hemisphere like a bowl (*Il.* 17, 425 χάλκεον οὐρανόν, cf. Pindar *N.* 6, 3–4; οὐρανὸν ἐς πολύχαλκον at *Il.* 5, 504, *Od.* 3, 2; σιδήρεον οὐρανόν at *Od.* 15, 329 and 17, 565. Solidity as well as brightness is presumably conveyed by these metallic epithets). It covers the round flat earth. The lower part of the gap between earth and sky, up to and including the clouds, contains ἀήρ or mist: the upper part (sometimes called the οὐρανός itself) is αἰθήρ, *aither*, the shining upper air, which is sometimes conceived as fiery. At *Il.* 14, 288 (ἐλάτη) δι' ἠέρος αἰθέρ' ἵκανεν, 'the fir-tree reached through the *aer* to the *aither*'. Below its surface, the earth stretches far downwards, and has its roots in or above Tartarus:

1 Homer *Il.* 8, 13 (Zeus speaks)

> ἤ μιν ἑλὼν ῥίψω ἐς Τάρταρον ἠερόεντα
> τῆλε μάλ', ἧχι βάθιστον ὑπὸ χθονός ἐστι βέρεθρον,
> ἔνθα σιδήρειαί τε πύλαι καὶ χάλκεος οὐδός,
> τόσσον ἔνερθ' Ἀίδεω ὅσον οὐρανός ἐστ' ἀπὸ γαίης.

2 Hesiod *Theogony* 726 (Τάρταρον)

> τὸν πέρι χάλκεον ἕρκος ἐλήλαται· ἀμφὶ δέ μιν νὺξ
> τριστοιχεὶ κέχυται περὶ δείρην· αὐτὰρ ὕπερθεν
> γῆς ῥίζαι πεφύασι καὶ ἀτρυγέτοιο θαλάσσης.

The circuit of Tartarus is thus 'brazen' (and so firm, unyielding) like the sky: the symmetry is reflected also in the equal

---

1 *Or seizing him I will hurl him into misty Tartaros, very far, where is the deepest gulf below earth; there are iron gates and brazen threshold, as far beneath Hades as sky is from earth.*

2 *Around it [Tartaros] a brazen fence is drawn; and all about it Night in three rows is poured, around the throat; and above are the roots of earth and unharvested sea.*

distance between sky and earth's surface, and earth's surface and its foundations—for 'Hades' in the last line of **1** seems to be an illogical variant upon an original 'earth', as in *Theogony* 720 τόσσον ἔνερθ' ὑπὸ γῆς ὅσον οὐρανός ἐστ' ἀπὸ γαίης ('as far below, under earth, as sky is distant from it'). There was a certain vagueness about the relationships of Hades, Erebos, and Tartarus, although Tartarus was certainly the lowest part of the underworld. The symmetry between underworld and overworld was not complete, of course: the shape of Tartarus was not normally conceived as hemispherical. A variant conception made the earth stretch downwards indefinitely:

3 Xenophanes fr. 28 (= **183**)

γαίης μὲν τόδε πεῖρας ἄνω παρὰ ποσσὶν ὁρᾶται
ἠέρι προσπλάζον, τὸ κάτω δ' ἐς ἄπειρον ἱκνεῖται.

(Cf. Strabo I, p. 12 Cas.)

This is a later formulation, but again a popular rather than an intellectual one. There is no great difference in the underlying thought; the difference is mainly that the mythological geography is not used here.

Round the edge of the earth-disc, according to the unsophisticated view, flowed the vast river of Okeanos. This concept was of considerable importance in pre-scientific Greek thought, and is discussed in the section which follows.

2. OKEANOS

(i) *As the river surrounding the earth, and source of all waters*

4 Homer *Il.* 18, 607 (Hephaistos)

ἐν δὲ τίθει ποταμοῖο μέγα σθένος Ὠκεανοῖο
ἄντυγα πὰρ πυμάτην σάκεος πύκα ποιητοῖο.

5 Homer *Il.* 21, 194 (Zeus)

τῷ οὐδὲ κρείων Ἀχελώιος ἰσοφαρίζει
οὐδὲ βαθυρρείταο μέγα σθένος Ὠκεανοῖο,
ἐξ οὗ περ πάντες ποταμοὶ καὶ πᾶσα θάλασσα
καὶ πᾶσαι κρῆναι καὶ φρείατα μακρὰ νάουσιν.

---

3 *Of earth this is the upper limit which we see by our feet, in contact with air; but its underneath continues indefinitely.*

4 *He put on it the great might of river Okeanos, along the well-made shield's outer rim.*

5 *Him not even Lord Acheloos equals, nor the great might of deep-flowing Okeanos, from whom, indeed, all rivers and all sea and all springs and deep wells flow.*

6 Herodotus IV, 8 τὸν δὲ Ὠκεανὸν λόγῳ μὲν λέγουσι (*sc.* Ἕλληνες) ἀπὸ ἡλίου ἀνατολέων ἀρξάμενον γῆν περὶ πᾶσαν ῥέειν, ἔργῳ δὲ οὐκ ἀποδεικνῦσι. (Cf. also *id.* II, 21; II, 23.)

That Okeanos surrounds the circular surface of the earth, though not explicitly stated in the Homeric poems, is suggested in **4** (where the shield made for Achilles is obviously thought of as round), in **9**, and by some of the epithets applied to Okeanos—especially ἀψόρροος, 'back-flowing' (which probably means 'flowing back into itself'). Passages in Euripides and others as well as in Herodotus (**6**) show that the idea of a circular surrounding Okeanos was widely accepted; though occasionally in Homer, especially in the *Odyssey*, a looser usage, as the broad outer sea, had already begun to appear. **4** describes Okeanos as a river, and this too was a commonly accepted view: references are frequent to the streams, ῥοαί, of Okeanos. As such, it was presumably composed of fresh water; and **5** (of which l. 195 was unwarrantably athetized by Zenodotus) describes it as the source of all waters, whether fresh or salt, which are enclosed within its orbit, on or under the earth. The idea that salt water is simply fresh water somehow flavoured by the earth was commonly held in the scientific period.

The earth-encircling river differs from other elements of the popular world-picture in that it cannot be obviously based upon experience. The sky *looks* hemispherical and, to some eyes, impenetrable; it is called 'brazen', therefore, and treated as ice-like or solid even by Anaximenes and Empedocles. The earth appears to be flat, and the horizon to be circular. Yet experience cannot so easily suggest that the ultimate horizon is bounded by a fresh-water river. Voyagers may have brought back reports of vast seas beyond the Mediterranean, but these would be salt. Springs bubbling up from the earth may suggest underground rivers, but these need not entail a surrounding river. The possibility must be considered, then, that this particular conception originated further east, in the great river-civilizations of Egypt and Mesopotamia, and was somehow introduced into Greece and given a specific Hellenic form. It will be seen (pp. 90f.) that Thales' idea of the earth floating on water was probably so borrowed; and the coincidences in detail between Greek versions of certain myths,

---

6 *They [the Greeks] affirm in words that Okeanos, beginning from the sun's risings, flows round the whole earth, but they give no effective demonstration of this.*

and Babylonian or Hittite versions, prove that conceptions not native either to the Aegean area, or to the proximate culture-centres of the Greek-speaking peoples before their entry into Greece, had embedded themselves in Greek thought even by the time of Hesiod (which we guess to be the seventh century B.C.), and probably much earlier. These coincidences are briefly discussed on pp. 33f. and 36f. In the second part of the present section on Okeanos, pp. 18f., the isolated Homeric references to Okeanos as origin of all things will also appear as a probable allusion to non-Greek mythological ideas. In Babylonian accounts, and in some Egyptian versions, the earth was regarded as drying out, or thrusting itself up, in the midst of the primeval waters.[1] The development of such an idea is not surprising in Mesopotamia, where the land had indeed been formed from the marshlands between the two rivers; nor in Egypt, where the fertile land emerged each year as the Nile floods receded. The earth that emerges from an indefinite expanse of primeval water will still be *surrounded* by water. This does seem to provide a plausible, though not a certain, motive for the formation of the Greek concept of Okeanos. In this popular development of the primeval-water motif the earth is regarded as being solidly rooted, once it has emerged, and the indefinite waste of water (which seems always to have been conceived as having an upper limit, a surface) is contracted into a vast but not necessarily illimitable river.[2] Thales, on the other hand, postulated a floating earth and so was not simply rationalizing the quasi-mythological Okeanos-interpretation.[3]

[1] Cf. the Babylonian Creation-epic, which originated probably in the 2nd millennium B.C.: tablet I, 1–6 (Pritchard, *Ancient Near Eastern Texts*, 60f.), 'When on high the heaven had not been named, Firm ground below had not been called by name, Naught but primordial Apsu, their begetter, (And) Mummu-Tiamat, she who bore them all, Their waters commingling as a single body; No reed-hut had been matted, no marshland had appeared....' (Trans. E. A. Speiser. Apsu and Tiamat were the male and female principles of primeval water. Sometimes, but perhaps not here, they represent fresh and salt water respectively.) For Egypt cf. e.g. the 24th-century B.C. text from Heliopolis, *ANET* p. 3: 'O Atum-Khepre, thou wast on high on the (primeval) hill....' (The primeval hillock was the first patch of land to rise above the boundless waters; it was located in many different cult-centres, and is symbolized by the pyramid.) Also another version, from the Book of the Dead (in this form, latter part of 2nd millennium): 'I am Atum when I was alone in Nun; I am Re in his (first) appearances, when he began to rule that which he had made.'

(Trans. J. A. Wilson. Atum was the creator-god worshipped at Heliopolis and equated with the sun-god Re. Nun is the primeval expanse of waters.)

[2] Okeanos has a further bank in the (probably late) underworld-episode in the *Odyssey*, and in Hesiod.

[3] In origin Ὠκεανός was perhaps a non-personal descriptive term, conceivably related to Hittite 'uginna', meaning 'circle', or Sanskrit 'a-çáyāna-ḥ', meaning 'that which surrounds'. Its development as a mythological figure, as sometimes in Homer and Hesiod, must have been comparatively late; but for Thales it would represent the crude mythological past.

The encircling river was presupposed in the myth that the sun, after crossing the sky with his horses and chariot, sails in a golden bowl round the stream of Okeanos, to the north (as is probably implied by 'the depths of night' in **8**), and so arrives back in the east just before dawn:

7 Mimnermus fr. 10 Diehl

Ἠέλιος μὲν γὰρ πόνον ἔλλαχεν ἤματα πάντα,
οὐδέ κοτ' ἄμπαυσις γίγνεται οὐδεμία
ἵπποισίν τε καὶ αὐτῷ, ἐπεὶ ῥοδοδάκτυλος Ἠὼς
Ὠκεανὸν προλιποῦσ' οὐρανὸν εἰσαναβῇ·
τὸν μὲν γὰρ διὰ κῦμα φέρει πολυήρατος εὐνὴ
κοίλη Ἡφαίστου χερσὶν ἐληλαμένη
χρυσοῦ τιμήεντος, ὑπόπτερος, ἄκρον ἐφ' ὕδωρ
εὕδονθ' ἁρπαλέως χώρου ἀφ' Ἑσπερίδων
γαῖαν ἐς Αἰθιόπων, ἵνα δὴ θοὸν ἅρμα καὶ ἵπποι
ἑστᾶσ', ὄφρ' Ἠὼς ἠριγένεια μόλῃ·
ἔνθ' ἐπεβή⟨σεθ' ἑ⟩ῶν ὀχέων Ὑπερίονος υἱός.

8 Stesichorus fr. 6, 1–4 Diehl

Ἀέλιος δ' Ὑπεριονίδας δέπας ἐσκατέβαινε
χρύσεον, ὄφρα δι' Ὠκεανοῖο περάσας
ἀφίκοιθ' ἱερᾶς ποτὶ βένθεα νυκτὸς ἐρεμνᾶς
ποτὶ ματέρα κουριδίαν τ' ἄλοχον παῖδάς τε φίλους.

---

7 *Helios gained a portion of toil for all his days, nor is there ever any rest for his horses and himself, when rosy-fingered Dawn, leaving Okeanos, mounts the sky; for him does his lovely bed bear across the wave, hollow and fashioned by the hands of Hephaestus out of precious gold, and winged; swiftly does it bear him sleeping over the surface of the water, from the dwelling of the Hesperides to the land of the Aithiopes, where his swift chariot and his horses stand till early-born Dawn shall come; there does the son of Hyperion mount his car.*

8 *Helios son of Hyperion descended into his golden cup, that, having passed over Okeanos, he might come to the depths of holy, dark night, to his mother and his wedded wife and his dear children.*

This detail is not mentioned in Homer.[1] In Egypt the sun was conceived as travelling from west to east in a ship, across the subterranean waters. This may or may not have been the origin of the Greek account; but the choice of a cup or bowl may be based upon the round shape of the sun itself, and suggests a more empirical and not wholly mythopoeic approach. In Heraclitus (**227**) the sun itself is described as a hollow bowl filled with fire, and there may have been a popular account of this kind which gave way to the more graphic conception of the sun as a charioteer.

[1] The sun rises *from* Okeanos (e.g. *Il.* 7, 422), but there is no suggestion of a vessel of any kind. Perhaps this was taken for granted; but it is also possible that the idea of the sun sailing round Okeanos is post-Homeric. At *Od.* 10, 191 the sun goes *under* the earth, but this is a unique occurrence in a passage that bears signs of lateness. The stars in Homer *bathe* in Okeanos (e.g. *Il.* 5, 6; 18, 489); they can hardly all have boats, and might be conceived as going through Okeanos and passing under the earth, though such details need not have been visualized.

(ii) *Okeanos as the source or origin of all things*

9 Homer *Il.* 14, 200 (repeated at 14, 301. Hera speaks)

εἶμι γὰρ ὀψομένη πολυφόρβου πείρατα γαίης,
Ὠκεανόν τε θεῶν γένεσιν καὶ μητέρα Τηθύν....

10 Homer *Il.* 14, 244 (Hypnos speaks)

ἄλλον μέν κεν ἔγωγε θεῶν αἰειγενετάων
ῥεῖα κατευνήσαιμι, καὶ ἂν ποταμοῖο ῥέεθρα
Ὠκεανοῦ, ὅς περ γένεσις πάντεσσι τέτυκται·
Ζηνὸς δ' οὐκ ἂν ἔγωγε Κρονίονος ἆσσον ἱκοίμην
οὐδὲ κατευνήσαιμ', ὅτε μὴ αὐτός γε κελεύοι.

The preceding section outlined the usual account of Okeanos in Homer. In the present passages the description of Okeanos as origin of the gods (**9**) and of all things (**10**) is unique and unexpected. Nowhere else in Homer is Okeanos mentioned in terms remotely resembling these; and it is notable that outside the particular episode in which these two passages occur, the Διὸς ἀπάτη or Deception of Zeus by Hera (*Il.* 14, 153–360 and 15,

---

9 *For I am going to see the limits of fertile earth, Okeanos begetter of gods and mother Tethys....*

10 *Another of the everlasting gods would I easily send to sleep, even the streams of river Okeanos who is the begetter of all: but Zeus son of Kronos would I not approach, nor send to sleep, except that he himself so bid me.*

init.), there is almost nothing in Homer that can reasonably be construed as specifically cosmogonical or cosmological in content; that is, as going beyond the accepted outline of what has been termed the popular world-picture. Even in this episode there is not very much.[1] Indeed, there is little which might not be explained without introducing cosmological interpretations, if a slight oddity of expression is allowed. This might apply even to Okeanos: **9** and **10** *could* imply no more than that the river of Okeanos is the source of all fresh water (as in **5**); water is necessary for life, therefore life must have originated, directly or indirectly, from Okeanos. This would not explain his parenthood of the gods in **9**; but that could be a poetical extension. It would also involve limiting the application of πάντεσσι in **10** to living creatures and plant-life, but again the same kind of poetic looseness might be presupposed. In any case the application of πάντεσσι is in doubt; it might be taken to apply simply to the gods, as in **9**, though without qualification its natural meaning is 'all things absolutely'. It must be admitted, however, that the references, if so understood, would be pointlessly abbreviated and give a somewhat bizarre effect.

[1] Namely **16** (Night); **18** (division of the world between Zeus, Poseidon, Hades); *Il.* 14, 203f., 274 (= 15, 225), 279 (the only Homeric references to Kronos, the Titans and Tartaros except for two important passages in bk. 8, *Il.* 8, 13ff. and 478ff.); *Il.* 14, 271; 15, 37f. (two of the four references in Homer to Styx as oath of the gods). The last two cases might be regarded as intrusions with Hesiodic affinities, though they are not derived from the Hesiodic poems that we know.

To Plato and Aristotle, however, **9** and **10** certainly seemed to have some kind of cosmological relevance:

11 Plato *Theaetetus* 152E ...Ὅμηρος, ⟨ὃς⟩ εἰπὼν ''Ὠκεανόν τε θεῶν γένεσιν καὶ μητέρα Τηθύν' πάντα εἴρηκεν ἔκγονα ῥοῆς τε καὶ κινήσεως. (Cf. also **14**.)

12 Aristotle *Met.* A3, 983b27 (following **87**) εἰσὶ δέ τινες οἳ καὶ τοὺς παμπαλαίους καὶ πολὺ πρὸ τῆς νῦν γενέσεως καὶ πρώτους θεολογήσαντας οὕτως οἴονται (*sc.* like Thales) περὶ τῆς φύσεως

---

11 *...Homer, who by saying 'Okeanos begetter of gods and mother Tethys' declared all things to be offspring of flux and motion.*

12 *There are some who think that the very ancient and indeed first speculators about the gods, long before the present age, made the same supposition about nature* (sc. *as Thales*);

ὑπολαβεῖν· Ὠκεανόν τε γὰρ καὶ Τηθὺν ἐποίησαν τῆς γενέσεως πατέρας καὶ τὸν ὅρκον τῶν θεῶν ὕδωρ, τὴν καλουμένην ὑπ' αὐτῶν Στύγα τῶν ποιητῶν· τιμιώτατον μὲν γὰρ τὸ πρεσβύτατον, ὅρκος δὲ τὸ τιμιώτατόν ἐστιν. (Cf. also **17**.)

Plato in **11** and elsewhere is obviously not entirely serious in his treatment of Homer as forerunner of the flux-idea assigned to Heraclitus, so we cannot be sure of the precise value he attached to the Homeric Okeanos-passage. Aristotle reports that it was interpreted rationalistically, as a possible anticipation of Thales. The form of the argument about the Styx in **12** reminds us not always to accept Aristotle's authority, as a historian of thought, without question; but later antiquity was persuaded through him to accept Okeanos and Tethys as representative of an early cosmogonical theory, since Eudemus adduced the same passage (obviously following Aristotle in **12**) in the Peripatetic history of theology.[1]

[1] As we know from the disagreement of Damascius, the Neoplatonist writer: **13** Damascius *de principiis* 124 ...οὐ γὰρ ἀποδεκτέον Εὐδήμου λέγοντος ὅτι ἀπὸ Ὠκεανοῦ καὶ Τηθύος ἄρχεται (*sc.* Ὅμηρος). (See **19**.) Cf. also Philodemus *de pietate* 47*a* (DK 3B5) and Athenagoras 18, p. 20 Schwartz (DK 1B13).

It has often been assumed that there is another and earlier class of testimony for the cosmogonical importance of Okeanos, namely early Orphic poetry:

14 Plato *Cratylus* 402B ...ὥσπερ αὖ Ὅμηρος 'Ὠκεανόν τε θεῶν γένεσίν' φησιν 'καὶ μητέρα Τηθύν'· οἶμαι δὲ καὶ Ἡσίοδος. λέγει δέ που καὶ Ὀρφεὺς ὅτι

Ὠκεανὸς πρῶτος καλλίρροος ἦρξε γάμοιο,
ὅς ῥα κασιγνήτην ὁμομήτορα Τηθὺν ὄπυιεν.

15 Plato *Timaeus* 40D–E ...πειστέον δὲ τοῖς εἰρηκόσιν ἔμπροσθεν, ἐκγόνοις μὲν θεῶν οὖσιν, ὡς ἔφασαν, σαφῶς δέ που τούς γε αὑτῶν

---

for they wrote that Okeanos and Tethys were the parents of coming-to-be, and the oath of the gods water—that which by the poets themselves is called Styx; for what is oldest is most honourable, and the most honourable thing is used as an oath.

13 *...for we must not accept it when Eudemus says that he* [*Homer*] *begins from Okeanos and Tethys.*

14 *...as Homer, again, says 'Okeanos begetter of gods and mother Tethys'; and I think Hesiod too. Orpheus, too, says somewhere that 'Fair-streamed Okeanos first began the marriages, who wed Tethys, his sister by the same mother'.*

15 *...we must believe those who formerly gave utterance, those who were, as they said, offspring of the gods, and must, I suppose, have truly known their own ancestors:... Okeanos*

προγόνους εἰδόσιν·...Γῆς τε καὶ Οὐρανοῦ παῖδες Ὠκεανός τε καὶ Τηθὺς ἐγενέσθην, τούτων δὲ Φόρκυς Κρόνος τε καὶ Ῥέα καὶ ὅσοι μετὰ τούτων....

But the Orphic verses of **14**, though established by Plato's time, are not necessarily as early in origin as the seventh or even the sixth century B.C. In any case, the view which they express does not necessarily differ greatly from that of the Hesiodic *Theogony*—as Plato may have perceived. There, Okeanos, Tethys and the other Titans are born to Gaia and Ouranos at a comparatively late stage from the point of view of cosmogonical production, but it is in their generation that the regular reproduction, by bisexual means, of fully personal figures (as opposed to world-constituents like Tartaros or Pontos) begins. **15**, in which 'offspring of the gods' shows that Plato is describing an Orphic view, indicates that according to one Orphic account Okeanos and Tethys were the *parents* of the Titans (including the theogonically vital pair Kronos and Rhea), and not their coevals as in the *Theogony*. That is probably another reason for πρῶτος in the Orphic verses of **14**: Okeanos and Tethys are the first fully anthropomorphized couple (though Okeanos, of course, is very much a border-line case), and prior even to Kronos and Rhea. Hesiod had assigned less importance to Okeanos than might reasonably have been expected, especially in view of the well-known Homeric passages **9** and **10**; so the Orphic versions presumably emended the Hesiodic account to the extent of putting Okeanos and Tethys one generation earlier than the Titans. Certainly there is no evidence here for assuming a peculiarly Orphic attribution of cosmogonical importance to Okeanos.

The evidence does not prove (or even, it might be felt, suggest) that there existed in Greece at a comparatively early date a systematic doctrine of the cosmogonical priority of Okeanos. Hesiod gives no indication of it, and later suppositions seem to be based on the two unusual Homeric passages, which are left as the only direct evidence for any such cosmogonical theory. They *might* have meant no more than that water is essential for life, though this would be rather odd. It was seen under section (i) that the idea of an encircling river Okeanos may well have been adapted

---

and Tethys were born as children of Ge [*earth*] *and Ouranos* [*sky*], *and their children were Phorkys, Kronos, Rhea and their companions....*

from Egyptian or Babylonian beliefs. It was part of those beliefs, too, that the world *originated* from primeval water (see n. 1 on p. 13); the isolated Homeric passages could, then, be a reference to that basic near-eastern assumption, as Plutarch assumed in **70**. The absence of any other such reference (at any rate until Thales) suggests that the Homeric ones were idiosyncratic—even, perhaps, pedantic; there are other indications that the composer of the episode in which they occur had special cosmogonical and theogonical interests. The concept of the encircling river had, of course, become assimilated in Greece at a far earlier date.

3. NIGHT

(i) *In Homer*

16 Homer *Il.* 14, 258 (Hypnos speaks)

. . . καί κέ μ' ἄιστον ἀπ' αἰθέρος ἔμβαλε πόντῳ (*sc.* Ζεύς)
εἰ μὴ Νὺξ δμήτειρα θεῶν ἐσάωσε καὶ ἀνδρῶν·
τὴν ἱκόμην φεύγων, ὁ δὲ παύσατο χωόμενός περ·
ἅζετο γὰρ μὴ Νυκτὶ θοῇ ἀποθύμια ἕρδοι.

This is the only place in the Homeric poems where Night is fully personified. Again, as with the two special Okeanos passages, it occurs in the episode of the Deceit of Zeus; and again there is an unusual implication of special power or priority among the gods. Zeus' respect for Night here is certainly strange, and quite unparalleled in Homer and Hesiod. In view of later interpretations it might suggest that the poet of this episode knew some story about Nyx as a cosmogonical figure. But the reference is an isolated one, and *could* be no more than a poetical development of the idea implicit in the phrase Νὺξ δμήτειρα θεῶν, 'Night subduer of the gods': even gods are overcome by sleep, hence even the virtually all-powerful Zeus hesitates to offend Night, the mother of sleep, lest she should subdue him on some unsuitable occasion. (It must be remarked, however, that he evidently had no hesitation about offending Hypnos himself, if he was prepared in the present passage to fling him out of heaven.)

---

16 *. . . and he [Zeus] would have cast me from the aither into the sea, out of sight, had not Night, subduer of gods and men, saved me; to her did I come in flight, and Zeus ceased, angry though he was; for he was in awe of doing what would be displeasing to swift Night.*

(ii) *An archaic cosmogonical concept according to Aristotle*

17 Aristotle *Met.* N4, 1091b4 ...οἱ δὲ ποιηταὶ οἱ ἀρχαῖοι ταύτῃ ὁμοίως, ᾗ βασιλεύειν καὶ ἄρχειν φασὶν οὐ τοὺς πρώτους οἷον Νύκτα καὶ Οὐρανὸν ἢ Χάος ἢ Ὠκεανόν, ἀλλὰ τὸν Δία. (Cf. *Met.* Λ6, 1071b27 οἱ θεολόγοι οἱ ἐκ Νυκτὸς γεννῶντες: also *ibid.* 1072a8.)

Aristotle thus accepted that there were poets and writers about the gods who put Night 'first', or who generated from Night. He may well have had the Homeric passage, **16**, in mind; but this alone would hardly motivate his inclusion of Night, and it seems probable that he was thinking primarily of the post-Hesiodic cosmogonies, compiled mainly in the sixth and fifth centuries, to be described under (iii). In these, Night, which was produced at a very early stage (though not the first) in the Hesiodic cosmogonical account (**24**), and was classed with Gaia, Okeanos and Ouranos in other more casual references in the *Theogony* (20 and 106f.), is elevated to the first stage of all, either by herself or jointly with other substances, Air or Tartaros. It is natural that both Day and Night should come into being as soon as Sky and Earth have separated, to occupy the gap between the two.[1] It is clear from *Met.* Λ6, 1071b27 that by τοὺς πρώτους in **17** Aristotle meant 'absolutely first', not simply 'at an early stage'; though all the four figures mentioned are important in the Hesiodic account, and we have no knowledge of any cosmogony which gave absolute priority to Ouranos.

[1] Among the offspring of Night in a subsequent passage of Hesiod, *Theog.* 211ff., are the Μοῖραι and Νέμεσις. This might seem to suggest that Night had a primordial *distributive* capacity (since the idea of distribution underlies both these personifications), in a διάταξις or assignment of parts of the cosmos to different gods. Such a distribution is mentioned in Homer (again associated with the Deceit of Zeus): **18** Homer *Il.* 15, 189

τριχθὰ δὲ πάντα δέδασται, ἕκαστος δ' ἔμμορε τιμῆς·
ἦτοι ἐγὼν (*sc.* Poseidon) ἔλαχον πολιὴν ἅλα ναιέμεν αἰεὶ
παλλομένων, Ἀίδης δ' ἔλαχε ζόφον ἠερόεντα,
Ζεὺς δ' ἔλαχ' οὐρανὸν εὐρὺν ἐν αἰθέρι καὶ νεφέλῃσι·
γαῖα δ' ἔτι ξυνὴ πάντων καὶ μακρὸς Ὄλυμπος.

---

17 *...the ancient poets similarly, inasmuch as they say that not the first figures have rule and kingship (Night and Ouranos or Chaos or Okeanos, for example), but Zeus.*—(*...those writers about the gods who generate from Night.*)

18 *In three parts were all things divided, and each got his share of honour: I indeed gained the grey sea to dwell in for ever, when the lots were shaken, and Hades gained misty darkness, and Zeus the broad sky among aither and clouds; but earth and tall Olympus belonged in common to all.*

So in Hesiod, *Theog.* 112f. and 881 ff. (the latter passage after the subjection of the Titans and the probably interpolated Typhoeus; cf. the division of the heavens by Marduk after the defeat of Tiamat in the Babylonian Creation-epic, *ANET* 67). Yet this happens at a relatively late stage in cosmogony; and Moira and Nemesis are probably associated with Night merely because, like her other children (Death, Grief, etc.), they can be regarded as baleful and intractable powers.

(iii) *Night in cosmogonies assigned to Orpheus, Musaeus, Epimenides*

19 Damascius *de principiis* 124 (DK 1 B 12) ἡ δὲ παρὰ τῷ Περιπατητικῷ Εὐδήμῳ ἀναγεγραμμένη ὡς τοῦ Ὀρφέως οὖσα θεολογία πᾶν τὸ νοητὸν ἐσιώπησεν...ἀπὸ δὲ τῆς Νυκτὸς ἐποιήσατο τὴν ἀρχήν, ἀφ' ἧς καὶ Ὅμηρος, εἰ καὶ μὴ συνεχῆ πεποίηται τὴν γενεαλογίαν, ἵστησιν· οὐ γὰρ ἀποδεκτέον Εὐδήμου λέγοντος ὅτι ἀπὸ Ὠκεανοῦ καὶ Τηθύος ἄρχεται....

20 Philodemus *de pietate* 47*a* (DK 3 B 5) ἐν δὲ τοῖς εἰς Ἐπιμενίδην (*sc.* ἀναφερομένοις ἔπεσιν) ἐξ Ἀέρος καὶ Νυκτὸς τὰ πάντα συστῆναι, ⟨ὥσπερ καὶ⟩ Ὅμηρος ⟨ἀποφαί⟩νετ' Ὠκεανὸν ἐκ Τηθύος τοὺς θεοὺς γεννᾶν.... (Cf. also **40**.)

21 Philodemus *de pietate* 137, 5 ἐν μέν τισιν ἐκ Νυκτὸς καὶ Ταρτάρου λέγεται τὰ πάντα, ἐν δέ τισιν ἐξ Ἅιδου καὶ Αἰθέρος· ὁ δὲ τὴν Τιτανομαχίαν γράψας ἐξ Αἰθέρος φησίν, Ἀκουσίλαος δὲ ἐκ Χάους πρώτου τἆλλα· ἐν δὲ τοῖς ἀναφερομένοις εἰς Μουσαῖον γέγραπται Τάρταρον πρῶτον ⟨καὶ Ν⟩ύκτα.

19 (on which see also pp. 40ff.) shows that Eudemus did not explain the priority of Night in the Orphic cosmogony as being dependent on the Homeric passage, **16**. This was because he considered that Homer clearly assigned cosmogonical priority to Okeanos and Tethys (**9**, **10**). Damascius here goes counter to Eudemus, and may mean to imply that the Orphic account was to some extent indebted to Homer.[1] But the crux of the matter

---

19 *The theology ascribed to Orpheus in Eudemus the Peripatetic kept silence about the whole intelligible realm...but he made the origin from Night, from whom Homer too (even though he does not describe the succession of generations as continuous) establishes the beginning of things; for we must not accept it when Eudemus says that Homer begins from Okeanos and Tethys....*

20 *In the verses ascribed to Epimenides all things are composed from Air and Night; as Homer, also, declared that Okeanos begets the gods from Tethys....*

21 *In some sources all things are said to come from Night and Tartaros, and in some from Hades and Aither; the author of the* Titanomachy *says they came from Aither, and Acusilaus says that the other things come from Chaos, which was the first; while in the verses ascribed to Musaeus it is written that Tartaros and Night were first.*

is the interpretation of **20** and **21**. These passages indicate that there were poetical accounts, composed probably in the 7th or 6th century B.C., which made Night (in association with Aer or Tartaros, both conveying the idea of darkness) the origin of the world. *If* there was an ancient, non-derivative theory of Night as a genuine cosmogonical figure (as Aristotle in **17** suggests), as opposed to post-Hesiodic learned variants, then these passages are likely to be our surest evidence for it: but only if they themselves appear to be non-Hesiodic in character. This, however, they do not appear (to the present writer at least) to be. With the exception of 'Ἀήρ in 'Epimenides'[2] the cosmic figures involved are all to be found in the Hesiodic cosmogony proper (**24**); and 'Ἀήρ, implying mist and darkness rather than the transparent stuff that we call 'air', is an essential element of the Hesiodic description although it does not happen to achieve personification—thus in the second stage of production, before Night, comes '*misty* Tartaros', Τάρταρά τ' ἠερόεντα (but see p. 25 n. 1). When we see from Damascius' reference to 'Epimenides' in **40** that Night and 'Ἀήρ *produce* Tartaros, it begins to look as though this account is working strictly within the limits of the Hesiodic formulation. In fact this is not entirely true, because later in **40** an *egg* is produced—a non-Hesiodic and conceivably primitive device (see pp. 44–8). Nevertheless, the first stages do not appear to be unaffected by the Hesiodic version; this impression is even stronger with 'Musaeus'[3] and the other accounts mentioned in **21**. Tartaros and Night belong to the second and third stages respectively of the Hesiodic cosmogony; they seemed to share the qualities which were sometimes assigned to Chaos itself, which was therefore suppressed—although Acusilaus of Argos (probably late sixth to early fifth century) retained the genuine Hesiodic order.[4]

[1] Night is described in the Orphic Rhapsodies (see p. 40) as a figure of great importance, the near-equal and successor of Phanes-Protogonos. So **22** Hermias in Plat. *Phaedr.* 247 C (Kern *Orphicorum Fragmenta* fr. 86, 1 f.) Πρωτόγονόν γε μὲν οὔτις ἐσέδρακεν ὀφθαλμοῖσιν / εἰ μὴ Νὺξ ἱερὴ μούνη. **23** Proclus in Plat. *Crat.* 396 B (Kern fr. 101) (Phanes) σκῆπτρον δ' ἀριδείκετον εἷο χέρεσσιν / θῆκε θεᾶς Νυκτός, ⟨ἵν' ἔχῃ⟩ βασιληίδα τιμήν.

---

22 *None gazed upon Protogonos ['First-born'] with their eyes, except holy Night alone.*

23 *(Phanes) placed his famous sceptre in the hands of goddess Night, so that she might have the prerogative of rulership.*

According to **33**, q.v., Night gave birth to Ouranos and Gaia: this seems to have been a secondary rebirth of some kind, see p. 40. The detail is not stressed, and in fact Phanes is the real creator-god; the relation of Night to sky and earth seems to be an incidental refinement. Another Orphic succession (Kern fr. 107) is Chaos-Okeanos-Nyx-Ouranos-Zeus. This, again, may merely imply a rearrangement of Hesiod in the light of Homer. Chrysippus, who is said to have 'accommodated' to Stoicism ideas ascribed to Orpheus and Musaeus, described Night as the first *goddess* (Chrys. *ap.* Philodemum *piet.* 13, 16; 14, 18, DK2B14).

[2] On Epimenides see pp. 44f.: the hexameter cosmogony and theogony to which his name was later attached was probably not by him (as Philodemus evidently suspected), but it may nevertheless have originated in the sixth century B.C. Damascius, too, stated that *Aer* and Night were Epimenides' first principles, and gave Eudemus as his source for this (**40**). Philodemus, therefore, who must also have relied on Eudemus' standard history of theology, provides in **20** an earlier confirmation of Damascius' reliability.

[3] The name of Musaeus, the mythical disciple of Orpheus and eponymous author of oracle-literature, tended to become attached to any kind of other-worldly verses—including, evidently, a theogonical poem like that assigned to Epimenides. The late sixth century B.C. is a plausible *terminus ante quem* for such a poem and ascription: compare the case of Onomacritus, who according to Herodotus VII, 6 (DK2B20*a*) was banished from Athens by Hipparchus when, having been entrusted with the collection and arrangement of Musaeus' oracles, he was found to have inserted a spurious one.

[4] Acusilaus was a genealogist who might well have given a summary, and of course unoriginal, account of the first ancestors; though some of the material assigned to him was later suspected. According to Damascius (DK9B1) he made a limited rearrangement of the Hesiodic figures which came after Chaos; but he is almost entirely irrelevant to the history of early Greek philosophy, and scarcely deserves the space accorded him in DK.

A new and important consideration may be introduced here. After the episode of the defeat of the Titans in the *Theogony* comes a series of passages (726–819) which have been widely recognized as additions to the 'original' text; they are in fact short variant descriptions of the underworld. These variants, or some of them, may of course be no later than the rest of the poem, though not composed for the place where they are now found. The probability is, however, that most of them were specially composed to 'improve' on the integral references to the underworld. If this is the case they belong to the later part of the seventh century at the earliest, while the early sixth century seems a likelier period for their composition. Now in most of these variants Night is, quite naturally, given some prominence: see for example **2**, where Night surrounds the 'throat' of Tartaros, and above are the roots of the earth (in itself probably a genuinely primitive conception). But in **27** (q.v., with discussion on pp. 30f.) this conception is further developed, and the sources and limits of all things are located in the great windy gap which is probably a later specification of Chaos in line 116 (**24**); the halls of dark night are said to be in or around this χάσμα. It is easy to see that this trend of thought could lead to the elevation of Night to be representative of the original, inchoate state of things. In the original cosmogonical account (**24**) Night comes at an early and important stage; the tendency to rearrange the Hesiodic figures is already indicated for the sixth century (probably); Homer provided one piece of cryptic encouragement for a further elevation of Night; and added elaborations of the Hesiodic picture of the underworld tended to reinterpret Tartaros and Night as local forms of an originative Χάος. These factors provide motive enough for Aristotle's judgement in **17**; and there seems to be little indication at present that the idea of an absolute priority of Night occurred early enough, or in a sufficiently independent form, to have had any effect on scientific cosmogonical thought. The isolated Homeric reference, **16**, cannot be assessed with any certainty: it may be simply a reference to the power of sleep, or it may be derived from a lost myth in which a personified Night had some special relationship to Zeus.

4. THE HESIODIC COSMOGONY, AND THE SEPARATION OF SKY AND EARTH

24 Hesiod *Theogony* 116

Ἦ τοι μὲν πρώτιστα Χάος γένετ', αὐτὰρ ἔπειτα 116
Γαῖ' εὐρύστερνος, πάντων ἕδος ἀσφαλὲς αἰεί, 117
Τάρταρά τ' ἠερόεντα μυχῷ χθονὸς εὐρυοδείης,[1] 119
ἠδ' Ἔρος, ὃς κάλλιστος ἐν ἀθανάτοισι θεοῖσι, 120
λυσιμελής, πάντων δὲ θεῶν πάντων τ' ἀνθρώπων
δάμναται ἐν στήθεσσι νόον καὶ ἐπίφρονα βουλήν.
ἐκ Χάεος δ' Ἔρεβός τε μέλαινά τε Νὺξ ἐγένοντο·
Νυκτὸς δ' αὖτ' Αἰθήρ τε καὶ Ἡμέρη ἐξεγένοντο,

---

24 *Verily first of all did Chaos come into being, and then broad-bosomed Gaia* [*earth*], *a firm seat of all things for ever, and misty Tartaros in a recess of broad-wayed earth, and Eros, who is fairest among immortal gods, looser of limbs, and subdues in their breasts the mind and thoughtful counsel of all gods and all men. Out of Chaos, Erebos and black Night came into being; and from Night, again, came Aither and Day, whom she conceived*

οὓς τέκε κυσαμένη Ἐρέβει φιλότητι μιγεῖσα.
Γαῖα δέ τοι πρῶτον μὲν ἐγείνατο ἶσον ἑαυτῇ
Οὐρανὸν ἀστερόενθ', ἵνα μιν περὶ πάντα καλύπτοι,
ὄφρ' εἴη μακάρεσσι θεοῖς ἕδος ἀσφαλὲς αἰεί.
γείνατο δ' Οὔρεα μακρά, θεῶν χαρίεντας ἐναύλους
Νυμφέων, αἳ ναίουσιν ἀν' οὔρεα βησσήεντα.
ἡ δὲ καὶ ἀτρύγετον πέλαγος τέκεν, οἴδματι θυῖον,
Πόντον, ἄτερ φιλότητος ἐφιμέρου· αὐτὰρ ἔπειτα
Οὐρανῷ εὐνηθεῖσα τέκ' Ὠκεανὸν βαθυδίνην,
Κοῖόν τε Κρῖόν θ' Ὑπερίονά τ' Ἰαπετόν τε....[2]

[1] Line 118, ἀθανάτων οἳ ἔχουσι κάρη νιφόεντος Ὀλύμπου, is inorganic and quite inappropriate here, and has been omitted. It occurs in the medieval mss., but is absent from quotations by Plato (*Symp.* 178B) and ps.-Aristotle (*MXG* 1, 975a11), as well as by Sextus Empiricus and Stobaeus. Line 119 was also omitted in these quotations (as, apparently, in the copy used by Zeno of Citium: *SVF* 1, 104–5), and a scholiast remarks ἀθετεῖται ('it is marked as spurious'); yet it is quoted in its correct place by Chalcidius (*in Tim.* 122), who omitted 118. Plato's continuation of 117 by 120 is not necessarily significant; he was solely interested in Eros, and quoted what was relevant to Eros and no more. The scholiast's doubt, and post-Platonic omissions, may have originated in Plato's omission; or the line may have been felt to be incongruous, having been added at the time when the variant descriptions of Hades accrued (p. 23).

[2] The list of Titans is completed in the lines that follow; Gaia's subsequent offspring are patently non-cosmological. At 154ff. comes the story of the mutilation of Kronos (**32**). At 211ff. there is a reversion to the production of personified abstractions, e.g. by Night and Strife, but they have no cosmological significance.

The author of the *Theogony* decided to trace back the ancestry of the gods to the beginning of the world, and **24** is his account of the earliest stages, in which the production of cosmic constituents like Ouranos (sky) gradually leads to the generation of vague but fully anthropomorphic mythical persons like the Titans. This poetical cosmogony, composed presumably at some time during the seventh century B.C., was not, however, *invented* by Hesiod: its occasional irrationality and reduplication of stages indicate that it is a

---

and bore after mingling in love with Erebos. And Earth first of all brought forth starry Ouranos [*sky*], *equal to herself, to cover her completely round about, to be a firm seat for the blessed gods for ever. Then she brought forth tall Mountains, lovely haunts of the divine Nymphs who dwell in the woody mountains. She also gave birth to the unharvested sea, seething with its swell, Pontos, without delightful love; and then having lain with Ouranos she bore deep-eddying Okeanos, and Koios and Krios and Hyperion and Iapetos....*

synthesis of at least two earlier variant accounts. For example, Erebos (which may be of Hittite etymology), although there is some vagueness about it in Homer, must be locally related to the whole complex Gaia-Hades-Tartaros (Ἐρέβεσφιν ὑπὸ χθονός at *Theogony* 669); yet it is produced a stage later than Gaia and Tartaros. It might be explained as a local differentiation, as Mountains and Sea (Pontos) are produced as local differentiations from Earth; but in that case it should naturally originate from Tartaros or Gaia and not from Chaos. It is grouped with Night, no doubt, because it shares a major characteristic (darkness), as Aither is grouped with Day. Generation is of opposites (e.g. of Aither and Day by Erebos—whose neuter gender does not inhibit parental activities—and Night), or of similars (Erebos and Night from Chaos, see p. 31), or of local differentiations. Some births, however, cannot be explained on any of these principles—notably that of Ouranos from Gaia. Again, there is inconsistency over the method of production. Eros is produced at the first stage of differentiation, presumably to provide an anthropomorphic, sexual explanation of subsequent differentiation. It is not, however, consistently used. Gaia produces Pontos 'without love' at 132; Night mates with Erebos at 125 but produces again 'without sleeping with anyone' at 213; Chaos at 123, and Gaia again at 126, produce independently though Love is already in existence. Immediately after producing Pontos independently at 132, Gaia produces the more fully personalized Okeanos by mating with her son and consort Ouranos.[1]

[1] In view of his cosmological importance as the surrounding river (§2) one would expect Okeanos to occur earlier, rather than later, than Pontos, which can properly be regarded as a detail of the earth. The production of Okeanos by *Gaia* and *Ouranos* may have a rationalistic motive, since the surrounding stream forms the point of contact between earth and the enclosing bowl of sky.

'First of all Chaos came-to-be': the primacy of Chaos is remarkable, and a careful enquiry must be made into what Hesiod is likely to have meant by Χάος here. Three interpretations may be rejected immediately: (i) Aristotle (*Phys.* Δ 1, 208b29) took it to mean space. But this concept is much later than the *Theogony*, occurring first, probably, in Pythagoras, then more clearly in Zeno of Elea, and most clearly in Plato's *Timaeus*. (ii) The Stoics followed Zeno of Citium (e.g. *SVF* 1, 103), who perhaps took the idea from Pherecydes of Syros (DK 7 B 1 *a*), in deriving χάος from χέεσθαι and therefore interpreting it as what is poured, i.e. water. (iii) The common modern sense of chaos as disorder can be seen e.g. in Lucian *Amores* 32, where Hesiod's χάος is interpreted as disordered, shapeless matter. This, again, may be Stoic in origin.

The noun is derived from √χα, meaning 'gape, gap, yawn', as in χαίνειν, χάσκειν, etc. Of the certain uses of the word before 400 B.C., one group simply refers to the cosmogonic Χάος of this passage (so Acusilaus in **21**, Aristophanes *Birds* 693, *Clouds* 627); the other group has the special meaning 'air', in the sense of the region between sky and earth, the region in which birds fly (so Bacchylides 5, 27, Euripides fr. 448 (Nauck²), Aristophanes *Clouds* 424, *Birds* 1218). One may suspect that Bacchylides' poetical and perhaps original use of the highly individual phrase ἐν ἀτρύτῳ χάει (as that in which the eagle flies—the free air, as opposed to earth or sea) was consciously imitated by Euripides and Aristophanes, either lyrically (*Birds* 1218) or as a convenient though not necessarily serious interpretation to be placed on the cosmogonical *chaos* of Hesiod. The evidence, then, does not point to an extensive use of χάος as the space between sky and earth, though such a use was certainly known. Here we must consider another instance of the word in the *Theogony* itself (in an episode which is possibly an expansion or addition, but which, even so, can hardly be later in date than the early sixth century):

25 Hesiod *Theogony* 695 (Zeus hurls thunderbolts at the Titans)

ἔζεε δὲ χθὼν πᾶσα καὶ Ὠκεανοῖο ῥέεθρα
πόντος τ' ἀτρύγετος· τοὺς δ' ἄμφεπε θερμὸς ἀυτμὴ
Τιτῆνας χθονίους, φλὸξ δ' αἰθέρα δῖαν ἵκανεν
ἄσπετος, ὄσσε δ' ἄμερδε καὶ ἰφθίμων περ ἐόντων
αὐγὴ μαρμαίρουσα κεραυνοῦ τε στεροπῆς τε.
καῦμα δὲ θεσπέσιον κατέχεν Χάος· εἴσατο δ' ἄντα
ὀφθαλμοῖσι ἰδεῖν ἠδ' οὔασι ὄσσαν ἀκοῦσαι
αὔτως ὡς εἰ Γαῖα καὶ Οὐρανὸς εὐρὺς ὕπερθε
πίλνατο· τοῖος γάρ κε μέγας ὑπὸ δοῦπος ὀρώρει....

25 *The whole earth boiled, and the streams of Okeanos, and the unharvested sea; and them, the earth-born Titans, did a warm blast surround, and flame unquenchable reached the holy aither, and the darting gleam of thunderbolt and lightning blinded the eyes even of strong men. A marvellous burning took hold of Chaos; and it was the same to behold with the eyes or to hear the noise with the ears as if earth and broad heaven above drew together; for just such a great din would have risen up....*

There has been dispute about which region of the world is represented by Χάος in line 700. Either (*a*) it represents the whole or part of the underworld: there is a parallel for this usage at *Theogony* 814 (**28**), in one of the added variants (see pp. 23f.); or (*b*) it represents the region between earth and aither. But (*a*) would be difficult: why should the *heat* penetrate to the underworld (the concussion of missiles does so at 681 ff., but that is natural and effective)? The Titans are not in the underworld, but on Mount Othrys (632); we have been told that the flash reaches the upper air, and it is relevant to add that the heat, also, filled the whole intermediate region. The following lines imagine earth and sky as clashing together—again, the emphasis is certainly not on the underworld. An objective judge would surely conclude that Χάος at line 700 describes the region between earth and sky.

In view of the basic meaning of χάος (as a gap, i.e. a bounded interval, not 'void' or anything like that),[1] and of one certain fifth-century usage as the region between sky and earth, and of another use of the word in the *Theogony* in which the meaning is probably the same, serious attention must be paid to an interpretation propounded most notably by Cornford (e.g. *Principium Sapientiae* 194f.), that Χάος γένετ' in the first line of **24** implies that *the gap between earth and sky came into being*; that is, that the first stage of cosmogony was the separation of earth and sky. This would not be consistent with one existing and indubitable feature of the cosmogony, the postponement of the birth of Ouranos until a second stage, at lines 126f. (Production from Chaos, lines 123ff., and from Gaia, 126ff., may take place simultaneously.) Apart from this peculiarity, the other conditions fit the proposed interpretation: earth, with its appendage Tartaros, appears directly the gap is made; so does Eros, which in its most concrete form as rain/semen exists between sky and earth according to poetical references.[2] It seems not improbable that in the Hesiodic scheme the explicit description of the formation of Ouranos has been delayed through the confused use of two separate accounts (a confusion which can be paralleled from other details of the scheme), and that it is implied in line 116 at the very first stage of cosmogony. The separation of sky and earth is certainly reduplicated in the *Theogony*, in a fully mythopoeic form, in the story of the mutilation of Kronos (**32**); though reduplication of accounts of a different logical character (quasi-rationalistic and mythopoeic) is easier to accept than reduplication on the same, quasi-rationalistic level.

[1] A comparison has often been drawn between χάος and *ginnunga-gap* in the Nordic cosmogony. This *gap* (which, however, preceded the creation of the giant from whom earth and sky were made) has been taken to imply simply an indefinite empty space: but it is important to observe that in Snorri's schematization it is conceived as being terminated by the realm of ice (*Niflheim*) to the north and that of fire (*Muspellsheim*) to the south. This certainly does not invalidate the supposition that χάος implies primarily a region of vast size, but secondarily and implicitly its boundaries.

[2] Not in Homer or Hesiod; most notably in **26** Aeschylus fr. 44, 1–5 (from the *Danaids*)

ἐρᾷ μὲν ἁγνὸς οὐρανὸς τρῶσαι χθόνα,
ἔρως δὲ γαῖαν λαμβάνει γάμου τυχεῖν.
ὄμβρος δ' ἀπ' εὐνατῆρος οὐρανοῦ πεσὼν
ἔκυσε γαῖαν· ἡ δὲ τίκτεται βροτοῖς
μήλων τε βοσκὰς καὶ βίον Δημήτριον.

This idea of the rain actually fertilizing the earth may be of great antiquity.

Cornford's interpretation may be helped by the verb used to describe the first stage of cosmogony: not ἦν but γένετ', perhaps implying that Χάος was not the eternal precondition of a differentiated world, but a modification of that precondition. (It is out of the question that Hesiod or his source was thinking of the originative substance as coming into being out of nothing.) The conception that earth and sky were originally one mass may have been so common (see pp. 32–4) that Hesiod could take it for granted, and begin his account of world-formation at the first stage of differentiation. This would be, undoubtedly, a cryptic and laconic procedure; and it seems probable that something more complicated was meant by Χάος γένετ' than, simply, 'sky and earth separated'—though I am inclined to accept that this was originally implicit in the phrase. The nature of the gap between sky and earth, after their first separation, may well have been somehow specified in the popular traditions on which Hesiod was presumably drawing. There was, conceivably, an attempt to imagine what would be the appearance of things when there was simply dark sky, and earth, and the gap between. Here we must turn for assistance to two of the variants (see p. 23) on the description of the underworld, appended to the Titanomachy in the *Theogony*.

---

26 *Holy sky passionately longs to penetrate the earth, and desire takes hold of earth to achieve this union. Rain from her bedfellow sky falls and impregnates earth, and she brings forth for mortals pasturage for flocks and Demeter's livelihood.*

27 Hesiod *Theogony* 736

ἔνθα δὲ γῆς δνοφερῆς καὶ Ταρτάρου ἠερόεντος
πόντου τ' ἀτρυγέτοιο καὶ οὐρανοῦ ἀστερόεντος
ἑξείης πάντων πηγαὶ καὶ πείρατ' ἔασιν
ἀργαλέ' εὐρώεντα, τά τε στυγέουσι θεοί περ,
χάσμα μέγ', οὐδέ κε πάντα τελεσφόρον· εἰς ἐνιαυτὸν
οὖδας ἵκοιτ', εἰ πρῶτα πυλέων ἔντοσθε γένοιτο.
ἀλλά κεν ἔνθα καὶ ἔνθα φέροι πρὸ θύελλα θυέλλῃ
ἀργαλέη· δεινὸν δὲ καὶ ἀθανάτοισι θεοῖσι
τοῦτο τέρας· Νυκτὸς δ' ἐρεβεννῆς οἰκία δεινὰ
ἕστηκεν νεφέλῃς κεκαλυμμένα κυανέῃσιν.

28 Hesiod *Theogony* 811 (following a repetition of ll. 736–9, *vide* **27**)

ἔνθα δὲ μαρμάρεαί τε πύλαι καὶ χάλκεος οὐδὸς
ἀστεμφής, ῥίζῃσι διηνεκέεσσιν ἀρηρώς,
αὐτοφυής· πρόσθεν δὲ θεῶν ἔκτοσθεν ἁπάντων
Τιτῆνες ναίουσι, πέρην Χάεος ζοφεροῖο.

Of these, **27** is evidently an attempt to improve 726–8 (**2**), where Tartaros (perhaps its upper part) is said to be surrounded by Night, and above it are the roots of earth and sea. In πείρατ' there is a more exact reversion to the apparent source of **2**, i.e. *Il.* 8, 478–9, τὰ νείατα πείραθ'. . .γαίης καὶ πόντοιο: while πηγαί (there is no reference, of course, to the ultimate originative sources of all things, as certain ingenious men have thought) is introduced as being especially appropriate to the sea. 740ff. are a special and peculiar development of 720ff. **28**, on the other hand, which follows a repetition of the first four lines of **27**, begins with a slightly altered line (*Il.* 8, 15) from the Homeric description of Tartaros (**1**), then with the 'roots' of **2**, quite vague this time, and ends with the χάσμα μέγ' of 740 repeated as Χάεος. Both passages contain inconsistencies and impossibilities, which indicate that they are somewhat superficial expansions by composers who were either

---

27 *There of murky earth and misty Tartaros and unharvested sea and starry sky, of all of them, are the springs in a row and the grievous, dank limits which even the gods detest; a great gulf, nor would one reach the floor for the whole length of a fulfilling year, if one were once within the gates. But hither and thither storm on grievous storm would carry one on; dreadful is this portent even for immortal gods; and the dreadful halls of gloomy Night stand covered with blue-black clouds.*

28 *There are gleaming gates, and brazen threshold unshaken, fixed with continuous roots, self-grown; and in front, far from all the gods, dwell the Titans, across murky Chaos.*

careless or stupid; for example, it is difficult to be favourably impressed by the alteration of the reasonable idea that the roots of the earth are above Tartaros to the idea that the 'sources and boundaries' of earth, sea, sky *and Tartaros* are in Tartaros (**27**). What is interesting is the further description of Tartaros as a χάσμα μέγ', a great gulf or chasm (cf. Euripides *Phoen.* 1605), full of storms and containing the halls of Night. In **28** this gulf is described as 'gloomy Chaos' (we need not concern ourselves with its peculiar geography, except to note that Chaos is not absolutely unbounded). This must contain a reference to the initial Χάος of line 116 (**24**), and it seems reasonable to suppose that the authors of these two additions understood the initial Χάος to be dark and windy, like Tartaros. This interpretation gains some support from the fact that in the original cosmogonical account Erebos and Night (both, presumably, gloomy) are produced from Chaos at the stage after the production of Gaia, Tartaros and Eros.

The evidence seems to point to the following conclusion. For Hesiod's source, at all events, the first stage in the formation of a differentiated world was the production of a vast gap between sky and earth. By Hesiod the emphasis is placed on the nature of the gap itself, not on the act of separation which produced it. The gap is conceived as dark and windy—dark, because aither and sun had not yet come into being, and windy, because this is the natural condition of the region (as can be perceived when one is away from shelter, e.g. on a high hillside). The same kind of description is applied, quite naturally, to the lightless gulfs of Tartaros; and in additions to the original poem Tartaros is considered in terms of, or actually as a part of, the original gap.[1]

[1] G. Vlastos (*Gnomon* 27 (1955) 74–5) finds **27** significant for the origin of Hesiod's cosmogonical Χάος, and even suggests that it was from here that Anaximander got the idea of τὸ ἄπειρον. U. Hölscher, too (*Hermes* 81 (1953) 391–401), has completely rejected the Cornford interpretation, and takes Χάος to be a dark and boundless waste. He supports this by the assumption that a cosmogony, attributed to Sanchuniathon (a Phoenician said to have lived before the Trojan war) by Philo of Byblus *ap.* Eusebium *P.E.* I, 10, is really of great antiquity, much older than Hesiod. According to the summary in Eusebius the first state of things was gloomy, boundless air and wind (χάος θολερόν, ἐρεβῶδες is one of its descriptions). When this 'passionately desired its own ἀρχαί' (whatever that may mean) there was intermixture. *Mot* (some kind of slime) was produced, and became the sowing of creation. Now it is true that the discoveries at Ras Shamra and elsewhere have shown (*a*) that some motifs in Greek mythology originated

long before Homer and Hesiod, and outside Greece; (*b*) that Phoenicia had its own versions of myths about the early history of the gods, in the second millennium B.C., and was a meeting-place of cultures. It is also true that in the theogony attributed to Sanchuniathon, after the cosmogonical summary, there is one detail (a deity, Eliun, in the generation before Ouranos) which does not correspond with Hesiod and does correspond with the cognate Hittite account of the 2nd millennium (see pp. 36f.). But this may be a detail of the genuine and ancient local cosmogonical tradition, which could be incorporated at any date: it does not prove that every part of the whole farrago assigned to Sanchuniathon (Hermes Trismegistus and all) has any claim to incorporate ancient material. In particular, it does not even begin to suggest that the cosmogonical account is anything but what it appears to be, i.e. a Hellenistic eclectic pastiche of Hesiod and later cosmogonical sources (there is a possible mention of an egg). To use it as a means of interpreting Χάος in the *Theogony*, and of showing that the idea of an originative windy darkness was already established for Hesiod to assimilate, must be considered interesting rather than scientific.

THE SEPARATION OF EARTH AND SKY IN GREEK LITERATURE

29 Euripides fr. 484 (from *Melanippe the Wise*)

κοὐκ ἐμὸς ὁ μῦθος ἀλλ' ἐμῆς μητρὸς πάρα,
ὡς οὐρανός τε γαῖά τ' ἦν μορφὴ μία·
ἐπεὶ δ' ἐχωρίσθησαν ἀλλήλων δίχα.
τίκτουσι πάντα κἀνέδωκαν εἰς φάος,
δένδρη, πετεινά, θῆρας, οὕς θ' ἅλμη τρέφει,
γένος τε θνητῶν.

30 Diodorus I, 7, I (DK 68 B 5, I) κατὰ γὰρ τὴν ἐξ ἀρχῆς τῶν ὅλων σύστασιν μίαν ἔχειν ἰδέαν οὐρανόν τε καὶ γῆν, μεμειγμένης αὐτῶν τῆς φύσεως· μετὰ δὲ ταῦτα διαστάντων τῶν σωμάτων ἀπ' ἀλλήλων τὸν μὲν κόσμον περιλαβεῖν ἅπασαν τὴν ὁρωμένην ἐν αὐτῷ σύνταξιν...[1]

31 Apollonius Rhodius I, 496

ἤειδεν δ' ὡς γαῖα καὶ οὐρανὸς ἠδὲ θάλασσα
τὸ πρὶν ἐπ' ἀλλήλοισι μιῇ συναρηρότα μορφῇ

---

29 *And the tale is not mine but from my mother, how sky and earth were one form; and when they had been separated apart from each other they bring forth all things, and gave them up into the light: trees, birds, beasts, the creatures nourished by the salt sea, and the race of mortals.*

30 *For by the original composition of the universe sky and earth had one form, their natures being mingled; after this their bodies parted from each other, and the world took on the whole arrangement that we see in it....*

31 *He sang how earth and sky and sea, being formerly connected with each other in one*

νείκεος ἐξ ὀλοοῖο διέκριθεν ἀμφὶς ἕκαστα·
ἠδ' ὡς ἔμπεδον αἰὲν ἐν αἰθέρι τέκμαρ ἔχουσιν
ἄστρα σεληναίη τε καὶ ἠελίοιο κέλευθοι....[2]

[1] The cosmogony and anthropogony in this first book of Diodorus (who, shortly after this passage, quoted **29**) were ascribed by Diels to Democritus. There is no mention of atoms, as Cornford noted; but some details of later stages may nevertheless come from the Μικρὸς διάκοσμος (p. 403 and n.). The development of society is similar to that described by Protagoras in the Platonic dialogue. The whole account is eclectic, but its main features are of fifth-century origin and predominantly Ionian character; as such it may well embody traditional cosmogonical ideas.

[2] Orpheus is the singer. The cosmogony has nothing in common with special 'Orphic' accounts (§5): Apollonius would naturally put into Orpheus' mouth the most primitive-sounding version that he knew.

It has been suggested above that the implied, although not emphasized, first stage of the Hesiodic cosmogony was the separation of sky and earth. That this idea was familiar enough in Greece is shown by **29–31**. Only **29**, admittedly, is even as early as the fifth century; but it is particularly important as explicitly describing the separation of sky and earth as being passed on from mother to child, i.e. as a popular and traditional account. No scientific parallel is known; though the idea may have been merged with specialized Ionian theories as in **30** and its continuation.

SEPARATION IN NON-GREEK SOURCES

The splitting of earth from sky is a cosmogonical mechanism that was widely used, long before the earliest known Greek cosmogonical ideas, in the mythological accounts of the great near-eastern cultures. (It is in fact common to many different cultures: cf., most notably, the Maori myth of the separation of Rangi (sky) and Papa (earth) by their constricted offspring, a close parallel to **32**.) Thus a gloss from the end of the first millennium B.C. on the Egyptian Book of the Dead explains that 'Re began to appear as a king, as one who was before the liftings of Shu had taken place, when he was on the hill which is in Hermopolis' (*ANET* 4). Shu is the air-god which is sputtered out by Re and lifts the sky-goddess, Nut, from the earth-god, Keb. In the Hurrian-Hittite 'Song of Ullikummi' (*ANET* 125; Gurney, *The Hittites*, 190–4) Upelluri,

---

form, through destructive strife separated apart each from the other; and how stars, moon and the sun's paths have forever in the aither a firm boundary....

a counterpart of Atlas, says: 'When heaven and earth were built upon me I knew nothing of it, and when they came and cut heaven and earth asunder with a cleaver I knew nothing of it.' In the Babylonian Creation-epic (IV, 137ff.; *ANET* 67) Marduk splits the body of the primeval water-goddess Tiamat and makes one half of it into sky (containing the celestial waters) and the other half into Apsu, the deep, and Esharra, the 'great abode' or firmament of earth. This is the first stage in the composition of the world as we know it, though a secondary stage in the far older history of the Babylonian pantheon. In another, later Semitic version, Genesis i, the primeval waters are similarly divided: 'And God said, Let there be a firmament in the midst of the waters, and let it divide the waters from the waters. And God made the firmament, and divided the waters which were under the firmament from the waters which were above the firmament; and it was so. And God called the firmament Heaven.' (Gen. i, 6–8.)[1]

[1] The opening words of the first chapter of Genesis, 'In the beginning God created the heaven and the earth. And the earth was without form, and void', are a confusing anticipation of what is to follow. The initial state is boundless, dark water; the first stage of differentiation is the separation of the waters into those of the sky and those of the earth. The anticipation in the initial summary provides a parallel for the reduplication involved in the Hesiodic cosmogony (p. 28).

The separation of sky and earth was implied, therefore, in various non-Greek mythological accounts older than Hesiod. It will be seen in the next section that Hesiod's description of the earliest generations of gods is a version of a basic near-eastern myth, which is also reproduced in an extant Hurrian-Hittite form. There is nothing surprising, therefore, in the separation-motif appearing in Hesiod—whether implicitly in the quasi-rationalistic Χάος γένετ' of the formal cosmogony, or more explicitly, but in fully mythopoeic guise, in the mutilation-story now to be considered.

THE MUTILATION-MYTH IN THE THEOGONY

32 Hesiod *Theogony* 154

ὅσσοι γὰρ Γαίης τε καὶ Οὐρανοῦ ἐξεγένοντο,
δεινότατοι παίδων, σφετέρῳ δ' ἤχθοντο τοκῆι

32 *All that came forth from Gaia and Ouranos, the most dire of children, from the beginning were hated by their own begetter; and just as soon as any of them came into*

ἐξ ἀρχῆς· καὶ τῶν μὲν ὅπως τις πρῶτα γένοιτο
πάντας ἀποκρύπτασκε, καὶ εἰς φάος οὐκ ἀνίεσκε,
Γαίης ἐν κευθμῶνι, κακῷ δ' ἐπετέρπετο ἔργῳ
Οὐρανός· ἡ δ' ἐντὸς στοναχίζετο Γαῖα πελώρη
στεινομένη· δολίην δὲ κακήν τ' ἐφράσσατο τέχνην.
. . . εἷσε δέ μιν (*sc.* Κρόνον) κρύψασα λόχῳ· ἐνέθηκε δὲ χερσὶν
ἅρπην καρχαρόδοντα, δόλον δ' ὑπεθήκατο πάντα.
ἦλθε δὲ Νύκτ' ἐπάγων μέγας Οὐρανός, ἀμφὶ δὲ Γαίῃ
ἱμείρων φιλότητος ἐπέσχετο καί ῥ' ἐτανύσθη
πάντῃ· ὁ δ' ἐκ λοχεοῖο πάις ὠρέξατο χειρὶ
σκαιῇ, δεξιτερῇ δὲ πελώριον ἔλλαβεν ἅρπην
μακρήν, καρχαρόδοντα, φίλου δ' ἀπὸ μήδεα πατρὸς
ἐσσυμένως ἤμησε, πάλιν δ' ἔρριψε φέρεσθαι
ἐξοπίσω. . . .

(The drops of blood fertilize Gaia and generate Furies, Giants and Melian nymphs; the severed parts fall into the sea, and from the foam Aphrodite is born.)

The details of the present version suggest that Ouranos *did* separate from Gaia, in the daytime at least: but why in this case could not Gaia emit her offspring during his absence? It is probable that in other versions of the story Ouranos covered Gaia continuously (as Rangi covers Papa in the Maori myth), so that in a manner of speaking 'sky and earth were one form'. There can be little doubt that this crude sexual account envisages, on another and less sophisticated plane, the same cosmogonical event that is implied first by Χάος γένετ' and second by Γαῖα. . .ἐγείνατο ἶσον ἑαυτῇ Οὐρανόν in the deliberate cosmogony of **24**.[1]

[1] The most obvious parallel for the repetition in mythopoeic form of an event that has already been accounted for in a quasi-rationalistic and much more sophisticated summary is seen in Genesis: the abstract Elohim of the first chapter is replaced by the fully anthropomorphic and much cruder

---

being he hid them all away and did not let them into the light, in the inward places of Gaia; and Ouranos rejoiced over the evil deed. And she, prodigious Gaia, groaned within, for she was crowded out; and she contrived a crafty, evil device. . . she sent him [*Kronos*] *into a hidden place of ambush, placed in his hands a jagged-toothed sickle, and enjoined on him the whole deceit. Great Ouranos came bringing Night with him, and over Gaia, desiring love, he stretched himself, and spread all over her; and he, his son, from his place of ambush stretched out with his left hand, and with his right he grasped the monstrous sickle, long and jagged-toothed, and swiftly sheared off the genitals of his dear father, and flung them behind him to be carried away. . . .*

Jahweh of the second, and the vague 'God created man in his own image' of chapter i is repeated in a far more graphic and more primitive form in the second chapter, where Jahweh creates man out of dust and breathes life into his nostrils. (For man formed from clay cf. e.g. the Old Babylonian text *ANET* 99 col. *b*, as well as the Greek Prometheus-myth.)

That some of the contents of the *Theogony* are of non-Greek origin and of a date far earlier than Hesiod's immediate predecessors is most strikingly shown by the parallelism between the Hesiodic account of the succession of oldest gods and the Hittite Kumarbi-tablet, of Hurrian origin and in its extant form dating from around the middle of the second millennium B.C.[1] In the Hittite version the first king in heaven is Alalu, who is driven out by the sky-god Anu (related to Sumerian AN = 'sky'); Anu is deposed by the father of the developed gods, Kumarbi (equivalent to Kronos 'father of the gods'). As Anu tries to escape into the sky Kumarbi bites off, and swallows, his member. On being told that he has become impregnated with the storm-god and two other 'terrible gods', Kumarbi spits out the member, which impregnates the earth with the two other gods; Kumarbi cannot, however, rid himself of the storm-god, and eventually gives birth to him. With the help of Anu, it is evident, the storm-god (to whom the Greek equivalent is obviously the thunder-and-lightning god Zeus) deposes Kumarbi and becomes king in heaven. The similarities to the Greek myth are obvious: the succession sky-god, father of gods, storm-god is common to each; so is the emasculation of the sky-god by Kumarbi/Kronos, and the impregnation of earth by the rejected member. There are, of course, significant differences too: the Hittite version (like other near-eastern accounts) has a god, Alalu, before the sky-god; what *Kronos* swallows is a stone (by mistake for the storm-god, *Theog.* 468 ff.); and it is Rhea, not he, that bears the storm-god Zeus. It is thought that in the broken part of the Hittite tablet there may have been some reference to Kumarbi eating a stone, but this is uncertain. It should be noted that in Hesiod, also, the sky-god (with Gaia) helps the storm-god to survive. The Hittite version carries no implication that the emasculation of the sky-god was concerned with the separation of sky from earth; indeed, no earth-goddess is involved. This is an important difference, but it suggests, not that the Greek separation-motive had no 2nd-millennium archetype, but that the Greek version incorporates variants which do not happen to be found in the Hittite account. The Greek version was not derived specifically from the Hittite, of course: there was a widely diffused common account, with many local variants, of which the Hittite tablet gives one version and Hesiod another—a version, moreover, which had suffered the vicissitudes of transmission to a younger and very different culture.

[1] For the Kumarbi-tablet see *ANET* 120–1; Gurney, *The Hittites*, 190–2; R. D. Barnett, *JHS* 65 (1945) 100f.; H. G. Güterbock, *Kumarbi* (Zürich 1946), 100ff.; *AJA* 52 (1948) 23ff. The 'Song of Ullikummi' (see pp. 33f.) records, on separate tablets, the further doings of Kumarbi while he is king in heaven; that sky and earth had been separated is plainly implied there.

5. ORPHIC COSMOGONIES

Several variations in cosmogony were ascribed to Ὀρφικοί, 'Orphics'. These might be described as people who, uniting elements from the cult of Apollo on the one hand (as Καθάρσιος, the purifier) and from Thracian reincarnation beliefs on the other, thought that the soul could survive if it were kept pure, and elaborated a partly individual mythology, with Dionysus as a central figure, to illustrate this theory. The Thracian Orpheus, with his sexual purity, his musical powers, and his power of prophecy after death, represented the combination of the two elements. Orphic beliefs were recorded in sacred accounts, ἱεροὶ λόγοι. Now this description would certainly be true, say, of the third century B.C.; but there has been much controversy about how early there appeared a distinct class of people with well-defined and individual beliefs of this kind. W. K. C. Guthrie has a sober discussion of the subject in chapter XI of *The Greeks and their Gods* (London, 1950): his view, which has many supporters, is that the Orphic doctrine was already set out in sacred books in the sixth century B.C. I. M. Linforth, however, in *The Arts of Orpheus* (Berkeley, 1941), analysed all the extant texts mentioning Orpheus and Orphics, and showed that, at any rate until 300 B.C., the description 'Orphic' was applied to all sorts of ideas connected with practically every kind of rite (τελετή). There were writings attributed to Orpheus, as indeed to Musaeus and Epimenides (see pp. 21ff.), as early as the sixth century B.C.; Herodotus knew of Orphics and Pythagoreans sharing a taboo in the fifth; Orphic oracle- and dispensation-mongers were familiar to Plato, and 'so-called Orphic accounts' to Aristotle. But the corpus of individual sectarian literature (of which descriptions of Hades, accounts of theogony and cosmogony, hymns, etc., are known to us) cannot for the most part be traced back earlier than the Hellenistic period, and in its present form mostly belongs to the Roman period. The inscribed metal sheets from graves in Magna Graecia and Crete, with instructions of an Orphic character for the soul of the dead man, again do not much precede Hellenistic times. The conclusion to be drawn from the available evidence seems to the present writer to be, as Linforth held, that there was no exclusively Orphic body of belief in the archaic period. However, Orpheus was then beginning to be treated as the patron saint of rites and ritual ways of life; and his name, like that of his legendary disciple Musaeus, became attached to theogonical literature of this period. Beliefs about reincarnation were becoming current in the Greek world, particularly in the west, and some adherents of these beliefs were calling themselves 'Ορφικοί by the fifth century. The formation of an exclusive sect with a definite body of relevant sacred literature came later.

In the present context, however, it is not necessary to try to establish a hypothesis on the Orphic question in general. The problem is primarily whether the *cosmogonical* ideas ascribed to the Orphics could have affected, or did affect, the development of philosophical thought in the sixth and fifth centuries.

Some elements of Orphic cosmogony were obviously derived from the Hesiodic *Theogony*, which influenced nearly all subsequent mythological thought on the subject. Thus both Chaos and Night will be seen to have had considerable importance in Orphic contexts. These elements passed through the medium of late archaic accounts like those of 'Epimenides', 'Musaeus' and Acusilaus (p. 23 nn. 2–4), and became gradually embedded in an individual Orphic mythological complex. Other elements are almost certainly later in origin, and in some cases show awareness of the details of oriental cult and iconography.[1] (This is a case of a learned adaptation of specific foreign information, not of the quite distinct process of the gradual assimilation of a widely-diffused general idea.) There are many scholars, however (including e.g. Gruppe, Mazon, Nestle), who have nevertheless followed an ancient tendency to regard all beliefs described as 'Orphic', including these cosmogonical beliefs, as of great antiquity. The evidence set out below should demonstrate the subjective nature of any such tendency. The one unusual idea is that of the *egg* as a secondary theogonical mechanism.

1 Most conspicuously, Time, Χρόνος, as a primary cosmogonical figure may derive from the Iranian hypostatization *Zvran Akarana* (unending time). But this Iranian concept finds its earliest testimony in a late 4th-century B.C. Greek reference, by Eudemus as reported in Damascius, and there is no reason to think that it was formulated as early as the Greek archaic period. 'Time' is a sophisticated cosmogonical concept in Plato's *Timaeus*; it was also personified, probably as an etymology of Kronos, by Pherecydes of Syros as early as the sixth century, though probably not with a profound abstract significance (see n. 1 on p. 46 and n. 1 on p. 56). Its oriental derivation in the Orphic accounts is indicated by its concrete shape as a multi-headed winged snake. Such multipartite monsters, as distinct from simpler fantasies like centaurs and perhaps gorgons, are orientalizing in character, mainly Semitic in origin, and begin to appear in Greek art around 700 B.C. They were, of course, extremely popular as decoration during the seventh and the first quarter of the sixth centuries. (Minoan art, too, had had its monsters, mainly dog-headed deities and other relatively simple theriomorphic creations.) That the winged-snake form of Time is much later, in its Greek appearances, than the Orientalizing period in art is chiefly suggested by the identification of an *abstraction* with such a form. This shows an acquaintance with rather complex oriental (especially Assyrian or Babylonian) modes of thought—something very different from the mere borrowing of a pictorial motif, or even the assimilation of a fully concrete myth-form. Such extravagances of the imagination evoked little sympathy in the Greek mind before the Hellenistic period. (It should be added, however, that some scholars see no objection to taking the winged-snake Chronos as archaic in date.)

NEOPLATONIST ACCOUNTS OF ORPHIC COSMOGONIES

The later Neoplatonists (fourth to sixth centuries A.D.), and in particular Damascius, with their long schematic allegorizations of earlier mythological accounts, are the main source for Orphic versions of the formation of the world. These writers are more reliable than appears at first sight, since much of their information was derived from summaries of Eudemus' great Peripatetic history of theology. In some cases fragments of late Orphic poetry can be adduced to confirm details of the Neoplatonic descriptions, which are tiresomely diffuse (and are therefore schematized in (ii) and (iii) below) and are expressed in the peculiar terminology of that school. Four different accounts of a cosmogony specifically named as Orphic are extant.

(i) *Derivation from Night*

Damascius in **19** (q.v.) stated that according to Eudemus 'the theology ascribed to Orpheus...made the origin of things from Night'. According to the Rhapsodies,[1] Night was the daughter of Phanes (see n. 1 on p. 22 and n. 3 on p. 41), himself descended from Chronos. She was given prophetic powers by Phanes, succeeded him as ruler, and seems somehow to have given birth for a second time to Gaia and Ouranos.[2] The secondary and repetitive nature of this production of sky and earth, and the obvious intention to make Phanes the ultimate creator of the world, suggest that Night's cosmogonical priority (as distinct from her undoubted position as a venerable figure among the gods) is here mainly the result of the derivative and syncretistic character of the Orphic theogony. Eudemus' judgement, however, is independent of these later developments, and must clearly be assessed in the light of Aristotle's references (**17**) to writers about the gods who generated from Night. On pp. 20 and 24 it is conjectured that these references are to sixth-century adaptations and elaborations of the Hesiodic *Theogony*, and that no earlier, autonomous doctrine is implied. Two such elaborations are ascribed to Epimenides and Musaeus in **20** and **21**; it was inevitable that similar systems should be associated also with Orpheus, if not in the sixth century B.C., then in the fifth or fourth. It appears probable that it was to this kind of derivative theogony that Eudemus referred.

[1] The so-called Orphic Rhapsodies (ἱεροὶ λόγοι ἐν ῥαψῳδίαις κδ̄ according to the Suda s.v. Ὀρφεύς), of which many fragments survive (Kern, frr. 59–235), mostly through quotation in Neoplatonist works, are a late compilation of hexameter verses of varying date of composition. None of them are certainly pre-Hellenistic and most are probably much later. Their name indicates their heterogeneous origin; it is significant that no author before the full Christian period seems to have heard of these verses, and it seems highly probable that their elaboration into an Orphic *Iliad* was not taken in hand until the third or fourth century A.D. Genuinely archaic beliefs might, of course, be embedded in some of these verses, late as they are in composition and collection.

[2] **33** Orph. Rhaps. fr. 109 Kern (from Hermias) (Νύξ) ἡ δὲ πάλιν Γαῖάν τε καὶ Οὐρανὸν εὐρὺν ἔτικτε / δεῖξέν τ' ἐξ ἀφανῶν φανεροὺς οἵ τ' εἰσὶ γενέθλην. But Phanes had already created Olympus, sun, moon and earth (frr. 89, 96, 91–3, 94 Kern, from the Rhapsodies), and sky is also presupposed.

---

33 *And she [Night], again, bore Gaia and broad Ouranos, and revealed them as manifest, from being unseen, and who they are by birth.*

(ii) '*The usual Orphic theology*' *in the Rhapsodies*

34 Damascius *de principiis* 123 (DK 1 B 12) ἐν μὲν τοίνυν ταῖς φερομέναις ταύταις Ῥαψῳδίαις Ὀρφικαῖς ἡ θεολογία ἥδε τίς ἐστιν ἡ περὶ τὸ νοητόν, ἣν καὶ οἱ φιλόσοφοι διερμηνεύουσιν, ἀντὶ μὲν τῆς μιᾶς τῶν ὅλων ἀρχῆς τὸν Χρόνον τιθέντες... (the full description, for which see DK, is long, and is expressed in difficult Neoplatonic terms. The substance of it is here given schematically:

Χρόνος < Αἰθήρ / Χάος }[1] ⟶ ᾠόν[2] [or ἀργὴς χιτών, or νεφέλη] → Φάνης[3] [~ Μῆτις, Ἠρικεπαῖος])

...τοιαύτη μὲν ἡ συνήθης Ὀρφικὴ θεολογία.

[1] Cf. **35** Orph. Rhaps. fr. 66 Kern (from Proclus) Αἰθέρα μὲν Χρόνος οὗτος ἀγήραος ἀφθιτόμητις / γείνατο, καὶ μέγα χάσμα πελώριον ἔνθα καὶ ἔνθα. Syrianus (fr. 107 Kern) also gave Aither and Chaos as the second stage, but after 'one and the good' as first. The μέγα χάσμα is taken directly from Hesiod *Theogony* 740 (**27**).

[2] Cf. **36** Orph. Rhaps. fr. 70 Kern (from Damascius) ἔπειτα δ' ἔτευξε μέγας Χρόνος αἰθέρι δίῳ / ὠεὸν ἀργύφιον.

[3] Phanes, connected by the Orphics with φαίνειν etc., is an exclusive Orphic development, of a comparatively late date, of the Hesiodic cosmogonical Eros (**24**). Winged, bisexual and self-fertilizing, bright and aitherial, he gives birth to the first generations of gods and is the ultimate creator of the cosmos.

(iii) *The version of Hieronymus and Hellanicus*

37 Damascius *de principiis* 123*bis* (DK 1 B 13) ἡ δὲ κατὰ τὸν Ἱερώνυμον φερομένη καὶ Ἑλλάνικον (*sc.* Ὀρφικὴ θεολογία),[1] εἴπερ μὴ καὶ ὁ αὐτός ἐστι, οὕτως ἔχει· ὕδωρ ἦν, φησίν, ἐξ ἀρχῆς καὶ ὕλη, ἐξ

---

34 *In these Orphic Rhapsodies, then, as they are known, this is the theology concerned with the intelligible; which the philosophers, too, expound, putting Chronos in place of the one origin of all...*

(*Chronos* < *Aither* / *Chaos* } → *egg* [or *shining tunic*, or *cloud*] → *Phanes* [~ *Metis*, *Erikepaios*])

...Such is the usual Orphic theology.

35 *This Chronos, unageing and of imperishable counsel, produced Aither, and a great, mighty gulf here and there.*

36 *Then great Chronos made in divine aither a silvery egg.*

37 *The Orphic Theology which is said to be according to Hieronymus and Hellanicus (if indeed he is not the same man) is as follows: water existed from the beginning, he says, and matter, from which earth was solidified....*

ἧς ἐπάγη ἡ γῆ.... See DK for full description, of which a summary is given here:

ὕδωρ } Χρόνος ἀγήραος ⟶ { Αἰθήρ, Χάος, Ἔρεβος }[2] →ᾠόν → θεὸς ἀσώματος
ὕλη → γῆ } (a winged, multi-headed, bisexual snake: also called Heracles, and accompanied by Ἀνάγκη and Ἀδράστεια) ... θεὸς ἀσώματος (having wings and animal heads)

[1] These authors cannot be identified with certainty. Damascius evidently suspected that they might be the same person, but more probably, for example, one was the epitomizer of the other. Hieronymus may be the author of Phoenician antiquities mentioned at Josephus *Ant.* I, 94; a winged symbol for El-Kronos comes in 'Sanchuniathon', Euseb. *P.E.* I, 10, 36 (see p. 31 n.). Hellanicus may have been the father (2nd–1st cent. B.C.) of one Sandon, probably of Tarsus, an Orphic writer mentioned in the Suda; this is much more likely than that he was the 5th-century B.C. Lesbian logographer.

[2] ἐν τούτοις ὁ Χρόνος ᾠὸν ἐγέννησεν, says Damascius—i.e. in Aither, Chaos and Erebos. It is not explicitly stated that the 'incorporeal god' comes out of the egg, but he obviously does so: compare **38**, and see next note for ἀσώματος.

(iv) *Athenagoras' variant of* (iii)

38 Athenagoras *pro Christianis* 18, p. 20 Schwartz (DK 1 B 13) ...ἦν γὰρ ὕδωρ ἀρχὴ κατ' αὐτὸν (*sc.* Ὀρφέα) τοῖς ὅλοις, ἀπὸ δὲ τοῦ ὕδατος ἰλὺς κατέστη, ἐκ δὲ ἑκατέρων ἐγεννήθη ζῷον, δράκων προσπεφυκυῖαν ἔχων κεφαλὴν λέοντος, διὰ μέσου δὲ αὐτῶν θεοῦ πρόσωπον, ὄνομα Ἡρακλῆς καὶ Χρόνος. (So far this is almost identical with the version of Hieronymus and Hellanicus.) οὗτος ὁ Ἡρακλῆς ἐγέννησεν ὑπερμέγεθες ᾠόν, ὃ συμπληρούμενον ὑπὸ βίας τοῦ γεγεννηκότος ἐκ παρατριβῆς εἰς δύο ἐρράγη. τὸ μὲν οὖν κατὰ

Water } *Unageing Chronos* → { *Aither*, *Chaos*, *Erebos* } → *Egg* → *an incorporeal god*
Matter → *Earth* } (*...with Necessity and Adrasteia*)

38 *...for water was the origin for the totality of things, according to him* [*Orpheus*], *and from water slime was established, and from both of them was generated a living creature, a snake with a lion's head growing on to it, and in the middle of them the face of a god, Heracles and Chronos by name. This Heracles generated a huge egg, which being completely filled by the force of its begetter burst into two through friction. So its top part ended up as*

κορυφὴν αὐτοῦ Οὐρανὸς εἶναι ἐτελέσθη, τὸ δὲ κάτω ἐνεχθὲν Γῆ· προῆλθε δὲ καὶ θεός τις δισώματος.[1] Οὐρανὸς δὲ Γῇ μιχθεὶς γεννᾷ θηλείας μὲν Κλωθὼ Λάχεσιν Ἄτροπον... (a theogony of the Hesiodic type follows).

[1] γη διὰ σώματος ms.; em. Lobeck, accep. Diels, Kranz; τρίτος ἤδη ἀσώματος Th. Gomperz.—In any case Phanes is meant. δισώματος and ἀσώματος are easily confused, and we cannot be certain that instances of the latter in the text of **37** are necessarily correct. δισώματος implies 'bisexual' (which Phanes was): 'incorporeal', of a being described as having more than its quota of bodily attributes, and those of a very peculiar sort, is perhaps odd even in a Neoplatonist.

Of these four types of Orphic-denominated cosmogony, (i) mentions a first stage, Night, that does not occur in the others. Night's importance in the Orphic pantheon probably depended, directly or indirectly, on modifications to the Hesiodic *schema* of cosmogony and theogony. Eudemus may have known Orphic accounts similar to the earlier versions associated with Epimenides and Musaeus. Much later, in one part of the heterogeneous Rhapsodies, Night was given a specific cosmogonical function as a secondary parent of Ouranos and Gaia. This detail may be indirectly developed from archaic cosmogonical motifs, but it cannot be considered strong evidence for an archaic *Orphic* cosmogonical Nyx. (ii) is termed the usual Orphic account presumably because it more or less corresponded with the broad picture given in the late Rhapsodies. (iii) is an elaboration of (ii). It cannot, as it stands, be pre-Hellenistic: its fantastic concrete description of the abstract Chronos is a sign of late origin, or at least of late remodelling. (iv) is quoted by a second-century Christian apologist of Neoplatonic leanings; it gives one significant detail, the splitting of the egg to form sky and earth, which is completely absent from the later Neoplatonic accounts. (iii) and (iv) have a first stage, slime in one form or another, which is no doubt an eclectic philosophical-physical intrusion. It might conceivably be taken directly from Ionian systems like that of Anaximander, but is much more likely to have come from derivative Stoic cosmogony.

Ouranos, and the underneath part as Ge; and a certain double-bodied god also came forth. And Ouranos having mingled with Ge begets, as female offspring, Clotho, Lachesis and Atropos....

THE EGG IN EARLIER GREEK SOURCES, NOT SPECIFICALLY ORPHIC

39 Aristophanes *Birds* 693 (the chorus of birds speak)

Χάος ἦν καὶ Νὺξ Ἔρεβός τε μέλαν πρῶτον καὶ Τάρταρος εὐρύς,
Γῆ δ' οὐδ' Ἀὴρ οὐδ' Οὐρανὸς ἦν· Ἐρέβους δ' ἐν ἀπείροσι κόλποις
τίκτει πρώτιστον ὑπηνέμιον Νὺξ ἡ μελανόπτερος ᾠόν,
ἐξ οὗ περιτελλομέναις ὥραις ἔβλαστεν Ἔρως ὁ ποθεινός,
στίλβων νῶτον πτερύγοιν χρυσαῖν, εἰκὼς ἀνεμώκεσι δίναις. 697
οὗτος δὲ Χάει πτερόεντι μιγεὶς νυχίῳ κατὰ Τάρταρον εὐρὺν
ἐνεόττευσεν γένος ἡμέτερον, καὶ πρῶτον ἀνήγαγεν ἐς φῶς.
πρότερον δ' οὐκ ἦν γένος ἀθανάτων πρὶν Ἔρως ξυνέμειξεν ἅπαντα·
ξυμμιγνυμένων δ' ἑτέρων ἑτέροις γένετ' Οὐρανὸς Ὠκεανός τε
καὶ Γῆ πάντων τε θεῶν μακάρων γένος ἄφθιτον. ὧδε μέν ἐσμεν
πολὺ πρεσβύτατοι πάντων μακάρων.

40 Damascius *de principiis* 124 (DK 3 B 5; from Eudemus) τὸν δὲ Ἐπιμενίδην δύο πρώτας ἀρχὰς ὑποθέσθαι Ἀέρα καὶ Νύκτα... ἐξ ὧν γεννηθῆναι Τάρταρον...ἐξ ὧν δύο Τιτᾶνας[1]...ὧν μιχθέντων ἀλλήλοις ᾠὸν γενέσθαι...ἐξ οὗ πάλιν ἄλλην γενεὰν προελθεῖν.

[1] The manuscript has δύο τινὰς, but Kroll's emendation to δύο Τιτᾶνας (accepted by Kranz in DK) is indicated by the etymology implied in the Neoplatonist parenthesis that follows the disputed word, τὴν νοητὴν μεσότητα οὕτω καλέσαντα, διότι ἐπ' ἄμφω 'διατείνει' τό τε ἄκρον καὶ τὸ πέρας. The other omissions in the text as printed above are Neoplatonic paraphrases which throw no light on the interpretation.

39 was written in 414 B.C. or shortly before. **40** lays claim to a still earlier date, but Philodemus in **20** evidently suspected the authenticity of the attribution of this verse theogony to Epimenides. There was considerable doubt about Epimenides' historical position,

---

39 *First of all was Chaos and Night and black Erebos and wide Tartaros, and neither Ge nor Aer nor Ouranos existed; in the boundless bosoms of Erebos black-winged Night begets, first, a wind-egg, from which in the fulfilment of the seasons ardent Eros burgeoned forth, his back gleaming with golden wings, like as he was to the whirling winds. Eros, mingling with winged, gloomy Chaos in broad Tartaros, hatched out our race and first brought it into the light. There was no race of immortals before Eros mingled all things together; but as one mingled with another Ouranos came into being, and Okeanos and Ge and the unfading race of all the blessed gods. Thus we are by far the oldest of all the blessed ones.*

40 *Epimenides posited two first principles, Air and Night...from which Tartaros was produced...from all of which two Titans were produced...from whose mutual mingling an egg came into being...from which, again, other offspring came forth.*

even in the fourth century B.C.: according to Plato he was active around 500 B.C., but Aristotle and the later tradition put him a century earlier (DK 3A 1–5). His name became a focus for magical and mystical anecdotes, and cosmogonical views might well have been expected of him. The only thing we can say with certainty about the date of **40** is that it is pre-Eudemian; but in view of the proliferation of mythological accounts in hexameters, concerned with genealogy and therefore liable to begin with a theogony, probably towards the end of the sixth century B.C., its content might be tentatively dated between then and the middle of the fifth century (see also nn. 1–3 on pp. 22f.). Thus an egg as an element in cosmogony, which is a typical feature of later Orphic accounts as recorded in the Neoplatonist tradition, is mentioned certainly near the end of the fifth century and probably before that. Were these earlier accounts specifically Orphic in character?

There are no necessarily significant differences in the manner of production of the egg in the earlier and in the later (definitely Orphic) accounts. In the latter, Chronos (in a late and bizarre form) begets the egg in Aither or in Aither-Chaos-Erebos (**36**, **37**). In **39** *Night* produces the egg in Erebos; in **40** it is begotten by two Titans—presumably Kronos (cf. **53**?) and Rhea—who are themselves the product of Air-Night and Tartaros. There is no mention of Chronos, of course, but Pherecydes of Syros (pp. 58f.) had probably already associated Kronos with Chronos, and there may be a connexion here with the later accounts:[1] see also **53** and discussion. There is a distinct similarity between what is produced from the egg in the birds' account and in the later Orphic versions: golden-winged Eros is an obvious prototype of the Orphic Phanes.[2] Yet most of Aristophanes' bird-cosmogony is indubitably derived from the Hesiodic *Theogony*, with appropriate modifications.[3] Chaos, Night, Erebos and Tartaros are involved in the first stages of both accounts; only Earth is postponed in Aristophanes, to be produced (in some ways more logically) simultaneously with Sky. The egg is a 'wind-egg', of course, partly to make it more bird-like, partly because of the traditional windiness of Tartaros (**27**). So Night, Chaos and Eros are all winged, because this is meant to be a birds' cosmogony. It is a parody of a traditional type of cosmogony; yet the original of a parody must be recognizable, and while the Hesiodic elements are clear enough the egg is non-Hesiodic. Eminently suited to bird-generation as it is, the device is unlikely to have been *invented* by Aristophanes for that reason. It must have been familiar as a means for producing, not necessarily a cosmogonical figure, but at least an important deity like Eros. Possibly the birth of Helen from an egg is significant here: connected with a tree-cult perhaps of Mycenean origin (M. Nilsson, *Gesch. d. griech. Religion* I, 211 and 315), she is a ward and representative of Aphrodite-Eros in Homer.

[1] The Kronos-Chronos identification was also made in Orphic circles: cf. e.g. Proclus *in* Plat. *Crat.* 396B (Kern fr. 68). This does not imply that Pherecydes was an Orphic, or took his ideas from early Orphic sources (though the Suda reports, probably on account of these similarities, that he 'collected Orpheus' writings'); rather it implies that the later Orphic eclectics used Pherecydes for source-material just as they used Hesiod and other early mythological writings.

[2] The language of the Rhapsodic account is indeed strongly reminiscent of Aristophanes: compare χρυσείαις πτερύγεσσι φορεύμενος ἔνθα καὶ ἔνθα (*sc.* Φάνης), 'Phanes...borne here and there by golden wings' (fr. 78 Kern), with line 697 of **39**. ἔνθα καὶ ἔνθα in the Orphic verse, as in **35**, recalls Hesiod *Theogony* 742 (**27**), part of the description of windy Tartarus; Hesiod is the chief linguistic and formal model for the Rhapsodies.

[3] So also in **40** the first stage, *Aer* and Night, is evolved from Hesiod: see p. 17. Philodemus in **20** did not mention the egg in Epimenides.

TENTATIVE CONCLUSIONS

The evidence is too sparse to lead to a final decision whether there existed specifically Orphic cosmogonical accounts early enough to have affected Presocratic ideas. Yet it seems probable that distinctively Orphic versions are not particularly early—earlier, say, than the fourth century B.C.; though the name of Orpheus, like that of Musaeus or Epimenides, may have been attached to fifth- or sixth-century theogonies. The ideas inherent in extant reports are eclectic in origin (Hesiod and the developments of Hesiod being the chief source), but in their present formulation are Hellenistic at the earliest. The one conceivably early characteristic is the use of an egg formed in Erebos or Aither, from which comes a deity who arranges the later stages of cosmic evolution. This device occurs in an Aristophanic parody, also in a very vague summary of verses ascribed to Epimenides and perhaps not later than the first half of the fifth century. Yet there is no reason for considering the device specifically Orphic, simply because it occurs in later Orphic accounts which are demonstrably eclectic. Once the metaphor of animal generation had been applied to cosmogony, as it certainly was by the time of Hesiod, the egg became a plausible genetic device. It is surprising, indeed, that we do not hear more of it in early Greek contexts: Nilsson (*Gesch.* I, 648) noted that the cosmic egg is a common feature in naïve mythology in many parts of the world (though it does not, as it happens, occur in near-eastern contexts except occasionally in Egypt and in the later Phoenician accounts). It could nevertheless have existed in Greece from quite early times as a folk-lore concept, which was excluded from many formal accounts because of its naïve quality and finds its only analogue in a tendency to treat the developing world embryonically. 'Epimenides' was attempting, without many natural advantages, to improve on Hesiod, and might well have welcomed the device just because it was not Hesiodic; while Aristophanes found it obviously appropriate for a comic bird-cosmogony. The later Orphism did not shun orientalizing novelties like the description of Time as a winged monster, and would certainly have no inhibitions about the egg-motif. There is a serious possibility that Aristophanes, far from depending on a hypothetical early Orphic tradition, was himself used as a source by the founders of a special Orphic literature.

One reason for doubting an early Orphic use of the egg-motif has been generally overlooked. If there were any such early use, one would expect later applications to be consistent with an earlier tradition, which in a sacred-book sect would be regarded as sacrosanct. Yet three quite different later uses are known. First, the egg simply produces Phanes (**34**, **37**). Secondly, in **38** the upper part of the egg forms the sky, the lower part the earth; the equivalent of Phanes emerges too, and sky and earth then mate as in Hesiod or the popular tradition. The same interpretation is outlined in Apion (early first century A.D.) *ap.* ps.-Clement *Hom.* VI (Kern fr. 56). Here the egg has a true cosmogonical function which can be paralleled from non-Greek myths. Thirdly, according to one extant source the Orphics used the arrangement of shell and skin (and presumably also of white and yolk) as an analogue for the arrangement of sky (outer heaven), aither and so on:

41 Achilles *Isag.* 4 (DK 1 B 12, Kern fr. 70) τὴν δὲ τάξιν ἣν δεδώκαμεν τῷ σφαιρώματι οἱ Ὀρφικοὶ λέγουσι παραπλησίαν εἶναι τῇ ἐν τοῖς ᾠοῖς· ὃν γὰρ ἔχει λόγον τὸ λέπυρον ἐν τῷ ᾠῷ, τοῦτον ἐν

---

41 *The arrangement which we have assigned to the celestial sphere the Orphics say is similar to that in eggs: for the relation which the shell has in the egg, the outer heaven has*

τῷ παντὶ ὁ οὐρανός, καὶ ὡς ἐξήρτηται τοῦ οὐρανοῦ κυκλοτερῶς ὁ αἰθήρ, οὕτως τοῦ λεπύρου ὁ ὑμήν.

This is, admittedly, a simile and not a cosmogonical device; it might be argued, also, that the formation of sky and earth from parts of the egg was just overlooked by the later Neoplatonists. Nevertheless it seems probable that there was considerable divergence in the use of the egg-motif, and that this divergence implies that no specific ancient Orphic tradition had been preserved. However, this special argument is less important than the general ones, from the eclectic nature of organized Orphism, which have already been adduced.

Thus this inevitably complex survey reaches the negative conclusion that there was probably no such thing as *Orphic* cosmogony either before or during the Presocratic period. It has, however, revealed birth from an egg as an archaic theogonical, not cosmogonical, device (one which perhaps played some part in Pherecydes too, see p. 59). The regular Orphic accounts kept this theogonical function; although one probably late variant made the egg truly cosmogonical, as the actual material of the cosmos.

6. PHERECYDES OF SYROS

This Pherecydes was a mythographer and theogonist, and must be distinguished from the fifth-century Athenian genealogist of the same name, also from a later and less important Lerian.[1] According to Aristotle he was not entirely mythological in his approach:

42 Aristotle *Met.* N4, 1091b8 ...ἐπεὶ οἵ γε μεμειγμένοι αὐτῶν (*sc.* τῶν θεολόγων) [καὶ] τῷ μὴ μυθικῶς ἅπαντα λέγειν, οἷον Φερεκύδης καὶ ἕτεροί τινες, τὸ γεννῆσαν πρῶτον ἄριστον τιθέασι, καὶ οἱ Μάγοι.

[1] F. Jacoby, *Mnemosyne* 13 (3rd series), 1947, 13ff., has finally discredited Wilamowitz's theory that 'Pherecydes' was a generic name attached to all early Ionian prose writing not specifically ascribed, as 'Hippocrates' became attached to all medical literature. The man of Syros and the Athenian were indeed carefully distinguished in many ancient sources, though not in all.

---

in the universe, and as the aither depends in a circle from the outer heaven, so does the membrane from the shell.

42 *...since the* '*mixed*' *theologians, those who do not say everything in mythical form, such as Pherecydes and certain of the others, and also the Magi, make the first generator the* best *thing.*

DATE

Pherecydes was active in the sixth century B.C., perhaps around the middle of it. Ancient authorities diverge: according to one tradition he was roughly contemporary with the Lydian king Alyattes (*c.* 605–560 B.C.) and the Seven Sages (conventionally dated around Thales' eclipse, 585/4, or the archonship of Damasias, 582/1); according to another, dependent on Apollodorus, his *acme* was in the 59th Olympiad, 544–541 B.C., and he was a contemporary of Cyrus.[1] The Apollodoran dating thus makes him a generation younger than Thales and a younger contemporary of Anaximander. It fits in with the later Pythagorean tradition which made Pythagoras bury Pherecydes (p. 51), though this event was itself probably fictitious. None of these chronological traditions looks particularly historical, and we know that such synchronisms were assigned by the Hellenistic chronographers largely on *a priori* grounds. Yet interest in Pherecydes was certainly alive in the fourth century B.C. (a crucial era for the transmission of information about the archaic period), and the broad limits of dating, i.e. in the sixth century, are unlikely to be wrong.

[1] The early dating is seen e.g. in the Suda (DK 7 A 2) and in Diog. L. I, 42 (DK 9 A 1, after Hermippus). The later dating appears e.g. in Diog. L. I, 118 (after Aristoxenus) and I, 121 (after Apollodorus)—see DK 7 A 1; also in Cicero *Tusc.* I, 16, 38 (DK 7 A 5), Pliny *N.H.* VII, 205, Eusebius *Chron.* (DK 7 A 1 *a*).

PHERECYDES' BOOK

43 Diogenes Laertius I, 119 σῴζεται δὲ τοῦ Συρίου τό τε βιβλίον ὃ συνέγραψεν οὗ ἡ ἀρχή· Ζὰς μὲν καὶ Χρόνος ἦσαν ἀεὶ καὶ Χθονίη... (for continuation see **50**).

44 Suda s.v. Pherecydes ἔστι δὲ ἅπαντα ἃ συνέγραψε ταῦτα· Ἑπτάμυχος ἤτοι Θεοκρασία ἢ Θεογονία. (ἔστι δὲ Θεολογία ἐν βιβλίοις ῑ ἔχουσα θεῶν γένεσιν καὶ διαδοχάς.)

45 Diogenes Laertius I, 116 τοῦτόν φησι Θεόπομπος πρῶτον περὶ φύσεως καὶ θεῶν γράψαι. Cf. Suda s.v. Pherecydes πρῶτον δὲ συγγραφὴν ἐξενεγκεῖν πεζῷ λόγῳ τινὲς ἱστοροῦσιν.

---

43 *There is preserved of the man of Syros the book which he wrote of which the beginning is: 'Zas and Chronos always existed and Chthonie...'.*

44 *Everything he wrote is as follows: Seven Recesses or Divine Mingling or Theogony. (And there is a Theology in ten books containing the birth and successions of the gods.)*

45 *This man is said by Theopompus to have been the first to write on nature and the gods.—Some relate that he was the first to bring out a book in prose.*

According to **43** Pherecydes' book (or what was taken for it) survived in Diogenes' time, the third century A.D. The opening words might be known well enough from the entry in Callimachus' catalogue of the Alexandrian library (the patronymic, omitted here, was given shortly before as Βάβυος, 'son of Babys'). That the book survived the burning of the Library in 47 B.C. may be confirmed by a longer quotation, **54**; though this and other fragments could have survived through the medium of handbooks or anthologies. The title is given in **44**. 'Επτάμυχος, '(of) seven recesses', seems to be the book's true title;[1] variants descriptive of the contents are added, as often, but are probably of later origin. The 'ten-volume theology' is probably a confusion with a ten-volume work on Attic history (itself beginning, no doubt, from gods and heroes) ascribed to the Athenian Pherecydes in the lines that follow in the Suda. The precise reference of the cryptic and unusual title '(of) seven recesses' is very obscure: see p. 58. **45** exemplifies the widespread tradition that this was the earliest prose book. What Theopompus (fourth century B.C.) must actually have said is that Pherecydes first wrote about the gods *in prose*, as opposed to e.g. Hesiod. Prose annals were presumably recorded before Pherecydes, but he and Anaximander (whose book may have been roughly contemporary, and might possibly be assigned to 547/6 B.C., p. 101) might well have been the first substantial prose writers to have survived; on the confusion over Thales as a writer see pp. 85 f.

[1] Some incline to accept '*five* recesses', from **51**, as the title, with Diels followed by Jaeger and others, on the sole strength of Damascius' statement there that the divine products of Chronos' seed, when disposed in five recesses, were called πεντέμυχος. Even if this is intended to give the title of the book, the five recesses mentioned just before provide a clear motive for writing five and not seven.

HIS LIFE AND LEGEND

(i) *The connexion with Pythagoras*

Many miracles were attributed to Pherecydes, e.g. predictions of an earthquake, a shipwreck, the capture of Messene. These were variously located: in Sparta, near Ephesus, in Samos, in Syros, and so on. The difficulty is that the same miracles were also attributed to Pythagoras. Apollonius the paradoxographer, not certainly using Aristotle, said that 'Pythagoras afterwards indulged in the miracle-working, τερατοποιΐα, of Pherecydes' (**259**); and it was certainly accepted in the Peripatetic circle that when Pherecydes fell ill of louse-disease in Delos his disciple Pythagoras came and cared for him until his death (Diog. L. I, 118, Diodorus x, 3, 4; DK 7A1 and 4). So Aristoxenus asserted, and Dicaearchus too according to Porphyry *Vit. Pythag.* 56. Porphyry also related (as quoted by Eusebius, DK 7A6) that according to the fourth-century B.C. writer Andron of Ephesus the miracles belonged properly to Pythagoras; but that Theopompus plagiarized the miracle-stories from Andron and, to disguise his theft, assigned them instead to Pherecydes and slightly altered the localities involved. Andron was far from critical, however, since he invented another Pherecydes of Syros, an astronomer (Diog. L. I, 119, DK 7A1); and Porphyry's explanation of the divergence is unconvincing. The confusion and disagreement which patently existed in the fourth century show that reliable details of the life of Pherecydes were lacking. If Pherecydes had been a sage of the type naturally to attract miracle-stories (as Pythagoras was), the connexion between two similar contemporaries would have been invented whether it existed or not; but apart from the feats otherwise attributed to Pythagoras, Pherecydes seems to have had little of the shaman or magician about him. It has been suggested that the whole tissue of legend might have arisen from a well-known fifth-century B.C. comment:

46 Ion of Chios *ap.* Diogenem Laertium I, 120 Ἴων δ' ὁ Χῖός φησι περὶ αὐτοῦ (*sc.* Φερεκύδου)·

(Fr. 4) ὣς ὁ μὲν ἠνορέῃ τε κεκασμένος ἠδὲ καὶ αἰδοῖ
καὶ φθίμενος ψυχῇ τερπνὸν ἔχει βίοτον,
εἴπερ Πυθαγόρης ἐτύμως ὁ σοφὸς περὶ πάντων
ἀνθρώπων γνώμας εἶδε καὶ ἐξέμαθεν.

As H. Gomperz maintained (*Wiener St.* 47 (1929) 14 n. 3), this probably means no more than 'If Pythagoras is right about the survival of the soul, then Pherecydes' soul should be enjoying a blessed existence'. It might have been misinterpreted, even in antiquity, to imply a friendship between the two men, and have encouraged the transference to Pherecydes of stories about Pythagoras.

---

46 *Ion of Chios says about him* [*Pherecydes*]: '*Thus did he excel in manhood and honour, and now that he is dead he has a delightful existence for his soul—if indeed Pythagoras the wise learned and knew true opinions above all men.*'

Elaborate biographical accounts were invented on the slightest pretext, especially in the third and second centuries B.C. (see e.g. p. 183); even so one hesitates to suppose that the fourth-century controversy can have been founded on evidence so slight as Ion's little encomium. Yet none of the evidence on this point looks at all convincing, and it is as well to preserve a certain scepticism about the relationship between the two men.

(ii) *Alleged access to Phoenician secret books*

47 Suda s.v. Pherecydes διδαχθῆναι δὲ ὑπ' αὐτοῦ Πυθαγόραν λόγος, αὐτὸν δὲ οὐκ ἐσχηκέναι καθηγητήν, ἀλλ' ἑαυτὸν ἀσκῆσαι κτησάμενον τὰ Φοινίκων ἀπόκρυφα βιβλία. (See also **61**.)

The assertion that Pherecydes was self-taught probably means no more than that no teacher could conveniently be supplied for him when his complete biography came to be written. That he used Phoenician secret books (an unlikely story indeed) is another piece of speculation of the type beloved by the biographical compilators. Yet it must have had some foundation, and may be based on apparently oriental motifs in his thought: he was later connected with Zoroastrianism (n. 2 on p. 65), and the battle of Kronos and Ophioneus, like that of Zeus and Typhoeus in Hesiod, had some Phoenician affinities (p. 68).

(iii) *The solstice-marker*

48 Diogenes Laertius I, 119 σῴζεται δὲ τοῦ Συρίου τό τε βιβλίον...(cf. **50**)...σῴζεται δὲ καὶ ἡλιοτρόπιον ἐν Σύρῳ τῇ νήσῳ.

49 Homer *Od.* 15, 403–4, with scholia

νῆσός τις Συρίη κικλήσκεται, εἴ που ἀκούεις,
Ὀρτυγίης καθύπερθεν, ὅθι τροπαὶ ἠελίοιο.

ὅθι τροπαὶ ἠελίοιο] ἔνθα φασὶν εἶναι ἡλίου σπήλαιον, δι' οὗ σημαιοῦνται τὰς τοῦ ἡλίου τροπάς (QV). οἷον ὡς πρὸς τὰς τροπὰς

---

47 *There is a story that Pythagoras was taught by him; but that he himself had no instructor, but trained himself after obtaining the secret books of the Phoenicians.*

48 *There is preserved of the man of Syros the book*...[cf. **50**]...*and there is preserved also a solstice-marker in the island of Syros.*

49 '*There is an island called Syrie—perhaps you have heard of it—above Ortygie, where are the turnings of the sun.*'

Where are the turnings of the sun] *They say there is a cave of the sun there, through which they mark the sun's turnings (QV). As it were toward the turnings of the*

ἡλίου, ὅ ἐστιν ἐπὶ τὰ δυτικὰ μέρη ὑπεράνωθεν τῆς Δήλου (BHQ).— οὕτως Ἀρίσταρχος καὶ Ἡρωδιανός (H).

The implication in **48** that a solstice-marker preserved in Syros in Diogenes' time had belonged to, or been used by, Pherecydes must be approached with caution. (A solstice-marker is a device to mark the point at which the sun 'turns' on the ecliptic, at midsummer or midwinter.) There seems to be some connexion with a cryptic couplet in Homer, **49**. The scholia show that two alternative interpretations of this couplet were known in Alexandria: either (*a*) ὅθι τροπαὶ ἠελίοιο describes Syrie (rather than Ortygie), and means that there was there a bearing-marker in the form of a cave; or (*b*) the meaning is that Syrie lies 'above', i.e. north of, Ortygie, and also west of it, where the sun 'turns' in the sense of setting.[1] Both (*a*) and (*b*) improbably assume that Ortygie represents Delos, and Sȳrie Sȳros (which lies some twenty miles slightly north of west from Delos).[2] Now whatever the intended meaning of the Homeric phrase,[3] there evidently was a sun-cave reported from Syros in the Alexandrian period, and this is presumably the form of marker that Diogenes referred to three or four centuries later. We hear of another type of natural solstice-marker from Itanos in Crete in the fourth century B.C., and such things must have been relatively common for calendar purposes. The sun-cave in Syros cannot, it seems, have been the original motive of the Homeric reference, but it was nevertheless seized upon at a later date (and certainly, one would think, later than Pherecydes) in an attempt to explain the description in the *Odyssey*. Whatever its antecedents, it would as a matter of course have become associated with the island's most notable inhabitant, Pherecydes. Although there is no other evidence that he was a practical scientist, many other sixth-century sages, especially the Milesians, were known to have had applied as well as theoretical interests; and it would be almost inevitable for an Alexandrian scholar, for instance, automatically to provide a historical association between the only two apparently scientific products of Syros—Pherecydes and the solstice-marker. Reluctant as one is, therefore, to disconnect such a pleasing device from such an intriguing man, extreme scepticism again seems desirable.

---

sun, which is in the westward direction, above Delos (BHQ).—So Aristarchus and Herodian (H).

[1] This sense of τροπαί is absolutely unparalleled and highly improbable, especially since τροπαὶ ἠελίοιο are mentioned three times in the Hesiodic *Works and Days*, always meaning solstice. But (*a*), as well as (*b*), is virtually impossible: for even though τροπαὶ ἠελίοιο can, and indeed does, mean 'solstice' or 'solstices', it cannot conceivably in any kind of Greek mean a device (whether a cave or anything else) for *marking* or *observing* solstices.

[2] There were other actual Ortygias as well as Delos (to which the name is only applied in contexts which could have been affected by learned speculation on **49**): notably the island forming part of Syracuse, and a precinct near Ephesus. 'Ορτυγίη means 'of the quail' (ὄρτυξ), and might be applied to any locality at which quails habitually rested in their migrations between Egypt and the north. A difficulty in identifying Ortygie with Delos is that the two places are distinguished in the Homeric Hymn to Apollo (16); but the passage is suspect on other grounds. A far more serious difficulty, and one that has been widely ignored, is that of identifying Συρίη, with a short upsilon, with Σῦρος, which has a long upsilon. The connexion of Syrie with Syracuse is also philologically improbable. Miss H. L. Lorimer (*Homer and the Monuments* 80ff.) argued for Συρίη referring to Sy̆ria (which, she maintained, might have been naïvely taken for an island), and for τροπαί meaning 'sunrise', i.e. the east. But it seems impossible that Syria should be termed an island; and the Phoenicians would hardly have been conceived as spending a whole year trading with a place so near their own country (cf. *Od.* 15, 455).

[3] ὅθι τροπαὶ ἠελίοιο could describe either Syrie or Ortygie. Here an observation of Miss Lorimer's is of great importance: the only other place in Homer where Ortygie is mentioned is *Od.* 5, 123, where Orion, having been carried off by Eos, is slain in Ortygie by Artemis. The implication is that Ortygie was the dwelling-place of Eos, the dawn, and therefore that it lies in the east. Miss Lorimer thought that solstices could not carry a directional meaning. But, since solstices would normally be observed at sunrise (by the bearing method), 'where the summer solstice is' would signify the general direction in which the sun rises at the summer solstice, namely north-east by east; while 'where the winter solstice is' would signify south-east by east. The summer solstice is the important one for record purposes, and the mention of the solstice, by itself, might naturally bring to mind the north-east by east direction. Thus the intention of the Homeric phrase is to indicate the general direction of this probably mythical Ortygie. It is worth adding that the dwelling-place of Eos was often conceived as being *Aia*, and that Aia was commonly identified with Colchis; and Colchis does in fact lie roughly north-east by east from the centre of the Ionian coastline.

THE CONTENTS OF PHERECYDES' BOOK

(i) *The primeval deities; initial creation by Chronos; the recesses*

50 Diogenes Laertius I, 119 σῴζεται δὲ τοῦ Συρίου τό τε βιβλίον ὃ συνέγραψεν οὗ ἡ ἀρχή· (Fr. 1) Ζὰς μὲν καὶ Χρόνος ἦσαν

---

50 *There is preserved of the man of Syros the book which he wrote of which the begin-*

ἀεὶ καὶ Χθονίη· Χθονίῃ δὲ ὄνομα ἐγένετο Γῆ, ἐπειδὴ αὐτῇ Ζὰς γῆν γέρας διδοῖ.

51 Damascius *de principiis* 124 *bis* Φερεκύδης δὲ ὁ Σύριος Ζάντα μὲν εἶναι ἀεὶ καὶ Χρόνον καὶ Χθονίαν τὰς τρεῖς πρώτας ἀρχάς...τὸν δὲ Χρόνον ποιῆσαι ἐκ τοῦ γόνου ἑαυτοῦ πῦρ καὶ πνεῦμα καὶ ὕδωρ... ἐξ ὧν ἐν πέντε μυχοῖς διῃρημένων πολλὴν ἄλλην γενεὰν συστῆναι θεῶν, τὴν πεντέμυχον καλουμένην, ταὐτὸν δὲ ἴσως εἰπεῖν πεντέκοσμον.

52 Porphyrius *de antro nymph.* 31 ...τοῦ Συρίου Φερεκύδου μυχοὺς καὶ βόθρους καὶ ἄντρα καὶ θύρας καὶ πύλας λέγοντος καὶ διὰ τούτων αἰνιττομένου τὰς τῶν ψυχῶν γενέσεις καὶ ἀπογενέσεις.

Zas and Chronos and Chthonie 'always existed': this resolves the difficulty of creation *ex nihilo.* An analogous declaration is seen, some two generations later, in Heraclitus' world-order, which no god or man made, but always was, and is, and shall be (**220**); also in Epicharmus fr. 1 (DK23 B 1—probably genuine), where the case is explicitly argued. But already in the sixth century B.C. the divinity assigned to Anaximander's ἄπειρον and Anaximenes' air probably implies that these, too, had always existed. It is surprising to find this concept stated so explicitly, and in a theogonical context, at this relatively early date. Yet the gods who always existed are probably conceived as original forms (by etymology) of conventional figures from the traditional theogony; and one of them is 'Time', which might naturally be felt, without any deep abstract reflexion, to have been unborn. Thus Pherecydes was not trying to solve a logical difficulty about creation so much as to substitute a new first stage, dependent on etymology and particularly on a new understanding of Kronos the father of the gods, for the imprecise, if more rationalistic, '*Chaos* came into being' of Hesiod.

The names are unusual. Ζάς (accusative Ζάντα) is obviously an etymological form of Ζεύς, and is perhaps intended to stress the

---

ning is: 'Zas and Chronos always existed and Chthonie; and Chthonie got the name of Ge, since Zas gave her Ge as a present [or *prerogative*].'

51 *Pherecydes of Syros said that Zas always existed, and Chronos and Chthonie, as the three first principles...and Chronos made out of his own seed fire and wind* [or *breath*] *and water...from which, when they were disposed in five recesses, were composed numerous other offspring of gods, what is called 'of the five recesses', which is perhaps the same as saying 'of five worlds'.*

52 *...when Pherecydes, the man of Syros, talks of recesses and pits and caves and doors and gates, and through these speaks in riddles of the becomings and deceases of souls.*

element ζα- (an intensive prefix), as in ζάθεος, ζαής; though there is some possibility that the form Zas is intended to link the sky-god Zeus with the earth-goddess Ge, whose Cyprian form is ζᾶ. Χθονίη, from χθών, is presumably intended to represent Earth in a primitive role, perhaps as the abode of chthonic daimons, and at all events with stress on the *underparts* of the earth. As for Χρόνος, it has been argued, notably by Wilamowitz, that the true reading must be Κρόνος: Kronos played an important part in Pherecydes' theogony according to one extant fragment, **58**, and 'Time' is a surprisingly sophisticated cosmogonical concept for the sixth century B.C. But Χρόνος, which is widely supported in the sources, is almost certainly correct; the other two figures are etymologizing variants of well-known theogonical figures, and we naturally anticipate a similar case with the third figure. The substitution of Χρόνος for Κρόνος is just what we should expect here.[1] It appears likely that by the later stages of the theogony the primeval trio assumed their familiar form as Zeus, Kronos and Hera.[2] That Pherecydes was addicted to etymologies emerges clearly from our scanty evidence: thus, in addition to the idiosyncratic derivations of names already discussed, Χάος was perhaps connected by him (as later by the Stoics) with χέεσθαι (p. 59 n.), and so interpreted as water; Rhea was called Ῥῆ (DK 7 B 9), and perhaps connected with ῥεῖν etc.; Okeanos was called Ogenos (**54**); the gods called a table θυωρός, 'watcher over offerings' (DK 7 B 12).

[1] Wilamowitz roundly declared that 'Time', as a cosmogonical god in the sixth century, was impossible. Certainly the abstraction implied in the χρόνου δίκη (Solon, see **113**), or τὴν τοῦ χρόνου τάξιν (Anaximander, see **112**), is less startling in its implications, as are the Χρόνος ὁ πάντων πατήρ of Pindar *Ol.* 2, 17 and the hypostatized Time of tragedy; though the two last instances provide some parallel. The Iranian cosmogonical Time, *Zvran Akarana*, was introduced as a refinement of Mazdaism and cannot be assumed earlier than the fourth century B.C. (n. on p. 39), though the possibility of oriental influence in this respect cannot be entirely discounted. The Chronos of the late Orphic cosmogonies was presented in a Hellenistic shape, and cannot be taken as any kind of parallel or precedent for the sixth century B.C. The connexion of Kronos with Chronos was certainly made by later Orphics (cf. e.g. Kern *Orph. Frag.* fr. 68), but according to Plutarch (*Is. Osir.* 32) this was a common Greek identification: we cannot say whether or not Pherecydes was the originator. That he did intend to relate them is stated by Hermias and Probus (DK 7 A 9), probably after Stoic sources. In any event one should not exaggerate (as Wilamowitz did) the depth of abstraction, and of metaphysical content, implied by the

presence of Chronos in **50**. Pherecydes probably took the Kronos of legend, asked himself what the etymology was, and arrived at the obvious answer, Chronos or Time—a familiar and simple concept which is plainly somehow involved in cosmogony.

[2] Chthonie gets the name of Ge, Earth, at a subsequent stage, presumably when Zas presents her with the cloth embroidered with earth in **54**. But at that point she apparently takes over the control and guardianship of marriages; this was Hera's prerogative (as Γαμηλία) according to the general view, and in so far as Chthonie-Ge is the wife of Zas-Zeus she is also thought of as becoming Hera. (Demeter, who is much closer to Ge, was in charge of certain female activities, as Θεσμοφόρος, but not of marriage; she may, however, provide a connecting link.) Hera was probably not an earth-goddess in origin, but there are other isolated cases where she replaces Gaia; for example, she appears to be the mother of Typhaon in the Homeric Hymn to Apollo, 351 f., also in Stesichorus (*Et. Magn.* 772. 50); cf. **53**, and Virgil *Aen.* IV, 166.

Damascius in **51** is following Eudemus. Chronos makes fire, wind and water out of his own seed,[1] and this is implied to take place at an early stage. The episode cannot be invented, though it would not be surprising if some details of it were distorted. One is reminded of Egyptian cosmogonical accounts in which the first world-constituents are produced by the onanism of a primeval god, notably that of Atum-Re mentioned in the Memphis theology (*ANET* 5); and also of the mutilation of Ouranos *by Kronos* in **32**, where certain mythological figures are begotten by Ouranos' member and the blood from it. The idea that the human seed is creative, and therefore that a primary deity's seed is cosmogonically creative, is neither surprising nor illogical. What is surprising here, however, is the things which are thus created: they smack of fifth-century four-element theory, earth being omitted because already accounted for in the very name of Chthonie-Ge. πνεῦμα looks suspiciously anachronistic, even though Anaximenes emphasized its importance at roughly this period (pp. 149 ff.). These substances cannot have formed the raw material of later cosmic arrangement: for according to **51** what they produce is not a world but deities of some kind. In fact, I would suggest that the seed producing fire, wind (πνεῦμα) and water is probably a later rationalizing interpretation, perhaps Stoic in origin but based on the Aristotelian concept (itself to some extent indebted to Diogenes of Apollonia, cf. **619** *fin.*) that the human σπέρμα, seed, contains σύμφυτον πνεῦμα, innate breath, which is also described as being 'hot' and aitherial (cf. e.g. *Generation of animals* B 3, 736 b 33 ff.). In accounts of early Stoic physiology, too, the seed is described as πνεῦμα μεθ' ὑγροῦ ('breath with moisture', Arius Didymus on Zeno) and is associated with πνεῦμα ἔνθερμον, 'warm breath'. It therefore seems probable that the three unexpected products of Chronos' seed—fire, wind and water—are an intrusive later interpretation of the nature of the seed itself, and that originally it was Chronos' semen itself that was placed in the recesses. As for these, the seven in the title as given in the Suda might be obtained by adding to the five recesses connected with Chronos in **51** the two other pre-existing deities Zas and Chthonie, the latter of which, certainly, had a local and indeed a recess-like connotation. Alternatively, all seven recesses could have been part of Chthonie: it is notable that the Babylonian world of the dead was conceived as having seven regions,[2] and in the myth of the Descent of Ishtar, Ishtar has to pass through seven gates (*ANET* 107f.); one thinks (though perhaps not significantly) of the doors and gates that Porphyry found in Pherecydes (**52**).

[1] Or possibly, if Kern's αὑτοῦ for ms. ἑαυτοῦ is right, out of Zas's. But there is no essential conflict with **42**, where τὸ γεννῆσαν πρῶτον must be Zas-Zeus: for it is Zas who first creates the parts of the world (**54**), while Chronos produces theogonical, not cosmogonical, constituents.

[2] In the first eleven chapters of the Hippocratic treatise Περὶ ἑβδομάδων the world is divided into seven parts to correspond with the seven parts of the human body. Some scholars date this fragmentary and unattractive work in the sixth century B.C. There seem to be no strong grounds for such an early date, and stylistically a late Hellenistic origin is far more probable.

A possible clue to the production by Chronos from his own seed appears in the following neglected passage:

53 Σ B *in* Homeri *Il.* 2, 783 Τυφωέος] φασὶ τὴν Γῆν ἀγανακτοῦσαν ἐπὶ τῷ φόνῳ τῶν Γιγάντων διαβαλεῖν Δία τῇ Ἥρᾳ· τὴν δὲ πρὸς Κρόνον ἀπελθοῦσαν ἐξειπεῖν· τὸν δὲ δοῦναι αὐτῇ δύο ᾠά, τῷ ἰδίῳ χρίσαντα θορῷ καὶ κελεύσαντα κατὰ γῆς ἀποθέσθαι, ἀφ' ὧν ἀναδοθήσεται δαίμων ὁ ἀποστήσων Δία τῆς ἀρχῆς. ἡ δέ, ὡς εἶχεν ὀργῆς, ἔθετο αὐτὰ ὑπὸ τὸ Ἄριμον τῆς Κιλικίας. ἀναδοθέντος δὲ τοῦ Τυφῶνος Ἥρα διαλλαγεῖσα Διὶ τὸ πᾶν ἐκφαίνει· ὁ δὲ κεραυνώσας Αἴτνην τὸ ὄρος ὠνόμασεν.

---

53 *They say that Ge in annoyance at the slaughter of the Giants slandered Zeus to Hera, and that Hera went off and told Kronos about this. He gave her two eggs, smearing them with his own semen, and telling her to store them underground: from them, he said, a daimon would be produced who would displace Zeus from power. And she in her anger put them under Arimon in Cilicia. But when Typhon had been produced, Hera had become reconciled to Zeus, and revealed everything; and Zeus blasted Typhon and named the mountain Aetna.*

This has to be used with caution: it may originate from the Pergamene editors of Homer (the first-hand scholia of B are anti-Aristarchean) and be based upon a genuinely ancient version, but it is in part eclectic, adding a Homeric element (Arimon) to those seen in 5th-century poetry (Pi. *P.* 1, 16 ff., Aesch. *Pr.* 351 ff.). It could therefore be distorted in places by later Orphic developments (cf. **34**, **37**); although it is evidently not directly dependent on the *Rhapsodies*, since the eggs are placed not in the windy wastes of Aither or Erebos (an essential element of the Rhapsodic account) but in Gaia. That Kronos not Chronos appears is not necessarily important (see p. 56). The notable thing is that Kronos impregnates two eggs (why two?) *with his own seed*, and that the eggs have to be placed *underground*, κατὰ γῆς, possibly in a recess of some kind—here, under a mountain. From the eggs, when fertilized by the seed, comes Typhon/Typhoeus, an analogue of Pherecydes' Ophioneus (pp. 66 ff.). There does seem to be a striking parallel with the cryptic mention of Chronos' seed in **51**; if so, it provides some confirmation of the speculation that some kind of theogonical figure or figures ('numerous other divine offspring') came directly from Chronos' seed.[1] It makes a faint possibility, too, that generation from an egg (but not of cosmological constituents) occurred in Pherecydes (see pp. 44–8)—though this device became so popular in Hellenistic and later accounts that it might well have been imposed on a simpler story.

[1] Porphyry (cf. DK 7 B 7) mentioned people who took what he called τὴν ἐκροήν, in Pherecydes, to refer to semen; though they applied the same interpretation to Hesiod's Styx and Plato's Ameles. H. Gomperz (*Wiener St.* 47 (1929), 19 n. 10) suggested that Chronos produced a generation of primeval deities from the ἐκροή, just as his later form Kronos did from Rhea; this would in fact fit in with the suggestion made above, that fire, wind and water are an intrusive gloss. The connexion of Rhea, called Ῥῆ by Pherecydes (DK 7 B 9), with ἐκροή seems quite possible. A further but more remote possibility is that Chronos' semen became primeval water. We are told in one source (Achilles *Isag.* 3, DK 7 B 1 *a*) that Pherecydes, like Thales, declared the element to be water, which he called χάος (presumably deriving it from χέεσθαι, if the whole thing is not Stoic accommodation). The Suda, too, says that 'he imitated the opinion of Thales' (DK 7 A 2); though Sextus, on the other hand, said that his principle was earth (DK 7 A 10). Great penetration is not to be sought in these interpretations; but it does seem probable that Pherecydes understood Hesiod's Chaos in a special sense, perhaps because of a specious etymology. The surviving fragments show that there was no question of water coming first; but the special interpretation of Chaos may have been connected with Chronos' seed at a relatively early stage of cosmic development.

The names listed by Porphyry in **52**—doors and gates as well as recesses, pits and caves—again suggest that something more elaborate than mere depressions in the earth was in question; though this may be just mythological decoration. Porphyry's interpretation, that these things were connected with the soul, is purely Neoplatonic and comes in a treatise in which every detail of the Cave of the Nymphs in the *Odyssey* is made to yield a similar psychic meaning. There is no good evidence for attributing any special interest in the soul to Pherecydes.[1]

[1] Cicero's remark at *Tusc.* I, 16, 38 (DK7A5), that Pherecydes was the first to call human souls eternal, is probably caused by the attribution of Pythagoras' ideas to his putative master; cf. the Suda, DK7A2. A similar statement occurs in Aponius (DK7A5); the addition that Pherecydes 'unum nobis de coelo spiritum, alterum credidit terrenis seminibus comparatum' seems to mean merely that the soul is aitherial, the body terrestrial, and not (as H. Gomperz and others have imagined) that Pherecydes postulated a double *spiritus*. That the soul is connected with aither is a view he might conceivably have held: see p. 200 and note.

(ii) *The wedding of Zas and Chthonie, and the embroidery of the cloth*

54 Grenfell and Hunt *Greek Papyri* Ser. II, no. 11, p. 23 (3rd cent. A.D.) (DK7B2) αὐ⟩τῷ ποιοῦσιν τὰ οἰκία πολλά τε καὶ μεγάλα. ἐπεὶ δὲ ταῦτα ἐξετέλεσαν πάντα καὶ χρήματα καὶ θεράποντας καὶ θεραπαίνας καὶ τἆλλα ὅσα δεῖ πάντα, ἐπεὶ δὴ πάντα ἑτοῖμα γίγνεται τὸν γάμον ποιεῦσιν. κἀπειδὴ τρίτη ἡμέρη γίγνεται τῷ γάμῳ, τότε Ζὰς ποιεῖ φᾶρος μέγα τε καὶ καλὸν καὶ ἐν αὐτῷ ⟨ποικίλλει Γῆν⟩ καὶ Ὠγη⟨νὸν καὶ τὰ Ὠ⟩γηνοῦ ⟨δώματα *** [col. 2] βουλόμενος⟩ γὰρ σέο τοὺς γάμους εἶναι τούτῳ σε τι⟨μῶ⟩. σὺ δέ μοι χαῖρε καὶ σύνισθι. ταῦτά φασιν ἀνακαλυπτήρια πρῶτον γενέσθαι· ἐκ τούτου δὲ ὁ νόμος ἐγένετο καὶ θεοῖσι καὶ ἀνθ⟨ρώποι⟩σιν. ἡ δέ μι⟨ν ἀμείβε⟩ται δεξαμ⟨ένη εὖ τὸ⟩ φᾶ⟨ρος . . .[1]

[1] The attribution to Pherecydes, and the supplements of ⟨ποικίλλει . . .⟩ to ⟨δώματα⟩, are confirmed by Clement of Alexandria *Strom.* VI, 9, 4, Φ. ὁ Σύριος λέγει· Ζὰς ποιεῖ φᾶρος . . . Ὠγηνοῦ δώματα. Other supplements by Blass, Weil, Diels; text as in DK, except for alterations to the slightly erroneous record there of gaps in the papyrus.

---

54 *His halls they make for him, many and vast. And when they had accomplished all these, and the furniture and manservants and maidservants and everything else necessary, when everything was ready, they hold the wedding. And on the third day of the wedding Zas makes a great and fair cloth and on it he decorates Ge and Ogenos and the halls of Ogenos *** 'for wishing* [or some such word] *marriages to be yours, I honour you with this. Hail to you, and be my consort.' And this they say was the first Anacalypteria: from this the custom arose both for gods and for men. And she replies, receiving from him the cloth ***.*

The marriage is between Zas and Chthonie, as is confirmed by **57**. Zas' declaration 'desiring [or some such word] marriages to belong to you' suggests strongly that Chthonie is here partially equated with Hera, the goddess of marriage (n. 2 on p. 57). The preparations are of a fairy-tale quality, and are carried out by unspecified agents. On the third day of the wedding festivities[1] Zas makes a great cloth, decorating it with Ge (earth) and Ōgēnos (evidently Pherecydes' name for Okeanos).[2] He presents it to Chthonie: the gift of this representation of Ge seems to be what was referred to in **50**, where Chthonie took the name Ge 'since Zas gave her earth as a gift [*or* prerogative]'. With the cloth he also gives her Ogenos, which may be regarded as a part of the earth's surface in the broad sense but is not a prerogative of Chthonie in the way that Ge is. Chthonie initially represents the solid substructure of earth rather than its variegated surface, Ge and Ogenos. Now the main question is whether the weaving or embroidering of earth and Okeanos is an allegory of an actual creation-act. It seems probable that it is; otherwise, what is the point of Zas undertaking this odd and unmasculine task—one very different, it may be noted, from Hephaestus' decoration of the shield of Achilles in *Iliad* book 18? Not simply to symbolize the gift of Ge, and as a mythological precedent for the Anacalypteria, the Unveiling of the bride; there is this aetiological element in the story, as is explicitly stated, but the gift need not have been of this bizarre kind if it had no more significance than that of an Unveiling-gift.[3] A more positive indication is provided in the following passage:

55 Proclus *in Tim.*, II, p. 54 Diehl ὁ Φερεκύδης ἔλεγεν εἰς Ἔρωτα μεταβεβλῆσθαι τὸν Δία μέλλοντα δημιουργεῖν, ὅτι δὴ τὸν κόσμον ἐκ τῶν ἐναντίων συνιστὰς εἰς ὁμολογίαν καὶ φιλίαν ἤγαγε καὶ ταυτότητα πᾶσιν ἐνέσπειρε καὶ ἕνωσιν τὴν δι' ὅλων διήκουσαν.

The whole of this from ὅτι δή onwards is palpably Stoic interpretation, with a slight Neoplatonic colouring, and tells us nothing about Pherecydes. The first statement, however, that Zeus turned into Eros when about to create, must be based on something in Pherecydes. It suggests first that Zas did undertake some kind of cosmogonical creation, and secondly that he did so as Eros, or at

---

55 *Pherecydes used to say that Zeus had changed into Eros when about to create, for the reason that, having composed the world from the opposites, he led it into agreement and peace and sowed sameness in all things, and unity that interpenetrates the universe.*

least in some erotic situation. This need mean no more than the liaisons and births of the *Theogony*; but that some particular description was envisaged is shown also by **57**, in which a specific Eros exists between Zas and Chthonie.[4] This tells us clearly that Zas' creation is concerned with an erotic situation between himself and Chthonie: the wedding itself may, therefore, be meant, and since we hear nothing of any offspring of cosmogonical relevance, while the depiction of earth and Okeanos (whether surrounding river, or sea in general) is the prelude to the consummation of the marriage and could well represent a cosmogonical act, we may provisionally accept that such is the case.

[1] The wedding ceremonies took three days in all, the final unveiling accompanied by gifts, and the consummation, taking place on the third: so Hesychius s.v., who put the ἀνακαλυπτήρια on the third day, though all other ancient authorities (none of them early) imply that the whole ceremony took only one day.

[2] Ogēnos (Ogĕnos in Lycophron and Stephanus of Byzantium) is an odd variant of Ὠκεανός, and is conceivably related to Akkadian *uginna* = circle. Pherecydes' use of it is another indication of his preference for archaizing or etymological forms.

[3] A πέπλος was given to Harmonia by Cadmus at their wedding (Apollodorus III, 4, 2), but we are not told that it was decorated in any particular way, and Cadmus did not make it. Nor does there seem to be more than an adventitious connexion with the ἱερὸς γάμος at Plataea (cf. Farnell, *Cults*, I, 244), in which a statue carved from an oak-tree was dressed as a bride to represent Hera.

[4] Cf. the golden-winged Eros who is imagined as groomsman at the wedding of Zeus and Hera in the hymeneal song in Aristophanes, *Birds* 1737 ff.

(iii) *The winged oak and the cloth*

56 Isidorus (the Gnostic, 1st–2nd cent. A.D.) *ap.* Clement. Al. *Strom.* VI, 53, 5 (DK 7B2) ...ἵνα μάθωσι τί ἐστιν ἡ ὑπόπτερος δρῦς καὶ τὸ ἐπ' αὐτῇ πεποικιλμένον φᾶρος, πάντα ὅσα Φερεκύδης ἀλληγορήσας ἐθεολόγησεν, λαβὼν ἀπὸ τῆς τοῦ Χὰμ προφητείας τὴν ὑπόθεσιν.

57 Maximus Tyrius IV, 4 p. 45, 5 Hobein ἀλλὰ καὶ τοῦ Συρίου τὴν ποίησιν σκόπει καὶ τὸν Ζῆνα καὶ τὴν Χθονίην καὶ τὸν ἐν τούτοις Ἔρωτα, καὶ τὴν Ὀφιονέως γένεσιν καὶ τὴν θεῶν μάχην καὶ τὸ δένδρον καὶ τὸν πέπλον.

---

56 *...that they may learn what is the winged oak and the decorated cloth upon it, all that Pherecydes said in allegory about the gods, taking his idea from the prophecy of Ham.*

57 *But consider also the work of the man of Syros, and Zas and Chthonie and the Eros between them, and the birth of Ophioneus and the battle of gods and the tree and the robe.*

We learn in **56** that the embroidered cloth (i.e. that given by Zas to Chthonie in **54**) was somehow on a winged oak: this must be what 'the tree and the robe' refer to in **57**. One modern suggestion (by H. Gomperz, *Wiener St.* 47 (1929) 22) is that the oak represents the frame of the loom on which Zas made the cloth. This involves taking ὑπόπτερος to mean simply 'swift', with total suppression of the concrete wing-image; there is no parallel for such a use with a concrete subject. More serious, a loom could hardly be called an *oak-tree*, simply, even in a fantastic context. According to another interpretation (Diels, *SB Ber.* 1897, 147f.) the oak resembles the mast on which Athene's *peplos* was carried in the Panathenaic procession. It is true that **57** uses the word πέπλον, and 'winged' might be explained as describing the cross-piece on which the robe was hung; but there is really no reason whatever for thinking of the Panathenaia, and to refer to the mast as an oak would be distinctly odd.[1] Both Diels and K. von Fritz (author of the article on Pherecydes in Pauly-Wissowa) believed that an allegorical version of *Anaximander* is also in question: the earth is shaped like a tree-trunk because it is cylindrical as in Anaximander (see **124**); it is described as a tree because Anaximander said that a sphere of flame fitted round air and earth like the bark round a tree (**123**); the earth is winged because it floats free in space (**125**); the embroidering of its surface is reminiscent of Anaximander's map (pp. 103f.); and the treatment of Okeanos as an integral part of the earth's surface is a new development found also in Anaximander. But none of these arguments is valid, let alone cogent: the shape of the earth cannot be represented by the shape of the trunk alone, which is not the only or even the most conspicuous part of an oak-tree; Anaximander's bark round a tree is a *simile*; 'winged', if it is to be given an abstract connotation at all, should mean 'swift-moving' and not 'floating'; Anaximander's map had no known connexion with his cosmology; and the tendency to integrate Okeanos with the inner seas is occasionally detectable even in Homer. Other alleged borrowings from Anaximander (Time, and γόνος ~ γόνιμον) are no more convincingly in favour of an interpretation which von Fritz had the temerity to call 'practically certain'. Further, there is little probability that a scientific account should, in the archaic period, receive a nearly contemporary allegorization.

[1] Diels, followed by e.g. Jaeger, Mondolfo and von Fritz, was groundlessly impressed by the whole context (DK 7 B 5) of **60** below, where Origen reports that Celsus interpreted certain rites and mythological incidents as symbolizing the subjection of matter by god. Two passages in Homer, then Pherecydes' description of Tartaros (**60**), and finally the Panathenaic *peplos* are so interpreted; the last is said to show 'that a motherless and immaculate deity prevails over the boastful Earthborn'. Here the robe represents Athene, the cart (later ship) in which the pole supporting it was carried represents the Earthborn: such ancient speculations about this particular ritual were rather common. The interpretation is quoted as a separate instance, parallel of course to the Pherecydes extract because adduced as another illustration of the same thesis; but there is nothing to suggest that Pherecydes should be interpreted in terms of the Panathenaia.

The following interpretation is proposed as more probable than any of those described above. The oak represents the solidly fixed substructure and foundations of the earth (the 'frame' of the earth, Zeller suggested). Its trunk and branches are the support and roots of the earth. That the earth has roots is part of the popular world-picture (pp. 10f.), and a tree's branches, in winter, appear as large inverted roots. That the roots of earth *and* sea were sometimes conceived as being above Tartarus, and that Tartarus itself could be imagined as a narrower pit beneath, is clearly shown by the important description at *Theogony* 726ff., already quoted as **2**: 'Around Tartarus a brazen fence is drawn; and all about it Night in three rows is poured, around the throat; and above are the roots of earth and unharvested sea.' The throat or neck that is Tartarus (or a part of it) corresponds with the trunk of the oak-tree, the roots which are above it correspond with the branches.[1] The oak is 'winged' partly, at least, because of the spreading, wing-like appearance of these same branches. On them Zas has laid the cloth embroidered with Earth and Ogenos: these represent the earth's surface, flat or slightly convex, as indeed it appears to be. We cannot say whether Ogenos is conceived as a surrounding river or as the sea. The oak is specified because it is associated more than any other tree with Zeus (cf. the prophetic oaks in his shrine at Dodona, *Od.* 14, 328), and because of its notable strength and the great spread of its branches. Thus according to the interpretation offered here Zas must have chosen, or magically grown, a broad oak as the foundation of the earth; or (following a suggestion by T. B. L. Webster) he summoned an oak from afar which magically flies to him, using its branches as wings. Zas then weaves a cloth, decorating it with earth and

Okeanos, and lays the decorated cloth on the outspread branches of the oak to form the earth's surface.[2]

[1] **60** mentions Tartaros below the earth, which suggests that Pherecydes broadly accepted the popular world-picture, not the rationalized construction of Anaximander. The kind of world-tree postulated above must be distinguished from e.g. the Scandinavian world-tree *Yggdrasil*, whose branches form *the heavens*, not the support for the earth's surface; though the roots of the tree are regarded as supporting the earth.

[2] A clue to the meaning of the winged oak and the cloth is apparently given by Isidorus' comment in **56** that Pherecydes 'took the supposition from the prophecy of Ham'. Unfortunately, little can be determined about this work. Harnack suggested that Ham in this context is a name for Zoroaster (Bidez and Cumont, *Les Mages Hellénisés* II, 62 n.); this identification was occasionally made, cf. *op. cit.* I, 43; II, 49–50. Zoroaster was well established as a sage by the early Hellenistic period, and Aristoxenus had stated that Pythagoras visited Zoroaster in Babylon (**294**). Of the vast mass of pseudo-Zoroastrian literature produced in the Hellenistic epoch, there was a work *On Nature* in four books, and special accounts of the magical properties of stones and plants, as well as descriptions of Hades. The book on nature seems to have contained nothing of cosmogonical interest, but, like the rest, to have dealt with astrology, minerals and so on. A second wave of Zoroastrian literature was produced in the first two centuries A.D. by various Gnostic sects—in the Clementine apocrypha, by the Sethians, by the disciples of Prodicus. More of genuine Zoroastrianism (dualism of good and evil, importance of fire) was to be found in these works than in the earlier group. It is a question to which group Isidorus was referring; though the facts that Isidorus' father Basilides inclined to Iranian dualism, and that the Ham-Zoroaster identification is probably first found in a Gnostic source, suggest that it was the later one. On the other hand Isidorus is less likely to have been taken in by a product of his own age. But in neither group can we detect anything which might have been regarded as a significant precedent for the winged oak or the embroidered cloth; we cannot even assume that Isidorus was struck by the oriental character of Pherecydes' allegory, since much of the Greek Zoroastrian literature was not oriental in origin or colouring. One cannot be certain that Pherecydes' allegory had not itself been absorbed into some pseudo-Zoroastrian source, and so misled Isidorus.

(iv) *The fight between Kronos and Ophioneus*

58 Celsus *ap.* Origen. *c. Celsum* VI, 42 (DK 7 B 4) Φερεκύδην δὲ πολλῷ ἀρχαιότερον γενόμενον Ἡρακλείτου μυθοποιεῖν στρατείαν στρατείᾳ παραταττομένην καὶ τῆς μὲν ἡγεμόνα Κρόνον ⟨ἀπο⟩διδόναι, τῆς ἑτέρας δ' Ὀφιονέα, προκλήσεις τε καὶ ἁμίλλας αὐτῶν ἱστορεῖν,

58 *Pherecydes, who lived much earlier than Heraclitus, related the myth that army was drawn up against army, and he gave Kronos as leader of one, Ophioneus of the other, and*

συνθήκας τε αὐτοῖς γίγνεσθαι ἵν' ὁπότεροι αὐτῶν εἰς τὸν 'Ωγηνὸν ἐμπέσωσι, τούτους μὲν εἶναι νενικημένους, τοὺς δ' ἐξώσαντας καὶ νικήσαντας, τούτους ἔχειν τὸν οὐρανόν.

59 Apollonius Rhodius I, 503 (following **31**)
('Ορφεύς) ἤειδεν δ' ὡς πρῶτον 'Οφίων Εὐρυνόμη τε
'Ωκεανὶς νιφόεντος ἔχον κράτος Οὐλύμποιο·
ὥς τε βίῃ καὶ χερσὶν ὁ μὲν Κρόνῳ εἴκαθε τιμῆς,
ἡ δὲ 'Ρέῃ, ἔπεσον δ' ἐνὶ κύμασιν 'Ωκεανοῖο·
οἱ δὲ τέως μακάρεσσι θεοῖς Τιτῆσιν ἄνασσον,
ὄφρα Ζεὺς ἔτι κοῦρος ἔτι φρεσὶ νήπια εἰδὼς
Δικταῖον ναίεσκεν ὑπὸ σπέος....

60 Celsus *ap.* Origen. *c. Celsum* VI, 42 (DK 7B5) ταῦτα δὲ τὰ 'Ομήρου ἔπη οὕτω νοηθέντα τὸν Φερεκύδην φησὶν (*sc.* Κέλσος) εἰρηκέναι τὸ (Fr. 5) Κείνης δὲ τῆς μοίρας ἔνερθέν ἐστιν ἡ Ταρταρίη μοῖρα· φυλάσσουσι δ' αὐτὴν θυγατέρες Βορέου "Αρπυιαί τε καὶ Θύελλα· ἔνθα Ζεὺς ἐκβάλλει θεῶν ὅταν τις ἐξυβρίσῃ.

Pherecydes evidently described in some detail an encounter between Kronos (probably derived from the primeval deity Chronos: see p. 56) and Ophioneus, the preliminaries of which appear in **58**. This must form part, at least, of 'the battle of gods' in Maximus' summary (**57**). Ophioneus is obviously connected with ὄφις, snake, and is a snake-like monster of the type of Typhoeus in the Hesiodic *Theogony* (line 825, Typhoeus had a hundred snake-heads). The battle with Kronos is otherwise known from rare Hellenistic references, of which the description in **59** is the most important. There, Ophion (as he is there called) has a consort, the Oceanid Eurynome, while Kronos is helped by Rhea. There are enough divergences to suggest that Apollonius is not merely copying Pherecydes,[1] and it seems that there was an old

---

recounted their challenges and struggles, and that they made an agreement that whichever of them fell into Ogenos, these were the vanquished, while those who thrust them out and were victorious were to possess the sky.

59 *He* [*Orpheus*] *sang how first of all Ophion and Eurynome, daughter of Okeanos, held sway over snowy Olympus; and how by strength of hands the former yielded his lordship to Kronos, the latter to Rhea, and they fell in the waves of Okeanos; and the other two meantime held sway over the blessed gods, the Titans, while Zeus, still a boy and still having childish thoughts in his heart, dwelt by the Dictaean cave....*

60 (*Celsus*) *says that with this interpretation of these Homeric lines in mind Pherecydes has said: 'Below that portion is the portion of Tartaros; the daughters of Boreas, the Harpies, and Storm, guard it; there Zeus expels whosoever of the gods behaves insolently.'*

story, not mentioned in Hesiod, which formed part of the manifold lost mythology of Kronos and related his encounter with a monster. In Pherecydes the victor is to have possession of the sky (and so become, or remain, supreme god); according to Apollonius in **59** (supported by a scholion on *Clouds* 247) Ophion and Eurynome had already ruled on Olympus and were trying to repel a challenge. There may be a reference here to the concept of Okeanos and Tethys as the first gods (**9**, **10**): Eurynome was a daughter of Okeanos,[2] and with Ophion may represent a second generation replacing, somehow, that of Ouranos and Gaia. Yet in Pherecydes there is nothing to suggest that Ophioneus had ever ruled the sky; Maximus in **57** mentions 'the birth of Ophioneus and the battle of gods', which may suggest that Ophioneus was, like Typhoeus in Hesiod, an unsuccessful challenger for power; and Tertullian (*de corona* 7, DK 7 B 4) asserted that according to Pherecydes Kronos was the first king of the gods. Further, Pherecydes cannot have accepted the usual view, seen in Apollonius, that Zeus was a child in Crete during part of the reign of Kronos. The primeval Zas probably turned into Zeus (*Zeus* not *Zas* occurs in **60**; though this could be due to carelessness in the transmission), just as Chronos probably turned into Kronos, and this would scarcely be by the medium of a birth. In Pherecydes, as in the common version, Kronos-Chronos must have eventually been deposed by Zas, to be despatched below the earth (as in Homer, *Il.* 14, 203f., and Hesiod). Unfortunately **60**, which locates the 'portion' of Tartaros below, presumably, that of Gaia (rather than of Hades in the sense of *Il.* 8, 16), does not mention Kronos; it seems to come from a description of the assignment of parts of the cosmos to different deities, which followed Zeus' final subjection of his adversaries in Homer and Hesiod also.

[1] Nor need we believe that Apollonius was reproducing an ancient Orphic account. There is a great deal in this cosmogony and theogony as sung by Orpheus in the *Argonautica* that is not Orphic (see also **31** and n. 2 on p. 33).

[2] Also at *Il.* 18, 398ff.; *Theog.* 358. At *Theog.* 295ff. another Oceanid, Callirhoe, produced the snake-woman Echidna, who mated with Typhaon.

The battle of Kronos against Ophion has obvious correspondences with that of Zeus against Typhoeus in the *Theogony*. The whole Typhoeus episode seems to have been interpolated into the Hesiodic poem; but this cannot have been long after the original composition, and is likely in any case to have been earlier than the date of Pherecydes. The cosmic fight with a snake-god is not, of course, exclusive to Greece, but is found all over the Near East long before Hesiod, in both Semitic and Indo-European contexts. Compare the fight of Marduk with the serpent-aided Tiamat in the Babylonian creation-myth (*ANET* 62 ff.); the victory of the storm-god over the dragon Illuyanka in the Hurrian-Hittite story of that name (*ANET* 125f.; Gurney, *The Hittites*, 181 ff.); and the nightly overcoming of the dragon Apophis by the Egyptian sun-god Re in his journey under the earth (*ANET* 6–7). The battle between Zeus and Typhoeus-Typhon (who was equated with the Egyptian Seth) was in later accounts, though not in Hesiod, located in Cilicia, especially on Mount Casius near the proto-Phoenician Minoan *entrepôt* of Ras-Shamra/Ugarit. It clearly coincided with a local version of the sky-god and snake-monster motif, and this correspondence may have been the chief motive for the assertion that Pherecydes borrowed from the Phoenicians:

61 Philo Byblius *ap.* Eusebium *P.E.* 1, 10, 50 παρὰ Φοινίκων δὲ καὶ Φερεκύδης λαβὼν τὰς ἀφορμὰς ἐθεολόγησε περὶ τοῦ παρ' αὐτῷ λεγομένου 'Οφιονέως θεοῦ καὶ τῶν 'Οφιονιδῶν.[1]

The earlier parallel of the Hesiodic Typhoeus makes it unnecessary to suppose that Pherecydes was borrowing directly from an oriental source, and one may wonder whether the reference in the Suda (**47**) to his access to Phoenician secret books was based on anything more than the Ophioneus-Typhon comparison.

[1] It is a question whether the 'Οφιονίδαι are literally 'the children of Ophioneus', or simply his army or supporters, cf. **58**. If the former, one may compare the monsters born to Typhaon by Echidna at *Theogony* 306 ff. —though these are not involved in the Typhoeus episode.

THE ORDER OF EVENTS IN PHERECYDES' BOOK

The extant evidence, reviewed in the preceding pages, presents us with a number of phases described by Pherecydes: (*a*) the three pre-existing deities; (*b*) the making by Chronos out of his own seed of things disposed in five recesses, which produce other generations of gods; (*c*) the making of the cloth by Zas, the depiction on it of Earth and Ogenos, the wedding of Zas and Chthonie, and the

---

61 *From the Phoenicians Pherecydes, too, took his impulse, when he wrote about him whom he called the god Ophioneus, and the children of Ophioneus.*

presentation of the cloth, followed (?) by the spreading of it over the winged oak; (*d*) the battle between Kronos and Ophioneus; (*e*) the assignment of portions to different deities, perhaps implied in **60**.

Several incidents must have taken place about which we possess no information: for example, Chronos-Kronos was presumably supplanted by Zas-Zeus, as in the common account, but Pherecydes' views here are unknown. Another problem is the birth of Ophioneus mentioned in Maximus' summary, **57**: who were the parents? It seems unlikely that Zas and Chthonie were (although all mythological weddings have offspring, and we do not know the offspring of this particular one), since it must be assumed that the battle of Kronos and Ophioneus, the reward of which is possession of the sky, takes place either during or as a prelude to the rule of Chronos-Kronos, which seems to have preceded the wedding of Zas and Chthonie and the assumed creation of earth and Okeanos. But a difficulty arises here. In the fight between Ophioneus and Kronos the loser is to be he who falls into Ogenos; but according to the creation-allegory interpretation Ogenos is made at the wedding of Zas and Chthonie, which should therefore precede and not follow the Ophioneus-fight. This difficulty applies to all reconstructions that make the weaving of the cloth a creation-allegory: for Chronos' mastery of the sky is suggested by all the other evidence (especially **51** and the analogy of the Homeric-Hesiodic account) to have preceded the period of Zas' activity. Either, therefore, Pherecydes was inconsistent in presupposing Ogenos before it had been formally created; or Ogenos existed *before* it was woven into or embroidered on the cloth; or Ogenos is not an original element in Celsus' account of the Kronos-Ophioneus fight. The last of these hypotheses is not impossible. A somewhat different version of this encounter is known from the Hellenistic period, and is best seen in **59**. There Ophion and his bride Eurynome, the daughter of Okeanos, ruled the sky, but were forcibly displaced by Kronos and Rhea and *fell into the waves of Okeanos*. Falling into Okeanos makes sense for an *Oceanid* and her consort; but in Pherecydes there seems to be no place for a female consort of any kind, let alone an Oceanid. It is possible, therefore, that Celsus or his source transferred into the Pherecydes version a detail from a rather different Hellenistic version, and adapted it to the known Pherecydean terminology.

Yet if Zas and Chthonie cannot *jointly* have produced Ophioneus after their wedding, it remains true that the earth-goddess Chthonie-Ge is the obvious parent for a snake (whose home is traditionally in the earth), just as Gaia is normally the mother of the snakeish Typhoeus. A liaison between Zas and Chthonie *before* their marriage (as suggested by *Il.* 14, 296) would fit the order of **57**: the passion of Zas and Chthonie, the birth of Ophioneus, the battle of gods, the tree and the robe (and, therefore, the marriage). But there is no strong reason for assuming that Maximus set down these themes in the exact order in which they occurred in Pherecydes' book; and the dramatic force of the description of the wedding, which has obvious literary pretensions, would undoubtedly be weakened if Zas and Chthonie had been living together for ages beforehand. It seems more probable that if Ophioneus was the child of Chthonie the father, if any, was other than Zas. Here Chronos springs to mind. His seed was placed in 'recesses', presumably in the earth, according to **51**; and there was a story, known only from **53** and not connected there with Pherecydes, that Kronos impregnated two eggs with his seed, gave the eggs to Hera to place underground, and so produced the snakish Typhoeus, to whom Ophioneus is similar. If this is the case, Chronos with Chthonie would produce Ophioneus and, perhaps, other monsters; Ophioneus would attack Chronos (already perhaps called Kronos) and be defeated; Zas in his turn would attack and overthrow Kronos, and would marry Chthonie, now to be called Ge and in some ways to become equivalent to Hera; in so doing he would create earth and sea as we know them (the existence of sky being somehow presupposed, perhaps implicit in Zas himself). How Zas subjected Kronos we do not know; it might be thought that Ophioneus was acting as his agent, but in view of **59** it *must* be assumed that Ophioneus was defeated and that Kronos was deposed by some other means. In this case the order of events might be: three pre-existing deities; Chronos rules the sky, plants his seed in Chthonie; birth of Ophioneus (with other chthonic creatures); Ophioneus challenges Kronos, but fails; Kronos somehow subjected by Zas; marriage of Zas and Chthonie-Ge-Hera, and creation of our world; apportionment of spheres, Zeus' enemies in Tartaros. But it must be emphasized that most of this is very speculative indeed.[1]

[1] Plato probably had Pherecydes in mind in **62** *Sophist* 242 C–D μῦθόν τινα ἕκαστος φαίνεταί μοι διηγεῖσθαι παισὶν ὡς οὖσιν ἡμῖν, ὁ μὲν ὡς τρία τὰ ὄντα, πολεμεῖ δὲ ἀλλήλοις ἐνίοτε αὐτῶν ἄττα πῃ, τοτὲ δὲ καὶ φίλα γιγνόμενα γάμους τε καὶ τόκους καὶ τροφὰς τῶν ἐκγόνων παρέχεται.... We cannot assume, however, that all the incidents mentioned here are consciously derived from Pherecydes.

CONCLUSION

In spite of all uncertainties, Pherecydes is clearly a notable figure in the history of Greek cosmogonical speculation. As Aristotle implied (**42**), he combines the mythological approach with a more objective one. The assertion that three deities always existed implies a rational amendment to the traditional genealogical pattern; yet the method of creation pursued by Chronos is as crudely anthropomorphic as anything in Hesiod. The details of the allegory of the decorated cloth, if correctly interpreted, are part of the stock of pure myth; at the same time the allegory itself, which is of the highest interest both for its originality and for its beauty, shows that Pherecydes accepted the naïve but not unempirical view of the structure of the world which was outlined in §1. His interest in etymology, and consequent handling of the first gods, is the first clear manifestation of a way of thinking conspicuous in Aeschylus and Heraclitus, and it evidently still impressed the Orphic eclectics of three and more centuries later. Pherecydes was an individualist both in his handling of the traditional stories of the gods and in his use of uncommon motifs. There is practically no indication of special near-eastern influence, except conceivably in the seven recesses. There is, however, one respect in which his narrative is closer to oriental accounts than to Greek ones. It is evident that in his book many incidents concerning the three pre-existing deities were related before the cosmogony proper (that is, the formation of earth and Ogenos) was reached. This may be compared with the Babylonian creation-myth, for example, where the splitting of Tiamat to form sky and earth comes only at the end of a long saga of the gods; and con-

---

62 *Each seems to me to tell us a kind of story, as though we were children, one saying that existing things are three, and that certain of them in some way fight with each other at times, and at times they become good friends and provide marriages and births and nurturings of their offspring....*

trasted with the Hesiodic *Theogony*, where the cosmic constituents are produced almost immediately, and as the *prelude* to the history of the gods. But this may be simply because Hesiod, and not Pherecydes and the Babylonian cosmogony, is quasi-rationalistic.

By no stretch of the imagination could the views of Pherecydes, or any of those described earlier in this chapter, be termed philosophical. They were, however, sometimes directed towards an explanation of the world as a whole, especially of how it came to be what it is; and they reveal on occasion a method not essentially different from that of Thales and the first Ionian philosophers, who are treated in the immediately following chapters. What gave these the title of philosopher was their abandonment of mythopoeic forms of thought, of personification and anthropomorphic theistic explanations, and their attempt to explain the seen world in terms of its seen constituents.

THE IONIAN THINKERS

It was in Ionia that the first completely rationalistic attempts to describe the nature of the world took place. There, material prosperity and special opportunities for contact with other cultures—with Sardis, for example, by land, and with the Pontus and Egypt by sea—were allied, for a time at least, with a strong cultural and literary tradition dating from the age of Homer. Within the space of a century Miletus produced Thales, Anaximander, and Anaximenes, each dominated by the assumption of a single primary material, the isolation of which was the most important step in any systematic account of reality. This attitude was clearly a development of the genetic or genealogical approach to nature exemplified by the Hesiodic *Theogony* and described in Chapter I. After the great Milesians, however, the attitude was moderated or abandoned. Xenophanes is here treated among the Ionians (chapter V), but in fact he does not fit into any general category. Born and brought up in Colophon, and strongly aware of Ionian ideas (more so, apparently, than Pythagoras), he moved to western Greece and was only incidentally interested in the details of cosmogony and cosmology. In Ephesus, meanwhile, the individualistic Heraclitus outstepped the limits of material monism, and, while retaining the idea of a basic (though not a cosmogonic) substance, discovered the most significant unity of things—a unity which he, too, assumed without question—in their structure or arrangement. Here there is a parallel with Pythagorean theories in the west of the Greek world. Pythagoreanism produced the reaction of Parmenides, and for a time the western schools were all-important; but the Ionian materialistic monism re-asserted itself, to a certain extent, in the compromises of some of the post-Parmenidean systems.

CHAPTER II

THALES OF MILETUS

DATE

Traditionally the earliest Greek physicist, or enquirer into the nature of things as a whole (**87**), Thales predicted an eclipse which took place in 585 B.C. (**76**). He was presumably not active, therefore, much earlier than the beginning of the sixth century.[1]

[1] The eclipse took place in Ol. 48, 4 (585/4) according to Pliny, *N.H.* II, 53 (DK 11 A 5), who presumably followed Apollodorus; and a year or more later according to the Eusebian scheme (DK 11 A 5). Modern calculations put it on 28 May 585 B.C., i.e. in Ol. 48, 3. Tannery's view that the eclipse predicted by Thales was that of 610 is now rejected. Apollodorus according to Diogenes Laertius I, 37–8 (DK 11 A 1) put Thales' birth in Ol. 35, 1 (640), his death in Ol. 58 (548–545) at the age of seventy-eight. There is a fault in the mathematics here: probably Ol. 35, 1 is a mistake, by the common confusion of ε̄ and θ̄, for Ol. 39, 1 (624). Apollodorus, then, characteristically placed Thales' death around the epoch-year of the capture of Sardis, his *acme* at the time of the eclipse, and his birth the conventional forty years earlier. This accords approximately with a different and slightly earlier dating authority: Demetrius of Phaleron, according to Diog. L. I, 22 (DK 11 A 1), placed the canonization of the Seven Sages (of whom Thales was a universally accepted member) in the archonship of Damasias at Athens, i.e. 582/1 B.C., the epoch-year of the first restored Pythian festival.

NATIONALITY

63 Diogenes Laertius I, 22 (DK 11 A 1 *init.*) ἦν τοίνυν ὁ Θαλῆς, ὡς μὲν Ἡρόδοτος καὶ Δοῦρις καὶ Δημόκριτός φασι, πατρὸς μὲν Ἐξαμύου μητρὸς δὲ Κλεοβουλίνης, ἐκ τῶν Θηλιδῶν, οἵ εἰσι Φοίνικες, εὐγενέστατοι τῶν ἀπὸ Κάδμου καὶ Ἀγήνορος...ἐπολιτογραφήθη δὲ (*sc.* Ἀγήνωρ) ἐν Μιλήτῳ ὅτε ἦλθε σὺν Νείλεῳ ἐκπεσόντι Φοινίκης. ὡς δ' οἱ πλείους φασίν, ἰθαγενὴς Μιλήσιος ἦν (*sc.* Θαλῆς) καὶ γένους λαμπροῦ.

---

63 *Now Thales, as Herodotus and Douris and Democritus say, was the son of Examyes as father and Cleobuline as mother, from the descendants of Theleus, who are Phoenicians, nobles from the line of Cadmus and Agenor...and he [Agenor] was enrolled as a citizen in Miletus when he came with Neileos, when the latter was exiled from Phoenicia. But most people say that Thales was a true Milesian by descent, and of high family.*

64 Herodotus I, 170 (from **66**) ...Θαλέω ἀνδρὸς Μιλησίου... τὸ ἀνέκαθεν γένος ἐόντος Φοίνικος....

The story of Thales' Phoenician ancestry, barely mentioned by Herodotus in **64** (though **63** makes it appear as though he had said more; the references in Douris and Democritus are otherwise unknown), was later much elaborated, partly, no doubt, to support the common theory of the eastern origins of Greek science. If Thales drew the attention of the Milesians to the navigational value of the Little Bear, used earlier by Phoenician sailors (see **80**), this would add to the force of Herodotus' comment. The probability is that Thales was as Greek as most Milesians.[1]

[1] Cf. **65** Herodotus I, 146 ...Μινύαι δὲ Ὀρχομένιοί σφι (*sc.* the Ionian colonists) ἀναμεμείχαται καὶ Καδμεῖοι καὶ Δρύοπες....Thus Thales' 'Phoenician' ancestors were probably Cadmeians from Boeotia and not full-blooded Semites. His father, Examyes, seems to have had a Carian name. Herodotus went on to say that even the ostensibly purest Ionian families were mixed by intermarriage with Carian women.

PRACTICAL ACTIVITIES

66 Herodotus I, 170 χρηστὴ δὲ καὶ πρὶν ἢ διαφθαρῆναι Ἰωνίην Θαλέω ἀνδρὸς Μιλησίου ἐγένετο (*sc.* ἡ γνώμη), τὸ ἀνέκαθεν γένος ἐόντος Φοίνικος, ὃς ἐκέλευε ἓν βουλευτήριον Ἴωνας ἐκτῆσθαι, τὸ δὲ εἶναι ἐν Τέῳ (Τέων γὰρ μέσον εἶναι Ἰωνίης), τὰς δὲ ἄλλας πόλιας οἰκεομένας μηδὲν ἧσσον νομίζεσθαι κατά περ εἰ δῆμοι εἶεν.

67 Herodotus I, 75 ὡς δὲ ἀπίκετο ἐπὶ τὸν Ἅλυν ποταμὸν ὁ Κροῖσος, τὸ ἐνθεῦτεν, ὡς μὲν ἐγὼ λέγω, κατὰ τὰς ἐούσας γεφύρας διεβίβασε τὸν στρατόν, ὡς δὲ ὁ πολλὸς λόγος Ἑλλήνων, Θαλῆς οἱ ὁ Μιλήσιος διεβίβασε. ἀπορέοντος γὰρ Κροίσου ὅκως οἱ διαβήσεται τὸν ποταμὸν ὁ στρατός (οὐ γὰρ δὴ εἶναί κω τοῦτον τὸν χρόνον τὰς γεφύρας ταύτας) λέγεται παρεόντα τὸν Θαλῆν ἐν τῷ

---

64 ...*of Thales, a man of Miletus...being a Phoenician by ultimate descent*....

65 ...*Minyans from Orchomenus are mixed with them* [*the Ionian colonists*], *and Cadmeians and Dryopes*....

66 *Useful also was the opinion, before the destruction of Ionia, of Thales, a man of Miletus, being a Phoenician by ultimate descent, who advised the Ionians to have a single deliberative chamber, saying that it should be in Teos, for this was in the middle of Ionia; the other cities should continue to be inhabited but should be regarded as if they were demes.*

67 *When he came to the Halys river, Croesus then, as I say, put his army across by the existing bridges; but, according to the common account of the Greeks, Thales the Milesian transferred the army for him. For it is said that Croesus was at a loss how his army should cross the river, since these bridges did not yet exist at this period; and that Thales, who was*

στρατοπέδῳ ποιῆσαι αὐτῷ τὸν ποταμὸν ἐξ ἀριστερῆς χειρὸς ῥέοντα τοῦ στρατοῦ καὶ ἐκ δεξιῆς ῥέειν, ποιῆσαι δὲ ὧδε· ἄνωθεν τοῦ στρατοπέδου ἀρξάμενον διώρυχα βαθέαν ὀρύσσειν ἄγοντα μηνοειδέα, ὅκως ἂν τὸ στρατόπεδον ἱδρυμένον κατὰ νώτου λάβοι, ταύτῃ κατὰ τὴν διώρυχα ἐκτραπόμενος ἐκ τῶν ἀρχαίων ῥεέθρων, καὶ αὖτις παραμειβόμενος τὸ στρατόπεδον ἐς τὰ ἀρχαῖα ἐσβάλλοι, ὥστε ἐπείτε καὶ ἐσχίσθη τάχιστα ὁ ποταμὸς ἀμφοτέρῃ διαβατὸς ἐγένετο.

Herodotus provides important evidence for Thales' activities as statesman and engineer (also as astronomer, **76**). Such versatility seems to have been typical of the Milesian thinkers, whom it is tempting to consider too exclusively as theoretical physicists. Thales, especially, became a symbol for ingenuity of a mathematical and geometrical kind: ἄνθρωπος Θαλῆς ('the man's a Thales'), says a character in Aristophanes (*Birds* 1009) of Meton the town-planner; and Plato (*Rep.* 600A) coupled him with Anacharsis. Herodotus, it is true, did not believe the story in **67** about Thales diverting the river Halys, but he did not deny that this is the sort of thing Thales might have done. There probably were crossings over the Halys, but Croesus' army might not have found them: Herodotus was rightly cautious, although the grounds of his suspicion were not certainly correct. He went on to mention a variant account by which the river was totally diverted into a new bed; the story, therefore, may have been widespread. The circumstantial and restrained nature of the version of **67** suggests that it contained a kernel of truth.

TRADITION OF A VISIT TO EGYPT

68 Aetius I, 3, 1 Θαλῆς...φιλοσοφήσας δὲ ἐν Αἰγύπτῳ ἦλθεν εἰς Μίλητον πρεσβύτερος.

69 Proclus *in Euclidem* p. 65 Friedl. (from Eudemus) (DK 11 A 11) Θαλῆς δὲ πρῶτον εἰς Αἴγυπτον ἐλθὼν μετήγαγεν εἰς τὴν Ἑλλάδα τὴν θεωρίαν ταύτην (*sc.* τὴν γεωμετρίαν)....

---

present in the army, made the river, which flowed on the left hand of the army, flow on the right hand also. He did so in this way: beginning upstream of the army he dug a deep channel, giving it a crescent shape, so that it should flow round the back of where the army was encamped, being diverted in this way from its old course by the channel, and passing the camp should flow into its old course once more. The result was that as soon as the river was divided it became fordable in both its parts.

68 *Thales...having practised philosophy in Egypt came to Miletus when he was older.*

69 *Thales, having first come to Egypt, transferred this study* [*geometry*] *to Greece....*

70 Plutarch *de Is. et Osir.* 34, 364D οἴονται δὲ καὶ Ὅμηρον ὥσπερ Θαλῆν μαθόντα παρ' Αἰγυπτίων ὕδωρ ἀρχὴν ἁπάντων καὶ γένεσιν τίθεσθαι.

It was the custom to credit the sixth-century sages (notably, for example, Solon) with visits to Egypt, the traditional fountain-head of Greek science. Thales as the earliest known Greek geometer had a special reason for being associated with the home of land-measurement.[1] The implication of **68** that he spent a considerable time there is unique and not persuasive. That he did visit Egypt, however, is possible enough: several of his achievements are quite plausibly located there (e.g. **81**; see also p. 86), and Miletus' relations with its colony Naucratis were so close as to make a visit by any prominent citizen, trader or not, perfectly feasible. The reference to Homer in **70** is, of course, to the Okeanos-passages **9** and **10**: Plutarch knew that in some Egyptian mythological cosmogonies water played an essential part, and we shall in fact see (pp. 90f.) that Thales probably derived his idea that the earth floats on water from earlier near-eastern, and possibly Egyptian, mythological accounts.

[1] Cf. **71** Herodotus II, 109 δοκέει δέ μοι ἐνθεῦτεν (*sc.* from re-measurement of holdings after the annual flood of the Nile) γεωμετρίη εὑρεθεῖσα εἰς τὴν Ἑλλάδα ἐπανελθεῖν.

Further, Thales appears in Aetius as the holder of a theory about the flooding of the Nile which is one of three already recorded by Herodotus:

72 Herodotus II, 20 (there are two particularly improbable theories about the cause of the flood) τῶν ἡ ἑτέρη μὲν λέγει τοὺς ἐτησίας ἀνέμους εἶναι αἰτίους πληθύειν τὸν ποταμόν, κωλύοντας ἐς θάλασσαν ἐκρέειν τὸν Νεῖλον.

73 Aetius IV, 1, 1 Θαλῆς τοὺς ἐτησίας ἀνέμους οἴεται πνέοντας τῇ Αἰγύπτῳ ἀντιπροσώπους ἐπαίρειν τοῦ Νείλου τὸν ὄγκον διὰ τὸ τὰς ἐκροὰς αὐτοῦ τῇ παροιδήσει τοῦ ἀντιπαρήκοντος πελάγους ἀνακόπτεσθαι.

---

70 *They think that Homer also, like Thales, made water principle and birth of all things through learning from the Egyptians.*

71 *It seems to me that geometry was discovered from this source* (sc. *re-measurement of holdings after the Nile flood*) *and so came to Greece.*

72 *Of these, one theory says that the Etesian winds are the cause of the river flooding, by preventing the Nile from running out into the sea.*

73 *Thales thinks that the Etesian winds, blowing straight on to Egypt, raise up the mass of the Nile's water through cutting off its outflow by the swelling of the sea coming against it.*

Aetius probably depends on a lost Peripatetic treatise, of which traces have survived in other sources (Diels *Doxographi Graeci* 226f.): therefore his information may be reliable and not, as is nevertheless possible, a purely speculative ascription. If Thales did advance this theory then he may have seen the Nile himself; though it should be remembered that he could easily have got the relevant information (that the Etesian winds blow in Egypt too), and even the idea, from Milesian traders.

ANECDOTES ABOUT THALES AS THE TYPICAL PHILOSOPHER

74 Plato *Theaetetus* 174A ...ὥσπερ καὶ Θαλῆν ἀστρονομοῦντα, ὦ Θεόδωρε, καὶ ἄνω βλέποντα, πεσόντα εἰς φρέαρ, Θρᾷττά τις ἐμμελὴς καὶ χαρίεσσα θεραπαινὶς ἀποσκῶψαι λέγεται, ὡς τὰ μὲν ἐν οὐρανῷ προθυμοῖτο εἰδέναι, τὰ δ' ὄπισθεν αὐτοῦ καὶ παρὰ πόδας λανθάνοι αὐτόν.

75 Aristotle *Politics* A 11, 1259a9 ὀνειδιζόντων γὰρ αὐτῷ διὰ τὴν πενίαν ὡς ἀνωφελοῦς τῆς φιλοσοφίας οὔσης, κατανοήσαντά φασιν αὐτὸν ἐλαιῶν φορὰν ἐσομένην ἐκ τῆς ἀστρολογίας, ἔτι χειμῶνος ὄντος, εὐπορήσαντα χρημάτων ὀλίγων ἀρραβῶνας διαδοῦναι τῶν ἐλαιουργείων τῶν τ' ἐν Μιλήτῳ καὶ Χίῳ πάντων, ὀλίγου μισθωσάμενον ἅτ' οὐδενὸς ἐπιβάλλοντος. ἐπειδὴ δ' ὁ καιρὸς ἧκε, πολλῶν ζητουμένων ἅμα καὶ ἐξαίφνης, ἐκμισθοῦντα ὃν τρόπον ἠβούλετο πολλὰ χρήματα συλλέξαντα ἐπιδεῖξαι ὅτι ῥᾴδιόν ἐστι πλουτεῖν τοῖς φιλοσόφοις ἂν βούλωνται, ἀλλ' οὐ τοῦτ' ἐστὶ περὶ ὃ σπουδάζουσιν. (Cf. also Diog. L. I, 26 (DK 11 A 1), from Hieronymus of Rhodes, and Cicero *Div.* I, 49, 111.)

Neither of these stories is likely to be strictly historical, even though they originated in the fourth century B.C. at the latest, before the great period of fictitious biography in the third and second

---

74 *...just as, Theodorus, a witty and attractive Thracian servant-girl is said to have mocked Thales for falling into a well while he was observing the stars and gazing upwards; declaring that he was eager to know the things in the sky, but that what was behind him and just by his feet escaped his notice.*

75 *For when they reproached him because of his poverty, as though philosophy were no use, it is said that, having observed through his study of the heavenly bodies that there would be a large olive-crop, he raised a little capital while it was still winter, and paid deposits on all the olive presses in Miletus and Chios, hiring them cheaply because no one bid against him. When the appropriate time came there was a sudden rush of requests for the presses; he then hired them out on his own terms and so made a large profit, thus demonstrating that it is easy for philosophers to be rich, if they wish, but that it is not in this that they are interested.*

centuries. They well demonstrate how at a comparatively early date Thales had become accepted as the typical philosopher: though **74**, one of the oldest versions of the absent-minded professor theme, would have had more point if applied to someone not so notoriously practical in his interests as Thales. The detail of the witty slave-girl is added to make the whole situation more piquant; possibly it is a vestige of a separate and mildly malicious joke at the philosopher's expense. Plato liked making fun of the Presocratics, a truth frequently overlooked in the interpretation of certain less obvious passages. The story in **75** may have gained currency, even before Aristotle, as a standard reply to the reproach of unpracticality implied in **74**. It might have had a slight basis of truth (though Aristotle did not think so): details like the addition of Chios to Miletus are possibly too elaborate for the wholly invented anecdote. At all events, anyone reading this book might draw some consolation from such a clear and influential formulation of one of the classical defences of abstruse studies.

THE PREDICTION OF THE ECLIPSE, AND OTHER ASTRONOMICAL ACTIVITIES

76 Herodotus I, 74 διαφέρουσι δέ σφι (*sc.* Medes and Lydians) ἐπ' ἴσης τὸν πόλεμον τῷ ἕκτῳ ἔτει συμβολῆς γενομένης συνήνεικε ὥστε τῆς μάχης συνεστεώσης τὴν ἡμέρην ἐξαπίνης νύκτα γενέσθαι. τὴν δὲ μεταλλαγὴν ταύτην τῆς ἡμέρης Θαλῆς ὁ Μιλήσιος τοῖσι Ἴωσι προηγόρευσε ἔσεσθαι, οὖρον προθέμενος ἐνιαυτὸν τοῦτον ἐν τῷ δὴ καὶ ἐγένετο ἡ μεταβολή.

77 Diogenes Laertius I, 23 δοκεῖ δὲ κατά τινας πρῶτος ἀστρολογῆσαι καὶ ἡλιακὰς ἐκλείψεις καὶ τροπὰς προειπεῖν, ὥς φησιν Εὔδημος ἐν τῇ περὶ τῶν ἀστρολογουμένων ἱστορίᾳ· ὅθεν αὐτὸν καὶ Ξενοφάνης καὶ Ἡρόδοτος θαυμάζει. μαρτυρεῖ δ' αὐτῷ καὶ Ἡράκλειτος καὶ Δημόκριτος.

---

76 *In the sixth year of the war, which they* [*Medes and Lydians*] *had carried on with equal fortunes, an engagement took place in which it turned out that when the battle was in progress the day suddenly became night. This alteration of the day Thales the Milesian foretold to the Ionians, setting as its limit this year in which the change actually occurred.*

77 *Some think he was the first to study the heavenly bodies and to foretell eclipses of the sun and solstices, as Eudemus says in his history of astronomy; for which reason both Xenophanes and Herodotus express admiration; and both Heraclitus and Democritus bear witness for him.*

78 Dercyllides *ap.* Theon. Smyrn. p. 198, 14 Hiller Εὔδημος ἱστορεῖ ἐν ταῖς Ἀστρολογίαις ὅτι Οἰνοπίδης εὗρε πρῶτος τὴν τοῦ ȝῳδιακοῦ λόξωσιν [Diels; διάȝωσιν ms.] καὶ τὴν τοῦ μεγάλου ἐνιαυτοῦ περίστασιν, Θαλῆς δὲ ἡλίου ἔκλειψιν καὶ τὴν κατὰ τὰς τροπὰς αὐτοῦ περίοδον, ὡς οὐκ ἴση ἀεὶ συμβαίνει.

The prediction of the eclipse must have been based on a long series of empirical observations, not upon a scientific theory of the true cause of eclipses. The cause was unknown to Thales' immediate successors in Miletus and therefore, presumably, to him. If the contrary was implied by Eudemus in **78** (it is asserted by Aetius, e.g. II, 24, 1, DK 11 A 17*a*), then Eudemus was guilty of drawing a wrong conclusion from the undoubted fact of Thales' prediction. The Babylonian priests had made observations of eclipses of the sun, both partial and total, for religious purposes, at any rate since 721 B.C.; and by the sixth century they had probably established a cycle of solstices (or less plausibly of lunations) within which eclipses might occur at certain points. It is overwhelmingly probable that Thales' feat depended on his access to these Babylonian records; we know that many cultivated Greeks visited Sardis at this period,[1] and relations with Ionia were naturally particularly close. Some scholars have argued that Thales' information more probably came from Egypt, with which he had other contacts; but there is no evidence that sufficiently detailed observations, over a long enough period, were made and recorded by the Egyptian priests. Even on the Babylonian data it could not be predicted that an eclipse would be visible at a particular point. Priests were despatched to different parts of the Babylonian empire when a possible eclipse was due, and even within this large area the expected phenomenon was sometimes not visible. Further, no precise date could be predicted, only broad limits of time. Thus Thales appears to have said that an eclipse was likely to occur within a certain year.[2] It was pure chance that it happened on the day of the battle and so seemed especially remarkable, and to some degree a matter of luck that it was visible near the Ionian area at all.

---

78 *Eudemus relates in the* Astronomy *that Oenopides first discovered the obliquity of the Zodiac and the cycle of the Great Year, and Thales the eclipse of the sun and the variable period of its solstices.*

[1] **79** Herodotus I, 29 ...ἀπικνέονται ἐς Σάρδις ἀκμαζούσας πλούτῳ ἄλλοι τε οἱ πάντες ἐκ τῆς Ἑλλάδος σοφισταί...καὶ δὴ καὶ Σόλων....

[2] Some scholars have felt a whole year to be too large a period, and have tried to restrict the meaning of ἐνιαυτόν in **76** to the summer solstice (by which the year-interval could be gauged); but there is no satisfactory evidence for such a usage.

The information added by Eudemus in **77** and **78**, that Thales predicted solstices and noted that their cycle is not always equal (by which is probably meant the slight variations in length of the solar seasons, as divided by solstices and equinoxes), is more straightforward. All that would be needed would be a rather long series of observations with a solstice-marker, a ἡλιοτρόπιον of some kind, such as was connected with Pherecydes (**48**), to mark the bearings of the sun at its most northerly and southerly points in the year—that is, the summer and winter solstices. Alternatively a *gnomon* or stable vertical rod, by which the length of the sun's shadow could be exactly recorded, would suffice. This was said by Herodotus to be a Babylonian invention (**99**), and its introduction was credited to Anaximander and not to Thales (**96**). However, measurement of shadows was certainly involved in the computation of the height of pyramids ascribed to Thales (p. 83), and one cannot be completely confident that the observation of the sun's zenith by similar means was unknown to him. The technique seems obvious to us now, and might be thought to have occurred to anyone who had reached Thales' by no means primitive stage of celestial observation. Diogenes (I, 24, DK 11 A 1) added that Thales discovered the passage of the sun from solstice to solstice, and the relation of the diameter of sun and moon to their orbits. The former phrase is very vague, and might imply no more than the knowledge that the sun moves between the tropics—which Thales obviously possessed. But it perhaps refers to the discovery of the inclination of the Zodiac, which Eudemus in **78** probably ascribed to Oinopides of Chios, over a century later; the assignment of detailed knowledge of the Zodiac to Thales and Pythagoras in Aetius (II, 12, 1, DK 11 A 13 *c*) is also speculative (see also p. 103 n.). Diogenes' second piece of information is quite anachronistic, for Thales cannot have thought that the heavenly bodies had orbits, since they did not pass under the earth (which

79 *...there arrived at Sardis in this bloom of its wealth all the sages from Greece...among whom came Solon....*

was not made free-swinging until Anaximander); at the most they had semi-orbits, and the ratio of diameter to celestial path would be twice that given.[1]

[1] The determination of this ratio was a recurrent problem in Greek astronomy, which might naturally come to be associated with the earliest known astronomer. The ratio suggested in Diogenes, 1/720th, implies a sexagesimal measurement of the circle of the ecliptic such as was adopted by the Babylonians: so A. Wasserstein, *JHS* 75 (1955) 114–16. Cf. Hdt. II, 109 (**99**), also II, 4.

One further observation is attributed to Thales, again with a possible implication that he may be indebted to foreign sources:

80 Callimachus *Iambus* I, 52, fr. 191 Pfeiffer (DK 11 A 3*a*)

. . . ἦν γὰρ ἡ νίκη
Θάλητος, ὅς τ' ἦν ἄλλα δεξιὸς γνώμην
καὶ τῆς 'Αμάξης ἐλέγετο σταθμήσασθαι
τοὺς ἀστερίσκους, ᾗ πλέουσι Φοίνικες.

This is part of the apocryphal story of the cup (in some versions, tripod) which had to be presented to the wisest man living: Thales was the first, and in some versions also the final, choice, but he modestly sent it on to Bias, and he to others of the Seven Sages. The 'little stars of the Wain' are the Little Bear (cf. Aratus *Phaen.* 39, with scholium); this constellation, because its revolution is smaller, provides a more accurate fixed point than the Great Bear or Wain as a whole (as opposed to the Pole star itself). σταθμᾶσθαι strictly means 'to measure', but sometimes, more vaguely, 'to mark out, define' (Σ on Pindar *Ol.* 10, 53). The probable meaning is that Thales defined the Little Bear, and drew the attention of Milesian sailors to its navigational usefulness. Diogenes Laertius, I, 23, interpreted the lines of Callimachus as meaning simply that Thales 'discovered' the Little Bear. Ionian sailors may previously have neglected it, since for all except long open-sea crossings the more conspicuous Great Bear was adequate.

Thus the ἀστρολογία, the study of heavenly bodies, mentioned as characteristic of Thales by Plato (**74**) and Aristotle (**75**),[1] seems to have comprised these activities: the lucky prediction of an eclipse, probably with the aid of Babylonian tables; the measurement of solstices and their variations, possibly undertaken in part

---

80 *. . . for the victory belonged to Thales, who was clever in judgement, not least because he was said to have measured out the little stars of the Wain, by which the Phoenicians sail.*

for calendar-making purposes; and the study of star-groups, perhaps mainly as a navigational aid.

[1] Cf. also **77**, where nothing is otherwise known of the references to Thales by Xenophanes, Heraclitus and Democritus.

MATHEMATICAL DISCOVERIES

81 Diogenes Laertius I, 27 ὁ δὲ Ἱερώνυμος καὶ ἐκμετρῆσαί φησιν αὐτὸν τὰς πυραμίδας ἐκ τῆς σκιᾶς, παρατηρήσαντα ὅτε ἡμῖν ἰσομεγέθης ἐστίν.

82 Proclus *in Euclidem* p. 352 Friedl. (DK 11 A 20) Εὔδημος δὲ ἐν ταῖς Γεωμετρικαῖς ἱστορίαις εἰς Θαλῆν τοῦτο ἀνάγει τὸ θεώρημα (*sc.* that triangles having one side and its adjacent angles equal are themselves equal)· τὴν γὰρ τῶν ἐν θαλάττῃ πλοίων ἀπόστασιν δι' οὗ τρόπου φασὶν αὐτὸν δεικνύναι τούτῳ προσχρῆσθαί φησιν ἀναγκαῖον.

In **81** Hieronymus of Rhodes attributes to Thales the simplest possible method of measuring the height of a pyramid. Thales might conceivably have learned this from the Egyptians; or it is not impossible that the pyramids were merely local colour, to fit the tradition of a visit to Egypt. Pliny (*N.H.* XXXVI, 82, DK 11 A 21) gave the same account, but a more complex variant appears in Plutarch, *Sept. Sap. Conv.* 2, 147A (DK 11 A 21), that the height of a pyramid is related to the length of its shadow exactly as the height of any mensurable vertical object is related to the length of *its* shadow at the same time of day. It is probable, though not certain, that Hieronymus is here dependent on his near-contemporary Eudemus (whose book on the history of geometry and mathematics, as opposed to his history of astronomy, Diogenes himself does not appear to have used for Thales); if so, there is a probability that Thales used the simpler method. On the other hand, the more complex one is based on an argument from similar triangles analogous to that ascribed to him by Eudemus in **82**, as a means of measuring the distance of ships out at sea. Provided the height of the observer above sea level were known, this calculation could be made with the aid of a primitive theodolite, two sticks (one as a sight-line, the other as an approximate level-line)

81 *Hieronymus says that he [Thales] actually measured the pyramids by their shadow, having observed the time when our own shadow is equal to our height.*

82 *Eudemus in the* History of geometry *refers this theorem to Thales; for the method by which they say he demonstrated the distance of ships out at sea must, he says, have entailed the use of this theorem.*

pivoting on a nail. It is to be observed that Eudemus only credited Thales with a knowledge of similar triangles on the *a priori* ground that he could not otherwise have performed this kind of calculation. Yet a man may make an empirical use of a rudimentary angle-measurer without forming an explicit theory about the principles involved, and certainly without stating those principles as a geometer.[1] Three other theorems attributed to Thales by Proclus following Eudemus, in the same commentary as **82** (DK 11 A 11),—circle bisected by diameter; angles at base of isosceles triangle are equal; vertically opposed angles are equal—are, again, probably just the neatest abstract solutions of particular practical problems associated with Thales. All this is very much a matter for conjecture: my own guess would be that Thales did gain a reputation with his contemporaries for carrying out various far from straightforward empirical feats of mensuration, without necessarily stating the geometry that lay behind them. This is perhaps confirmed by the fact that Thales' Milesian successors seem to have paid little attention to mathematical theory.

[1] Burnet, *EGP* 45f., observed that a knowledge of the Egyptian *seqt* ratio (a trigonometrical approximation) could have produced a solution of both problems. In view of the possibility of Thales' acquaintance with Egypt, and his analogous use (it is assumed) of an empirical Babylonian formula, this explanation can by no means be excluded.—Pamphile's report in Diog. L. I, 24 that Thales inscribed a right-angled triangle in a circle 'and sacrificed an ox' (cf. **281**) is entertaining, if not convincing.

WRITINGS

83 Simplicius *Phys.* p. 23, 29 Diels Θαλῆς δὲ πρῶτος παραδέδοται τὴν περὶ φύσεως ἱστορίαν τοῖς Ἕλλησιν ἐκφῆναι, πολλῶν μὲν καὶ ἄλλων προγεγονότων, ὡς καὶ Θεοφράστῳ δοκεῖ, αὐτὸς δὲ πολὺ διενεγκὼν ἐκείνων ὡς ἀποκρύψαι πάντας τοὺς πρὸ αὐτοῦ. λέγεται δὲ ἐν γραφαῖς μηδὲν καταλιπεῖν πλὴν τῆς καλουμένης Ναυτικῆς ἀστρολογίας.

84 Diogenes Laertius I, 23 καὶ κατά τινας μὲν σύγγραμμα κατέλιπεν οὐδέν· ἡ γὰρ εἰς αὐτὸν ἀναφερομένη Ναυτικὴ ἀστρολογία Φώκου λέγεται εἶναι τοῦ Σαμίου. Καλλίμαχος δ' αὐτὸν οἶδεν

83 *Thales is traditionally the first to have revealed the investigation of nature to the Greeks; he had many predecessors, as also Theophrastus thinks, but so far surpassed them as to blot out all who came before him. He is said to have left nothing in the form of writings except the so-called* Nautical star-guide.

84 *And according to some he left no book behind; for the* Nautical star-guide *ascribed to him is said to be by Phokos the Samian. Callimachus knew him as the discoverer of the*

εὑρετὴν τῆς ἄρκτου τῆς μικρᾶς λέγων ἐν τοῖς Ἰάμβοις οὕτως... [**80**, ll. 3–4], κατά τινας δὲ μόνα δύο συνέγραψε Περὶ τροπῆς καὶ Ἰσημερίας, τὰ ἄλλ' ἀκατάληπτα εἶναι δοκιμάσας.

85 Suda s.v. (from Hesychius) (DK 11 A 2) ...ἔγραψε περὶ μετεώρων ἐν ἔπεσι, περὶ ἰσημερίας, καὶ ἄλλα πολλά.

These passages show that there was profound doubt in antiquity about Thales' written works. It is plain, at all events, that there was no work by him in the Alexandrian library, except the dubious 'Nautical Star-guide' (cf. also **98**). Aristotle appears not to have seen any book by him, at least on cosmological matters; he was extremely cautious in ascribing opinions to him, using the expressions 'deriving the supposition perhaps from...', 'the account which they say Thales gave' (**87**, **86**), and 'from what they relate' (**91**). Aristotle was not necessarily conscientious in using original sources; Theophrastus, as a professed historian of earlier philosophy, should have been conscientious (though he was not always so, in fact), but he evidently had little to add to Aristotle about Thales (except for the minor amendment implied by the conjecture in **83** that Thales *did* have predecessors). Eudemus made some positive assertions about Thales as geometer and astronomer (**77**, **78**, **82**), but we have seen on **82** that these were sometimes very speculative; they were perhaps partly based on the quasi-legendary biographical tradition, and do not imply that Eudemus had seen written works by Thales.

Diogenes' doubt in **84** about the 'Nautical Star-guide' was shared by Plutarch, *de Pyth. or.* 18, 402 E (DK 11 B 1), who added that the work in question was in verse; we may thus conjecture that this was the verse work described by Hesychius in **85** as περὶ μετεώρων. Lobon of Argos (a disreputable stichometrist of the second century B.C.), according to Diog. L. I, 34, said that Thales wrote 200 hexameters. Only mild suspicion is expressed in **83**, where any uncertainty implied by καλουμένης is perhaps restricted to the nature of the title. But this last sentence almost certainly contains Simplicius' own judgement and not that of Theophrastus, the paraphrase of whom seems to end before λέγεται. Diogenes'

Little Bear, and wrote as follows in his Iambs... [**80**, ll. 3–4]*; while according to some he wrote only two works,* On the solstice *and* On the equinox, *considering the rest to be incomprehensible.*

85 *...he wrote on celestial matters in epic verse, on the equinox, and much else.*

information in **84**, that the work was also ascribed to one Phokos of Samos, almost settles the matter: any astronomical work of archaic appearance might naturally be ascribed to Thales, but works actually by Thales would not be alternatively ascribed to men of comparative obscurity. It is possible that the 'Nautical star-guide' was a genuine sixth-century work similar to the hexameter Ἀστρολογία of Cleostratus of Tenedos (DK ch. 6) or the so-called Hesiodic Ἀστρονομίη (DK ch. 4): so Diels and others have assumed. It is also possible that it was a Hellenistic forgery. Diogenes in **84** is a little worried by Callimachus' mention in **80** of a particular nautical star-aid ascribed to Thales; but this need not have been described by Thales in writing. However, there is nothing inherently improbable in Thales having recorded such aids to navigation, a plausible enough activity for a practical sage in a maritime centre: but it was probably not in the 'Nautical Star-guide' known to the Hellenistic world that he did so. The other works mentioned in **84**, on the solstice and the equinox (only the latter in **85**), are unlikely, from their similar contents, to have been separate books. Simplicius in **83**, and those recorded in **84** who thought that Thales left no book, evidently did not accept this work as genuine. Thales studied the solstices according to Eudemus in **77** and **78**, and it would be on the ground of this known interest that such a work would be ascribed to him. Once again, however, it must be remembered that observations of solstices and of star-risings and -settings were widely made in the archaic period, and also set down in verse, partly in the attempt to establish a satisfactory calendar: see Cleostratus fr. 4 (DK 6 B 4) and the Hesiodic *Astronomy* (DK 4 B 1–5). Observations about the Hyades and the setting of the Pleiades were also attributed to Thales (Σ on Aratus 172, Pliny *N.H.* XVIII, 213; DK 11 B 2, 11 A 18); the latter observation, incidentally, was accurate for the latitude of Egypt, not that of Greece.

The evidence does not allow a certain conclusion, but the probability is that Thales did not write a book; though the ancient holders of this view might have been misled by the absence of a genuine work from the Alexandrian library, and also by the apophthegmatic nature of the wisdom assigned to the Seven Sages in general.

COSMOLOGY

(i) *The earth floats on water, which is in some way the source of all things*

86 Aristotle *de caelo* B 13, 294a28 οἱ δ' ἐφ' ὕδατος κεῖσθαι (*sc.* φασὶ τὴν γῆν). τοῦτον γὰρ ἀρχαιότατον παρειλήφαμεν τὸν λόγον, ὅν φασιν εἰπεῖν Θαλῆν τὸν Μιλήσιον, ὡς διὰ τὸ πλωτὴν εἶναι μένουσαν ὥσπερ ξύλον ἤ τι τοιοῦτον ἕτερον (καὶ γὰρ τούτων ἐπ' ἀέρος μὲν οὐθὲν πέφυκε μένειν, ἀλλ' ἐφ' ὕδατος), ὥσπερ οὐ τὸν αὐτὸν λόγον ὄντα περὶ τῆς γῆς καὶ τοῦ ὕδατος τοῦ ὀχοῦντος τὴν γῆν.

87 Aristotle *Met.* A3, 983b6 τῶν δὴ πρώτων φιλοσοφησάντων οἱ πλεῖστοι τὰς ἐν ὕλης εἴδει μόνας ᾠήθησαν ἀρχὰς εἶναι πάντων· ἐξ οὗ γὰρ ἔστιν ἅπαντα τὰ ὄντα, καὶ ἐξ οὗ γίγνεται πρώτου καὶ εἰς ὃ φθείρεται τελευταῖον, τῆς μὲν οὐσίας ὑπομενούσης τοῖς δὲ πάθεσι μεταβαλλούσης, τοῦτο στοιχεῖον καὶ ταύτην ἀρχήν φασιν εἶναι τῶν ὄντων, καὶ διὰ τοῦτο οὔτε γίγνεσθαι οὐδὲν οἴονται οὔτ' ἀπόλλυσθαι, ὡς τῆς τοιαύτης φύσεως ἀεὶ σῳζομένης...δεῖ γὰρ εἶναί τινα φύσιν ἢ μίαν ἢ πλείους μιᾶς ἐξ ὧν γίγνεται τἆλλα σῳζομένης ἐκείνης. τὸ μέντοι πλῆθος καὶ τὸ εἶδος τῆς τοιαύτης ἀρχῆς οὐ τὸ αὐτὸ πάντες λέγουσιν, ἀλλὰ Θαλῆς μὲν ὁ τῆς τοιαύτης ἀρχηγὸς φιλοσοφίας ὕδωρ εἶναί φησιν (διὸ καὶ τὴν γῆν ἐφ' ὕδατος ἀπεφαίνετο εἶναι), λαβὼν ἴσως τὴν ὑπόληψιν ταύτην ἐκ τοῦ πάντων ὁρᾶν τὴν τροφὴν ὑγρὰν οὖσαν καὶ αὐτὸ τὸ θερμὸν ἐκ τούτου γιγνόμενον καὶ τούτῳ ζῶν (τὸ δ' ἐξ οὗ γίγνεται, τοῦτ' ἐστὶν ἀρχὴ πάντων), διά τε δὴ τοῦτο τὴν ὑπόληψιν λαβὼν ταύτην καὶ διὰ τὸ πάντων τὰ σπέρματα τὴν φύσιν ὑγρὰν ἔχειν· τὸ δ' ὕδωρ ἀρχὴ τῆς φύσεώς ἐστι τοῖς ὑγροῖς.

---

86 *Others say that the earth rests on water. For this is the most ancient account we have received, which they say was given by Thales the Milesian, that it stays in place through floating like a log or some other such thing (for none of these rests by nature on air, but on water)—as though the same argument did not apply to the water supporting the earth as to the earth itself.*

87 *Most of the first philosophers thought that principles in the form of matter were the only principles of all things: for the original source of all existing things, that from which a thing first comes-into-being and into which it is finally destroyed, the substance persisting but changing in its qualities, this they declare is the element and first principle of existing things, and for this reason they consider that there is no absolute coming-to-be or passing away, on the ground that such a nature is always preserved...for there must be some natural substance, either one or more than one, from which the other things come-into-being, while it is preserved. Over the number, however, and the form of this kind of principle they do not all agree; but Thales, the founder of this type of philosophy, says that it is water (and therefore declared that the earth is on water), perhaps taking this supposition from seeing the nurture of all things to be moist, and the warm itself coming-to-be from this and living by this (that from which they come-to-be being the principle of all things)—taking the supposition both from this and from the seeds of all things having a moist nature, water being the natural principle of moist things.*

Our knowledge of Thales' cosmology depends virtually completely on these two passages, with the cryptic addition of **91–93**. Apart from Aristotle's own criticism and conjecture, they assign two propositions to Thales: (1) the earth floats on water (like a piece of wood or something of the sort); (2) the 'principle' of all things is water (in Aristotle's sense of ἀρχή as explained in the first half of **87**, i.e. the original constituent material of things, which persists as a substratum and into which they will perish). (1) was professedly known to Aristotle only indirectly, on the information of others; further, it is impossible to tell whether the supporting argument (solid things do not rest on air, but they do on water, therefore the earth floats on water) was also derived from the reports of Thales, or whether it was entirely supplied by Aristotle. His final objection, that Thales has solved nothing because he would still have to find something to support the water that supports the earth, shows how little Aristotle understood the probable nature of Thales' way of thinking: Thales would almost certainly still accept the popular conception of the earth (or, in this case, its immediate support) stretching down so far that the problem almost disappeared, as in Homer (**1**) and long after Thales in Xenophanes (**3**). The probable direct origin of Thales' idea of the earth floating on water was from non-Greek mythological accounts (pp. 90f.); the device might have attracted him in part because it provided support for the earth, but it is by no means certain that Thales felt this to be a serious problem, and most improbable in any case that he worked out the theory for himself as a conscious answer to that problem. As for proposition (2), Aristotle evidently knew nothing beyond what he wrote, since the reasons given for Thales' choice of water are professedly conjectural (λαβὼν ἴσως...). The first half of **87** is quoted to show the kind of analysis and terminology which Aristotle (and following him Theophrastus[1] and thus the subsequent doxographical tradition) applied to the early physicists or natural philosophers, the φυσικοί —those who, according to Aristotle, posited solely, or primarily, the first (material) of his four causes. His application of a single rigid analysis to his predecessors, while justly and usefully emphasizing certain resemblances between them, is also a source of confusion. Thus Thales' 'principle' (in Aristotle's sense) and Heraclitus' 'principle' (fire according to Aristotle) were clearly, for Thales and for Heraclitus themselves, very different kinds of thing.

In fact, all we know about Thales' views on water (apart from that the earth floats on it) is that, in a hearsay and probably much abbreviated and somewhat distorted form, they appeared to the not over-discriminating Aristotle to fit his own idea of a material ἀρχή. Yet it is possible, contrary to Aristotle's automatic assumption, that Thales declared earth to *come from* water (i.e. to be solidified out of it in some way) without therefore thinking that the earth and its contents *are* somehow water, that they have any continuing relation to it (beyond the fact that the earth floats on water) except that of a man to his remote ancestors: for Thales, we may conjecture, was still to some extent influenced by the genealogical view of cosmogony best exemplified in Hesiod (**24**). See further pp. 92 f.

[1] Theophrastus' abbreviated account of Thales' material principle is given by Simplicius, *Phys.* p. 23, 21 Diels (= Theophr. *Phys. Op.* fr. 1), DK 11 A 13. It is a close parallel of Aristotle in **87**, using in many parts the same phraseology. It adds one more conjectural reason for Thales' choice of water, that corpses dry up (τὰ νεκρούμενα ξηραίνεται): this perhaps came from Hippon (see next n.), who is probably credited with a similar argument in Anon. Lond. XI, 22 (DK 38 A 11), i.e. in a Peripatetic source. The addition occurs also in Aetius.

The reasons conjectured by Aristotle in **87** for the importance attached by Thales to water as a constituent of things are mainly physiological.[1] From the analogy of his immediate successors we might have expected Thales to have adduced meteorological reasons, more conspicuously, in support of the cosmic importance of water.[2] Yet we must beware of exaggerated generalizations like that implied in Burnet's view that sixth-century thinkers were almost exclusively interested in meteorological (in the strict sense, including astronomical) phenomena. It is undoubtedly true that the *scientific* study of medicine began in the fifth century B.C., and that analogies between the world and details of human structure become much commoner then. Yet chapter I has shown the strongly genealogical colouring of much pre-philosophical Greek speculation, and also the importance of the analogy of physiological reproduction. In the case of Thales there are reasons for thinking that his explanation of the world was influenced not only by this variegated traditional background of earlier Greek quasi-mythological cosmogonical versions, but also by a specific cosmological idea derived directly, perhaps, from further east.

[1] It seems more probable than not that Aristotle took them from Hippon of Samos (or of Rhegium, Croton, or Metapontium), who in the second half of the fifth century B.C. revived and modified the idea of water as constituent material of things. Hippon, whose intellect Aristotle did not admire, evidently had strong physiological interests. Cf. in particular **88** Aristotle *de an.* A2, 405b1 τῶν δὲ φορτικωτέρων καὶ ὕδωρ τινὲς ἀπεφήναντο (*sc.* τὴν ψυχήν), καθάπερ Ἵππων· πεισθῆναι δ' ἐοίκασιν ἐκ τῆς γονῆς, ὅτι πάντων ὑγρά· καὶ γὰρ ἐλέγχει τοὺς αἷμα φάσκοντας τὴν ψυχήν, ὅτι ἡ γονὴ οὐχ αἷμα. Note that there is a good deal of conjecture in this, too. Against the assumption that Aristotle's conjectured reasons for Thales' choice of water were derived from Hippon is that the additional reason given in Theophrastus (see previous note) probably did come from Hippon, and might therefore have been expected to be included by Aristotle.

[2] As in **89** Heraclitus Homericus *Quaest. Hom.* 22 ἡ γὰρ ὑγρὰ φύσις, εὐμαρῶς εἰς ἕκαστα μεταπλαττομένη, πρὸς τὸ ποικίλον εἴωθε μορφοῦσθαι· τό τε γὰρ ἐξατμιζόμενον αὐτῆς ἀεροῦται, καὶ τὸ λεπτότατον ἀπὸ ἀέρος αἰθὴρ ἀνάπτεται, συνιζάνον τε τὸ ὕδωρ καὶ μεταβαλλόμενον εἰς ἰλὺν ἀπογαιοῦται· διὸ δὴ τῆς τετράδος τῶν στοιχείων ὥσπερ αἰτιώτατον ὁ Θαλῆς ἀπεφήνατο στοιχεῖον εἶναι τὸ ὕδωρ. These reasons certainly stem from a Stoic source—there is much Stoic phraseology—and may well be entirely conjectural. According to Theophrastus, evidently, Thales used water and its products to explain earthquakes (**90**: this depends on the special conception that the earth *rests on* water), also winds and movements of stars (Hippolytus *Ref.* I, I); but these would scarcely provide the reason for Thales adopting the theory in the first place.

The near-eastern origin of part of Thales' cosmology is indicated by his conception that the earth floats or rests on water. In Egypt the earth was commonly conceived as a flat, rimmed dish resting upon water, which also filled the sky; the sun sailed each day across the sky in a boat, and also sailed under the earth each night (not round it, as in the Greek legend, e.g. 7). In the Babylonian creation-epic Apsu and Tiamat represent the primeval waters, and Apsu remains as the waters under the earth after Marduk has split the body of Tiamat to form sky (with its waters) and earth. In the story of Eridu (seventh century B.C. in its youngest extant version),

---

88 *Of the cruder thinkers some actually declared it* (sc. *the soul*) *to be water, like Hippon; they seem to have been persuaded by the seed of all things being moist. In fact he refutes those who say that the soul is blood; because the seed is not blood.*

89 *For moist natural substance, since it is easily formed into each different thing, is accustomed to undergo very various changes: that part of it which is exhaled is made into air, and the finest part is kindled from air into aither, while when water is compacted and changes into slime it becomes earth. Therefore Thales declared that water, of the four elements, was the most active, as it were, as a cause.*

in the beginning 'all land was sea'; then Marduk built a raft on the surface of the water, and on the raft a reed-hut which became the earth. An analogous view is implied in the Psalms (where also Leviathan is an analogue of Tiamat), where Jahweh 'stretched out the earth above the waters' (136, 6), 'founded it upon the seas, and established it upon the floods' (24, 2). Similarly Tehom is 'the deep that lieth under' (Gen. xlix. 25), 'the deep that coucheth beneath' (Deut. xxxiii. 13).[1] Against this profusion of parallel material, from the east and south-east, for the waters under the earth, there is no comparable Greek material apart from Thales. The naïve Greek conception of a river Okeanos *surrounding* the earth (ch. 1 §2) is not strictly comparable (for it is clear that there is no Okeanos under the earth), although it was probably a much earlier development, in a different direction, of the widely-diffused near-eastern generic concept of the earth rising in the midst of the primeval waters—a concept almost certainly not native to the Greek-speaking peoples, whose home before the migrations into the Greek peninsula lay far from the sea. Similarly, although the isolated references in *Iliad* book 14 (**9** and **10**) to Okeanos as origin of all things were also probably based upon the same near-eastern concept, from a slightly different aspect, they contain no implication of the special idea that the earth floats on water, and so are unlikely to have been the origin of Thales' assertion of this idea. For any more general contention that the earth came from, or is maintained by, water, Thales would no doubt be encouraged and gratified to have the apparently native Homeric precedents. Thus Thales' view that the earth floats on water seems to have been most probably based upon direct contact with near-eastern mythological cosmology. We have already seen that he had associations both with Babylonia and with Egypt. The idea that the earth actually floats upon water was more clearly and more widely held in the latter of these countries; and the conjecture might be hazarded that Thales was indebted to Egypt for this element of his world-picture.[2]

[1] These instances are cited by U. Hölscher in his convincing discussion of Thales, *Hermes* 81 (1953) 385–91. Some of the material is treated in ch. 1, especially pp. 12 ff. For the idea of Nun, the Egyptian primeval ocean, supporting the earth, see also the remarks of J. A. Wilson, *Before Philosophy* 59 ff., and H. Frankfort, *Ancient Egyptian Religion* (N.Y., 1948) 114.

[2] This was, indeed, the opinion of later Greek critics about the origin of

Thales' ideas on water in general: cf. Plutarch in **70** (who was acquainted with the Nun-myth), and, less dogmatically, Simplicius *de caelo* 522, 14 (DK 11 A 14). Both, however, are conjectural judgements.

Thales evidently used the floating-earth idea to explain earthquakes:

90 Seneca *Qu. Nat.* III, 14 (presumably from Theophrastus, through a Posidonian source): ait enim (*sc.* Thales) terrarum orbem aqua sustineri et vehi more navigii mobilitateque eius fluctuare tunc cum dicitur tremere.

The cosmological scope of the idea is, however, limited; and it seems reasonable to conclude from Aristotle's information in **87** that Thales also thought that the world *originated* from water, since this is implicit in the near-eastern mythologies and is stated in the Homeric Okeanos-passages which are thought to be based on those mythologies. Thales may have rationalized the idea from a Greek mythological form like the Homeric one; he may also have been directly influenced (as he seems to have been for the special detail that the earth floats on water) by foreign, perhaps Egyptian versions. Even more uncertainty attaches to a problem that has already been foreshadowed: are we justified in inferring from the Peripatetic identification of Thales' water as 'material principle' that he believed the visible, developed world to *be* water in some way? This is the normal interpretation of Thales; but it is important to realize that it rests ultimately on the Aristotelian formulation, and that Aristotle, knowing little about Thales, and that indirectly, would surely have found the mere information that the world originated from water sufficient justification for saying that water was Thales' material principle or ἀρχή, with the implication that water is a persistent substrate. It must be emphasized once more that no such development was necessary, and that it was not implicit in the near-eastern concepts which were ultimately Thales' archetype. Thales might have held that the world originated from an indefinite expanse[1] of primeval water, on which it still floats and which is still responsible for certain natural phenomena, without also believing that earth, rocks, trees or men are in any way *made of* water or a form of water. There would be a remote ancestral connexion, no more. On the other hand Thales

---

90 *For he [Thales] said that the world is held up by water and rides like a ship, and when it is said to 'quake' it is actually rocking because of the water's movement.*

could have made the entirely new inference that water is the continuing, hidden constituent of all things. Certainly his near successor Anaximenes believed that all things were made of air (but he had thought of a way in which this could be so: air takes on different forms when compressed or rarefied), and it is invariably assumed that he was extending and refining a line of thought initiated by Thales. It would be imprudent entirely to reject this assumption, which goes back to Theophrastus and Aristotle. The physiological reasons instanced by Aristotle, that all living things depend on water for nourishment, that the sperm is moist, and so on, although conjectural, are of a kind that might well have struck Thales. With other indications (e.g. the Homeric statement that the surrounding Okeanos is the source of all springs and rivers, **5**) they could have led him to the conclusion that water, as well as being the cosmogonical source, is also involved in the very essence of the developed world. On the other hand, one must remain aware of the possibility that Aristotle was simply making his own kind of inference, in the absence of other information, from Thales' belief that the world originated from water and that water still plays a major part in the cosmos by supporting the earth.

[1] Thales would have accepted Simplicius' judgement (*Phys.* 458, 23, DK 11 A 13) that water was, for him, ἄπειρον; though for Thales this would mean 'limitless', i.e. of indefinite extent, and not 'infinite', and be a natural assumption rather than a consciously propounded theory. Simplicius was more seriously misleading in asserting (*Phys.* 180, 14) that Thales, like Anaximenes, generated by means of the condensation and rarefaction of his material principle. This is a purely schematic judgement based on an over-rigid dichotomy in Aristotle (**106**). Theophrastus only found the device explicitly used in Anaximenes: see **145**.

Two things, then, have emerged from the present discussion: (i) 'all things are water' is not necessarily a reliable summary of Thales' cosmological views; and (ii) even if we do accept Aristotle's account (with some allowance, in any event, for his inevitably altered viewpoint), we have little idea of *how* things were felt to be essentially related to water.

(ii) *Even apparently inanimate things can be 'alive'; the world is full of gods*

91 Aristotle *de an.* A 2, 405 a 19 ἔοικε δὲ καὶ Θαλῆς, ἐξ ὧν ἀπομνημονεύουσι, κινητικόν τι τὴν ψυχὴν ὑπολαβεῖν, εἴπερ τὴν λίθον ἔφη ψυχὴν ἔχειν ὅτι τὸν σίδηρον κινεῖ.

---

91 *Thales, too, seems, from what they relate, to have supposed that the soul was something kinetic, if he said that the (Magnesian) stone possesses soul because it moves iron.*

92 Diogenes Laertius I, 24 Ἀριστοτέλης δὲ καὶ Ἱππίας φασὶν αὐτὸν καὶ τοῖς ἀψύχοις μεταδιδόναι ψυχῆς, τεκμαιρόμενον ἐκ τῆς λίθου τῆς μαγνήτιδος καὶ τοῦ ἠλέκτρου.

93 Aristotle *de an.* A 5, 411a7 καὶ ἐν τῷ ὅλῳ δέ τινες αὐτὴν (*sc.* τὴν ψυχὴν) μεμεῖχθαί φασιν, ὅθεν ἴσως καὶ Θαλῆς ᾠήθη πάντα πλήρη θεῶν εἶναι.

The two passages from Aristotle's *de anima* allow us to conjecture, but no more, about Thales' vision of the whole world as somehow alive and animated. Aristotle himself was reporting second-hand evidence, and his statements are jejune and cautious (although in **91** εἴπερ need not, and probably does not, express doubt, while ἴσως in **93** qualifies ὅθεν and not the assertion that follows). The concluding words of **93**, 'all things are full of gods', occur also in Plato, in a probably conscious but unattributed quotation.[1] **92** cites the sophist and polymath Hippias as an earlier source than Aristotle for Thales' attribution of motive power to Magnesian (magnetic) stone, to which is added amber, which becomes magnetic when rubbed. Presumably the addition is from Hippias, who may well have been Aristotle's source here.[2]

[1] **94** Plato *Laws* 10, 899B ἔσθ' ὅστις ταῦτα ὁμολογῶν ὑπομενεῖ μὴ θεῶν εἶναι πλήρη πάντα; The context deals with souls being called gods, but contains no explicit reference to Thales. It is quite in Plato's style to introduce, rather laboriously, a familiar phrase to enlighten an unfamiliar argument of his own, without naming the author. His use of the words in question is important, in any case, because it shows that they are not simply an Aristotelian summary. They could (in direct speech) be a genuine quotation from Thales; they have a totally different appearance from the banal apophthegms hopefully assigned to Thales in Demetrius of Phaleron's collection (*ap.* Stob. III, 1, 172, DK 10, 3). Aristotle repeated them, with the substitution of ψυχῆς for θεῶν and without attribution, at *G.A.* Γ 11, 762a21.

[2] Snell, in an important and elusive article, *Philologus* 96 (1944) 170–82, shows that Hippias was quite possibly the source of Aristotle's other remarks on Thales, including the comparison with older ideas on Okeanos etc. (**12**, cf. **14**). The fragment of Hippias quoted by Clement, DK 86 B 6, shows that he made a collection of key passages on similar topics from Homer, Hesiod, Orphic writings, and Greek and other prose-sources. He was therefore the earliest systematic doxographer.

---

92 *Aristotle and Hippias say that he gave a share of soul even to inanimate* [lit. *soulless*] *objects, using Magnesian stone and amber as indications.*

93 *And some say that it* [*soul*] *is intermingled in the universe, for which reason, perhaps, Thales also thought that all things are full of gods.*

94 *Is there anyone who will accept this and maintain that all things are* not *full of gods?*

All that Aristotle seems to have known in **91** was that Thales thought that magnetic stone possesses soul because it is able to move iron; but the further inference, that for Thales the soul was something motive, is clearly legitimate. Soul, whether it was associated with breath, blood, or spinal fluid, was universally regarded as the source of consciousness and life. A man is alive, he can move his limbs and so move other things; if he faints, it means that his soul has withdrawn or become incapacitated; if he dies, it has become permanently so, and the 'soul' that goes squeaking down to Hades in Homer is a mere shadow, because it is dissociated from the body and can no longer produce life and movement. It is a common primitive tendency to regard rivers, trees and so on as somehow animated or inhabited by spirits: this is partly, though not wholly, because they seem to possess the faculty of self-movement and change, they differ from mere stocks and stones. Thales' attitude was not primitive, of course, but there is a connexion with that entirely unphilosophical animism. It should be noted, however, that his examples are of a different order: magnetic stone looks as unalive as could be, and cannot move or change itself, only a certain kind of external object. Thus Thales appears to have made explicit, in an extreme form, a way of thinking that permeated Greek mythology but whose ultimate origins were almost prearticulate. Now it is possible that our second piece of specific information, **93**, is a generalization based on this very conclusion that certain kinds of apparently inanimate object are alive, possess soul, because they have a limited power of movement. 'All things are full of gods':[1] the chief distinguishing marks of the gods are that they are immortal, they enjoy perpetual life, and that their power (their life-force, as it were) is unlimited, it extends both over the animate and over the inanimate world. Thus the assertion may well imply (since even apparently dead things like stone may possess soul of a kind) that the world as a whole manifests a power of change and motion which is certainly not even predominantly human, and must, both because of its permanence and because of its extent and variation, be regarded as divine, as due to the inherence of some form of immortal ψυχή.[2]

[1] Or of daimons, according to the paraphrase in Aetius after Theophrastus:

95 Aetius I, 7, 11 Θαλῆς νοῦν τοῦ κόσμου τὸν θεόν, τὸ δὲ πᾶν ἔμψυχον

---

95 *Thales said that the mind of the world is god, and that the sum of things is besouled,*

ἅμα καὶ δαιμόνων πλῆρες· διήκειν δὲ καὶ διὰ τοῦ στοιχειώδους ὑγροῦ δύναμιν θείαν κινητικὴν αὐτοῦ. The juxtaposition of the two statements from Aristotle is not significant. The last sentence is Stoic in form and content; the first clause (Θαλῆς...θεόν), too, is entirely anachronistic, and probably due to Stoic reinterpretation. It was repeated by Cicero, *N.D.* I, 10, 25, who added that god, as mind, made the world out of water. A considerable number of recognizably fictitious opinions, like this one, were attributed to Thales by puzzled or unscrupulous doxographers and biographers. Compare, perhaps, the 30,000 daimons of Hesiod *Erga* 252 ff.

[2] The claim by Choerilus of Iasus (3rd–2nd c. B.C.) and others, recorded in Diog. L. I, 24 (DK 11 A 1), that according to Thales the soul was immortal, obviously arose as an illegitimate conclusion from this kind of argument, and is again due to Stoic perversion (primarily) of the type of **95**. Thales could have distinguished clearly between the human ψυχή and the divine life-force in the world as a whole, at the same time as implicitly recognizing their underlying connexion.

The precise nature of Thales' belief that all things are full of gods is obviously not determinable. Even along the line of interpretation suggested above there is one notable uncertainty: did Thales make the bold induction, from the observation about Magnesian stone and amber, that *all* apparently inanimate things really possess soul to some degree? Or was Burnet right in maintaining (*EGP* 50) that 'to say the magnet and amber are alive is to imply, if anything, that other things are not'? Formally this is an illegitimate contention (since only a part of what Thales said is known), and in itself the fragmentary observation implies nothing either way. Nor does the assertion that all things are full of gods, even if it is closely connected with the observation about magnetic stone, necessarily imply that the universal induction was made; for just as one can say in English 'this book is full of absurdities' without meaning that every single thing in it is absurd, so πλήρης in Greek could mean 'containing a great number of', as well as 'absolutely filled out by'. *A priori*, it perhaps seems more probable that Thales meant that all things in sum (rather than each single thing) were interpenetrated by some kind of life-principle; although there would be many kinds of matter from which this life-principle, with its kinetic power, might be absent. The point was that the range of soul, or of life, was much greater than it appeared to be. Thales was giving an explicit and individual statement of a broad presupposition common to all the early physicists, that the world

---

and full of daimons; right through the elemental moisture there penetrates a divine power that moves it.

was somehow alive, that it underwent spontaneous change, and (what irritated Aristotle) that there was therefore no need to give any special account of natural change. This presupposition is still sometimes called 'hylozoism'; but this name implies too strongly that it is something uniform, determinable, and conscious. In fact the term applies to at least three possible and distinct attitudes of mind: (*a*) the assumption (conscious or not) that all things absolutely are in some way alive; (*b*) the belief that the world is interpenetrated by life, that many of its parts which appear inanimate are in fact animate; (*c*) the tendency to treat the world as a whole, whatever its detailed constitution, as a single living organism. (*a*) is an extreme, but in view of the universalizing tendency of Greek thought not an impossible, form of the general presupposition; in a way it might be said to be exemplified by Xenophanes. Thales' belief, it has been suggested, approaches closer to (*b*). (*c*) is implicit in the old genealogical view of the world's history described in chapter 1, which still persisted to a large extent under the new rationalized form of philosophical cosmogony. Aristotle is seen at his most perspicuous in **118**, where, perhaps with Thales especially in mind, he shows himself aware of the possibility of this kind of attitude.[1]

[1] The spears in the *Iliad* (11, 574 etc.) which are 'eager to devour flesh', and other similar cases, are sometimes cited as an indication that the animistic view was an old one. Animism is, of course, as old as man himself, and it arises out of the failure to objectify one's experience of the outside world, a technique which requires some practice. The Homeric expressions are better described as a literary conceit, like the pathetic fallacy—a deliberate rejection of the technique.

CONCLUSION

Thales was chiefly known for his prowess as a practical astronomer, geometer, and sage in general. His prediction of the eclipse was probably made feasible by his use of Babylonian records, perhaps obtained at Sardis; he also probably visited Egypt. His theory that the earth floats on water seems to have been derived from near-eastern cosmogonical myths, perhaps directly; water as the origin of things was also a part of these myths, but had been mentioned in a Greek context long before Thales. His development of this concept may in itself have seemed to Aristotle sufficient warrant for saying that Thales held water to be the ἀρχή, in its Peripatetic sense of a persisting substrate. Yet Thales could indeed have felt that since water is essential for the maintenance of plant and animal life—we do not know what meteorological arguments he used—it remains still as the basic constituent of things. Although these ideas were strongly affected, directly or indirectly, by mythological precedents, Thales evidently abandoned mythic formulations: this alone justifies the claim that he was the first philosopher, naïve though his thought still was. Further, he noticed that even certain kinds of stone could have a limited power of movement and therefore, he thought, of life-giving soul; the world as a whole, consequently, was somehow permeated (though probably not completely) by a life-force which might naturally, because of its extent and its persistence, be called divine. Whether he associated this life-force with water, the origin and perhaps the essential constituent of the world, we are not told. The concluding word must be that the evidence for Thales' cosmology is too slight and too imprecise for any of this to be more than speculative; what has been aimed at is reasonable speculation.

CHAPTER III

ANAXIMANDER OF MILETUS

DATE, BOOK, AND SCIENTIFIC ACTIVITIES

96 Diogenes Laertius II, 1–2 (DK 12 A 1) Ἀναξίμανδρος Πραξιάδου Μιλήσιος· οὗτος ἔφασκεν ἀρχὴν καὶ στοιχεῖον τὸ ἄπειρον, οὐ διορίζων ἀέρα ἢ ὕδωρ ἢ ἄλλο τι...εὗρεν δὲ καὶ γνώμονα πρῶτος καὶ ἔστησεν ἐπὶ τῶν σκιοθήρων ἐν Λακεδαίμονι, καθά φησι Φαβωρῖνος ἐν Παντοδαπῇ ἱστορίᾳ, τροπάς τε καὶ ἰσημερίας σημαίνοντα, καὶ ὡροσκοπεῖα κατεσκεύασε. καὶ γῆς καὶ θαλάσσης περίμετρον πρῶτος ἔγραψεν, ἀλλὰ καὶ σφαῖραν κατεσκεύασε. τῶν δὲ ἀρεσκόντων αὐτῷ πεποίηται κεφαλαιώδη τὴν ἔκθεσιν, ᾗ που περιέτυχεν καὶ Ἀπολλόδωρος ὁ Ἀθηναῖος· ὅς καί φησιν αὐτὸν ἐν τοῖς Χρονικοῖς τῷ δευτέρῳ ἔτει τῆς πεντηκοστῆς ὀγδόης ὀλυμπιάδος (547/6 B.C.) ἐτῶν εἶναι ἑξήκοντα τεττάρων καὶ μετ᾽ ὀλίγον τελευτῆσαι (ἀκμάσαντά πη μάλιστα κατὰ Πολυκράτη τὸν Σάμου τύραννον).

97 Suda s.v. Ἀναξίμανδρος Πραξιάδου Μιλήσιος φιλόσοφος συγγενὴς καὶ μαθητὴς καὶ διάδοχος Θάλητος. πρῶτος δὲ ἰσημερίαν εὗρε καὶ τροπὰς καὶ ὡρολογεῖα, καὶ τὴν γῆν ἐν μεσαιτάτῳ κεῖσθαι. γνώμονά τε εἰσήγαγε καὶ ὅλως γεωμετρίας ὑποτύπωσιν ἔδειξεν. ἔγραψε Περὶ φύσεως, Γῆς περίοδον καὶ Περὶ τῶν ἀπλανῶν καὶ Σφαῖραν καὶ ἄλλα τινά.

---

96 *Anaximander son of Praxiades, of Miletus: he said that the principle and element is the Indefinite, not distinguishing air or water or anything else...he was the first to discover a* gnomon, *and he set one up on the Sundials* (?) *in Sparta, according to Favorinus in his* Universal history, *to mark solstices and equinoxes; and he also constructed hour-indicators. He first drew an outline of earth and sea, but he also constructed a (celestial) globe. Of his opinions he made a summary exposition, which I suppose Apollodorus the Athenian, also, encountered. Apollodorus says in his* Chronicles *that Anaximander was sixty-four years old in the second year of the fifty-eighth Olympiad, and that he died shortly afterwards (having been near his prime approximately during the time of Polycrates, tyrant of Samos).*

97 *Anaximander son of Praxiades, of Miletus, philosopher, was a kinsman, pupil and successor of Thales. He first discovered the equinox and solstices and hour-indicators, and that the earth lies in the centre. He introduced the* gnomon *and in general made known an outline of geometry. He wrote* On nature, Circuit of the earth *and* On the fixed stars *and a* Celestial globe *and some other works.*

(i) *Date*

If Thales earned the title of the first Greek philosopher mainly because of his abandonment of mythological formulations, Anaximander is the first of whom we have concrete evidence that he made a comprehensive and detailed attempt to explain all aspects of the world of man's experience. He was younger than Thales, but probably not by much. Burnet (*EGP* 51) inferred from the latter part of **96** that the chronographer Apollodorus found definite evidence, perhaps in a summary version of his book, that Anaximander was sixty-four in 547/6 B.C.; and that his death 'soon afterwards' was placed by Apollodorus in the next year, the epoch-year of the capture of Sardis. (The last clause of **96** is presumably a mistake: Polycrates did not come to power until *ca.* 540 B.C. and died *ca.* 522.) If this is so, then Thales and Anaximander died in the same Olympiad, and Anaximander was only fourteen years younger than Thales (n. on p. 74).[1] Anaximander was called the 'successor and pupil' of Thales by Theophrastus (**103** A), also his kinsman, companion, acquaintance or fellow-citizen in the later doxographical tradition. In most cases this kind of statement need only imply that the one was thought to come from the same city as, and to be somewhat younger than, the other.[2] If there were fixed dates both for Thales (the prediction of the eclipse in 585/4) and for Anaximander (for the information that he was sixty-four in 547/6 was presumably available also to Theophrastus), the *a priori* basis for Theophrastus' conjecture would be a reasonable one.

[1] That Thales and Anaximander are not separated by the conventional Apollodoran 40-year interval (see next note) is in favour of 547/6 being a non-arbitrary date. It is true that, if Anaximander could be made the master of Pythagoras, then his birth should be eighty years earlier than the latter's *floruit* (which Apollodorus placed in 532/1), and he would be very close to 64 (in fact 65) in 547/6. According to the evidence of Hippolytus (*Ref.* I, 6, 7, DK 12 A 11) even Apollodorus was wrong by one year, since Hippolytus gives the birth-year as Ol. 42, 3 (610/9 B.C.) instead of Ol. 42, 2. What is significant, however, is that Anaximander's age was known for a particular year which was not his *floruit* and not necessarily that of his death, although it was close to his death. Further, no connexion of Pythagoras with Anaximander is known in the great majority of our sources (only in Porphyry *V.P.* 2, after the imaginative 3rd-century B.C. biographer Neanthes of Cyzicus, and in Apuleius, *Florida* 15, 20). Nevertheless, the possibility cannot be entirely excluded that Apollodorus' dating of Anaximander was arbitrarily hinged to his Polycrates-Pythagoras system. This might help to account for the last clause of **96**.

[2] The arrangement of the early philosophers into 'schools', and into masters and pupils within these schools, was initiated by Theophrastus and systematically applied in the *Successions* of Sotion, *ca.* 200 B.C. Apollodorus used the latter work, and normally assumed a 40-year interval in age between master and pupil.

(ii) *Anaximander's book*

The book-titles ascribed to Anaximander in **97**, presumably from Hesychius, should be regarded with reserve. It was the custom with Alexandrian writers to supply titles, in the absence of definite evidence, to suit an early thinker's known interests. 'On nature' was a standard comprehensive title which tended to be assigned to all those whom Aristotle called φυσικοί, that is, to almost all the Presocratics.[1] That Anaximander certainly wrote a book of some kind is shown both by Theophrastus' incontrovertible quotation in **103** A, and possibly by Diogenes' information in **96** that there was a 'summary exposition', which he took to be by the philosopher himself. What Diogenes knew of may have been a later summary (produced either by a pupil or, more probably, in the fourth century B.C. or later); or it may have been the original work, whose short, perhaps discontinuous, and apophthegmatic nature was not what was normally expected of a philosophical book.[2] It is not clear whether it was from this source that Apollodorus determined the year in which Anaximander was sixty-four; it seemed probable to Diogenes, though that age is considerably greater than the average for authorship. The elder Pliny (*N.H.* II, 31, DK 12 A 5) stated that Anaximander discovered the obliquity of the Zodiac in this same Olympiad, the fifty-eighth; but the ascription of this discovery is probably false (p. 103 n.), and Pliny perhaps merely misapplied Apollodorus' dating. Diogenes' term περιέτυχεν, 'came upon', might imply that the so-called summary exposition was a rarity in Apollodorus' time. Theophrastus, almost two centuries before, had access to at least one original sentence, but seems to have lacked full information about Anaximander's originative substance. The possibility cannot be ignored that he, too, used a summary or handbook, partly at least in the form of a collection of excerpts, and one which concentrated on cosmology, anthropology and so on rather than on the nature of the parent-material. On the other hand, Anaximander himself might have offered little information on the originative substance.

[1] Cf. **98** Themistius *Or.* 26 p. 383 Dindorf ('Αναξίμανδρος) ἐθάρρησε πρῶτος ὧν ἴσμεν Ἑλλήνων λόγον ἐξενεγκεῖν περὶ φύσεως συγγεγραμμένον. Thales was thought not to have written a book, at any rate one of a general cosmological kind: see pp. 85 ff. One of the objections to Περὶ φύσεως as a genuine sixth-century book-title is that φύσις is probably not used in the collective sense, 'Nature', before about the middle of the fifth century (cf. Kirk, *Heraclitus, the Cosmic Fragments*, 227 ff.). Gorgias' sardonic title Περὶ φύσεως ἢ περὶ τοῦ μὴ ὄντος implies that Περὶ φύσεως was common *in his time*, but no more than that. On the other hand, the addition of a word like χρημάτων or ἁπάντων to φύσεως would make the usage possible. The fact remains that Περὶ φύσεως was indiscriminately applied to any work of a vaguely physical nature: cf. e.g. pp. 166f., for Xenophanes' poetry.

[2] We do not know how many words a papyrus roll is likely to have held in the sixth century B.C. The letters were probably large (papyrus should have been relatively cheap in Miletus, from Naucratis), and the total product quite short. See p. 266 for an estimate of the length of Parmenides' poem; and p. 366 and n. 2 for Anaxagoras' book.

(iii) *Scientific activities: (a) the gnomon*

Anaximander did not *discover* the gnomon, as **96** claims (the gnomon is a set-square or any vertical rod whose shadow indicates the sun's direction and height): compare

99 Herodotus II, 109 πόλον μὲν γὰρ καὶ γνώμονα καὶ τὰ δυώδεκα μέρεα τῆς ἡμέρης παρὰ Βαβυλωνίων ἔμαθον οἱ Ἕλληνες.

97 may be correct, nevertheless, in suggesting that Anaximander *introduced* the gnomon into Greece. We cannot be sure, however, that Thales did not use some form of the instrument (p. 81), and it is possible that Anaximander gained the credit by accident, or because his use of the gnomon was more conspicuous. No special discoveries involving its use were assigned to him which were not also assigned to Thales; but he may have gained notoriety by the incident referred to by Favorinus in **96**. The statement that Anaximander set up a gnomon in Sparta ἐπὶ τῶν σκιοθήρων is mysterious. A σκιόθηρον (or σκιοθήρης) was a sun-dial, but the prepositional phrase cannot mean anything like 'for a sun-dial' or 'for the benefit of the sun-dials', and the suggestion might be made that there was a prominence in Sparta later known as 'the sun-dials', from the gnomon or gnomons that existed there; ἐπί, then, would be local. ὡροσκοπεῖα in **96** and ὡρολογεῖα in **97** imply that

---

98 *(Anaximander) was the first of the Greeks whom we know who ventured to produce a written account on nature.*

99 *The Greeks learned from the Babylonians of the celestial sphere and the* gnomon *and the twelve parts of the day.*

the ground near the gnomon was calibrated so as to give the time of day, as well as the position of the sun on the ecliptic and so the season of the year. For another association of Anaximander with Sparta see n. on p. 104.[1]

[1] Pliny, *N.H.* II, 187 (DK 13 A 14*a*), held that it was Anaximenes who first demonstrated in Sparta the 'horologium quod appellant sciothericon', and who discovered the use of the gnomon. This is probably a mistake by Pliny, who tended to confound his facts in writing about early astronomy. He attributed the discovery of the obliquity of the Zodiac to Anaximander (p. 101), but Eudemus in **78** probably assigned this to Oinopides. The full comprehension of the ecliptic doubtless belonged to the fifth century; that the sun moves from north to south and back was known much earlier—and certainly, for example, by Thales.

(iii) *Scientific activities: (b) the map*

100 Agathemerus I, I Ἀναξίμανδρος ὁ Μιλήσιος ἀκουστὴς Θαλέω πρῶτος ἐτόλμησε τὴν οἰκουμένην ἐν πίνακι γράψαι· μεθ' ὃν Ἑκαταῖος ὁ Μιλήσιος ἀνὴρ πολυπλανὴς διηκρίβωσεν, ὥστε θαυμασθῆναι τὸ πρᾶγμα.

101 Strabo I, p. 7 Casaubon ...τοὺς πρώτους μεθ' Ὅμηρον δύο φησὶν Ἐρατοσθένης, Ἀναξίμανδρόν τε Θαλοῦ γεγονότα γνώριμον καὶ πολίτην καὶ Ἑκαταῖον τὸν Μιλήσιον. τὸν μὲν οὖν ἐκδοῦναι πρῶτον γεωγραφικὸν πίνακα, τὸν δὲ Ἑκαταῖον καταλιπεῖν γράμμα πιστούμενον ἐκείνου εἶναι ἐκ τῆς ἄλλης αὐτοῦ γραφῆς.

These passages are obviously based on the same one statement by Eratosthenes, as is Diogenes' remark in **96** that 'Anaximander first drew an outline of land and sea'. Diogenes' addition, 'but he also constructed a sphere' (that is, a map of the heaven), is unsubstantiated and, in the light of Anaximander's theory of the heavenly bodies (pp. 135 ff.), improbable. The general nature of his map may perhaps be inferred from the following passage:

102 Herodotus IV, 36 γελῶ δὲ ὁρῶν γῆς περιόδους γράψαντας πολλοὺς ἤδη καὶ οὐδένα νόον ἐχόντως ἐξηγησάμενον· οἳ Ὠκεανόν

---

100 *Anaximander the Milesian, a disciple of Thales, first dared to draw the inhabited world on a tablet; after him Hecataeus the Milesian, a much-travelled man, made the map more accurate, so that it became a source of wonder.*

101 *...Eratosthenes says that the first to follow Homer were two, Anaximander, who was an acquaintance and fellow-citizen of Thales, and Hecataeus the Milesian. The former was the first to publish a geographical map, while Hecataeus left behind a drawing believed to be his from the rest of his writings.*

102 *I smile when I see that many have drawn circuits of the earth, up to now, and none*

τε ῥέοντα γράφουσι πέριξ τὴν γῆν, ἐοῦσαν κυκλοτερέα ὡς ἀπὸ τόρνου, καὶ τὴν Ἀσίην τῇ Εὐρώπῃ ποιεύντων ἴσην.

It is a reasonable assumption that the (probably Ionian) maps referred to here resembled that of Anaximander as improved by his fellow-citizen Hecataeus; and therefore that Anaximander produced a circular plan in which the known regions of the world formed roughly equal segments. His empirical knowledge of geography was presumably based in part on seafarers' reports, which in Miletus, as a commercial centre and founder of colonies, would be both accessible and varied. The philosopher himself was said to have led a colonizing expedition to Apollonia (the city on the Black Sea, presumably), cf. Aelian *V.H.* III, 17 (DK 12A3). Otherwise his only known foreign contacts are with Sparta.[1]

[1] Apart from the sun-indicator story in **96**, Cicero related (*de divinat.* I, 50, 112, DK 12A5*a*) that Anaximander warned the Spartans to move into the fields when an earthquake was imminent. One is reminded of miraculous predictions assigned to Pherecydes and Pythagoras (pp. 50f.); but as a citizen of Miletus, in the earthquake belt, Anaximander would have had special experience. The modern Thessalians, for example, know that an earthquake is imminent when the storks become agitated. At all events Anaximander seems to have visited Sparta, otherwise two separate anecdotes about him would hardly be located there.

THE NATURE OF ANAXIMANDER'S ORIGINATIVE SUBSTANCE, τὸ ἄπειρον (THE INDEFINITE)

Part of Theophrastus' account of Anaximander's originative material is preserved by Simplicius. It is disputed whether Simplicius derived this and similar doxographical extracts direct from a version of Theophrastus, or by the medium of Alexander's lost commentary on the *Physics*; some extracts certainly came from this source. A more important question is whether Simplicius, or Alexander, was using the full edition of Theophrastus, or the two-volume summary, or an even shorter compendious account. The long surviving fragment on sensation, also in Simplicius, is on a very much larger scale than the extremely cursory extracts on the material principle, which suggests that they were derived from different versions of Theophrastus; the latter probably do not come from the complete edition. Hippolytus and the author of the pseudo-Plutarchean *Stromateis* also have doxographical summaries

of them has explained the matter sensibly: they draw Okeanos running around the earth, which is drawn as though with a compass, and make Asia equal to Europe.

of Anaximander; they follow Theophrastus less closely than does Simplicius, but provide confirmation and expansion at certain points. They also cover a greater range of subjects, some of which (e.g. zoogony, astronomy) are dealt with at greater length than the question of the ἀρχή. Simplicius' extract is printed in the left-hand column of **103**, with the corresponding parts of the two subsidiary versions alongside. Briefer and less accurate versions of this doxography appear in **96** and in Aetius (I, 3, 3, DK 12 A 14). It should be remembered that the passages in **103** are versions of *Theophrastus*' view of Anaximander; it will be seen that, so far as the material principle was concerned, he differed little from Aristotle, from whom some of his phraseology is directly derived. He quoted one original sentence (bold type in **103** A; see pp. 117f.); this need not imply that he had seen the whole of Anaximander's book, as is almost invariably assumed. If he did see the whole, either it was very obscure about the originative stuff or he was untypically obtuse.

103 Versions of Theophrastus' account of Anaximander's originative substance:

A. Simplicius *Phys.* 24, 13; DK 12 A 9	B. Hippolytus *Ref.* I, 6, 1–2; DK 12 A 11	C. Ps.-Plutarch *Strom.* 2; DK 12 A 10
τῶν δὲ ἓν καὶ κινούμενον καὶ ἄπειρον λεγόντων Ἀναξίμανδρος μὲν Πραξιάδου Μιλήσιος Θαλοῦ γενόμενος διάδοχος καὶ μαθητὴς	Θαλοῦ τοίνυν Ἀναξίμανδρος γίνεται ἀκροατής. Ἀ. Πραξιάδου Μιλήσιος· . . .	. . . Ἀναξίμανδρον Θάλητος ἑταῖρον γενόμενον
ἀρχήν τε καὶ στοιχεῖον εἴρηκε τῶν ὄντων τὸ ἄπειρον,	οὗτος μὲν ἀρχὴν καὶ στοιχεῖον εἴρηκε τῶν ὄντων τὸ ἄπειρον,	τὸ ἄπειρον φάναι τὴν πᾶσαν αἰτίαν ἔχειν τῆς τοῦ παντὸς γενέσεώς τε καὶ φθορᾶς,

---

A	B	C
Of those who say that it is one, moving, and infinite, Anaximander, son of Praxiades, a Milesian, the successor and pupil of Thales,	*Now Anaximander was the disciple of Thales. Anaximander, son of Praxiades, of Miletus:* . . .	. . . *Anaximander, who was the companion of Thales,*
said that the principle and element of existing things was the apeiron [*indefinite*, or *infinite*],	*he said that the principle and element of existing things was the* apeiron,	*said that the* apeiron *contained the whole cause of the coming-to-be and destruction of the world,*

103 (*cont.*)

πρῶτος τοῦτο τοὔνομα κομίσας τῆς ἀρχῆς.	πρῶτος ⟨τοῦτο⟩ τοὔνομα καλέσας τῆς ἀρχῆς.	
	(πρὸς δὲ τούτῳ κίνησιν ἀίδιον εἶναι, ἐν ᾗ συμβαίνει γίνεσθαι τοὺς οὐρανούς.)	
λέγει δ' αὐτὴν μήτε ὕδωρ μήτε ἄλλο τι τῶν καλουμένων εἶναι στοιχείων, ἀλλ' ἑτέραν τινὰ φύσιν ἄπειρον,	. . . οὗτος ἀρχὴν ἔφη τῶν ὄντων φύσιν τινὰ τοῦ ἀπείρου,	
ἐξ ἧς ἅπαντας γίνεσθαι τοὺς οὐρανοὺς καὶ τοὺς ἐν αὐτοῖς κόσμους.	ἐξ ἧς γίνεσθαι τοὺς οὐρανοὺς καὶ τὸν ἐν αὐτοῖς κόσμον.	ἐξ οὗ δή φησι τούς τε οὐρανοὺς ἀποκεκρίσθαι καὶ καθόλου τοὺς ἅπαντας ἀπείρους ὄντας κόσμους.
	ταύτην δ' ἀίδιον εἶναι καὶ ἀγήρω, ἣν καὶ πάντας περιέχειν τοὺς κόσμους.	
ἐξ ὧν δὲ ἡ γένεσίς ἐστι τοῖς οὖσι, καὶ τὴν	λέγει δὲ χρόνον ὡς ὡρισμένης τῆς γενέσεως	ἀπεφήνατο δὲ τὴν φθορὰν γίνεσθαι καὶ πολὺ

---

being the first to introduce this name of the material principle.	*being the first to use this name of the material principle.*	
	(*In addition to this he said that motion was eternal, in which it results that the heavens come into being.*)	
He says that it is neither water nor any other of the so-called elements, but some other apeiron *nature,*	. . . *he said that the material principle of existing things was some nature coming under the heading of the* apeiron,	
from which come into being all the heavens and the worlds in them.	*from which come into being the heavens and the world in them.*	*from which he says that the heavens are separated off, and in general all the worlds, being* apeirous [*innumerable*].
	This nature is eternal and unageing, and it also surrounds all the worlds.	
And the source of coming-to-be for existing	*He talks of Time as though coming-to-be and*	*He declared that destruction, and much earlier*

103 (*cont.*)

φθορὰν εἰς ταῦτα γίνεσθαι **κατὰ τὸ χρεών·**

διδόναι γὰρ αὐτὰ δίκην καὶ τίσιν ἀλλήλοις τῆς ἀδικίας κατὰ τὴν τοῦ χρόνου τάξιν, ποιητικωτέροις οὕτως ὀνόμασιν αὐτὰ λέγων. (What follows is Simpl., not Theophrastus.)

καὶ τῆς οὐσίας καὶ τῆς φθορᾶς.

(λέγει δὲ χρόνον...)

πρότερον τὴν γένεσιν ἐξ ἀπείρου αἰῶνος ἀνακυκλουμένων πάντων αὐτῶν.

(i) *Did Anaximander call the originative substance* ἀρχή?

Most modern critics think that Theophrastus named Anaximander as the first to have used ἀρχή (literally 'beginning' or 'source') as a special term for the originative substance. They infer this from πρῶτος τοῦτο τοὔνομα κομίσας τῆς ἀρχῆς in **103**A, its equivalent in **103**B, and one further context in Simplicius (*Phys.* 150, 23) where Anaximander is described as πρῶτος αὐτὸς ἀρχὴν ὀνομάσας τὸ ὑποκείμενον. Burnet, however (*EGP* 54 n. 2), maintained that what Theophrastus said was simply that Anaximander was the first to call the material principle (ἀρχή in its normal Peripatetic sense) by the name τὸ ἄπειρον, without further qualification. This, indeed, is the obvious sense of the extract from Theophrastus, **103**A, while in **103**B τοῦτο has presumably dropped out by haplography before τοὔνομα. The other passage of Simplicius is more difficult: its most obvious meaning is 'being the first to call the substratum of the opposites ἀρχή', but Burnet explained it as meaning 'being the first to name the substratum of the opposites as the material cause' (that is, because according to Aristotle the opposites in Anaximander were specifically produced from the

---

things is that into which destruction, too, happens 'according to necessity;

for they pay penalty and retribution to each other for their injustice according to the assessment of Time',

as he describes it in these rather poetical terms.

existence and destruction were limited.

(*He talks of Time...*)

coming-to-be, happen from infinite ages, since they are all occurring in cycles.

originative stuff). Burnet's interpretation, while admittedly not the most apparent meaning of the clause in isolation, is certainly more relevant to the trend of Simplicius' argument. Further, Theophrastus had used the word ἀρχή in his remarks on Thales as already reported by Simplicius (*Phys.* 23, 23, DK 11 A 13), with no special note that Thales himself did not actually use this word—a note that would perhaps have been natural if Theophrastus had gone on to assert that Anaximander was its originator. It is possible, of course, that Simplicius misunderstood Theophrastus' comment about ἀρχή and ἄπειρον. The whole question is of minor importance; it does seem, however, that no technical use of ἀρχή by Anaximander was implied *by Theophrastus*—the use he referred to was of τὸ ἄπειρον.

(ii) *What did Anaximander mean by* τὸ ἄπειρον?

104 Aristotle *Phys.* Γ4, 203a16 οἱ δὲ περὶ φύσεως πάντες ὑποτιθέασιν ἑτέραν τινὰ φύσιν τῷ ἀπείρῳ τῶν λεγομένων στοιχείων, οἷον ὕδωρ ἢ ἀέρα ἢ τὸ μεταξὺ τούτων.

First, it is advisable to isolate the Peripatetic, and so also the doxographical, interpretation of τὸ ἄπειρον. Aristotle, curiously enough, mentioned Anaximander by name only four times, but made several probable references to his primary substance (e.g. **111** *fin.*). There is little doubt that he took ἄπειρον in Anaximander, and in the monists in general, to mean primarily 'spatially infinite'. This is suggested in **110**. In **104**, part of his discussion of the concept of infinity, Aristotle attributes some specific quality, presumably that of the intermediate in the case of Anaximander (pp. 110ff.), to the material principles of all the φυσικοί who recognize the infinite. Theophrastus seems to have felt that Anaximander had given his primary substance a name which described its spatial property, but which said nothing except by implication (that it was not identified with any of the later 'elements') about its qualitative properties. Thus in **103** A l. 2, and in other such classifications, ἄπειρον means 'infinite'; it is 'neither water nor any other of the so-called elements, but some other infinite nature from which come all the heavens...' (Anaximander's heavens being infinite in number for Theophrastus).[1]

104 *All the physicists make the infinite a property of some other nature belonging to the so-called elements, such as water or air or that which is intermediate between these.*

[1] The words ἑτέραν τινὰ φύσιν ἄπειρον seem to echo Aristotle's radically different ἑτέραν τινὰ φύσιν τῷ ἀπείρῳ in **104**; especially since the wider contexts of the two phrases have much in common. This superficial similarity of phraseology suggests that Theophrastus had made himself familiar with his master's discussion of infinity in the *Physics* before he set about summarizing the theories of Anaximander.

It is, however, uncertain that Anaximander himself intended τὸ ἄπειρον to mean precisely 'the spatially infinite'. We may legitimately doubt whether the concept of infinity was apprehended before questions of continuous extension and continuous divisibility were raised by Melissus and Zeno. ἄπειρον means 'without boundary, limit, definition'; this indefiniteness is spatial in early usages, as in the ἀπείρονα πόντον of Homer (Anaximander's ἄπειρον is presumably from ἄπειρος, of which ἀπείρων is a more poetical equivalent), and as in Xenophanes (**3**), who said that the earth went down ἐς ἄπειρον, indefinitely, i.e. beyond the imagination or the concern of men. Now Anaximander certainly assumed the original stuff to have been indefinitely huge in extent; but he perhaps gave formal expression to this idea by saying that this stuff 'surrounded all things' (**110**), and might not have felt this characteristic (which must have been assumed as a matter of course by Thales, see n. on p. 93) to be sufficiently remarkable to be applied as sole description, that is as 'the spatially indefinite'. We might expect any such single description to refer first to the *kind* of substance, not to its commonly assumed vastness of extent. Thus Cornford (e.g. *C.A.H.* IV, 542) and others have argued that τὸ ἄπειρον meant 'that which is internally unbounded, without internal distinctions', i.e. that which is indistinct, indefinite in kind. There is no need to stress *internal* divisions,[1] but the general point seems not improbable: for Anaximander the original world-forming stuff was indefinite, it resembled no one kind of matter in the developed world. Yet no parallel early use of ἄπειρος in a certainly non-spatial sense can be cited, and this is in favour of retaining the interpretation 'spatially indefinite'. In any case the lack of positive identification was conspicuously implied. Either τὸ ἄπειρον meant 'the spatially indefinite', and was implied to be indefinite in kind because it was not formally identified as fire, air, water or earth (to use Theophrastus' terms of **103** A); or Anaximander intended it to mean primarily 'that which is indefinite in kind', but naturally assumed it also to be of unlimited extent and duration—properties which, when expressed, would be expressed in terms of all-inclusiveness and divine immortality.[2]

[1] Nor is it easy to accept Diels' and Cornford's view that the ἄπειρον was conceived as circular or spherical, cf. ἄπειρον ἀμφίβληστρον at Aeschylus *Ag.* 1382, ἄπειρος of a ring in Aristophanes and Aristotle, etc. It is impossible to prove that any particular application of the word that was feasible in the archaic period was entirely absent from Anaximander's mind; but the intention seems to have been to deny any fixed determination.

[2] Cherniss, *Aristotle's Criticism of Presocratic Philosophy* 377 f., maintained that Anaximander meant ἄπειρον ⟨τὸ πλῆθος⟩, i.e. 'with an indeterminate number of internal divisions'. But in this case ἄπειρον would have to be expressly qualified by a word implying number, as in Anaxagoras frr. 1 and 2 (**495**, **515**).

(iii) *The Indefinite as an intermediate substance in Aristotle*

105 Aristotle *de gen. et corr.* B5, 332a19 ...οὐκ ἔστιν ἓν τούτων (*sc.* fire, air, water, earth) ἐξ οὗ τὰ πάντα· οὐ μὴν οὐδ' ἄλλο τί γε παρὰ ταῦτα, οἷον μέσον τι ἀέρος καὶ ὕδατος ἢ ἀέρος καὶ πυρός, ἀέρος μὲν παχύτερον καὶ πυρός, τῶν δὲ λεπτότερον· ἔσται γὰρ ἀὴρ καὶ πῦρ ἐκεῖνο μετ' ἐναντιότητος· ἀλλὰ στέρησις τὸ ἕτερον τῶν ἐναντίων· ὥστ' οὐκ ἐνδέχεται μονοῦσθαι ἐκεῖνο οὐδέποτε, ὥσπερ φασί τινες τὸ ἄπειρον καὶ τὸ περιέχον.

106 Aristotle *Phys.* A4, 187a12 ὡς δ' οἱ φυσικοὶ λέγουσι, δύο τρόποι εἰσίν. οἱ μὲν γὰρ ἓν ποιήσαντες τὸ σῶμα τὸ ὑποκείμενον, ἢ τῶν τριῶν τι ἢ ἄλλο ὅ ἐστι πυρὸς μὲν πυκνότερον ἀέρος δὲ λεπτότερον, τἆλλα γεννῶσι πυκνότητι καὶ μανότητι πολλὰ ποιοῦντες.... οἱ δ' ἐκ τοῦ ἑνὸς ἐνούσας τὰς ἐναντιότητας ἐκκρίνεσθαι, ὥσπερ Ἀναξίμανδρός φησι καὶ ὅσοι δ' ἓν καὶ πολλά φασιν εἶναι, ὥσπερ Ἐμπεδοκλῆς καὶ Ἀναξαγόρας· ἐκ τοῦ μίγματος γὰρ καὶ οὗτοι ἐκκρίνουσι τἆλλα.

---

105 ...*There is no* one *of these things* [*fire, air, water, earth*] *from which come all things; and certainly nothing else beside these, such as something half-way between air and water, or air and fire, being thicker than air and fire and finer than the others: for that will be air and fire, simply, together with contrariety; but one of the two opposites is a privation—so that it is impossible for the intermediate ever to exist in isolation, as some say the infinite* [apeiron] *and the surrounding does.*

106 *Two types of explanation are given by the physicists. Those who have made the subsisting body* one, *either one of the three or something else which is thicker than fire and finer than air, generate the rest by condensation and rarefaction, making it into many.... But the others say that the opposites are separated out from the One, being present in it, as Anaximander says and all who say there are one and many, like Empedocles and Anaxagoras; for these, too, separate out the rest from the mixture.*

Aristotle, when listing various monistic theories of the φυσικοί, on a number of occasions speaks of a substance *between* the elements—normally between fire and air or between air and water.[1] In three or four of these passages it looks as though Anaximander is meant as the proponent of an intermediate substance, not because he is directly named but because the substance is implied to have been called simply τὸ ἄπειρον. In **105** the people who said that 'the ἄπειρον and the surrounding' existed on its own, in isolation from the elements, appear from the terminology (cf. **110**) to be Anaximander and followers; see also **111**, where the intermediate between water and air is said to 'surround all the heavens, being boundless'. Now Aristotle in **104** declared that all the φυσικοί who envisaged it gave some specific description of the infinite (τὸ ἄπειρον): we may ask what description Anaximander was deemed by Aristotle, when he wrote those words, to have given, if not as an intermediate—which is, indeed, actually mentioned in that passage as a typical description. Were it not for one passage, namely **106**, there would be no difficulty in accepting that Aristotle had Anaximander in mind in most, at any rate, of his references to an intermediate material principle. One of Aristotle's most acute ancient commentators, Alexander of Aphrodisias, did in fact accept this; so, usually, did Simplicius. Yet in **106**, on the only possible interpretation, Aristotle placed the intermediate substance and Anaximander in opposed groups.[2] Various unenlightening guesses have been made about the historical author of the intermediate-substance theory; but a careful study of all Aristotle's references indicates that Anaximander was, after all, in his mind—although Anaximander in fact held no such theory. Aristotle evidently felt that Anaximander's (for Aristotle) 'infinite' ἀρχή must have had *some* expressible relationship to the so-called elements; and there are some passages (e.g. **107**) in which he wrote simply of τὸ παρὰ τὰ στοιχεῖα, 'that which is beside the elements', not identifiable with any one of them, and not of τὸ μεταξύ or τὸ μέσον. By this formulation one possibility was that it was intermediate between two elements; another, that it was a mixture of them all. In **106** Aristotle seems to take the latter view;[3] but he elsewhere considered the former possibility, and had arrived at the theoretical hypothesis of an intermediate (a hypothesis which he himself, of course, regarded as untenable: cf. **105**) as a by-product of his reflexions on Anaximander. That he had no explicit historical example in mind, however, is shown by his variation of the elements between which the intermediate came. My suggestion is, then, that Aristotle, puzzled about the nature of Anaximander's ἄπειρον, thought that, if not an element, it must be either an intermediate or a mixture. Usually when he mentioned an intermediate in lists of possible primary substances he had Anaximander in mind, though he also tended to add the intermediate indiscriminately to any such list for the sake of exhaustivity. It is so added in **106**, where, as the result of a different type of critique, he applies the mixture-interpretation to Anaximander by name.

[1] Apart from **104**, **105**, **106**, **111**, cf. *Met.* A7, 988a30; 989a14; *Phys.* A6, 189b1; Γ4, 203a18; *GC* B1, 328b35.

[2] It might be argued that τὸ ἕν, the One, is common to both groups, therefore that Anaximander might occur in each. But the contrast is really between those who retain the One as a substratum, and those who (like Anaximander) do not.

[3] That Aristotle could regard Anaximander's ἄπειρον as a mixture is shown for certain in **122**. For a fuller discussion of the whole topic see Kirk, 'Some problems in Anaximander', *CQ* N.S. 5 (1955) 24ff.

(iv) *Why 'the Indefinite' and not a specific originative substance?*

107 Aristotle *Phys.* Γ5, 204b22 ἀλλὰ μὴν οὐδὲ ἓν καὶ ἁπλοῦν εἶναι ἐνδέχεται τὸ ἄπειρον σῶμα, οὔτε ὡς λέγουσί τινες τὸ παρὰ τὰ στοιχεῖα, ἐξ οὗ ταῦτα γεννῶσιν, οὔθ' ἁπλῶς. εἰσὶ γάρ τινες οἳ τοῦτο ποιοῦσι τὸ ἄπειρον, ἀλλ' οὐκ ἀέρα ἢ ὕδωρ, ὡς μὴ τἆλλα φθείρηται ὑπὸ τοῦ ἀπείρου αὐτῶν· ἔχουσι γὰρ πρὸς ἄλληλα ἐναντίωσιν, οἷον ὁ μὲν ἀὴρ ψυχρός, τὸ δ' ὕδωρ ὑγρόν, τὸ δὲ πῦρ θερμόν· ὧν εἰ ἦν ἓν ἄπειρον ἔφθαρτο ἂν ἤδη τἆλλα. νῦν δ' ἕτερον εἶναί φασι ἐξ οὗ ταῦτα.

108 Aristotle *Phys.* Γ4, 203b15 τοῦ δ' εἶναί τι ἄπειρον ἡ πίστις ἐκ πέντε μάλιστ' ἂν συμβαίνοι σκοποῦσιν...ἔτι τῷ οὕτως ἂν μόνως μὴ ὑπολείπειν γένεσιν καὶ φθοράν, εἰ ἄπειρον εἴη ὅθεν ἀφαιρεῖται τὸ γιγνόμενον.

---

107 *But yet, nor can the infinite body be one and simple, whether it be, as some say, that which is beside the elements, from which they generate the elements, or whether it be expressed simply. For there are some people who make what is beside the elements the infinite, and not air or water, so that the rest be not destroyed by their infinite substance; for the elements are opposed to each other (for example, air is cold, water moist, and fire hot), and if one of those were infinite the rest would already have been destroyed. But, as it is, they say that the infinite is different from these, and that they come into being from it.*

108 *Belief in infinity would result, for those who consider the matter, for the most part from five factors...further, because only so would generation and destruction not fail, if there were an infinite source from which that which is coming-to-be is derived.*

These passages present two possible motives for the postulation of the Indefinite as primary substance. The reason in **107**—that the infinite primary substance, if identified with a specific world-constituent, would swamp the other world-constituents and never allow them to develop—is assigned to those who posited an ἄπειρον substance 'beside the elements', i.e. not identical with any of them. When Aristotle used this formulation he usually, though not necessarily invariably, had Anaximander in mind (pp. 110ff.), and Simplicius in his comment on the passage (*Phys.* 479, 33) ascribed this reason to Anaximander. On the other hand the totally different reason suggested in **108**—that an infinite source-material ensures that coming-to-be within the world shall not fail for want of material—is given as Anaximander's by Aetius (I, 3, 3, DK 12 A 4) and by Simplicius in one passage (*de caelo* 615, 15, DK 12 A 17). Aetius' attribution suggests that Theophrastus applied the motive of **108** to Anaximander; but we cannot be sure that he did not apply that of **107** also, and in either case he was probably working from what Aristotle had said.

Most modern critics have accepted **108** as giving Anaximander's true motive, and many have rejected **107** as not (in spite of appearances) applying to Anaximander. Thus Cherniss called the argument in **107** 'the peculiarly Aristotelian argument of the necessary equilibrium of contrary forces'. It is true that it is expressed, naturally enough, in an Aristotelian form. But Anaximander had postulated a comprehensive balance between opposed substances (see **112** with discussion), and might well have reasoned in some such way as this: 'Thales said that all things originated from water; but water (which we see in the form of rain, sea and rivers) is opposed to fire (the sun, the fiery aither, volcanoes etc.), and these things are mutually destructive. How then can fire have become such a prominent part of our world, if it were from the beginning constantly opposed by the whole indefinitely-extended mass of its very opposite? How, indeed, can it have appeared at all, for a single moment? The warring constituents of our world, then, must have developed from a substance different from any of them—something indefinite or indeterminable.' (Aristotle's interpretation of ἄπειρον as 'infinite' does not affect this issue.)

As for **108**, Aristotle himself pointed out its fallacy:

109 Aristotle *Phys.* Γ8, 208a8 οὔτε γάρ, ἵνα ἡ γένεσις μὴ ἐπιλείπῃ, ἀναγκαῖον ἐνεργείᾳ ἄπειρον εἶναι σῶμα αἰσθητόν· ἐνδέχεται γὰρ τὴν θατέρου φθορὰν θατέρου εἶναι γένεσιν, πεπερασμένου ὄντος τοῦ παντός.

But this was precisely Anaximander's view of physical change—that there is no wastage: opposed substances make retribution *to each other* for their encroachments (pp. 118ff.), and provided the balance is maintained all change in the developed world takes place between the same original quantity of separate, opposed substances. (It may be noted that **107** gives a reason for postulating a *qualitatively* indefinite primary substance, while **108** gives one for postulating a *spatially* indefinite, or infinite, substance; cf. pp. 108ff.)

(v) *The Indefinite is all-enfolding and all-controlling*(?), *divine and immortal*

110 Aristotle *Phys.* Γ4, 203b7 ...τοῦ δὲ ἀπείρου οὐκ ἔστιν ἀρχή...ἀλλ' αὕτη τῶν ἄλλων εἶναι δοκεῖ, καὶ περιέχειν ἅπαντα καὶ πάντα κυβερνᾶν, ὥς φασιν ὅσοι μὴ ποιοῦσι παρὰ τὸ ἄπειρον ἄλλας αἰτίας οἷον νοῦν ἢ φιλίαν· καὶ τοῦτ' εἶναι τὸ θεῖον· ἀθάνατον γὰρ καὶ ἀνώλεθρον, ὥσπερ φησὶν ὁ Ἀναξίμανδρος καὶ οἱ πλεῖστοι τῶν φυσιολόγων.

111 Aristotle *de caelo* Γ5, 303b10 ἔνιοι γὰρ ἓν μόνον ὑποτίθενται, καὶ τοῦτο οἱ μὲν ὕδωρ, οἱ δ' ἀέρα, οἱ δὲ πῦρ, οἱ δ' ὕδατος μὲν λεπτότερον ἀέρος δὲ πυκνότερον· ὃ περιέχειν φασὶ πάντας τοὺς οὐρανοὺς ἄπειρον ὄν.

The assertion in **110** that the primary substance 'enfolds all and steers all' is assigned to those physicists who according to Aristotle postulated an infinite primary stuff but no separate cause of

---

109 *Nor, in order that generation may not fail, is it necessary for perceptible body to be* actually *infinite: for it is possible for the destruction of one thing to be the generation of the other, the sum of things being limited.*

110 ...*of the infinite there is no beginning*...*but this seems to be the beginning of the other things, and to surround all things and steer all, as all those say who do not postulate other causes, such as mind or love, above and beyond the infinite. And this is the divine; for it is immortal and indestructible, as Anaximander says and most of the physical speculators.*

111 *For some posit one substance only, and this some posit as water, some as air, some as fire, some as finer than water and thicker than air; which they say surrounds all the heavens, being infinite.*

motion—certainly, therefore, to the Milesians, Heraclitus, and Diogenes of Apollonia. 'Steers all' obviously reproduces Presocratic terminology, and the whole phrase 'enfolds all things and steers all' may form a single rhythmical unit. Anaximander, who is mentioned below in connexion with another phrase describing the same subject, and who is probably referred to in **111** in connexion with περιέχειν, could have been its author.[1]

[1] περιέχει is presumably genuine in Anaximenes fr. 2 (**163**), even if some of its context is re-worded; Anaxagoras (who is not in question in the Aristotelian passage) certainly used τὸ περιέχον in fr. 2 (**515**). κυβερνᾶν, of the steering of cosmic constituents or events, occurs in Heraclitus fr. 41 (**230**), Parmenides fr. 12, 3 (**358**), Diogenes of Apollonia fr. 5 (**606**). The two words could, of course, have been combined by Aristotle from different sources.

It is not easy, however, to see what manner of control could be exercised on all things by Anaximander's Indefinite. The Greek does not necessarily mean that the steering is due to the enfolding—both properties independently are natural ones for something conceived as divine—but it probably implies it. Again, the metaphor of steering does not necessarily entail a conscious and intelligent agent, for the steering of a ship can be regarded as a purely mechanical process, with reference to changes of direction imposed by the steering mechanism and not to the intentions of the navigator. Yet the archaic theomorphic, and thus to some extent anthropomorphic, conception of the primary stuff favours the assumption of purposeful action. Possible methods of control are the following: (1) by means of surrounding or enfolding: either (*a*) by preventing the further expansion of the differentiated world ('all things'), or (*b*) by making good the waste involved in change in the world; (2) by being immanent in all things, or some things, and providing either (*a*) motive power or life-force, or (*b*) a principle or rule or law of change; (3) by having initiated the world in such a way as to provide a continuing rule or law of change.—(1, *b*) was implied in **108**, but it was argued on pp. 113f. that this is unlikely to be valid for Anaximander; the same argument applies to (1, *a*). (2, *a*) would perhaps apply to Thales; (2, *b*), rather than (3), to Heraclitus (pp. 188, 200). (2), as well as (1), seems unlikely for Anaximander, for the Indefinite clearly cannot have been imagined as *immanent* in the developed world, even in the way that Thales' world was somehow interpenetrated with a divine life-substance: the Indefinite was probably so named because it was not identical with anything in nature. (3), however, could apply to Anaximander: it is feasible that the control exercised on all things was through the law of retribution between opposites, a law (or manner of behaviour) which was initiated when the first opposed substances appeared within the Indefinite and which still governs all change in the world. Nevertheless, it remains true that Aristotle *could* have had in mind someone other than Anaximander—Heraclitus, perhaps, or Diogenes of Apollonia—in the first part of **110**, and particularly, perhaps, in the phrase 'steers all things'.

The ascription of the idea of περιέχειν to the monists is repeated in **111**; here again the infinite material suggests Anaximander, though it surrounds not 'all things' but 'all the heavens'. This statement seems to have been taken up by Theophrastus (**103**), who evidently thought that it implied separate first heavens, each enclosing a separate world: see pp. 121 ff. for the idea of innumerable worlds. But Aristotle's phrase could be due to his using οὐρανοί in a special sense, as the spheres of the sun, moon and stars (cf. *de caelo* A9, 278b9); he might naturally apply his own analysis of the cosmos (based on the Eudoxan-Callippean scheme) to Anaximander, with his separate circles for the heavenly bodies (pp. 135 ff.), and intend nothing more than one complex world.

In the latter part of **110** we are told that the enfolding stuff 'is the divine; for it is immortal and indestructible, as Anaximander says and most of the physicists'. It is legitimate to suppose that the words 'immortal and indestructible' were intended to belong to Anaximander himself, though others said something similar. According to Theophrastus as reported in **103B**, however, the phrase was ἀίδιον καὶ ἀγήρω. There is a Homeric formula used of gods or their appurtenances, 'immortal and free from old age': so at *Od.* 5, 218 (to Calypso), ἡ μὲν γὰρ βροτός ἐστι, σὺ δ' ἀθάνατος καὶ ἀγήρως (cf. also *Il.* 2, 447). Short epic formulas often found their way into archaic prose, and it seems likely that this, rather than the somewhat repetitive equivalent in Aristotle, was the original form.[1] At all events Anaximander seems to have applied to the Indefinite the chief attributes of the Homeric gods, immortality and boundless power (connected in his case with boundless extent); it seems not improbable that he actually called it 'divine', and in this he was typical of the Presocratic thinkers in general.

[1] Especially since the two words are applied to the structure of the natural world, in a description of philosophical contemplation, by Euripides (fr. 910 Nauck[2]): 'observing the unageing structure of immortal Nature', ἀθανάτου καθορῶν φύσεως κόσμον ἀγήρω.

(vi) *The Indefinite is not in eternal motion, nor is it a mixture*

(These further points concerning the Indefinite are discussed under 'Cosmogony', pp. 126ff.)

THE EXTANT FRAGMENT OF ANAXIMANDER

112 Simplicius *Phys.* 24, 17 (repeated from **103** A) ...ἑτέραν τινὰ φύσιν ἄπειρον, ἐξ ἧς ἅπαντας γίνεσθαι τοὺς οὐρανοὺς καὶ τοὺς ἐν αὐτοῖς κόσμους. ἐξ ὧν δὲ ἡ γένεσίς ἐστι τοῖς οὖσι, καὶ τὴν φθορὰν εἰς ταῦτα γίνεσθαι 'κατὰ τὸ χρεών· διδόναι γὰρ αὐτὰ δίκην καὶ τίσιν ἀλλήλοις τῆς ἀδικίας κατὰ τὴν τοῦ χρόνου τάξιν', ποιητικωτέροις οὕτως ὀνόμασιν αὐτὰ λέγων.

(i) *Extent*

Simplicius is undoubtedly quoting from a version of Theophrastus' history of earlier philosophy, and from the section on the material principle, περὶ ἀρχῆς. The concluding clause, a judgement on Anaximander's style, shows that what immediately precedes is still a direct quotation. Thus κατὰ τὴν τοῦ χρόνου τάξιν, which many have held to be a Theophrastean paraphrase of κατὰ τὸ χρέων, should provisionally be accepted as original.[1] διδόναι – ἀδικίας is certainly original, and well exemplifies the poetical style noted by Theophrastus. κατὰ τὸ χρεών, too, should probably be accepted as by Anaximander: χρεών retained a marked poetical colouring (except in the special usage χρεών ἐστι) until the expression τὸ χρεών became popular in the Hellenistic period as a circumlocution for death. It is the most plausible restoration in Heraclitus fr. 80, κατ' ἔριν καὶ χρεών (for χρεώμενα), to give a similar phrase to the one under discussion. The preceding words, ἐξ ὧν – εἰς ταῦτα γίνεσθαι, have been much disputed. The use of the abstracts γένεσις and φθορά, well established in Peripatetic but not (from the other extant evidence) in Presocratic vocabulary,

---

112 ...*some other* apeiron *nature, from which come into being all the heavens and the worlds in them. And the source of coming-to-be for existing things is that into which destruction, too, happens, 'according to necessity; for they pay penalty and retribution to each other for their injustice according to the assessment of Time', as he describes it in these rather poetical terms.*

suggests that these belong to Theophrastus. The sentiment, too, looks Peripatetic: it is a close restatement of one of Aristotle's basic dogmas about the primary substance of the physical monists, 'all things are destroyed into that from which they came-to-be' (*Phys.* Γ 5, 204 b 33; cf. also **87** line 3). Theophrastus was given to quoting single words or phrases; thus he could have quoted the concluding phrase of a sentence, the rest of which he had paraphrased, in order to emphasize the connexion with the following sentence which he quotes in full. See further under §v.

[1] Theophrastus certainly used similar phraseology himself, notably τάξιν τινὰ καὶ χρόνον ὡρισμένον (of Heraclitus). But this is very different from the bold personification of τὴν τοῦ χρόνου τάξιν.

(ii) *The meaning of the main assertion*

The context shows that Theophrastus regarded the quotation as appropriate to the view he had just attributed to Anaximander, that 'all the heavens and the worlds in them' came from the Indefinite. ἐξ ὧν... (the plural is generic) adds that, since they came from the Indefinite, they will also return to it 'of necessity; for they pay penalty and retribution to each other...'. It appears from the version of ps.-Plutarch, **103** C, that by 'the heavens and the worlds in them' Theophrastus was referring to ἄπειροι κόσμοι, innumerable worlds. But there is a very strong objection to understanding the words quoted from Anaximander to refer to innumerable worlds coming-to-be from, and being destroyed into, the Indefinite. ἀλλήλοις shows that retribution is made *mutually* between the parties who are the subject of the sentence. Can we really believe that the divine Indefinite commits *injustice* on its own products, and has to pay them recompense? This, surely, is intolerable; but if so, then Theophrastus (who was not infallible in such matters of interpretation, any more than Aristotle) mistook the proper application of Anaximander's dictum. It has long been observed that the things which commit injustice on each other must be equals, different but correlative; and that these are most likely to be the opposed substances which make up the differentiated world.[1]

[1] G. Vlastos, *CP* 42 (1947) 171 f., following Cherniss, tried to show how the ultimate balance between opposites could be reconciled with the reabsorption of the world into the Indefinite: when this happens, he said, the opposites finally settle up accounts with each other (not with the

Indefinite). But if the principle of justice applies in the present world, it is not easy to see how such a drastic change, affecting all its constituents, as the return of the world to the Indefinite could ever come about.

(iii) *The opposites*

It will be seen later (**120**, **123**) that the production of opposites was an essential stage of cosmogony for Anaximander; it is therefore reasonable to assume that they played an important part in the developed world. The interplay of opposites is basic in Heraclitus, who seems to have deliberately corrected Anaximander by his paradox 'strife is *justice*' (fr. 80, **214**). Anaximander is the first in whom the concept of opposed natural substances (which recurs in Heraclitus, Parmenides, Empedocles, Anaxagoras, and in the Pythagoreans certainly as early as Alcmaeon) clearly appears. Doubtless he was influenced by observation of the main seasonal changes, in which heat and drought in summer seem to be pitted against cold and rain in winter. The constant interchange between opposed substances is explained by Anaximander in a legalistic metaphor derived from human society: the prevalence of one substance at the expense of its contrary is 'injustice', and a reaction takes place through the infliction of punishment by the restoration of equality—of more than equality, since the wrong-doer is deprived of part of his original substance, too. This is given to the victim in addition to what was his own, and in turn leads (it might be inferred) to κόρος, surfeit, on the part of the former victim, who now commits injustice on the former aggressor. Thus both the continuity and the stability of natural change were motivated, for Anaximander, by means of this anthropomorphic metaphor. The main opposites in cosmogony were the hot substance and the cold substance—flame or fire and mist or air. These, with which are associated dryness and moisture, are also the main cosmological opposites, most notably involved in the large-scale changes in the natural world. They were probably isolated by Heraclitus (fr. 126) before ever they were elevated to the form of standard irreducible elements by Empedocles. Caution must be shown, to be sure, about the opposites in Anaximander: it is possible, for example, that the Peripatetics substituted their own more abstract formulations, the hot and the cold and so on, for much more concrete expressions by Anaximander himself. For him, the world may have been made up of substances which, while they each possessed individual tendencies contrary to those of some of the others, need not have been formally described as opposites, that is, for example, as the hard and the soft; but simply as fire, wind, iron, water, man, woman and so on.

(iv) '*The assessment of Time*'

The concluding phrase of the quotation, 'according to the assessment of Time', elaborates the injustice-metaphor. What kind of assessment does Time make? The word τάξις suggests the ordaining of punishment by a judge or, more aptly, the assessment of tribute (as in the Athenian tribute-lists). In these cases what is ordained or assessed is the *amount* of the punishment or payment; this can hardly be the primary purpose of *Time's* assessment. Time must presumably control the time-limit for payment; the amount would be fixed, as total restitution plus a proportionate *amende*. The idea of a time-limit is appropriate: the injustice of summer has to be made good within the roughly equal period of winter, that of night during the period of day, and so on. No uniform period can be meant: Time makes the assessment to meet the particular case. That the additional idea of inevitability is implicit in the remarkable personification of Time here may be indicated by the strikingly similar 'trial conducted by Time' in Solon, roughly a generation before Anaximander:

113 Solon fr. 24 Diehl, lines 1–7

ἐγὼ δὲ τῶν μὲν οὕνεκα ξυνήγαγον
δῆμον, τί τούτων πρὶν τυχεῖν ἐπαυσάμην;
συμμαρτυροίη ταῦτ' ἂν ἐν δίκῃ Χρόνου
μήτηρ μεγίστη δαιμόνων 'Ολυμπίων
ἄριστα, Γῆ μέλαινα, τῆς ἐγώ ποτε
ὅρους ἀνεῖλον πολλαχῇ πεπηγότας·
πρόσθεν δὲ δουλεύουσα, νῦν ἐλευθέρα.

Here Earth justifies Solon's claim because *with the lapse of time* she has become free; that is what Time's trial signifies. No predetermined time-limit is intended here. Elsewhere in Solon, too, it is the inevitability of retribution that is stressed again and again;

---

113 *Why did I cease before I gained the objects for whose sake I brought together the people? The great mother of the Olympian deities would be my best supporting witness for this in the court of Time—black Earth, whose boundary-stones, fixed in many places, I once removed; formerly was she enslaved, now is she free.*

so in Anaximander, we may infer, injustice must *inevitably* be punished, sooner or later in time—but here the periods, since they are those of the great seasonal changes, as well as other less important ones, must be supervised and assessed appropriately to each case.

(v) *The original of Theophrastus' paraphrase*

It has been suggested on pp. 117f. that 'from what things coming-to-be is for the things that are, destruction also takes place into these' may be a paraphrase by Theophrastus of something in Anaximander which Theophrastus thought could be recast into the common Aristotelian formula. If that statement in Anaximander immediately preceded his dictum about the retribution of opposites (as the transitional phrase κατὰ τὸ χρεών may suggest), then it too was presumably concerned with the behaviour of opposites in the developed world. One sentiment, I suggest, which Anaximander might have expressed in this context, and which could have deceived Theophrastus in the way indicated, was that opposite substances pay recompense each to its own opposite and to no other; for example the hot substance to the cold, and not to the heavy or the hard. This is a necessary hypothesis for Anaximander's theory of cosmic stability, obvious to us but not so obvious then, since Heraclitus also emphasized it for his own special purposes. The axiom may have been stated in terms so general, and possibly in a context so isolated, that Theophrastus was able to mistake its proper reference.

INNUMERABLE WORLDS

(i) *Successive rather than coexistent*

Plural worlds of some kind were attributed to Anaximander by Theophrastus: '...some other substance of infinite spatial extent, from which come into being all the heavens and the worlds in them' (**103**A). The fragment, about things paying to each other the penalty for injustice, was adduced as somehow relevant to this process; in this Theophrastus seems to have been mistaken (pp. 118ff.). In the doxographical versions of Theophrastus we learn that these plural worlds were ἄπειροι, i.e. infinite or innumerable. There has been much controversy as to whether these innumerable worlds were successive in time (so that our world will eventually pass away, to be succeeded by another, and so on), or coexistent. Zeller supported the former interpretation, Burnet the latter; Cornford demonstrated the fallacy of many of Burnet's arguments and reinstated the Zellerian interpretation in general favour (see *CQ* 28 (1934) 1 ff., and *Principium Sapientiae* 177 ff.). It may be accepted that if Anaximander believed in innumerable worlds it was in a series of successive single worlds and not in any form of coexistent worlds: as Cornford argued, there is 'nothing in the appearance of nature' to suggest the latter (except the heavenly bodies, which, however, were described by Anaximander not as worlds but simply as gaps in fire-filled circles of air: see pp. 135 ff.). Nor, it may be added, was there any mythological or other conceivable motive or precedent which might have persuaded him to elaborate here an anti-empirical theory.

(ii) *But are even successive worlds plausible in Anaximander?*

I have elsewhere suggested (*CQ* N.S. 5 (1955) 28 ff.) that Anaximander may in reality have believed in *no* type of innumerable worlds; and this suggestion is further argued here. The reader should be aware that the generally accepted view is that he believed in a succession of single worlds, each being produced by and destroyed into the Indefinite. This is not unlike what Theophrastus believed, and it possesses a *prima facie* credibility. If it is true, it is still worth emphasizing what a remarkable idea this was.

If coexistent worlds might be suggested to some people (though not, as it happens, to Anaximander) by the heavenly bodies, there is nothing whatever in 'the appearance of nature' to suggest *successive* worlds—successive separate worlds, that is (for such are clearly meant by both Theophrastus and his modern followers), as distinct from successive changes in the state of the one continuing world. These last are envisaged in the mythical catastrophes by fire and flood described in Plato's *Timaeus*, 22 C–E, and were to some extent suggested by natural phenomena; cf. pp. 139 f. We may take it that the Milesians were trying to account for the world as they experienced it; their explanations were often fanciful and dogmatic, but were none the less attempts to account for observed phenomena. Now there was no reason whatever to assume that the world was going to be destroyed, or that if destroyed it would be succeeded by another—an idea equally foreign to the naïve mythopoeic view (it was not suggested in any Greek mythological source) and to the empirical analytic view.

It is true that the world may at times have been treated as a kind of living organism—but the life was the immortal life of the gods, who are born, as the world was born, but who live for ever. It would be entirely contrary to the whole mythical background of Greek thought, and to the dictates of common sense, to believe in a cycle of separate worlds; and their appearance in Anaximander is extraordinary. But to anyone already familiar with Empedocles' radical changes of the σφαῖρος (pp. 326ff.) and with the atomist theory of Leucippus and Democritus, of innumerable worlds coming-to-be and passing away throughout infinite space (pp. 409ff.), and already perhaps prone to misinterpret Heraclitus as having postulated a succession of worlds (p. 202 n.), the oddity would not be conspicuous. Given a specific motive Theophrastus might, therefore, have made a false and anachronistic attribution. Such a motive, it is suggested, was provided by the atomists' arguments for innumerable worlds, as succinctly and influentially re-stated by Aristotle.

(iii) *Atomist arguments applied by Theophrastus to Anaximander?*

114 Aristotle *Phys.* Γ4, 203b23 ...διὰ γὰρ τὸ ἐν τῇ νοήσει μὴ ὑπολείπειν καὶ ὁ ἀριθμὸς δοκεῖ ἄπειρος εἶναι καὶ τὰ μαθηματικὰ μεγέθη καὶ τὸ ἔξω τοῦ οὐρανοῦ· ἀπείρου δ' ὄντος τοῦ ἔξω, καὶ σῶμα ἄπειρον εἶναι δοκεῖ καὶ κόσμοι· τί γὰρ μᾶλλον τοῦ κενοῦ ἐνταῦθα ἢ ἐνταῦθα;

This passage gives the fifth and most important motive, according to Aristotle, for the development of a concept of infinity. The argument that if what is outside the heaven is infinite then body is infinite, and that if body is infinite then worlds are infinite, is derived from the atomists, of whom Aristotle was undoubtedly thinking here. But the infinite worlds are necessitated by the postulate of infinite body, whether or not this is in turn argued (as by the atomists) from infinite void. On this reasoning Theophrastus might have been impelled to assume that the first and most notable believer in infinite body (as he thought)—namely Anaximander—also posited infinite worlds. These worlds would

---

114 ...*through not giving out in our thought, both number seems to be infinite and mathematical magnitudes and what lies outside the heaven. But if what lies outside is infinite, body also seems to be infinite, and worlds too: for why should they exist more in one part of the void than in another?*

behave like the atomists' in that they would be coexistent and also successive—that is, coming-to-be and passing away continually. The assumption that all innumerable worlds are of this kind appears to be made by Aristotle in the latter part of **118**. If we find evidence that Theophrastus treated Anaximander's worlds as both coexistent and successive, this will suggest strongly that he was applying atomistic reasoning to Anaximander.

(iv) *The doxographical evidence may suggest that Theophrastus applied atomist-type worlds to Anaximander*

If one turns to the doxographical sources for further elucidation of Theophrastus' views, the evidence is found to be confused and to some extent corrupt. Thus one of our twin sources for Aetius (ps.-Plutarch; cf. Aetius II, 1, 3, DK 12 A 17) assigns innumerable worlds only to the atomists, while the other (Stobaeus) assigns them in addition to Anaximander, Anaximenes, Archelaus, Xenophanes(!), and Diogenes of Apollonia. Neither version can correctly represent Theophrastus: but both could have arisen from a generalization of the atomistic arguments. There was a further confusion in Aetius (I, 7, 12, DK 12 A 17) between the innumerable-world hypothesis and the common opinion that the stars were gods. These confusions (which are seen also in Cicero) are unlikely to have been caused by a simple statement in Theophrastus that Anaximander postulated successive worlds. Two important witnesses had quite definite views:

115 Simplicius *Phys.* 1121, 5 οἱ μὲν γὰρ ἀπείρους τῷ πλήθει τοὺς κόσμους ὑποθέμενοι, ὡς οἱ περὶ Ἀναξίμανδρον καὶ Λεύκιππον καὶ Δημόκριτον καὶ ὕστερον οἱ περὶ Ἐπίκουρον, γινομένους αὐτοὺς καὶ φθειρομένους ὑπέθεντο ἐπ' ἄπειρον, ἄλλων μὲν ἀεὶ γινομένων ἄλλων δὲ φθειρομένων, καὶ τὴν κίνησιν ἀίδιον ἔλεγον....

This comment on **114** is probably Simplicius' own, and does not directly reproduce Theophrastus. Simplicius might, however, be expected to be influenced by the Theophrastean interpretation; though we cannot be sure that *he* was not misapplying the atomist arguments, as Cornford thought. Yet the same interpretation

---

115 *For those who supposed the worlds to be infinite in number, like the associates of Anaximander and Leucippus and Democritus and afterwards those of Epicurus, supposed them to be coming-to-be and passing away for an infinite time, with some of them always coming-to-be and others passing away; and they said that motion was eternal....*

appears in a source earlier than Simplicius, and one which is dependent on the Theophrastean tradition through a different channel (there is a confusion with Anaxagoras in the first part):

116 Augustinus *C.D.* VIII, 2 non enim ex una re sicut Thales ex umore, sed ex suis propriis principiis quâsque res nasci putavit (*sc.* Anaximander). quae rerum principia singularum esse credidit infinita, et innumerabiles mundos gignere et quaecumque in eis oriuntur; eosque mundos modo dissolvi modo iterum gigni existimavit, quanta quisque aetate sua manere potuerit.

Worlds coming-to-be and passing away throughout space (or the Indefinite) are surely intended here; 'quanta...potuerit' suggests an irregularity which is foreign to the idea of a sequence of single worlds, but which is essential to the atomistic conception.[1]

[1] A passage in Cicero (*N.D.* I, 10, 25, DK 12 A 17) which ascribes to Anaximander worlds rising and setting 'longis intervallis' *might* point in the same direction, though certainty is impossible because of the ambiguity of 'intervallis' (spatial or temporal?).

Thus two sources independent of each other, the one indirectly (here) and the other directly influenced by the tradition from Theophrastus, assigned atomistic worlds to Anaximander. Further, such an ascription by Theophrastus himself, of worlds both coexistent and successive, would at least provide a possible motive for the confusion between the two in some parts of the dependent doxographical tradition on Anaximander.

(v) *Further considerations against and for the hypothesis*

Two difficulties of this interpretation must be mentioned.

(*a*) It is possible from **111** that Aristotle meant to attribute plural worlds to the monistic physicists in general: the infinite primary substance, they said, 'surrounds all the heavens (οὐρανούς)'. To meet this, it was proposed on p. 116 that Aristotle was using οὐρανοί in his special sense of 'celestial spheres': he meant 'everything enclosed by the first heaven' and (perhaps because of the analogy of Anaximander's circles) expressed this concept in language appropriate to his own cosmology. Certainly in **110** the

---

116 *For he [Anaximander] thought that things were born not from one substance, as Thales thought from water, but each from its own particular principles. These principles of individual things he believed to be infinite, and to give birth to innumerable worlds and whatsoever arises in them; and those worlds, he thought, are now dissolved, now born again, according to the age to which each is able to survive.*

infinite primary substance is said to enclose simply 'all things', and there is no suggestion elsewhere in Aristotle of innumerable separate worlds before the atomists.

(*b*) If Theophrastus thought that anyone who postulated infinite material should also postulate innumerable worlds like the atomists, why did Simplicius write in **150** (the continuation of **115**) that *Anaximenes*, whose primary substance was described as infinite by Theophrastus and Simplicius, believed in successive *single* worlds? The distinction from Anaximander is puzzling on any interpretation. But Heraclitus and Diogenes are mentioned as sharing the belief; Simplicius certainly ascribed successive worlds to Heraclitus, and he may have thought that Anaximenes should be classed with him, as a believer in a specific primary substance, rather than with Anaximander and the atomists, whose ἀρχή was undifferentiated. There is also a possibility that Anaximenes does not belong here at all: see n. on p. 151. Nevertheless these two pieces of evidence, puzzling as they are, cannot be regarded as neutralized. On the other side there were three special characteristics of Anaximander's cosmology which might well have encouraged an innumerable-world interpretation: (1) the theory that the earth was surrounded by a number—perhaps an indefinite number—of rings of the celestial bodies (pp. 135ff.); (2) the theory that the earth was drying up, which was probably part of a wider theory of cycles of change on the earth's surface—a succession of κόσμοι in the sense of local arrangements (pp. 139f.); (3) the potential ambiguity of the fragment known to Theophrastus. This fragment seems properly to have described the interaction of substances within the world, but Theophrastus misapplied it to interaction between the world and the Indefinite. Thus (1) might help to suggest coexistent worlds, (2) and (3) successive ones. Theophrastus may have applied atomistic arguments and imposed upon Anaximander worlds that were both.

COSMOGONY

(i) '*Eternal motion*' *and vortex: are they relevant to Anaximander?*

117 Hippolytus *Ref.* 1, 6, 2 (from **103** B) ...κίνησιν ἀίδιον εἶναι, ἐν ᾗ συμβαίνει γίνεσθαι τοὺς οὐρανούς.

---

117 *...motion was eternal, in which it results that the heavens come into being.*

118 Aristotle *Phys.* Θ 1, 250b11 Πότερον γέγονέ ποτε κίνησις... ἢ οὔτ' ἐγένετο οὔτε φθείρεται ἀλλ' ἀεὶ ἦν καὶ ἀεὶ ἔσται, καὶ τοῦτ' ἀθάνατον καὶ ἄπαυστον ὑπάρχει τοῖς οὖσιν, οἷον ζωή τις οὖσα τοῖς φύσει συνεστῶσι πᾶσιν;...ἀλλ' ὅσοι μὲν ἀπείρους τε κόσμους εἶναί φασι, καὶ τοὺς μὲν γίγνεσθαι τοὺς δὲ φθείρεσθαι τῶν κόσμων, ἀεί φασιν εἶναι κίνησιν...ὅσοι δ' ἕνα, ⟨ἢ ἀεὶ⟩ ἢ μὴ ἀεί, καὶ περὶ τῆς κινήσεως ὑποτίθενται κατὰ λόγον.[1]

119 Aristotle *de caelo* B 13, 295a7 ἀλλὰ μὴν εἴ γε ἔστι κίνησίς τις κατὰ φύσιν, οὐκ ἂν ἡ βίαιος εἴη φορὰ μόνον οὐδ' ἠρέμησις· ὥστ' εἰ βίᾳ νῦν ἡ γῆ μένει, καὶ συνῆλθεν ἐπὶ τὸ μέσον φερομένη διὰ τὴν δίνησιν. ταύτην γὰρ τὴν αἰτίαν πάντες λέγουσιν ἐκ τῶν ἐν τοῖς ὑγροῖς καὶ περὶ τὸν ἀέρα συμβαινόντων· ἐν τούτοις γὰρ ἀεὶ φέρεται τὰ μείζω καὶ τὰ βαρύτερα πρὸς τὸ μέσον τῆς δίνης. διὸ δὴ τὴν γῆν πάντες ὅσοι τὸν οὐρανὸν γεννῶσιν ἐπὶ τὸ μέσον συνελθεῖν φασίν.

[1] ⟨ἢ ἀεὶ⟩ (Ross) is supported by the comments of both Themistius and Simplicius. The sense is that those who postulate one eternal world also postulate eternal motion; those who postulate one non-eternal world do not. Note that successive single worlds (which would require eternal motion) are not included in this analysis.

Theophrastus evidently stated that the Indefinite was characterized by an eternal motion, which was somehow responsible for the innumerable worlds. He likewise attributed eternal motion to Anaximenes, presumably because, like Anaximander, Anaximenes did not specify anything that could obviously act as a cause of change. Aristotle frequently rebuked the monists for this very fault; but **118** shows that he could on occasion understand their ways of thinking better than his pupil Theophrastus. There he considers an ungenerated motion which is 'deathless', which inheres in things as a kind of life. He was thinking of Thales,

---

118 *Did motion come into being at some time...or did it neither come-to-be nor is it destroyed, but did it always exist and will it go on for ever, and is it immortal and unceasing for existing things, being like a kind of life for all natural objects?...But all who say that there are infinite worlds, and that some of them are coming-to-be and others passing away, say that motion always exists...while all who say that there is one world, whether eternal or not, make an analogous supposition about motion.*

119 *Yet if indeed there is some kind of natural motion, there would not be enforced motion only, or enforced rest; so that if the earth now stays in place by force, it also came together to the centre by being carried there because of the vortex.* (*For this is the cause that everyone gives, through what happens in water and in air: for in these the larger and heavier objects are always carried toward the centre of the vortex.*) *Therefore all who generate the heaven say that the earth came together to the centre.*

perhaps (p. 97); but the phrase 'immortal and unceasing' reminds one of the phraseology which he attributed to Anaximander, among others, in **110**: he probably realized, then, that for Anaximander change in the cosmos was bound up with the divinity, the power of life and movement, of the Indefinite. What Theophrastus had in mind as Anaximander's 'eternal motion' was probably some more explicit, mechanical kind of motion like that of the atomists, who are mentioned indirectly in the latter part of **118**; we have seen (pp. 123ff.) that Theophrastus may well have grouped Anaximander with the atomists over the question of innumerable worlds. Some modern scholars (e.g. Burnet) have held that Anaximander postulated a confused agitation like the winnowing motion in Plato's *Timaeus*; others (e.g. Tannery) have assigned a circular motion to the Indefinite. Both are equally unlikely. It is highly improbable that Anaximander himself ever isolated this question of motion; the Indefinite was divine, and naturally possessed the power to move what and where it willed. To define its properties further would defeat Anaximander's purpose.

One often reads of a vortex or vortices in Anaximander. There is in fact no evidence for this apart from Aristotle in **119**, a highly involved piece of *a priori* reasoning in which the reference of 'therefore' at the beginning of the last sentence is unclear. But in any case Anaximander was certainly not in Aristotle's mind when he wrote this passage; for shortly afterwards (**125**) Anaximander is distinguished from the majority of the physicists on the ground that his earth remained at the centre by equilibrium and not by conventional kinds of 'force'. This distinction and the subsequent discussion come as an appendix to the discussion of vortex-action, which is no longer under consideration; thus it may be accepted that Aristotle was talking loosely in saying in **119** that 'all who generate the heaven say that the earth came together to the centre', if this implies more than accretion. Vortices are not associated in our doxographical sources with anyone before Empedocles, though Aristotle's generalization in **119** would surely have led Theophrastus to mention earlier occurrences, had he been able to find them. It is, nevertheless, just possible that what was separated off from the Indefinite in the first stage of Anaximander's cosmogony was a vortex, see p. 132; what is quite out of the question is either that the whole Indefinite was in vortex-motion, or that the diurnal movement of the heavenly bodies is due to this cause (which would not suit the earth's equilibrium in **125**). The tendency of heavy bodies to the centre is assumed in most early cosmogonies. This may have been due in part, as implied in **119**, to the observation of vortex-action in everyday experience; but in part it simply reflected the obvious arrangement of the components of the visible cosmos.

(ii) *How did the opposites come from the Indefinite?*

120 Aristotle *Phys.* A4, 187a20 (from **106**) οἱ δ' ἐκ τοῦ ἑνὸς ἐνούσας τὰς ἐναντιότητας ἐκκρίνεσθαι, ὥσπερ Ἀναξίμανδρός φησι καὶ ὅσοι δ' ἓν καὶ πολλά φασιν εἶναι, ὥσπερ Ἐμπεδοκλῆς καὶ Ἀναξαγόρας· ἐκ τοῦ μίγματος γὰρ καὶ οὗτοι ἐκκρίνουσι τἆλλα.

121 Simplicius *Phys.* 24, 21 (continuing **103**A) δῆλον δὲ ὅτι τὴν εἰς ἄλληλα μεταβολὴν τῶν τεττάρων στοιχείων οὗτος θεασάμενος οὐκ ἠξίωσεν ἕν τι τούτων ὑποκείμενον ποιῆσαι, ἀλλά τι ἄλλο παρὰ ταῦτα· οὗτος δὲ οὐκ ἀλλοιουμένου τοῦ στοιχείου τὴν γένεσιν ποιεῖ, ἀλλ' ἀποκρινομένων τῶν ἐναντίων διὰ τῆς ἀιδίου κινήσεως.

It is almost certain from the first sentence of **121** that Simplicius is no longer quoting Theophrastus, but giving his own paraphrase of what he has just quoted. In the second sentence he partly depends on the analysis by Aristotle in **106**. There are two notable differences between his comment and the Aristotelian original: (*a*) the opposites are separated *out* (ἐκκρίνεσθαι) in Aristotle, separated *off* (ἀποκρινομένων) in Simplicius; (*b*) Simplicius, but not Aristotle, said that the separation was due to the eternal motion. Now it has been argued by U. Hölscher (*Hermes* 81 (1953) 258ff.) that Simplicius in the second sentence of **121** (as at *Phys.* 150, 22) is simply and solely enlarging on Aristotle, and reproduces no Theophrastean interpretation whatever; this passage, therefore, is not good evidence for Anaximander unless Aristotle is reliable in **120**. But, the argument continues, Aristotle was prone to read his

---

120 *But the others say that the opposites are separated out from the One, being present in it, as Anaximander says and all who say there are one and many, like Empedocles and Anaxagoras; for these, too, separate out the rest from the mixture.*

121 *It is clear that he* [*Anaximander*], *seeing the changing of the four elements into each other, thought it right to make none of these the substratum, but something else beside these; and he produces coming-to-be not through the alteration of the element, but by the separation off of the opposites through the eternal motion.*

own simple bodies, and two pairs of basic opposites, into everything, and he perverted Anaximander by substituting separating *out* for separating *off* from the Indefinite, thus making this into a mixture of opposites. Theophrastus attributed separating *off* to Anaximander, but of the innumerable worlds and not of opposites (ἀποκεκρίσθαι in **103** C); and this, according to Hölscher, was the proper application of the word. Against this ingenious theory the following points may be made. The mention of the eternal motion by Simplicius is Theophrastean and not Aristotelian in source (see **117**); so, apparently, is his use of the verb for separating *off*. Therefore, while it is agreed that he was not here quoting Theophrastus, he probably did have Theophrastus' assessment of Anaximander in mind. Further, Hölscher has not succeeded in convincingly destroying a most damaging piece of evidence, passage **123**. This continuation of Ps.-Plutarch's doxography in **103** C states that 'the productive from the eternal of hot and cold was separated off at the beginning of this world', and continues with details of the cosmogony. This, though garbled, represents Theophrastus, and shows that Theophrastus accepted separation off from the Indefinite, and opposites, as involved in Anaximander's cosmogony. Since the extant fragment (**112**) suggests that the world is still composed of opposites, it seems legitimate to accept from both Theophrastus and Aristotle that opposites were involved in cosmogony.

Nevertheless, we may accept the warning about ἐκκρίνεσθαι in Aristotle: it seems quite likely that this is a distortion of ἀποκρίνεσθαι. And according to **123** what was separated off was not opposite substances (flame and mist) but something that produced them. This might have been a kind of seed, it might have been a vortex; there was perhaps a confusion in the tradition (see p. 133). At all events we have no right to assume with Aristotle that the opposites were *in* (ἐνούσας) the Indefinite, and were separated *out* of it; still less may we define the Indefinite as a mixture, as Aristotle undoubtedly did.[1] The Indefinite was not clearly defined and analysed by Anaximander; but this does not mean, of course, that he might not have been making it behave, in respect of its products, in some way like a compound—either a mechanical mixture or a fusion.[2] If the opposites arose directly from the Indefinite by being separated off, as Simplicius states in **121**, then the Indefinite was being unconsciously treated as unhomogeneous;

for separation off cannot simply imply the isolation of one part of the Indefinite, that part which becomes the world: it implies this *and* some change in the isolated part. If this change was not the appearance of opposites, but of something productive of them, then one might infer that the Indefinite was the kind of thing that contained, for example, sperms or embryos: but that still does not mean that Anaximander thought of it as being of a specific character.

[1] Cf. **122** Aristotle *Met.* Λ 1, 1069b20 ...καὶ τοῦτ' ἐστὶ τὸ 'Αναξαγόρου ἓν (βέλτιον γὰρ ἢ ὁμοῦ πάντα) καὶ 'Εμπεδοκλέους τὸ μίγμα καὶ 'Αναξιμάνδρου, καὶ ὡς Δημόκριτός φησιν. If **120** is doubtful, this passage certainly seems to attribute a mixture to Anaximander. This used to be thought very scandalous. G. Calogero suggests 'Αναξιμάνδρου ⟨τὸ ἄπειρον⟩.

[2] As suggested by Cornford and by Vlastos (*CP* 42 (1947) 170–2). Theophrastus is quoted by Simplicius (**507**) as saying that the mixture of all things in Anaxagoras could be regarded as 'one substance indefinite both in kind and in size', and that he would resemble Anaximander—but whether in the idea of *mixture* is not clear.

(iii) *The actual formation of the cosmos*

123 Ps.-Plutarch *Strom.* 2 (continuing **103** C and **124** A; DK 12 A 10) φησὶ δὲ τὸ ἐκ τοῦ ἀιδίου γόνιμον θερμοῦ τε καὶ ψυχροῦ κατὰ τὴν γένεσιν τοῦδε τοῦ κόσμου ἀποκριθῆναι καὶ τινα ἐκ τούτου φλογὸς σφαῖραν περιφυῆναι τῷ περὶ τὴν γῆν ἀέρι ὡς τῷ δένδρῳ φλοιόν· ἧστινος ἀπορραγείσης καὶ εἴς τινας ἀποκλεισθείσης κύκλους ὑποστῆναι τὸν ἥλιον καὶ τὴν σελήνην καὶ τοὺς ἀστέρας. (Continues at **137**.)

This passage (supplemented, for the heavenly bodies, by Hippolytus in **127**) is virtually our only authority for Theophrastus' report of the details of the cosmogonical process in Anaximander. The *Stromateis* are usually less accurate than either Simplicius or Hippolytus in reproducing Theophrastus (cf. **103**); but it cannot be doubted that the present passage is based on him, and the citation of the bark-simile, which looks as though it is derived

---

122 *...and this is the One of Anaxagoras (for this is a better description than 'all things together') and the mixture of Empedocles and of Anaximander, and what Democritus describes.*

123 *He says that that which is productive from the eternal of hot and cold was separated off at the coming-to-be of this world, and that a kind of sphere of flame from this was formed round the air surrounding the earth, like bark round a tree. When this was broken off and shut off in certain circles, the sun and the moon and the stars were formed.*

from Anaximander himself, suggests that in places, at least, the passage follows Theophrastus fairly closely.

Theophrastus had previously stated (**103** A, B, C) that innumerable worlds came out of the Indefinite; the present passage describes the emergence of our world, and is unaffected by whether or not Anaximander accepted successive worlds. The phrase ἐκ τοῦ ἀιδίου, 'from the eternal', perhaps means 'from the Indefinite', which was described as immortal.[1] 'The productive from the eternal of hot and cold...was separated off' is still difficult. γόνιμος (productive) was a favourite Peripatetic word, which usually retained some flavour, if only a slight one, of biological generation. In the fifth century, on the other hand, γόνιμος only occurs twice, in Euripides and Aristophanes—the latter use being a weakened metaphor—except for a special medical-technical use (of critical periods in disease; the biological meaning is almost suppressed) in the Hippocratic *Visits*. It seems unlikely, therefore, that it is an Anaximandrean word; and in view of occurrences of the word, especially in Plutarch, as a dead metaphor with no biological implications we cannot be sure that it was here intended to represent generation of a biological kind, however remotely. This must be emphasized because of the popularity of Cornford's suggestion that this stage in Anaximander corresponds with the production of a cosmogonical egg in 'Orphic' accounts (on which see pp. 41–8). It would not be surprising to find that Anaximander resorted to the old mythological medium of sexual generation to account for the most difficult stage in world-formation—the production of heterogeneous plurality out of a single source, and that, here, an Indefinite one. One would not, however, expect a crude and explicit device like the egg; and the evidence is not certainly in favour of any such sexual device, however metaphorical. A completely different suggestion was made by Vlastos (*CP* 42 (1947) 171 n. 140), that τὸ γόνιμον was not a thing so much as a process. A vortex, for instance, might well account for the appearance of opposites; for the phraseology we may compare Democritus fr. 167, δῖνον ἀπὸ τοῦ παντὸς ἀποκριθῆναι ('a vortex was separated off from the whole').[2] Yet why did Theophrastus not simply use the word δῖνος or δίνη to describe a process completely familiar to him, and one which would further have emphasized the resemblance of Anaximander and Anaxagoras (n. 2 on p. 131)? If he had used the word, we should not have this vague circumlocution in ps.-Plutarch. It is at least a possibility that Theophrastus himself was in doubt about this first stage, perhaps through lack of full information, and used a vague expression to cover himself; but he would not have *invented* an intermediary between the Indefinite and the opposites (which could have been more easily produced, as in **120**, directly), and judgement must be reserved on its character.

[1] Another possibility is that the whole phrase means 'that which was capable from all time of producing...'. In this case we should expect ἐξ ἀιδίου, without the article. But the insertion of ἐκ τοῦ ἀιδίου between τὸ and γόνιμον, on the other interpretation, is almost as strange. In any case, the tortuosity of expression is not immediately due to Anaximander, and the obscure meaning is not greatly affected either way.

[2] That 'separating off' can be applied to the products of a vortex, as well as to the vortex itself, is demonstrated by Anaxagoras fr. 9 *init.*, οὕτω τούτων περιχωρούντων τε καὶ ἀποκρινομένων ὑπὸ βίης τε καὶ ταχυτῆτος... ('these things thus revolving and being separated off by force and speed...').

The nature of the hot (substance) and cold (substance) thus cryptically produced appears from what follows: they are flame and air-mist (the inner part of which is assumed to have condensed into earth). The ball of flame fits closely round the air, as closely as bark grows round a tree; this can be the point of the simile, which does not necessarily suggest that the flame is annular (though the eventual shape of the earth is cylindrical, see **124**). So far, then, something has been isolated in the Indefinite which produces flame and air-mist; earth condenses at the core, flame fits closely round the air. Now the ball of flame bursts, breaks up into circles which are enclosed by mist which has also expanded (cf. **127**), and forms the heavenly bodies. From **134** and **135** we learn that the moist earth is dried by the sun, the remnants of the moisture being sea.[1]

[1] It is possible that **123** contains other signs of biological-embryological language, apart from the dubious γόνιμον. H. C. Baldry (*CQ* 26 (1932) 27 ff.) pointed out that ἀπόκρισις was used in embryological treatises to describe the separation of the seed from the parent; φλοιός could be used of a caul, and was perhaps used in a similar sense by Anaximander—see **136**; ἀπορρήγνυσθαι is sometimes used of a new growth detaching itself from the parent body (which it can hardly mean here, *contra* Heidel and Baldry). But none of these words has an exclusively embryological sense; they are common terms (except φλοιός, which most frequently means 'bark') which would naturally be applied to both embryology and cosmogony.

COSMOLOGY: THE PRESENT STRUCTURE OF THE WORLD

(i) *The earth*

124 (A) Ps.-Plutarch *Strom.* 2 ὑπάρχειν δέ φησι τῷ μὲν σχήματι τὴν γῆν κυλινδροειδῆ, ἔχειν δὲ τόσουτον βάθος ὅσον ἂν εἴη τρίτον πρὸς τὸ πλάτος.

(B) Hippolytus *Ref.* 1, 6, 3 τὸ δὲ σχῆμα αὐτῆς (*sc.* τῆς γῆς) γυρόν, στρογγύλον, κίονος λίθῳ παραπλήσιον·[1] τῶν δὲ ἐπιπέδων ᾧ μὲν ἐπιβεβήκαμεν, ὃ δὲ ἀντίθετον ὑπάρχει.

125 Aristotle *de caelo* B13, 295b10 εἰσὶ δέ τινες οἳ διὰ τὴν ὁμοιότητά φασιν αὐτὴν (*sc.* τὴν γῆν) μένειν, ὥσπερ τῶν ἀρχαίων Ἀναξίμανδρος. μᾶλλον μὲν γὰρ οὐθὲν ἄνω ἢ κάτω ἢ εἰς τὰ πλάγια φέρεσθαι προσήκει τὸ ἐπὶ τοῦ μέσου ἱδρυμένον καὶ ὁμοίως πρὸς τὰ ἔσχατα ἔχον· ἅμα δ᾽ ἀδύνατον εἰς τἀναντία ποιεῖσθαι τὴν κίνησιν, ὥστ᾽ ἐξ ἀνάγκης μένειν.

126 Hippolytus *Ref.* 1, 6, 3 (preceding **124B**) τὴν δὲ γῆν εἶναι μετέωρον ὑπὸ μηδενὸς κρατουμένην, μένουσαν δὲ διὰ τὴν ὁμοίαν πάντων ἀπόστασιν.

[1] ὑγρόν, χίονι mss.; κίονι Aetius III, 10, 2 (DK 12A25). γυρόν (Roeper) is plausible for the impossible ὑγρόν: originally meaning 'curved' (e.g. of a hook, or of hunched shoulders), it came to mean also 'round'. στρογγύλον, then, may be an interpolated gloss. I have emended χίονι to κίονος, *exempli gratia*; the sense is not in doubt.

The earth is shaped like a column-drum; men live on its upper surface. It is three times as wide as it is deep—a ratio which is analogous to the distances of the heavenly bodies (pp. 136f.). Its evident stability is explained in a new way which represents a radical advance on Thales' idea that it *floated* on water (an idea revived and modified by Anaximenes, p. 153). What the earth is at the centre of, presumably, is the rings of the heavenly bodies, of

---

124 (A) *He says that the earth is cylindrical in shape, and that its depth is a third of its width.* (B) *Its shape is curved, round, similar to the drum of a column; of its flat surfaces we walk on one, and the other is on the opposite side.*

125 *There are some who say, like Anaximander among the ancients, that it [the earth] stays still because of its equilibrium. For it behoves that which is established at the centre, and is equally related to the extremes, not to be borne one whit more either up or down or to the sides; and it is impossible for it to move simultaneously in opposite directions, so that it stays fixed by necessity.*

126 *The earth is on high, held up by nothing, but remaining on account of its similar distance from all things.*

which the sun's is the largest (**127**). Anaximander was not talking of the world as a whole, or saying that *it* was at the centre of the Indefinite, though he would doubtless have accepted this if the idea were put to him. At all events he completely broke away from the popular idea that the earth must be supported by something concrete, that it must have 'roots'; his theory of equilibrium was a brilliant leap into the realms of the *a priori*—one which he would not have been tempted to take, it might be suggested, if vortex-action had been applied in his cosmogony and was at hand, as it were, to explain the stability of the earth.

(ii) *The heavenly bodies*

127 Hippolytus *Ref.* I, 6, 4–5 τὰ δὲ ἄστρα γίνεσθαι κύκλον πυρὸς ἀποκριθέντα τοῦ κατὰ τὸν κόσμον πυρός, περιληφθέντα δ' ὑπὸ ἀέρος (cf. **123**). ἐκπνοὰς δ' ὑπάρξαι, πόρους τινὰς αὐλώδεις, καθ' οὓς φαίνεται τὰ ἄστρα· διὸ καὶ ἐπιφρασσομένων τῶν ἐκπνοῶν τὰς ἐκλείψεις γίνεσθαι. τὴν δὲ σελήνην ποτὲ μὲν πληρουμένην φαίνεσθαι ποτὲ δὲ μειουμένην παρὰ τὴν τῶν πόρων ἐπίφραξιν ἢ ἄνοιξιν. εἶναι δὲ τὸν κύκλον τοῦ ἡλίου ἑπτακαιεικοσαπλασίονα ⟨τῆς γῆς, ὀκτωκαιδεκαπλασίονα δὲ τὸν⟩ τῆς σελήνης, καὶ ἀνωτάτω μὲν εἶναι τὸν ἥλιον, κατωτάτω δὲ τοὺς τῶν ἀπλανῶν ἀστέρων κύκλους.

128 Aetius II, 20, I 'Αναξίμανδρος (*sc.* τὸν ἥλιόν φησι) κύκλον εἶναι ὀκτωκαιεικοσαπλασίονα τῆς γῆς, ἁρματείῳ τροχῷ παραπλήσιον, τὴν ἁψῖδα ἔχοντα κοίλην, πλήρη πυρός, κατά τι μέρος ἐκφαίνουσαν διὰ στομίου τὸ πῦρ ὥσπερ διὰ πρηστῆρος αὐλοῦ. (Cf. Aetius II, 25, I, DK 12 A 22, for the moon.)

129 Aetius II, 21, I 'Αναξίμανδρος (*sc.* φησὶ) τὸν μὲν ἥλιον ἴσον εἶναι τῇ γῇ, τὸν δὲ κύκλον ἀφ' οὗ τὴν ἐκπνοὴν ἔχει καὶ ὑφ' οὗ περιφέρεται ἑπτακαιεικοσαπλασίω τῆς γῆς.

---

127 *The heavenly bodies come into being as a circle of fire separated off from the fire in the world, and enclosed by air. There are breathing-holes, certain pipe-like passages, at which the heavenly bodies show themselves; accordingly eclipses occur when the breathing-holes are blocked up. The moon is seen now waxing, now waning according to the blocking or opening of the channels. The circle of the sun is 27 times the size of ⟨the earth, that of⟩ the moon ⟨18 times⟩; the sun is highest, and the circles of the fixed stars are lowest.*

128 *Anaximander says the sun is a circle 28 times the size of the earth, like a chariot wheel, with its felloe hollow and full of fire, and showing the fire at a certain point through an aperture as though through the nozzle of a bellows.*

129 *Anaximander says that the sun is equal to the earth, but that the circle from which it has its breathing-hole and by which it is carried round is 27 times the size of the earth.*

130 Aetius II, 16, 5 Ἀναξίμανδρος ὑπὸ τῶν κύκλων καὶ τῶν σφαιρῶν ἐφ' ὧν ἕκαστος βέβηκε φέρεσθαι (*sc.* τοὺς ἀστέρας φησίν).

The sun and moon are each an aperture in separate solid rings like the felloes of cartwheels. These rings consist of fire surrounded by air (regarded as concealing mist), and out of the single aperture in each of them fire emerges like air from the nozzle of a bellows; the similes of the cartwheels and the bellows perhaps derive from Anaximander himself. Eclipses, and phases of the moon, are due to a total or partial blocking of the aperture; typically, no motive is given for this blockage. The aperture of the sun is the same size as the surface (presumably) of the earth (**129**)—a remarkable view contradicted by Heraclitus in fr. 3; the diameter of its wheel is twenty-seven times as great as this (twenty-eight times in **128**).[1] The moon-wheel is nineteen earth-diameters (or eighteen, presumably) across; the obvious lacuna in **127** has been filled after Aetius II, 25, 1, which gives the corresponding information to **128** for the moon, only adding that the circles of sun and moon lie obliquely. The star-wheels (on which see below), although we are not told so, were presumably of nine (or ten) earth-diameters, being nearest to the earth (**127** *fin.*). Thus Anaximander gave the structure of the world a mathematical basis, developing the assumption (seen already in Homer and Hesiod, cf. **1** with comment) that it is orderly and determinable. His proportionate distances may have influenced Pythagoras.

[1] This larger figure (28*x*) cannot represent the distance from the outer, as opposed to the inner, edges of the celestial circle if diameters are meant; for 2, not 1, should then be added to the multiple, to give 29*x*. If the radius and not the diameter were intended the figures given would hold: but 'the circle of the sun is twenty-seven times that of the earth' (**127**, **128**)—the earth whose 'breadth' is specified in **124**—implies clearly enough that the diameter is really meant. In that case the larger figure might represent the diameter from outer edge to outer edge, the smaller one that from points half-way between the outer and inner edges of the actual felloe of air—assuming, what seems reasonable, that the felloe is one earth-diameter thick.

The stars present certain difficulties. (*a*) **127** *fin.* mentions the fixed stars as closest to the earth. Possibly, as Diels thought, there is another lacuna here and the planets were mentioned too. That

---

130 *Anaximander says that the heavenly bodies are carried by the circles and spheres on which each one goes.*

the fixed stars and the planets were at the same distance from the earth is perhaps implied by Aetius II, 15, 6 (DK 12 A 18), and is suggested by the series of proportionate distances: 1 (diameter of earth)—*x*—18 (moon-ring)—27 (sun-ring). Here *x*, the missing distance, must be that of the stars and planets: it must be 9, to fit into the series, and there is no vacant number to allow a different distance for stars and planets. (*b*) **130** mentions both circles and spheres of the stars (while **127** has a circle of stars at the beginning, circles at the end). The two are incompatible; possibly a sphere for the fixed stars, rings for the planets were meant. But this is inconsistent with the argument that fixed stars and planets must be at the same distance from the earth; there would not be room for both a sphere and rings. Indeed a sphere, although the simplest explanation of the fixed stars, is impossible: the cosmogonical account (**123**) showed that a ball of flame broke up, or broke away from the mist round the earth, and was then shut into circles (obviously of air-mist) which composed sun, moon and stars. There is no possibility, let alone any mention, of part of the sphere of flame remaining as a sphere after it had broken away. Thus it must be assumed that each star, including the planets, has its own wheel; these wheels are equal in diameter and are inclined on countless different planes. They do not obscure the sun and moon (cf. e.g. Homer *Il.* 20, 444 ff.; 21, 549). If their centre is the same as the centre of the earth, the circum-polar stars (which do not set) are unexplained—as they would be even by a sphere; and yet if their centres were at different distances up and down the earth's axis, which could account for some stars not setting, they would be likely to infringe the equilibrium described in **125** and **126**. Probably Anaximander did not think of these difficulties. The movement of the sun on the ecliptic, the declination of the moon, and the wanderings of the planets were probably explained as due to wind (see **134** and **135**); the east-to-west movements were due to rotation of the wheels (cf. φέρεσθαι in **130**) in the planes of their circumferences.

(iii) *Meteorological phenomena*

131 Hippolytus *Ref.* I, 6, 7 ἀνέμους δὲ γίνεσθαι τῶν λεπτοτάτων ἀτμῶν τοῦ ἀέρος ἀποκρινομένων καὶ ὅταν ἀθροισθῶσι κινουμένων,

---

131 *Winds occur when the finest vapours of the air are separated off and when they are*

ὑετοὺς δὲ ἐκ τῆς ἀτμίδος τῆς ἐκ τῶν ὑφ' ἥλιον ἀναδιδομένης· ἀστραπὰς δὲ ὅταν ἄνεμος ἐκπίπτων διιστᾷ τὰς νεφέλας.[1]

132 Aetius III, 3, 1–2 (περὶ βροντῶν ἀστραπῶν κεραυνῶν πρηστήρων τε καὶ τυφώνων.) Ἀναξίμανδρος ἐκ τοῦ πνεύματος ταυτὶ πάντα συμβαίνειν· ὅταν γὰρ περιληφθὲν νέφει παχεῖ βιασάμενον ἐκπέσῃ τῇ λεπτομερείᾳ καὶ κουφότητι, τότε ἡ μὲν ῥῆξις τὸν ψόφον, ἡ δὲ διαστολὴ παρὰ τὴν μελανίαν τοῦ νέφους τὸν διαυγασμὸν ἀποτελεῖ.

133 Seneca *Qu. Nat.* II, 18 Anaximandrus omnia ad spiritum rettulit: tonitrua, inquit, sunt nubis ictae sonus... (see DK 12 A 23).

[1] ἐκ τῆς ἀτμίδος—ἀναδιδομένης Cedrenus; the mss. give an obviously corrupt reading (DK 1 p. 84 n.) which implies if anything that the exhalation is from the earth. A dual exhalation was imposed also on Heraclitus (p. 204 n. 1); it was probably a refinement by Aristotle. Cedrenus (11th cent. A.D.) is sometimes correct: e.g. his ἐκπίπτων in **131** is shown by **132** to be correct against mss. ἐμπίπτων.

These passages suggest that Anaximander shared in, and perhaps to a large degree originated, a more or less standard Ionian way of accounting for meteorological (in our sense) events. The chief elements of this scheme are wind, the evaporation from the sea, and the condensed masses of vapour which form the clouds. All testimonies on the subject are, of course, based on Theophrastus, whom we may suspect of not always resisting the temptation to supply 'appropriate' explanations, where none existed, of certain natural phenomena which he thought interested all Presocratics. The explanation of wind in **131** (cf. also Aetius III, 7, 1, DK 12 A 24) is very involved; note that it is somehow due to 'separation off' of the finest part of air. Rain is caused by the condensation (presumably) of moist vapours evaporated by the sun; wind causes most other phenomena (**132**, **133**), including, probably, the movements north and south of sun and moon (see **134**, **135**). The emphasis on wind, a product of air, might suggest partial conflation with Anaximenes; he gave the same explanation of lightning as

---

set in motion by congregation; rain occurs from the exhalation that issues upwards from the things beneath the sun, and lightning whenever wind breaks out and cleaves the clouds.

132 (*On thunder, lightning, thunderbolts, whirlwinds and typhoons.*) *Anaximander says that all these things occur as a result of wind: for whenever it is shut up in a thick cloud and then bursts out forcibly, through its fineness and lightness, then the bursting makes the noise, while the rift against the blackness of the cloud makes the flash.*

133 *Anaximander referred everything to wind: thunder, he said, is the noise of smitten cloud....*

Anaximander, but in an appendix to **132** is distinguished as having cited a special parallel (oars flash in water; see **161**).

(iv) *The earth is drying up*

134 Aristotle *Meteor.* B1, 353b6 εἶναι γὰρ τὸ πρῶτον ὑγρὸν ἅπαντα τὸν περὶ τὴν γῆν τόπον, ὑπὸ δὲ τοῦ ἡλίου ξηραινόμενον τὸ μὲν διατμίσαν πνεύματα καὶ τροπὰς ἡλίου καὶ σελήνης φασὶ ποιεῖν, τὸ δὲ λειφθὲν θάλατταν εἶναι· διὸ καὶ ἐλάττω γίνεσθαι ξηραινομένην οἴονται καὶ τέλος ἔσεσθαί ποτε πᾶσαν ξηράν.

135 Alexander *in Meteor.* p. 67, 11 (DK12A27) (commenting on **134**) ...ταύτης τῆς δόξης ἐγένετο, ὡς ἱστορεῖ Θεόφραστος, Ἀναξίμανδρός τε καὶ Διογένης.

Alexander in **135** must mean the attribution by Theophrastus to apply to the whole of **134**, not merely to the last sentence, since a little later (commenting on *Meteor.* 355a22) he associates Anaximander and Diogenes again with the idea that winds cause the turnings of the sun. (In paraphrasing **134** he had become confused and described another theory.) It is helpful to have Theophrastus' attribution, although it must be noted that the only name mentioned by *Aristotle* in connexion with the drying up of the sea is that of Democritus (*Meteor.* B3, 356b10, DK68A100). Aristotle had previously mentioned (*Meteor.* A14, 352a17) that those who believed the sea to be drying up were influenced by local examples of this process (which, we may note, was conspicuous around sixth-century Miletus); he himself rebuked them for their false inference, and pointed out that in other places the sea was gaining; also, there were long-term periods of comparative drought and flood which Aristotle called the 'great summer' and 'great winter' in a 'great year'.[1]

[1] Here Aristotle may be aiming particularly at Democritus, who thought that the sea was drying up *and that the world would come to an end.* Anaximander need not have thought this any more than Xenophanes did; in fact Aristotle might have been rebuking Democritus in terms of the earlier cyclical theory.—There may well be a special reference to Anaxi-

---

134 *For first of all the whole area round the earth is moist, but being dried by the sun the part that is exhaled makes winds and turnings of the sun and moon, they say, while that which is left is sea; therefore they think that the sea is actually becoming less through being dried up, and that some time it will end up by all being dry.*

135 *...of this opinion, as Theophrastus relates, were Anaximander and Diogenes.*

mander in Aristotle's words (*Meteor.* B2, 355a22) 'those who say...that when the world around the earth was heated by the sun, air came into being and the whole heaven *expanded*...' (cf. **123**).

It is clear that if Anaximander thought that the sea would dry up once and for all this would be a serious betrayal of the principle enunciated in the extant fragment (**112**), that things are punished for their injustice: for land would have encroached on sea without suffering retribution. Further, although only the sea is mentioned, it is reasonable to conclude that, since rain was explained as due to the condensation of evaporation (**131**), the drying up of the sea would lead to the drying up of the whole earth. But could our whole interpretation of the fragment as an assertion of cosmic stability be wrong; could the drying up of the earth be the prelude to re-absorption into the Indefinite? This it could not be, since if the earth were destroyed by drought that would implicitly qualify the Indefinite itself as dry and fiery, thus contradicting its very nature; and, in addition, the arguments from the form of the fragment still stand. The principle of the fragment could, however, be preserved if the diminution of the sea were only one part of a cyclical process: when the sea is dry a 'great winter' (to use Aristotle's term, which may well be derived from earlier theories) begins, and eventually the other extreme is reached when all the earth is overrun by sea and turns, perhaps, into slime. That this is what Anaximander thought is made more probable by the fact that Xenophanes, another Ionian of a generation just after Anaximander's, postulated cycles of the earth drying out and turning into slime: see pp. 177ff. Xenophanes was impressed by fossils of plant and animal life embedded in rocks far from the present sea, and deduced that the earth was once mud. But he argued, not that the sea will dry up even more, but that everything will turn back into mud; men will be destroyed, but then the cycle will continue, the land will dry out, and men will be produced anew. For Anaximander, too, men were born ultimately from mud (**136**, **138**). The parallelism is not complete, but it is extremely close: Xenophanes may have been correcting or modifying Anaximander. Anaximander, too, was familiar with the great legendary periods of fire and flood, in the ages of Phaethon and Deucalion; impressed by the recession of the sea from the Ionian coast-line he might well have applied such periods to the whole history of the earth.

ZOOGONY AND ANTHROPOGONY

136 Aetius v, 19, 4 Ἀναξίμανδρος ἐν ὑγρῷ γεννηθῆναι τὰ πρῶτα ζῷα φλοιοῖς περιεχόμενα ἀκανθώδεσι, προβαινούσης δὲ τῆς ἡλικίας ἀποβαίνειν ἐπὶ τὸ ξηρότερον καὶ περιρρηγνυμένου τοῦ φλοιοῦ ἐπ' ὀλίγον χρόνον μεταβιῶναι.

137 Ps.-Plutarch *Strom.* 2 ἔτι φησὶν ὅτι κατ' ἀρχὰς ἐξ ἀλλοειδῶν ζῴων ὁ ἄνθρωπος ἐγεννήθη, ἐκ τοῦ τὰ μὲν ἄλλα δι' ἑαυτῶν ταχὺ νέμεσθαι, μόνον δὲ τὸν ἄνθρωπον πολυχρονίου δεῖσθαι τιθηνήσεως· διὸ καὶ κατ' ἀρχὰς οὐκ ἄν ποτε τοιοῦτον ὄντα διασωθῆναι.

138 Censorinus *de die nat.* 4, 7 Anaximander Milesius videri sibi ex aqua terraque calefactis exortos esse sive pisces seu piscibus simillima animalia; in his homines concrevisse fetusque ad pubertatem intus retentos; tunc demum ruptis illis viros mulieresque qui iam se alere possent processisse.

139 Hippolytus *Ref.* I, 6, 6 τὰ δὲ ζῷα γίνεσθαι ⟨ἐξ ὑγροῦ⟩ ἐξατμιζομένου [Diels, -όμενα mss.] ὑπὸ τοῦ ἡλίου. τὸν δὲ ἄνθρωπον ἑτέρῳ ζῴῳ γεγονέναι, τουτέστι ἰχθύι, παραπλήσιον κατ' ἀρχάς.

140 Plutarch *Symp.* VIII, 730E (DK 12A30) διὸ καὶ σέβονται (*sc.* Σύροι) τὸν ἰχθῦν ὡς ὁμογενῆ καὶ σύντροφον, ἐπιεικέστερον Ἀναξιμάνδρου φιλοσοφοῦντες· οὐ γὰρ ἐν τοῖς αὐτοῖς ἐκεῖνος ἰχθῦς καὶ ἀνθρώπους, ἀλλ' ἐν ἰχθύσιν ἐγγενέσθαι τὸ πρῶτον ἀνθρώπους ἀποφαίνεται καὶ τραφέντας, ὥσπερ οἱ γαλεοί,[1] καὶ γενομένους ἱκανοὺς ἑαυτοῖς βοηθεῖν ἐκβῆναι τηνικαῦτα καὶ γῆς λαβέσθαι.

---

136 *Anaximander said that the first living creatures were born in moisture, enclosed in thorny barks; and that as their age increased they came forth on to the drier part and, when the bark had broken off, they lived a different kind of life for a short time.*

137 *Further he says that in the beginning man was born from creatures of a different kind; because other creatures are soon self-supporting, but man alone needs prolonged nursing. For this reason he would not have survived if this had been his original form.*

138 *Anaximander of Miletus conceived that there arose from heated water and earth either fish or creatures very like fish; in these man grew, in the form of embryos retained within until puberty; then at last the fish-like creatures burst and men and women who were already able to nourish themselves stepped forth.*

139 *Living creatures came into being from moisture evaporated by the sun. Man was originally similar to another creature—that is, to a fish.*

140 *Therefore they* [*the Syrians*] *actually revere the fish as being of similar race and nurturing. In this they philosophize more suitably than Anaximander; for he declares, not that fishes and men came into being in the same parents, but that originally men came into being inside fishes, and that having been nurtured there—like sharks—and having become adequate to look after themselves, they then came forth and took to the land.*

[1] Emperius' γαλεοί for the impossible mss. παλαιοί is a brilliant emendation based on another passage in Plutarch, *de soll. an.* 33, 982A, where the shark is said to produce an egg, then to nurture the young inside itself until it is bigger; Aristotle had noted this at *H.A.* Z10, 565b1. But 'like sharks' may well be a parenthetical remark by Plutarch (note the case: nominative not accusative), who knew about them indirectly from Aristotle; he would naturally quote them as an illustration of Anaximander's idea.

This is virtually all the information we have about Anaximander's brilliant conjectures on the origins of animal and human life. The first living creatures are generated from slime (elsewhere called ἰλύς) by the heat of the sun: this became a standard account, and even Aristotle accepted spontaneous generation in such cases. The observation behind the theory was perhaps that of mud-flies and sand-worms which abound in the hot sand at the edge of the sea. Yet the first creatures were not of that kind, but were surrounded by prickly barks—like sea-urchins, Cornford suggested. Aetius (**136**) seems to preserve special information about these first creatures, which presumably were prior to the fish-like creatures in which men were reared. The use of φλοιός here reminds one of the bark-simile in the cosmogonical account (**123**); both ball of flame and prickly shell broke away from round the core (here περι- not ἀπορρήγνυσθαι).

The meaning of the concluding words of **136** is disputed; but μετα- in new late-Greek compounds usually implies change rather than succession, and the sense is probably that the creatures, emerged from their husks, lived a different life (i.e. on land) for a short time longer. Possibly Anaximander had some conception of the difficulties of adaptation to environment. This would be no more startling than his intelligent observation that man (with nine months' gestation and many years' helplessness) could not have survived in primitive conditions without protection of some kind. This consideration led to the conjecture that man was reared in a kind of fish—presumably because the earth was originally moist, and the first creatures were of the sea.

Anaximander's is the first attempt of which we know to explain the origin of man, as well as of the world, rationally. Not all his successors concerned themselves with man's history (they were more interested in his present condition), and none surpassed him in the thoughtful ingenuity of his theories. Incomplete and sometimes inconsistent as our sources are, they show that Anaximander's account of Nature, though among the earliest, was one of the broadest in scope and most imaginative of all.

CHAPTER IV

ANAXIMENES OF MILETUS

HIS DATE, LIFE AND BOOK

141 Diogenes Laertius II, 3 Ἀναξιμένης Εὐρυστράτου Μιλήσιος ἤκουσεν Ἀναξιμάνδρου, ἔνιοι δὲ καὶ Παρμενίδου φασὶν ἀκοῦσαι αὐτόν. οὗτος ἀρχὴν ἀέρα εἶπε καὶ τὸ ἄπειρον. κινεῖσθαι δὲ τὰ ἄστρα οὐχ ὑπὸ γῆν ἀλλὰ περὶ γῆν. κέχρηταί τε λέξει Ἰάδι ἁπλῇ καὶ ἀπερίττῳ. καὶ γεγένηται μέν, καθά φησιν Ἀπολλόδωρος, περὶ τὴν Σάρδεων ἅλωσιν, ἐτελεύτησε δὲ τῇ ἑξηκοστῇ τρίτῃ ὀλυμπιάδι (528–525 B.C.).

It may be doubted whether the chronographical tradition knew more about Anaximenes' date than the statement of Theophrastus (**143**) that he was an associate of Anaximander. The Succession-writers would establish him in the next philosophical generation to Anaximander, and Eratosthenes, followed by Apollodorus, would choose a suitable epoch-year for his *acme*, i.e. the age of forty. The obvious epoch-year was that of the capture of Sardis by Cyrus, 546/5 B.C. (= Ol. 58, 3; Hippolytus *Ref.* I, 7, 9, DK 13A7, gave Ol. 58, 1, complicated in the Suda, 13A2). This puts his birth around the *acme* of Thales, his death around the commonly-chosen age of sixty, and makes him twenty-four years younger than Anaximander. This is all quite hypothetical; but we may accept what seems likely from his thought, that he was younger than Anaximander; while his active life can scarcely have continued far into the fifth century (Miletus was destroyed in 494 B.C.).[1]

[1] The mss. of Diogenes in **141** reverse the position of περὶ τὴν Σάρδεων ἅλωσιν and τῇ ἑξηκοστῇ τρίτῃ ὀλυμπιάδι. Diels emended (as printed here). G. B. Kerferd points out (*Mus. Helvet.* 11 (1954) 117ff.) that if the capture of Sardis were that of 498 B.C., and γεγένηται meant (as it certainly can, and perhaps should) 'was born' rather than 'flourished', then the ms. text could be correct *if* Anaximenes died at the age of 30 or

---

141 *Anaximenes son of Eurystratus, of Miletus, was a pupil of Anaximander; some say he was also a pupil of Parmenides. He said that the material principle was air and the infinite; and that the stars move, not under the earth, but round it. He used simple and economical Ionic speech. He was active, according to what Apollodorus says, around the time of the capture of Sardis, and died in the 63rd Olympiad.*

less. This seems unlikely in itself and, if true, would probably have earned comment in our sources. Further, it is unlikely that Apollodorus would have ignored Theophrastus' connexion of Anaximenes with Anaximander (who according to Apollodorus was dead by 528); or that he would have used two separate captures of Sardis as epochs (he certainly uses that of 546/5). Further, Hippolytus (DK 13 A 7) supports a *floruit* at or near 546/5.

About Anaximenes' life, and his practical activities, we know nothing (cf. n. on p. 103). From the stylistic judgement in **141**, however, it is known that he wrote a book, a part of which at least must have been known to Theophrastus, from whom the criticism presumably emanates. The 'simple and unsuperfluous' Ionic may be contrasted with the 'rather poetical terminology' of Anaximander (**112**).

AIR IN ANAXIMENES

(i) *Air is the originative substance and basic form of matter; it changes by condensation and rarefaction*

142 Aristotle *Met.* A 3, 984 a 5 Ἀναξιμένης δὲ ἀέρα καὶ Διογένης πρότερον ὕδατος καὶ μάλιστ' ἀρχὴν τιθέασι τῶν ἁπλῶν σωμάτων.

143 Theophrastus *ap.* Simplicium *Phys.* 24, 26 Ἀναξιμένης δὲ Εὐρυστράτου Μιλήσιος, ἑταῖρος γεγονὼς Ἀναξιμάνδρου, μίαν μὲν καὶ αὐτὸς τὴν ὑποκειμένην φύσιν καὶ ἄπειρόν φησιν ὥσπερ ἐκεῖνος, οὐκ ἀόριστον δὲ ὥσπερ ἐκεῖνος ἀλλὰ ὡρισμένην, ἀέρα λέγων αὐτήν· διαφέρειν δὲ μανότητι καὶ πυκνότητι κατὰ τὰς οὐσίας. καὶ ἀραιούμενον μὲν πῦρ γίνεσθαι, πυκνούμενον δὲ ἄνεμον, εἶτα νέφος, ἔτι δὲ μᾶλλον ὕδωρ, εἶτα γῆν, εἶτα λίθους, τὰ δὲ ἄλλα ἐκ τούτων. κίνησιν δὲ καὶ οὗτος ἀίδιον ποιεῖ, δι' ἣν καὶ τὴν μεταβολὴν γίνεσθαι.

144 Hippolytus *Ref.* 1, 7, 1 Ἀναξιμένης...ἀέρα ἄπειρον ἔφη τὴν ἀρχὴν εἶναι, ἐξ οὗ τὰ γινόμενα καὶ τὰ γεγονότα καὶ τὰ ἐσόμενα καὶ θεοὺς καὶ θεῖα γίνεσθαι, τὰ δὲ λοιπὰ ἐκ τῶν τούτου ἀπογόνων. (2) τὸ

---

142 *Anaximenes and Diogenes make air, rather than water, the material principle above the other simple bodies.*

143 *Anaximenes son of Eurystratus, of Miletus, a companion of Anaximander, also says that the underlying nature is one and infinite like him, but not undefined as Anaximander said but definite, for he identifies it as air; and it differs in its substantial nature by rarity and density. Being made finer it becomes fire, being made thicker it becomes wind, then cloud, then (when thickened still more) water, then earth, then stones; and the rest come into being from these. He, too, makes motion eternal, and says that change, also, comes about through it.*

144 *Anaximenes...said that infinite air was the principle, from which the things that are becoming, and that are, and that shall be, and gods and things divine, all come into*

δὲ εἶδος τοῦ ἀέρος τοιοῦτον· ὅταν μὲν ὁμαλώτατος ᾖ, ὄψει ἄδηλον, δηλοῦσθαι δὲ τῷ ψυχρῷ καὶ τῷ θερμῷ καὶ τῷ νοτερῷ καὶ τῷ κινουμένῳ. κινεῖσθαι δὲ ἀεί· οὐ γὰρ μεταβάλλειν ὅσα μεταβάλλει, εἰ μὴ κινοῖτο. (3) πυκνούμενον γὰρ καὶ ἀραιούμενον διάφορον φαίνεσθαι· ὅταν γὰρ εἰς τὸ ἀραιότερον διαχυθῇ, πῦρ γίνεσθαι, ἀνέμους δὲ πάλιν εἶναι ἀέρα πυκνούμενον, ἐξ ἀέρος ⟨δὲ⟩ νέφος ἀποτελεῖσθαι κατὰ τὴν πίλησιν, ἔτι δὲ μᾶλλον ὕδωρ, ἐπὶ πλεῖον πυκνωθέντα γῆν καὶ εἰς τὸ μάλιστα πυκνότατον λίθους. ὥστε τὰ κυριώτατα τῆς γενέσεως ἐναντία εἶναι, θερμόν τε καὶ ψυχρόν.

142, together with **153** and **162**, is all that Aristotle had to say about Anaximenes by name, and our tradition depends on Theophrastus, who according to Diogenes Laertius v, 42 wrote a special monograph on him (see p. 4). A short version of Theophrastus' account of the material principle is preserved by Simplicius in **143**. In the present case Hippolytus' version is longer than Simplicius'; but an inspection of **144** shows that this is mainly due to wordy expansion and additional (sometimes non-Theophrastean) interpretation. However, the expression πίλησις (πιλεῖσθαι), 'felting', for the condensation of air, is found also in Ps.-Plutarch's summary (**151**) and was probably used by Theophrastus; it was a common fourth-century term and need not have been used in this form by Anaximenes himself, contrary to what Diels and others say.

For Anaximenes the originative stuff was explicitly the basic form of material in the differentiated world, since he had thought of a way in which it could become other components of the world, like sea or earth, without losing its own nature. It was simply condensed or rarefied—that is, it altered its appearance according to how much there was of it in a particular place. This met the objection which Anaximander may well have felt against Thales' water (pp. 112ff.), and which encouraged him to postulate an

---

being, and the rest from its products. The form of air is of this kind: whenever it is most equable it is invisible to sight, but is revealed by the cold and the hot and the damp and by movement. It is always in motion: for things that change do not change unless there be movement. Through becoming denser or finer it has different appearances; for when it is dissolved into what is finer it becomes fire, while winds, again, are air that is becoming condensed, and cloud is produced from air by felting. When it is condensed still more, water is produced; with a further degree of condensation earth is produced, and when condensed as far as possible, stones. The result is that the most influential components of generation are opposites, hot and cold.

indefinite originative material. Anaximenes' air, too, was indefinitely vast in extent—it surrounded all things (**110** and **163**), and was thus described as ἄπειρον, infinite, by Theophrastus. It is questionable exactly what he meant by air. ἀήρ in Homer and sometimes in later Ionic prose meant 'mist', something visible and obscuring; if Anaximander really talked of 'the cold' in cosmogony he probably meant a damp mist, part of which congealed to form a slimy kind of earth. Anaximenes probably said (**163**) that all things were surrounded by πνεῦμα καὶ ἀήρ, 'wind (or breath) and air', and that the soul is related to this air; which suggests that for him ἀήρ was not mist but, as Hippolytus in **144** assumed, the invisible atmospheric air. This is confirmed by the fact that he evidently described winds as a slightly condensed form of air (**143**, **144**). Now atmospheric air was certainly not included as a world-component by Heraclitus (e.g. **221**), and its substantiality—that is, corporeality—needed to be emphasized by Empedocles (**453**). It looks, then, as though Anaximenes simply assumed that some part, at least, of the atmospheric air was substantial, and indeed the basic form of substance; although he did not offer any notable demonstration of its substantiality and so convince his immediate successors. This assumption would be a very remarkable one; though it must be remembered that πνεῦμα in the sense of breath was certainly regarded as existing, and yet it was invisible. It was not, however, totally insensible; its presence was revealed by tangible properties—in Hippolytus' terms by 'the cold and the hot and the moist and the moving'. Atmospheric air, on occasions, makes itself known by none of these things; probably in that state Anaximenes would not recognize it as air, or as existing at all.

The main forms assumed by air as a result of condensation and rarefaction were outlined by Theophrastus. They are obvious enough, and were clearly based on observation of natural processes—rain coming from clouds, water apparently condensing into earth, evaporation, and so on. Such changes were accepted by all the Presocratics; it was only Anaximenes who explained them solely in terms of the density of a single material.[1] It may be asked why *air* was specified as the normal or basic form of matter; from the point of view of natural change within the world, water, equally, might be basic, with air as a rarefied variant. In view of **163** (pp. 158ff.), where cosmic air is compared with the πνεῦμα or breath which is traditionally conceived as the breath-soul or life-giving ψυχή, it seems that Anaximenes regarded air as the breath of the world, and so as its ever-living, and therefore divine, source; see also p. 161. Further, air might have seemed to possess some of the *indefinite* qualities of Anaximander's originative stuff (not being naturally characterized by any particular opposite); in addition it had the advantage of occupying a large region of the developed world. Anaximenes seems at first sight to have abandoned the principle of general opposition in the world (it was shortly to be revived in a more Anaximandrean form, though with some modification, by Heraclitus), and so to have lost even the metaphorical motives of injustice and retribution, for natural change. Yet one pair of opposites, the rare and the dense, took on a new and special significance, and it could legitimately be argued that all changes are due to the reaction of these two: see further p. 149. In addition, no doubt, Anaximenes shared Thales' assumption that matter was somehow alive, which would be confirmed by the constant mobility of air—especially if this was only accepted as being air when it was perceptible. Theophrastus, as usual, reduced these assumptions to the formula of 'eternal motion', adding that all change would depend on this motion.

[1] Cf. **145** Simplicius *Phys.* 149, 32 ἐπὶ γὰρ τούτου (*sc.* Anaximenes) μόνου Θεόφραστος ἐν τῇ Ἱστορίᾳ τὴν μάνωσιν εἴρηκε καὶ πύκνωσιν, δῆλον δὲ ὡς καὶ οἱ ἄλλοι τῇ μανότητι καὶ πυκνότητι ἐχρῶντο. There is no difficulty here (and no need for drastic expedients like the supposition that μόνου means πρώτου): 'the others' (e.g. Hippasus and Heraclitus in DK 22 A 5) were loosely described by Theophrastus as using condensation, but only Anaximenes explicitly used the rare and the dense as an essential part of his theory. Simplicius then slightly misunderstood Theophrastus' comment on Anaximenes, which may indeed have been carelessly phrased.

It appears that according to Theophrastus ('the other things, from these' in **143** *fin.*, also in a vague and inaccurate paraphrase in **144** *init.*; cf. Cicero *Acad.* II, 37, 118, DK 13 A 9) Anaximenes did not think that every kind of natural substance could be explained as a direct form of air, but that there were certain basic forms (fire, air, wind, cloud, water, earth, stone) of which other kinds were compounds. If true, this is important, since it makes Anaximenes the pioneer of the idea that there are elements from which other

---

145 *For in the case of him [Anaximenes] alone did Theophrastus in the* History *speak of rarefaction and condensation, but it is plain that the others, also, used rarity and density.*

objects are compounded—an idea first formally worked out by Empedocles. Yet it seems questionable whether this interpretation is justified. There is no other evidence that anyone before Empedocles tried to give a detailed account of any but the main cosmic substances; having invented a device to explain diversity, it would be more in the Milesian character for Anaximenes to have adhered to it; and Theophrastus was prone to add just such generalizing summaries, often slightly misleading, to a specific list.[1]

[1] Another probably false interpretation is that which makes Anaximenes the forerunner of atomism. He cannot have conceived of matter as continuous, it is argued; therefore, since there can be more or less of it in the same space, it must have been composed of particles which can be more or less heavily concentrated. But it seems unlikely that anyone before Pythagoras or Heraclitus bothered about the formal constitution of matter, or about precisely what was involved in condensation, which could be simply an objective description of certain observed processes.

(ii) *Hot and cold are due to rarefaction and condensation*

146 Plutarch *de prim. frig.* 7, 947F (DK 13B1) ...ἢ καθάπερ Ἀναξιμένης ὁ παλαιὸς ᾤετο, μήτε τὸ ψυχρὸν ἐν οὐσίᾳ μήτε τὸ θερμὸν ἀπολείπωμεν, ἀλλὰ πάθη κοινὰ τῆς ὕλης ἐπιγιγνόμενα ταῖς μεταβολαῖς· τὸ γὰρ συστελλόμενον αὐτῆς καὶ πυκνούμενον ψυχρὸν εἶναί φησι, τὸ δ' ἀραιὸν καὶ τὸ 'χαλαρόν' (οὕτω πως ὀνομάσας καὶ τῷ ῥήματι) θερμόν. ὅθεν οὐκ ἀπεικότως λέγεσθαι τὸ καὶ θερμὰ τὸν ἄνθρωπον ἐκ τοῦ στόματος καὶ ψυχρὰ μεθιέναι· ψύχεται γὰρ ἡ πνοὴ πιεσθεῖσα καὶ πυκνωθεῖσα τοῖς χείλεσιν, ἀνειμένου δὲ τοῦ στόματος ἐκπίπτουσα γίγνεται θερμὸν ὑπὸ μανότητος. τοῦτο μὲν οὖν ἀγνόημα ποιεῖται τοῦ ἀνδρὸς ὁ Ἀριστοτέλης.... (Cf. *Problemata* 34, 7, 964a10.)

Plutarch seems to have had access to a genuine citation from Anaximenes: the word χαλαρός, 'slack', if no more, is definitely said to be his, and there is no reason to doubt it. Conceivably Plutarch depends on a lost passage of Aristotle; the passage from

---

146 ...*or as Anaximenes thought of old, let us leave neither the cold nor the hot as belonging to substance, but as common dispositions of matter that supervene on changes; for he says that matter which is compressed and condensed is cold, while that which is fine and 'relaxed' (using this very word) is hot. Therefore, he said, the dictum is not an unreasonable one, that man releases both warmth and cold from his mouth: for the breath is chilled by being compressed and condensed with the lips, but when the mouth is loosened the breath escapes and becomes warm through its rarity. This theory Aristotle claims to be due to the man's* [sc. *Anaximenes'*] *ignorance*....

the Aristotelian *Problems* discusses the phenomenon in the manner suggested in the continuation of **146**, but without naming Anaximenes. The example of breath was evidently cited by Anaximenes as showing that rarefaction and condensation of air can produce, not merely obvious variations like those of hardness and softness, thickness and thinness, but a variation of the hot and the cold which seems to have little directly to do with density. On this evidence alone one would expect the instance to be part of an argument that condensation and rarefaction can produce quite unexpected alterations, and so could be responsible for every kind of diversity. Hippolytus in **144**, however, suggests that hot and cold play a vital part in coming-to-be: in other words Anaximenes still attributed special importance to the chief cosmogonical substances in Anaximander, the hot stuff and the cold stuff. There is no mention of this in Simplicius' extract from Theophrastus (**143**), but Hippolytus or his immediate source is unlikely to be entirely responsible for it. It is, however, difficult to see how these opposed substances could be basic in Anaximenes' scheme of things, and it seems highly probable that Theophrastus, seeing that some prominence was given to hot and cold in Anaximenes, suggested that they were for him, as they were for Aristotle and for Theophrastus himself, one of the essential elements of γένεσις. (The Peripatetic simple bodies were composed of prime matter informed by either hot or cold and either wet or dry.) This interpretation is anachronistic, and leaves us free to accept the natural one suggested by Plutarch himself, expressed though it still is in Peripatetic terms. But can even Anaximenes have thought that temperature varied directly with density? There is such a thing, for example, as hot stone or cold air. This difficulty might not have occurred to him, since in general it is true that the ascending scale of density represents also a descending scale of temperature, from fire down to stones; air itself normally not striking one (at any rate in the Mediterranean) as consistently either hot or cold. Alternatively, the instance of breath compressed by the lips might seem to illustrate that density *can* affect temperature, without implying that it always does so to the same degree.[1]

[1] The instance of the breath is one of the first recorded Greek uses of a detailed observation to support a physical theory. Note, however, (i) that it is not strictly an 'experiment', i.e. the deliberate production of a chain of events the unknown conclusion of which will either confirm or deny a

prior hypothesis; (ii) that because of lack of control and of thoroughness the conclusion drawn from the observation is the exact opposite of the truth; (iii) that the word λέγεσθαι may suggest that the observation was a common one, not made for the first time by Anaximenes.

(iii) *Air is divine*

147 Cicero *N.D.* I, 10, 26 post Anaximenes aera deum statuit eumque gigni esseque immensum et infinitum et semper in motu, quasi aut aer sine ulla forma deus esse possit...aut non omne quod ortum sit mortalitas consequatur.

148 Aetius I, 7, 13 Ἀναξιμένης τὸν ἀέρα (*sc.* θεὸν εἶναί φησι)· δεῖ δ' ὑπακούειν ἐπὶ τῶν οὕτως λεγομένων τὰς ἐνδιηκούσας τοῖς στοιχείοις ἢ τοῖς σώμασι δυνάμεις.

149 Augustinus *C.D.* VIII, 2 iste (*sc.* Anaximander) Anaximenen discipulum et successorem reliquit, qui omnes rerum causas aeri infinito dedit, nec deos negavit aut tacuit; non tamen ab ipsis aerem factum, sed ipsos ex aere ortos credidit.

The first and third of these passages assert that according to Anaximenes a god or gods came into being from the primal air; Hippolytus also, in the first sentence of **144**, wrote that 'gods and things divine' arose from air. Theophrastus, therefore, probably said more than that Anaximenes' primal air itself was divine (cf. Aristotle's assertion in **110** that Anaximander and most of the physicists considered their originative stuff to be divine). It is probable, then, that Anaximenes himself said something about gods: it may be reasonably inferred that this was to the effect that such gods as there were in the world were themselves derived from the all-encompassing air, which was truly divine. If so, Anaximenes might be a precursor of Xenophanes and Heraclitus in their criticisms of the deities of conventional religion; though there is no evidence that Anaximenes went so far as actually to deny their existence, any more than Heraclitus did. That air itself was divine

---

147 *Afterwards, Anaximenes determined that air is a god, and that it comes into being, and is measureless and infinite and always in motion; as though either formless air could be a god...or mortality did not attend upon everything that has come into being.*

148 *Anaximenes (says that) the air (is god): one must understand, in the case of such descriptions, the powers which interpenetrate the elements or bodies.*

149 *He [Anaximander] left Anaximenes as his disciple and successor, who attributed all the causes of things to infinite air, and did not deny that there were gods, or pass them over in silence; yet he believed not that air was made by them, but that they arose from air.*

is implied both by Aristotle's generalization and by Aetius in **148**, who gives a Stoicizing description of the kind of divinity involved as 'powers permeating elements or bodies', i.e. a motive and organizing capacity that inheres in varying degrees in the constituents of the world.[1]

[1] It has sometimes been maintained in the past (e.g. by Burnet, *EGP* 78) that Anaximenes' gods are innumerable worlds. This is because according to Aetius I, 7, 12 and Cicero *N.D.* I, 10, 25 *Anaximander's* innumerable worlds were called gods (DK 12 A 17). These statements seem to have arisen from a confusion of the innumerable worlds with the stars; and Cicero cannot possibly have had the same kind of evidence for Anaximenes, since in the very next sentence, **147**, he only mentions *one* god as coming into being (and confusedly describes it as infinite, i.e. as primal air). There are in fact only two doxographical indications that Anaximenes postulated innumerable worlds: Aetius II, 1, 3 (Stob. only; see p. 124) and **150** Simplicius *Phys.* 1121, 12 γενητὸν δὲ καὶ φθαρτὸν τὸν ἕνα κόσμον ποιοῦσιν ὅσοι ἀεὶ μέν φασιν εἶναι κόσμον, οὐ μὴν τὸν αὐτὸν ἀεί, ἀλλὰ ἄλλοτε ἄλλον γινόμενον κατά τινας χρόνων περιόδους, ὡς Ἀναξιμένης τε καὶ Ἡράκλειτος καὶ Διογένης καὶ ὕστερον οἱ ἀπὸ τῆς Στοᾶς. Here Simplicius appears to assign *successive* worlds to Anaximenes. One possible reason for this is given on p. 126; but Simplicius' passage is very closely based on Aristotle *de caelo* A 10, 279 b 12 (DK 22 A 10), in which Empedocles, not Anaximenes, precedes Heraclitus; and the possibility of contamination cannot be excluded. There is far less reason to assign innumerable worlds to Anaximenes than to Anaximander, from the state of the doxographical evidence; though something was probably said on the subject by Theophrastus, on the grounds that Anaximenes, too, postulated what Theophrastus considered to be an infinite originative stuff (see pp. 123 ff.).

COSMOGONY

151 Ps.-Plutarch *Strom.* 3 (cf. DK 13 A 6) ...γεννᾶσθαί τε πάντα κατά τινα πύκνωσιν τούτου (*sc.* ἀέρος) καὶ πάλιν ἀραίωσιν. τήν γε μὴν κίνησιν ἐξ αἰῶνος ὑπάρχειν· πιλουμένου δὲ τοῦ ἀέρος πρώτην γεγενῆσθαι λέγει τὴν γῆν πλατεῖαν μάλα· διὸ καὶ κατὰ λόγον αὐτὴν ἐποχεῖσθαι τῷ ἀέρι· καὶ τὸν ἥλιον καὶ τὴν σελήνην καὶ τὰ λοιπὰ ἄστρα τὴν ἀρχὴν τῆς γενέσεως ἐκ γῆς ἔχειν. ἀποφαίνεται γοῦν

---

150 *All those make the one world born and destructible who say that there is always a world, yet it is not always the same but becoming different at different times according to certain periods of time, as Anaximenes and Heraclitus and Diogenes said, and later the Stoics.*

151 *...and all things are produced by a kind of condensation, and again rarefaction, of this* [sc. *air*]. *Motion, indeed, exists from everlasting; he says that when the air felts, there first of all comes into being the earth, quite flat—therefore it accordingly rides on the air; and sun and moon and the remaining heavenly bodies have their source of generation*

τὸν ἥλιον γῆν, διὰ δὲ τὴν ὀξεῖαν κίνησιν καὶ μάλ' ἱκανῶς θερμότητα λαβεῖν [Zeller; θερμοτάτην κίνησιν λαβεῖν codd. plurimi].

152 Hippolytus *Ref.* 1, 7, 5 γεγονέναι δὲ τὰ ἄστρα ἐκ γῆς διὰ τὸ τὴν ἰκμάδα ἐκ ταύτης ἀνίστασθαι, ἧς ἀραιουμένης τὸ πῦρ γίνεσθαι, ἐκ δὲ τοῦ πυρὸς μετεωριζομένου τοὺς ἀστέρας συνίστασθαι.

Anaximenes presumably gave an account of the development of the world from undifferentiated air; as with Anaximander, only ps.-Plutarch summarizes the subject in general, and he does little more than apply the obvious changes of air (outlined by Theophrastus with reference to continuing natural processes, cf. the present tense of γίνεσθαι in **143**) to what could be an *a priori* cosmogonical pattern. Only in the case of the formation of the heavenly bodies is there detailed information; here Hippolytus in **152** is almost certainly right as against the last sentence of **151**, which seems to impose on Anaximenes ideas from Xenophanes (ignition through motion) and Anaxagoras (the same, and sun made of earth; cf. pp. 155 ff. for another confusion). The heavenly bodies (ἄστρα) certainly originate from the earth, but only in that moist vapour is exhaled or evaporated from (the moist parts of) earth; this is further rarefied and so becomes fire, of which the heavenly bodies are composed. The formation of the earth had occurred by the condensation of a part of the indefinitely-extended primal air. No reason is even suggested for this initial condensation, except possibly the 'eternal motion'; as with Anaximander, this was Theophrastus' way of expressing the capacity of the divine originative stuff to initiate change and motion where it willed: see p. 128.[1]

[1] As with Anaximander, there is no ground for postulating a vortex in Anaximenes except Aristotle's generalization in **119**; in Anaximenes' case there is not even the mysterious 'producer of the hot and the cold' to be accounted for. Yet Anaximenes was not implicitly excepted from the generalization, as Anaximander may have been (p. 128). However, Aristotle had reason a few lines earlier, **153**, to class Anaximenes with Anaxagoras and Democritus (they all assumed that the earth remains stable because of its breadth); the two others certainly postulated a

---

from earth. At least, he declares the sun to be earth, but that through the rapid motion it obtains heat in great sufficiency.

152 *The heavenly bodies have come into being from earth through the exhalation arising from it; when the exhalation is rarefied fire comes into being, and from fire raised on high the stars are composed.*

vortex, and so Aristotle might have been content to class Anaximenes with them in this respect too—if he was not simply being careless in his use of 'all', πάντες, in **119**. Of course, as Zeller pointed out, vortex-action would produce the variations of pressure required for a cosmos; though Anaximenes did not in fact explain the heavenly bodies by direct rarefaction of the extremities.

COSMOLOGY

(i) *The earth is flat and rides on air*

153 Aristotle *de caelo* B13, 294b13 (DK 13A20) Ἀναξιμένης δὲ καὶ Ἀναξαγόρας καὶ Δημόκριτος τὸ πλάτος αἴτιον εἶναί φασι τοῦ μένειν αὐτήν (*sc.* τὴν γῆν)· οὐ γὰρ τέμνειν ἀλλ' ἐπιπωματίζειν τὸν ἀέρα τὸν κάτωθεν, ὅπερ φαίνεται τὰ πλάτος ἔχοντα τῶν σωμάτων ποιεῖν· ταῦτα γὰρ καὶ πρὸς τοὺς ἀνέμους ἔχει δυσκινήτως διὰ τὴν ἀντέρεισιν.

Anaximenes seems to have consolidated the conception of the earth as broad, flat and shallow in depth—'table-like' according to Aetius III, 10, 3 (DK 13A20)—and as being supported by air. This idea was closely followed by Anaxagoras and the atomists (**529** *init.* and p. 412), who in details of cosmology conservatively selected from the Ionian tradition. That the earth was supported by air was obviously an adaptation, encouraged no doubt by the observation of leaves floating in the air, of Thales' idea that the earth floated on water. Aristotle in the continuation of **153** was wrong in suggesting that support is provided because the air underneath is trapped and cannot withdraw: for Anaximenes the surrounding air was unbounded in any way, and was doubtless unthinkingly supposed to support the earth because of its indefinite depth—and because leaves do float on air. Theophrastus, judging from **151**, **154**, and Aetius III, 15, 8 (DK 13A20), wrote that according to Anaximenes the earth *rides*, ἐποχεῖσθαι, on air: the verb occurs in Homer and could well have been used by Anaximenes. Aristotle's 'covers the air below like a lid' is probably his own expression, an improvement perhaps on Plato's reference (*Phaedo* 99B) to an unnamed physicist—Anaximenes or Anaxagoras or the atomists or all of them—who 'puts air underneath as a support for the earth, which is like a broad kneading-trough'.

---

153 *Anaximenes and Anaxagoras and Democritus say that its* [*the earth's*] *flatness is responsible for it staying still: for it does not cut the air beneath but covers it like a lid, which flat bodies evidently do; for they are hard to move even for the winds, on account of their resistance.*

(ii) *The heavenly bodies*

154 Hippolytus *Ref.* I, 7, 4 τὴν δὲ γῆν πλατεῖαν εἶναι ἐπ' ἀέρος ὀχουμένην, ὁμοίως δὲ καὶ ἥλιον καὶ σελήνην καὶ τὰ ἄλλα ἄστρα πάντα πύρινα ὄντα ἐποχεῖσθαι τῷ ἀέρι διὰ πλάτος.

155 Aetius II, 13, 10 'Αναξιμένης πυρίνην μὲν τὴν φύσιν τῶν ἄστρων, περιέχειν δέ τινα καὶ γεώδη σώματα συμπεριφερόμενα τούτοις ἀόρατα.

156 Aetius II, 23, 1 'Αναξιμένης ὑπὸ πεπυκνωμένου ἀέρος καὶ ἀντιτύπου ἐξωθούμενα τὰ ἄστρα τὰς τροπὰς ποιεῖσθαι.

157 Aetius II, 14, 3–4 'Αναξιμένης ἥλων δίκην καταπεπηγέναι τὰ ἄστρα τῷ κρυσταλλοειδεῖ· ἔνιοι δὲ πέταλα εἶναι πύρινα ὥσπερ ȝωγραφήματα.

158 Aetius II, 22, 1 'Αναξιμένης πλατὺν ὡς πέταλον τὸν ἥλιον.

159 Hippolytus *Ref.* I, 7, 6 οὐ κινεῖσθαι δὲ ὑπὸ γῆν τὰ ἄστρα λέγει, καθὼς ἕτεροι ὑπειλήφασιν, ἀλλὰ περὶ γῆν, ὡσπερεὶ περὶ τὴν ἡμετέραν κεφαλὴν στρέφεται τὸ πιλίον. κρύπτεσθαί τε τὸν ἥλιον οὐχ ὑπὸ γῆν γενόμενον ἀλλ' ὑπὸ τῶν τῆς γῆς ὑψηλοτέρων μερῶν σκεπόμενον καὶ διὰ τὴν πλείονα ἡμῶν αὐτοῦ γενομένην ἀπόστασιν.

160 Aristotle *Meteor.* B 1, 354a28 πολλοὺς πεισθῆναι τῶν ἀρχαίων μετεωρολόγων τὸν ἥλιον μὴ φέρεσθαι ὑπὸ γῆν ἀλλὰ περὶ τὴν γῆν καὶ τὸν τόπον τοῦτον, ἀφανίȝεσθαι δὲ καὶ ποιεῖν νύκτα διὰ τὸ ὑψηλὴν εἶναι πρὸς ἄρκτον τὴν γῆν.

---

154 *The earth is flat, being borne upon air, and similarly sun, moon and the other heavenly bodies, which are all fiery, ride upon the air through their flatness.*

155 *Anaximenes says that the nature of the heavenly bodies is fiery, and that they have among them certain earthy bodies that are carried round with them, being invisible.*

156 *Anaximenes says that the heavenly bodies make their turnings through being pushed out by condensed and opposing air.*

157 *Anaximenes says that the stars are implanted like nails in the crystalline; but some say they are fiery leaves like paintings.*

158 *Anaximenes says the sun is flat like a leaf.*

159 *He says that the heavenly bodies do not move under the earth, as others have supposed, but round it, just as if a felt cap turns round our head; and that the sun is hidden not by being under the earth, but through being covered by the higher parts of the earth and through its increased distance from us.*

160 *Many of the old astronomers were convinced that the sun is not carried under the earth, but round the earth and this region; and that it is obscured, and makes night, through the earth being high towards the north.*

That the heavenly bodies were created by the rarefaction into fire of vapour from the earth was asserted in **152**. Like the earth, they ride on air (**154**); though since they are made of fire, as **154** and **155** confirm, and since fire is more diffuse than air, there is a difficulty which Anaximenes may not have seen in making them rest on air in the same way as the denser earth does. That the movements of the sun on the ecliptic, of the moon in declination, and perhaps of the planets, are caused by winds (which are slightly condensed air, cf. **143**) is suggested by **156**; Aristotle had referred at *Meteor.* B 1, 353 b 5 and B 2, 355 a 21 (**612**) to old writers who had explained the first two of these three celestial motions in just this way. **157** creates a difficulty, however, in stating that the ἄστρα (which can mean all the heavenly bodies, or the fixed stars and the planets, or just the fixed stars) are attached like studs to the ice-like outer heaven (which according to **159** would be hemispherical), and not floating free. This could only apply to the fixed stars; but we hear nothing more about the 'ice-like', and indeed the concept of a solid outer heaven is foreign to the little that is known of Anaximenes' cosmogony and to the other details of cosmology. The same term was applied three times by Aetius to Empedocles' heaven (which would be spherical), and at II, 13, 11 (**437**) he said that Empedocles' fixed stars were bound to the ice-like, while the planets were free. It appears that this concept may have been mistakenly transferred to Anaximenes. The second part of **157** is introduced as an opinion held by 'some people'; but since Anaximenes certainly held the heavenly bodies to be fiery, and since **158** compares the sun to a leaf, it looks as though he is the author of the opinion that they were fiery leaves, and as if the text is astray. What the comparison to paintings implies is quite uncertain. If Anaximenes *is* meant, the ἄστρα in question could be the heavenly bodies in general, or (if the first part is accepted) they could be the planets, which would be distinguished, as by Empedocles, from the fixed stars on the 'ice-like'. Presumably this last term refers to the apparent transparency of the sky; it represents an improvement, from the empirical point of view, on the Homeric solid metal bowl (p. 10). Such an improvement would not be uncharacteristic of Anaximenes; but the attribution of this view to him remains very doubtful.[1] The inaccuracy of doxographical attributions, particularly in Aetius, is probably demonstrated by the second part of **155**. It is usually assumed that

Anaximenes postulated these invisible celestial bodies in order to explain eclipses; but according to Hippolytus I, 8, 6 (DK 59 A 42) Anaxagoras, too, believed in them. Yet Anaxagoras knew the true cause of eclipses, therefore he cannot have postulated the invisible bodies for this purpose. The previous sentence in Aetius explains all: Diogenes of Apollonia postulated these bodies to explain meteorites like the famous one which fell at Aegospotami in 467 B.C. (**611**). Anaxagoras, too, had probably been persuaded by this notable event to account for meteorites; but Anaximenes had no such good reason, and the theory was probably projected on to him from his assumed follower Diogenes. In any case the theory concerned meteorites and not eclipses.[2]

[1] W. K. C. Guthrie (*CQ* N.S. 6 (1956) 40 ff.) suggests that the simile might conceivably be a physiological one, since in Galen's time, at least, ἧλος could be used for a spot or lump growing on the pupil of the eye, while the cornea itself was sometimes described as 'the ice-like membrane'. This membrane was regarded as viscous, not as solid; which removes one difficulty of the attribution to Anaximenes. The date of such terminology is not known; the simile might possibly have been supplied by Aetius or his immediate source, though this seems unlikely.

[2] Eudemus(?) in the sequel to **78** (DK 13 A 16) assigns to Anaximenes the discovery that the moon shines by reflected light. This is incompatible with the belief that the moon is fiery, and is probably due to another backward projection, this time of a belief common to Parmenides (DK 28 A 42), Empedocles (**435**), and Anaxagoras (**527**).

The heavenly bodies do not pass under the earth, but (as in the pre-philosophical world-picture, where the sun, at least, floats round river Okeanos to the north: see pp. 14 f.) they move round it, like a cap revolving round our head as Hippolytus adds in **159**. This image is scarcely likely to have been invented by anyone except Anaximenes. The cap in question is a close-fitting, roughly hemispherical felt cap; conceivably it supports the dubious implication of **157** that the heaven can be regarded as a definite (though perhaps a viscous) hemisphere, carrying the fixed stars. As has been remarked, this is merely a refinement of the naïve view of the sky as a metal bowl. The second part of **159** adds that the sun is hidden (that is, in its passage from the west back again to the east) 'by the higher parts of the earth' (also by its greater distance; this may be a doxographical addition). If the sun does not go under the earth, some explanation has to be given of why it is not visible at night. But do the 'higher parts' refer to high mountains in the north—the mythical Rhipaean mountains, that is—or to the actual tilting of the flat earth on its horizontal axis? The latter explanation was certainly ascribed to Anaxagoras, Leucippus, and Diogenes, who were strongly influenced by Anaximenes in cosmological matters. This tilting would explain how the stars could set, supposing that they are somehow fixed in the heaven: they rotate on the hemisphere (whose pole is the Wain) and pass below the upper, northern edge of the earth but not below its mean horizontal axis. Yet attractive as this interpretation is, it is made very doubtful by **160**: here Aristotle refers to the theory of 'higher parts' (again, in ambiguous terms) as being held by many of the old astronomers. But his context, which is concerned with showing that the greatest rivers flow from the greatest mountains, in the north, makes it quite clear that he understands 'the earth being high to the north' to refer to its northern mountain ranges. It must be assumed that Aristotle was thinking in part of Anaximenes, details of whose cosmological views were known to him (cf. **153**, **162**); Anaxagoras and Leucippus, then, either made an advance on Anaximenes here or were themselves misinterpreted later. A serious difficulty in the tilted-earth hypothesis is that the earth would not thus float on air, but would slip downwards as leaves do; this applies also to Leucippus' earth. The cap-image must illustrate the hemispherical shape of the sky, not its obliquity; it is difficult, indeed, to see why the cap should be imagined as being tilted on the head. Thus Anaximenes appears to have accepted the broad structure of the naïve world-picture, but to have purged it of its more obviously mythological details like the sun's golden bowl (which presumably helped to conceal its light during the voyage north).

(iii) *Meteorological phenomena*

161 Aetius III, 3, 2 Ἀναξιμένης ταὐτὰ τούτῳ (*sc.* Ἀναξιμάνδρῳ), προστιθεὶς τὸ ἐπὶ τῆς θαλάσσης, ἥτις σχιζομένη ταῖς κώπαις παραστίλβει. III, 4, 1 Ἀναξιμένης νέφη μὲν γίνεσθαι παχυνθέντος ἐπὶ πλεῖον τοῦ ἀέρος, μᾶλλον δ' ἐπισυναχθέντος ἐκθλίβεσθαι τοὺς

---

161 *Anaximenes said the same as he* [*Anaximander*], *adding what happens in the case of sea, which flashes when cleft by oars.—Anaximenes said that clouds occur when the air is further thickened; when it is compressed further rain is squeezed out, and hail occurs*

ὄμβρους, χάλαζαν δὲ ἐπειδὰν τὸ καταφερόμενον ὕδωρ παγῇ, χιόνα δ' ὅταν συμπεριληφθῇ τι τῷ ὑγρῷ πνευματικόν.

162 Aristotle *Meteor.* B7, 365b6 'Αναξιμένης δέ φησι βρεχομένην τὴν γῆν καὶ ξηραινομένην ῥήγνυσθαι καὶ ὑπὸ τούτων τῶν ἀπορρηγνυμένων κολωνῶν ἐμπιπτόντων σείεσθαι· διὸ καὶ γίγνεσθαι τοὺς σεισμοὺς ἔν τε τοῖς αὐχμοῖς καὶ πάλιν ἐν ταῖς ὑπερομβρίαις· ἔν τε γὰρ τοῖς αὐχμοῖς, ὥσπερ εἴρηται, ξηραινομένην ῥήγνυσθαι καὶ ὑπὸ τῶν ὑδάτων ὑπερυγραινομένην διαπίπτειν.

Anaximenes is said to have given the same explanation of thunder and lightning, in terms of wind, as Anaximander: see **132** and comment. The oar-image may be original. Clouds, rain, hail and snow are mainly due to the condensation of air, as one would expect; this was indicated by Theophrastus in **143**, and Aetius (also Hippolytus, *Ref.* I, 7, 7–8, DK 13A7) adds further details. Winds, too, are slightly condensed air (**143**), and according to Hippolytus the rainbow was due to the reflexion of different sunbeams by air. Aristotle in **162** gives a relatively full account of Anaximenes' explanation of earthquakes: note that air plays no part in this whatever.

THE COMPARISON BETWEEN COSMIC AIR AND THE BREATH-SOUL

163 Aetius I, 3, 4 'Αναξιμένης Εὐρυστράτου Μιλήσιος ἀρχὴν τῶν ὄντων ἀέρα ἀπεφήνατο· ἐκ γὰρ τούτου πάντα γίγνεσθαι καὶ εἰς αὐτὸν πάλιν ἀναλύεσθαι. οἷον ἡ ψυχή, φησίν, ἡ ἡμετέρα ἀὴρ οὖσα συγκρατεῖ ἡμᾶς, καὶ ὅλον τὸν κόσμον πνεῦμα καὶ ἀὴρ περιέχει· λέγεται δὲ συνωνύμως ἀὴρ καὶ πνεῦμα. ἁμαρτάνει δὲ καὶ οὗτος ἐξ ἁπλοῦ καὶ μονοειδοῦς ἀέρος καὶ πνεύματος δοκῶν συνεστάναι τὰ ζῷα.... (For continuation see DK 13B2.)

---

when the descending water coalesces, snow when some windy portion is included together with the moisture.

162 *Anaximenes says that the earth, through being drenched and dried off, breaks asunder, and is shaken by the peaks that are thus broken off and fall in. Therefore earthquakes happen in periods both of drought and again of excessive rains; for in droughts, as has been said, it dries up and cracks, and being made over-moist by the waters it crumbles apart.*

163 *Anaximenes son of Eurystratus, of Miletus, declared that air is the principle of existing things; for from it all things come-to-be and into it they are again dissolved. As our soul, he says, being air holds us together and controls us, so does wind* [*or breath*] *and air enclose the whole world.* (*Air and wind are synonymous here.*) *He, too, is in error in thinking that living creatures consist of simple and homogeneous air and wind....*

The underlined words here are commonly accepted as a direct quotation from Anaximenes. There must, however, have been some alteration and some re-wording: for the sentence is not in Ionic (cf. **141**), and it contains one word, συγκρατεῖ, which could not possibly have been used by Anaximenes, and another, κόσμον, which is unlikely to have been used by him in precisely this sense.[1] That the sentence does, however, represent some kind of reproduction of a statement by Anaximenes is shown by Aetius' comment that 'air' and 'breath [*or* wind]' have the same meaning here, and also by the fact that the comparison with the soul complicates the simple Aristotelian criticism which Aetius is reproducing, that Anaximenes did not specify a moving cause. On the other hand the use of φησί, 'he says', does not guarantee a direct quotation in this kind of writing. περιέχει, of air enfolding all things, is quite likely to be Anaximenean, cf. **110**; while the concept of the soul as breath (one suspects that πνεῦμα, not ἀήρ, originally stood in the first clause) is certainly an archaic one—compare the Homeric distinction between the life-soul, which normally seems to be identified with the breath, and the sensory and intellectual soul normally called θυμός. τὸν κόσμον could have replaced e.g. simply ἅπαντα, 'all things'. The degree of re-wording, then, probably is not very great; unfortunately we cannot determine whether, or how far, it affected the exact point and degree of comparison.

[1] συγκρατεῖν is otherwise first used in Plutarch (twice), then in 2nd-cent. A.D. medical writers and Diog. L. (of restraining the breath etc.); also in the *Geoponica* and the Christian fathers. It is an unnatural compound which could only have occurred in the Κοινή; it is really a compendium for συνέχειν καὶ κρατεῖν. This is illustrated in Plut. *Vit. Phoc.* 12, συνεκράτει τὸ μαχιμώτατον τῆς δυνάμεως: he kept control of his troops by keeping them together (on a hill-top). κόσμος originally means 'order', and it is probably not established in the meaning 'world-order' until the second half of the fifth century B.C. It must have been used in *descriptions* of the order apparent in nature much before then, and probably by early Pythagoreans; Pythagoras himself is credited with using κόσμος = οὐρανός, but this is perhaps an over-simplification (Diog. L. VIII, 48). Heraclitus' κόσμον τόνδε (**220**) is probably transitional to the later and widely accepted usage, which appears unequivocally for the first time in Empedocles fr. 134, 5. (This passage was omitted by an oversight from the discussion in Kirk, *Heraclitus, the Cosmic Fragments* 312–14, and the conclusions there should be modified accordingly.)

As it stands the comparison is not very clear: 'Breath and air enclose (surround) the whole world in the way that our soul, being breath, holds us (i.e. our bodies) together and controls us.' The similarity in the two cases cannot just be that of the subject, air, without further implication; it would be pointless to say, for example, 'just as air dries moisture, so does it fill balloons'. Four possibilities, out of many, may be mentioned: (i) συγκρατεῖ in Aetius has replaced a simple notion like συνέχει, and the meaning is 'air holds us together, from inside, and the world together, from outside, ⟨and therefore man and the world are more alike than at first appears⟩, *or* ⟨and therefore air is operative in the most diverse kinds of object⟩'. (ii) περιέχει carries with it the implication of καὶ κυβερνᾷ, cf. **110**. The meaning would then be 'as our soul holds the body together and so controls it, so the originative substance (which is basically the same stuff as soul) holds the world together and so controls *it*', supporting the inference 'holds together therefore controls'. (iii) 'The soul, which is breath, holds together and controls man; therefore what holds together and controls the world must also be breath or air, because the world is like a large-scale man or animal.' (iv) 'The life-principle and motive force of man is, traditionally, πνεῦμα or the breath-soul; ⟨πνεῦμα is seen in the outside world, as wind;⟩ therefore the life-principle of the outside world is πνεῦμα; ⟨therefore wind, breath, or air is the life and substance of all things⟩.'—Now it has been seen that the form συγκρατεῖ is impossible for Anaximenes, but the question also arises whether even a verb like συνέχει could, for him, have described the relation of the soul to the body. The fact is that the idea of the soul *holding together* the body has no other parallel in a Presocratic source, or indeed in any Greek source earlier than Stoic ones and some of the later Hippocratic works. The concept involved is admittedly not a complex one: for when the life-soul departs, the body, or most of it, obviously disintegrates, it is no longer held together. Nevertheless the absence of parallels, together with the knowledge that Anaximenes' terminology has certainly been tampered with at this point, makes it unwise to accept the sense even of συνέχει here. This damages (ii), but not (i) and (iii); their main arguments can be re-stated with the substitution of 'possess', for example, in place of 'hold together (and control)': for Anaximenes could certainly have held that the soul *possesses*, ἔχει, the body, meaning that it permeates the whole of it (cf. e.g. Heraclitus fr. 67*a*); and possibly, even, that it controls it. (iv) avoids emphasizing συγκρατεῖ, and depends in part on the fact that Anaximenes' is the first extant use of the word πνεῦμα, which became common (both for breath and for gust of wind) with the tragedians; its possible dual application *could* have led Anaximenes to the parallelism of man and the world. Indeed all three remaining interpretations, (iv) and the revised forms of (i) and (iii), express this parallelism in one form or another: it is the essence of the statement to be interpreted. Beyond that, to the particular form of the inference that must have been based upon it, we can hardly hope to penetrate with certainty. Yet the fully developed and clear-cut use of the inference from the known microcosm, man, to the unknown macrocosm, the world as a whole, does not otherwise appear until the latter part of the fifth century, under the influence, it is thought, of the new interest in theoretical medicine at that time; it is perhaps unlikely to occur in such a plain form as (iii) so early as Anaximenes. It is possible, moreover, that he did not argue so logically as even (i) or (iv) suggest; rather that a conjecture about the world was *illustrated* by reference to man and the soul, just as a dogma about the cause of lightning was illustrated by the example of the oar-blade, or that about the heavenly bodies by that of the cap on the head. This would be more plausible as the first stage in the development of the man-world argument, and accords with Anaximenes' known use of imagery.

All this is necessarily very conjectural. It remains uncertain to what extent Anaximenes was tending to treat the world itself as alive, as a kind of huge animal organism; it has been noticed that, although he introduced a thoroughly rational description of change, Anaximenes in some respects clung to the framework of the popular, non-philosophical world-construction, and so might retain more of the old anthropomorphic attitude than at first sight seems probable. However, his perception that air is the cosmic equivalent of the life-soul in man goes far beyond that attitude; it must, in fact, have been an important motive for his choice of air as the originative substance.[1] The mention of soul is important in itself; apart from **91** it is the first Presocratic psychological statement to survive—though the actual structure of the soul envisaged, as breath, belonged to an age-old popular tradition. Another conception of the soul, as made of the fiery aither which also fills the outer sky, was accepted from another channel of the popular tradition by Heraclitus, who was also to develop the assumption, probably implicit in Anaximenes, that man and the outside world are made of the same material and behave according to similar rules.

[1] It is perhaps odd that Aristotle did not name Anaximenes at *de an.* A 2, 405 a 21, where 'Diogenes and some others' are named as holding the view that the soul is air: Aristotle is arguing that the Presocratics made the soul out of their ἀρχή. Plato, *Phaedo* 96 B (what we think with is air), was probably referring to Diogenes of Apollonia (cf. pp. 437 f.), who held that soul was *warm* air, thus perhaps conjoining the view of soul as aither or fire. There is no reason to think with Vlastos (*AJP* 76 (1955) 364 and n. 56) that Diogenes was here exclusively indebted to Anaximenes.

CONCLUSION

Anaximenes is the last of the great Milesian thinkers. He was obviously indebted to Anaximander, but also probably to Thales, to whose concept of the originative stuff as an actual component of the world he was enabled to return by his great idea of condensation and rarefaction—an observable means of change by which quantity controls kind. This idea was probably accepted by Heraclitus and submerged in a system of a rather different nature: for after the Milesians the old cosmogonical approach, according to which the most important object was to name a single kind of material from which the whole differentiated world could have grown, was enlarged and moderated. New problems, of theology and of unity in the arrangement, rather than the material, of things, exercised Anaximenes' successors Xenophanes and Heraclitus—although they too (even though the former migrated) were Ionians; still more basic departures from the Milesian tradition were made in the west. But when the fifth-century thinkers of the east and the mainland (Anaxagoras, Diogenes, Leucippus and Democritus) had recovered from the western elenchus of the Eleatics, it was to the Milesians, and particularly to Anaximenes, that they chiefly turned for details of cosmology; doubtless because those details had been in part adapted from, and were still protected by, the popular, non-scientific tradition.

CHAPTER V

XENOPHANES OF COLOPHON

DATE AND LIFE

164 Diogenes Laertius IX, 18 (DK21A1) Ξενοφάνης Δεξίου ἤ, ὡς Ἀπολλόδωρος, Ὀρθομένους Κολοφώνιος...οὗτος ἐκπεσὼν τῆς πατρίδος ἐν Ζάγκλῃ τῆς Σικελίας διέτριβε καὶ ἐν Κατάνῃ....γέγραφε δὲ ἐν ἔπεσι καὶ ἐλεγείας καὶ ἰάμβους καθ' Ἡσιόδου καὶ Ὁμήρου, ἐπικόπτων αὐτῶν τὰ περὶ θεῶν εἰρημένα. ἀλλὰ καὶ αὐτὸς ἐρραψῴδει τὰ ἑαυτοῦ. ἀντιδοξάσαι τε λέγεται Θαλῇ καὶ Πυθαγόρᾳ, καθάψασθαι δὲ καὶ Ἐπιμενίδου. μακροβιώτατός τε γέγονεν, ὥς που καὶ αὐτός φησιν·

(Fr. 8) ἤδη δ' ἑπτά τ' ἔασι καὶ ἑξήκοντ' ἐνιαυτοὶ
βληστρίζοντες ἐμὴν φροντίδ' ἀν' Ἑλλάδα γῆν·
ἐκ γενετῆς δὲ τότ' ἦσαν ἐείκοσι πέντε τε πρὸς τοῖς,
εἴπερ ἐγὼ περὶ τῶνδ' οἶδα λέγειν ἐτύμως.

...(20) καὶ ἤκμαζε κατὰ τὴν ἑξηκοστὴν ὀλυμπιάδα.

165 Clement *Strom.* I, 64, 2 τῆς δὲ Ἐλεατικῆς ἀγωγῆς Ξενοφάνης ὁ Κολοφώνιος κατάρχει, ὅν φησι Τίμαιος κατὰ Ἱέρωνα τὸν Σικελίας δυνάστην καὶ Ἐπίχαρμον τὸν ποιητὴν γεγονέναι, Ἀπολλόδωρος δὲ κατὰ τὴν τεσσαρακοστὴν ὀλυμπιάδα γενόμενον παρατετακέναι ἄχρι Δαρείου τε καὶ Κύρου χρόνων.

Xenophanes, as opposed to the Milesians, wrote in verse; and a number of fragments of his work have survived. If we assume that

---

164 *Xenophanes son of Dexios or, according to Apollodorus, of Orthomenes, of Colophon...he, being expelled from his native land, passed his time in Zancle in Sicily and in Catana....He wrote in epic metre, also elegiacs and iambics, against Hesiod and Homer, reproving them for what they said about the gods. But he himself also recited his own original poems. He is said to have held contrary opinions to Thales and Pythagoras, and to have rebuked Epimenides too. He had an extremely long life, as he himself somewhere says: 'Already there are seven and sixty years tossing my thought up and down the land of Greece; and from my birth there were another twenty-five to add to these, if I know how to speak truly about these things.'...And he was at his prime in the 60th Olympiad.*

165 *Of the Eleatic school Xenophanes the Colophonian is the pioneer, who Timaeus says lived in the time of Hieron, tyrant of Sicily, and the poet Epicharmus, while Apollodorus says that he was born in the 40th Olympiad and lasted until the times of Darius and Cyrus.*

he left Colophon in Ionia about the time of its capture by the Medes in 546/5 B.C. (he certainly knew it before this time, since in fr. 3, DK21B3, he referred to the corruption of the Colophonians by Lydian luxury), then from his own words in **164** he would have been born around 570 B.C., twenty-five years earlier. Even if this assumption is made, his great age—at least 92 from his words in **164**—makes it impossible to assign his extant poetry to any narrow period. He referred to Pythagoras (**268**) and Simonides (DK21B21), as well as to Thales and Epimenides—no more is known than the bare fact of his reference to the last three—and was himself referred to by Heraclitus (**193**); and Parmenides was later supposed to be his pupil. All this is possible enough if he lived from *ca.* 570 to *ca.* 475 B.C. The statement of Timaeus (the 4th/3rd century B.C. historian of Sicily) in **165** is compatible with this assumption, since Hiero reigned from 478 to 467 B.C. and Epicharmus was at Syracuse during this time. Apollodorus is perhaps wrongly reported in **165**: Ol. 40 (620–617 B.C.) is improbably early for Xenophanes' birth, and 'until the times of Cyrus and Darius' is curious, since Cyrus died in 529 and Darius gained power in 521. Yet there is no absolutely positive evidence that Xenophanes died later than e.g. 525, when Pythagoras had not been long in Italy. However, Diogenes in **164**, after mentioning Apollodorus, put Xenophanes' *floruit* in Ol. 60 (540–537 B.C.); this seems to be the true Apollodoran dating, based on the epoch-year of the foundation of Elea (on which Xenophanes was said to have written a poem) in 540.

The details of Xenophanes' life are even more uncertain. Born and brought up in Ionia, and obviously acquainted with the trends of Ionian thought, he was compelled to leave when a young man, and from then on lived a wandering life, chiefly perhaps in Sicily; his connexion with Elea may have been a later invention (see pp. 165 f.). He was a poet and sage, a singer of his own songs rather than those of others: he was certainly not, as some have mistakenly assumed from **164**, a Homeric rhapsode. In the longest of his extant elegies (fr. 1, which has no immediate philosophical relevance) he has authority enough to outline the rules of behaviour for the symposium that is to follow; he seems therefore to have been honourably received in aristocratic households.

THE ASSOCIATION OF XENOPHANES WITH ELEA

166 Plato *Sophist* 242 D (DK 21 A 29) τὸ δὲ παρ' ἡμῖν Ἐλεατικὸν ἔθνος, ἀπὸ Ξενοφάνους τε καὶ ἔτι πρόσθεν ἀρξάμενον, ὡς ἑνὸς ὄντος τῶν πάντων καλουμένων οὕτω διεξέρχεται τοῖς μύθοις.

167 Aristotle *Met.* A 5, 986 b 18 Παρμενίδης μὲν γὰρ ἔοικε τοῦ κατὰ τὸν λόγον ἑνὸς ἅπτεσθαι, Μέλισσος δὲ τοῦ κατὰ τὴν ὕλην· διὸ καὶ ὁ μὲν πεπερασμένον, ὁ δ' ἄπειρόν φησιν εἶναι αὐτό· Ξενοφάνης δὲ πρῶτος τούτων ἑνίσας (ὁ γὰρ Παρμενίδης τούτου λέγεται γενέσθαι μαθητής) οὐθὲν διεσαφήνισεν.... (For continuation see **177**.)

It is commonly assumed in the doxographers that Xenophanes spent a part at least of his life in Elea, and that he was the founder of the Eleatic school of philosophy. This is exemplified in **165**. That he was Parmenides' master stems from Aristotle in **167**, and was categorically asserted by Theophrastus according to Simplicius (**168**). Yet Aristotle's judgement possibly arises from Plato's remark in **166**. This remark was not necessarily intended as a serious historical judgement (one may compare the statements in the *Theaetetus* (152 D–E, 160 D) that Homer and Epicharmus were the founders of the Heraclitean tradition), as is confirmed by the addition of the words καὶ ἔτι πρόσθεν, 'and even before'. The connexion between Xenophanes and Parmenides obviously depends on the superficial similarity between the motionless one deity of the former and the motionless sphere of Being in the latter—although it will be seen that Parmenides' theoretical construction was reached in a quite different way from Xenophanes', a way which is in fact incompatible. The extreme example of the treatment of Xenophanes as an Eleatic is seen in the pseudo-Aristotelian *de Melisso Xenophane Gorgia* (DK 21 A 28), a treatise written probably about the time of Christ in which Xenophanes' god is explained in fully Eleatic terms, and the inference is drawn from Aristotle's judgement in **167** that it was neither limited as in

---

166 *Our Eleatic tribe, beginning from Xenophanes and even before, explains in its myths that what we call all things are actually one.*

167 *For Parmenides seems to fasten on that which is one in definition, Melissus on that which is one in material; therefore the former says that it is limited, the latter that it is unlimited. But Xenophanes, the first of these to postulate a unity (for Parmenides is said to have been his pupil), made nothing clear....*

Parmenides nor unlimited as in Melissus. Unfortunately Simplicius, who could not find at least some physical parts of Xenophanes' poetry (*de caelo* 522, 7, DK21A47), relied on this treatise and quoted far less than usual from Theophrastus. Other evidence connecting Xenophanes with Elea is slight: he is said by Diogenes Laertius (IX, 20, DK21A1) to have written 2000 lines on the foundation of Colophon and the colonization of Elea, but this probably comes from the stichometrist and forger Lobon of Argos and is unreliable; while Aristotle (*Rhet.* B23, 1400b5, DK21A13) told an anecdote of some advice of his to the Eleans—but this was a 'floating' anecdote also connected with Heraclitus and others. It is not improbable that Xenophanes visited Elea; that was perhaps the extent of his connexion with it. He was not in any way typical of the new western trend in philosophy initiated by Pythagoras; nor was he typically Ionian, but since his ideas were a direct reaction from Ionian theories and from the originally Ionian Homer he is placed in this book with the Ionians, and not in his probable chronological place after Pythagoras—like him an emigrant from eastern to western Greece.

HIS POEMS

Some of Xenophanes' extant fragments are in elegiac metre, some are hexameters; while **170** consists of an iambic trimeter followed by a hexameter. This accords with Diogenes' mention of these three metres in **164**. Some at any rate of his poems were called Σίλλοι, 'squints' or satires, and the third-century B.C. 'sillographer' Timon of Phlius is said by Sextus (DK21A35) to have dedicated his own Σίλλοι to Xenophanes, about whom he certainly wrote; see also DK21A20–23. According to three late sources, Stobaeus (from an allegorizing author), the Geneva scholiast on the *Iliad*, and Pollux (DK21A36, 21B30, 21B39), there was a physical work by Xenophanes called Περὶ φύσεως, 'On nature'. The value of this title has already been discussed (p. 101 and n. 1 on p. 102), and it is only to be expected that at least some later references to physical opinions in Xenophanes should occur in this form. It is notable that Aetius, who also quoted the passages cited in the first two cases above, said nothing about a Περὶ φύσεως (DK21A36 and 46). That Xenophanes wrote a formal work on physical matters seems questionable—though not so impossible as Burnet would have us believe (*EGP* 115f.). Theophrastus, we may observe, said that

Xenophanes' monistic conception was not 'physical' in the normal sense.[1] Xenophanes was not, like Anaximenes or Heraclitus, primarily engaged in giving a comprehensive explanation of the natural world. He was interested, without doubt, particularly in theology, and many of his remarks on physical topics are connected with that; others may have been ironical rejections of previous theories, and others again would naturally reflect the interest which many educated Greeks must have felt about natural problems at this time. Such remarks, together with comments on particular poets and thinkers (e.g. **169**; cf. also DK 21 A 22), could have been expressed in separate poems in a variety of metres—though the extant theological and physical fragments are nearly all in hexameters. There may have been a separate collection of convivial songs in elegiacs.

[1] Cf. **168** Simplicius *Phys.* 22, 26 μίαν δὲ τὴν ἀρχὴν ἤτοι ἓν τὸ ὂν καὶ πᾶν (καὶ οὔτε πεπερασμένον οὔτε ἄπειρον οὔτε κινούμενον οὔτε ἠρεμοῦν) Ξενοφάνην τὸν Κολοφώνιον τὸν Παρμενίδου διδάσκαλον ὑποτίθεσθαί φησιν ὁ Θεόφραστος, ὁμολογῶν ἑτέρας εἶναι μᾶλλον ἢ τῆς περὶ φύσεως ἱστορίας τὴν μνήμην τῆς τούτου δόξης. Theophrastus is here misled by Aristotle in **177** into thinking that Xenophanes' one god is definitely non-physical, and is the whole of existence like the Parmenidean Being. But he can hardly have thought this if there was a poem which in any way resembled the works of the Milesians.

HIS IMPORTANCE

Widely different views have been held on the intellectual importance of Xenophanes. Thus Jaeger (*Theology* 52) writes of his 'enormous influence on later religious development', while Burnet (*EGP* 129) maintained that 'he would have smiled if he had known that one day he was to be regarded as a theologian'. Burnet's depreciation is certainly much exaggerated. Yet it is plain that Xenophanes differed considerably from the Milesians or Heraclitus or Parmenides. He was a poet with thoughtful interests, especially about religion and the gods, which led him to react against the archetype of poets and the mainstay of contemporary education, Homer. His attacks on Homeric theology must have had a deep influence both on ordinary men who heard his poems and on other

---

168 *Theophrastus says that Xenophanes the Colophonian, the teacher of Parmenides, supposed the principle to be single, or that the whole of existence was one (and neither limited nor unlimited, neither in motion nor at rest); and Theophrastus agrees that the record of Xenophanes' opinion belongs to another study rather than that of natural philosophy.*

thinkers; Heraclitus' attack on blood-purification and images (**244**), for example, was presumably influenced by him. His positive description of deity conceivably lay behind Aeschylus' description of divine power in the *Supplices* (**176**). The assessment of the true relative merits of poets and athletes (fr. 2) was developed by Euripides in the *Autolycus* (fr. 282 Nauck, DK 21 C 2); this is a less specialized instance of Xenophanes' rational intellectualism. Nor is it safe to exaggerate his non-scientific character on the grounds of his theological interest; the study of gods was not divorced from that of nature, and the deduction from fossils (pp. 177 ff.), whether or not it reflects original observation, shows careful and by no means implausible argument from observed fact to general hypothesis—a procedure notoriously rare among the Presocratics. Some of his other physical statements are unutterably bizarre, but we cannot tell how serious they were meant to be. He was a critic rather than an original dogmatic, not a specialist but a true σοφιστής or sage, prepared to turn his intelligence upon almost any problem (though as it happens we know of no political pronouncements)—which is why Heraclitus attacked him in **193**. His opinions on almost all subjects deserve careful attention.

THEOLOGY

(i) *Attacks on* (*a*) *the immorality*, (*b*) *the anthropomorphic nature*, *of the gods of the conventional religion*

169 Fr. 11, Sextus *adv. math.* IX, 193

πάντα θεοῖς ἀνέθηκαν Ὅμηρός θ' Ἡσίοδός τε
ὅσσα παρ' ἀνθρώποισιν ὀνείδεα καὶ ψόγος ἐστίν,
κλέπτειν μοιχεύειν τε καὶ ἀλλήλους ἀπατεύειν.

170 Fr. 14, Clement *Strom.* V, 109, 2

ἀλλ' οἱ βροτοὶ δοκέουσι γεννᾶσθαι θεούς,
τὴν σφετέρην δ' ἐσθῆτα ἔχειν φωνήν τε δέμας τε.

171 Fr. 16, Clement *Strom.* VII, 22, 1

Αἰθίοπές τε ⟨θεοὺς σφετέρους⟩ σιμοὺς μέλανάς τε
Θρῆκές τε γλαυκοὺς καὶ πυρρούς ⟨φασι πέλεσθαι⟩.

---

169 *Homer and Hesiod have attributed to the gods everything that is a shame and reproach among men, stealing and committing adultery and deceiving each other.*

170 *But mortals consider that the gods are born, and that they have clothes and speech and bodies like their own.*

171 *The Ethiopians say that their gods are snub-nosed and black, the Thracians that theirs have light blue eyes and red hair.*

172 Fr. 15, Clement *Strom.* v, 109, 3

ἀλλ' εἰ χεῖρας ἔχον βόες ⟨ἵπποι τ'⟩ ἠὲ λέοντες,
ἢ γράψαι χείρεσσι καὶ ἔργα τελεῖν ἅπερ ἄνδρες,
ἵπποι μέν θ' ἵπποισι βόες δέ τε βουσὶν ὁμοίας
καί ⟨κε⟩ θεῶν ἰδέας ἔγραφον καὶ σώματ' ἐποίουν
τοιαῦθ' οἷόν περ καὐτοὶ δέμας εἶχον ⟨ἕκαστοι⟩.[1]

[1] **171** is convincingly reconstructed by Diels from an unmetrical quotation in Clement. The supplements in **172** are respectively by Diels, Sylburg and Herwerden; the text as in DK. Line 1 of **170** is an iambic trimeter.

Xenophanes' criticisms are clear enough: first, the gods of Homer and Hesiod are often immoral—this is patently true; second, and more fundamental, there is no good reason for thinking that the gods are anthropomorphic at all. Xenophanes brilliantly perceives, first that different races credit the gods with their own particular characteristics (this is an early example of the new anthropological approach which is seen in Herodotus and culminated in the φύσις–νόμος distinction); second, as a *reductio ad absurdum*, that animals would also do the same. The conclusion is that such assessments are subjective and without value, and that the established picture in Homer ('according to whom all have learned', fr. 10) of gods as men and women must be abandoned.

(ii) *Constructive theology: there is a single non-anthropomorphic deity*

173 Fr. 23, Clement *Strom.* v, 109, 1

εἷς θεός, ἔν τε θεοῖσι καὶ ἀνθρώποισι μέγιστος,
οὔτι δέμας θνητοῖσιν ὁμοίιος οὐδὲ νόημα.

174 Fr. 26+25, Simplicius *Phys.* 23, 11+23, 20

αἰεὶ δ' ἐν ταὐτῷ μίμνει κινούμενος οὐδέν
οὐδὲ μετέρχεσθαί μιν ἐπιπρέπει ἄλλοτε ἄλλῃ,
ἀλλ' ἀπάνευθε πόνοιο νόου φρενὶ πάντα κραδαίνει.

---

172 *But if cattle and horses or lions had hands, or were able to draw with their hands and do the works that men can do, horses would draw the forms of the gods like horses, and cattle like cattle, and they would make their bodies such as they each had themselves.*

173 *One god, greatest among gods and men, in no way similar to mortals either in body or in thought.*

174 *Always he remains in the same place, moving not at all; nor is it fitting for him to go to different places at different times, but without toil he shakes all things by the thought of his mind.*

175 Fr. 24, Sextus *adv. math.* IX, 144

οὖλος ὁρᾷ, οὖλος δὲ νοεῖ, οὖλος δέ τ' ἀκούει.[1]

[1] Diog. L. IX, 19 (DK 21 A 1) implies that the words οὐ μέντοι ἀναπνεῖ, 'but does not breathe', formed part of the quotation. This is probably a later version by someone interested in Pythagorean cosmology.

'Greatest among gods and men' in **173** should not be taken literally; men are mentioned by a 'polar' usage, as in Heraclitus fr. 30 (**220**), where this world-order was made by 'none of gods or men'. This is simply an emphatic device, and for the same reason the plural of 'gods' need not be intended literally. In fact Xenophanes wrote of 'gods' in other places also, e.g. in **191**; partly, no doubt, this was a concession, perhaps not a fully conscious one, to popular religious terminology. It seems very doubtful whether Xenophanes would have recognized other, minor deities as being in any way related to the 'one god', except as dim human projections of it. The one god is unlike men in body and thought—it has, therefore (and also in view of **175**), a body; but it is motionless,[1] for the interesting reason that it is 'not fitting' for it to move around. Xenophanes thus accepts the well-established Greek criterion of *seemliness*. Not only is it unfitting for the god to move, but movement is actually unnecessary, for the god 'shakes all things by the active will proceeding from his insight'.[2] This insight is related to seeing and hearing, but like them is accomplished not by special organs but by the god's whole unmoving body. This remarkable description was reached, probably, by taking the very antithesis of the characteristics of a Homeric god. That thought or intelligence can affect things outside the thinker, without the agency of limbs, is a development—but a very bold one—of the Homeric idea that a god can accomplish his end merely by implanting, for example, Infatuation (Ἄτη) in a mortal. That it was nevertheless a possible idea is shown by its acceptance and expansion by Aeschylus.[3]

[1] It was probably because of its motionless unity that Xenophanes' god was identified with Parmenides' Being, and later absorbed some of its properties. As early as Timon of Phlius it is called 'equal in every way' (ἶσον ἁπάντη, cf. μεσσόθεν ἰσοπαλὲς πάντῃ in Parmenides, **351**), and so becomes credited with spherical shape. Xenophanes may have described it as 'all alike' (ὁμοίην in Timon fr. 59, DK 21 A 35), since this is implicit in the whole of it functioning in a particular way as in **175**; its sphericity goes beyond the fragments and is perhaps debatable.

---

175 *All of him sees, all thinks, and all hears.*

[2] This translation is based on K. von Fritz, *CP* 40 (1945) 230, who has a good discussion of the sense of νόος and φρήν. The phrase νόου φρενί looks more curious than it is: it is obviously based on νόει φρεσί and νοέω φρεσί at *Iliad* 9, 600 and 22, 235 respectively. Further, κραδαίνει can only mean 'shakes', which suggests that Xenophanes had in mind *Il.* 1, 530, where Zeus shakes great Olympus with a nod of his head. These are other indications that Xenophanes' god is more Homeric (in a negative direction) than it seems.

[3] **176** Aeschylus *Supplices* 96–103 (Ζεύς) / ἰάπτει δ' ἐλπίδων / ἀφ' ὑψιπύργων πανώλεις / βροτούς, βίαν δ' οὔτιν' ἐξοπλίζει. / πᾶν ἄπονον δαιμονίων. / ἥμενος ὃν φρόνημά πως / αὐτόθεν ἐξέπραξεν ἔμ-/πας ἑδράνων ἀφ' ἁγνῶν. In some ways this reminds one of Solon; we cannot be quite sure that Xenophanes' view of deity was as original as it now seems to be.

(iii) *Is the one god coextensive with the world?*

177 Aristotle *Met.* A5, 986b21 (for what precedes see **167**) ...Ξενοφάνης δὲ πρῶτος τούτων ἑνίσας (ὁ γὰρ Παρμενίδης τούτου λέγεται γενέσθαι μαθητής) οὐθὲν διεσαφήνισεν, οὐδὲ τῆς φύσεως τούτων οὐδετέρας (*sc.* formal or material unity) ἔοικε θιγεῖν, ἀλλ' εἰς τὸν ὅλον οὐρανὸν ἀποβλέψας τὸ ἓν εἶναί φησι τὸν θεόν.

Xenophanes arrived at the concept of one god by reaction from Homeric anthropomorphic polytheism; Parmenides arrived at the sphere of Being by logical inference from a purely existential axiom. The processes are absolutely different, and, as has already been emphasized, Parmenides is unlikely to have been a pupil of Xenophanes, even though he might have noted the older poet's view with some interest. Aristotle obviously could not understand what Xenophanes meant by his one motionless god, but complained that he 'made nothing clear' and went on to dismiss both him and Melissus as being 'rather too uncouth' (μικρὸν ἀγροικότεροι). This puzzlement of Aristotle's suggests that Xenophanes did not produce a discursive elaboration of his theological views, which might not, indeed, have gone very far beyond the extant fragments on the subject. Aristotle's implication that the one god was neither immaterial (as he thought Parmenides' One to be) nor

---

176 *(Zeus) hurls mortals in destruction from their high-towered expectations, but puts forth no force: everything of gods is without toil. Sitting, he nevertheless at once accomplishes his thought, somehow, from his holy resting-place.*

177 *...but Xenophanes, the first of these to postulate a unity (for Parmenides is said to have been his pupil), made nothing clear, nor does he seem to have touched the nature of either of these* [sc. *Parmenides' formal unity or Melissus' material unity*]*; but with his eye on the whole heaven he says that the One is god.*

material like Melissus' One (cf. **167**) was due to the presence of both corporeal and apparently non-corporeal elements in Xenophanes' description—the body, δέμας, on the one hand (**173**), and the shaking of all things by intellect on the other (**174**). It is significant here that Aristotle did not adduce Anaxagoras' Nous (which was the ultimate source of movement and the finest kind of body, and which permeated some but not all things) in illustration of Xenophanes' deity. Instead he made the cryptic remark that Xenophanes 'with his eye on the whole world said that the One was god' (for οὐρανός can hardly mean 'first heaven' here). This clearly implies that god is identical with the world, which is what Theophrastus seems to have assumed (**168**). But Aristotle must be wrong here: how could the god be motionless if it is identical with a world which is itself implied to move (**174**)? It is probable, indeed, that although Xenophanes' god is not a direct development from the cosmogonical tradition, yet it is to some extent based upon the Milesian idea of a divine substance which, in the case of Thales and Anaximenes, was regarded as somehow permeating objects in the world and giving them life and movement. Yet Xenophanes cannot have precisely worked out the local relationship of the god on the one hand and the manifold world (which he cannot have intended to reject) on the other. Aristotle, by treating him as a primitive Eleatic, misled the whole ancient tradition on this point. If Xenophanes had even implied that the god lay *outside* the world, then Aristotle or his elaborators could have seized upon this as an anticipation of the Prime Mover. The conclusion seems to be that Xenophanes' god was conceived as the negation of Homeric divine properties, and was not precisely located—any more than the old Homeric gods were thought by Xenophanes' contemporaries to be necessarily located on Olympus. It had a body of sorts because totally incorporeal existence was inconceivable, but that body, apart from its perceptual-intellectual activity, was of secondary importance, and so perhaps was its location.

PHYSICAL IDEAS

(i) *The heavenly bodies*

178 Hippolytus *Ref.* I, 14, 3 τὸν δὲ ἥλιον ἐκ μικρῶν πυριδίων ἀθροιζομένων γίνεσθαι καθ' ἑκάστην ἡμέραν, τὴν δὲ γῆν ἄπειρον

---

178 *The sun comes into being each day from little pieces of fire that are collected, and the*

εἶναι καὶ μήτε ὑπ' ἀέρος μήτε ὑπὸ τοῦ οὐρανοῦ περιέχεσθαι. καὶ ἀπείρους ἡλίους εἶναι καὶ σελήνας, τὰ δὲ πάντα εἶναι ἐκ γῆς.

179 Ps.-Plutarch *Strom.* 4 (DK21A32) τὸν δὲ ἥλιόν φησι καὶ τὰ ἄστρα ἐκ τῶν νεφῶν γίνεσθαι.

180 Aetius II, 20, 3 Ξενοφάνης ἐκ νεφῶν πεπυρωμένων εἶναι τὸν ἥλιον. Θεόφραστος ἐν τοῖς Φυσικοῖς γέγραφεν ἐκ πυριδίων μὲν τῶν συναθροιζομένων ἐκ τῆς ὑγρᾶς ἀναθυμιάσεως, συναθροιζόντων δὲ τὸν ἥλιον.

181 Fr. 32, Σ BLT *in Iliadem* 11, 27

ἥν τ' Ἶριν καλέουσι, νέφος καὶ τοῦτο πέφυκε,
πορφύρεον καὶ φοινίκεον καὶ χλωρὸν ἰδέσθαι.

182 Aetius II, 24, 9 Ξενοφάνης πολλοὺς εἶναι ἡλίους καὶ σελήνας κατὰ κλίματα τῆς γῆς καὶ ἀποτομὰς καὶ ζώνας, κατὰ δέ τινα καιρὸν ἐκπίπτειν τὸν δίσκον εἴς τινα ἀποτομὴν τῆς γῆς οὐκ οἰκουμένην ὑφ' ἡμῶν καὶ οὕτως ὥσπερ κενεμβατοῦντα ἔκλειψιν ὑποφαίνειν· ὁ δ' αὐτὸς τὸν ἥλιον εἰς ἄπειρον μὲν προϊέναι, δοκεῖν δὲ κυκλεῖσθαι διὰ τὴν ἀπόστασιν.

There is a divergence in the doxographical accounts of the constitution of the heavenly bodies: were they a concentration of fiery particles as the sun is said to be in **178**, the second part of **180**, and ps.-Plutarch a few sentences before **179**; or ignited clouds as is said of sun and stars in **179**, of the sun in **180**, and of the stars, which are said to re-kindle at night like embers, in Aetius II, 13, 14, DK21A38? Theophrastus is named in **180** as supporting the former view, but the latter also, which is widely represented in the

---

earth is infinite and enclosed neither by air nor by the heaven. There are innumerable suns and moons, and all things are made of earth.

179 *He says that the sun and the stars come from clouds.*

180 *Xenophanes says that the sun is made of ignited clouds. Theophrastus in the* Physical philosophers *wrote that it is made of little pieces of fire collected together from the moist exhalation, and themselves collecting together the sun.*

181 *What they call Iris [rainbow], this too is cloud, purple and red and yellow to behold.*

182 *Xenophanes said there are many suns and moons according to regions, sections and zones of the earth, and that at a certain time the disc is banished into some section of the earth not inhabited by us, and so treading on nothing, as it were, produces the phenomenon of an eclipse. The same man says that the sun goes onwards* ad infinitum, *but seems to move in a circle because of the distance.*

doxographers, must somehow stem from him. It seems possible that the idea of the sun, at least, as a concentration of fire, which arose from the exhalation from the sea, is in part due to a conflation of Xenophanes with Heraclitus, who probably thought that the bowls of the heavenly bodies were filled with fire nourished in their courses by the exhalation (**227**). Heraclitus also thought that the sun was new every day, which accords with Xenophanes in **178**. But Heraclitus was certainly influenced in other respects by Xenophanes, and the similarity here might be so caused. Yet are the two theories as different as they appear to be at first sight? It is conceivable that the concentrations of fire *resemble* fiery clouds, and that some such statement in Theophrastus became dissected in the epitomes. Alternatively, the sun alone, because of its special brightness, might be a 'concentration' of fire, the other heavenly bodies being merely ignited clouds. That Xenophanes explained the rainbow as a cloud (a development, perhaps, of Anaximenes, cf. p. 158) is demonstrated by **181**; according to Aetius II, 18, 1 (DK 21 A 39) what we term St Elmo's fire was due to little clouds ignited by motion, and perhaps this explains the καί in **181** l. 1. It is not safe to deduce from this particle that some heavenly bodies were clouds; though it seems possible that this was in fact Xenophanes' view. It is notable that this (as opposed to some of his other ideas) is an entirely reasonable physical theory, which proves that Xenophanes cannot be classified solely as a theologian; though it is possible enough that his motive for giving physical explanations of the heavenly bodies was to disprove the popular conception of them as gods. This is certainly implied by the phrase 'what men call Iris' in **181**.

Hippolytus' statement in **178** that there are 'innumerable suns and moons' seems to refer to the re-kindling of the sun (and presumably also of the moon) each day; but in **182** a completely different and much more bizarre explanation is given. There are many suns and moons in different regions, zones, or segments of the earth; eclipses of the sun are caused by our sun as it were treading on nothing and being forced into another segment not inhabited by 'us'. The concluding sentence of **182**, however, accords with the view of **178** that the sun is new every day. There is certainly a confusion here by Aetius or his source. It seems probable that the plurality of suns and moons is simply due to their being renewed each day; that Xenophanes explained eclipses as caused by the sun withdrawing to another region of the earth; and that the two ideas became confused. That the sun continues westward indefinitely looks like a deliberately naïve statement of the anti-scientific viewpoint (Heraclitus perhaps reacted in a similar way to excessive dogmatism about astronomy, cf. fr. 3). It is possible that the segments of the earth were regarded as hollow depressions, as in the *Phaedo* myth; this might seem to account for the sun's apparent rising and setting, though not its disappearance at eclipses. Whatever is the true explanation, it is clear that Xenophanes permitted himself a certain degree of fantasy here (and possibly, judging by the expression 'treading on nothing', of humour). Perhaps there was some kind of irony; at any rate the explanation of eclipses must be plainly distinguished from his more empirical, if not necessarily original, views on the actual constitution of the heavenly bodies.[1]

[1] The same combination of a bizarre original statement by Xenophanes and misunderstanding by the doxographers probably accounts for Aetius' mention (II, 24, 4, DK 21 A 41) of a month-long, and a continuous, eclipse.

(ii) *The earth's roots*

183 Fr. 28, Achilles *Isag.* 4, p. 34, 11 Maass

γαίης μὲν τόδε πεῖρας ἄνω παρὰ ποσσὶν ὁρᾶται
ἠέρι προσπλάζον, τὸ κάτω δ' ἐς ἄπειρον ἱκνεῖται.[1]

[1] ἠέρι Diels, αἰθέρι Karsten, καὶ ῥεῖ mss. Both suggested emendations are possible, but the former is in every respect preferable: -ει was written for -ι by a common mis-spelling, and then καὶ was substituted for what appeared to be an impossible disjunctive ἠὲ.

Here Xenophanes gives an extreme kind of common-sense account, based upon the Hesiodic description of Tartarus as being as far below the earth as sky is above it (*Theog.* 720, cf. *Il.* 8, 16 and see p. 11). At *Theogony* 726f. (**2**) the roots of earth and unharvested sea are above Tartarus. Thus in the Hesiodic picture the earth stretched a defined distance downwards, but in reality this distance was obviously thought of as indefinitely vast—the height of the sky, in fact. Xenophanes was not seriously emending it in calling it 'indefinite'. That the earth does stretch downwards indefinitely is

---

183 *Of earth this is the upper limit which we see by our feet, in contact with air; but its underneath continues indefinitely.*

a naïve but understandable view which Xenophanes probably intended as an implied criticism of the dogmatic theories of the Milesians on this subject. Aristotle (*de caelo* B 13, 294a21, DK 21 A 47) criticized Xenophanes and others for holding this view, on the grounds that they were being idle in not seeking a proper explanation. The first part of **183** is such an obvious statement of fact that it cannot have been intended as anything else; which confirms our interpretation of the second part. Ps.-Plutarch (*Strom.* 4, DK 21 A 32) and Hippolytus in **178** state that the earth is not totally enclosed (περιέχεσθαι) by air. This is presumably a further deduction from **183**.

(iii) *Water, or sea, and earth*

184 Fr. 29, Simplicius *Phys.* 189, 1

γῆ καὶ ὕδωρ πάντ' ἐσθ' ὅσα γίνοντ' ἠδὲ φύονται.

185 Fr. 33, Sextus *adv. math.* x, 34

πάντες γὰρ γαίης τε καὶ ὕδατος ἐκγενόμεσθα.

186 Fr. 30, Σ Genav. *in Iliadem* 21, 196

πηγὴ δ' ἐστὶ θάλασσ' ὕδατος, πηγὴ δ' ἀνέμοιο·
οὔτε γὰρ ἐν νέφεσιν ⟨γίνοιτό κε ἶς ἀνέμοιο
ἐκπνείοντος⟩ ἔσωθεν ἄνευ πόντου μεγάλοιο
οὔτε ῥοαὶ ποταμῶν οὔτ' αἰ⟨θέρος⟩ ὄμβριον ὕδωρ,
ἀλλὰ μέγας πόντος γενέτωρ νεφέων ἀνέμων τε
καὶ ποταμῶν.

The idea that everything, men included, is composed of and originates from water and earth is a naïve popular one: flesh and bone may be compared with earth and stone, blood with water. Compare our burial service, 'earth to earth, ashes to ashes, dust to dust'; and *Iliad* 7, 99, 'but may you all become earth and water'. Further, the surface of the earth, that which lies by our feet (**183**), is obviously broadly composed of earth and sea. Xenophanes takes this simple apprehension and develops it into a rudimentary

---

184 *All things that come-to-be and grow are earth and water.*

185 *For we all came forth from earth and water.*

186 *Sea is the source of water, and source of wind; for neither ⟨would there be the force of wind blowing forth from⟩ inside clouds without the great ocean, nor river-streams nor the showery water from the upper air: but the great ocean is begetter of clouds and winds and rivers.*

physical theory in **186** (where the main supplement is by Diels): sea, which is the most extensive form of water, is noted as the source of all rivers as in Homer (see **5**)—but also of rain and of clouds (which Anaximander had assumed to be condensations of the exhalation from the sea) and of the winds which appear to issue from clouds. This importance attached to the sea gains significance from the observation and deduction to be described in the next section, that the earth's surface in its present form must have developed from sea.

(iv) *The earth's surface becomes sea once again*

187 Hippolytus *Ref.* I, 14, 5 ὁ δὲ Ξενοφάνης μίξιν τῆς γῆς πρὸς τὴν θάλασσαν γίνεσθαι δοκεῖ καὶ τῷ χρόνῳ ὑπὸ τοῦ ὑγροῦ λύεσθαι, φάσκων τοιαύτας ἔχειν ἀποδείξεις, ὅτι ἐν μέσῃ γῇ καὶ ὄρεσιν εὑρίσκονται κόγχαι, καὶ ἐν Συρακούσαις δὲ ἐν ταῖς λατομίαις λέγει εὑρῆσθαι τύπον ἰχθύος καὶ φυκῶν [Gomperz; φωκῶν mss.], ἐν δὲ Πάρῳ τύπον δάφνης ἐν τῷ βάθει τοῦ λίθου, ἐν δὲ Μελίτῃ πλάκας συμπάντων τῶν θαλασσίων. (6) ταῦτα δέ φησι γενέσθαι ὅτε πάντα ἐπηλώθησαν πάλαι, τὸν δὲ τύπον ἐν τῷ πηλῷ ξηρανθῆναι. ἀναιρεῖσθαι δὲ τοὺς ἀνθρώπους πάντας ὅταν ἡ γῆ κατενεχθεῖσα εἰς τὴν θάλασσαν πηλὸς γένηται, εἶτα πάλιν ἄρχεσθαι τῆς γενέσεως, καὶ ταύτην πᾶσι τοῖς κόσμοις γίνεσθαι καταβολήν [H. Lloyd-Jones; καταβάλλειν mss., μεταβολήν Diels, DK].

188 Fr. 37, Herodian π. μον. λέξ. 30, 30

καὶ μὲν ἐνὶ σπεάτεσσί τεοις καταλείβεται ὕδωρ.

The deduction based upon fossils is a remarkable and impressive one. The enumeration of different occurrences is in itself unusually scientific; the assertion ascribed to Xenophanes in the Aristotelian *Mirabilia* (DK 21 A 48), that Stromboli tended to erupt in the seventeenth year, shows a similar method. Not that the poet himself need have observed fossils in all three places—fossil-impressions

---

187 *Xenophanes thinks that a mixture of the earth with the sea is going on, and that in time the earth is dissolved by the moist. He says that he has demonstrations of the following kind: shells are found inland, and in the mountains, and in the quarries in Syracuse he says that an impression of a fish and of seaweed has been found, while an impression of a bay-leaf was found in Paros in the depth of the rock, and in Malta flat shapes of all marine objects. These, he says, were produced when everything was long ago covered with mud, and the impression was dried in the mud. All mankind is destroyed whenever the earth is carried down into the sea and becomes mud; then there is another beginning of coming-to-be, and this foundation happens for all the worlds.*

188 *And in some caves water drips down.*

might naturally arouse popular curiosity, and so become known; though it is notable that two of the three places were in Xenophanes' Sicilian orbit. (Paros has been doubted on geological grounds; but its north-eastern part is neither marble nor schist, and could have contained fossils. The Director of the Institute for Geology, Athens, confirms that plant fossils have recently been found there.) We cannot even be sure that the observations were first made in Xenophanes' lifetime; they might conceivably have been available to Anaximander. However, Xenophanes may reasonably be accepted as the first to draw attention to their real significance. The conjecture that the earth's surface had once been mud or slime was again not new; this was a Milesian theory possibly originating with Thales and certainly held by Anaximander, who believed that life started from mud. The fossils, however, seemed to be positive proof. It has been seen (pp. 139f.) that Alexander attributed to Anaximander (as well as to Diogenes) the belief that the sea is diminishing and will eventually dry up. In Anaximander, however, there is no positive information that the process is a cyclical one. Hippolytus in **187** *ad fin.* definitely ascribes a cyclical theory to Xenophanes: the earth must once have been mud because plants once existed in what is now rock, fishes in what is now dry land, and men are destroyed when it turns back to mud; then they are produced anew, and this happens for all the arrangements of the earth's surface. Thus Xenophanes accepted that living creatures come from mud, after Anaximander; but while Anaximander seems to have seen their destruction as arising from extreme drought, for Xenophanes it was due to flood; it has already been suggested that myths of great catastrophes, notably the flood of Deucalion and Pyrrha and the earth-scorching of Phaethon, may have provided a precedent for this kind of theory. This divergence between the two thinkers was connected with divergent interpretations of the present trend of change in the earth's surface: for Anaximander it was drying up, for Xenophanes it was already turning back into sea or mud. This might have been a conscious correction on the part of the latter; it may not be coincidence that the sea was receding round Miletus, but in Sicily was supposed to have engulfed the land-bridge which became the Messina strait.

The cyclical transformations between earth and sea—neither of which, however, can have been completely eliminated—were clearly related to the assertions in **184** and **185** that things come from earth and sea; while the products of sea in **186** showed that sea is surprisingly potent. **188**, fragmentary as it is, may be intended to illustrate the passage between the two basic materials: Diels and others have thought of stalactitic caves, i.e. of water turning to earth (rock not being clearly differentiated), while Deichgräber (*Rh. M.* 87 (1938) 16) thought that both this and the reverse process might be meant; certainly, damp caves can appear to produce moisture from earth. This, like much else, remains uncertain (for example, at what stage is the drying-up of the sea reversed?). The clear exposition of a cyclical theory supported by concrete evidence is indisputable, and once again shows that Xenophanes must be seriously reckoned with. The way in which such a cyclical theory could encourage the doxographers in an innumerable-world interpretation is demonstrated by the ambiguous use of κόσμοις in **187** (there properly 'world-arrangements', i.e. of the earth's surface, but appearing to mean 'separate worlds').

XENOPHANES' EMPHASIS ON THE LIMITATIONS OF HUMAN KNOWLEDGE

189 Fr. 34, Sextus *adv. math.* VII, 49 and 110, cf. Plutarch *aud. poet.* 2, 17E

καὶ τὸ μὲν οὖν σαφὲς οὔτις ἀνὴρ ἴδεν οὐδέ τις ἔσται
εἰδὼς ἀμφὶ θεῶν τε καὶ ἅσσα λέγω περὶ πάντων·
εἰ γὰρ καὶ τὰ μάλιστα τύχοι τετελεσμένον εἰπών,
αὐτὸς ὅμως οὐκ οἶδε· δόκος δ' ἐπὶ πᾶσι τέτυκται.

190 Fr. 35, Plutarch *Symp.* IX, 7, 746B

ταῦτα δεδοξάσθω μὲν ἐοικότα τοῖς ἐτύμοισι....

191 Fr. 18, Stobaeus *Anth.* I, 8, 2

οὔτοι ἀπ' ἀρχῆς πάντα θεοὶ θνητοῖσ' ὑπέδειξαν,
ἀλλὰ χρόνῳ ζητοῦντες ἐφευρίσκουσιν ἄμεινον.

---

189 *No man knows, or ever will know, the truth about the gods and about everything I speak of: for even if one chanced to say the complete truth, yet oneself knows it not; but seeming is wrought over all things* [or *fancy is wrought in the case of all men*].

190 *Let these things be opined as resembling the truth....*

191 *Yet the gods have not revealed all things to men from the beginning; but by seeking men find out better in time.*

192 Fr. 38, Herodian π. μον. λέξ. 41, 5

εἰ μὴ χλωρὸν ἔφυσε θεὸς μέλι, πολλὸν ἔφασκον
γλύσσονα σῦκα πέλεσθαι.

It has been suggested by K. Deichgräber (*Rh. M.* 87 (1938) 23 ff.) that Xenophanes in his utterances on the shortcomings of human knowledge is developing a common poetical contrast between the comparative ignorance of the poet and the all-knowledge of the Muse whom he calls on to assist him: cf. e.g. Homer *Il.* 2, 485 f., Pindar *Paean* 6, 51 ff. Yet this contrast is merely a special form of that between the capacity of the gods in general and the limitations of men, which is re-stated, after Xenophanes, by Heraclitus in fr. 78 (**208**) and by Alcmaeon in fr. 1 (**285**). In Xenophanes himself it is implicit, too, in the assertion of **173** that the one god is unlike men either in body or in thought. Parmenides, when he came to propose dogmatic views which could not be corroborated from human experience, gave them the form of a divine revelation. Yet there is no indication that Xenophanes claimed anything like a revelation; **191** suggests that arduous investigation is rewarded, and the probability is that he, like Heraclitus, felt himself to be in a special state of knowledge for this reason. Deichgräber also thought that **189** was intended as the prooemium of the physical doctrine, not of the constructive theology; but it seems most unlikely that the plural of ἀμφὶ θεῶν should be taken literally to mean 'about the gods of conventional religion'; the phrase means simply 'about theology'. The assumption of two distinct poems is, it has been suggested, a dubious one; and this is confirmed by the linking of 'theology' and 'what I say about all things'. The constructive description of the one god must ultimately have come within the scope of **189**: it was the antithesis of the mistaken Homeric concept, but, though it might be 'like the truth', in the words of **190**, it could not be taken as absolutely certain. Even Xenophanes' special position as one who had given much attention to the subject could not ensure that. However, Xenophanes did not suggest that one could not be certain that a belief was *wrong*; and his destructive criticism of the Homeric gods, based as it was on a demonstrated subjectivity, might be accepted as true.

192 shows that Xenophanes thought about problems of relationship, which were to be especially significant for Heraclitus

---

192 *If god had not made yellow honey, men would consider figs far sweeter.*

(pp. 189f.). For Xenophanes the observation about honey (which may have been proverbial) presumably confirmed his beliefs about the limitation of knowledge—again the contrast between god, or gods, and men is perhaps present. Once again Xenophanes was developing an idea already implicit in popular literature and giving it a special philosophical significance. After the dogmatism of the Milesians (and also of Pythagoras, mocked by Xenophanes in **268** for his extravagant theory of metempsychosis) an appeal to caution was salutary, and from this time on there was certainly more verbal reference to the broadest aspects of epistemology. Unfortunately Xenophanes' revival of the traditional doctrine of human limitations, this time in a partly philosophical context, did little else that is noticeable to curb the naturally over-dogmatic tendency of Greek philosophy in its first buoyant stages.

CHAPTER VI

HERACLITUS OF EPHESUS

DATE AND LIFE

193 Diogenes Laertius IX, 1 (DK22A1) Ἡράκλειτος Βλόσωνος ἤ, ὥς τινες, Ἡράκωντος Ἐφέσιος. οὗτος ἤκμαζε μὲν κατὰ τὴν ἐνάτην καὶ ἑξηκοστὴν ὀλυμπιάδα. μεγαλόφρων δὲ γέγονε παρ᾽ ὁντιναοῦν καὶ ὑπερόπτης, ὡς καὶ ἐκ τοῦ συγγράμματος αὐτοῦ δῆλον, ἐν ᾧ φησι· (Fr. 40) Πολυμαθίη νόον ἔχειν οὐ διδάσκει· Ἡσίοδον γὰρ ἂν ἐδίδαξε καὶ Πυθαγόρην αὖτίς τε Ξενοφάνεά τε καὶ Ἑκαταῖον....(3)...καὶ τέλος μισανθρωπήσας καὶ ἐκπατήσας ἐν τοῖς ὄρεσι διῃτᾶτο, πόας σιτούμενος καὶ βοτάνας. καὶ μέντοι καὶ διὰ τοῦτο περιτραπεὶς εἰς ὕδερον κατῆλθεν εἰς ἄστυ καὶ τῶν ἰατρῶν αἰνιγματωδῶς ἐπυνθάνετο εἰ δύναιντο ἐξ ἐπομβρίας αὐχμὸν ποιῆσαι· τῶν δὲ μὴ συνιέντων αὑτὸν εἰς βούστασιν κατορύξας τῇ τῶν βολίτων ἀλέᾳ ἤλπισεν ἐξατμισθήσεσθαι. οὐδὲν δὲ ἀνύων οὐδ᾽ οὕτως ἐτελεύτα βιοὺς ἔτη ἑξήκοντα.

The information that Heraclitus was at his *acme*, i.e. aged forty, in Ol. 69 (504–501 B.C.) was doubtless taken from the chronographer Apollodorus: Heraclitus' middle age is placed about forty years after Anaximenes' assumed *acme* and Xenophanes' departure from Colophon. (According to Sotion (Diog. L. IX, 5, DK22A1) some people said that Heraclitus 'heard' Xenophanes. That there was some influence is probable enough, but the critical tone of fr. 40, quoted in **193**, does not suggest a formal master-pupil relationship.) There is no need seriously to doubt Apollodorus' dating here, since Heraclitus mentioned Pythagoras and Hecataeus as well as Xeno-

---

193 *Heraclitus son of Bloson (or, according to some, of Herakon) of Ephesus. This man was at his prime in the 69th Olympiad. He grew up to be exceptionally haughty and supercilious, as is clear also from his book, in which he says: 'Learning of many things does not teach intelligence; if so it would have taught Hesiod and Pythagoras, and again Xenophanes and Hecataeus.'...Finally he became a misanthrope, withdrew from the world, and lived in the mountains feeding on grasses and plants. However, having fallen in this way into a dropsy he came down to town and asked the doctors in a riddle if they could make a drought out of rainy weather. When they did not understand he buried himself in a cow-stall, expecting that the dropsy would be evaporated off by the heat of the manure; but even so he failed to effect anything, and ended his life at the age of sixty.*

phanes,[1] and was perhaps indirectly referred to by Parmenides (**345**, cf. p. 272; also fr. 8, 55ff., **353**). Attempts have sometimes been made to place Heraclitus' philosophical activity later than the Apollodoran dating would reasonably suggest, after 478 B.C. (and even, most improbably, after Parmenides); but they have not won acceptance, and rest on implausible hypotheses such as that no trace of self-government (suggested by the information of fr. 121 that the Ephesians had exiled Heraclitus' friend Hermodorus) would be possible in Ephesus until after its liberation from Persia around 478. Heraclitus might have lived longer than Apollodorus' sixty years (at which age Anaximenes also, and Empedocles according to Aristotle, were said to die); but we may nevertheless provisionally accept that he was in his middle years at the end of the sixth century and that his main philosophical activity had ended by about 480.

[1] The past tense in fr. 40, 'would have taught', need not mean that all those mentioned were dead (Xenophanes at any rate lived until after 478), but it implies that they were all widely known at the time of writing. Another fragment, 129 (**261**; it may be to some extent re-worded but is not spurious, see p. 219n.), implies that Pythagoras was already dead; he is said to have 'flourished' in 532/1 B.C. (p. 217), and perhaps died between 510 and 505. The Suda places Hecataeus' birth as late as 520–516 B.C.

The rest of **193** is quoted as a sample of the kind of biographical fiction that proliferated round the name of Heraclitus. We are also told by Diogenes that he refused to make laws for the Ephesians but preferred playing with children in the temple of Artemis. Most of these stories are based on well-known sayings of Heraclitus; many were intended to make him look ridiculous, and were invented with malicious intent by Hellenistic pedants who resented his superior tone. For example, extreme misanthropy is deduced from his criticisms of the majority of men (e.g. **197**), vegetarianism from a mention of blood-pollution in **244**, the fatal dropsy from his assertion 'it is death for souls to become water' in **232**. He was known as an obscure propounder of riddles, and this is made out to have cost him his life: the doctors, whom he appeared to criticize in fr. 58 (p. 190), do nothing to save him. He is said to have buried himself in dung because he had said in fr. 96 that corpses are more worthless than dung; 'being exhaled' refers to his theory of exhalations from the sea. The only details about Heraclitus' life which it might be safe to accept as true are that he spent it in

Ephesus, that he came of an old aristocratic family,[1] and that he was on bad terms with his fellow-citizens.

[1] Cf. **194** Diog. L. IX, 6 σημεῖον δ' αὐτοῦ τῆς μεγαλοφροσύνης 'Αντισθένης φησὶν ἐν Διαδοχαῖς· ἐκχωρῆσαι γὰρ τἀδελφῷ τῆς βασιλείας. There is no apparent reason why this information should be fictitious. Strabo, 14, p. 633 Cas. (DK 22 A 2), said that the descendants of Androclus founder of Ephesus were still called 'kings', and had certain privileges like that of front seats at the games.

'THE OBSCURE'

Timon of Phlius, the third-century B.C. satirist, called Heraclitus αἰνικτής, 'riddler' (Diog. L. IX, 6). This legitimate criticism of his style later gave rise to the almost invariable epithet σκοτεινός, *obscurus* in Latin (Cicero *de finibus* II, 5, 15, etc.). Another common description in the Roman period was 'the weeping philosopher'. This latter judgement is entirely trivial, being founded partly on humorous references to the idea that all things flow like rivers (cf. e.g. Plato *Crat.* 440 C, believers in flux are like people with catarrh), and partly on Theophrastus' well-known attribution to Heraclitus of μελαγχολία (Diog. L. IX, 6), by which, however, he meant 'impulsiveness' (see Aristotle's description at *Eth. Nic.* H 8, 1150 b 25) and not 'melancholy' in its later and its modern sense.

HERACLITUS' BOOK

195 Diogenes Laertius IX, 5 τὸ δὲ φερόμενον αὐτοῦ βιβλίον ἐστὶ μὲν ἀπὸ τοῦ συνέχοντος Περὶ φύσεως, διῄρηται δὲ εἰς τρεῖς λόγους, εἴς τε τὸν περὶ τοῦ παντὸς καὶ πολιτικὸν καὶ θεολογικόν. (6) ἀνέθηκε δ' αὐτὸ εἰς τὸ τῆς 'Αρτέμιδος ἱερόν, ὡς μέν τινες, ἐπιτηδεύσας ἀσαφέστερον γράψαι ὅπως οἱ δυνάμενοι προσίοιεν αὐτῷ καὶ μὴ ἐκ τοῦ δημώδους εὐκαταφρόνητον ᾖ. . . . τοσαύτην δὲ δόξαν ἔσχε τὸ σύγγραμμα ὡς καὶ αἱρετιστὰς ἀπ' αὐτοῦ γενέσθαι τοὺς κληθέντας 'Ηρακλειτείους.

Ancient biographers and historians of philosophy assumed that all the Presocratics wrote one or more books (though there was doubt

---

194 *Antisthenes in his* Successions *quotes as a sign of his [Heraclitus'] arrogance that he resigned the hereditary 'kingship' to his brother.*

195 *The book said to be his is called 'On Nature', from its chief content, and is divided into three discourses: On the Universe, Politics, Theology. He dedicated it and placed it in the temple of Artemis, as some say, having purposely written it rather obscurely so that only those of rank and influence should have access to it, and it should not be easily despised by the populace. . . . The work had so great a reputation that from it arose disciples, those called Heracliteans.*

over Thales, see pp. 84ff.). They certainly assumed that Heraclitus wrote one, and Diogenes tells us that its title was 'On nature'. This title was regularly assigned to works by those whom Aristotle and the Peripatetics called 'natural philosophers', and cannot be regarded as necessarily authentic in all cases: see n. on p. 102. The division into three sections is unlikely to have been original, and suggests that Diogenes or his source was thinking of an edition or collection of sayings, probably made in Alexandria, which followed a Stoic analysis of the parts of philosophy. Diels maintained that Heraclitus wrote no consecutive book, but merely gave repeated utterance to a series of carefully-formulated opinions or γνῶμαι. This view has found few supporters, but could be correct. The surviving fragments have very much the appearance of oral pronouncements put into a concise and striking, and therefore easily memorable, form; they do not resemble extracts from a continuous written work. The obstacle to this view is fr. 1 (**197**), a structurally complicated sentence which looks very like a written introduction to a book. Possibly when Heraclitus achieved fame as a sage a collection of his most famous utterances was made, for which a special prologue was composed. In any event the fragments we possess (and not all those in DK are fully authentic) were for the most part obviously framed as oral apophthegms rather than as parts of a discursive treatise; this was in keeping with Heraclitus' oracular intentions (see p. 212). The suggestion in **195** that the 'Heracliteans', also mentioned by Plato and Aristotle, were devotees of the book is almost certainly guesswork; its importance lies in its implication that there was no 'school' of direct followers at Ephesus.[1] No follower of note is known until Cratylus, an older contemporary (probably) of Plato, who developed a debased form of Heracliteanism by exaggerating, and combining together, the Ephesian's belief in the inevitability of change and his belief (quite a common one in his time) in the significance of names.

[1] In spite of **196** Plato *Theaet.* 179D πολλοῦ καὶ δεῖ φαύλη εἶναι (*sc.* ἡ μάχη), ἀλλὰ περὶ μὲν τὴν Ἰωνίαν καὶ ἐπιδίδωσι πάμπολυ. οἱ γὰρ τοῦ Ἡρακλείτου ἑταῖροι χορηγοῦσι τούτου τοῦ λόγου μάλα ἐρρωμένως. (Cf. *ibid.* 179E, ...αὐτοῖς μὲν τοῖς περὶ τὴν Ἔφεσον.) This whole passage is intentionally humorous, as indeed are most of Plato's remarks about

196 (*The battle*) *is far from being a slight one, but in the region of Ionia it is even greatly increasing. For the companions of Heraclitus minister to this argument with might and main.* (Cf. ...*to those around Ephesus.*)

Heraclitus, and the local references need not be intended literally; anyone using what Plato would consider to be a Heraclitean type of argument might be ironically associated with Ephesus. Plato's most extreme Heraclitean acquaintance, at any rate, namely Cratylus, was neither an Ephesian nor from Ionia.

SPECIAL DIFFICULTIES OF INTERPRETATION

As has been seen, Heraclitus was renowned in antiquity for his obscurity: his pronouncements were undeniably often cryptic, probably intentionally so, and little serious attempt seems to have been made by Plato and Aristotle to penetrate to his real meaning. Theophrastus, on whom the later doxographical tradition depends, unfortunately based his interpretation on Aristotle's. He does not appear to have had access to a complete book by Heraclitus, or even (to judge, for example, from the omission of all but the barest reference to Heraclitus in Theophrastus' *de sensu*) to a fully representative collection of separate utterances; in fact he complained that Heraclitus' pronouncements were either unfinished or inconsistent. The Stoics further distorted the account. They adopted Heraclitus as their ancient authority, chiefly on physical matters, and in some respects produced an accurate development of his ideas; for example in their ideal of ὁμολογουμένως ζῆν, living in accord with Nature (cf. e.g. **198**). In other respects, however, they radically re-adapted his views to meet special requirements of their own—for example in their attribution to him of the idea of *ecpyrosis*, the periodical consumption of the whole world by fire. Our sources subsequent to the founder of Stoicism, Zeno of Citium, accepted this particular interpretation of Heraclitus, which can be reconciled with some of the extant sayings and may have been encouraged by Theophrastus, but is incompatible with others and wholly at variance with the basic Heraclitean concept of measure in natural change: see further pp. 196–9 and n. on p. 202.

As for Plato and Aristotle, there is little *verbatim* quotation of Heraclitus in either, nor were they really interested in the accurate *objective* assessment of early predecessors. Plato occasionally mentions him, mainly in a humorous or ironical way and with emphasis on a view freely attributed to him in the dialogues, that 'all things are in flux'—πάντα ῥεῖ or πάντα χωρεῖ. According to Aristotle at *Met.* A6, 987a32, Plato was influenced in youth by the emphasis laid by Cratylus on this kind of view. But all Presocratic thinkers were struck by the dominance of change in the world of our experience. Heraclitus was obviously no exception, indeed he probably expressed the universality of change more clearly than his predecessors; but for him it was the obverse idea of the *measure* inhering in change, the stability that persists through it, that was of vital importance. Plato may have been genuinely misled, especially by fifth-century sophistic exaggerations, in his distortion of Heraclitus' emphasis here; and Aristotle accepted the Platonic flux-interpretation and carried it still further. Other references to Heraclitus in Aristotle attack him for denying the law of contradiction in his assertions that opposites are 'the same'. Again, this is a misinterpretation by Aristotle, who applied his own high logical standards anachronistically: by 'the same' Heraclitus evidently meant not 'identical' so much as 'not essentially separate', or 'belonging to one single complex'.

In view of these defects in the authors of the ancient assessment it is safer to attempt the reconstitution of Heraclitus' thought, in the first instance, on the basis of the extant genuine fragments. Even so one cannot hope for more than a very limited understanding, partly because Heraclitus, as Aristotle found, did not use the categories of formal logic, and tended to describe the same thing (or roughly the same thing) now as a god, now as a form of matter, now as a rule of behaviour or principle which was nevertheless a physical constituent of things.

HERACLITUS' THOUGHT

(1) *Men should try to comprehend the underlying coherence of things: it is expressed in the Logos, the formula or element of arrangement common to all things*

197 Fr. 1, Sextus *adv. math.* VII, 132 τοῦ δὲ λόγου τοῦδ' ἐόντος ἀεὶ ἀξύνετοι γίνονται ἄνθρωποι καὶ πρόσθεν ἢ ἀκοῦσαι καὶ ἀκούσαντες τὸ πρῶτον· γινομένων γὰρ πάντων κατὰ τὸν λόγον τόνδε ἀπείροισιν ἐοίκασι, πειρώμενοι καὶ ἐπέων καὶ ἔργων τοιούτων ὁκοίων ἐγὼ διηγεῦμαι κατὰ φύσιν διαιρέων ἕκαστον καὶ φράζων ὅκως ἔχει· τοὺς δὲ ἄλλους ἀνθρώπους λανθάνει ὁκόσα ἐγερθέντες ποιοῦσιν ὅκωσπερ ὁκόσα εὕδοντες ἐπιλανθάνονται.

---

197 *Of the Logos which is as I describe it men always prove to be uncomprehending, both before they have heard it and when once they have heard it. For although all things happen according to this Logos men are like people of no experience, even when they experience such words and deeds as I explain, when I distinguish each thing according to its constitution and declare how it is; but the rest of men fail to notice what they do after they wake up just as they forget what they do when asleep.*

198 Fr. 2, Sextus *adv. math.* VII, 133 διὸ δεῖ ἕπεσθαι τῷ ⟨ξυνῷ⟩· τοῦ λόγου δ' ἐόντος ξυνοῦ ζώουσιν οἱ πολλοὶ ὡς ἰδίαν ἔχοντες φρόνησιν.[1]

199 Fr. 50, Hippolytus *Ref.* IX, 9, 1 οὐκ ἐμοῦ ἀλλὰ τοῦ λόγου ἀκούσαντας ὁμολογεῖν σοφόν ἐστιν ἓν πάντα εἶναι.

[1] διὸ δεῖ ἕπεσθαι τῷ κοινῷ· ξυνὸς γὰρ ὁ κοινός· τοῦ... mss. ξυνός and κοινός are different words for the same idea, the former being the normal epic and Ionic form and that used by Heraclitus. The later form was evidently given in a gloss, and then this gloss replaced the original word, though the appended explanation remained.

These sayings make it plain that Heraclitus regarded himself as having access to, and trying vainly to propagate, an all-important truth about the constitution of the world of which men are a part. The great majority fail to recognize this truth,[1] which is 'common'—that is, both valid for all things and accessible for all men, if only they use their observation and their understanding[2] and do not fabricate a private and deceptive intelligence. What they should recognize is the *Logos*, which is perhaps to be interpreted as the unifying formula or proportionate method of arrangement of things, what might almost be termed the structural plan of things both individual and in sum. The technical sense of λόγος in Heraclitus is probably related to the general meaning 'measure', 'reckoning' or 'proportion'; it cannot be simply Heraclitus' own 'account' that is in question (otherwise the distinction in **199** between ἐμοῦ and τοῦ λόγου is meaningless), although the Logos was revealed in that account. The effect of arrangement according to a common plan or measure is that all things, although apparently plural and totally discrete, are really united in a coherent complex (**199**) of which men themselves are a part, and the comprehension of which is therefore logically necessary for the adequate enactment of their own lives. Yet 'formula', 'proportionate arrangement' and so on are misleadingly abstract as translations of this technical sense of λόγος: the Logos was probably conceived by Heraclitus as an actual constituent of things, and in many respects it is co-extensive with the primary cosmic constituent, fire (see p. 200). It must constantly be remembered that no firm distinc-

---

198 *Therefore it is necessary to follow the common; but although the Logos is common the many live as though they had a private understanding.*

199 *Listening not to me but to the Logos it is wise to agree that all things are one.*

tion between different modes of existence had yet been envisaged, and that what to us is obviously non-concrete and immaterial, like an arrangement, might be regarded before Plato as possessing the assumed ultimate characteristic of 'being', that is, concrete bulk. To put it in another way, the arrangement would not be fully distinguished from the thing arranged, but would be felt to possess the same concreteness and reality as the thing itself.

[1] Men are attacked for this failure in many other extant fragments: see frr. 17, 19, 28, 34, 56, 72. But nothing substantial is added there to the content of **197**, **198**, **199**. Analogous rebukes are also hurled at individuals—Homer, Hesiod, Xenophanes, Hecataeus, Archilochus and Pythagoras: see e.g. **193**, where the ground of criticism is that such men (of whom Pythagoras comes in for special attack elsewhere, cf. e.g. **261**) pursued the wrong kind of knowledge, πολυμαθίη or the mere collection of disparate and unrelated facts.

[2] Cf. **200** Fr. 55, Hippolytus *Ref.* IX, 9, 5 ὅσων ὄψις ἀκοὴ μάθησις, ταῦτα ἐγὼ προτιμέω. But observation must be checked by understanding, φρόνησις: this is shown by **201** Fr. 107, Sextus *adv. math.* VII, 126 κακοὶ μάρτυρες ἀνθρώποισιν ὀφθαλμοὶ καὶ ὦτα βαρβάρους ψυχὰς ἐχόντων. Here 'barbarian souls' are those that cannot understand the language of, cannot correctly interpret, the senses, but are misled by superficial appearances. An analogous distinction between mere sensation and the intelligent interpretation of sense-data was later made by Democritus (pp. 423f.).

(2) *Different types of example of the essential unity of opposites*

202 Fr. 61, Hippolytus *Ref.* IX, 10, 5 θάλασσα ὕδωρ καθαρώτατον καὶ μιαρώτατον, ἰχθύσι μὲν πότιμον καὶ σωτήριον, ἀνθρώποις δὲ ἄποτον καὶ ὀλέθριον.

203 Fr. 60, Hippolytus *Ref.* IX, 10, 4 ὁδὸς ἄνω κάτω μία καὶ ὡυτή.

204 Fr. 111, Stobaeus *Anth.* III, 1, 177 νοῦσος ὑγιείην ἐποίησεν ἡδὺ καὶ ἀγαθόν, λιμὸς κόρον, κάματος ἀνάπαυσιν.

205 Fr. 88, [Plutarch] *Cons. ad Apoll.* 10, 106E ταὐτό τ' ἔνι ζῶν καὶ τεθνηκὸς καὶ τὸ ἐγρηγορὸς καὶ τὸ καθεῦδον καὶ νέον καὶ γηραιόν·

---

200 *The things of which there is seeing and hearing and perception, these do I prefer.*

201 *Evil witnesses are eyes and ears for men, if they have souls that do not understand their language.*

202 *Sea is the most pure and the most polluted water; for fishes it is drinkable and salutary, but for men it is undrinkable and deleterious.*

203 *The path up and down is one and the same.*

204 *Disease makes health pleasant and good, hunger satiety, weariness rest.*

205 *And as the same thing there exists in us living and dead and the waking and the*

τάδε γὰρ μεταπεσόντα ἐκεῖνά ἐστι κἀκεῖνα [πάλιν] μεταπεσόντα ταῦτα.

These fragments exemplify four different kinds of connexion between evident opposites:

(i) In **202** the same thing produces opposite effects upon different classes of animate object; so also fr. 13 (pigs like mud ⟨but men do not⟩) and fr. 9 (donkeys prefer rubbish to gold, ⟨men gold to rubbish⟩).

(ii) In **203**[1] different aspects of the same thing may justify opposite descriptions; so also fr. 58 (cutting and burning ⟨which are normally bad⟩ call for a fee when done by a surgeon) and fr. 59 (the act of writing combines straight, in the whole line, and crooked, in the shape of each letter).

(iii) In **204** good and desirable things like health or rest are seen to be possible only if we recognize their opposites, sickness or weariness; so probably fr. 23 (there would be no right without wrong).

(iv) In **205** certain opposites are said to be essentially connected (literally, to be 'the same', a pregnant expression) because they succeed, and are succeeded by, each other and nothing else. So in fr. 126 the hot substance and the cold form what we might call a hot-cold continuum, a single entity (i.e. temperature). So also fr. 57: night and day, which Hesiod had made parent and child, are, and must always have been, essentially connected and co-existent.

These four kinds of connexion between opposites can be further classed under two main headings: (*a*) i–iii, opposites which inhere in, or are simultaneously produced by, a single subject; (*b*) iv, opposites which are not susceptible of simultaneous distinction in relation to different objects, or parts of the subject, but are connected through being different stages in a single invariable process.

[1] This seems the most probable interpretation of 'the road up and down'. Theophrastus and a few of his followers applied the phrase to the interchanges between world-masses in the cosmic process, and most modern scholars have done the same. But the same words 'one and the same' are used of evident opposites in the formally similar fr. 59; and Hippolytus, a reliable source of *verbatim* quotations from Heraclitus who seems to have

---

sleeping and young and old: for these things having changed round are those, and those having changed round are these.

used a good handbook in which sayings of Heraclitus were grouped by subject, certainly took 'the road up and down' as another illustration of the unity of opposites and not as a cosmological metaphor, to which indeed it is not completely appropriate. We should think of an actual road or path, which is called 'the road up' by those who live at the bottom, 'the road down' by those at the top. Vlastos, *AJP* 76 (1955) 349 n. 26, objects to this interpretation on the grounds of its 'banality'; but it only appears banal to us because of its familiarity, and fr. 59, for example, undoubtedly has precisely the same quality.

These and similar reflexions (cf. also frr. 103, 48, 126, 99), on objects conventionally treated as entirely separate from and opposed to each other, evidently persuaded Heraclitus that there is *never* any real absolute division of opposite from opposite. (For a re-statement of this view by Anaxagoras see p. 381.)

(3) *Each pair of opposites thus forms both a unity and a plurality. Different pairs are also found to be inter-connected*

206 Fr. 10, [Aristotle] *de mundo* 5, 396b20 συλλάψιες ὅλα καὶ οὐχ ὅλα, συμφερόμενον διαφερόμενον, συνᾷδον διᾷδον· ἐκ πάντων ἓν καὶ ἐξ ἑνὸς πάντα.[1]

207 Fr. 67, Hippolytus *Ref.* IX, 10, 8 ὁ θεὸς ἡμέρη εὐφρόνη, χειμὼν θέρος, πόλεμος εἰρήνη, κόρος λιμός [τἀναντία ἅπαντα, οὗτος ὁ νοῦς]· ἀλλοιοῦται δὲ ὅκωσπερ ⟨πῦρ⟩ ὁπόταν συμμιγῇ θυώμασιν ὀνομάζεται καθ' ἡδονὴν ἑκάστου. [πῦρ suppl. Diels.]

[1] συλλάψιες is textually slightly preferable to συνάψιες, which would mean 'things in contact'. A more important question is whether the word is subject or predicate. Snell showed that it is subject, contrary to the common view; neither 'wholes' and 'not wholes' nor 'in tune' and 'out of tune' are typical pairs of Heraclitean opposites, nor indeed are they connected by Heraclitus' regular principles.

In **206** 'things taken together' must be, primarily, opposites: what one takes together with night, for example, is day. (Here we may note that Heraclitus expresses what we should call 'quality' always in terms of simple extremes, which he can then classify as opposites; so that all change can thus be regarded as that between

---

206 *Things taken together are whole and not whole, something which is being brought together and brought apart, which is in tune and out of tune; out of all things there comes a unity, and out of a unity all things.*

207 *God is day night, winter summer, war peace, satiety hunger [all the opposites, this is the meaning]; he undergoes alteration in the way that fire, when it is mixed with spices, is named according to the scent of each of them.*

opposites.) Such 'things taken together' are truly described in one sense as 'whole', that is, forming one continuum, or in another sense as 'not whole', that is, when acting as single components. Applying these alternative analyses to the conglomeration of 'things taken together', we can see that 'from all things a unity is formed', and also that from this unity (ἐξ ἑνός) there can be separated the superficial, discrete, plural aspect of things (πάντα).

207 asserts a relationship between god and a number of pairs of opposites, each pair separately connected by automatic succession; these, as the glossator saw, probably stand for all pairs of opposites however connected. The relationship in question is a loose predicative one; and Heraclitus, perhaps enlarging on Xenophanes, seems to have regarded 'god' as in some probably undefined way immanent in things, or as the sum total of things.[1] One recalls the Milesian view that the originative material, which may still be represented in the world, is divine. Heraclitus, although not so explicitly corporealistic in his conception of divinity, was little more 'religious' than the Milesians in that he did not associate 'god' with the need for cult and worship (although he did not utterly reject all cult, see p. 212). The particular point of **207** is that every opposite can be expressed in terms of god: because peace is divine it does not follow that war is not equally divine, is not equally permeated by the directive and formulaic constituent which is on occasions equated with the whole ordered cosmos (pp. 188, 200). God cannot here be essentially different from Logos; and the Logos is the constituent of things which makes them opposed, and which ensures that change between opposites will be proportional and balanced overall. God, then, is said to be the common connecting element in all extremes, just as fire is the common element of different vapours (because these were conceived as a compound of fire with different kinds of incense); change from one to another brings about a total change of name, which is misleading, because only a superficial component has altered and the most important constituent remains. This difficult saying implies that, while each separate pair of contraries forms a single continuum, the several continua, also, are connected with each other, though in a different manner. Thus the total plurality of things forms a single, coherent, determinable complex—what Heraclitus called 'unity'.

[1] The superiority of god to man, and of the divine 'synthetic' view of things to the human chaotic view, is heavily stressed by Heraclitus: e.g. **208** Fr. 78, Origen *c. Celsum* VI, 12 ἦθος γὰρ ἀνθρώπειον μὲν οὐκ ἔχει γνώμας, θεῖον δὲ ἔχει. See also frr. 79, 82–3, and compare the Hebrew concept: 'As the heavens are higher than the earth, so are my ways higher than your ways, and my thoughts than your thoughts'—Isaiah lv. 8f. One saying specifically asserts that for god the separateness implied by opposites does not exist: **209** Fr. 102, Porphyrius *in Iliadem* 4, 4 τῷ μὲν θεῷ καλὰ πάντα καὶ ἀγαθὰ καὶ δίκαια, ἄνθρωποι δὲ ἃ μὲν ἄδικα ὑπειλήφασιν ἃ δὲ δίκαια.

(4) *The unity of things lies beneath the surface; it depends upon a balanced reaction between opposites*

210 Fr. 54, Hippolytus *Ref.* IX, 9, 5 ἁρμονίη ἀφανὴς φανερῆς κρείττων.

211 Fr. 123, Themistius *Or.* 5, p. 69 D. φύσις κρύπτεσθαι φιλεῖ.

212 Fr. 51, Hippolytus *Ref.* IX, 9, 1 οὐ ξυνιᾶσιν ὅκως διαφερόμενον ἑωυτῷ ξυμφέρεται· παλίντονος ἁρμονίη ὅκωσπερ τόξου καὶ λύρης.[1]

[1] Hippolytus, the fullest source here, and usually a reliable one, has ὁμολογέειν (for ὁμολογέει) and παλίντροπος. ξυμφέρεται is a probable restoration from Plato's version, *Symp.* 187A, and avoids a difficult use of ὁμολογεῖν—a verb which could easily have been repeated accidentally, since Hippolytus used it twice in the infinitive just before he quoted the fragment. παλίντονος has as much support as παλίντροπος in the versions (of the second part only) by Plutarch and Porphyry, and is preferred because it gives a fully intelligible sense. G. Vlastos, *AJP* 76 (1955) 348ff., defends παλίντροπος: his strongest point is that Diog. L. IX, 7, a summary and often imprecise version of Theophrastus, has the phrase διὰ τῆς ἐναντιοτροπῆς ἡρμόσθαι. This certainly appears at first sight to be based upon παλίντροπος ἁρμονίη; yet the ἐναντιοτροπή (which would have to be ἐναντιοτροπία if derived from an adjectival form -τροπος) probably refers to the τροπαί of **221**, combined (as they certainly were by Theophrastus, cf. the fuller account of him in Diog. L. IX, 8) with the 'way up and down' interpreted as change between opposites. ἡρμόσθαι could be a general application of the concept of ἁρμονίη, cf. **210**. It is also possible

---

208 *Human disposition does not have true judgement, but divine disposition does.*

209 *To god all things are beautiful and good and just, but men have supposed some things to be unjust, others just.*

210 *An unapparent connexion is stronger than an apparent one.*

211 *The real constitution of things is accustomed to hide itself.*

212 *They do not apprehend how being at variance it agrees with itself* [literally, *how being brought apart it is brought together with itself*]*: there is a back-stretched connexion, as in the bow and the lyre.*

that there was doubt about the form of the epithet as early as Theophrastus, as there certainly was later. Objections to παλίντροπος are (i) can 'a turning-back connexion' really be said, even by Heraclitus, for 'a connexion *achieved by* contrary changes'? Perhaps it can—it would be possible, certainly, in Aeschylus. If this is accepted, the meaning given fits in well enough with Heraclitus' theory of natural change. Unfortunately (ii) it does not make any intelligible sense when applied, as it is, to the bow and the lyre. Vlastos suggests that the sequence of tension and relaxation of the string, which discharges the arrow or makes the note, is meant: but this sequence cannot be described as an 'adjustment' or 'connexion', in any kind of Greek. The παλίντροπος κέλευθος in Parmenides fr. 6 (**345**) is, of course, perfectly intelligible, and does not necessarily contain a reference to Heraclitus (cf. p. 272), or at any rate to this fragment.

What is stated in **210** is a general rule; comparison with **211** (where φύσις probably means not 'Nature' but 'a thing's true constitution'), and also with **212**, suggests that the rule is intended to apply to the working of the world as a whole, as a sum of constituent parts whose connexion is not apparent at first sight. The unseen connexion of opposites is in fact stronger than other, more obvious types of connexion.[1] **212**, one of Heraclitus' most familiar sayings, contains a characteristic looseness in predication: the subject of ξυμφέρεται is probably not ⟨τὸ⟩ διαφερόμενον, i.e. another example of a specific opposite, but a generalizing διαφερόμενόν ⟨τι⟩, where 'anything being carried apart' means something like 'any discrete pair of opposites'. Thus the sense given is similar to that implicit in συμφερόμενον διαφερόμενον in **206**: any pair, or sum of pairs, can be regarded either (*a*) as heterogeneous and analysable in terms of separate extremes, or (*b*) as tending together with itself to form a unity. Now comes an important addition: there is (*sc.* in it, i.e. it exemplifies) a connexion or means of joining (the literal sense of ἁρμονίη) through opposite tensions,[2] which ensures this coherence—just as the tension in the string of bow or lyre, being exactly balanced by the outward tension exerted by the arms of the instrument, produces a coherent, unified, stable and efficient complex. We may infer that if the balance between opposites were *not* maintained, for example if 'the hot' (i.e. the sum of hot substances) began seriously to outweigh the cold, or night day, then the unity and coherence of the world would cease, just as, if the tension in the bow-string exceeds the tension in the arms, the whole complex is destroyed.

[1] A number of fragments imply that it needs both faith and persistence to find the underlying truth. So e.g. **213** Fr. 18, Clement *Strom.* II, 17, 4

ἐὰν μὴ ἔλπηται ἀνέλπιστον οὐκ ἐξευρήσει, ἀνεξερεύνητον ἐὸν καὶ ἄπορον. See also **247**, and frr. 22, 86; compare Xenophanes (**191**).

[2] παλίντονος = 'counter-stretched', i.e. tending equally in opposite directions. A tension in one direction automatically produces an equivalent tension in the other; if not, the system collapses.

(5) *The total balance in the cosmos can only be maintained if change in one direction eventually leads to change in the other, that is, if there is unending 'strife' between opposites*

214 Fr. 80, Origen *c. Celsum* VI, 42 εἰδέναι χρὴ τὸν πόλεμον ἐόντα ξυνόν, καὶ δίκην ἔριν, καὶ γινόμενα πάντα κατ' ἔριν καὶ χρεών.[1]

215 Fr. 53, Hippolytus *Ref.* IX, 9, 4 πόλεμος πάντων μὲν πατήρ ἐστι, πάντων δὲ βασιλεύς, καὶ τοὺς μὲν θεοὺς ἔδειξε τοὺς δὲ ἀνθρώπους, τοὺς μὲν δούλους ἐποίησε τοὺς δὲ ἐλευθέρους.

[1] χρεών Diels, χρεώμενα ms. The emendation is not certain, but is hard to improve; the three extra letters may be connected with the omission of three letters just before, where the unique Vatican ms. has εἰ δέ for the obvious original εἰδέναι.

Strife or war is Heraclitus' metaphor for the dominance of change in the world. It is obviously related to the reaction between opposites; most kinds of change (except for e.g. growth, which is the accretion of like to like), it may be inferred, could be resolved into change between opposites. At all events, change from one extreme to the other might seem to be the most radical possible. The 'war' which underlies all events, and is responsible for different and indeed opposed conditions of men and for their fate after death (cf. **239** and **242** for the difficult assertion about men and gods), is called δίκη, the 'indicated way' (from the same root as δείκνυμι), or the normal rule of behaviour. This must be a deliberate amendment of Anaximander's dictum (**112**) that things pay retribution to each other for the *injustice* of their alternate encroachments in the processes of natural change. Heraclitus points out that if strife—that is, the action and reaction between

---

213 *If one does not expect the unexpected one will not find it out, since it is not to be searched out, and difficult to compass.*

214 *It is necessary to know that war is common and right is strife and that all things happen by strife and necessity.*

215 *War is the father of all and king of all, and some he shows as gods, others as men; some he makes slaves, others free.*

opposed substances—were to cease, then the victor in every contest of extremes would establish a permanent domination, and the world as such would be destroyed.[1] Yet just as in a battle there are temporary local stoppages, or deadlocks produced by the exact balance of opposing forces, so Heraclitus must have allowed that temporary stability is to be found here and there in the cosmic battlefield, so long as it is only temporary and is balanced by a corresponding state elsewhere. This would not diminish the validity of the domination of strife (which, as for Anaximander, provides a metaphorical motive for change), but it allows the principle to be applied to the world of our actual experience, in which all things must eventually change but some things are for the time being obviously stable.

[1] Cf. **216** Aristotle *Eth. Eudem.* H 1, 1235a25 καὶ Ἡράκλειτος ἐπιτιμᾷ τῷ ποιήσαντι Ὡς ἔρις ἔκ τε θεῶν καὶ ἀνθρώπων ἀπόλοιτο (=*Il.* 18, 107)· οὐ γὰρ ἂν εἶναι ἁρμονίαν μὴ ὄντος ὀξέος καὶ βαρέος οὐδὲ τὰ ζῷα ἄνευ θήλεος καὶ ἄρρενος ἐναντίων ὄντων. Here ἁρμονία has its special sense of 'musical scale'.

(6) *The river-image illustrates the kind of unity that depends on the preservation of measure and balance in change*

217 Fr. 12, Arius Didymus *ap.* Eusebium *P.E.* xv, 20, +fr. 91, Plutarch *de E* 18, 392B ποταμοῖσι τοῖσιν αὐτοῖσιν ἐμβαίνουσιν ἕτερα καὶ ἕτερα ὕδατα ἐπιρρεῖ (=fr. 12).[1]...σκίδνησι καὶ...συνάγει...συνίσταται καὶ ἀπολείπει...πρόσεισι καὶ ἄπεισι (=fr. 91).

[1] The words καὶ ψυχαὶ δὲ ἀπὸ τῶν ὑγρῶν ἀναθυμιῶνται, which follow ὕδατα ἐπιρρεῖ in Arius, are counted as part of fr. 12 by most editors; but they are out of place here and are almost certainly part of an attempt by Cleanthes to find an exhalation of soul in Heraclitus as in Zeno: see Kirk, *Heraclitus, the Cosmic Fragments* 367ff. The pairs of verbs which form fr. 91 occur in Plutarch immediately after a summary by him (in Platonic terms) of the main river-statement; see further p. 198.

According to the Platonic interpretation, accepted and expanded by Aristotle, Theophrastus, and the doxographers, this river-image was cited by Heraclitus to emphasize the absolute con-

---

216 *Heraclitus rebukes the author of the line 'Would that strife might be destroyed from among gods and men': for there would be no musical scale unless high and low existed, nor living creatures without female and male, which are opposites.*

217 *Upon those that step into the same rivers different and different waters flow....It scatters and...gathers...it comes together and flows away...approaches and departs.*

tinuity of change in every single thing: everything is in perpetual flux like a river. So **218** Plato *Cratylus* 402 A λέγει που Ἡράκλειτος ὅτι πάντα χωρεῖ καὶ οὐδὲν μένει, καὶ ποταμοῦ ῥοῇ ἀπεικάζων τὰ ὄντα λέγει ὡς δὶς ἐς τὸν αὐτὸν ποταμὸν οὐκ ἂν ἐμβαίης. It is to this interpretation that Aristotle refers in **219** Aristotle *Phys.* Θ3, 253b9 καί φασί τινες κινεῖσθαι τῶν ὄντων οὐ τὰ μὲν τὰ δ' οὔ, ἀλλὰ πάντα καὶ ἀεί, ἀλλὰ λανθάνειν τοῦτο τὴν ἡμετέραν αἴσθησιν. Aristotle here makes explicit what is implicit in Plato, that many things (those that appear to be stable) must be undergoing *invisible* or unnoticed changes. Can Heraclitus really have thought that a rock or a bronze cauldron, for example, was invariably undergoing invisible changes of material? Perhaps so; but nothing in the extant fragments suggests that he did, and his clearly-expressed reliance on the senses, provided they be interpreted intelligently, suggests that he did not.[1] It cannot be too strongly emphasized that before Parmenides and his apparent proof that the senses were completely fallacious—a proof that was clearly a tremendous shock to his contemporaries—gross departures from common sense must only be accepted when the evidence for them is extremely strong. In the present case it is quite conceivable that Plato was misled by post-Heraclitean exaggerations and distortions of Heraclitus' emphasis on eventual change; in particular, perhaps, by Cratylus, who thought that you could not step even *once* into the same river (Aristotle *Met.* Γ5, 1010a13), and who is said by Aristotle to have influenced Plato as a young man (*Met.* A6, 987a32).[2]

[1] See **200, 201.** It is true that Melissus in fr. 8 (**392**) drew attention to the appearance that some 'stable' things do change: iron is worn away by the finger, and so on. This observation occurs in a context which perhaps has verbal references to Heraclitus (e.g. τό τε θερμὸν ψυχρὸν γίνεσθαι καὶ τὸ ψυχρὸν θερμόν, cf. fr. 126). Yet there is no reason whatever to think that Melissus meant that change must in this case be *continuous*, even though it can be *invisible*. Every time the finger rubs, it rubs off an invisible portion of iron; yet when it does not rub, what reason is there to think that the iron is still changing? Melissus' point is rather that appearances show that

---

218 *Heraclitus somewhere says that all things are in process and nothing stays still, and likening existing things to the stream of a river he says that you would not step twice into the same river.*

219 *And some say not that some existing things are moving, and not others, but that all things are in motion all the time, but that this escapes our perception.*

everything, even the apparently stable, is *subject to change*. This is precisely what Heraclitus must have thought; he may or may not have mentioned infra-visible changes, but in any case would only accept them when they were deducible—and continuous change is *not* deducible in many apparently stable objects. Melissus' argument, of course, was that the senses must be fallacious; for between Heraclitus and himself had come Parmenides. With Empedoclean effluences (p. 343) the situation changes.

[2] Vlastos, *AJP* 76 (1955) 338ff., argues that Cratylus' rejoinder as reported by Aristotle implies a previous statement just like that in Plato (**218**), that you could not step twice into the same river; in fact what Heraclitus said was not fr. 12 (**217**) but something very like Plato's version, and the Platonic interpretation of universal flux is correct.—But (i) Aristotle's formulation of Cratylus' emendation of Heraclitus is likely enough to be based on Plato's summary, rather than on the exact form of statements by Cratylus or Heraclitus; and (ii) in any case, the river-statement could have been slightly distorted by other sophists even before Cratylus; or he (who certainly grossly exaggerated Heraclitus' belief about names) could have altered its formal expression himself. As for the question of which is the more original form of the river-statement, fr. 12 or Plato's version, the former has every appearance of belonging to Heraclitus, being in natural and unforced Ionic and having the characteristic rhythm of archaic prose; while the latter looks Platonic, and could more easily be a misunderstanding of fr. 12 than *vice versa*. See further Kirk, *Heraclitus, the Cosmic Fragments* 367ff., as well as Vlastos, *loc. cit.*

Cratylus' 'improvement' of Heraclitus is implicit in a saying ascribed, as I consider wrongly, to Heraclitus, fr. 49*a* in DK: 'We step and do not step into the same rivers; we are and are not.' This last existential aphorism is particularly improbable, and the whole sentence can be explained as a development of fr. 12, where the mention of the human standard ('those who step...') probably has as its chief purpose the provision of an animate point by which the flow can be gauged.

In **217** the tentative addition to fr. 12 of the verbs which compose fr. 91 (which the context, and their own nature, seem to indicate as describing the flow of water, with special attention to the regularity of its replacement) brings out what is implicit in fr. 12: that the *unity* of the river as a whole is dependent upon the *regularity* (also perhaps suggested by the repetition ἕτερα καὶ ἕτερα) of the flux of its constituent waters. The river provides an image of the balance of constituents in the world. The river-statement does not suggest for one moment that everything singly behaves like a river. Obviously, a rock or a mountain or a table is temporarily static, and will remain so, perhaps, for a long time: what matters for Heraclitus' theory of balanced reaction and strife is that *eventually* it should change and so help to maintain the process of world-constituents. Meanwhile the stability of a mountain, for example, is balanced by a corresponding stability elsewhere of corresponding masses of sea, and of fire or aither (the mountain being mostly earth); on which see the next section.

(7) *The world is an ever-living fire, parts of which are always extinguished to form the two other main world-masses, sea and earth. Changes between fire, sea and earth balance each other; pure, or aitherial, fire has a directive capacity*

220 Fr. 30, Clement *Strom.* v, 104, 1 κόσμον τόνδε [τὸν αὐτὸν ἁπάντων][1] οὔτε τις θεῶν οὔτε ἀνθρώπων ἐποίησεν, ἀλλ' ἦν ἀεὶ καὶ ἔστιν καὶ ἔσται· πῦρ ἀείζωον, ἁπτόμενον μέτρα καὶ ἀποσβεννύμενον μέτρα.

221 Fr. 31, Clement *Strom.* v, 104, 3 πυρὸς τροπαί· πρῶτον θάλασσα, θαλάσσης δὲ τὸ μὲν ἥμισυ γῆ τὸ δὲ ἥμισυ πρηστήρ... ⟨γῆ⟩ θάλασσα διαχέεται, καὶ μετρέεται εἰς τὸν αὐτὸν λόγον ὁκοῖος πρόσθεν ἦν ἢ γενέσθαι γῆ.

222 Fr. 90, Plutarch *de E* 8, 388 D πυρός τε ἀνταμοιβὴ τὰ πάντα καὶ πῦρ ἁπάντων ὅκωσπερ χρυσοῦ χρήματα καὶ χρημάτων χρυσός.

223 Fr. 64, Hippolytus *Ref.* ix, 10, 6 τὰ δὲ πάντα οἰακίζει κεραυνός.

[1] Vlastos, *op. cit.* 344 ff., argues that 'the same of all' is original, and contrasts the real physical world of common experience with the deceptive private imaginings of men who do not follow the Logos (cf. **198** etc.). This would be possible enough if (what does not seem particularly probable) fr. 30 followed directly upon a reference to men's delusions; but neither Plutarch nor Simplicius, who also quote the first part of the fragment, gives the debated phrase. More important, Vlastos does not mention that Clement in the context of the quotation is following some Stoic source in endeavouring to explain away this fragment's inconsistency with the Stoic *ecpyrosis*-interpretation, by arguing that 'this world-order' in Heraclitus is the all-inclusive, eternal system, τὸν ἐξ ἁπάσης τῆς οὐσίας ἰδίως ποιὸν κόσμον as Clement had just said, and not this particular world. Thus the interpolation is very strongly motivated; see further Kirk, *Heraclitus, the Cosmic Fragments* 307 ff.

---

220 *This world-order* [*the same of all*] *did none of gods or men make, but it always was and is and shall be: an everliving fire, kindling in measures and going out in measures.*

221 *Fire's turnings: first sea, and of sea the half is earth, the half 'burner'* [i.e. *lightning or fire*]*...⟨earth⟩ is dispersed as sea, and is measured so as to form the same proportion as existed before it became earth.*

222 *All things are an equal exchange for fire and fire for all things, as goods are for gold and gold for goods.*

223 *Thunderbolt steers all things.*

Fire is the archetypal form of matter. The world-order as a whole can be described as a fire of which measures are being extinguished, corresponding measures being re-kindled; not all of it is burning at the same time. It always has been, and always will be, in this condition (**220**). Cosmogony in the Milesian sense is therefore not to be found in Heraclitus. Fire cannot be an originative stuff in the way that water or air was for Thales or Anaximenes, and according to Aristotle and his followers it is no longer indefinite or infinite (cf. Theophrastus *ap.* Simpl. *Phys.* 24, 1, DK 22 A 5); it is nevertheless the continuing source of the natural processes in **221**. Regarded as *a part* of the cosmos, fire is on a par with sea (presumably representing water in general, as in Xenophanes) and earth, as one of the three obvious world-masses. The pure cosmic fire was probably identified by Heraclitus with αἰθήρ (aither), the brilliant fiery stuff which fills the shining sky and surrounds the world: this aither was widely regarded both as divine and as a place of souls.[1] The apprehension that the soul may be fire or aither, not breath as Anaximenes had thought, must have helped to determine the choice of fire as the controlling form of matter (cf. p. 161). **223** shows that Heraclitus' fire—the purest and brightest sort, that is, as of the aitherial and divine thunderbolt—has a directive capacity. In part this reflects the divinity assigned to aither in the popular conception; more important, perhaps, is the fact that all fire (even the lower, mundane sort), by the regularity with which it absorbs fuel and emits smoke, while maintaining a kind of stability between them, patently embodies the rule of measure in change which inheres in the world process, and of which the Logos is an expression (pp. 188f.). Thus it is naturally conceived as the very constituent of things which actively determines their structure and behaviour—which ensures not only the opposition of opposites, but also their unity through 'strife'.

[1] Cf. e.g. **224** Aristotle *de caelo* B 1, 284a 11 τὸν δ' οὐρανὸν καὶ τὸν ἄνω τόπον οἱ μὲν ἀρχαῖοι τοῖς θεοῖς ἀπένειμαν ὡς ὄντα μόνον ἀθάνατον.... **225** *Inscriptiones Graecae*[2] I, 945, 6 (Athens, 5th c. B.C.) αἰθὴρ μὲν ψυχὰς ὑπεδέξατο, σώμ[ατα δὲ χθών]. **226** [Hippocrates] *de carnibus* 2 δοκέει δέ

---

224 *The ancients assigned to the gods the heaven and the upper region as being the only immortal place....*

225 *Aither received their souls, earth their bodies.*

μοι ὃ καλέομεν θερμὸν ἀθάνατόν τε εἶναι καὶ νοέειν πάντα καὶ ὁρῆν καὶ ἀκούειν καὶ εἰδέναι πάντα, ἐόντα τε καὶ ἐσόμενα. τοῦτο οὖν τὸ πλεῖστον, ὅτε ἐταράχθη ἅπαντα, ἐξεχώρησεν εἰς τὴν ἀνωτάτω περιφορήν, καὶ αὐτό μοι δοκέει αἰθέρα τοῖς παλαιοῖς εἰρῆσθαι. Cf. also Euripides fr. 839, 9ff., fr. 941 (Nauck[2]), *Helen* 1014 ff.; Aristophanes *Peace* 832f. None of these passages, of course, is as early as Heraclitus, and **226** clearly shows the influence of Anaxagoras and Diogenes of Apollonia. But the belief is described as ancient in **224** and **226**, and is so widely represented in fifth-century poetry that it must have been well established and widely known by then. It is comparable with the belief in the divinity of the sun, which must be of great antiquity.

The cosmos consists, broadly, of the masses of earth (interpenetrated with secondary fire, as in volcanos) and sea, surrounded by the bright integument of fire or aither. This fire, we may conjecture on the basis of **221**, was regarded by Heraclitus as the motive point of the cosmological processes: from its region appears to come rain, which ultimately nourishes the sea, and it is itself replenished (for fire 'consumes' moisture) by the moist evaporation ascending from the sea. Sea, as Xenophanes had shown, turns into earth, and earth at other times and places changes to water. Thus sea and earth are what cosmic or aitherial fire 'turns to' (**221**).[1] Changes between the three world-masses are going on simultaneously in such a way that the total of each always remains the same. If a quantity of earth dissolves into sea, an equivalent quantity of sea in other parts is condensing into earth, and so with changes between sea and 'burner' (fire): this seems to be the sense of **221**. The λόγος or proportion remains the same—again it is the measure and regularity of change, this time of large-scale cosmological change, that is stressed. The only surprising thing about this cosmology is its apparent avoidance of analysis into opposites and of the relation of opposites to fire-sea-earth. The probable explanation is that the opposites are invoked in the logical examination of change, but that in the examination of large-scale changes a more empirical description can be retained, particularly as the Logos is closely related to fire. The connexion between the two types of analysis is the underlying concept of measure and proportion.

---

226 *What we call 'hot' seems to me to be immortal and to apprehend all things and to see and hear and know all things, both present and future. This, then, the most of all, when all things became confused, went out to the furthermost revolution, and seems to me to have been what was called aither by the men of old.*

[1] Or 'is exchanged for' in the phrase of **222**. Note that **220** and **222** both tend to invalidate the Stoic ascription to Heraclitus of a periodic ἐκπύρωσις or consumption of the world by fire. The world-order *is and shall be* an ever-living fire kindling and going out in measures (simultaneously, that is): and in the trade-image of goods and gold the situation could not arise that all the goods (the manifold world) are simultaneously absorbed into gold (fire), so that there is all gold and no goods. Theophrastus, after referring to this image, added 'He makes an order and a definite time of the change of the world according to some destined necessity' (Simpl. *Phys.* 24, 4ff., DK 22 A 5). It seems probable that Theophrastus was here misapplying Aristotle's dictum that 'things are destroyed into that from which they came'; influenced in addition, perhaps, by Aristotle's curious remark (*de caelo* A 10, 279 b 14, DK 22 A 10) that Empedocles and Heraclitus made the world fluctuate between its present condition and destruction. Aristotle may have been thinking of a great-year cycle of 10,800 years apparently mentioned by Heraclitus (DK 22 A 13); this may have applied to a cycle of favoured souls, or conceivably to the time taken for a single portion of fire to pass through all its stages, and in either case could have been misleading if presented incompletely. Plato (*Soph.* 242 D, DK 22 A 10) clearly distinguished between Heraclitus' *simultaneous* unity and plurality of the cosmos and Empedocles' separate *periods* of Love and Strife. At the same time, they *are* mentioned together as both alike believing in the unity and plurality of the cosmos; and Aristotle's coupling of the two might conceivably have been motivated by the Platonic comparison, the important distinction between them being overlooked.

(8) *Astronomy. The heavenly bodies are bowls of fire, nourished by exhalations from the sea; astronomical events, too, have their measures*

227 Diogenes Laertius IX, 9–10 (DK 22 A 1) τὸ δὲ περιέχον ὁποῖόν ἐστιν οὐ δηλοῖ· εἶναι μέντοι ἐν αὐτῷ σκάφας ἐπεστραμμένας κατὰ κοῖλον πρὸς ἡμᾶς, ἐν αἷς ἀθροιζομένας τὰς λαμπρὰς ἀναθυμιάσεις ἀποτελεῖν φλόγας, ἃς εἶναι τὰ ἄστρα. (10) λαμπροτάτην δὲ εἶναι τὴν τοῦ ἡλίου φλόγα καὶ θερμοτάτην....ἐκλείπειν τε ἥλιον καὶ σελήνην ἄνω στρεφομένων τῶν σκαφῶν· τούς τε κατὰ μῆνα τῆς σελήνης σχηματισμοὺς γίνεσθαι στρεφομένης ἐν αὐτῇ κατὰ μικρὸν τῆς σκάφης.

228 Fr. 6, Aristotle *Meteor.* B 2, 355 a 13 ὁ ἥλιος...νέος ἐφ' ἡμέρῃ ἐστίν.

---

227 *He does not reveal the nature of the surrounding; it contains, however, bowls turned with their hollow side towards us, in which the bright exhalations are collected and form flames, which are the heavenly bodies. Brightest and hottest is the flame of the sun.... And sun and moon are eclipsed when the bowls turn upwards; and the monthly phases of the moon occur as its bowl is gradually turned.*

228 *The sun...is new each day.*

229 Fr. 94, Plutarch *de exil.* 11, 604A Ἥλιος οὐχ ὑπερβήσεται μέτρα· εἰ δὲ μή, Ἐρινύες μιν Δίκης ἐπίκουροι ἐξευρήσουσιν.

No extant fragment clearly reveals Heraclitus' ideas on the nature of the heavenly bodies; but Theophrastus evidently gave a moderately detailed if subjective account of his views, the non-Peripatetic parts of which there is no reason to disbelieve. Diogenes preserves the fullest version of this account, of which **227** is a part; for the rest (the stars are further from the earth than the sun, the moon nearer) see DK22A1. The heavenly bodies are solid bowls filled with fire. This fire is maintained by moist exhalations or evaporations from the sea, which are somehow collected in them and burned as fuel.[1] This is presumably the way in which water changes into fire in the balanced interaction between world-masses described in **221**. The idea that, since moisture is evaporated by fire, fire is physically nourished by it is a naïve and popular one. Similarly the solid celestial bowls are probably a quasi-scientific elaboration of the popular myth that the sun each night sails from west to east *in a golden bowl* round the northern stream of Okeanos (see **7**, **8**). Eclipses and phases of the moon were explained by the turning away of the bowls: but no true cause (as opposed to a mere mechanism) was given, and Diogenes (IX, 11, DK22A1), presumably still following Theophrastus, stated that Heraclitus said nothing about the constitution of the bowls. Heraclitus was probably not interested in astronomy for its own sake, and seems to have been content with adaptations of popular accounts so long as his general theory of cosmological change was preserved. **228** is consonant with Theophrastus' account of the celestial bowls: the sun is 'new' every day in the sense that its fire is replenished each night with entirely fresh exhalations. Naturally, this replenishment and consumption form a regular cycle, though one which could admit slight variations. The principle of measure in natural change is illustrated also in **229**, where the sun is restrained by Dike, the personification of normality and therefore regularity, from exceeding its measures—for example from coming too close to the earth or shining beyond its proper time.

---

229 *Sun will not overstep his measures; otherwise the Erinyes, ministers of Justice, will find him out.*

[1] Theophrastus and his followers usually attributed *two* exhalations, a moist and a dry one, to Heraclitus: this is most probably a misunderstanding based upon Aristotle's own dual-exhalation explanation of meteorological (as opposed, in his case, to astronomical) events. Aristotle seems to have elaborated this theory out of Heraclitus' ideas on the importance of the exhalation from the sea and other terrestrial waters; but it appears from passages in his *Meteorologica* that Aristotle considered the dry exhalation from the earth to be his own discovery (Kirk, *Heraclitus, the Cosmic Fragments* 273 ff.). Yet, because it is kindled, he can treat Heraclitus' exhalation as fiery: see p. 207 n. 1. The explanation of night and day (as well as winter and summer) as due to the alternating prevalence of the dark and bright exhalations, ascribed to Heraclitus in Diogenes' Theophrastean account, is suspect: Heraclitus knew as well as anyone that day is due to the sun, and declared in fr. 99 that 'if there were no sun, it would be night'.

(9) *Wisdom consists in understanding the way the world works*

230 Fr. 41, Diogenes Laertius IX, 1 ἓν τὸ σοφόν· ἐπίστασθαι γνώμην, ὅκῃ κυβερνᾶται πάντα διὰ πάντων.[1]

231 Fr. 32, Clement *Strom.* V, 115, 1 ἓν τὸ σοφὸν μοῦνον λέγεσθαι οὐκ ἐθέλει καὶ ἐθέλει Ζηνὸς ὄνομα.

[1] ὀτέη κυβερνῆσαι P[1]B, ὀτ' ἐγκυβερνῆσαι F; ὀτέη ἐκυβέρνησε Diels, DK, ὀπῇ κυβερνᾶται Gigon, Walzer, ὀτέῃ κυβερνᾶται Vlastos, ὅκῃ κυβερνᾶται scripsi. The feminine form ὀτέη is not, in fact, found; ὅκῃ is one obvious source of corruption. This involves taking γνώμην as internal accusative with ἐπίστασθαι, after Heidel: 'to be acquainted with true judgement how all things are steered through all'. This would be a development of Solon fr. 16 Diehl: γνωμοσύνης δ' ἀφανὲς χαλεπώτατόν ἐστι νοῆσαι / μέτρον, ὃ δὴ πάντων πείρατα μοῦνον ἔχει ('Most hard is it to apprehend the unapparent measure of judgement, which alone holds the limits of all things'). On the other hand the Stoics took γνώμην in Heraclitus' saying as direct object of ἐπίστασθαι (cf. Cleanthes *Hymn to Zeus* 34 f.), as representing their own familiar idea of divine Reason; that they should place this interpretation on the dictum is not surprising, in any case. But that *Heraclitus* should have used γνώμη by itself, with no definite article and no possessor expressed, to stand for Fire or Logos (cf. **223**), has seemed improbable to some. Each of the two alternative interpretations has its difficulties, but the resulting sense in each case is not very different: wisdom consists in understanding how the world works—which in any event involves understanding the divine Logos.

230 gives the real motive of Heraclitus' philosophy: not mere curiosity about nature (although this was doubtless present too)

---

230 *The wise is one thing, to be acquainted with true judgement, how all things are steered through all.*

231 *One thing, the only truly wise, does not and does consent to be called by the name of Zeus.*

but the belief that man's very life is indissociably bound up with his whole surroundings. Wisdom—and therefore, it might be inferred, satisfactory living—consists in understanding the Logos, the analogous structure or common element of arrangement in things, embodying the μέτρον or measure which ensures that change does not produce disconnected, chaotic plurality. Absolute understanding here can only be achieved by god (**231**; cf. also **209**), who in some respects, therefore (but not of course in anthropomorphism and in the demand for cult), resembles the Zeus of the conventional religion. God, with his synoptic view, is thus 'the only thing that is (completely) wise'. Fire (**223**) and the Logos itself (**199**) are to a large degree co-extensive with, or different aspects of, this completely wise thing.

It remains to describe Heraclitus' views about men—their soul, institutions and ideas. But for Heraclitus this subject was in no way separate from the study of the outside world; the same materials and the same laws are found in each sphere. **230** clearly depends upon this assumption, which is implicit also in **197** (fr. 1).

(10) *The soul is composed of fire; it comes from, and turns into, moisture, total absorption by which is death for it. The soul-fire is related to the world-fire*

232 Fr. 36, Clement *Strom.* VI, 17, 2 ψυχῇσιν θάνατος ὕδωρ γενέσθαι, ὕδατι δὲ θάνατος γῆν γενέσθαι· ἐκ γῆς δὲ ὕδωρ γίνεται, ἐξ ὕδατος δὲ ψυχή.

233 Fr. 118, Stobaeus *Anth.* III, 5, 8 αὔη ψυχὴ σοφωτάτη καὶ ἀρίστη.

234 Fr. 117, Stobaeus *Anth.* III, 5, 7 ἀνὴρ ὁκόταν μεθυσθῇ ἄγεται ὑπὸ παιδὸς ἀνήβου, σφαλλόμενος, οὐκ ἐπαΐων ὅκη βαίνει, ὑγρὴν τὴν ψυχὴν ἔχων.

235 Fr. 45, Diogenes Laertius IX, 7 ψυχῆς πείρατα ἰὼν οὐκ ἂν ἐξεύροιο, πᾶσαν ἐπιπορευόμενος ὁδόν· οὕτω βαθὺν λόγον ἔχει.

---

232 *For souls it is death to become water, for water it is death to become earth; from earth water comes-to-be, and from water, soul.*

233 *A dry soul is wisest and best.*

234 *A man when he is drunk is led by an unfledged boy, stumbling and not knowing where he goes, having his soul moist.*

235 *You would not find out the boundaries of soul, even by travelling along every path: so deep a measure does it have.*

Anaximenes had probably drawn cosmological conclusions from the nature of the soul, which, following the Homeric view, he envisaged as breath. Heraclitus abandoned this idea in favour of another popular conception of the soul, that it was made of fiery aither. On this foundation he built up a rationalistic psychological theory, in which for the first time (unless Pythagoras himself went further in this direction than we suspect) the structure of the soul is related not only to that of the body, but also to that of the world as a whole.

The soul in its true and effective state is made of fire: in **232** soul replaces fire in a list of what might otherwise be taken for the main interactions of the world-masses (cf. **221**). The implication is not only that soul is fiery, but also that it plays some part in the great cycle of natural change. It comes into being from moisture (and, if it is analogous to cosmic fire, is maintained, at least in part, by some kind of moisture—see p. 203), and is destroyed when it turns entirely into water.[1] The efficient soul is dry (**233**), that is, fiery. A soul that is moistened, for example by excessive drinking as in **234** (which well illustrates the still naïve character of Heraclitus' psychology), is diminished in capacity and makes its owner behave childishly, without either wits or physical strength. Thus intellect is explicitly placed in the soul. The soul, which can move to all parts of the body at need,[2] has limits that cannot be reached (**235**); probably the thought here is not so much of the problem of self-consciousness as of the soul being a representative portion of the cosmic fire—which, compared with the individual, is obviously of vast extent. Thus it could be conceived as an adulterated fragment of the surrounding cosmic fire,[3] and so as the possessor in some degree of that fire's directive power (**223**). All this, as has been indicated, is a development of what may be reasonably taken as a popular conception of the nature of aither (cf. n. 1 on p. 200); but a simpler and more empirical indication of the fiery nature of soul was at hand, since it must have been commonly observed that warmth is associated with the living body and that the dead, soulless body is cold (so Vlastos, *op. cit.* 364f.).

[1] A Stoic re-formulation of **232**, in which air is characteristically added to the three genuinely Heraclitean world-masses (to produce the four 'elements' of post-Empedoclean speculation), gives 'the death of fire is the birth of air', etc.; this appears as fr. 76 in DK, but is totally misleading

for Heraclitus. He appears to have ignored air as a major cosmic constituent, in spite of Anaximenes; though the exhalation from the sea, by which sea turns to fire, might have been termed ἀήρ. Aristotle (*de an.* A2, 405a24, DK22A15) wrote that Heraclitus made soul the same as the material principle, namely 'the exhalation from which he compounds the other things'. Aristotle himself accepted two kinds of exhalation, one being fiery, so that the 'exhalation' here represents fire.

[2] According to the scholiast on Chalcidius (fr. 67*a* in DK) Heraclitus compared the soul to a spider which rushes to any part of its web which is damaged. The soul is described as 'firme et proportionaliter iuncta' to the body; the idea of proportion is appropriate to Heraclitus. Cf. on Anaximenes, pp. 158ff.

[3] So Macrobius *S. Scip.* 14, 19 (DK22A15), 'Heraclitus said that the soul is a spark of the essential substance of the stars' (*scintillam stellaris essentiae*)—the stars being no doubt conceived as concentrations of aither.

(11) *Waking, sleeping and death are related to the degree of fieriness in the soul. In sleep the soul is partly cut off from the world-fire, and so decreases in activity*

236 Fr. 26, Clement *Strom.* IV, 141, 2 ἄνθρωπος ἐν εὐφρόνῃ φάος ἅπτεται ἑαυτῷ [ἀποθανὼν] ἀποσβεσθεὶς ὄψεις, ζῶν δὲ ἅπτεται τεθνεῶτος εὕδων [ἀποσβεσθεὶς ὄψεις], ἐγρηγορὼς ἅπτεται εὕδοντος. (Text as in DK, after Wilamowitz.)

237 Sextus *adv. math.* VII, 129 (DK22A16) τοῦτον οὖν τὸν θεῖον λόγον καθ' Ἡράκλειτον δι' ἀναπνοῆς σπάσαντες νοεροὶ γινόμεθα, καὶ ἐν μὲν ὕπνοις ληθαῖοι, κατὰ δὲ ἔγερσιν πάλιν ἔμφρονες· ἐν γὰρ τοῖς ὕπνοις μυσάντων τῶν αἰσθητικῶν πόρων χωρίζεται τῆς πρὸς τὸ περιέχον συμφυΐας ὁ ἐν ἡμῖν νοῦς, μόνης τῆς κατὰ ἀναπνοὴν προσφύσεως σῳζομένης οἱονεί τινος ῥίζης, χωρισθείς τε ἀποβάλλει ἣν πρότερον εἶχε μνημονικὴν δύναμιν. (130) ἐν δὲ ἐγρηγόρσει πάλιν διὰ τῶν αἰσθητικῶν πόρων ὥσπερ διά τινων θυρίδων προκύψας καὶ τῷ περιέχοντι συμβαλὼν λογικὴν ἐνδύεται δύναμιν....

---

236 *A man in the night kindles a light for himself when his vision is extinguished; living, he is in contact with the dead, when asleep, and with the sleeper, when awake.*

237 *According to Heraclitus we become intelligent by drawing in this divine reason* [logos] *through breathing, and forgetful when asleep, but we regain our senses when we wake up again. For in sleep, when the channels of perception are shut, our mind is sundered from its kinship with the surrounding, and breathing is the only point of attachment to be preserved, like a kind of root; being sundered, our mind casts off its former power of memory. But in the waking state it again peeps out through the channels of perception as though through a kind of window, and meeting with the surrounding it puts on its power of reason....*

The light kindled at night in **236** must be what a man sees in dreaming, when the actual darkness seems to be illuminated; we are also told that 'sleepers are workers' (fr. 75) and that 'what we see when asleep is sleep' (fr. 21). Naturally this light is deceptive: see the last sentence of fr. 1 (**197**). It is an individual, private illumination which supplants the real illumination of the Logos which is common to all (**198**). In sleep a man is 'in contact with' death (there is a typical Heraclitean word-play in **236** between the two senses of ἅπτεσθαι, 'kindle' and 'touch'): his soul-fire is burning low, is almost extinguished, and in most respects he resembles a dead man. Sleep, then, is a medial state between waking life and death.

Sextus' information in **237** is obviously important, but must be treated with caution: he naturally imposed Sceptic epistemological interpretations upon Heraclitus, for whom his sources were, in addition, Stoic-influenced. Yet he goes on to make clearly accurate quotations of the long fr. 1 and of fr. 2 (**197** and **198**). It is to be expected from **232** that the soul-fire has some kind of physical affinity, and therefore connexion, with the cosmic fire outside. Sextus tells us that in the waking state the connexion is provided by a direct contact through the senses with the external fire—with the 'surrounding', in his own terminology, by which it may be inferred that the surrounding aither is meant; or rather the Logos-element in things, which may be envisaged as a direct offshoot of the pure aitherial fire. Sight is presumably of particular importance among the senses, since it receives and absorbs the fiery impressions of light. In sleep the only possible contact is provided by breathing; it may be wondered whether this draws in fire so much as moisture (though cf. n. 3 on p. 211), since 'souls come from water' (**232**) and should draw nourishment from moisture. According to Aetius IV, 3, 12, DK22A15 (where there is some Stoic influence), souls are nourished by both external and internal exhalations: the internal exhalations, if they exist, would be from blood and other bodily liquids; the external ones would be those absorbed by breathing, and likewise moist. Unfortunately the extant fragments are no help here.[1] It is possible that in sleep the moist nourishment of the soul-fire, no longer balanced by the direct fiery accretions received in waking through the senses, subdues the soul and brings it into a death-like state. It may be noted that the intelligent condition consequent upon the apprehension of the Logos (see fr. 1, **197**) would mean in psychological terms that the active, fiery part of the soul has made contact with the fiery Logos-constituent of the objective situation, and has been increased by it.[2]

[1] Sextus went on to compare the resuscitation of the soul-fire by restored contact with the universal Logos (here expressed in Stoic-Sceptic terms) with the way in which embers glow again when brought near to a live fire. This image, already perhaps used by Xenophanes (p. 173), may well have been re-used by Heraclitus. Conceivably the word ἀγχιβασίη, 'going near to', which Heraclitus used (fr. 122) according to the Suda, belonged to the same image.

[2] Chalcidius, probably after Posidonius, ascribed to Heraclitus a view quite different from Sextus', according to which the soul only has contact with the cosmic reason when free in sleep from the interruption of the senses (*in Tim.* ch. 251, DK 22 A 20). The 'cosmic reason' is Stoic, and the rest is quite obviously (*pace* A. Delatte) Platonic; though cf. Pi. fr. 131 b.

(12) *Virtuous souls do not become water on the death of the body, but survive to join, eventually, the cosmic fire*

238 Fr. 25, Clement *Strom.* IV, 49, 3 μόροι γὰρ μέζονες μέζονας μοίρας λαγχάνουσι καθ' Ἡράκλειτον.

239 Fr. 63, Hippolytus *Ref.* IX, 10, 6 †ἔνθα δ' ἐόντι† ἐπανίστασθαι καὶ φύλακας γίνεσθαι ἐγερτὶ ζώντων καὶ νεκρῶν.

240 (Fr. 136), Σ Bodl. ad Epictetum, p. lxxxiii Schenkl
ψυχαὶ ἀρηίφατοι καθαρώτεραι ἢ ἐνὶ νούσοις.

The 'better portions' which are won in **238** must belong to the soul alone, since after death the body is 'more fit to be cast out than dung' (fr. 96). Therefore not all souls can equally undergo the 'death' (**232**) of becoming water, that is, of ceasing to be soul, which is essentially fiery. **239** (whose first words are probably corrupt) seems to suggest that certain souls survive death and become daimons; this is manifestly developed from a famous passage in Hesiod.[1] The key to Heraclitus' belief here is, I think, provided by **240**, which is clearly not a *verbatim* quotation but a verse summary of perhaps considerably later date than Heraclitus himself (although we know from Diogenes Laertius IX, 16,

---

238 *For better deaths gain better portions according to Heraclitus.*

239 †*To him* [or *it*], *being there,*† *they rise up and become guardians, wakefully, of living and dead.*

240 *Souls slain in war are purer than those* (*that perish*) *in diseases.*

DK 22 A 1, that Scythinus made a metrical version of Heraclitus in the late fourth or third century B.C.). It probably owes something to fr. 24, 'Gods and men honour those slain in battle', but the comparison with those who die from illness is quite new, and is unlikely to have been simply invented *after* Heraclitus. How can the souls of those dying in battle, it may be asked, be 'purer' than the souls of those dying from disease? The answer I suggest is that the latter are moistened and inefficient, and their possessors are in a semi-conscious and sleep-like condition; those slain in battle, on the contrary, are cut off at their most active, when their souls are fiery from virtuous and courageous activity.[2] At the moment of death the enfeebled souls of the sick lose their last residue of fieriness and become completely watery, so that they cease to exist as souls; while the souls of those slain in battle (almost instantaneously, for the most part) are predominantly fiery. It seems plausible, then, that the latter avoid the soul-death of becoming water.[3] They leave the body and, we may guess, are re-united with the aitherial fire. Before this happens they probably remain for a time as disembodied daimons, after the Hesiodic pattern. But there can be no idea of individual survival apart from this, or indeed of perpetual survival as aitherial fire: for measures of that fire are constantly being drawn into the cosmological process, and undergo the changes of **221** (see n. on p. 202 for a possible soul-period of some kind). Thus Heraclitus does not appear to be indebted here to Pythagoras.

[1] **241** Hesiod *Erga* 121 ff. (of the golden race) αὐτὰρ ἐπεὶ δὴ τοῦτο γένος κατὰ γαῖ' ἐκάλυψε / τοὶ μὲν δαίμονές εἰσι Διὸς μεγάλου διὰ βουλὰς / ἐσθλοί, ἐπιχθόνιοι φύλακες θνητῶν ἀνθρώπων. See also *ibid.* 252 ff. Another saying of Heraclitus preserved by Hippolytus is very obscure: it evidently has some connexion with the doctrine of opposites, but also suggests the deification of some souls (cf. **216**): **242** Fr. 62, Hippolytus *Ref.* IX, 10, 6 ἀθάνατοι θνητοί, θνητοὶ ἀθάνατοι, ζῶντες τὸν ἐκείνων θάνατον τὸν δὲ ἐκείνων βίον τεθνεῶτες.

[2] Though it has been ingeniously suggested by W. J. Verdenius that one saying implies that θυμός, anger or emotion, entails a fiery expenditure or *decrease* of the soul-fire (compare 'flashing eyes', 'breathing fire', etc. in

---

241 *But when the earth hid this race, they are noble daimons through the counsels of great Zeus, guardians on earth of mortal man.*

242 *Immortal mortals, mortal immortals* [or *mortal immortals, immortal mortals;* or *immortals are mortal, mortals are immortal;* or *immortals are mortals, mortals are immortals*, etc.], *living their death and dying their life.*

our own idiom): **243** Fr. 85, Plutarch *Coriol.* 22 θυμῷ μάχεσθαι χαλεπόν· ὃ γὰρ ἂν θέλῃ ψυχῆς ὠνεῖται. It is difficult to control anger because the soul-fire (which presumably does the controlling) has been diminished *by* anger. This is probably correct: but in virtuous anger or emotion (as in the heroic conception of battle) this loss might be more than made up by an increase of fire.

[3] Fr. 98 describes souls as 'using smell in Hades': this, too, suggests that some souls, at least, exist after the death of the body. 'Hades' should not be taken too literally. The point of this cryptic saying is perhaps that those souls which survive death are surrounded by dry matter (in other words, fire); for it was a common view that the sense of smell operates on objects drier than the smelling organ (*de carnibus* 16; Aristotle *de sensu* 5, 444a22). It is possible, however, that the fragment is quite naïve in implication: simply that soul is (according to one popular view) breath, that smell is inhaled with the breath, and therefore that smell is the sense used by the soul when the other organs have perished with the body. If this is so the saying could be ironic, or an attack on the idea of the breath-soul.

(13) *The uses of conventional religion are foolish and illogical, although on occasion they accidentally point to the truth*

244 Fr. 5, Aristocritus *Theosophia* 68 καθαίρονται δ' ἄλλως ⟨αἷμα⟩ αἵματι μιαινόμενοι οἷον εἴ τις εἰς πηλὸν ἐμβὰς πηλῷ ἀπονίζοιτο. μαίνεσθαι δ' ἂν δοκοίη, εἴ τις αὐτὸν ἀνθρώπων ἐπιφράσαιτο οὕτω ποιέοντα. καὶ τοῖς ἀγάλμασι δὲ τουτέοισιν εὔχονται, ὁκοῖον εἴ τις δόμοισι λεσχηνεύοιτο, οὔ τι γινώσκων θεοὺς οὐδ' ἥρωας οἵτινές εἰσι. [⟨αἷμα⟩ D. S. Robertson.]

245 Fr. 14, Clement *Protrepticus* 22 τὰ νομιζόμενα κατ' ἀνθρώπους μυστήρια ἀνιερωστὶ μυεῦνται.

246 Fr. 15, Clement *Protrepticus* 34 εἰ μὴ γὰρ Διονύσῳ πομπὴν ἐποιοῦντο καὶ ὕμνεον ᾆσμα αἰδοίοισιν, ἀναιδέστατα εἴργαστ' ἄν· ὡυτὸς δὲ Ἀίδης καὶ Διόνυσος, ὁτέῳ μαίνονται καὶ ληναΐζουσιν.

247 Fr. 93, Plutarch *de Pyth. or.* 21, 404 E ὁ ἄναξ οὗ τὸ μαντεῖόν ἐστι τὸ ἐν Δελφοῖς οὔτε λέγει οὔτε κρύπτει ἀλλὰ σημαίνει.

---

243 *It is hard to fight with anger; for what it wants it buys at the price of soul.*

244 *They vainly purify themselves of blood-guilt by defiling themselves with blood, as though one who had stepped into mud were to wash with mud; he would seem to be mad, if any of men noticed him doing this. Further, they pray to these statues, as if one were to carry on a conversation with houses, not recognizing the true nature of gods or demi-gods.*

245 *The secret rites practised among men are celebrated in an unholy manner.*

246 *For if it were not to Dionysus that they made the procession and sung the hymn to the shameful parts, the deed would be most shameless; but Hades and Dionysus, for whom they rave and celebrate Lenaean rites, are the same.*

247 *The lord whose oracle is in Delphi neither speaks out nor conceals, but gives a sign.*

Heraclitus followed Xenophanes in ridiculing the anthropomorphism and idolatry of the contemporary Olympian religion. Yet the last words of **244** (and also, e.g., **207** and **239**) show that he did not reject the idea of divinity altogether, or even some conventional descriptions of it. **245** implies that mysteries would not be utterly worthless if they were correctly celebrated. **246** suggests how this is so: such rituals can possess (and sometimes accidentally do possess) a positive value, because they guide men indirectly to the apprehension of the Logos. The precise grounds on which Hades and Dionysus are here identified are not known, but presumably the former represents death, the latter exuberant life; and it is the implied identification of these especially significant opposites (cf. **205**, **242**) that prevents the cult from being utterly shameful. It may be observed that the participants themselves could hardly be expected to see the significance of what they do, at least before Heraclitus revealed it—or rather hinted at it: the method adopted by Apollo in his Delphic pronouncements is praised in **247**, because a *sign* may accord better than a misleadingly explicit *statement* with the nature of the underlying truth, that of the Logos (cf. **210**–**212**). Probably Heraclitus intended by this kind of parallel to justify his own oracular and obscure style.[1]

[1] Cf. **248** Fr. 92, Plutarch *de Pyth. or.* 6, 397 A Σίβυλλα δὲ μαινομένῳ στόματι καθ' Ἡράκλειτον ἀγέλαστα καὶ ἀκαλλώπιστα καὶ ἀμύριστα φθεγγομένη χιλίων ἐτῶν ἐξικνεῖται τῇ φωνῇ διὰ τὸν θεόν. It is impossible to determine precisely how much of this is a *verbatim* quotation; H. Fränkel, for example, thinks that only down to στόματι is. I would conjecture that down to φθεγγομένη (with the possible exception of καὶ ἀκαλλώπιστα καὶ ἀμύριστα) is by Heraclitus, the rest is a very loose paraphrase by Plutarch. The saying looks like a justification of the unadorned oracular method of exegesis; but precise interpretation is impossible. Heraclitus himself certainly combined the terseness of the gnomic style with the obscurity of the related oracular style; his underlying meaning was sometimes reinforced by word-plays (e.g. ξὺν νόῳ–ξυνῷ in **253**) and etymological periphrases. A similar use is seen in Aeschylus, whose choral style, especially in the *Oresteia*, has some affinities with Heraclitus.

(14) *Ethical and political advice; self-knowledge, common sense and moderation are ideals which for Heraclitus had a special grounding in his account of the world as a whole*

249 Fr. 101, Plutarch *adv. Colot.* 20, 1118 C ἐδιζησάμην ἐμεωυτόν.

---

248 *The Sibyl with raving mouth, according to Heraclitus, uttering things mirthless, unadorned and unperfumed, reaches over a thousand years with her voice through the god.*

249 *I searched out myself.*

250 Fr. 119, Stobaeus *Anth.* IV, 40, 23 ἦθος ἀνθρώπῳ δαίμων.

251 Fr. 43, Diogenes Laertius IX, 2 ὕβριν χρὴ σβεννύναι μᾶλλον ἢ πυρκαϊήν.

252 Fr. 44, Diogenes Laertius IX, 2 μάχεσθαι χρὴ τὸν δῆμον ὑπὲρ τοῦ νόμου ὅκωσπερ τείχεος.

253 Fr. 114, Stobaeus *Anth.* III, 1, 179 ξὺν νόῳ λέγοντας ἰσχυρίζεσθαι χρὴ τῷ ξυνῷ πάντων, ὅκωσπερ νόμῳ πόλις καὶ πολὺ ἰσχυροτέρως· τρέφονται γὰρ πάντες οἱ ἀνθρώπειοι νόμοι ὑπὸ ἑνὸς τοῦ θείου· κρατεῖ γὰρ τοσοῦτον ὁκόσον ἐθέλει καὶ ἐξαρκεῖ πᾶσι καὶ περιγίνεται.

Heraclitus' ethical advice is gnomic in form, and for the most part similar in general content to that of his predecessors and contemporaries; sometimes it is expressed more graphically and often more savagely.[1] It stresses the importance of moderation, which itself depends upon a correct assessment of one's capacities. But this kind of advice (with which one naturally compares the Delphic maxims 'Know thyself' and 'Nothing too much') has a deeper significance in Heraclitus because of its grounding (not explicitly stated but clearly implied in **197** etc.) in his physical theories, and because of his belief that only by understanding the central pattern of things can a man become wise and fully effective: see **197**, **199**, **230**, **237**. That is the real moral of Heraclitus' philosophy, in which ethics is for the first time formally interwoven with physics.

[1] Heraclitus was undoubtedly of a strongly critical temperament, and his abuse can hardly have made him popular with his unfortunate fellow-citizens: cf. e.g. **254** Fr. 29, Clement *Strom.* V, 59, 5 αἱρεῦνται γὰρ ἓν ἀντὶ ἁπάντων οἱ ἄριστοι, κλέος ἀέναον θνητῶν· οἱ δὲ πολλοὶ κεκόρηνται ὅκωσπερ κτήνεα. His political ideas seem to have been anti-democratic, though perhaps from empirical rather than ideological motives: 'One man is as ten thousand for me, if he is best', he said (fr. 49), and abused the

---

250 *Man's character is his daimon.*

251 *Insolence is more to be extinguished than a conflagration.*

252 *The people must fight on behalf of the law as though for the city wall.*

253 *Those who speak with sense must rely on what is common to all, as a city must rely on its law, and with much greater reliance. For all the laws of men are nourished by one law, the divine law; for it has as much power as it wishes and is sufficient for all and is still left over.*

254 *The best choose one thing in place of all else, 'everlasting' glory among mortals; but the majority are glutted like cattle.*

Ephesians for exiling his friend Hermodorus on the ground of his exceptional ability (fr. 121). Himself of noble birth, he refused his traditional privileges (**194**).

Thus 'searching out oneself' in **249** leads, it may be inferred, to the discovery that the soul ranges outside oneself (see **235**, **237**). **250** is a denial of the view, common in Homer, that the individual often cannot be held responsible for what he does. δαίμων here means simply a man's personal destiny; this is determined by his own character, over which he has some control, and not by external and often capricious powers acting perhaps through a 'genius' allotted to each individual by chance or Fate. Helen blamed Aphrodite for her own weakness; but for Heraclitus (as indeed for Solon, who had already reacted against the moral helplessness of the heroic mentality) there was a real point in intelligent and prudent behaviour. **251** has no special overtones: it shows how conventional the practical side of Heraclitus' ethics often was, and also that he did not always think of human behaviour in terms of the *fiery* nature of the soul (for ὕβρις should involve a moistening of the soul, not its conflagration). By contrast, the insistence on respect for law in **252**, though again expressed in conventional terms, takes on a far deeper significance, and is given a profound justification, in the light of **253** (which should be compared with **197**, **198** and **199**). Human laws are nourished by the divine universal law; they accord with the Logos, the formulaic constituent of the cosmos. 'Nourished' is mainly, but not completely, metaphorical: the contact between human laws and the Logos is indirect, though not without material basis, since good laws are the product of wise men with fiery souls (**233**) who thereby understood, as Heraclitus himself does, the proper relation of men with the world.

CONCLUSION

In spite of much obscurity and uncertainty of interpretation, it does appear that Heraclitus' thought possessed a comprehensive unity which (conceivably because of the lack of information about Anaximander and Pythagoras) seems completely new. Practically all aspects of the world are explained systematically, in relation to a central discovery—that natural changes of all kinds are regular and balanced, and that the cause of this balance is fire, the common constituent of things that was also termed their

Logos. Human behaviour, as much as changes in the external world, is governed by the same Logos: the soul is made of fire, part of which (like part of the whole world-order) is extinguished. Understanding of the Logos, of the true constitution of things, is necessary if our souls are not to be excessively moistened and rendered ineffective by private folly. Heraclitus' relation of the soul to the world was more credible than that of Pythagoras, since it was more rational; it pointed a direction which was not, on the whole, followed until the atomists and, later, Aristotle; in the intervals a new tendency, towards the rejection of Nature, flourished with the Eleatics, Socrates and Plato.

THE ITALIAN SCHOOLS

The second main stage in the history of Presocratic speculation consists of the two great Italian schools, the Pythagorean and the Eleatic. The original motive and character of Italian thought differ widely from those of the Milesians. Whereas the Milesians were impelled by innate intellectual curiosity and dissatisfaction with the old mythological accounts to attempt a rational explanation of physical phenomena, the impulse underlying Pythagoreanism seems to have been a religious or emotional one. Plato himself refers to Pythagoras (*Republic* 600 A–B, DK 14, 10) as 'presiding over a band of intimate disciples who loved him for the inspiration of his society and handed down a way of life which to this day distinguishes the Pythagoreans from the rest of the world'. Such a eulogy would be scarcely appropriate to the Milesians. Again, while the Milesians sought a purely naturalistic explanation of the world, and Heraclitus represents an intermediate stage, the Pythagoreans, this time in the words of Aristotle (*Metaphysics* A 8, 989 b 29, DK 58 B 22), 'employ stranger principles and elements than the physicists, the reason being that they took them from non-sensible things'. The Pythagorean cosmology is concerned, at the outset at any rate, more with the form or structure of the world than with its mere matter.

But, as Aristotle adds in the next breath, having chosen their apparently abstract principles, 'they still concern themselves wholly with nature; they generate the universe and watch what happens to its various parts and affections and activities; and they use up their first principles and causes on these things, as if they agreed with the other physicists that Being is just so much as is sensible and is embraced within what they call the universe. And yet, as I said, they maintain causes and first principles that are adequate to lead up to the higher kinds of reality—that are indeed better fitted to them than to discussions about nature.' These sentences state very clearly what is probably the most important of all facts about the Italian schools. While the Pythagoreans were only secondarily, and the Eleatics hardly at all, interested in the material aspect of the world, and while both groups therefore start from first principles which in these days would be called abstract, both groups of thinkers alike, thanks merely to the date at which they lived, were so subject to the universal preconception that 'Being is just so much as is sensible' that they end in a corporealism hardly less total, if much more difficult to understand, than that of the Milesians. Many modern scholars find this conclusion so repugnant that they read into the Italian philosophers' theories philosophical distinctions of which all the evidence, including sometimes the actual words of the philosopher in question, seems to show that they were unaware. In the opinion of the present writer, it is only on the supposition that the only form of existence recognized by the Presocratics was existence in space, and that consequently the distinction between the corporeal and the incorporeal had not yet been clearly and explicitly drawn, that it is possible to understand what the early Italian philosophers meant.

CHAPTER VII

PYTHAGORAS OF SAMOS

LIFE AND DATE

While the developments already described were taking place in Ionia, an independent movement, initiated by Pythagoras, was gaining strength in southern Italy. Of the life of Pythagoras himself, though there are several late and unreliable works on the subject, we can be said to know very little indeed. He passed his early life in the island of Samos,[1] flourishing, according to Apollodorus, in 532/1 B.C., during the reign of the tyrant Polycrates. He is said to have left Samos to escape from the tyranny[2] and to have settled at Croton in southern Italy, where he appears to have risen to a position of great authority.[3] Eventually, however, the Crotoniates rose in revolt against him and he withdrew to the neighbouring city of Metapontium, where he died.[4]

[1] Cf. **255** Herodotus IV, 95 (DK 14, 2) ὡς δὲ ἐγὼ πυνθάνομαι τῶν τὸν Ἑλλήσποντον οἰκεόντων Ἑλλήνων καὶ Πόντον, τὸν Σάλμοξιν τοῦτον ἐόντα ἄνθρωπον δουλεῦσαι ἐν Σάμῳ, δουλεῦσαι δὲ Πυθαγόρῃ τῷ Μνησάρχου... δοκέω δὲ πολλοῖσι ἔτεσι πρότερον τὸν Σάλμοξιν τοῦτον γενέσθαι Πυθαγόρεω.

[2] **256** Porphyrius *V.P.* 9 (DK 14, 8) γεγονότα δ' ἐτῶν τεσσαράκοντά φησιν ὁ Ἀριστόξενος καὶ ὁρῶντα τὴν τοῦ Πολυκράτους τυραννίδα συντονωτέραν οὖσαν...οὕτως δὴ τὴν εἰς Ἰταλίαν ἄπαρσιν ποιήσασθαι.

[3] **257** Diog. L. VIII, 3 ...ἀπῆρεν εἰς Κρότωνα τῆς Ἰταλίας, κἀκεῖ νόμους θεὶς τοῖς Ἰταλιώταις ἐδοξάσθη σὺν τοῖς μαθηταῖς, οἳ πρὸς τοὺς τριακοσίους ὄντες ᾠκονόμουν ἄριστα τὰ πολιτικά, ὥστε σχεδὸν ἀριστοκρατίαν εἶναι τὴν πολιτείαν.

[4] **258** Iamblichus *V.P.* 249 (DK 14, 16) ὁ μὲν οὖν Πυθαγόρας διὰ ταύτην τὴν αἰτίαν ἀπῆλθεν εἰς τὸ Μεταπόντιον κἀκεῖ λέγεται καταστρέψαι τὸν βίον. Cf. Diog. L. VIII, 15.

---

255 *According to my information from the Greeks who live beside the Hellespont and Pontus, this Salmoxis, a real man, was a slave in Samos to Pythagoras son of Mnesarchus ...but I believe that this Salmoxis lived many years before Pythagoras.*

256 *Aristoxenus says that at the age of forty, seeing that the tyranny of Polycrates had grown more intense,...he eventually emigrated to Italy.*

257 *...He emigrated to Croton in Italy and there, by legislating for the Italians, won renown together with his pupils. They numbered nearly 300, and they administered the affairs of state so well that the constitution was virtually an aristocracy.*

258 *For this reason Pythagoras departed to Metapontium, where he is said to have died.*

OBSCURITY OF THE TRADITION

Both Plato and Aristotle are remarkably chary of mentioning Pythagoras by name,[1] and neither tells us, in the extant works, anything of the slightest value about him. Moreover, from the way in which they speak of later Pythagorean doctrine,[2] it would appear that they are both alike sceptical about the historical origins of Pythagoreanism. Probably the name of Pythagoras was already, as it certainly was later, enveloped in a mist of legend.[3]

[1] Plato mentions him once only, at *Rep.* 600 A–B, Aristotle in his extant works (but cf. note 2 below) only twice, at *Met.* A 5, 986 a 30 (where, however, the name of Pythagoras is probably only a later addition: cf. Ross, note *ad loc.*) and *Rhet.* B 23, 1398 b 14.

[2] Plato uses the word Πυθαγόρειος with equal reserve: it occurs only at *Rep.* 530 D. Elsewhere he cites what we know to be Pythagorean doctrine anonymously. Aristotle, though he is not so shy of the word Πυθαγόρειος, frequently prefers to describe the Pythagoreans as either οἱ Ἰταλικοί, οἱ περὶ Ἰταλίαν or (as at *Met.* 985 b 23, 989 b 29 etc.) οἱ καλούμενοι Πυθαγόρειοι. Aristotle, however, was sufficiently interested in Pythagoreanism to write a treatise, which is unfortunately lost, entitled Περὶ τῶν Πυθαγορείων.

[3] Certainly the surviving fragments of Aristotle's lost work on the Pythagoreans already incorporate several miraculous tales; cf. also **259** Apollonius *Hist. Mir.* 6 (DK 14, 7) Πυθαγόρας Μνησάρχου υἱὸς τὸ μὲν πρῶτον διεπονεῖτο περὶ τὰ μαθήματα καὶ τοὺς ἀριθμούς, ὕστερον δέ ποτε καὶ τῆς Φερεκύδου τερατοποιΐας οὐκ ἀπέστη. This is probably not a quotation from Aristotle (=fr. 191 Rose), as Heidel showed (*AJP* 61 (1940) 8f.); but it may be based on Aristotle. For Pherecydes cf. pp. 50 ff.

EARLY EVIDENCE ABOUT PYTHAGORAS

260 Heraclitus fr. 40, Diogenes Laertius IX, 1 πολυμαθίη νόον ἔχειν οὐ διδάσκει· Ἡσίοδον γὰρ ἂν ἐδίδαξε καὶ Πυθαγόρην αὖτίς τε Ξενοφάνεά τε καὶ Ἑκαταῖον.

261 Heraclitus fr. 129, Diogenes Laertius VIII, 6 Πυθαγόρης Μνησάρχου ἱστορίην ἤσκησεν ἀνθρώπων μάλιστα πάντων καὶ

---

259 *Pythagoras son of Mnesarchus at first worked strenuously at mathematics and numbers, but later could not resist the miracle-mongering of Pherecydes.*

260 *The learning of many things does not teach intelligence; if so it would have taught Hesiod and Pythagoras, and again Xenophanes and Hecataeus.*

261 *Pythagoras, son of Mnesarchus, practised scientific enquiry beyond all other men*

ἐκλεξάμενος ταύτας τὰς συγγραφὰς (*sc.* e.g. Hesiod?) ἐποιήσατο ἑαυτοῦ σοφίην, πολυμαθίην, κακοτεχνίην.[1]

262 Herodotus IV, 95 (DK 14, 2) ...τὸν Σάλμοξιν τοῦτον... Ἕλλησί τε ὁμιλήσαντα καὶ Ἑλλήνων οὐ τῷ ἀσθενεστάτῳ σοφιστῇ Πυθαγόρῃ....

263 Porphyrius *Vita Pythagorae* 30 (DK 31 B 129) (=Empedocles fr. 129) τούτοις καὶ Ἐμπεδοκλῆς μαρτυρεῖ λέγων περὶ αὐτοῦ (*sc.* Pythagoras)

ἦν δέ τις ἐν κείνοισιν ἀνὴρ περιώσια εἰδώς,
ὃς δὴ μήκιστον πραπίδων ἐκτήσατο πλοῦτον
παντοίων τε μάλιστα σοφῶν ⟨τ'⟩ ἐπιήρανος ἔργων·
ὁππότε γὰρ πάσῃσιν ὀρέξαιτο πραπίδεσσιν,
ῥεῖ' ὅ γε τῶν ὄντων πάντων λεύσσεσκεν ἕκαστον
καί τε δέκ' ἀνθρώπων καί τ' εἴκοσιν αἰώνεσσιν.

[1] The authenticity of this fragment has been long doubted, and it was regarded by Diels (though not by Kranz) as spurious; but since the case against it rests on a misunderstanding of the word ἐκλεξάμενος, which was taken to imply that Pythagoras wrote rather than read books, there is no good reason why it should not be substantially genuine.

Despite the silence of Plato and Aristotle these fifth-century passages, to which should be added also **268** and **269**, amply suffice to prove that Pythagoras was in fact a historical, not merely a legendary, figure. The difficulty lies in establishing anything more than his bare existence; but we shall find that on the basis of what little contemporary or early evidence survives it is possible to reconstruct at least the rough outlines of his system.

THE EARLY PYTHAGOREAN COMMUNITY

Little as we know of Pythagoras himself, of his immediate followers we know even less. There can be no doubt that Pythagoras founded in Croton a sort of religious fraternity or order;[1] but there

---

and, making a selection of these writings, claimed for his own a wisdom which was really dilettantism and malpractice.

262 ...*This Salmoxis...who had associated with the Greeks, and especially with Pythagoras, who was not the weakest sage among the Greeks....*

263 *Empedocles too bears witness to this, writing of him: 'And there was among them a man of rare knowledge, most skilled in all manner of wise works, a man who had won the utmost wealth of wisdom; for whensoever he strained with all his mind, he easily saw everything of all the things that are, in ten, yea, twenty lifetimes of men.'* (Empedocles trans. Burnet)

is no good evidence for the widely held view that it was modelled on Orphic cult-societies. It is true that Orphic and Pythagorean doctrines and practices are often compared, as they are first in the following passage:

264 Herodotus II, 81 οὐ μέντοι ἔς γε τὰ ἱρὰ ἐσφέρεται εἰρίνεα οὐδὲ συγκαταθάπτεταί σφι (*sc.* the Egyptians)· οὐ γὰρ ὅσιον. ὁμολογέουσι δὲ ταῦτα τοῖσι Ὀρφικοῖσι καλεομένοισι καὶ Βακχικοῖσι, ἐοῦσι δὲ Αἰγυπτίοισι, καὶ Πυθαγορείοισι· οὐδὲ γὰρ τούτων τῶν ὀργίων μετέχοντα ὅσιόν ἐστι ἐν εἰρινέοισι εἵμασι θαφθῆναι. ἔστι δὲ περὶ αὐτῶν ἱρὸς λόγος λεγόμενος. (Cf. also **270**.)

Even such a relatively early passage cannot, however, be safely taken as evidence for the existence of the Orphics (or of the Pythagoreans) before, say, the middle of the fifth century B.C., and it throws no light on the question which of the two communities, if either, was indebted to the other. Of Pythagoras' earliest adherents very few are even known to us by name—a state of affairs which seems to have come about from two main reasons. In the first place, there was apparently a rule of secrecy in the community,[2] by which the offence of divulging Pythagorean doctrine to the uninitiated is said by later authorities to have been severely punished—with the result that there were evidently no Pythagorean writings before, at earliest, the time of Philolaus[3] (i.e. the end of the fifth century B.C.). And second, even within the school itself, such was the respect paid to its founder that later discoveries made by members of the fraternity seem not to have been claimed as individual achievements but rather attributed indiscriminately to Pythagoras himself[4]—with the result that much that can hardly have been the work of Pythagoras, especially in the mathematical field, must remain anonymous. The most, therefore, that can be even attempted in the case of the Pythagoreans is to divide their doctrine into three sections, two of which cover the period from the founder to Parmenides, while the third is concerned with the generation of Pythagoreans which flourished, under the leadership of Philolaus, at the end of the fifth century.[5]

---

264 *But woollen articles are never taken into temples, nor are they buried with them; that is not lawful. They agree in this with the so-called Orphic and Bacchic practices, which are really Egyptian, and with the Pythagorean; for it is not lawful for one who partakes in these rites to be buried in woollen clothes. There is a sacred account given on this subject.*

[1] We hear much of the rules of the society in late and (except when quoting from a reputable source) unreliable authors (cf. e.g. Diog. L. VIII, 10; Iambl. *V.P.* 81), but such evidence should be treated with reserve. It will, however, become clear from what follows that the society must have been, in part at least, a religious fraternity.

[2] **265** Porphyrius *Vita Pythagorae* 19 (DK 14, 8*a*)· γενομένων δὲ τούτων μεγάλη περὶ αὐτοῦ (*sc.* Pythagoras) ηὐξήθη δόξα, καὶ πολλοὺς μὲν ἔλαβεν ἐξ αὐτῆς τῆς πόλεως (*sc.* Croton) ὁμιλητάς, οὐ μόνον ἄνδρας ἀλλὰ καὶ γυναῖκας, ὧν μιᾶς γε Θεανοῦς καὶ διεβοήθη τοὔνομα, πολλοὺς δ' ἀπὸ τῆς σύνεγγυς βαρβάρου χώρας βασιλεῖς τε καὶ δυνάστας. ἃ μὲν οὖν ἔλεγε τοῖς συνοῦσιν, οὐδὲ εἷς ἔχει φράσαι βεβαίως· καὶ γὰρ οὐδ' ἡ τυχοῦσα ἦν παρ' αὐτοῖς σιωπή. (See **271** for continuation.) This passage derives from Dicaearchus of Messene, a pupil of Aristotle. There seem to have been two motives for silence: first (see Iambl. *V.P.* 94), to insure that initiates could 'hold their peace' (ἐχεμυθεῖν); and second (see Diog. L. VIII, 15), to discourage 'the utterance of all things to all men'. Diogenes is here quoting Aristoxenus of Tarentum, another pupil of Aristotle, of whose book on Pythagoreanism relatively substantial fragments are preserved by later writers, especially Iamblichus.

[3] **266** Iambl. *V.P.* 199 (DK 14, 17) θαυμάζεται δὲ καὶ ἡ τῆς φυλακῆς ἀκρίβεια· ἐν γὰρ τοσαύταις γενεαῖς ἐτῶν οὐδεὶς οὐδενὶ φαίνεται τῶν Πυθαγορείων ὑπομνημάτων περιτετευχὼς πρὸ τῆς Φιλολάου ἡλικίας, ἀλλ' οὗτος πρῶτος ἐξήνεγκε τὰ θρυλούμενα ταῦτα τρία βιβλία, ἃ λέγεται Δίων ὁ Συρακούσιος ἑκατὸν μνῶν πρίασθαι Πλάτωνος κελεύσαντος.... (For the story of Plato's plagiarism, see p. 308.) Cf. **267** Plutarch *Alex. fort.* I, 4, 328: οὐδὲ Πυθαγόρας ἔγραψεν οὐδὲν οὐδὲ Σωκράτης οὐδὲ 'Αρκεσίλαος οὐδὲ Καρνεάδης.

[4] Hence arose, presumably, the favourite Pythagorean expression αὐτὸς ἔφα, 'he himself said so'; see Diog. L. VIII, 46.

[5] Iambl. *V.P.* 267 (DK 58 A) gives us, it is true, a long list of the names of Pythagoreans, some few of whom are probably early; but the failure to distinguish between different generations of the school, illustrated by the inclusion in the same list of, for instance, Alcmaeon (see p. 232) and Plato's contemporary, Archytas, renders it almost worthless.

---

265 *After this his fame grew great, and he won many followers from the city itself (not only men but women also, one of whom, Theano, became very well known too) and many princes and chieftains from the barbarian territory around. What he said to his associates, nobody can say for certain; for silence with them was of no ordinary kind.*

266 *The strictness of their secrecy is astonishing; for in so many generations evidently nobody ever encountered any Pythagorean notes before the time of Philolaus; he first published those three notorious books, which Dion of Syracuse is said to have bought, at Plato's request, for 100 minae....*

267 *Pythagoras wrote nothing, nor did Socrates nor Arcesilaus nor Carneades.*

THE MYSTICAL SIDE OF PYTHAGORAS' TEACHING

(1) *Transmigration of souls*

268 Diogenes Laertius VIII, 36 (= Xenophanes fr. 7) περὶ δὲ τοῦ ἄλλοτ' ἄλλον γεγενῆσθαι Ξενοφάνης ἐν ἐλεγείᾳ προσμαρτυρεῖ, ἧς ἀρχή,

νῦν αὖτ' ἄλλον ἔπειμι λόγον, δείξω δὲ κέλευθον.

ὃ δὲ περὶ αὐτοῦ (*sc.* Pythagoras) φησιν οὕτως ἔχει·

καί ποτέ μιν στυφελιζομένου σκύλακος παριόντα
φασὶν ἐποικτῖραι καὶ τόδε φάσθαι ἔπος·
Παῦσαι μηδὲ ῥάπιζ', ἐπεὶ ἦ φίλου ἀνέρος ἐστὶν
ψυχή, τὴν ἔγνων φθεγξαμένης ἀΐων.

269 Diogenes Laertius I, 120 (= Ion fr. 4) Ἴων δ' ὁ Χῖός φησι περὶ αὐτοῦ (*sc.* Pherecydes)·

ὣς ὁ μὲν ἠνορέῃ τε κεκασμένος ἠδὲ καὶ αἰδοῖ
καὶ φθίμενος ψυχῇ τερπνὸν ἔχει βίοτον,
εἴπερ Πυθαγόρης ἐτύμως ὁ σοφὸς περὶ πάντων
ἀνθρώπων γνώμας εἶδε καὶ ἐξέμαθεν... (= **46**).

270 Herodotus II, 123 πρῶτοι δὲ καὶ τόνδε τὸν λόγον Αἰγύπτιοί εἰσιν οἱ εἰπόντες ὡς ἀνθρώπου ψυχὴ ἀθάνατός ἐστι, τοῦ σώματος δὲ καταφθίνοντος ἐς ἄλλο ζῷον αἰεὶ γινόμενον ἐσδύεται, ἐπεὰν δὲ πάντα περιέλθῃ τὰ χερσαῖα καὶ τὰ θαλάσσια καὶ τὰ πετεινὰ αὖτις ἐς ἀνθρώπου σῶμα γινόμενον ἐσδύνειν, τὴν περιήλυσιν δὲ αὐτῇ γίνεσθαι ἐν τρισχιλίοισι ἔτεσι. τούτῳ τῷ λόγῳ εἰσὶ οἳ Ἑλλήνων ἐχρήσαντο, οἱ μὲν πρότερον οἱ δὲ ὕστερον, ὡς ἰδίῳ ἑωυτῶν ἐόντι· τῶν ἐγὼ εἰδὼς τὰ οὐνόματα οὐ γράφω.

---

268 *On the subject of reincarnation Xenophanes bears witness in an elegy which begins: 'Now I will turn to another tale and show the way.' What he says about Pythagoras runs thus: 'Once they say that he was passing by when a puppy was being whipped, and he took pity and said: "Stop, do not beat it; for it is the soul of a friend that I recognized when I heard it giving tongue."'*

269 *Ion of Chios says about him (Pherecydes): 'Thus did he excel in manhood and honour, and now that he is dead he has a delightful existence for his soul—if indeed Pythagoras the wise learned and knew true opinions above all men.'*

270 *Moreover, the Egyptians are the first to have maintained the doctrine that the soul of man is immortal, and that, when the body perishes, it enters into another animal that is being born at the time, and when it has been the complete round of the creatures of the dry land and of the sea and of the air it enters again into the body of a man at birth; and its cycle is completed in 3000 years. There are some Greeks who have adopted this doctrine, some in former times, and some in later, as if it were their own invention; their names I know but refrain from writing down.*

Herodotus' refusal to mention names in **270** has been taken to indicate that he is speaking not of Pythagoras himself but of contemporaries of his own; Stein suggested Empedocles, but it seems more plausible to suppose that it was people in Athens whom Herodotus preferred not to name. It is, however, likely that the phrase οἱ μὲν πρότερον, 'some in former times', was intended to embrace both Pythagoras and certain others who were already known as Orphics (cf. **264**). That Pythagoras himself did indeed believe in the transmigration of souls is anyhow pretty conclusively proved by **268**. He is even said by Diogenes Laertius (VIII, 4–5, DK 14, 8) to have claimed to remember his own four previous incarnations.

(2) *Kinship of all living things*

The fragment of Xenophanes (**268**) shows that souls could be reincarnated in the form of other living things than man, and this in turn suggests the kinship of all living things.

265, where Porphyry is drawing on Aristotle's follower Dicaearchus, continues as follows:

271 Porphyrius, *Vita Pythagorae* 19 (DK 14, 8*a*) μάλιστα μέντοι γνώριμα παρὰ πᾶσιν ἐγένετο πρῶτον μὲν ὡς ἀθάνατον εἶναί φησι (*sc.* Pythagoras) τὴν ψυχήν, εἶτα μεταβάλλουσαν εἰς ἄλλα γένη ζῴων, πρὸς δὲ τούτοις ὅτι κατὰ περιόδους τινὰς τὰ γενόμενά ποτε πάλιν γίνεται, νέον δ' οὐδὲν ἁπλῶς ἐστι,[1] καὶ ὅτι πάντα τὰ γινόμενα ἔμψυχα ὁμογενῆ δεῖ νομίζειν. φαίνεται γὰρ εἰς τὴν Ἑλλάδα τὰ δόγματα πρῶτος κομίσαι ταῦτα Πυθαγόρας.

[1] It was presumably in connexion with the cycle of reincarnation that the Pythagoreans held the remaining doctrine here attributed to them, that of the periodic recurrence of events. The most reliable statement of this belief is in the following fragment of Eudemus: **272** Eudemus *ap.* Simplic. *Phys.* 732, 30 (DK 58 B 34) εἰ δέ τις πιστεύσειε τοῖς Πυθαγορείοις, ὥστε πάλιν τὰ αὐτὰ ἀριθμῷ, κἀγὼ μυθολογήσω τὸ ῥαβδίον ἔχων ὑμῖν καθημένοις οὕτω, καὶ τὰ ἄλλα πάντα ὁμοίως ἕξει, καὶ τὸν χρόνον εὔλογόν ἐστι τὸν αὐτὸν

---

271 *None the less the following became universally known: first, that he maintains that the soul is immortal; next, that it changes into other kinds of living things; also that events recur in certain cycles, and that nothing is ever absolutely new; and finally, that all living things should be regarded as akin. Pythagoras seems to have been the first to bring these beliefs into Greece.*

272 *If one were to believe the Pythagoreans, with the result that the same individual things will recur, then I shall be talking to you again sitting as you are now, with this pointer in my hand, and everything else will be just as it is now, and it is reasonable to suppose that the time then is the same as now.*

εἶναι. A passage in the *Theologumena Arithmeticae* (p. 52, 8 de Falco; DK 14, 8) tells us that certain later Pythagoreans, working on the basis of the intervals between Pythagoras' own earlier incarnations, believed that the human soul was reincarnated every 216 years—the precise number 216 being characteristically chosen as the cube of 6. Though such embellishments of the doctrine are doubtless late, it is not impossible that Pythagoras himself did indeed hold the belief, later adopted by the Stoics, in the periodic cycle; but it is at least as likely that the later Pythagoreans borrowed it from Empedocles (see pp. 326f.).

Unfortunately, despite the definite suggestion in the last sentence that Pythagoras had learnt these doctrines abroad, the question of their origin is hopelessly shrouded in legend. He is said by different late writers to have visited, and to have learnt from, peoples as various as the Chaldaeans, the Indian Brahmins, the Jews and even the Druids and the Celts; but all that such traditions tell us is that certain similarities were later detected between the teaching of Pythagoras and the beliefs held in countries other than Greece. Even Herodotus' suggestion in **270** that the doctrine of transmigration came from Egypt is demonstrably false—the Egyptians never held such a doctrine; and none of the other guesses about its origin are as well attested as that.

Nor are the details of the two closely related doctrines, the transmigration of souls and the kinship of all living things, at all easy to fill in. Empedocles' version, as his fr. 117 (**476**) proves, included at least some plants among living things, and presumably for that reason involved abstention from laurel leaves (fr. 140) and beans (fr. 141). Since, as we shall see in the next section, similar rules of abstinence are attributed to Pythagoras, it may well be that he too thought it was possible to be reincarnated as a plant; but such relatively reliable and explicit evidence as exists, most of which has already been cited, proves only that a human soul can sink as low in the scale of living things as a dog (**268**). It is possible, but no more than that, that in a world which he regarded as dualistic (see pp. 240ff.) Pythagoras believed that ψυχή, 'life', was somehow a unity, a single mass, a part of which was scattered in an impure form throughout the world, while another part, into which the individual soul would be reabsorbed after its final incarnation, retained its purity. Such a doctrine, however, even if it was held, seems to have had little effect on the cosmological side of Pythagoreanism (see pp. 250ff.), in which the place of the immortal soul is by no means clear.

(3) *Rules of abstinence and other prohibitions*

Arising in part from his belief in the kinship of all living things, but with a clear admixture of other motives and influences, various forms of abstinence are attributed by later writers to Pythagoras. Two typical passages, chosen from many others like them, are:

273 Porphyrius *Vita Pythagorae* 7 (DK 14, 9) ...μὴ μόνον τῶν ἐμψύχων ἀπέχεσθαι, ἀλλὰ καὶ μαγείροις καὶ θηράτορσι μηδέποτε πλησιάζειν.

274 Diogenes Laertius VIII, 19 παντὸς δὲ μᾶλλον ἀπηγόρευε μήτ' ἐρυθῖνον ἐσθίειν μήτε μελάνουρον· καρδίας τ' ἀπέχεσθαι καὶ κυάμων· Ἀριστοτέλης δέ φησι καὶ μήτρας καὶ τρίγλης ἐνίοτε... (20)...θυσίαις τε ἐχρῆτο ἀψύχοις· οἱ δέ φασιν ὅτι ἀλέκτορσι μόνον καὶ ἐρίφοις γαλαθηνοῖς καὶ τοῖς λεγομένοις ἁπαλίαις, ἥκιστα δὲ ἀρνάσιν.

It would appear from **273** that the primary motive (but not, as some of the instances in **274** show, the only one) for the Pythagorean rules and prohibitions was the belief in the kinship of all living things: butchers and huntsmen are presumably alike defiled by the murder of their own kin. Unfortunately, as **274** again serves to show, there is great inconsistency between the various authorities about the details of the Pythagorean rules of abstinence.[1] The fuller accounts are clearly unreliable, and perhaps all that can be safely concluded from them is that certain rules of abstinence arising from the belief in kinship were an early feature of the Pythagorean way of life.

[1] The conflicting nature of the evidence is in part due to Aristoxenus, who, being a friend of the Pythagoreans of his day and anxious to justify their neglect of the religious side of Pythagoras' teaching, was intent on eliminating, or at least rationalizing, all such rules. But that some at least of these rules are of a certain age is proved by Herodotus' mention in **264** of the ban on burying the dead in woollen shrouds.

---

273 *...not only to abstain from living things, but also never to approach butchers and huntsmen.*

274 *Above all else he forbade the eating of red mullet and black-tail; and he enjoined abstinence from the heart and from beans; also, according to Aristotle, on certain occasions, from the womb and from mullet....He sacrificed only inanimate things; but others say that he used only cocks and sucking kids and piglings, as they are called, and never lambs.*

Besides the rules that can be explained in this way there are also, however, in the various lists handed down to us, others of at least four different types. A few, such as 'be not possessed of irrepressible mirth' or 'disbelieve nothing strange about the gods or about religious beliefs', would seem to be nothing more than common ethical or religious reflexions. A larger group, some of which have already appeared in **274**, are probably descended from primitive folk-taboo. Others again, such as 'sacrifice and worship without shoes on' or 'cut not your finger-nails at a sacrifice', clearly concern ritual purity. And finally some, such as 'when you rise from bed, roll the bed-clothes together and smoothe out the place where you lay', seem to owe their origin to sympathetic magic.[1]

[1] The list from which these examples are taken is perhaps of sufficient interest to deserve extensive quotation: **275** Iamblichus *Protr.* 21 (DK 58 c 6) ἔστω δὲ τὰ φρασθησόμενα Σύμβολα ταῦτα· α̅. εἰς ἱερὸν ἀπιὼν προσκυνῆσαι, μηδὲν ἄλλο μεταξὺ βιωτικὸν μήτε λέγε μήτε πρᾶττε. β̅. ὁδοῦ πάρεργον οὔτε εἰσιτέον εἰς ἱερὸν οὔτε προσκυνητέον τὸ παράπαν, οὐδ' εἰ πρὸς ταῖς θύραις αὐταῖς παριὼν γένοιο. γ̅. ἀνυπόδητος θῦε καὶ προσκύνει. δ̅. τὰς λεωφόρους ὁδοὺς ἐκκλίνων διὰ τῶν ἀτραπῶν βάδιζε.... ς̅. γλώσσης πρὸ τῶν ἄλλων κράτει θεοῖς ἑπόμενος....η̅. πῦρ μαχαίρῃ μὴ σκάλευε....ι̅. ἀνδρὶ ἐπανατιθεμένῳ μὲν φορτίον συνέπαιρε, μὴ συγκαθαίρει δὲ ἀποτιθεμένῳ. ι̅α̅. εἰς μὲν ὑπόδησιν τὸν δεξιὸν πόδα προπάρεχε, εἰς δὲ ποδόνιπτρον τὸν εὐώνυμον. ι̅β̅. περὶ Πυθαγορείων ἄνευ φωτὸς μὴ λάλει. ι̅γ̅. ζυγὸν μὴ ὑπέρβαινε. ι̅δ̅. ἀποδημῶν τῆς οἰκείας μὴ ἐπιστρέφου, Ἐρινύες γὰρ μετέρχονται....ι̅ζ̅. ἀλεκτρυόνα τρέφε μέν, μὴ θῦε δέ. Μηνὶ γὰρ καὶ Ἡλίῳ καθιέρωται. ι̅η̅. ἐπὶ χοίνικι μὴ καθέζου....κ̅α̅. χελιδόνα οἰκίᾳ μὴ δέχου.

---

275 *Let the rules to be pondered be these:*

1\. *When you are going out to a temple, worship first, and on your way neither say nor do anything else connected with your daily life.*

2\. *On a journey neither enter a temple nor worship at all, not even if you are passing the very doors.*

3\. *Sacrifice and worship without shoes on.*

4\. *Turn aside from highways and walk by footpaths....*

6\. *Follow the gods and restrain your tongue above all else....*

8\. *Stir not the fire with iron....*

10\. *Help a man who is loading freight, but not one who is unloading.*

11\. *Putting on your shoes, start with the right foot; washing your feet, with the left.*

12\. *Speak not of Pythagorean matters without light.*

13\. *Never step over a cross-bar.*

14\. *When you are out from home, look not back, for the Furies come after you....*

17\. *Rear a cock, but do not sacrifice it; for it is dedicated to Moon and Sun.*

18\. *Do not sit on a quart measure....*

21\. *Let not a swallow nest under your roof.*

κβ̄. δακτύλιον μὴ φόρει....κδ̄. παρὰ λύχνον μὴ ἐσοπτρίζου. κε̄. περὶ θεῶν μηθὲν θαυμαστὸν ἀπίστει μηδὲ περὶ θείων δογμάτων. κς̄. ἀσχέτῳ γέλωτι μὴ ἔχεσθαι. κζ̄. παρὰ θυσίᾳ μὴ ὀνυχίζου....κθ̄. στρωμάτων ἀναστὰς συνέλισσε αὐτὰ καὶ τὸν τόπον συνστόρνυε. λ̄. καρδίαν μὴ τρῶγε....λβ̄. ἀποκαρμάτων σῶν καὶ ἀπονυχισμάτων κατάπτυε....λδ̄. χύτρας ἴχνος ἀπὸ σποδοῦ ἀφάνιζε....λζ̄. κυάμων ἀπέχου....λθ̄. ἐμψύχων ἀπέχου. For other such lists, and rationalizations of the various ἀκούσματα they contain, cf. Porph. *V.P.* 42 (DK58C6) and Diog. L. VIII, 17–18.

After the death of Pythagoras, his school apparently split into two sects, one of which, the so-called 'Acousmatics' or 'Pythagorists', preserved the mystical side of his teaching, while the other, the 'Mathematicians', concentrated on the scientific side.[1] There is no telling how many of the Pythagorean rules and prohibitions—ἀκούσματα or σύμβολα, as they were called—actually go back to the founder himself, but certainly many of them look like primitive survivals.

[1] Porphyry suggests that this division goes back to Pythagoras himself: **276** Porph. *V.P.* 37 διττὸν γὰρ ἦν αὐτοῦ τῆς διδασκαλίας τὸ σχῆμα· καὶ τῶν προσιόντων οἱ μὲν ἐκαλοῦντο μαθηματικοὶ οἱ δ' ἀκουσματικοί, καὶ μαθηματικοὶ μὲν οἱ τὸν περιττότερον καὶ πρὸς ἀκρίβειαν διαπεπονημένον τῆς ἐπιστήμης λόγον ἐκμεμαθηκότες, ἀκουσματικοὶ δ' οἱ μόνας τὰς κεφαλαιώδεις ὑποθήκας τῶν γραμμάτων ἄνευ ἀκριβεστέρας διηγήσεως ἀκηκοότες. But this is probably no more than a misguided attempt to account for the later cleavage.

PYTHAGORAS' CONCERN WITH SCIENCE

So far, of course, there is little to distinguish Pythagoreanism from a mere mystery religion: the only reliable traces, in the evidence so

---

22. *Do not wear a ring....*
24. *Do not look in a mirror beside a lamp.*
25. *Disbelieve nothing strange about the gods or about religious beliefs.*
26. *Be not possessed by irrepressible mirth.*
27. *Cut not your finger-nails at a sacrifice....*
29. *When you rise from bed roll the bed-clothes together and smoothe out the place where you lay.*
30. *Eat not the heart....*
32. *Spit upon the trimmings of your hair and finger-nails....*
34. *Leave not the mark of the pot in the ashes....*
37. *Abstain from beans....*
39. *Abstain from living things.*

276 *The form of his instruction was twofold: one group of his followers were called the Mathematicians, the other the Acousmatics. The Mathematicians were those who had learnt the more detailed and exactly elaborated version of his knowledge, the Acousmatics those who had heard only the summary headings of his writings, without the more exact exposition.*

far cited, of another side to Pythagoras' teaching are Heraclitus' references, in **260** and **261**, to his πολυμαθίη and ἱστορίη ('polymathy' and 'scientific enquiry'), and Herodotus' description of him in **262** as 'by no means the weakest sage among the Hellenes'. These passages alone, however, do suggest—what is evident also from the fact that in the fifth century the Pythagoreans were among the leading scientists—that Pythagoras was interested in science as well as in the fate of the soul. Clearly too religion and science were, to Pythagoras, not two separate departments between which there was no contact, but rather the two inseparable factors in a single way of life.[1] Unfortunately there is no reliable evidence whatever concerning the nature of Pythagoras' scientific teaching: any reconstruction must be conjectural, merely attributing to Pythagoras himself such of the later Pythagorean doctrines as could without anachronism have been held in the sixth century B.C. and may plausibly account for the subsequent spread and development of Pythagoreanism. The central notions, which held together the two strands that were later to fall apart, seem to have been those of θεωρία (contemplation),[2] κόσμος (an orderliness found in the arrangement of the universe)[3] and κάθαρσις (purification).[4] By contemplating the principle of order revealed in the universe—and especially in the regular movements of the heavenly bodies—and by assimilating himself to that orderliness, man himself was progressively purified until he eventually escaped from the cycle of birth and attained immortality.

[1] The widening of the basis of mathematics is suggested by **277** Proclus *in Eucl.* p. 65 Friedl. (DK 14, 6*a*) ἐπὶ δὲ τούτοις Πυθαγόρας τὴν περὶ αὐτὴν (*sc.* γεωμετρίαν) φιλοσοφίαν εἰς σχῆμα παιδείας ἐλευθέρου μετέστησεν ἄνωθεν τὰς ἀρχὰς αὐτῆς ἐπισκοπούμενος.... Several passages in Aristotle even suggest a close connexion in Pythagoreanism between mathematics and ethics.

[2] The supremacy of the contemplative life is illustrated by the parable of the Festival in **278** Diog. L. VIII, 8 καὶ τὸν βίον ἐοικέναι πανηγύρει· ὡς οὖν εἰς ταύτην οἱ μὲν ἀγωνιούμενοι, οἱ δὲ κατ' ἐμπορίαν, οἱ δέ γε βέλτιστοι ἔρχονται θεαταί, οὕτως ἐν τῷ βίῳ οἱ μὲν ἀνδραποδώδεις, ἔφη, φύονται δόξης καὶ πλεονεξίας θηραταί, οἱ δὲ φιλόσοφοι τῆς ἀληθείας.

---

277 *So Pythagoras turned geometrical philosophy into a form of liberal education by seeking its first principles in a higher realm of reality....*

278 *Life, he said, is like a festival; just as some come to the festival to compete, some to ply their trade, but the best people come as spectators, so in life the slavish men go hunting for fame or gain, the philosophers for the truth.*

[3] Pythagoras is said by Aetius, in a much debated passage (II, 1, 1; DK 14, 21), to have been the first to use the word κόσμος of the universe; but if the passage has any foundation in fact, it is most likely that Pythagoras used the word, not, as Aetius said, to mean ἡ τῶν ὅλων περιοχή, 'that which embraces all things', but with a special emphasis on the element of orderliness, or the arrangement: cf. p. 159 n. Pythagoras is also said by Diog. L. (I, 12), who is here quoting Heraclides, to have coined the word 'philosophy'; cf. Kirk, *Heraclitus, the Cosmic Fragments*, 395.

[4] The notion of κάθαρσις was linked especially with music: see **279** Cramer, *An. Par.* I, 172 ...οἱ Πυθαγορικοί, ὡς ἔφη Ἀριστόξενος, καθάρσει ἐχρῶντο τοῦ μὲν σώματος διὰ τῆς ἰατρικῆς, τῆς δὲ ψυχῆς διὰ τῆς μουσικῆς. Cf. Iambl. *V.P.* 110 and Porph. *V.P.* 30.

SCIENTIFIC ACHIEVEMENTS

The two most fundamental and universal of Pythagorean scientific doctrines are, first, the ultimate dualism between Limit and Unlimited, and second, the equation of things with numbers (see pp. 240–50). What is required, therefore, is a plausible explanation of how these two doctrines, by no means obviously interdependent, should have occurred to Pythagoras or his followers. There seems no reason to doubt the tradition that Pythagoras himself discovered—probably by measuring the appropriate lengths of string on a monochord—that the chief musical intervals are expressible in simple numerical ratios between the first four integers.[1] This single discovery would account naturally for all the most characteristic of Pythagorean doctrines. If the musical scale depends simply upon the imposition of definite proportions on the indefinite continuum of sound between high and low, might not the same principles, Limit and the Unlimited, underlie the whole universe? If numbers alone are sufficient to explain the 'consonances', might not everything else be likewise expressible as a number or a proportion? Moreover, since the first four integers contain the whole secret of the musical scale, their sum, the number 10 or the Dècad, might well 'seem to embrace', as Aristotle puts it, 'the whole nature of number' (see **289**) and so come to be regarded, as it certainly was, with veneration.[2] It is not surprising, therefore, that both mathematics and music should have played from the outset so vital a part in Pythagoreanism. Of the various mathematical discoveries attributed to Pythagoras it is not unlikely that

---

279 *The Pythagoreans, according to Aristoxenus, practised the purification of the body by medicine, that of the soul by music.*

some—notably, the theorem that still bears his name, and its corollary, the incommensurability of the diagonal and the side of a square[3]—are genuinely his. It is also a remote possibility, in view of his interest in the musical scale, that he himself invented the well-known doctrine of the 'Harmony of the Spheres' (see **330**). Some authorities maintained that he first discovered that the morning and the evening star are one and the same, while others attributed the discovery to Parmenides. There is, unfortunately, no means of assessing the relative strength of the two claims—though it might perhaps be thought that Pythagoras' interests would have inclined him more towards astronomy than would those of Parmenides. All such details, however, rest on no reliable evidence; all that can be said with confidence of the scientific achievements of Pythagoras himself is that they must have been sufficient to give the original impetus to the Pythagoreanism of the fifth century which Aristotle describes.

[1] Octave=2:1, fifth=3:2, fourth=4:3. An elaborate story that Pythagoras made his discovery by noticing that the hammers in a smithy happened to produce these intervals and therefore weighing the hammers is found in several late authors (e.g. Iambl. *V.P.* 115ff., Boethius *de mus.* 1, 10); but it is proved to be unreliable by the fact that Pythagoras' alleged experiments could not have yielded the results attributed to them.

[2] The number 10 was represented by ten dots or alphas arranged in an equilateral triangle so:

•

• •

• • •

• • • •

This diagram, which shows at a glance that 10=1+2+3+4, was known to the Pythagoreans as the Tetractys of the Decad, and by it they swore their most binding oaths. So **280** Aetius 1, 3, 8 (DK 58 B 15) εἶναι δὲ τὴν φύσιν τοῦ ἀριθμοῦ δέκα. μέχρι γὰρ τῶν δέκα πάντες Ἕλληνες, πάντες βάρβαροι ἀριθμοῦσιν, ἐφ' ἃ ἐλθόντες πάλιν ἀναποδοῦσιν ἐπὶ τὴν μονάδα. καὶ τῶν δέκα πάλιν, φησίν (*sc.* Pythagoras), ἡ δύναμίς ἐστιν ἐν τοῖς τέσσαρσι καὶ τῇ τετράδι. τὸ δὲ αἴτιον· εἴ τις ἀπὸ τῆς μονάδος [ἀναποδῶν] κατὰ πρόσθεσιν τιθείη τοὺς ἀριθμοὺς ἄχρι τῶν τεσσάρων προελθὼν ἐκπληρώσει τὸν ⟨τῶν⟩ δέκα ἀριθμόν· ἐὰν δὲ ὑπερβάλῃ τις τὸν τῆς τετράδος, καὶ τῶν δέκα ὑπερεκπεσεῖται· οἷον εἴ τις θείη ἓν καὶ δύο προσθείη καὶ τρία καὶ τούτοις τέσσαρα, τὸν

---

280 *Ten is the very nature of number. All Greeks and all barbarians alike count up to ten, and having reached ten revert again to the unit. And again, Pythagoras maintains, the power of the number ten lies in the number four, the tetrad. This is the reason: if one starts at the unit and adds the successive numbers up to four, one will make up the number ten; and if one exceeds the tetrad, one will exceed ten too. If, that is, one takes the unit, adds*

τῶν δέκα ἐκπληρώσει ἀριθμόν. ὥστε ὁ ἀριθμὸς κατὰ μὲν μονάδα ἐν τοῖς δέκα, κατὰ δὲ δύναμιν ἐν τοῖς τέσσαρσι. διὸ καὶ ἐπεφθέγγοντο οἱ Πυθαγόρειοι ὡς μεγίστου ὅρκου ὄντος τῆς τετράδος·

> οὐ μὰ τὸν ἁμετέρᾳ γενεᾷ παραδόντα τετρακτύν,
> παγὰν ἀενάου φύσεως ῥίζωμά τ' ἔχουσαν.

Cf. Theo Smyrnaeus 94, 6 Hiller; Sextus *adv. math.* VII, 94ff.

3 **281** Proclus *in Eucl.* p. 426 Friedl. (ἐν τοῖς ὀρθογωνίοις τριγώνοις τὸ ἀπὸ τῆς τὴν ὀρθὴν γωνίαν ὑποτεινούσης πλευρᾶς τετράγωνον ἴσον ἐστὶ τοῖς ἀπὸ τῶν τὴν ὀρθὴν γωνίαν περιεχουσῶν πλευρῶν τετραγώνοις)· †τῶν μὲν ἱστορεῖν τὰ ἀρχαῖα βουλομένων ἀκούοντας τὸ θεώρημα τοῦτο εἰς Πυθαγόραν ἀναπεμπόντων ἔστιν εὑρεῖν καὶ βουθυτεῖν λεγόντων αὐτὸν ἐπὶ τῇ εὑρέσει.†

According to one version of a very variable story Hippasus of Metapontium, an early Pythagorean, was expelled from the school, or even drowned at sea, for revealing to the uninitiated, in defiance of the rule of secrecy, the irrational or incommensurable (i.e. that some geometrical quantities cannot be expressed in terms of whole numbers). See Iambl. *V.P.* 247 (DK 18, 4).

---

two, then three and then four, one will make up the number ten. So that number by the unit resides in the number ten, but potentially in the number four. And so the Pythagoreans used to invoke the tetrad as their most binding oath: 'Nay, by him that gave to our generation the tetractys, which contains the fount and root of eternal nature.'

281 (*The square on the hypotenuse of a right-angled triangle is equal to the sum of the squares on the sides enclosing the right angle.*) The text of the next sentence is corrupt, but the sense is: *If we pay any attention to those who like to recount ancient history, we may find some of them referring this theorem to Pythagoras, and saying that he sacrificed an ox in honour of his discovery.*

CHAPTER VIII

ALCMAEON OF CROTON

DATE AND RELEVANCE

Of the generation of Pythagoreans contemporary with or immediately following Pythagoras very few are even known to us by name, and, with the possible exception of Hippasus (cf. p. 231 n. 3), nothing of importance is known about any of them. The only Italian thinker between Pythagoras and Parmenides of whose opinions there is sufficient evidence to justify his inclusion in this book is Alcmaeon of Croton, who flourished, probably, early in the fifth century B.C.[1]

282 Diogenes Laertius VIII, 83 (DK 24 A 1) Ἀλκμαίων Κροτωνιάτης. καὶ οὗτος Πυθαγόρου διήκουσε. καὶ τὰ πλεῖστά γε [τὰ] ἰατρικὰ λέγει, ὅμως δὲ καὶ φυσιολογεῖ ἐνίοτε λέγων· 'δύο τὰ πολλά ἐστι τῶν ἀνθρωπίνων'. δοκεῖ δὲ πρῶτος φυσικὸν λόγον συγγεγραφέναι.

This brief passage contains several important pieces of information. The statement that he 'heard Pythagoras' doubtless means, as it usually does, no more than that he was in some sort of contact with the Pythagorean school.[2] The following sentence, on the other hand, is certainly accurate; but, though Alcmaeon's interests were primarily medical and physiological,[3] his theories even in these specialized fields exercised a considerable influence on later philosophers. The alleged quotation, whether or not it preserves Alcmaeon's own words, certainly preserves one of the most important of his views, his dualism. And finally, though the suggestion that he was the first to do so is of doubtful value (cf., e.g., **45**, **98**), he does indeed seem to have written a book on natural science, of which a few possibly genuine fragments survive.[4]

[1] The evidence on which this dating relies is **283** Aristotle *Met.* A 5, 986 a 29 καὶ γὰρ ἐγένετο τὴν ἡλικίαν Ἀλκμαίων ἐπὶ γέροντι Πυθαγόρᾳ....

---

282 *Alcmaeon of Croton: another pupil of Pythagoras. For the most part his theories are medical, but sometimes he treats of natural philosophy too, maintaining that 'the majority of human affairs are in pairs'. He seems to have been the first to write an account of nature.*

283 Diels' text means: *Alcmaeon was a young man in Pythagoras' old age....*

The text, however, is obviously corrupt. While Diels inserts νέος before ἐπί, Ross regards the words ἐγένετο τὴν ἡλικίαν and ἐπὶ γέροντι Πυθαγόρᾳ, which are omitted by one ms. and ignored by Alexander, as a later addition (see his note *ad loc.*). It is true that Iamblichus *V.P.* 104 lists Alcmaeon among 'the contemporaries of Pythagoras, his young pupils in his old age'; but since the same list contains also the names of Philolaus, Archytas and Leucippus, it clearly has no value as evidence. All that can safely be said, therefore, is that there is no reason why this dating, whether it represents Aristotle's own opinion or that of an interpolator, should not be approximately correct.

[2] Aristotle mentions Alcmaeon by name on several occasions, but, though in **289** he guesses either that Alcmaeon borrowed from the Pythagoreans or they from him, he never suggests that Alcmaeon himself was a member of the school. Later writers are, as usual, less cautious.

[3] Alcmaeon's physiological research was directed chiefly towards determining the nature of sense-perception. His theories are summed up by Theophrastus in a passage of which the most important sentences are the following: **284** Theophr. *de sensu* 25f. (DK 24 A 5) τῶν δὲ μὴ τῷ ὁμοίῳ ποιούντων τὴν αἴσθησιν Ἀλκμαίων μὲν πρῶτον ἀφορίζει τὴν πρὸς τὰ ζῷα διαφοράν. ἄνθρωπον γάρ φησι τῶν ἄλλων διαφέρειν ὅτι μόνον ξυνίησι, τὰ δ' ἄλλα αἰσθάνεται μέν, οὐ ξυνίησι δέ, ὡς ἕτερον ὂν τὸ φρονεῖν καὶ αἰσθάνεσθαι, καὶ οὔ, καθάπερ Ἐμπεδοκλῆς, ταὐτόν· ἔπειτα περὶ ἑκάστης λέγει....ἁπάσας δὲ τὰς αἰσθήσεις συνηρτῆσθαί πως πρὸς τὸν ἐγκέφαλον· διὸ καὶ πηροῦσθαι κινουμένου καὶ μεταλλάττοντος τὴν χώραν· ἐπιλαμβάνειν γὰρ τοὺς πόρους, δι' ὧν αἱ αἰσθήσεις. The view that the brain is the seat of sensations was taken over from Alcmaeon in the Hippocratic treatise *de morbo sacro*, 14 and 17 (DK 24 A 11). The existence of the πόροι is said by Chalcidius (*in Tim.* ch. 237, DK 24 A 10) to have been proved by Alcmaeon's dissection of the eye.

[4] The book is said by Diog. L. (with only one brief sentence between **282** and this passage) to have begun as follows: **285** Diog. L. VIII, 83 Ἀλκμαίων Κροτωνιήτης τάδε ἔλεξε Πειρίθου υἱὸς Βροτίνῳ καὶ Λέοντι καὶ Βαθύλλῳ· περὶ τῶν ἀφανέων, περὶ τῶν θνητῶν σαφήνειαν μὲν θεοὶ ἔχοντι, ὡς δὲ ἀνθρώποις τεκμαίρεσθαι....The fact that Brotinus (or Brontinus, as other ancient sources call him) was evidently connected with Pythagoras by some marriage tie is one of the indications that Alcmaeon was in close contact with the Pythagorean school. Leon and Bathylaus (not Bathyllus) are to be found in the list of Pythagoreans in Iambl. *V.P.* 267 (DK 58 A).

---

284 *Of those who think perception is of unlike by unlike Alcmaeon first defined the difference between man and animals. For man, he says, differs from other animals in that 'he only understands, while the rest perceive but do not understand', thought and perception being different, not, as Empedocles maintains, the same. Thereafter he discusses each of the senses severally....Collectively he maintains that the senses are somehow connected with the brain; and so they are incapacitated when it moves or changes its position; for it stops the passages through which sensations come.*

285 *Alcmaeon of Croton, son of Peirithous, spoke these words to Brotinus and Leon and Bathyllus. Concerning things unseen and things mortal the gods see clearly, but so far as men may conjecture....*

ALCMAEON'S INFLUENCE ON HIS SUCCESSORS

(1) *His theory of health*

Alcmaeon, like the Pythagoreans, was a dualist; but whereas the Pythagoreans recognized certain particular pairs of opposites as ultimate (notably Limit and Unlimited, Odd and Even; see **289**, p. 238), Alcmaeon, presumably owing to his medical approach to cosmology, seems merely to have asserted that contrariety was fundamental without specifying any ultimate pair or pairs. His most influential doctrine, his theory of health, illustrates his dualism, and is summarized by Aetius as follows:

286 Aetius v, 30, 1 Ἀλκμαίων τῆς μὲν ὑγιείας εἶναι συνεκτικὴν τὴν 'ἰσονομίαν' τῶν δυνάμεων, ὑγροῦ, ξηροῦ, ψυχροῦ, θερμοῦ, πικροῦ, γλυκέος καὶ τῶν λοιπῶν, τὴν δ' ἐν αὐτοῖς 'μοναρχίαν' νόσου ποιητικήν· φθοροποιὸν γὰρ ἑκατέρου μοναρχίαν. καὶ νόσον συμπίπτειν ὡς μὲν ὑφ' οὗ ὑπερβολῇ θερμότητος ἢ ψυχρότητος, ὡς δὲ ἐξ οὗ διὰ πλῆθος τροφῆς ἢ ἔνδειαν, ὡς δ' ἐν οἷς ἢ ⟨περὶ Diels⟩ αἷμα ἢ μυελὸν ἢ ἐγκέφαλον. ἐγγίνεσθαι δὲ τούτοις ποτὲ κἀκ τῶν ἔξωθεν αἰτιῶν, ὑδάτων ποιῶν ἢ χώρας ἢ κόπων ἢ ἀνάγκης ἢ τῶν τούτοις παραπλησίων. τὴν δ' ὑγίειαν τὴν σύμμετρον τῶν ποιῶν κρᾶσιν.

This doctrine, though here restricted to the medical field, may perhaps have suggested the theory put forward by Simmias in Plato's *Phaedo* (85E–86D) that the soul is merely an 'attunement' of the physical opposites that compose the body; and since Plato is there probably citing a Pythagorean view, it seems quite likely that at this point at least Alcmaeon exercised an influence on the Pythagoreans (see pp. 261 f.).[1]

[1] Once again, despite the general similarity between Alcmaeon's views and those of the Pythagoreans, the ἰσονομία theory involves a significant difference of detail from the Pythagorean doctrine of ἁρμονίη. G. Vlastos

---

286 *Alcmaeon maintains that the bond of health is the 'equal balance' of the powers, moist and dry, cold and hot, bitter and sweet, and the rest, while the 'supremacy' of one of them is the cause of disease; for the supremacy of either is destructive. Illness comes about directly through excess of heat or cold, indirectly through surfeit or deficiency of nourishment; and its centre is either the blood or the marrow or the brain. It sometimes arises in these centres from external causes, moisture of some sort or environment or exhaustion or hardship or similar causes. Health on the other hand is the proportionate admixture of the qualities.*

(*Gnomon* 25 (1953) 33–4) writes: 'It is well known that the general norm of κρᾶσις in Greek cosmology and medicine was ἰσονομία (Alcmaeon B4) or ἰσομοιρία (περὶ ἀέρων 12), i.e. the 1/1 ratio....Over against this wide-spread view, the Pythagorean discovery of the formulae for musical harmony introduced an entirely new idea, for it depicted patterns of good κρᾶσις which did not conform to ἰσονομία but involved pairs of unequal (and, in each case, odd-even) numbers: 1/2, 2/3, 3/4.' See p. 230 n. 1.

(2) *The composition of the soul*

287 Aristotle *de anima* A2, 405a29 παραπλησίως δὲ τούτοις (*sc.* Thales, Diogenes of Apollonia and Heraclitus) καὶ Ἀλκμαίων ἔοικεν ὑπολαβεῖν περὶ ψυχῆς· φησὶ γὰρ αὐτὴν ἀθάνατον εἶναι διὰ τὸ ἐοικέναι τοῖς ἀθανάτοις· τοῦτο δ' ὑπάρχειν αὐτῇ ὡς ἀεὶ κινουμένῃ· κινεῖσθαι γὰρ καὶ τὰ θεῖα πάντα συνεχῶς ἀεί, σελήνην, ἥλιον, τοὺς ἀστέρας καὶ τὸν οὐρανὸν ὅλον.

288 [Aristotle] *Probl.* 17, 3, 916a33 τοὺς ἀνθρώπους φησὶν Ἀλκμαίων διὰ τοῦτο ἀπόλλυσθαι, ὅτι οὐ δύνανται τὴν ἀρχὴν τῷ τέλει προσάψαι.

These two passages, despite their apparent dissimilarity, have been thought to refer to the same doctrine. The heavenly bodies have the property of continuous motion in a circle, and the soul, too, according to **287**, is endowed with continuous motion; but whereas the movement of the heavenly bodies is circular, 'man', according to **288**, 'is unable to join the beginning to the end'—in other words the soul's motion cannot long remain circular—and so dies. This curious doctrine recalls fr. 103 of Heraclitus, 'on a circle beginning and end are the same'; but its details are obscure and there is no reliable evidence to enable us to reconstruct them. Here again, however, it seems possible that Alcmaeon exercised an influence on Plato, since the doctrine in the *Timaeus* of circles revolving in the soul seems to bear some relation to the theory of Alcmaeon and may perhaps have been borrowed directly from him.

---

287 *Alcmaeon also seems to have held much the same view about the soul as these others; for he says that it is immortal owing to its similarity to the immortal; and it has this quality because it is always in motion; for everything divine is in continual motion—the sun, the moon, the stars and the whole heavens.*

288 *Alcmaeon says that men die for this reason, that they cannot join the beginning to the end.*

CHAPTER IX

PRE-PARMENIDEAN PYTHAGOREANISM

THE PROBLEM OF DATING

In his numerous references to Pythagoreanism Aristotle very seldom either names individual Pythagoreans or distinguishes between different generations of the school. However much Pythagorean doctrine may have evolved during the fifth and early fourth centuries, Aristotle is content to summarize the main features of the system as a whole; and since there is no ancient authority of comparable weight with Aristotle, very various views have been taken of the development of the Pythagorean cosmology.[1] The most that we can hope to achieve is to divide the Pythagoreanism of the fifth century into two main periods, one before Parmenides, the other after Zeno; and since the primary means by which even so much may be achieved consists in considering which Pythagorean doctrines seem to be attacked by Parmenides and which look like a reply to either Parmenides or Zeno, any such reconstruction must of necessity be hazardously conjectural. None the less the attempt seems worth the making, for otherwise the only possible course is to follow Aristotle and group all the Pythagorean doctrines of more than a century of development into one indiscriminate amalgam.

[1] For three widely different reconstructions of 5th-century Pythagoreanism see (i) Burnet, *EGP*; (ii) F. M. Cornford, *CQ* XVI and XVII (1922 and 1923), and introductory chapters of *Plato and Parmenides*; (iii) J. E. Raven, *Pythagoreans and Eleatics*.

ARISTOTLE'S GENERAL SUMMARY

The longest and most helpful of Aristotle's summaries of Pythagoreanism, which must first be read and considered *in extenso*, is:

289 Aristotle *Metaphysics* A5, 985b23 ἐν δὲ τούτοις καὶ πρὸ τούτων (*sc.* Leucippus and Democritus) οἱ καλούμενοι Πυθαγόρειοι[1] τῶν μαθημάτων ἁψάμενοι πρῶτοι ταῦτα προήγαγον, καὶ

---

289 *Contemporaneously with these philosophers, and before them, the Pythagoreans, as they are called, devoted themselves to mathematics; they were the first to advance this study,*

ἐντραφέντες ἐν αὐτοῖς τὰς τούτων ἀρχὰς τῶν ὄντων ἀρχὰς ᾠήθησαν εἶναι πάντων. ἐπεὶ δὲ τούτων οἱ ἀριθμοὶ φύσει πρῶτοι, ἐν δὲ τοῖς ἀριθμοῖς ἐδόκουν θεωρεῖν ὁμοιώματα πολλὰ τοῖς οὖσι καὶ γιγνομένοις, μᾶλλον ἢ ἐν πυρὶ καὶ γῇ καὶ ὕδατι, ὅτι τὸ μὲν τοιονδὶ τῶν ἀριθμῶν πάθος δικαιοσύνη, τὸ δὲ τοιονδὶ ψυχὴ καὶ νοῦς, ἕτερον δὲ καιρὸς καὶ τῶν ἄλλων ὡς εἰπεῖν ἕκαστον ὁμοίως, ἔτι δὲ τῶν ἁρμονιῶν ἐν ἀριθμοῖς ὁρῶντες τὰ πάθη καὶ τοὺς λόγους, ἐπεὶ δὴ τὰ μὲν ἄλλα τοῖς ἀριθμοῖς ἐφαίνετο τὴν φύσιν ἀφωμοιῶσθαι πᾶσαν, οἱ δ' ἀριθμοὶ πάσης τῆς φύσεως πρῶτοι, τὰ τῶν ἀριθμῶν στοιχεῖα τῶν ὄντων στοιχεῖα πάντων ὑπέλαβον εἶναι, καὶ τὸν ὅλον οὐρανὸν ἁρμονίαν εἶναι καὶ ἀριθμόν· καὶ ὅσα εἶχον ὁμολογούμενα δεικνύναι ἔν τε τοῖς ἀριθμοῖς καὶ ταῖς ἁρμονίαις πρὸς τὰ τοῦ οὐρανοῦ πάθη καὶ μέρη καὶ πρὸς τὴν ὅλην διακόσμησιν, ταῦτα συνάγοντες ἐφήρμοττον. κἂν εἴ τί που διέλειπε, προσεγλίχοντο τοῦ συνειρομένην πᾶσαν αὐτοῖς εἶναι τὴν πραγματείαν. λέγω δ' οἷον, ἐπειδὴ τέλειον ἡ δεκὰς εἶναι δοκεῖ καὶ πᾶσαν περιειληφέναι τὴν τῶν ἀριθμῶν φύσιν, καὶ τὰ φερόμενα κατὰ τὸν οὐρανὸν δέκα μὲν εἶναί φασιν, ὄντων δὲ ἐννέα μόνον τῶν φανερῶν διὰ τοῦτο δεκάτην τὴν ἀντίχθονα ποιοῦσιν. διώρισται δὲ περὶ τούτων ἐν ἑτέροις ἡμῖν ἀκριβέστερον....[2] (986a15) φαίνονται δὴ καὶ οὗτοι τὸν ἀριθμὸν νομίζοντες ἀρχὴν εἶναι καὶ ὡς ὕλην τοῖς οὖσι καὶ ὡς πάθη τε καὶ ἕξεις, τοῦ δὲ ἀριθμοῦ στοιχεῖα τό τε ἄρτιον καὶ τὸ περιττόν, τούτων δὲ τὸ μὲν ἄπειρον, τὸ δὲ πεπερασμένον, τὸ

---

and having been brought up in it they thought its principles were the principles of all things. Since of these principles numbers are by nature the first, and in numbers they seemed to see many resemblances to the things that exist and come into being—more than in fire and earth and water (such and such a modification of numbers being justice, another being soul and reason, another being opportunity—and similarly almost all other things being numerically expressible); since, again, they saw that the attributes and the ratios of the musical scales were expressible in numbers; since, then, all other things seemed in their whole nature to be modelled after numbers, and numbers seemed to be the first things in the whole of nature, they supposed the elements of numbers to be the elements of all things, and the whole heaven to be a musical scale and a number. And all the properties of numbers and scales which they could show to agree with the attributes and parts and the whole arrangement of the heavens, they collected and fitted into their scheme; and if there was a gap anywhere, they readily made additions so as to make their whole theory coherent. E.g. as the number 10 is thought to be perfect and to comprise the whole nature of numbers, they say that the bodies which move through the heavens are ten, but as the visible bodies are only nine, to meet this they invent a tenth—the 'counter-earth'. We have discussed these matters more exactly elsewhere....

Evidently, then, these thinkers also consider that number is the principle both as matter for things and as forming their modifications and their permanent states, and hold that the elements of number are the even and the odd, and of these the former is unlimited, and the

δ' ἓν ἐξ ἀμφοτέρων εἶναι τούτων (καὶ γὰρ ἄρτιον εἶναι καὶ περιττόν), τὸν δ' ἀριθμὸν ἐκ τοῦ ἑνός, ἀριθμοὺς δέ, καθάπερ εἴρηται, τὸν ὅλον οὐρανόν.

ἕτεροι δὲ τῶν αὐτῶν τούτων τὰς ἀρχὰς δέκα λέγουσιν εἶναι τὰς κατὰ συστοιχίαν λεγομένας·

πέρας καὶ ἄπειρον
περιττὸν καὶ ἄρτιον
ἓν καὶ πλῆθος
δεξιὸν καὶ ἀριστερόν
ἄρρεν καὶ θῆλυ
ἠρεμοῦν καὶ κινούμενον
εὐθὺ καὶ καμπύλον
φῶς καὶ σκότος
ἀγαθὸν καὶ κακόν
τετράγωνον καὶ ἑτερόμηκες·

ὅνπερ τρόπον ἔοικε καὶ Ἀλκμαίων ὁ Κροτωνιάτης ὑπολαβεῖν, καὶ ἤτοι οὗτος παρ' ἐκείνων ἢ ἐκεῖνοι παρὰ τούτου παρέλαβον τὸν λόγον τοῦτον· καὶ γὰρ ἐγένετο τὴν ἡλικίαν Ἀλκμαίων ἐπὶ γέροντι Πυθαγόρᾳ, ἀπεφήνατο δὲ παραπλησίως τούτοις.[3] φησὶ γὰρ εἶναι δύο τὰ πολλὰ τῶν ἀνθρωπίνων, λέγων τὰς ἐναντιότητας οὐχ ὥσπερ οὗτοι διωρισμένας ἀλλὰ τὰς τυχούσας, οἷον λευκὸν μέλαν, γλυκὺ πικρόν, ἀγαθὸν κακόν, μέγα μικρόν.[4] οὗτος μὲν οὖν ἀδιορίστως ἀπέρριψε περὶ τῶν λοιπῶν, οἱ δὲ Πυθαγόρειοι καὶ πόσαι καὶ τίνες αἱ ἐναντιώσεις ἀπεφήναντο. παρὰ μὲν οὖν τούτων ἀμφοῖν τοσοῦτον ἔστι λαβεῖν ὅτι τἀναντία ἀρχαὶ τῶν ὄντων· τὸ δὲ ὅσαι, παρὰ τῶν ἑτέρων, καὶ τίνες αὗταί εἰσιν. πῶς μέντοι πρὸς τὰς εἰρημένας αἰτίας

---

latter limited; and the 1 proceeds from both of these (for it is both even and odd), and number from the 1; and the whole heaven, as has been said, is numbers.

Other members of this same school say there are ten principles, which they arrange in two columns of cognates—limit and unlimited, odd and even, one and plurality, right and left, male and female, resting and moving, straight and curved, light and darkness, good and bad, square and oblong. In this way Alcmaeon of Croton seems also to have conceived the matter, and either he got this view from them or they got it from him; . . . for he expressed himself similarly to them. For he says most human affairs go in pairs, meaning not definite contrarieties such as the Pythagoreans speak of, but any chance contrarieties, e.g. white and black, sweet and bitter, good and bad, great and small. He threw out indefinite suggestions about the other contrarieties, but the Pythagoreans declared both how many and which their contrarieties are.

From both these schools, then, we can learn this much, that the contraries are the principles of things; and how many these principles are and which they are, we can learn from one of the two schools. But how these principles can be brought together under the

ἐνδέχεται συναγαγεῖν, σαφῶς μὲν οὐ διήρθρωται παρ' ἐκείνων, ἐοίκασι δ' ὡς ἐν ὕλης εἴδει τὰ στοιχεῖα τάττειν· ἐκ τούτων γὰρ ὡς ἐνυπαρχόντων συνεστάναι καὶ πεπλάσθαι φασὶ τὴν οὐσίαν.

[1] For Aristotle's caution in speaking of the Pythagoreans see note 2 on p. 218.

[2] Alexander, in his comments on this passage (*Met.* 41, 1, DK58B4), refers to the *de caelo* (i.e. **329**) and the lost Πυθαγορικῶν δόξαι for Aristotle's fuller treatment of this topic.

[3] On the text of this sentence see note 1 on p. 232.

[4] See p. 234.

This long passage, though it is one of the few in which Aristotle recognizes (in the words ἕτεροι δὲ τῶν αὐτῶν τούτων, 'others of these same thinkers') distinctions within the school, is evidently intended as a summary of the main features of Pythagoreanism as a whole.[1] It accordingly refers in passing to most of the doctrines which Aristotle elsewhere examines in greater detail. At the same time it is by itself far from self-explanatory: almost every sentence in it needs corroboration, amplification or elucidation. The most convenient course will be to take this passage as a text for the whole of this chapter, expanding in turn each of the most important sentences in their logical order rather than in the order in which Aristotle presents them. Since Pythagoreanism is evidently based on an ultimate dualism, it will be best to start from the two first principles (which are first not only in the list but also, as the previous paragraph shows, in cosmology), Limit and Unlimited and Odd and Even. Next, since the unit is derived from these two principles, we must examine the nature of the Pythagorean units and of number in general. That will enable us to see what the Pythagoreans meant by the equation of things with numbers. Finally we can attempt to reconstruct the cosmogony of these early Pythagoreans, against which the criticisms of the Eleatics seem to have been primarily directed.

[1] The opening words of the passage, ἐν δὲ τούτοις καὶ πρὸ τούτων, show that Aristotle has in mind, at least among others, the generation of Pythagoreans which flourished at the end of the fifth century B.C. and of which Philolaus was the most prominent member. When, however, he

---

causes we have named has not been clearly and articulately stated by them; they seem, however, to range the elements under the head of matter; for out of these as immanent parts they say substance is composed and moulded. (Trans. Ross)

passes in the following paragraph to 'others of this same school', his suggestion that either Alcmaeon borrowed from them or they from him seems to indicate that he is passing from a later to an earlier generation. But since the entire passage is clearly intended as a summary of the salient features of Pythagoreanism as a whole, no reliance can safely be placed upon this unusual distinction.

DUALISM

290 Aristotle *Met.* A5, 986b2, from **289** παρὰ μὲν οὖν τούτων ἀμφοῖν τοσοῦτον ἔστι λαβεῖν ὅτι τἀναντία ἀρχαὶ τῶν ὄντων· τὸ δὲ ὅσαι, παρὰ τῶν ἑτέρων, καὶ τίνες αὗταί εἰσιν.

291 Aristotle *Met.* A5, 987a13 (DK58B8) οἱ δὲ Πυθαγόρειοι δύο μὲν τὰς ἀρχὰς κατὰ τὸν αὐτὸν εἰρήκασι τρόπον, τοσοῦτον δὲ προσεπέθεσαν ὃ καὶ ἴδιόν ἐστιν αὐτῶν, ὅτι τὸ πεπερασμένον καὶ τὸ ἄπειρον [καὶ τὸ ἓν] οὐχ ἑτέρας τινὰς ᾠήθησαν εἶναι φύσεις, οἷον πῦρ ἢ γῆν ἤ τι τοιοῦτον ἕτερον, ἀλλ' αὐτὸ τὸ ἄπειρον καὶ αὐτὸ τὸ ἓν οὐσίαν εἶναι τούτων ὧν κατηγοροῦνται, διὸ καὶ ἀριθμὸν εἶναι τὴν οὐσίαν πάντων.

292 Aristotle *Eth. Nic.* A4, 1096b5 πιθανώτερον δ' ἐοίκασιν οἱ Πυθαγόρειοι λέγειν περὶ αὐτοῦ, τιθέντες ἐν τῇ τῶν ἀγαθῶν συστοιχίᾳ τὸ ἕν.

293 Aristotle *Eth. Nic.* B5, 1106b29 τὸ γὰρ κακὸν τοῦ ἀπείρου, ὡς οἱ Πυθαγόρειοι εἴκαζον, τὸ δ' ἀγαθὸν τοῦ πεπερασμένου.

These passages make it plain that in Aristotle's opinion not only was Pythagoreanism fundamentally dualistic[1] but also the Table of Opposites, attributed in **289** to only one section or generation of the school, was a characteristic feature of that dualism.[2] What that Table in fact represents is, as Cornford says (*Plato and Parmenides* 7), 'ten different manifestations of the two primary

---

290 *From both these schools, then, we can learn this much, that the contraries are the principles of things; and how many these principles are and which they are, we can learn from one of the two schools.*

291 *But the Pythagoreans have said in the same way that there are two principles, but added this much, which is peculiar to them, that they thought finitude and infinity [and unity] were not attributes of certain other things, e.g. of fire or earth or anything else of this kind, but that infinity itself and unity itself were the substance of the things of which they are predicated. This is why number was the substance of all things.* (Trans. Ross)

292 *The Pythagoreans seem to have a more plausible view on the subject, when they put the One in the column of goods.*

293 *For evil belongs to the unlimited, as the Pythagoreans conjectured, and good to the limited.*

opposites in various spheres; in each pair there is a good and an answering evil'. The principle of Limit, in other words, is represented in the appropriate sphere by oddness, unity, rest, goodness and so on, while the principle of the Unlimited is represented by their opposites. Moreover, as is clear from the phrases αὐτὸ τὸ ἕν, 'unity itself', in **291**, and ἐν τῇ τῶν ἀγαθῶν συστοιχίᾳ, 'in the column of goods', in **292**, unity and goodness at least—and the same is presumably true of the rest—are not only 'manifestations' of Limit but rather, each within its appropriate field, actually synonymous with Limit: in arithmetic Unity, in ethics Good take upon themselves the function of the primary principle.[3]

[1] This is denied by Cornford (*op. cit.*), who, on the basis of two very unreliable passages (Alexander Polyhistor *ap.* Diog. L. VIII, 24 (DK 58 B 1 *a*), on which see Festugière, *Rev. des Ét. Grecques* 58 (1945) 1 ff., and Eudorus *ap.* Simpl. *Phys.* 181, 10, on which see Raven, *Pyth. and El.* 15), argues against Aristotle that Pythagoreanism was fundamentally monistic. There can, however, be no doubt that on this question in particular Aristotle is by far our most reliable authority. Moreover, if we elect to follow him, we can immediately see the motive for the tradition preserved in **294** Hippolytus *Ref.* I, 2, 12 Διόδωρος δὲ ὁ Ἐρετριεὺς καὶ Ἀριστόξενος ὁ μουσικός φασι πρὸς Ζαράταν τὸν Χαλδαῖον ἐληλυθέναι Πυθαγόραν. Zoroastrianism, like Pythagoreanism, was based upon a dualism between a good principle, Ormazd, and a bad, Ahriman; and all that this tradition proves is that already in the 4th century B.C. the similarity between the two systems had been observed.

[2] It has been maintained, by Zeller and others (see Ross, *Ar. Met.* note *ad loc.*), that the Table of Opposites belongs to the time of Philolaus. We shall see, however, when we come to Parmenides, that Aristotle's implication that it belongs rather to the time of Alcmaeon is probably reliable.

[3] Cf. also **295** Aristotle *Met.* A6, 987b22 (DK 58 B 13) τὸ μέντοι γε ἓν οὐσίαν εἶναι, καὶ μὴ ἕτερόν γέ τι ὂν λέγεσθαι ἕν, παραπλησίως τοῖς Πυθαγορείοις ἔλεγε (*sc.* Plato), καὶ τὸ τοὺς ἀριθμοὺς αἰτίους εἶναι τοῖς ἄλλοις τῆς οὐσίας ὡσαύτως ἐκείνοις· τὸ δὲ ἀντὶ τοῦ ἀπείρου ὡς ἑνὸς δυάδα ποιῆσαι, τὸ δὲ ἄπειρον ἐκ μεγάλου καὶ μικροῦ, τοῦτ' ἴδιον. Here again τὸ ἕν clearly stands for πέρας and as such is contrasted with τὸ ἄπειρον.

---

294 *Diodorus of Eretria and Aristoxenus the musical scholar say that Pythagoras visited Zaratas the Chaldaean.*

295 *But he agreed with the Pythagoreans in saying that the One is substance and not a predicate of something else; and in saying that the Numbers are the causes of the reality of other things, he also agreed with them; but positing a dyad and constructing the infinite out of great and small, instead of treating the infinite as one, is peculiar to him.* (Trans. Ross)

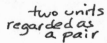

LIMIT AND UNLIMITED, ODD AND EVEN

296 Aristotle *Met.* A5, 985b23, from **289** ἐν δὲ τούτοις καὶ πρὸ τούτων οἱ καλούμενοι Πυθαγόρειοι τῶν μαθημάτων ἁψάμενοι πρῶτοι ταῦτα προήγαγον, καὶ ἐντραφέντες ἐν αὐτοῖς τὰς τούτων ἀρχὰς τῶν ὄντων ἀρχὰς ᾠήθησαν εἶναι πάντων. ἐπεὶ δὲ τούτων οἱ ἀριθμοὶ φύσει πρῶτοι...τὰ τῶν ἀριθμῶν στοιχεῖα τῶν ὄντων στοιχεῖα πάντων ὑπέλαβον εἶναι....τοῦ δὲ ἀριθμοῦ στοιχεῖα τό τε ἄρτιον καὶ τὸ περιττόν, τούτων δὲ τὸ μὲν ἄπειρον, τὸ δὲ πεπερασμένον....

In these sentences Aristotle first tells us that the Pythagoreans were led to adopt their primary principles by their study of 'mathematics', and then suggests, by the stress he lays on 'the elements of number', that he is thinking only of arithmetic. There is, however, no doubt that from the outset the Pythagoreans studied geometry as well as arithmetic. Indeed Diogenes Laertius (VIII, 12) tells us that Pythagoras himself studied especially 'the arithmetical form of geometry', τὸ ἀριθμητικὸν εἶδος αὐτῆς. But whereas the opposition of Odd and Even is clearly appropriate in arithmetic, it is equally clear that it is not applicable to geometry. Evidently, therefore, when the Pythagoreans wished to find a similar pair of opposites to underlie geometry, they had recourse to the pair which Pythagoras himself had already presumably discovered in his study of harmonics (see p. 229), namely Limit and the Unlimited. Every geometrical figure can be naturally enough regarded as a parcel of unlimited space bounded by limiting points, lines or surfaces. At the same time it was clearly undesirable to have two unrelated pairs of opposites underlying respectively arithmetic and geometry. The Pythagoreans therefore simply equated Odd with Limit and Even with Unlimited, and proceeded to rationalize these by no means self-evident equations by a number of curiously unconvincing arguments which we must next consider.

---

296 *Contemporaneously with these philosophers and before them, the Pythagoreans, as they are called, devoted themselves to mathematics; they were the first to advance this study, and having been brought up in it they thought its principles were the principles of all things. Since of these principles numbers are by nature the first...they supposed the elements of numbers to be the elements of all things....The elements of number are the even and the odd, and of these the former is unlimited, and the latter limited....*

THE NATURE OF NUMBER

The early Pythagoreans, having no simple form of numerical notation, chose to express numbers in the form of patterns similar to those now found on dominoes or dice. Thus the number 10 was represented, as we have already seen (p. 230 note 2), by ten dots or alphas arranged in an equilateral triangle. Aristotle is certainly referring to two other such figures when he explains the Pythagorean equation of Even with Unlimited as follows:

297 Aristotle *Physics* Γ4, 203a10 (DK58B28) καὶ οἱ μὲν (*sc.* φασὶ) τὸ ἄπειρον εἶναι τὸ ἄρτιον (τοῦτο γὰρ ἐναπολαμβανόμενον καὶ ὑπὸ τοῦ περιττοῦ περαινόμενον παρέχειν τοῖς οὖσι τὴν ἀπειρίαν· σημεῖον δ' εἶναι τούτου τὸ συμβαῖνον ἐπὶ τῶν ἀριθμῶν· περιτιθεμένων γὰρ τῶν γνωμόνων περὶ τὸ ἓν καὶ χωρὶς ὅτε μὲν ἄλλο ἀεὶ γίγνεσθαι τὸ εἶδος, ὅτε δὲ ἕν). Πλάτων δὲ....

Difficult as are the words καὶ χωρίς (which are usually taken to mean 'and in the other case'), there can be no doubt that the two figures to which Aristotle is here referring are these:

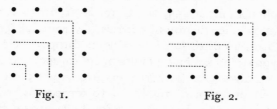

Fig. 1. Fig. 2.

Either of these figures can, of course, be extended, by the addition of more 'gnomons',[1] *ad infinitum*. In Figure 1, where 'the gnomons are being placed around the one', each successive addition marks the next in the series of odd numbers, while Figure 2 similarly represents the series of even numbers. But whereas Figure 1 remains, with each addition, always the same figure, a square, Figure 2 on the contrary changes with each addition the ratio of its length to its height. Hence, of course, the inclusion of τετράγωνον καὶ ἑτερόμηκες in the Table of Opposites; for ἑτερόμηκες, as

297 *Further, the Pythagoreans identify the infinite with the even. For this, they say, when it is taken in and limited by the odd, provides things with the element of infinity. An indication of this is what happens with numbers. If the gnomons are placed round the one, and without the one, in the one construction the figure that results is always different, in the other it is always the same. But Plato....* (After Hardie)

we are told in many passages in later mathematical writers,[2] refers properly to a rectangle in which one side exceeds the other by a single unit. And Aristotle is no doubt right in giving this as one of the arguments by which the equations of Odd with Limit and of Even with Unlimited were justified. Figure 1 representing the Odd is uniform, ἕν, Figure 2 representing the Even is infinitely variable, ἄλλο ἀεί.

[1] As Ross says in his note on this passage (*Aristotle, Physics* 542–5): 'The stricter meaning of the word (*sc.* "gnomon") is "the figure which remains of a square when a smaller square is cut out of it"....But in a wider sense γνώμων can stand for any number which when added to a figurate number gives the next number of the same figure (Iamb. *in Nic.* 58, 19 Pistelli; Hero *Deff.* 58).'

[2] E.g. **298** Nicomachus *Introd. Arithm.* II, 17 (108, 8 Hoche) ἑτερομήκης ἀριθμὸς λέγεται οὗ ἐπιπέδως σχηματογραφέντος τετράπλευρος μὲν καὶ τετραγώνιος γίνεται ἡ καταγραφή, οὐ μὴν ἴσαι ἀλλήλαις αἱ πλευραὶ οὐδὲ τὸ μῆκος τῷ πλάτει ἴσον, ἀλλὰ παρὰ μονάδα. Cf. Theo 31, 20 Hiller.

It seems probable, too, that the same two figures were used to justify these equations in another way. Simplicius, commenting on the first words of this passage, writes as follows:

299 Simplicius *Physics* 455, 20 οὗτοι δὲ τὸ ἄπειρον τὸν ἄρτιον ἀριθμὸν ἔλεγον 'διὰ τὸ πᾶν μὲν ἄρτιον, ὥς φασιν οἱ ἐξηγηταί, εἰς ἴσα διαιρεῖσθαι, τὸ δὲ εἰς ἴσα διαιρούμενον ἄπειρον κατὰ τὴν διχοτομίαν· ἡ γὰρ εἰς ἴσα καὶ ἡμίση διαίρεσις ἐπ' ἄπειρον· τὸ δὲ περιττὸν προστεθὲν περαίνει αὐτό· κωλύει γὰρ αὐτοῦ τὴν εἰς ἴσα διαίρεσιν'. οὕτως μὲν οὖν οἱ ἐξηγηταὶ τῷ ἀρτίῳ τὸ ἄπειρον ἀνατιθέασι κατὰ τὴν εἰς ἴσα διαίρεσιν, καὶ δηλονότι οὐκ ἐπ' ἀριθμῶν ἀλλ' ἐπὶ μεγεθῶν λαμβάνουσι τὴν ἐπ' ἄπειρον τομήν....ὅλως δὲ οὐδὲ ὁ Ἀριστοτέλης φαίνεται τὴν εἰς ἴσα διαίρεσιν αἰτιασάμενος τοῦ ἀπείρου.

Whatever these commentators whom Simplicius quotes may have meant, they clearly cannot have meant that every even

---

298 *An 'oblong number' is one which, when represented diagrammatically, has a four-sided rectangular figure, but its sides are not equal, its length differing from its breadth by a single unit.*

299 *They meant by infinity even numbers, 'since everything even', as the commentators say, 'is divisible into equal parts, and what is divisible into equal parts is infinite in respect of division into two; for division into halves goes on* ad infinitum, *while the addition of the odd limits it by putting an end to halving'. So the commentators refer the unlimited to the even in respect of divisibility into halves, and it is plain that they conceive of infinite divisibility in terms not of numbers but of magnitudes....But Aristotle evidently does not regard divisibility into halves as in any way an explanation of infinity.*

number is divisible *ad infinitum* into halves; for it is an axiom common to all Greek mathematicians that the unit is indivisible and that such fractions as $\frac{1}{4}$ or $\frac{1}{16}$ represent one unit out of a total of 4 or 16. The easiest way to make sense of their comment can in fact be represented diagrammatically so:

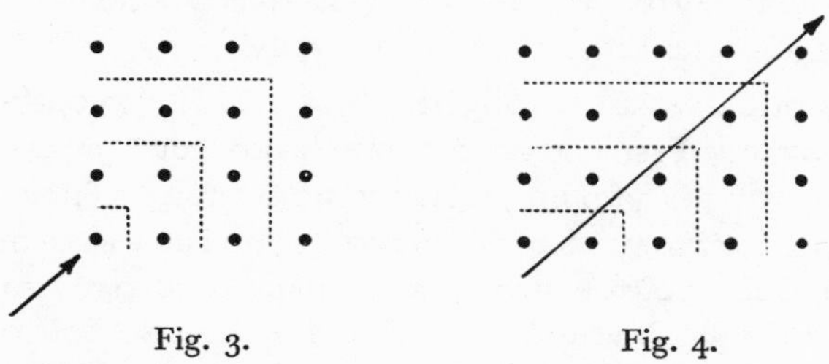

Fig. 3. Fig. 4.

Whereas in Figure 4 ἡ εἰς ἴσα καὶ ἡμίση διαίρεσις ἐπ' ἄπειρον, 'division into halves goes on *ad infinitum*', in Figure 3 on the contrary τὸ περιττὸν προστεθὲν περαίνει αὐτό· κωλύει γὰρ αὐτοῦ τὴν εἰς ἴσα διαίρεσιν,[1] 'the addition of the unit prevents division into halves'. Odd number in general, and the number 3 in particular, were defined by the Pythagoreans (and Aristotle himself was evidently familiar with the definition, see **388**) as 'that which has a beginning, a middle and an end'. Even number on the other hand, as Figure 4 shows, has no 'middle'; and the absence of a 'middle' may well have provided the Pythagoreans with another rationalization, however naïve and artificial, for the equation of Even with Unlimited.

[1] Cf. with this passage from Simplicius four others cited by Ross in his note (p. 542) on Aristotle *Phys.* 203a10–11, and also especially **300** Nicomachus *I.A.* I, 7 (13, 10 Hoche) ἔστι δὲ ἄρτιον μὲν ὃ οἷόν τε εἰς δύο ἴσα διαιρεθῆναι μονάδος μέσον μὴ παρεμπιπτούσης, περιττὸν δὲ τὸ μὴ δυνάμενον εἰς δύο ἴσα μερισθῆναι διὰ τὴν προειρημένην τῆς μονάδος μεσιτείαν.

UNITS HAVE MAGNITUDE

301 Aristotle *Met.* A5, 986a15 (from **289**) φαίνονται δὴ καὶ οὗτοι τὸν ἀριθμὸν νομίζοντες ἀρχὴν εἶναι καὶ ὡς ὕλην τοῖς οὖσι....

---

300 *Even is that which admits of division into halves without the interposition of the unit, odd is that which does not admit of division into halves because the unit is interposed as described.*

301 *Evidently, then, these thinkers also consider that number is the principle both as matter for things....*

302 Aristotle *Met.* M6, 1080b16 καὶ οἱ Πυθαγόρειοι δ' ἕνα, τὸν μαθηματικόν (*sc.* ἀριθμόν φασιν εἶναι), πλὴν οὐ κεχωρισμένον ἀλλ' ἐκ τούτου τὰς αἰσθητὰς οὐσίας συνεστάναι φασίν. τὸν γὰρ ὅλον οὐρανὸν κατασκευάζουσιν ἐξ ἀριθμῶν, πλὴν οὐ μοναδικῶν, ἀλλὰ τὰς μονάδας ὑπολαμβάνουσιν ἔχειν μέγεθος·...μοναδικοὺς τοὺς ἀριθμοὺς εἶναι πάντες τιθέασι πλὴν τῶν Πυθαγορείων·...ἐκεῖνοι δ' ἔχοντας μέγεθος, καθάπερ εἴρηται πρότερον.

303 Aristotle *Met.* M8, 1083b8 ὁ δὲ τῶν Πυθαγορείων τρόπος τῇ μὲν ἐλάττους ἔχει δυσχερείας τῶν πρότερον εἰρημένων, τῇ δὲ ἰδίας ἑτέρας. τὸ μὲν γὰρ μὴ χωριστὸν ποιεῖν τὸν ἀριθμὸν ἀφαιρεῖται πολλὰ τῶν ἀδυνάτων· τὸ δὲ τὰ σώματα ἐξ ἀριθμῶν εἶναι συγκείμενα, καὶ τὸν ἀριθμὸν τοῦτον εἶναι μαθηματικόν, ἀδύνατόν ἐστιν. οὔτε γὰρ ἄτομα μεγέθη λέγειν ἀληθές, εἴ θ' ὅτι μάλιστα τοῦτον ἔχει τὸν τρόπον, οὐχ αἵ γε μονάδες μέγεθος ἔχουσιν. μέγεθος δὲ ἐξ ἀδιαιρέτων πῶς δυνατόν; ἀλλὰ μὴν ὅ γ' ἀριθμητικὸς ἀριθμὸς μοναδικός ἐστιν. ἐκεῖνοι δὲ τὸν ἀριθμὸν τὰ ὄντα λέγουσιν. τὰ γοῦν θεωρήματα προσάπτουσι τοῖς σώμασιν ὡς ἐξ ἐκείνων ὄντων τῶν ἀριθμῶν.[1]

[1] Aristotle has been discussing before this passage, and in the second sentence quoted is referring to, the theory held by Plato and some of the Platonists that number exists as a separate entity apart from sensible things. On this theory see Ross, *Ar. Met.* liii–lvii.

The unfortunate consequence of their diagrammatic representation of numbers was that the Pythagoreans, thinking of numbers as spatially extended and confusing the point of geometry with

---

302 *Now the Pythagoreans also believe in one kind of number—the mathematical; only they say it is not separate but sensible substances are formed out of it. For they construct the whole universe out of numbers—only not numbers consisting of abstract units; they suppose the units to have spatial magnitude....All...suppose numbers to consist of abstract units, except the Pythagoreans; but* they *suppose the numbers to have magnitude, as has been said before.* (Trans. Ross)

303 *The doctrine of the Pythagoreans in one way affords fewer difficulties than those before named, but in another way has others peculiar to itself. For not thinking of number as capable of existing separately removes many of the impossible consequences; but that bodies should be composed of numbers, and that this should be mathematical number, is impossible. For it is not true to speak of indivisible spatial magnitudes; and however much there might be magnitudes of this sort, units at least have not magnitude; and how can a magnitude be composed of indivisibles? But arithmetical number, at least, consists of abstract units, while these thinkers identify number with real things; at any rate they apply their propositions to bodies as if they consisted of those numbers.* (Trans. Ross)

the unit of arithmetic, tended to imagine both alike as possessing magnitude. It is true that Aristotle, in discussing the views of earlier thinkers, often confronts them with such logical consequences of their doctrines as they themselves never either enunciated or foresaw; and no doubt in **303** he is, to some extent at least, pursuing this usual practice. But **302** leaves no doubt that the Pythagoreans did indeed assume, even though the assumption was only tacit,[1] that units are spatially extended; and when we come to consider the paradoxes of Zeno we shall find that it is against this assumption, along with the confusion of points and units, that they have their greatest force (see pp. 289ff.).

[1] This is, I believe, a point of great importance. In his review of J. E. Raven, *Pythagoreans and Eleatics*, G. Vlastos (*Gnomon* 25 (1953) 29–35), following Heidel (*AJP* 61 (1940) 29 n. 58), cites **304** Aetius I, 3, 19 Ἔκφαντος Συρακούσιος, εἷς τῶν Πυθαγορείων, πάντων τὰ ἀδιαίρετα σώματα καὶ τὸ κενόν (*sc.* ἀρχὰς εἶναι)· τὰς γὰρ Πυθαγορικὰς μονάδας οὗτος πρῶτος ἀπεφήνατο σωματικάς. He then writes (p. 32): 'Whatever may be the date of Ecphantus, this statement definitely implies that number-atomism was not regarded by the tradition stemming from Theophrastus as an original feature of Pythagoreanism.' Even if we accept, as we doubtless should, the view of both Heidel and Vlastos that Ecphantus 'was, at most, no earlier than the atomists and, more probably, a fourth-century figure' (Vlastos, p. 32 n. 1), I cannot myself accept the implication which the statement of Aetius is said to carry. All that the statement seems to me to imply is that Ecphantus was the first Pythagorean explicitly to acknowledge the consequences of Zeno's attack upon the tacit confusion of the earlier Pythagoreans. The phrase 'number-atomism' too easily suggests (as it was meant to do by Cornford, who used it freely) a system in which units were explicitly stated to possess magnitude. It is not therefore appropriate to the present reconstruction of Pythagoreanism, which suggests only that the earlier Pythagoreans, like all the rest of the Presocratics, failed to distinguish between the corporeal and the incorporeal. See further on Melissus, pp. 302 ff.

Nor, indeed, is that the full extent of the confusion. These unit-points functioned also as the basis of physical matter: they were regarded in fact as a primitive form of atom. When, therefore, Aristotle speaks of number as ὡς ὕλην τοῖς οὖσι, 'functioning as the material element in things', or when, as he often does, he asserts that the Pythagoreans regarded the universe as consisting

---

304 *Ecphantus of Syracuse, one of the Pythagoreans, held that the principles of all things are indivisible bodies and void. For he was the first to say that the Pythagorean units were corporeal.*

of numbers, he means that concrete objects were literally composed of aggregations of unit-point-atoms. Two such passages are:

305 Aristotle *Met.* A8, 990a18 (DK58B22) ἔτι δὲ πῶς δεῖ λαβεῖν αἴτια μὲν εἶναι τὰ τοῦ ἀριθμοῦ πάθη καὶ τὸν ἀριθμὸν τῶν κατὰ τὸν οὐρανὸν ὄντων καὶ γιγνομένων καὶ ἐξ ἀρχῆς καὶ νῦν, ἀριθμὸν δ' ἄλλον μηθένα εἶναι παρὰ τὸν ἀριθμὸν τοῦτον ἐξ οὗ συνέστηκεν ὁ κόσμος;

306 Aristotle *Met.* N3, 1090a20 οἱ δὲ Πυθαγόρειοι, διὰ τὸ ὁρᾶν πολλὰ τῶν ἀριθμῶν πάθη ὑπάρχοντα τοῖς αἰσθητοῖς σώμασιν, εἶναι μὲν ἀριθμοὺς ἐποίησαν τὰ ὄντα, οὐ χωριστοὺς δέ, ἀλλ' ἐξ ἀριθμῶν τὰ ὄντα.

THINGS EQUAL NUMBERS

307 Aristotle *Met.* A5, 985b26, from **289** ἐπεὶ δὲ τούτων οἱ ἀριθμοὶ φύσει πρῶτοι, ἐν δὲ τοῖς ἀριθμοῖς ἐδόκουν θεωρεῖν ὁμοιώματα πολλὰ τοῖς οὖσι καὶ γιγνομένοις, μᾶλλον ἢ ἐν πυρὶ καὶ γῇ καὶ ὕδατι, ὅτι τὸ μὲν τοιονδὶ τῶν ἀριθμῶν πάθος δικαιοσύνη, τὸ δὲ τοιονδὶ ψυχὴ καὶ νοῦς, ἕτερον δὲ καιρὸς καὶ τῶν ἄλλων ὡς εἰπεῖν ἕκαστον ὁμοίως....

308 [Aristotle] *Magna Moralia* A1, 1182a11 πρῶτος μὲν οὖν ἐνεχείρησε Πυθαγόρας περὶ ἀρετῆς εἰπεῖν, οὐκ ὀρθῶς δέ· τὰς γὰρ ἀρετὰς εἰς τοὺς ἀριθμοὺς ἀνάγων οὐκ οἰκείαν τῶν ἀρετῶν τὴν θεωρίαν ἐποιεῖτο· οὐ γάρ ἐστιν ἡ δικαιοσύνη ἀριθμὸς ἰσάκις ἴσος. (Cf. Ar. *Eth. Nic.* E8, 1132b21, DK58B4.)

---

305 *Further, how are we to combine the belief that the modifications of number, and number itself, are causes of what exists and happens in the heavens both from the beginning and now, and that there is no other number than this number out of which the world is composed?* (Trans. Ross)

306 *But the Pythagoreans, because they saw many attributes of numbers belonging to sensible bodies, supposed real things to be numbers—not separable numbers, however, but numbers of which real things consist.* (Trans. Ross)

307 *Since of these principles numbers are by nature the first, and in numbers they seemed to see many resemblances to the things that exist and come into being—more than in fire and earth and water (such and such a modification of numbers being justice, another being soul and reason, another being opportunity—and similarly almost all other things being numerically expressible)....*

308 *Pythagoras first attempted to discuss goodness, but not in the right way; for by referring the virtues to numbers he made his study of them inappropriate; for justice is not a square number.*

309 Aristotle *Met.* M4, 1078b21 (DK58B4) οἱ δὲ Πυθαγόρειοι πρότερον περί τινων ὀλίγων, ὧν τοὺς λόγους εἰς τοὺς ἀριθμοὺς ἀνῆπτον, οἷον τί ἐστι καιρὸς ἢ τὸ δίκαιον ἢ γάμος, ἐκεῖνος [i.e. Socrates, not, as in DK, Democritus] δ' εὐλόγως ἐζήτει τὸ τί ἐστιν.

310 Aristotle *Met.* A8, 990a22 (DK58B22), continuing **305** ὅταν γὰρ ἐν τῳδὶ μὲν τῷ μέρει δόξα καὶ καιρὸς αὐτοῖς ᾖ, μικρὸν δὲ ἄνωθεν ἢ κάτωθεν ἀδικία καὶ κρίσις ἢ μῖξις, ἀπόδειξιν δὲ λέγωσιν ὅτι τούτων μὲν ἕκαστον ἀριθμός ἐστι, συμβαίνει δὲ κατὰ τὸν τόπον τοῦτον ἤδη πλῆθος εἶναι τῶν συνισταμένων μεγεθῶν διὰ τὸ τὰ πάθη ταῦτα ἀκολουθεῖν τοῖς τόποις ἑκάστοις, πότερον οὗτος ὁ αὐτός ἐστιν ἀριθμός, ὁ ἐν τῷ οὐρανῷ, ὃν δεῖ λαβεῖν ὅτι τούτων ἕκαστόν ἐστιν, ἢ παρὰ τοῦτον ἄλλος;

We have seen in the last paragraph what the Pythagoreans meant by their equation of concrete objects with numbers: they meant that each such object consisted of a definite number of unit-point-atoms. Accordingly we often find Aristotle protesting against the Pythagoreans, as he does, for instance, at **311** *de caelo* Γ1, 300a17 (DK58B38): τὰ μὲν γὰρ φυσικὰ σώματα φαίνεται βάρος ἔχοντα καὶ κουφότητα, τὰς δὲ μονάδας οὔτε σῶμα ποιεῖν οἷόν τε συντιθεμένας οὔτε βάρος ἔχειν. In **308**, **309** and **310**, however, we are concerned with equations of, to us at least, a very different type: the equation of justice with ἀριθμὸς ἰσάκις ἴσος—i.e. the first square number, 4—seems clearly symbolical rather than literal. It must once again be remembered, however, that Greek thinkers were very slow to apprehend that anything could exist without spatial extension. Empedocles, as we shall see (**424**),

---

309 *The Pythagoreans had before this treated of a few things, whose definitions they connected with numbers—e.g. opportunity, justice or marriage. But it was natural that Socrates should seek the essence.* (Trans. Ross)

310 *When in one particular region they place opinion and opportunity, and, a little above or below, injustice and sifting or mixture, and allege as proof of this that each one of these is a number, and that in this place there is already a plurality of the extended bodies composed of numbers* just because *the qualities of number that constitute these are connected with these groups of places,—this being so, is this number, which we must suppose each of these abstractions to be, the same number which is exhibited in the material universe, or is it another than this?* (Trans. Ross, altered in accordance with his notes on Ar. *Met.* 990a25 and 26, pp. 184–5)

311 *For natural bodies are manifestly endowed with weight and lightness, but an assemblage of units can neither be composed to form a body nor possess weight.* (Trans. Stocks)

still speaks of his moving principles (as we might call them), Love and Strife, as 'equal in length and breadth to the four elements', and likewise Anaxagoras describes his Nous as 'the finest and purest of substances' (**503**). Plato seems to have been the first Greek to have consciously thought that anything could exist otherwise than in space, and he was followed in this respect by Aristotle.[1] But that these two were the exception rather than the rule is suggested by the fact that the Stoics still regarded justice, for instance, as extended in space. It seems most probable, therefore, that these early Pythagoreans had not clearly distinguished in their own minds between such equations as, on the one hand, 'A man = 250' and, on the other, 'Justice = 4'. The question in **310**, whether it is the same kind of number in each case, is not only, in fact, perfectly legitimate, but should probably be answered (though here again the Pythagoreans' assumption was doubtless only tacit rather than explicit) in the affirmative. Aristotle himself, having learnt the distinction between the concrete and the abstract, fails to see the confusion underlying the Pythagorean equations of abstracts with numbers. But even if those equations had been intended, as Cornford supposes (*Plato and Parmenides* 26), to be merely symbolical, they would still have had little appeal to a mind such as Aristotle's.

[1] Both Plato's Ideas and Aristotle's Unmoved Mover are explicitly stated by their authors to be not in space. See Plato *Tim.* 52 c and Aristotle *Met.* Λ7, 1073 a 5.

COSMOGONY

(i) *The first unit*

312 Aristotle *Met.* N3, 1091 a 12 ἄτοπον δὲ καὶ γένεσιν ποιεῖν ἀιδίων ὄντων, μᾶλλον δ' ἕν τι τῶν ἀδυνάτων. οἱ μὲν οὖν Πυθαγόρειοι πότερον οὐ ποιοῦσιν ἢ ποιοῦσι γένεσιν οὐδὲν δεῖ διστάζειν· φανερῶς γὰρ λέγουσιν ὡς τοῦ ἑνὸς συσταθέντος, εἴτ' ἐξ ἐπιπέδων εἴτ' ἐκ χροιᾶς εἴτ' ἐκ σπέρματος εἴτ' ἐξ ὧν ἀποροῦσιν εἰπεῖν, εὐθὺς τὸ ἔγγιστα τοῦ ἀπείρου ὅτι εἵλκετο καὶ ἐπεραίνετο ὑπὸ τοῦ πέρατος.

---

312 *It is strange also to attribute generation to eternal things, or rather this is one of the things that are impossible. There need be no doubt whether the Pythagoreans attribute generation to them or not; for they obviously say that when the one had been constructed, whether out of planes or of surface or of seed or of elements which they cannot express, immediately the nearest part of the unlimited began to be drawn in and limited by the limit.* (After Ross)

313 Aristotle *Met.* M6, 1080b20 (DK58B9) (omitted from the middle of **302**) ὅπως δὲ τὸ πρῶτον ἓν συνέστη ἔχον μέγεθος, ἀπορεῖν ἐοίκασιν.

The mode of generation of 'the first unit with magnitude' is indeed, as Aristotle complains, one of the most mysterious features of the Pythagorean cosmology, and there is no reliable evidence apart from Aristotle's own words to enable us to solve the problem. Fortunately, however, Aristotle's three suggestions in **312**, which 'must have been prompted', as Cornford says (*Plato and Parmenides* 19; cf. Ross's note *ad loc.*), 'by known features of the system', give us something to go on. Surfaces do certainly play a large part in Pythagorean cosmology; and χροιά is to the Pythagoreans, as Aristotle himself tells us, so inseparable an aspect of surface that the two words are actually synonymous:

314 Aristotle *de sensu* 3, 439a30 τὸ γὰρ χρῶμα ἢ ἐν τῷ πέρατί ἐστιν ἢ πέρας. διὸ καὶ οἱ Πυθαγόρειοι τὴν ἐπιφάνειαν χροιὰν ἐκάλουν.

Since, however, surfaces do not appear to be generated till a later stage in cosmogony (see pp. 253 ff.), it is the third suggestion that appears the most plausible. 'This biological conception', as Cornford again wrote (*ibid.*), 'fits the notion of the world as a living and breathing creature' (cf. **312** and also **316** below), 'which, like other living things, would grow from a seed to its full form. It also fits in with the position of the male principle under Limit, the female under Unlimited, in the Table of Opposites.' This notion of the seed certainly looks like an early doctrine (cf. the genealogical concept of cosmogony exemplified in ch. 1), and its connexion with another Pythagorean view which there is reason to regard as early, namely the Table of Opposites (see p. 241 note 2), serves perhaps to confirm what we might anyhow suspect.

The early Pythagoreans may well, therefore, have initiated the cosmogonical process by representing the male principle of Limit as somehow implanting in the midst of the surrounding Unlimited the seed which, by progressive growth, was to develop into the visible universe. Here once again, however, it is possible that they

---

313 *But how the first unit with magnitude was constructed, they seem at a loss to describe.*

314 *For colour is either contained in the limit or actually is limit; and so the Pythagoreans regarded surface and colour as synonymous.*

felt no need, and consequently, as Aristotle's words in both **312** and **313** certainly suggest, simply omitted, to explain this mysterious beginning of cosmogony.

(ii) *The void*

315 Aristotle *Physics* Δ6, 213b22 εἶναι δ' ἔφασαν καὶ οἱ Πυθαγόρειοι κενόν, καὶ ἐπεισιέναι αὐτῷ[1] τῷ οὐρανῷ ἐκ τοῦ ἀπείρου πνεῦμά τε[1] ὡς ἀναπνέοντι καὶ τὸ κενόν, ὃ διορίζει τὰς φύσεις, ὡς ὄντος τοῦ κενοῦ χωρισμοῦ τινος τῶν ἐφεξῆς καὶ τῆς διορίσεως· καὶ τοῦτ' εἶναι πρῶτον ἐν τοῖς ἀριθμοῖς· τὸ γὰρ κενὸν διορίζειν τὴν φύσιν αὐτῶν.

316 Stobaeus *Anth.* I, 18, 1*c* (quoting Aristotle) ἐν δὲ τῷ περὶ τῆς Πυθαγόρου φιλοσοφίας πρώτῳ γράφει τὸν μὲν οὐρανὸν εἶναι ἕνα, ἐπεισάγεσθαι δὲ ἐκ τοῦ ἀπείρου χρόνον τε καὶ πνοὴν καὶ τὸ κενόν, ὃ διορίζει ἑκάστων τὰς χώρας ἀεί.

317 Alexander *Met.* 512, 37 (commenting on Ar. *Met.* Z11, 1036b8, **406**) ἐπειδὴ γὰρ δυάς ἐστι τὸ πρῶτον διάστατον (εἰς πρώτην γὰρ τὴν δυάδα ἡ μονὰς διέστη, καὶ οὕτως εἰς τὴν τριάδα καὶ τοὺς ἑξῆς ἀριθμούς), εἴπερ ὁριζόμεθα, φασί (*sc.* the Pythagoreans), τὴν γραμμήν, οὐ χρὴ λέγειν αὐτὴν πόσον ἐφ' ἓν διάστατον, ἀλλὰ γραμμή ἐστι τὸ πρῶτον διάστατον.

[1] The text and precise meaning of this sentence are doubtful: αὐτῷ G Philoponus Stobaeus, αὐτὸ EFIJ; πνεύματος codd. Philoponus *in lemmate* Stobaeus, πνεῦμα Simplicius Tennemann Heidel, πνεῦμά τε Diels, fortasse E[1].—Ross prints αὐτὸ and πνεύματος, with some hesitation; but the paraphrases of Philoponus (610, 8; 615, 23) and Simplicius (to whom Themistius is here closely similar) say nothing about infinite *breath*, but merely mention 'the surrounding infinite' or 'that which lies outside': so **318** Simplicius *Phys.* 651, 26 ...τὸ κενὸν ἐπεισιέναι τῷ κόσμῳ οἷον ἀναπνέοντι ἤτοι εἰσπνέοντι αὐτῷ ὥσπερ πνεῦμα ἀπὸ τοῦ ἔξωθεν περικεχυ-

---

315 *The Pythagoreans, too, held that void exists and that breath(?) and void enter from the Unlimited into the heaven itself which, as it were, inhales; the void distinguishes the natures of things, being a kind of separating and distinguishing factor between terms in series. This happens primarily in the case of numbers; for the void distinguishes their nature.*

316 *In the first book of his work* On the philosophy of Pythagoras *he writes that the universe is one, and that from the unlimited there are drawn into it time, breath and the void, which constantly distinguishes the places of the various classes of thing.*

317 *For since the dyad is the first extension (for the unit first extended into the dyad, so to the triad and the numbers in succession), if we define the line, the Pythagoreans say, we should not call it quantity extended in one dimension, but the line is the first extension.*

318 *...The void enters the universe, which, as it were, inhales or breathes it in, just like breath, from that which surrounds it.*

μένου. This suggests that Simplicius read πνεῦμα in his text of Aristotle, and that πνεῦμα belongs to the inhalation image (according to Simplicius, though not to Philoponus and Themistius, it is explicitly a simile, i.e. ὡς in **315** means οἷον). If Simplicius is correct we must accept αὐτῷ and πνεῦμα in Aristotle, and the meaning will be: '...and there enters into the universe itself out of the infinite, as though the universe were inhaling breath, even the void'. This eliminates the surprising idea (which is anyhow irrelevant to Aristotle's point) that the world draws in *breath* as well as the void; though the idea was accepted by Stobaeus in **316**, perhaps through an ambiguity of Aristotle's language.

However it came into being, the first unit seems forthwith to have begun, as it were, to inhale the surrounding Unlimited. Exactly as, in **297**, the Even was said to be 'taken in and limited by the Odd', so in **312** 'the nearest part of the Unlimited was drawn in and limited by Limit'—or rather, to be precise, by the first unit functioning as Limit. And now, in **315** and **316**, we learn something of the consequences of this progressive 'inhalation': whether or not breath and time came with it, at all events the void entered in from outside. The function of the void is to keep things apart—and things include the units of arithmetic. Unfortunately Aristotle himself nowhere in his extant works tells us anything at all of the first consequence of this 'inhalation' of the void by the first unit; but **317**, which, in the opinion of Ross, 'was probably derived from Aristotle's lost work on the Pythagoreans' (note on Ar. *Met.* Z 11, 1036b8), seems to fill the gap. Apparently the first unit, like other living things, began at once to grow, and somehow as the result of its growth burst asunder into two; whereupon the void, fulfilling its proper function, keeps the two units apart, and thus, owing to the confusion of the units of arithmetic with the points of geometry, brings into existence not only the number 2 but also the line. So the process is begun which, continuing indefinitely, is to result in the visible universe as we know it.

(iii) *Points, lines, planes and solids*

319 Speusippus *ap. Theologumena Arithmeticae* p. 84, 10 de Falco (DK 44 A 13) τὸ μὲν γὰρ ἓν στιγμή, τὰ δὲ δύο γραμμή, τὰ δὲ τρία τρίγωνον, τὰ δὲ τέσσαρα πυραμίς. ταῦτα δὲ πάντα ἐστὶ πρῶτα καὶ ἀρχαὶ τῶν καθ' ἕκαστον ὁμογενῶν...τὰ αὐτὰ δὲ καὶ

---

319 *For 1 is the point, 2 the line, 3 the triangle and 4 the pyramid. All these are primary, the first principles of individual things of the same class...and the same holds in generation*

ἐν τῇ γενέσει· πρώτη μὲν γὰρ ἀρχὴ εἰς μέγεθος στιγμή, δευτέρα γραμμή, τρίτη ἐπιφάνεια, τέταρτον στερεόν.

320 Aristotle *Met.* N3, 1090b5 (with which cf. *ib.* Z2, 1028b15, **405**) εἰσὶ δέ τινες οἳ ἐκ τοῦ πέρατα εἶναι καὶ ἔσχατα τὴν στιγμὴν μὲν γραμμῆς, ταύτην δ' ἐπιπέδου, τοῦτο δὲ τοῦ στερεοῦ, οἴονται εἶναι ἀνάγκην τοιαύτας φύσεις εἶναι.

317 has already told us that, having generated the number 2, which equals the line, the first unit 'proceeds in the same way to the number 3 and the other numbers in succession'; and just as 2 equals the line, so also, we learn from **319**, 3 equals the triangle, the simplest plane figure, and 4 the tetrahedron, the simplest solid. By the time of Aristotle there were already two different accounts given of the way in which the first unit proceeded to generate in turn the line, the plane and the solid. Besides the apparently primitive method with which we are at present concerned, by which the 'inhalation' of the void resulted in the division of the first unit into 2, 3 and 4 in succession, there was also a more sophisticated view by which the first unit 'flowed' into a line, the line into a plane and the plane into a solid. By this method, however, which looks like a later refinement of the other, the resulting figures are obviously not, as in **319**, the triangle and the tetrahedron, but rather the square and the cube.[1] There is little doubt that the view of the early generation of Pythagoreans we are now considering is that preserved by Speusippus in **319**;[2] and if, as is usually assumed, **320** also refers to the Pythagoreans, then we have Aristotle's authority for the conclusion that points, lines and planes, being regarded as φύσεις, i.e. separate entities, played a vital part in Pythagorean cosmogony.

[1] Aristotle himself mentions this more sophisticated method at **321** *de an.* A4, 409a4 ἐπεί φασι κινηθεῖσαν γραμμὴν ἐπίπεδον ποιεῖν, στιγμὴν δὲ γραμμήν, καὶ αἱ τῶν μονάδων κινήσεις γραμμαὶ ἔσονται. ἡ γὰρ στιγμὴ μονάς ἐστι θέσιν ἔχουσα. Whoever it was who first held this view, therefore,

---

too; for the first principle in magnitude is the point, the second the line, the third surface and the fourth the solid.

320 *There are some who, because the point is the limit and extreme of the line, the line of the plane, and the plane of the solid, think there must be real things of this sort.* (Trans. Ross)

321 *For they say that the movement of a line creates a plane and that of the point a line; and likewise the movements of units will be lines. For the point is a unit having position.*

it is at least pre-Aristotelian. But in any case Sextus is probably right when, in the course of a long discussion of the two methods, he first describes that with which we are concerned and then proceeds as follows: **322** Sextus *adv. math.* x, 281 τινὲς δ' ἀπὸ ἑνὸς σημείου τὸ σῶμά φασι συνίστασθαι· τουτὶ γὰρ τὸ σημεῖον ῥυὲν γραμμὴν ἀποτελεῖν, τὴν δὲ γραμμὴν ῥυεῖσαν ἐπίπεδον ποιεῖν, τοῦτο δὲ εἰς βάθος κινηθὲν τὸ σῶμα γεννᾶν τριχῇ διάστατον. διαφέρει δὲ ἡ τοιαύτη τῶν Πυθαγορικῶν στάσις τῆς τῶν προτέρων. In the present chapter we need consider in detail only the method resulting in the tetrahedron rather than the cube.

[2] The extract from Speusippus is introduced by the author of *Theol. Arithm.* as follows: **323** *Theol. Arithm.* 82, 10 de Falco Σπεύσιππος...ἐκ τῶν ἐξαιρέτως σπουδασθεισῶν ἀεὶ Πυθαγορικῶν ἀκροάσεων, μάλιστα δὲ τῶν Φιλολάου συγγραμμάτων, βιβλίδιόν τι συντάξας γλαφυρὸν ἐπέγραψε μὲν αὐτὸ Περὶ Πυθαγορικῶν ἀριθμῶν....Though the extant fragments ascribed to Philolaus are of very doubtful authenticity (see pp. 308 ff.), there can be little doubt that Speusippus is here at least preserving a genuinely early Pythagorean doctrine. Cf. also the sixth of the list of eleven Tetractyes preserved by Theo, where all but the second—that consisting of the 'numbers by which Plato constructs the soul in the *Timaeus*'—would seem to be derived from a Pythagorean source: **324** Theo Smyrnaeus 97, 17 Hiller ἕκτη δὲ (*sc.* τετρακτὺς) τῶν φυομένων. τὸ μὲν σπέρμα ἀνάλογον μονάδι καὶ σημείῳ, ἡ δὲ εἰς μῆκος αὔξη δυάδι καὶ γραμμῇ, ἡ δὲ εἰς πλάτος τριάδι καὶ ἐπιφανείᾳ, ἡ δὲ εἰς πάχος τετράδι καὶ στερεῷ. This passage is of interest as confirming two points already made: first, that the first unit may have been deposited in the Unlimited like a seed (cf. **312** and comment); and second, that the generation of numbers, geometrical figures and physical bodies is achieved by one and the same process (cf. pp. 246 ff.).

So far, then, thanks to the tacit confusion between the unit of arithmetic and the point of geometry, the first unit has by one and the same process generated both the next three numbers in the series and the three dimensions. But once again the confusion does not stop there. Just as the number 4, being composed of four unit-points, is equated with the simplest geometrical solid, so also that geometrical solid, being composed of four point-atoms, is itself a

---

322 *Some say that the solid body is constructed from a single point; this point, by fluxion, creates the line, the line, by fluxion, makes the plane, and it in turn, by moving upwards or downwards, generates the three-dimensional body. But this section of the Pythagoreans differs from the earlier.*

323 *Speusippus...drawing on the Pythagorean doctrines that have always been particularly valued, and especially the writings of Philolaus, compiled an accomplished treatise which he entitled 'On Pythagorean numbers'....*

324 *The sixth tetractys is of things that grow. The seed is analogous to the unit and point, growth in length to the dyad and the line, growth in breadth to the triad and the plane, growth in depth to the tetrad and the solid.*

physical body. The generation of the number-series is to the Pythagoreans, in other words, both the generation of the objects of geometry and also cosmogony. Since things equal numbers, the first unit, in generating the number series, is generating also the physical universe.

(iv) *Qualitative distinctions*

325 Aristotle *Met.* A5, 986a15, from **289** φαίνονται δὴ καὶ οὗτοι τὸν ἀριθμὸν νομίζοντες ἀρχὴν εἶναι καὶ ὡς ὕλην τοῖς οὖσι καὶ ὡς πάθη τε καὶ ἕξεις....

326 Aristotle *Met.* A8, 990a12 (DK58B22) (immediately preceding **305**) ἔτι δὲ εἴτε δοίη τις αὐτοῖς ἐκ τούτων εἶναι τὸ μέγεθος εἴτε δειχθείη τοῦτο, ὅμως τίνα τρόπον ἔσται τὰ μὲν κοῦφα τὰ δὲ βάρος ἔχοντα τῶν σωμάτων; ἐξ ὧν γὰρ ὑποτίθενται καὶ λέγουσιν, οὐθὲν μᾶλλον περὶ τῶν μαθηματικῶν λέγουσι σωμάτων ἢ περὶ τῶν αἰσθητῶν· διὸ περὶ πυρὸς ἢ γῆς ἢ τῶν ἄλλων τῶν τοιούτων σωμάτων οὐδ' ὁτιοῦν εἰρήκασιν, ἅτε οὐθὲν περὶ τῶν αἰσθητῶν οἶμαι λέγοντες ἴδιον.

327 Aristotle *Met.* N5, 1092b8 οὐθὲν δὲ διώρισται οὐδὲ ὁποτέρως οἱ ἀριθμοὶ αἴτιοι τῶν οὐσιῶν καὶ τοῦ εἶναι, πότερον ὡς ὅροι, οἷον αἱ στιγμαὶ τῶν μεγεθῶν...(see **402**), ἢ ὅτι [ὁ] λόγος ἡ συμφωνία ἀριθμῶν, ὁμοίως δὲ καὶ ἄνθρωπος καὶ τῶν ἄλλων ἕκαστον; τὰ δὲ δὴ πάθη πῶς ἀριθμοί, τὸ λευκὸν καὶ γλυκὺ καὶ τὸ θερμόν;

On their implicit assumption that units, points and atoms are identical, the Pythagoreans have now succeeded in explaining the bare existence of physical bodies. But they have not yet begun to explain the fact, which they can hardly have overlooked, that one such physical body differs in appearance and behaviour from

---

325 *Evidently, then, these thinkers also consider that number is the principle both as matter for things and as forming their modifications and their permanent states....*

326 *Further, if we either granted them that spatial magnitude consists of these elements, or this were proved, still how would some bodies be light, and others have weight? To judge from what they assume and maintain, they speak no more of mathematical bodies than of perceptible; hence they have said nothing whatever about fire or earth or the other bodies of this sort, I suppose because they have nothing to say which applies* peculiarly *to perceptible things.* (Trans. Ross)

327 *Once more, it has in no sense been determined in which way numbers are the causes of substances and of being—whether (1) as limits (as points are of spatial magnitudes)... or (2) is it because harmony is a ratio of numbers, and so is man and everything else? But how are the attributes—white and sweet and hot—numbers?* (Trans. Ross)

another. The question that Aristotle asks in **326** is not, perhaps, very difficult to answer: presumably bodies are light when they contain a high proportion of void, and heavy when the proportions are reversed. But the question at the end of **327** (even if anachronistic, since the distinction had not yet been drawn between qualities and things) is by no means so simple and can only be answered with a conjecture. Every body consists, in varying proportions, of the two fundamental components, Limit and Unlimited; and those two fundamental components have each, as the Table of Opposites shows, their respective manifestations in different spheres. According, therefore, as either Limit or Unlimited prevails in the constitution of a thing, so presumably will that thing reveal more of the one principle's manifestations—more, for instance, of rest, straightness, goodness or light—and less of the other. This is admittedly a very unsatisfactory explanation of so important a factor in cosmology as qualitative distinctions. But this particular deficiency in the Pythagorean system should surprise us the less when we find, as we do, that this is one of the grounds on which Aristotle most strongly and repeatedly criticizes the Pythagoreans.

(v) *Astronomy*

328 Aristotle *Met.* A5, 986a8, from **289** ...ἐπειδὴ τέλειον ἡ δεκὰς εἶναι δοκεῖ καὶ πᾶσαν περιειληφέναι τὴν τῶν ἀριθμῶν φύσιν, καὶ τὰ φερόμενα κατὰ τὸν οὐρανὸν δέκα μὲν εἶναί φασιν, ὄντων δὲ ἐννέα μόνον τῶν φανερῶν διὰ τοῦτο δεκάτην τὴν ἀντίχθονα ποιοῦσιν. διώρισται δὲ περὶ τούτων ἐν ἑτέροις ἡμῖν ἀκριβέστερον.

329 Aristotle *de caelo* B13, 293a18 τῶν πλείστων ἐπὶ τοῦ μέσου κεῖσθαι λεγόντων (*sc.* τὴν γῆν)...ἐναντίως οἱ περὶ τὴν Ἰταλίαν, καλούμενοι δὲ Πυθαγόρειοι, λέγουσιν. ἐπὶ μὲν γὰρ τοῦ μέσου πῦρ εἶναί φασι, τὴν δὲ γῆν ἓν τῶν ἄστρων οὖσαν κύκλῳ φερομένην περὶ τὸ μέσον νύκτα τε καὶ ἡμέραν ποιεῖν. ἔτι δ' ἐναντίαν ἄλλην ταύτῃ

---

328 *As the number 10 is thought to be perfect and to comprise the whole nature of numbers, they say that the bodies which move through the heavens are ten, but as the visible bodies are only nine, to meet this they invent a tenth—the 'counter-earth'. We have discussed these matters more exactly elsewhere.*

329 *Most people say that the earth lies at the centre of the universe,...but the Italian philosophers known as Pythagoreans take the contrary view. At the centre, they say, is fire, and the earth is one of the stars, creating night and day by its circular motion about the centre. They further construct another earth in opposition to ours to which they give the*

κατασκευάζουσι γῆν, ἣν ἀντίχθονα ὄνομα καλοῦσιν, οὐ πρὸς τὰ φαινόμενα τοὺς λόγους καὶ τὰς αἰτίας ζητοῦντες, ἀλλὰ πρός τινας λόγους καὶ δόξας αὑτῶν τὰ φαινόμενα προσέλκοντες καὶ πειρώμενοι συγκοσμεῖν. πολλοῖς δ' ἂν καὶ ἑτέροις συνδόξειε μὴ δεῖν τῇ γῇ τὴν τοῦ μέσου χώραν ἀποδιδόναι, τὸ πιστὸν οὐκ ἐκ τῶν φαινομένων ἀθροῦσιν ἀλλὰ μᾶλλον ἐκ τῶν λόγων. τῷ γὰρ τιμιωτάτῳ οἴονται προσήκειν τὴν τιμιωτάτην ὑπάρχειν χώραν, εἶναι δὲ πῦρ μὲν γῆς τιμιώτερον, τὸ δὲ πέρας τοῦ μεταξύ, τὸ δ' ἔσχατον καὶ τὸ μέσον πέρας· ὥστ' ἐκ τούτων ἀναλογιζόμενοι οὐκ οἴονται ἐπὶ τοῦ μέσου τῆς σφαίρας κεῖσθαι αὐτήν, ἀλλὰ μᾶλλον τὸ πῦρ. (b 1) ἔτι δ' οἵ γε Πυθαγόρειοι καὶ διὰ τὸ μάλιστα προσήκειν φυλάττεσθαι τὸ κυριώτατον τοῦ παντός· τὸ δὲ μέσον εἶναι τοιοῦτον· ὃ Διὸς φυλακὴν ὀνομάζουσι, τὸ ταύτην ἔχον τὴν χώραν πῦρ, ὥσπερ τὸ μέσον ἁπλῶς λεγόμενον καὶ τὸ τοῦ μεγέθους μέσον καὶ τοῦ πράγματος ὂν μέσον καὶ τῆς φύσεως. καίτοι καθάπερ ἐν τοῖς ζῴοις οὐ ταὐτὸν τὸ τοῦ ζῴου καὶ τοῦ σώματος μέσον, οὕτως ὑποληπτέον μᾶλλον καὶ περὶ τὸν ὅλον οὐρανόν.[1]

330 Aristotle *de caelo* B 9, 290b 12 φανερὸν δ' ἐκ τούτων ὅτι καὶ τὸ φάναι γίνεσθαι φερομένων (*sc.* τῶν ἄστρων) ἁρμονίαν, ὡς συμφώνων γινομένων τῶν ψόφων, κομψῶς μὲν εἴρηται καὶ περιττῶς ὑπὸ τῶν εἰπόντων, οὐ μὴν οὕτως ἔχει τἀληθές. δοκεῖ γάρ τισιν ἀναγκαῖον εἶναι τηλικούτων φερομένων σωμάτων γίγνεσθαι ψόφον, ἐπεὶ καὶ τῶν παρ' ἡμῖν οὔτε τοὺς ὄγκους ἐχόντων ἴσους οὔτε

---

name counter-earth. In all this they are not seeking for theories and causes to account for observed facts, but rather forcing their observations and trying to accommodate them to certain theories and opinions of their own. But there are many others who would agree that it is wrong to give the earth the central position, looking for confirmation rather to theory than to the facts of observation. Their view is that the most precious place befits the most precious thing: but fire, they say, is more precious than earth, and the limit than the intermediate, and the circumference and the centre are limits. Reasoning on this basis they take the view that it is not earth that lies at the centre of the sphere, but rather fire. (b 1) *The Pythagoreans have a further reason. They hold that the most important part of the world, which is the centre, should be most strictly guarded, and name it, or rather the fire which occupies that place, the 'Guard-house of Zeus', as if the word 'centre' were quite unequivocal, and the centre of the mathematical figure were always the same with that of the thing or the natural centre. But it is better to conceive of the case of the whole heaven as analogous to that of animals, in which the centre of the animal and that of the body are different.* (After Stocks)

330 *From all this it is clear that the theory that the movement of the stars produces a harmony, i.e. that the sounds they make are concordant, in spite of the grace and originality with which it has been stated, is nevertheless untrue. Some thinkers suppose that the motion of bodies of that size must produce a noise, since on our earth the motion of bodies far inferior in size and in speed of movement has that effect. Also, when the sun and the moon,*

τοιούτῳ τάχει φερομένων· ἡλίου δὲ καὶ σελήνης, ἔτι τε τοσούτων τὸ πλῆθος ἄστρων καὶ τὸ μέγεθος φερομένων τῷ τάχει τοιαύτην φοράν, ἀδύνατον μὴ γίγνεσθαι ψόφον ἀμήχανόν τινα τὸ μέγεθος. ὑποθέμενοι δὲ ταῦτα καὶ τὰς ταχυτῆτας ἐκ τῶν ἀποστάσεων ἔχειν τοὺς τῶν συμφωνιῶν λόγους, ἐναρμόνιόν φασι γίγνεσθαι τὴν φωνὴν φερομένων κύκλῳ τῶν ἄστρων. ἐπεὶ δ' ἄλογον δοκεῖ τὸ μὴ συνακούειν ἡμᾶς τῆς φωνῆς ταύτης, αἴτιον τούτου φασὶν εἶναι τὸ γιγνομένοις εὐθὺς ὑπάρχειν τὸν ψόφον, ὥστε μὴ διάδηλον εἶναι πρὸς τὴν ἐναντίαν σιγήν· πρὸς ἄλληλα γὰρ φωνῆς καὶ σιγῆς εἶναι τὴν διάγνωσιν, ὥστε καθάπερ τοῖς χαλκοτύποις διὰ συνήθειαν οὐθὲν δοκεῖ διαφέρειν, καὶ τοῖς ἀνθρώποις ταὐτὸ συμβαίνειν.

There is unfortunately no sure means of precisely dating either of these celebrated doctrines, the Counter-Earth (**328** and **329**[1]) and the 'Harmony of the Spheres' (**330**). The former is explicitly attributed by Aetius to Philolaus;[2] but despite the relative reliability of its source the attribution has often been doubted. On the whole it seems legitimate provisionally to accept the attribution of the Counter-Earth doctrine to Philolaus (see pp. 307 ff.), while the doctrine of the 'Harmony of the Spheres', which is considerably less complicated, may perhaps be surmised to have originated early in the fifth century B.C., when, thanks to Pythagoras' own discovery that the intervals of the musical scale could be expressed as numerical ratios (see pp. 229 f.), the Pythagoreans seem, in Aristotle's words in **289**, to have 'collected and fitted into their scheme all the properties of numbers and scales which they could show to agree with the attributes and parts and the whole arrangement of the heavens'.

[1] Simplicius, paraphrasing, expanding, and commenting on this passage, adds just sufficient detail, derived in part from Aristotle's lost work *On the Pythagoreans*, to be worth quoting at some length: **331** Simplicius *de caelo*

---

they say, and all the stars, so great in number and in size, are moving with so rapid a motion, how should they not produce a sound immensely great? Starting from this argument and from the observation that their speeds, as measured by their distances, are in the same ratios as musical concordances, they assert that the sound given forth by the circular movement of the stars is a harmony. Since, however, it appears unaccountable that we should not hear this music, they explain this by saying that the sound is in our ears from the very moment of birth and is thus indistinguishable from its contrary silence, since sound and silence are discriminated by mutual contrast. What happens to men, then, is just what happens to coppersmiths, who are so accustomed to the noise of the smithy that it makes no difference to them. (Trans. Stocks)

331 *In the centre of the universe they say there is fire, and round the centre moves the*

511, 26 ἐν μὲν τῷ μέσῳ τοῦ παντὸς πῦρ εἶναί φασι, περὶ δὲ τὸ μέσον τὴν ἀντίχθονα φέρεσθαί φασι γῆν οὖσαν καὶ αὐτήν, ἀντίχθονα δὲ καλουμένην διὰ τὸ ἐξ ἐναντίας τῇδε τῇ γῇ εἶναι, μετὰ δὲ τὴν ἀντίχθονα ἡ γῆ ἥδε φερομένη καὶ αὐτὴ περὶ τὸ μέσον, μετὰ δὲ τὴν γῆν ἡ σελήνη· οὕτω γὰρ αὐτὸς (*sc.* Aristotle) ἐν τῷ περὶ τῶν Πυθαγορικῶν ἱστορεῖ· τὴν δὲ γῆν ὡς ἓν τῶν ἄστρων οὖσαν κινουμένην περὶ τὸ μέσον κατὰ τὴν πρὸς τὸν ἥλιον σχέσιν νύκτα καὶ ἡμέραν ποιεῖν. ἡ δὲ ἀντίχθων κινουμένη περὶ τὸ μέσον καὶ ἑπομένη τῇ γῇ ταύτῃ οὐχ ὁρᾶται ὑφ' ἡμῶν διὰ τὸ ἐπιπροσθεῖν ἡμῖν ἀεὶ τὸ τῆς γῆς σῶμα....τέλειον γὰρ ἀριθμὸν ὑποθέμενοι τὴν δεκάδα ἐβούλοντο καὶ τῶν κυκλοφορητικῶν σωμάτων τὸν ἀριθμὸν εἰς δεκάδα συνάγειν. θέντες οὖν, φησί, τὴν ἀπλανῆ μίαν καὶ τὰς πλανωμένας ἑπτὰ καὶ τὴν γῆν ταύτην τῇ ἀντίχθονι τὴν δεκάδα συνεπλήρωσαν. καὶ οὕτω μὲν αὐτὸς τὰ τῶν Πυθαγορείων ἀπεδείξατο· οἱ δὲ γνησιώτερον αὐτῶν μετασχόντες πῦρ μὲν ἐν τῷ μέσῳ λέγουσι τὴν δημιουργικὴν δύναμιν τὴν ἐκ μέσου πᾶσαν τὴν γῆν ζωογονοῦσαν καὶ τὸ ἀπεψυγμένον αὐτῆς ἀναθάλπουσαν· διὸ οἱ μὲν Ζηνὸς πύργον αὐτὸ καλοῦσιν, ὡς αὐτὸς ἐν τοῖς Πυθαγορικοῖς ἱστόρησεν, οἱ δὲ Διὸς φυλακήν, ὡς ἐν τούτοις, οἱ δὲ Διὸς θρόνον, ὡς ἄλλοι φασίν. Hilda Richardson (*CQ* 20 (1926) 119) argues, on the basis of this passage and a number of other less definite indications, that 'the earliest generations of the Pythagorean school conceived of fire as existing at the heart of their central, spherical earth'. But whether this is so or not, Simplicius himself evidently believed that the earlier Pythagorean theory was geocentric, and that the more sophisticated doctrine was a later refinement.

[2] **332** Aetius II, 7, 7 (DK 44 A 16) Φιλόλαος πῦρ ἐν μέσῳ περὶ τὸ κέντρον ὅπερ ἑστίαν τοῦ παντὸς καλεῖ καὶ Διὸς οἶκον καὶ μητέρα θεῶν βωμόν τε καὶ συνοχὴν καὶ μέτρον φύσεως. καὶ πάλιν πῦρ ἕτερον ἀνωτάτω τὸ περιέχον. πρῶτον δ' εἶναι φύσει τὸ μέσον, περὶ δὲ τοῦτο δέκα σώματα θεῖα χορεύειν, [οὐρανόν] ⟨μετὰ τὴν τῶν ἀπλανῶν σφαῖραν⟩ τοὺς ē πλανήτας, μεθ' οὓς ἥλιον,

---

counter-earth, being itself an earth, and called the counter-earth because it is opposite this earth of ours; and after the counter-earth comes our earth, which also moves around the centre; and after the earth comes the moon; for so Aristotle records in his work On the Pythagoreans. *The earth, being one of the stars and moving around the centre, makes day and night in accordance with its position relative to the sun. The counter-earth, as it moves around the centre following our earth, is invisible to us because the bulk of the earth is always in the way... For on their assumption that the decad is the perfect number, they wished to bring the number of bodies revolving in a circle also up to ten. And so, Aristotle says, positing the sphere of the fixed stars as one, the planets as seven, and then this earth of ours, they completed the decad with the counter-earth. So Aristotle expounded the Pythagoreans' views; but the more genuine members of the school regard fire at the centre as the creative force which gives life to the whole earth from the centre and warms its cold parts; and so some call it the 'Tower of Zeus', as Aristotle recorded in* On the Pythagoreans, *others the 'Guard-house of Zeus', as he says here, others again the 'Throne of Zeus', as other authorities tell us.*

332 *Philolaus places fire around the centre of the universe, and calls it the 'Hearth of the world', the 'House of Zeus', 'Mother of the Gods', 'altar, bond and measure of nature'. Then again there is another fire enveloping the universe at the circumference. But he says that the centre is by nature primary, and around the centre ten divine bodies dance—first the sphere of the fixed stars, then the five planets, next the sun, then the moon, then the earth,*

ὑφ' ᾧ σελήνην, ὑφ' ᾗ τὴν γῆν, ὑφ' ᾗ τὴν ἀντίχθονα, μεθ' ἃ σύμπαντα τὸ πῦρ ἑστίας περὶ τὰ κέντρα τάξιν ἐπέχον. The supplement μετὰ...σφαῖραν is by Diels, οὐρανόν being presumably a marginal gloss.

(vi) *The soul*

333 Aristotle *Met.* A5, 985b29, from **289** ...τὸ μὲν τοιονδὶ τῶν ἀριθμῶν πάθος δικαιοσύνη, τὸ δὲ τοιονδὶ ψυχὴ καὶ νοῦς....

334 Aristotle *de anima* A2, 404a16 ἔοικε δὲ καὶ τὸ παρὰ τῶν Πυθαγορείων λεγόμενον τὴν αὐτὴν ἔχειν διάνοιαν· ἔφασαν γάρ τινες αὐτῶν ψυχὴν εἶναι τὰ ἐν τῷ ἀέρι ξύσματα, οἱ δὲ τὸ ταῦτα κινοῦν. περὶ δὲ τούτων εἴρηται, διότι συνεχῶς φαίνεται κινούμενα, κἂν ᾖ νηνεμία παντελής.

335 Aristotle *de anima* A4, 407b27 καὶ ἄλλη δέ τις δόξα παραδέδοται περὶ ψυχῆς...ἁρμονίαν γάρ τινα αὐτὴν λέγουσι· καὶ γὰρ τὴν ἁρμονίαν κρᾶσιν καὶ σύνθεσιν ἐναντίων εἶναι καὶ τὸ σῶμα συγκεῖσθαι ἐξ ἐναντίων. Cf. Ar. *Pol.* Θ5, 1340b18 (DK58B41) and Plato *Phaedo* 86B–C.

336 Aristotle *de anima* A3, 407b20 οἱ δὲ μόνον ἐπιχειροῦσι λέγειν ποῖόν τι ἡ ψυχή, περὶ δὲ τοῦ δεξομένου σώματος οὐθὲν ἔτι προσδιορίζουσιν, ὥσπερ ἐνδεχόμενον κατὰ τοὺς Πυθαγορικοὺς μύθους τὴν τυχοῦσαν ψυχὴν εἰς τὸ τυχὸν ἐνδύεσθαι σῶμα.

Here we have at least four different (though not necessarily mutually exclusive) views of the soul, each of which is said by Aristotle to be Pythagorean. Once again the attempt to date them can rest only upon conjecture. It seems probable that the view in **334**, that the soul is either the motes in the air or that which

---

then the counter-earth, and finally the fire of the 'Hearth', which has its station around the centre.

333 *...such and such a modification of numbers being justice, another being soul and reason....*

334 *The theory held by the Pythagoreans seems to have the same purport; for some of them said that the soul is the motes in the air, others that it is what moves them. They spoke of motes because they are evidently in continual motion, even when there is a complete calm.*

335 *Another theory has been handed down to us about the soul.... They say that it is a kind of attunement; for attunement is a blending and composing of opposites, and the body is constituted of opposites.*

336 *But they only attempt to say what sort of a thing the soul is, while concerning the body that is to receive it they specify nothing further, as if it were possible, by the Pythagorean tales, for any chance soul to enter into any chance body.*

moves them, belongs to the early and unwittingly corporealist generation which thought that units were extended in space. The doctrine in **335**, on the other hand, that the soul is an attunement (which is of course reconcilable with the view mentioned in **333** that it is a πάθος ἀριθμῶν) may have originated from the ἰσονομία view of health introduced by Alcmaeon (see pp. 234 f.), and in that case would not have been held before his time. Finally, the familiar belief in transmigration, to which Aristotle is clearly referring in **336**, is a belief of a different order, not being concerned with the nature of the soul as such but rather with what befalls it. This is one of the few traces of the religious side of Pythagoreanism that are to be found in Aristotle's extant writings; and it is noteworthy that in this unusual context he uses, not the familiar form Πυθαγόρειος, but the variant, very seldom found in his works, Πυθαγορικός. The belief in transmigration goes back, as we saw (pp. 222 f.), to Pythagoras himself, but was certainly preserved, throughout the whole of the fifth century at least, by the Acousmatics (see p. 227).

It would be possible, if perhaps dangerously conjectural, to fit all these theories into a consistent picture, as follows. The earliest Pythagoreans might well have maintained that between its various incarnations the soul, separated from a body, hovered in the air like the motes in a sunbeam; and in that case others of the school, feeling perhaps that this was too humble a part, preferred to regard it rather as that which moved the motes (conceivably even as the πνεῦμα or πνοή ('breath') of **315** and **316**). Alcmaeon could then have borrowed from these earliest Pythagoreans the belief, which underlies also his own peculiar view of the soul (cf. p. 235), that the soul is always in motion. Finally the next generation of Pythagoreans, borrowing in their turn from Alcmaeon, may have based upon his theory of health their own doctrine, by far the most influential of those under discussion, that the soul was an attunement of the bodily constituents.

CHAPTER X

PARMENIDES OF ELEA

DATE

337 Plato *Parmenides* 127A ἔφη δὲ δὴ ὁ Ἀντιφῶν λέγειν τὸν Πυθόδωρον ὅτι ἀφίκοιντό ποτε εἰς Παναθήναια τὰ μεγάλα Ζήνων τε καὶ Παρμενίδης. τὸν μὲν οὖν Παρμενίδην εὖ μάλα δὴ πρεσβύτην εἶναι, σφόδρα πολιόν, καλὸν δὲ κἀγαθὸν τὴν ὄψιν, περὶ ἔτη μάλιστα πέντε καὶ ἑξήκοντα· Ζήνωνα δὲ ἐγγὺς ἐτῶν τετταράκοντα τότε εἶναι, εὐμήκη δὲ καὶ χαρίεντα ἰδεῖν· καὶ λέγεσθαι αὐτὸν παιδικὰ τοῦ Παρμενίδου γεγονέναι. καταλύειν δὲ αὐτοὺς ἔφη παρὰ τῷ Πυθοδώρῳ ἐκτὸς τείχους ἐν Κεραμεικῷ· οἷ δὴ καὶ ἀφικέσθαι τόν τε Σωκράτη καὶ ἄλλους τινὰς μετ' αὐτοῦ πολλούς, ἐπιθυμοῦντας ἀκοῦσαι τῶν τοῦ Ζήνωνος γραμμάτων—τότε γὰρ αὐτὰ πρῶτον ὑπ' ἐκείνων κομισθῆναι —Σωκράτη δὲ εἶναι τότε σφόδρα νέον. (Cf. Plato *Theaetetus* 183E and *Sophist* 217C (both DK28A5), each of which refers briefly to the meeting of the young Socrates with the old Parmenides.)

338 Diogenes Laertius IX, 23 (DK28A1) ἤκμαζε δὲ (*sc.* Parmenides) κατὰ τὴν ἐνάτην καὶ ἑξηκοστὴν ὀλυμπιάδα (i.e. 504–501 B.C.).

Whether or not Parmenides and Zeno ever visited Athens and met there the young Socrates, Plato need not have been so precise about their respective ages. The fact that he gives these details strongly suggests that he is writing with chronological accuracy. Socrates was just over seventy when he was put to death in 399 B.C., which means that he was born in 470/469. If we assume that the words σφόδρα νέον, 'very young', mean that he was under twenty-five, then the meeting might have taken place between 450 and 445 B.C. This places Parmenides' birth at about 515–

---

337 *According to Antiphon's account, Pythodorus said that Parmenides and Zeno once came to Athens for the Great Panathenaea. Parmenides was well advanced in years—about sixty-five—and very grey, but a fine-looking man. Zeno was then nearly forty, and tall and handsome; he was said to have been Parmenides' favourite. They were staying at Pythodorus' house outside the city-wall in the Ceramicus. Thither went Socrates, and several others with him, in the hope of hearing Zeno's treatise; for this was the first time Parmenides and Zeno had brought it to Athens. Socrates was still very young at the time.*

338 *Parmenides flourished in the sixty-ninth Olympiad.*

510 B.C. and Zeno's at about 490–485. It is of course true that the date given by Diogenes, which he probably derived from Apollodorus, does not nearly square with this; but, as Burnet points out (*EGP* 170), 'the date given by Apollodorus depends solely on that of the foundation of Elea (540 B.C.), which he had adopted as the *floruit* of Xenophanes. Parmenides is born in that year, just as Zeno is born in the year when Parmenides "flourished".' Unsatisfactory as a late Platonic dialogue may be as evidence for chronology, it can hardly be doubted that it is more reliable than this. But in any case what really matters is not so much Parmenides' precise dates as his relation to the other Presocratics. We shall see as we proceed that his poem certainly contains references to Anaximenes (see p. 275) and perhaps also to Heraclitus (see pp. 183 and 272), while both Empedocles and Anaxagoras refer often and obviously to Parmenides (cf. **414–416**, **497**).

LIFE

339 Diogenes Laertius IX, 21–3 (DK28A1) Παρμενίδης Πύρητος Ἐλεάτης διήκουσε Ξενοφάνους. (τοῦτον (*sc.* Xenophanes) Θεόφραστος ἐν τῇ Ἐπιτομῇ Ἀναξιμάνδρου φησὶν ἀκοῦσαι.) ὅμως δ' οὖν ἀκούσας καὶ Ξενοφάνους οὐκ ἠκολούθησεν αὐτῷ. ἐκοινώνησε δὲ καὶ Ἀμεινίᾳ Διοχαίτα τῷ Πυθαγορικῷ, ὡς ἔφη Σωτίων, ἀνδρὶ πένητι μέν, καλῷ δὲ καὶ ἀγαθῷ. ᾧ καὶ μᾶλλον ἠκολούθησε καὶ ἀποθανόντος ἡρῷον ἱδρύσατο γένους τε ὑπάρχων λαμπροῦ καὶ πλούτου, καὶ ὑπ' Ἀμεινίου, ἀλλ' οὐχ ὑπὸ Ξενοφάνους εἰς ἡσυχίαν προετράπη...(23)...λέγεται δὲ καὶ νόμους θεῖναι τοῖς πολίταις, ὥς φησι Σπεύσιππος ἐν τῷ Περὶ φιλοσόφων.[1]

340 Strabo 6, p. 252 Cas. (DK28A12) ...Ἐλέαν..., ἐξ ἧς Παρμενίδης καὶ Ζήνων ἐγένοντο ἄνδρες Πυθαγόρειοι. δοκεῖ δέ μοι καὶ δι' ἐκείνους καὶ ἔτι πρότερον εὐνομηθῆναι.

---

339 *Parmenides of Elea, son of Pyres, was a pupil of Xenophanes (and he, according to Theophrastus in his* Epitome, *of Anaximander). But though a pupil of Xenophanes, he did not follow him. He associated also, as Sotion recorded, with the Pythagorean Ameinias, son of Diochaitas, a poor but noble man, whom he preferred to follow. When Ameinias died Parmenides, who came of a distinguished family and was rich, built a shrine to him. It was by Ameinias rather than Xenophanes that he was converted to the contemplative life....He is said also to have legislated for the citizens of Elea, as Speusippus records in his work* On the philosophers.

340 *...Elea..., whence Parmenides and Zeno came, both Pythagoreans. I believe that through their agency the city was well governed, as it had also been even earlier.*

[1] Cf. **341** Plutarch *adv. Colot.* 32, 1126A Παρμενίδης δὲ τὴν ἑαυτοῦ πατρίδα διεκόσμησε νόμοις ἀρίστοις, ὥστε τὰς ἀρχὰς καθ' ἕκαστον ἐνιαυτὸν ἐξορκοῦν τοὺς πολίτας ἐμμενεῖν τοῖς Παρμενίδου νόμοις.

These two passages, though both from late authors, preserve two traditions which are likely enough, on other grounds, to be true. That Parmenides should have taken an active part in the politics of his city is in no way surprising: several of the Presocratic philosophers did. And that he should originally have been a Pythagorean is not only not unlikely in itself, Elea being no great distance from Croton and Metapontium, but is borne out by internal evidence in his poem (see especially p. 277). Again, the statement in **339** that it was not Xenophanes but the otherwise unknown Pythagorean Ameinias who 'converted' Parmenides to the philosophic life is not the sort of thing to be invented. Aristotle himself, possibly misled by a remark of Plato's in the *Sophist* (242C–D, cf. **166**) which is not to be taken seriously, says of Parmenides that 'he is supposed to have been a pupil of Xenophanes' (*Met.* A5, 986b22, DK28A6); and Sotion, whom Diogenes is quoting in **339**, must have had some good reason—possibly the existence of the shrine erected by Parmenides in memory of Ameinias—for rejecting Aristotle's guidance and substituting for Xenophanes so obscure a figure. When it is remembered, finally, that these traditions are probably derived from such earlier authorities as the fourth-century historian Timaeus, there seems to be no good ground for rejecting the scanty evidence we possess about the life of Parmenides.

THE NATURE OF PARMENIDES' POEM

Parmenides wrote exclusively in hexameter verse—in which he was followed by Empedocles. With the exception of the allegory of the proem (and perhaps also certain passages in the 'Way of Seeming', in which divine figures were introduced), his subject-matter is of the most prosaic order. His diction, moreover, besides being far from poetical, is often exceedingly obscure: the precise meaning of some of his sentences will probably never be unanimously agreed. Thanks to Simplicius, who, knowing that the original work was already in his day rare, transcribed large

---

341 *Parmenides set his own state in order with such admirable laws that the government yearly swears its citizens to abide by the laws of Parmenides.*

sections of it into his commentaries on Aristotle, we possess, probably, a higher proportion of the writings of Parmenides than of any other Presocratic philosopher. After the allegorical introduction the poem is in two parts, the 'Way of Truth' and the 'Way of Seeming'. The former, of which Diels estimated that we possess about nine-tenths, presents an unprecedented exercise in logical deduction: starting from the premise ἔστι, 'it is',—in much the same way as Descartes started from the premise 'cogito'—Parmenides proceeds, by the sole use of reason unaided by the senses, to deduce all that can be known about Being, and he ends by denying any truthful validity to the senses or any reality to what they appear to perceive. Then in the 'Way of Seeming', unexpectedly reinstating the world of appearances that he has so vehemently demolished, he appends what seems, from the relatively scanty fragments that survive, to have been a cosmogony of the traditional type. The relation between the two parts of the poem is by no means obvious and has, as we shall see, been very variously interpreted; but fortunately it is the 'Way of Truth', of which so large a proportion survives, that made Parmenides the most influential of all the Presocratics, while the 'Way of Seeming', whatever the motive that prompted Parmenides to write it, seems to have exercised comparatively little influence upon his successors (but see p. 283).

THE PROEM

342 Fr. 1, Sextus *adv. math.* VII, 111 and Simplicius *de caelo* 557, 25

ἵπποι ταί με φέρουσιν ὅσον τ' ἐπὶ θυμὸς ἱκάνοι
πέμπον, ἐπεί μ' ἐς ὁδὸν βῆσαν πολύφημον ἄγουσαι
δαίμονος, ἣ κατὰ πάντ' ἄστη[1] φέρει εἰδότα φῶτα·
τῇ φερόμην· τῇ γάρ με πολύφραστοι φέρον ἵπποι
ἅρμα τιταίνουσαι, κοῦραι δ' ὁδὸν ἡγεμόνευον.
ἄξων δ' ἐν χνοίῃσιν ἵει σύριγγος ἀυτὴν
αἰθόμενος (δοιοῖς γὰρ ἐπείγετο δινωτοῖσιν
κύκλοις ἀμφοτέρωθεν), ὅτε σπερχοίατο πέμπειν

---

342 *The steeds that carry me took me as far as my heart could desire, when once they had brought me and set me on the renowned way of the goddess, who leads the man who knows through every town. On that way was I conveyed; for on it did the wise steeds convey me, drawing my chariot, and maidens led the way. And the axle blazing in the socket—for it was urged round by well-turned wheels at each end—was making the holes in the naves sing,*

Ἡλιάδες κοῦραι, προλιποῦσαι δώματα Νυκτός,
εἰς φάος, ὠσάμεναι κράτων ἄπο χερσὶ καλύπτρας.
ἔνθα πύλαι Νυκτός τε καὶ Ἤματός εἰσι κελεύθων,
καί σφας ὑπέρθυρον ἀμφὶς ἔχει καὶ λάινος οὐδός.
αὐταὶ δ' αἰθέριαι πλῆνται μεγάλοισι θυρέτροις·
τῶν δὲ Δίκη πολύποινος ἔχει κληῖδας ἀμοιβούς.
τὴν δὴ παρφάμεναι κοῦραι μαλακοῖσι λόγοισιν
πεῖσαν ἐπιφραδέως, ὥς σφιν βαλανωτὸν ὀχῆα
ἀπτερέως ὤσειε πυλέων ἄπο· ταὶ δὲ θυρέτρων
χάσμ' ἀχανὲς ποίησαν ἀναπτάμεναι πολυχάλκους
ἄξονας ἐν σύριγξιν ἀμοιβαδὸν εἰλίξασαι
γόμφοις καὶ περόνῃσιν ἀρηρότε· τῇ ῥα δι' αὐτέων
ἰθὺς ἔχον κοῦραι κατ' ἀμαξιτὸν ἅρμα καὶ ἵππους.
καί με θεὰ πρόφρων ὑπεδέξατο, χεῖρα δὲ χειρὶ
δεξιτερὴν ἕλεν, ὧδε δ' ἔπος φάτο καί με προσηύδα·
ὦ κοῦρ' ἀθανάτοισι συνάορος ἡνιόχοισιν,
ἵπποις ταί σε φέρουσιν ἱκάνων ἡμέτερον δῶ,
χαῖρ', ἐπεὶ οὔτι σε μοῖρα κακὴ προὔπεμπε νέεσθαι
τήνδ' ὁδόν (ἦ γὰρ ἀπ' ἀνθρώπων ἐκτὸς πάτου ἐστίν),
ἀλλὰ θέμις τε δίκη τε. χρεὼ δέ σε πάντα πυθέσθαι
ἠμὲν Ἀληθείης εὐκυκλέος ἀτρεμὲς ἦτορ
ἠδὲ βροτῶν δόξας, ταῖς οὐκ ἔνι πίστις ἀληθής.
ἀλλ' ἔμπης καὶ ταῦτα μαθήσεαι, ὡς τὰ δοκοῦντα
χρῆν δοκίμως εἶναι διὰ παντὸς πάντα περῶντα.[2]

[1] πάντ' ἄστη Sextus N, πάντ' ἄτη L, πάντα τῇ E, ς. κατὰ πάντα τατὴ Barnett Wilamowitz (='stretched through all things') seems improbable, since τατός occurs elsewhere only once, in Aristotle's *Hist. An.* The reading

---

while the daughters of the Sun, hasting to convey me into the light, threw back the veils from off their faces and left the abode of night. There are the gates of the ways of Night and Day, fitted above with a lintel and below with a threshold of stone. They themselves, high in the air, are closed by mighty doors, and avenging Justice controls the double bolts. Her did the maidens entreat with gentle words and cunningly persuade to unfasten without demur the bolted bar from the gates. Then, when the doors were thrown back, they disclosed a wide opening, when their brazen posts fitted with rivets and nails swung in turn on their hinges. Straight through them, on the broad way, did the maidens guide the horses and the car. And the goddess greeted me kindly, and took my right hand in hers, and spake to me these words: 'Welcome, o youth, that comest to my abode on the car that bears thee, tended by immortal charioteers. It is no ill chance, but right and justice, that has sent thee forth to travel on this way. Far indeed does it lie from the beaten track of men. Meet it is that thou shouldst learn all things, as well the unshaken heart of well-rounded truth, as the opinions of mortals in which is no true belief at all. Yet none the less shalt thou learn these things also—how the things that seem, as they all pass through everything, must gain the semblance of being.' (After Burnet)

of N, by its suggestion that Parmenides was an itinerant philosopher, accords with the statement of Plato that Parmenides and Zeno visited Athens.

[2] δοκίμως Simpl. mss., δοκιμῶσ' Diels, admitting an elision unknown in hexameters. But, coming so soon after δοκοῦντα, δοκίμως surely means 'seemingly', which resolves the difficulty. περῶντα Simpl. A; περ ὄντα DEF.

This proem is not only of the utmost interest as a whole but also contains a number of important points of detail. Parmenides is clearly describing his escape from error to enlightenment, and it is most likely that, as Diels suggested, the allegorical form is borrowed from oracle- and mystery-literature. 'It is clear', writes Bowra (*Problems in Greek Poetry* 47), 'that this Proem is intended to have the importance and seriousness of a religious revelation.' Not only the passage from darkness into light but many minor details throughout the poem suggest that Parmenides desired, particularly in the Proem, to arm himself in advance, by stressing the religious nature of his revelation, with an answer to his potential critics. Bowra is probably right in concluding that these potential critics were 'his fellow Pythagoreans'.

Two points of detail call for comment. It is to be noted, in the first place, that the goddess is made to address Parmenides (l. 24) as κοῦρε, 'youth', a word which provides us with our only clue as to the date of the poem's composition. If we take this to mean that Parmenides was, at the most, not much over thirty when he wrote his poem, that would fix its date somewhere between, say, 490 and 475 B.C.; and if this estimate is right, then we have an approximate *terminus ad quem*, not only for several of the Pythagorean views already described, against which we shall see that Parmenides especially aims many of his arguments, but also, possibly, for the publication of the fundamental doctrine of Heraclitus.

The other important point concerns the phrase (l. 29) Ἀληθείης εὐκυκλέος, 'well-rounded Truth'. Truth is described as well-rounded because, presumably, wherever you pick up the chain of Parmenides' reasoning, you can follow it round in a circle, passing through each of its links in turn, back to your starting-point. Parmenides himself says almost exactly that in fragment 5:

343 Fr. 5, Proclus *in Parm.* I, 708, 16 Cousin

. . . ξυνὸν δέ μοί ἐστιν
ὁππόθεν ἄρξωμαι· τόθι γὰρ πάλιν ἵξομαι αὖθις.

Every attribute of reality can be deduced from every other.

---

343 *It is all one to me where I begin; for I shall come back there again in time.*

THE WAY OF TRUTH

(i) *The premise*

344 Fr. 2, Proclus *in Tim.* I, 345, 18 Diehl

εἰ δ᾽ ἄγ᾽ ἐγὼν ἐρέω, κόμισαι δὲ σὺ μῦθον ἀκούσας,
αἵπερ ὁδοὶ μοῦναι διζήσιός εἰσι νοῆσαι·
ἡ μὲν ὅπως ἔστιν τε καὶ ὡς οὐκ ἔστι μὴ εἶναι,
πειθοῦς ἐστι κέλευθος (Ἀληθείῃ γὰρ ὀπηδεῖ),
ἡ δ᾽ ὡς οὐκ ἔστιν τε καὶ ὡς χρεών ἐστι μὴ εἶναι,
τὴν δή τοι φράζω παναπευθέα ἔμμεν ἀταρπόν·
οὔτε γὰρ ἂν γνοίης τό γε μὴ ἐόν (οὐ γὰρ ἀνυστόν)
οὔτε φράσαις. (Fr. 3) τὸ γὰρ αὐτὸ νοεῖν ἔστιν τε καὶ εἶναι.

The goddess begins her instruction by defining 'the only two conceivable ways of enquiry', which are directly contrary one to the other: if you accept one premise, then logic compels you to reject the other. The choice in fact, as Parmenides later puts it in its briefest form (**347** l. 16), is simply this: ἔστιν ἢ οὐκ ἔστιν. Unfortunately even to translate these apparently simple words is liable to be misleading, because of the ambiguity, of which Parmenides himself was unconscious, between the predicative and the existential senses of the Greek word ἐστι.[1] The usual translation, 'It is or it is not', too easily gives rise to the question what 'it' is. So Burnet, for instance, at the beginning of his discussion of the Way of Truth (*EGP* 178), writes: '...it is not quite obvious at first sight what it is precisely that *is*....There can be no real doubt that this is what we call body....The assertion that *it is* amounts just to this, that the universe is a *plenum*.' Such a conclusion is at best premature. At this early stage in his poem Parmenides' premise ἔστι has no definite subject at all: if it is necessary to translate the sentence ἔστιν ἢ οὐκ ἔστιν, then perhaps the least misleading rendering is: 'Either a thing is or it is not.' Parmenides is attacking those who believe, as all men always had believed,

---

344 *Come now, and I will tell thee—and do thou hearken and carry my word away—the only ways of enquiry that can be thought of* [literally, *that exist for thinking*, the old dative sense of the infinitive]*: the one way, that it* is *and cannot not-be, is the path of Persuasion, for it attends upon Truth; the other, that it* is-not *and needs must not-be, that I tell thee is a path altogether unthinkable. For thou couldst not know that which is-not* (*that is impossible*) *nor utter it; for the same thing can be thought as can be* [construction as above, literally *the same thing exists for thinking and for being*].

that it is possible to make a significant negative predication; but he is enabled to attack them only because of his own confusion between a negative predication and a negative existential judgement. The gist of this difficult and important fragment is therefore this: 'Either it is right only to think or say of a thing, "it is..." (i.e. "it is so-and-so, e.g. white"), or else it is right to think or say only "it is not..." (i.e. "it is not something else, e.g. black"). The latter is to be firmly rejected on the ground [a mistaken one, owing to the confusion between existential and predicative] that it is impossible to conceive of Not-Being, the non-existent. Any propositions about Not-Being are necessarily meaningless; the only significant thoughts or statements concern Being.'

[1] Owing to this undetected ambiguity it is often difficult to decide how the word ἐστι should be accented in Parmenides' poem. I have for the most part, but not always, followed DK; where I have diverged, see the parentheses in the translation.

A page or two after the sentences quoted in the last paragraph Burnet, in discussing the effects of Parmenides' 'thorough-going dialectic', adds (p. 180): 'Philosophy must now cease to be monistic or cease to be corporealist. It could not cease to be corporealist; for the incorporeal was still unknown.' This too seems an over-simplification. It is true that the incorporeal was still unknown; but it does not follow from that that Parmenides was wishing to describe 'body' or 'a *plenum*'. On the contrary, the chief difficulty about Parmenides is that, while the incorporeal was still unknown, and no vocabulary therefore existed to describe it, he was none the less, as were the Pythagoreans in the choice of their first principles, feeling his way towards it. We shall see (pp. 302 ff.) that Melissus carried the advance a stage further; but it seems probable, even in the case of Parmenides, that had he been asked whether his 'Being' was solid (or 'body') his answer would have been a hesitant negative.

(ii) *Two false premises*

345 Fr. 6, Simplicius *Phys.* 117, 4

χρὴ τὸ λέγειν τε νοεῖν τ' ἐὸν ἔμμεναι· ἔστι γὰρ εἶναι,
μηδὲν δ' οὐκ ἔστιν· τά σ' ἐγὼ φράζεσθαι ἄνωγα.

---

345 *That which can be spoken and thought needs must be* [construction as in **344**]*; for it is possible for it, but not for nothing, to be; that is what I bid thee ponder. This is*

πρώτης γάρ σ' ἀφ' ὁδοῦ ταύτης διζήσιος ⟨εἴργω⟩,
αὐτὰρ ἔπειτ' ἀπὸ τῆς, ἣν δὴ βροτοὶ εἰδότες οὐδὲν
πλάττονται, δίκρανοι· ἀμηχανίη γὰρ ἐν αὐτῶν
στήθεσιν ἰθύνει πλακτὸν νόον· οἱ δὲ φοροῦνται
κωφοὶ ὁμῶς τυφλοί τε, τεθηπότες, ἄκριτα φῦλα,
οἷς τὸ πέλειν τε καὶ οὐκ εἶναι ταὐτὸν νενόμισται
κοὐ ταὐτόν, πάντων δὲ παλίντροπός ἐστι κέλευθος.

346 Fr. 7, Plato *Sophist* 237A and Sextus *adv. math.* VII, 114

οὐ γὰρ μήποτε τοῦτο δαμῇ εἶναι μὴ ἐόντα·
ἀλλὰ σὺ τῆσδ' ἀφ' ὁδοῦ διζήσιος εἶργε νόημα
μηδέ σ' ἔθος πολύπειρον ὁδὸν κατὰ τήνδε βιάσθω
νωμᾶν ἄσκοπον ὄμμα καὶ ἠχήεσσαν ἀκουὴν
καὶ γλῶσσαν, κρῖναι δὲ λόγῳ πολύδηριν ἔλεγχον
ἐξ ἐμέθεν ῥηθέντα.

Though Parmenides has, in **344**, suggested that there are only two 'conceivable ways of enquiry', either a thing is or it is not, it now appears from these two fragments (which seem to present a continuous passage) that in addition to the true premise there are actually two premises that must be rejected. One of these, of course, is that already defined in fr. 2, the premise οὐκ ἔστι, and described as παναπευθέα, 'altogether inconceivable'; misguided as men may be, no man could confine himself to negative judgements and negative statements only. But for all that, the goddess (in **345** l. 3) warns Parmenides against treading this path, because, as she goes on to suggest (in ll. 8–9), this utterly false way can be, and constantly is, so combined with the true way that a third way, a compromise between the other two, a thing both is and is not, comes into the picture. This third way is the way on which 'ignorant mortals wander two-faced'; and they are two-faced because, as Simplicius puts it (*Phys.* 117, 3; DK28B6), εἰς ταὐτὸ συνάγουσι τὰ ἀντικείμενα, 'they combine contraries'. It is in fact

---

the first way of enquiry from which I hold thee back, and then from that way also on which mortals wander knowing nothing, two-headed; for helplessness guides the wandering thought in their breasts; they are carried along, deaf and blind at once, altogether dazed—hordes devoid of judgement, who are persuaded that to be and to be-not are the same, yet not the same, and for whom the path of all things is backward-turning.

346 *For never shall this be proved, that things that are not are; but do thou hold back thy thought from this way of enquiry, nor let custom, born of much experience, force thee to let wander along this road thy aimless eye, thy echoing ear or thy tongue; but do thou judge by reason the strife-encompassed proof that I have spoken.*

this very combination of contraries that is the basis of 'the opinions of mortals' (**342** l. 30 and **353** l. 51) which provide the content of the Way of Seeming; the premise upon which the whole Way of Seeming rests is just this compromise between the true way and the utterly false way, a thing both is and is not. It has often been suggested that the last clause of **345**, πάντων δὲ παλίντροπός ἐστι κέλευθος (translated 'of all things the path is backward-turning'), contains a special reference to the doctrines of Heraclitus; and so translated, it certainly is particularly appropriate to the Heraclitean belief that all things eventually change into their opposites (see pp. 195 f.).[1] But it is by no means the case that unless we see such a reference, then the last two lines of the fragment are meaningless. They need not necessarily mean anything more than that mortals as a whole (note ἄκριτα φῦλα, '*hordes* devoid of judgement') 'have made up their minds to believe that to be and not to be are the same and yet not the same' (i.e. they believe that that which *is* can change and become *not* what it was before. To be and not to be are the same in that they are both found in any event; and yet they are obviously opposites and are therefore, in a more exact sense, not the same), 'and they imagine that all things pass back and forth between being and not-being' (i.e. all things change from being so-and-so, e.g. hot, to not being so-and-so, and then change back again).

[1] A quite different interpretation of this last clause is attractive, taking πάντων as masculine and κέλευθος (as in **344** l. 4) as a 'way of thought', which is described as παλίντροπος because, having started out promisingly by saying ἔστι, these muddlers turn back on their tracks by adding οὐκ ἔστι. If this interpretation were adopted, the case for seeing here a reference to Heraclitus (which anyhow was largely based on the doubtful reading παλίντροπος for παλίντονος in **212**) would be further weakened.

(iii) *Deductions from the true premise:*

(*a*) *denial of time, the void, plurality*

The premise ἔστι is by now established as the only possibility: the only significant thought or statement is that a thing *is*. At this stage, therefore, Parmenides proceeds to consider precisely what must be the nature of the subject of the only true statement that can be made. From now onwards until the end of the Way of Truth he is concerned, in other words, to deduce all that can be deduced from his chosen premise about the properties of Being.

347 Fr. 8, Simplicius *Phys.* 145, 1 (continuing **346**)

μόνος δ' ἔτι μῦθος ὁδοῖο
λείπεται ὡς ἔστιν· ταύτῃ δ' ἔπι σήματ' ἔασι
πολλὰ μάλ', ὡς ἀγένητον ἐὸν καὶ ἀνώλεθρόν ἐστιν,
ἔστι γὰρ οὐλομελές τε καὶ ἀτρεμὲς ἠδ' ἀτέλεστον·
οὐδέ ποτ' ἦν οὐδ' ἔσται, ἐπεὶ νῦν ἔστιν ὁμοῦ πᾶν,
ἕν, συνεχές· τίνα γὰρ γένναν διζήσεαι αὐτοῦ;
πῇ πόθεν αὐξηθέν; οὐδ' ἐκ μὴ ἐόντος ἐάσσω
φάσθαι σ' οὐδὲ νοεῖν· οὐ γὰρ φατὸν οὐδὲ νοητὸν
ἔστιν ὅπως οὐκ ἔστι. τί δ' ἄν μιν καὶ χρέος ὦρσεν
ὕστερον ἢ πρόσθεν, τοῦ μηδενὸς ἀρξάμενον, φῦν;
οὕτως ἢ πάμπαν πελέναι χρεών ἐστιν ἢ οὐχί.
οὐδέ ποτ' ἐκ μὴ ἐόντος ἐφήσει πίστιος ἰσχὺς
γίγνεσθαί τι παρ' αὐτό· τοῦ εἵνεκεν οὔτε γενέσθαι
οὔτ' ὄλλυσθαι ἀνῆκε Δίκη χαλάσασα πέδῃσιν,
ἀλλ' ἔχει· ἡ δὲ κρίσις περὶ τούτων ἐν τῷδ' ἔστιν·
ἔστιν ἢ οὐκ ἔστιν· κέκριται δ' οὖν, ὥσπερ ἀνάγκη,
τὴν μὲν ἐᾶν ἀνόητον ἀνώνυμον (οὐ γὰρ ἀληθὴς
ἔστιν ὁδός), τὴν δ' ὥστε πέλειν καὶ ἐτήτυμον εἶναι.
πῶς δ' ἂν ἔπειτ' ἀπόλοιτο ἐόν; πῶς δ' ἄν κε γένοιτο;
εἰ γὰρ ἔγεντ', οὐκ ἔστ', οὐδ' εἴ ποτε μέλλει ἔσεσθαι.
τὼς γένεσις μὲν ἀπέσβεσται καὶ ἄπυστος ὄλεθρος.

This passage, though it presents a continuous argument and is impossible to subdivide, leads Parmenides none the less to more than one conclusion; and each of his affirmations involves a corresponding denial. The selected premise ἔστι, being the only

---

347 *One way only is left to be spoken of, that it is; and on this way are full many signs that what is is uncreated and imperishable, for it is entire, immovable and without end.* *It* was *not in the past, nor* shall *it be, since it is now, all at once, one, continuous; for what creation wilt thou seek for it? how and whence did it grow? Nor shall I allow thee to say or to think, 'from that which is not'; for it is not to be said or thought that it is not. And what need would have driven it on to grow, starting from nothing, at a later time rather than an earlier? Thus it must either completely be or be not. Nor will the force of true belief allow that, beside what is, there could also arise anything from what is not; wherefore Justice looseth not her fetters to allow it to come into being or perish, but holdeth it fast; and the decision on these matters rests here: it is or it is not. But it has surely been decided, as it must be, to leave alone the one way as unthinkable and nameless (for it is no true way), and that the other is real and true. How could what is thereafter perish? and how could it come into being? For if it came into being, it is not, nor if it is going to be in the future. So coming into being is extinguished and perishing unimaginable.*

true premise, must, Parmenides first argues, be eternally true; there cannot ever have been a time in the past, nor will there ever be a time in the future, when the statement ἔστι is anything but true. It follows, therefore, that past and future are alike meaningless, the only time is a perpetual present time, and Being must of necessity be both uncreated and imperishable. Parmenides actually adds in the course of this argument that Being must also be both ἀτρεμές, 'immovable', and ἕν, συνεχές, 'one, continuous'; but unless each of these epithets is interpreted (not very plausibly, since συνεχές unquestionably refers to space, not time, in **348** l. 25) to mean only that Being exists unalterably in one continuous present, then he is here anticipating—for 'it is all one to him where he begins' (**343**)—conclusions which he does not establish until later in the present fragment.

The next step in the argument, which occupies ll. 6–11, is the demolition of the concept of the void. The cosmogony of the Pythagoreans had made great use of the void: the first unit, once generated, had proceeded forthwith to take in from the surrounding Unlimited, possibly time (which Parmenides has just demolished), and certainly the void (to which he now turns his attention); and the void had from the outset fulfilled its vitally important function of keeping units apart (see pp. 252 f.). It is tempting to suppose that Parmenides, whom there is reason to suspect of being a dissident Pythagorean (cf. p. 265), aims the three questions that these lines contain at the very cosmogony that he had come to reject. At all events the Pythagoreans' answer to the second of these questions (πῇ πόθεν αὐξηθέν;) could only be that their first unit had grown by 'inhaling' the void; and Parmenides' immediate demolition of that concept effectually destroys, therefore, the very basis of their cosmogony. Moreover, even granting that the first unit had indeed so developed, as the Pythagoreans maintained, into the universe as we know it, why should the process have ever begun at one moment rather than another? Being must either exist as a whole or not exist at all: that (as ll. 15–18 repeat) has already been established. Yet the Pythagoreans assert that more and more of Being is constantly coming into existence from the unreal void.

The last point established in this passage before Parmenides rounds it off with a summary is that contained in lines 12–13. Unfortunately this particular sentence is ambiguous. It could perhaps mean simply that nothing can come from τὸ μὴ ὄν, 'that which does not exist', except Not-Being; but in view of the fact that it follows, in its context, immediately after nine lines that are concerned entirely with τὸ ὄν, 'Being' (in one of which, l. 6, τὸ ὄν is referred to as αὐτό), it seems preferable to follow Cornford (*Plato and Parmenides* 37) and translate: 'Nor will the force of belief suffer to arise out of what is not something over and above it (viz. what is).' In any case, as Cornford points out, this latter sense is unquestionably contained in another brief sentence further on in the same fragment (**352** ll. 36–7).

(*b*) *Reality is indivisible*

348 Fr. 8, l. 22, Simplicius *Phys.* 145, 23 (continuing **347**)

οὐδὲ διαιρετόν ἐστιν, ἐπεὶ πᾶν ἐστιν ὁμοῖον·
οὐδέ τι τῇ μᾶλλον, τό κεν εἴργοι μιν συνέχεσθαι,
οὐδέ τι χειρότερον, πᾶν δ' ἔμπλεόν ἐστιν ἐόντος.
τῷ ξυνεχὲς πᾶν ἐστιν· ἐὸν γὰρ ἐόντι πελάζει.

With these four lines should be read also the following fragment, the place of which in the poem as a whole is not clear:

349 Fr. 4, Clement *Strom.* v, 15, 5

λεῦσσε δ' ὅμως ἀπεόντα νόῳ παρεόντα βεβαίως·
οὐ γὰρ ἀποτμήξει τὸ ἐὸν τοῦ ἐόντος ἔχεσθαι
οὔτε σκιδνάμενον πάντῃ πάντως κατὰ κόσμον
οὔτε συνιστάμενον.

In these two short passages Parmenides reinforces his earlier denial of the void by a fresh argument which appears to be aimed both at Anaximenes and at the Pythagoreans. Anaximenes by his doctrine of condensation and rarefaction (see pp. 145ff.), the Pythagoreans by their view of the void as χωρισμός τις τῶν ἐφεξῆς καὶ διόρισις, 'a kind of separation and definition of things in proximity' (see **315**), had both alike been guilty of assuming the existence of what is not. Being, Parmenides maintains against them, is both indivisible and homogeneous.

---

348 *Nor is it divisible, since it is all alike; nor is there more here and less there, which would prevent it from cleaving together, but it is all full of what is. So it is all continuous; for what is clings close to what is.*

349 *Yet look at things which, though far off, are firmly present to thy mind; for thou shalt not cut off what is from clinging to what is, neither scattering itself everywhere in order nor crowding together.*

(*c*) *Reality is motionless, finite, like a sphere*

350 Fr. 8, l. 26, Simplicius *Phys.* 145, 27 (continuing **348**)

αὐτὰρ ἀκίνητον μεγάλων ἐν πείρασι δεσμῶν
ἔστιν ἄναρχον ἄπαυστον, ἐπεὶ γένεσις καὶ ὄλεθρος
τῆλε μάλ' ἐπλάχθησαν, ἀπῶσε δὲ πίστις ἀληθής.
ταὐτόν τ' ἐν ταὐτῷ τε μένον καθ' ἑαυτό τε κεῖται
χοὔτως ἔμπεδον αὖθι μένει· κρατερὴ γὰρ Ἀνάγκη
πείρατος ἐν δεσμοῖσιν ἔχει, τό μιν ἀμφὶς ἐέργει,
οὕνεκεν οὐκ ἀτελεύτητον τὸ ἐὸν θέμις εἶναι·
ἔστι γὰρ οὐκ ἐπιδευές· [μὴ] ἐὸν δ' ἂν παντὸς ἐδεῖτο.

351 Fr. 8, l. 42, Simplicius *Phys.* 146, 15 (after **352**)

αὐτὰρ ἐπεὶ πεῖρας πύματον, τετελεσμένον ἐστὶ
πάντοθεν, εὐκύκλου σφαίρης ἐναλίγκιον ὄγκῳ,
μεσσόθεν ἰσοπαλὲς πάντῃ· τὸ γὰρ οὔτε τι μεῖζον
οὔτε τι βαιότερον πελέναι χρεόν ἐστι τῇ ἢ τῇ.
οὔτε γὰρ οὐκ ἐὸν ἔστι, τό κεν παύοι μιν ἱκνεῖσθαι
εἰς ὁμόν, οὔτ' ἐὸν ἔστιν ὅπως εἴη κεν ἐόντος
τῇ μᾶλλον τῇ δ' ἧσσον, ἐπεὶ πᾶν ἐστιν ἄσυλον·
οἷ γὰρ πάντοθεν ἶσον, ὁμῶς ἐν πείρασι κύρει.

These two passages are actually separated by eight lines of summary, but by temporarily omitting those eight lines the argument is shown to be so continuous that they are best treated together. Parmenides is of course inevitably repetitive, because, as we saw (**343**), his arguments are so closely linked one with another that each attribute of Being can be deduced from any other. But even allowing for his habitual repetitiveness, we can

---

350 *But, motionless within the limits of mighty bonds, it is without beginning or end, since coming into being and perishing have been driven far away, cast out by true belief. Abiding the same in the same place it rests by itself, and so abides firm where it is; for strong Necessity holds it firm within the bonds of the limit that keeps it back on every side, because it is not lawful that what is should be unlimited; for it is not in need—if it were, it would need all.*

351 *But since there is a furthest limit, it is bounded on every side, like the bulk of a well-rounded sphere, from the centre equally balanced in every direction; for it needs must not be somewhat more here or somewhat less there. For neither is there that which is not, which might stop it from meeting its like, nor can what is be more here and less there than what is, since it is all inviolate; for being equal to itself on every side, it rests uniformly within its limits.*

hardly fail to notice, in these sixteen lines, the recurrent emphasis placed on the conception of limit, πεῖρας. Now Limit, as one of the two fundamental Pythagorean principles, stood at the top of the left-hand column in the Table of Opposites (see **289**); and among the concepts listed in that column was one, namely unity, which Parmenides has already accepted as consistent with his premise. Moreover, there is another point in these two passages that Parmenides is evidently concerned to stress: Being—or the One—is ἀκίνητον, 'motionless', ἐν ταὐτῷ μένον, 'resting in the same place', ἔμπεδον, 'stable', and ἰσοπαλές, 'equally poised'. It is in fact, in Pythagorean terminology, ἠρεμοῦν, 'at rest', as opposed to κινούμενον, 'in motion'. It begins to look almost as if Parmenides, having been reared in the Pythagorean school, had come to feel that the fatal flaw in Pythagoreanism was its dualism. At all events he seems so far, while denying the existence of those two manifestations of the Unlimited, time and the void, to be applying to his Being those attributes from the left-hand column of the Table of Opposites that can be apprehended by the sole use of reason as opposed to the senses.

SUMMARY OF THE WAY OF TRUTH

352 Fr. 8, l. 34, Simplicius *Phys.* 146, 7 (continuing **350**)

ταὐτὸν δ' ἔστι νοεῖν τε καὶ οὕνεκεν ἔστι νόημα.
οὐ γὰρ ἄνευ τοῦ ἐόντος, ἐν ᾧ πεφατισμένον ἐστίν,
εὑρήσεις τὸ νοεῖν· οὐδὲν γὰρ ⟨ἢ⟩ ἔστιν ἢ ἔσται
ἄλλο πάρεξ τοῦ ἐόντος, ἐπεὶ τό γε Μοῖρ' ἐπέδησεν
οὖλον ἀκίνητόν τ' ἔμεναι· τῷ πάντ' ὄνομ' ἔσται
ὅσσα βροτοὶ κατέθεντο πεποιθότες εἶναι ἀληθῆ,
γίγνεσθαί τε καὶ ὄλλυσθαι, εἶναί τε καὶ οὐχί,
καὶ τόπον ἀλλάσσειν διά τε χρόα φανὸν ἀμείβειν.

These eight lines, which belong properly between **350** and **351**, give a summary recapitulation of the main steps in the argument

---

352 *What can be thought is only the thought that it is.* [The infinitive by itself seldom bears the sense of the infinitive with article—i.e. '*thinking*'; the construction must be the same as in **344** and **345**—that is: *the only thing that exists for thinking is the thought that it is.*] *For you will not find thought without what is, in relation to which it is uttered; for there is not, nor shall be, anything else besides what is, since Fate fettered it to be entire and immovable. Wherefore all these are mere names which mortals laid down believing them to be true—coming into being and perishing, being and not being* [i.e. both at once], *change of place and variation of bright colour.*

of the Way of Truth. Lines 34–6 repeat the conclusion reached at the end of **344**; lines 36–7 confirm lines 12–13 of fragment 8, **347**; lines 37–8 summarize very briefly the content of **350** and **351**; and lines 38–40 revert to lines 19–21 of this same fragment, **347**. It is only in the last clause, διά τε χρόα φανὸν ἀμείβειν, 'and change of bright colour', that we find a new point. Change of colour is presumably specified as being a type of change that does not involve change of place; both locomotion and qualitative change are 'mere names'.

TRANSITION TO WAY OF SEEMING

353 Simplicius *Phys.* 30, 14 μετελθὼν δὲ ἀπὸ τῶν νοητῶν ἐπὶ τὰ αἰσθητὰ ὁ Παρμενίδης, ἤτοι ἀπὸ ἀληθείας, ὡς αὐτός φησιν, ἐπὶ δόξαν, ἐν οἷς λέγει

(Fr. 8, l. 50) ἐν τῷ σοι παύω πιστὸν λόγον ἠδὲ νόημα
ἀμφὶς ἀληθείης· δόξας δ' ἀπὸ τοῦδε βροτείας
μάνθανε κόσμον ἐμῶν ἐπέων ἀπατηλὸν ἀκούων,

τῶν γενητῶν ἀρχὰς καὶ αὐτὸς στοιχειώδεις μὲν τὴν πρώτην ἀντίθεσιν ἔθετο, ἣν φῶς καλεῖ καὶ σκότος ⟨ἢ⟩ πῦρ καὶ γῆν ἢ πυκνὸν καὶ ἀραιὸν ἢ ταὐτὸν καὶ ἕτερον, λέγων ἐφεξῆς τοῖς πρότερον παρακειμένοις ἔπεσιν

(Fr. 8, l. 53) μορφὰς γὰρ κατέθεντο δύο γνώμας ὀνομάζειν,
τῶν μίαν οὐ χρεών ἐστιν—ἐν ᾧ πεπλανημένοι εἰσίν—
τἀντία δ' ἐκρίναντο δέμας καὶ σήματ' ἔθεντο
χωρὶς ἀπ' ἀλλήλων, τῇ μὲν φλογὸς αἰθέριον πῦρ,
ἤπιον ὄν, μέγ' [ἀραιὸν] ἐλαφρόν, ἑωυτῷ πάντοσε τωὐτόν,
τῷ δ' ἑτέρῳ μὴ τωὐτόν· ἀτὰρ κἀκεῖνο κατ' αὐτὸ
τἀντία νύκτ' ἀδαῆ, πυκινὸν δέμας ἐμβριθές τε.[1]

---

353 *Parmenides effects the transition from the objects of reason to the objects of sense, or, as he himself puts it, from truth to seeming, when he writes: 'Here I end my trustworthy discourse and thought concerning truth; henceforth learn the beliefs of mortal men, listening to the deceitful ordering of my words'; and he then himself makes the elemental principles of created things the primary opposition of light and darkness, as he calls them, or fire and earth, or dense and rare, or sameness and difference; for he says immediately after the lines quoted above: 'For they made up their minds to name two forms, of which they must not name one only—that is where they have gone astray—and distinguished them as opposite in appearance and assigned to them manifestations different one from the other—to one the aitherial flame of fire, gentle and very light, in every direction identical with itself, but not with the other; and that other too is in itself just the opposite, dark night, dense in appear-*

τόν σοι ἐγὼ διάκοσμον ἐοικότα πάντα φατίζω,
ὡς οὐ μή ποτέ τίς σε βροτῶν γνώμη παρελάσσῃ.

[1] This passage of Simplicius actually ends here, at l. 59, but elsewhere (*Phys.* 39, 8) he appends also the next two lines. [ἀραιὸν] secl. Diels.

Parmenides has now, in the Way of Truth, taught us all that reason, unaided by the senses, can deduce about Being. It is like a sphere, single, indivisible and homogeneous, timeless, changeless and, since motion is itself one form of change, motionless as well. It has in fact no perceptible qualities whatever. If Parmenides had taken the left-hand column of the Pythagorean Table of Opposites and selected from it those concepts which could be apprehended by reason alone, the result would be much what his One is; while to the right-hand column, the various manifestations of the Unlimited, he has denied any reality whatever. Such are the consequences of the exercise of reason. Now, however, in passing from the Way of Truth to the Way of Seeming, Parmenides passes, as Simplicius saw, ἀπὸ τῶν νοητῶν ἐπὶ τὰ αἰσθητά, 'from the objects of reason to the objects of sense'; and just as in the Way of Truth the objects of sense have been altogether excluded, so also, as we shall see, the Way of Seeming will exclude altogether the objects of reason. Since all objects of sense are, to Parmenides, 'mere names' without substantial existence, he is obviously compelled to base his survey of them upon the false assumptions which he himself declines to share with mortals; but at the same time his survey does not cover *all* those false assumptions. Besides allowing existence to non-existent phenomena, most men went so far as to confuse them with the objects of reason. Parmenides will not, even in what he knows and avows to be 'a deceitful ordering of words' (l. 52), follow them as far as that in their error.

The significance and purpose of the Way of Seeming has been very variously interpreted. Whereas Zeller for instance, following, as he thought, a suggestion by Theophrastus,[1] regarded it as a review of popular beliefs, Burnet (*EGP* 184–5) concluded that 'in the absence of evidence to the contrary' it should be regarded rather as 'a sketch of contemporary Pythagorean cosmology'. Against any such view there are several strong arguments. The

---

ance and heavy. The whole ordering of these I tell thee as it seems likely, that so no thought of mortal men shall ever outstrip thee.'

Way of Seeming, contrary to Burnet's view, bears no discernible trace of the two fundamental Pythagorean doctrines—the opposition of Limit and Unlimited, and the equation, in whatever sense, of things with numbers; nor do the remarks of the ancient commentators indicate that there ever was any trace of these doctrines anywhere in the whole poem. It does, on the other hand, contain at least one doctrine, that of the στεφάναι in **358** and **359**, of which there is no trace in the Pythagorean cosmology, nor indeed anywhere else except possibly in Anaximander (see pp. 135 ff.). Finally, it is surely inconceivable that all the ancient commentators should have regarded the cosmology of the Way of Seeming, as they all, including Theophrastus, almost invariably did, as Parmenides' own invention, if it was in reality nothing but a summary of either popular beliefs or contemporary Pythagoreanism.

[1] **354** Theophrastus *Phys. Op.* fr. 6 *ap.* Alexandrum *Met.* 31, 12 (DK 28 A 7) ...κατὰ δόξαν δὲ τῶν πολλῶν εἰς τὸ γένεσιν ἀποδοῦναι τῶν φαινομένων δύο ποιῶν τὰς ἀρχάς.... Burnet also (*EGP* 182–4), to this extent following Zeller, used this passage to show that in the opinion of Theophrastus Parmenides meant to give the belief of 'the many'. It is, however, open to doubt whether Theophrastus here meant any more than that in the opinion of the many it is the *phenomenal* world that has to be explained. Cf. **355** Aristotle *Met.* A 5, 986 b 31 (DK 28 A 24) ...ἀναγκαζόμενος δ' ἀκολουθεῖν τοῖς φαινομένοις, καὶ τὸ ἓν μὲν κατὰ τὸν λόγον πλείω δὲ κατὰ τὴν αἴσθησιν ὑπολαμβάνων εἶναι, δύο τὰς αἰτίας καὶ δύο τὰς ἀρχὰς πάλιν τίθησι.... At all events this passage from Aristotle seems to show that he regarded the cosmology of the Way of Seeming as Parmenides' own; and that Theophrastus usually took the same view is evident from **357** below. The real value of these two passages is that they emphasize what was evidently the most important characteristic of the Way of Seeming: *two* constituents (and two only) are named, not one only. Parmenides' predecessors, other than the Pythagoreans and Alcmaeon, had run into difficulties by trying to generate the opposites out of one ἀρχή.

The foregoing interpretation of the Way of Truth will have suggested quite a different interpretation of the Way of Seeming. The essential difference between the objects of reason and the objects of sense is evidently, to Parmenides, just this: that whereas, in the case of the objects of reason, acceptance of one of a pair of

---

354 ...*to give an account, in accordance with popular opinion, of the coming into being of sensible things, he makes the first principles two....*

355 ...*but being forced to comply with sensible things, and supposing the existence of that which is one in formula but more than one according to our sensations, he now posits two causes and two first principles....* (After Ross)

contraries logically involves the rejection of the other, in the case of the objects of sense the acceptance of one involves the acceptance of the other as well. Light, for instance, can only be seen to exist in its contrast with darkness; a heavy body cannot be heavy unless there is a lighter body with which to compare it; and so with all sensible contraries.[1] The fundamental error of which men are guilty is that they have agreed to recognize the existence of these sensible opposites; and this is, of course, the error which Parmenides himself must knowingly perpetrate if he is to give an account of phenomena. Accordingly, even as he perpetrates it he declares it to be an error: 'that', he says (**353**, fr. 8 l. 54), 'is where they have gone astray'. But at least he will follow misguided mortals no further. If he is to introduce these sensible contraries he will not confuse them with intelligible; and so, instead of the primary pair of Pythagorean opposites, Limit and Unlimited (the former of which has been shown in the Way of Truth to be intelligible), he selects as his own primary pair one of their perceptible manifestations, φῶς and σκότος (or, as he himself calls it, νύξ), 'light' and 'darkness' (or 'night').

[1] This consideration seems sufficient to establish Simplicius' interpretation of the clause τῶν μίαν οὐ χρεών ἐστιν, 'two forms, of which it is not right to name one only (i.e. without the other)', as the most convincing. It is true that Cornford's translation, 'of which it is not right to name so much as one' (*Plato and Parmenides* 46), avoids the obvious difficulty of taking μίαν in the sense of ἑτέρην, and may therefore be right. But if we suppose Parmenides to mean that, whereas in the Way of Truth it is right to name one opposite and one only (the other being ἀνώνυμον, **347** l. 17), in the Way of Seeming you must not name one only without also naming the other, then we not only give the sentence an additional point, of which the structure of the whole poem seems to show that Parmenides himself was fully aware, but we also give to the crucial word μίαν the significance which its obvious contrast with δύο seems to suggest.

What Parmenides has in fact done, in passing from the Way of Truth to the Way of Seeming, is to take his own sphere of reality, the One, and fill it, quite illegitimately, with the sensible opposites of light and darkness; and once he has taken that forbidden step, then he can proceed, as had the Pythagoreans with Limit and Unlimited, to broaden the scope of each of these primary opposites by describing their various manifestations.[1] Light is rare, night dense, and so on. Once one pair of sensible opposites has been admitted, then there is no insuperable difficulty in giving an

explanation of phenomena; and if only because it avoids the confusion between reason and sense, Parmenides' own explanation, even though deliberately based on error, is at least such that 'no thought of mortal men shall ever outstrip him' (**353**, fr. 8 l. 61).

[1] Cf. Fr. 9, which according to Simplicius comes μετ' ὀλίγα (i.e. soon after Fr. 8): **356** Simplicius *Phys.* 180, 9

αὐτὰρ ἐπειδὴ πάντα φάος καὶ νὺξ ὀνόμασται
καὶ τὰ κατὰ σφετέρας δυνάμεις ἐπὶ τοῖσί τε καὶ τοῖς,
πᾶν πλέον ἐστὶν ὁμοῦ φάεος καὶ νυκτὸς ἀφάντου,
ἴσων ἀμφοτέρων, ἐπεὶ οὐδετέρῳ μέτα μηδέν.

THE SENSIBLE OPPOSITES

357 Theophrastus *de sensu* 1 ff. (DK 28 A 46) περὶ δ' αἰσθήσεως αἱ μὲν πολλαὶ καὶ καθόλου δόξαι δύ' εἰσιν· οἱ μὲν γὰρ τῷ ὁμοίῳ ποιοῦσιν, οἱ δὲ τῷ ἐναντίῳ. Παρμενίδης μὲν καὶ Ἐμπεδοκλῆς καὶ Πλάτων τῷ ὁμοίῳ, οἱ δὲ περὶ Ἀναξαγόραν καὶ Ἡράκλειτον τῷ ἐναντίῳ....(3) Παρμενίδης μὲν γὰρ ὅλως οὐδὲν ἀφώρικεν ἀλλὰ μόνον ὅτι δυοῖν ὄντοιν στοιχείοιν κατὰ τὸ ὑπερβάλλον ἐστὶν ἡ γνῶσις. ἐὰν γὰρ ὑπεραίρῃ τὸ θερμὸν ἢ τὸ ψυχρόν, ἄλλην γίνεσθαι τὴν διάνοιαν, βελτίω δὲ καὶ καθαρωτέραν τὴν διὰ τὸ θερμόν· οὐ μὴν ἀλλὰ καὶ ταύτην δεῖσθαί τινος συμμετρίας·

(Fr. 16) ὡς γὰρ ἕκαστος (φησίν) ἔχει κρᾶσιν μελέων πολυπλάγκτων,
τὼς νόος ἀνθρώποισι παρίσταται· τὸ γὰρ αὐτὸ
ἔστιν ὅπερ φρονέει μελέων φύσις ἀνθρώποισιν
καὶ πᾶσιν καὶ παντί· τὸ γὰρ πλέον ἐστὶ νόημα.

τὸ γὰρ αἰσθάνεσθαι καὶ τὸ φρονεῖν ὡς ταὐτὸ λέγει· διὸ καὶ τὴν μνήμην καὶ τὴν λήθην ἀπὸ τούτων γίνεσθαι διὰ τῆς κράσεως· ἂν

---

356 *And when all things have been named light and night, and things corresponding to their powers have been assigned to each, everything is full of light and of obscure night at once, both equal, since neither has any share of nothingness.*

357 *The majority of general views about sensation are two: some make it of like by like, others of opposite by opposite. Parmenides, Empedocles and Plato say it is of like by like, the followers of Anaxagoras and of Heraclitus of opposite by opposite....Parmenides gave no clear definition at all, but said only that there were two elements and that knowledge depends on the excess of one or the other. Thought varies according to whether the hot or the cold prevails, but that which is due to the hot is better and purer; not but what even that needs a certain balance; for, says he, 'According to the mixture that each man has in his wandering limbs, so thought is forthcoming to mankind; for that which thinks is the same thing, namely the substance of their limbs, in each and all men; for that of which there is more is thought'—for he regards perception and thought as the same. So too memory and forgetfulness arise from these causes, on account of the mixture; but he never*

δ' ἰσάζωσι τῇ μίξει, πότερον ἔσται φρονεῖν ἢ οὔ, καὶ τίς ἡ διάθεσις, οὐδὲν ἔτι διώρικεν. ὅτι δὲ καὶ τῷ ἐναντίῳ καθ' αὑτὸ ποιεῖ τὴν αἴσθησιν, φανερὸν ἐν οἷς φησι τὸν νεκρὸν φωτὸς μὲν καὶ θερμοῦ καὶ φωνῆς οὐκ αἰσθάνεσθαι διὰ τὴν ἔκλειψιν τοῦ πυρός, ψυχροῦ δὲ καὶ σιωπῆς καὶ τῶν ἐναντίων αἰσθάνεσθαι. καὶ ὅλως δὲ πᾶν τὸ ὂν ἔχειν τινὰ γνῶσιν.

This passage, which sets forth the most influential of the doctrines that survive from the Way of Seeming, contains two points in particular that are of interest and importance. It is noteworthy in the first place how completely Parmenides must, in the Way of Seeming, have suppressed his real convictions: the equation of perception and thought comes strangely from the author of the Way of Truth. At the same time the whole of this passage again makes clear how prominent a place was taken in the Way of Seeming by the sensible opposites: if we can trust Theophrastus' interpretation, even thought derives from the preponderance of one opposite in the body over the other. Here once again, as in the ψυχὴ ἁρμονία theory of the Pythagoreans (see pp. 261 f.), it is probable that we see the influence of Alcmaeon; but be that as it may, Parmenides' own theory of the perception of like by like was not without influence on his successors (cf. especially Empedocles, pp. 343 ff.).

ASTRONOMY

358 Fr. 12, Simplicius *Phys.* 39, 14 and 31, 13

αἱ γὰρ στεινότεραι (*sc.* στεφάναι) πλῆντο πυρὸς ἀκρήτοιο,
αἱ δ' ἐπὶ ταῖς νυκτός, μετὰ δὲ φλογὸς ἵεται αἶσα·
ἐν δὲ μέσῳ τούτων δαίμων ἣ πάντα κυβερνᾷ·
πάντα γὰρ ⟨ἣ⟩ στυγεροῖο τόκου καὶ μίξιος ἄρχει
πέμπουσ' ἄρσενι θῆλυ μιγῆν τό τ' ἐναντίον αὖτις
ἄρσεν θηλυτέρῳ.

---

made clear whether, if they are equally mixed, there will be thought or not, or, if so, what its character will be. But that he regards perception as also due to the opposite as such he makes clear when he says that a corpse does not perceive light, heat or sound owing to its deficiency of fire, but that it does perceive their opposites, cold, silence and so on. And he adds that in general everything that exists has some measure of knowledge.

358 *The narrower rings were filled with unmixed fire, those next to them with night, and after them rushes their share of flame; and in the midst of them is the goddess who steers all; for she it is that begins all the works of hateful birth and begetting, sending female to mix with male and male in turn with female.*

359 Aetius II, 7, 1 Παρμενίδης στεφάνας εἶναι περιπεπλεγμένας ἐπαλλήλους, τὴν μὲν ἐκ τοῦ ἀραιοῦ, τὴν δὲ ἐκ τοῦ πυκνοῦ· μικτὰς δὲ ἄλλας ἐκ φωτὸς καὶ σκότους μεταξὺ τούτων. καὶ τὸ περιέχον δὲ πάσας τείχους δίκην στερεὸν ὑπάρχειν, ὑφ' ᾧ πυρώδης στεφάνη, καὶ τὸ μεσαίτατον πασῶν στερεόν, περὶ ὃ πάλιν πυρώδης (*sc.* στεφάνη). τῶν δὲ συμμιγῶν τὴν μεσαιτάτην ἁπάσαις ⟨ἀρχήν⟩ τε καὶ ⟨αἰτίαν⟩ κινήσεως καὶ γενέσεως ὑπάρχειν, ἥντινα καὶ δαίμονα κυβερνῆτιν καὶ κληδοῦχον ἐπονομάζει Δίκην τε καὶ Ἀνάγκην. καὶ τῆς μὲν γῆς ἀπόκρισιν εἶναι τὸν ἀέρα διὰ τὴν βιαιοτέραν αὐτῆς ἐξατμισθέντα πίλησιν, τοῦ δὲ πυρὸς ἀναπνοὴν τὸν ἥλιον καὶ τὸν γαλαξίαν κύκλον. συμμιγῆ δ' ἐξ ἀμφοῖν εἶναι τὴν σελήνην, τοῦ τ' ἀέρος καὶ τοῦ πυρός. περιστάντος δ' ἀνωτάτω πάντων τοῦ αἰθέρος ὑπ' αὐτῷ τὸ πυρῶδες ὑποταγῆναι τοῦθ' ὅπερ κεκλήκαμεν οὐρανόν, ὑφ' ᾧ ἤδη τὰ περίγεια.

It is fortunate that, since he neither believed in it himself nor, apparently, succeeded in influencing others by it, Parmenides' astronomical system is of little importance; for it is virtually impossible to reconstruct. These two passages are quoted now chiefly because they give us what little reliable information we possess about the very obscure doctrine, to which reference has already been made (p. 280), of the στεφάναι or 'bands'.[1] Two other points of interest do, however, arise from these passages. First, we see yet again how prominent are the sensible opposites in the cosmology of the Way of Seeming; and in addition to the two familiar pairs in **359**, dense and rare, light and darkness, we meet also in **358** with the new pair—another, incidentally, which figures in the Pythagorean table—male and female.[2] And second, we learn again, from the fact that Justice or Necessity is now described as the 'cause of movement and becoming', how totally irreconcilable are the two parts of Parmenides' poem (cf. **347** l. 14 and **350** l. 30). We

---

359 *Parmenides said that there were rings wound one around the other, one formed of the rare, the other of the dense; and that there were others between these compounded of light and darkness. That which surrounds them all like a wall is, he says, by nature solid; beneath it is a fiery ring; and likewise what lies in the middle of them all is solid; and around it is again a fiery ring. The middlemost of the mixed rings is the primary cause of movement and of coming into being for them all, and he calls it the goddess that steers all, the holder of the keys, Justice and Necessity. The air, he says, is separated off from the earth, vaporized owing to earth's stronger compression; the sun is an exhalation of fire, and so is the circle of the Milky Way. The moon is compounded of both air and fire. Aither is outermost, surrounding all; next comes the fiery thing that we call the sky; and last comes the region of the earth.*

should not waste time in the hopeless attempt to reconcile the two parts. For Parmenides, such inconsistency is inevitably involved in any attempt to explain, what deserves only to be negated, the evidence of the illusory senses.

[1] Aetius' account in **359**, which probably summarises Theophrastus, is so condensed that the most we can safely conclude from it is as follows. Surrounding the whole system 'like a wall' is a solid firmament, and there is another solid at the centre; immediately inside the former and immediately outside the latter are two 'bands' of fire; between these two are a number of 'bands' made up of the rare and the dense, light and darkness; and in the midst of these, according to Parmenides' own words in **358** as well as Aetius' summary, is 'the goddess who steers all'. J. S. Morrison (*JHS* 75 (1955) 59ff.) has lately published a new reconstruction of the system, which reaches the conclusion that 'Parmenides' general scheme... whereby an upper firmament and system of elementary masses in rings is repeated below the earth is only another and more precise form of the Hesiodic picture in which the lower world, like the upper, has its firmament of bronze, and holds a reservoir of the elementary masses' (but see p. 30f.). No such reconstruction can carry complete conviction, if only because it must inevitably be based on many conjectures. A full discussion of the many problems involved would run to a length out of all proportion, in a book such as this, to the importance of the topic. Whereas the astronomy of Anaximander is an appreciable part of his contribution to thought, that of Parmenides is not.

[2] Fr. 17, a single line concerned with embryology, **360** Galen *in Epid.* VI, 48

δεξιτεροῖσιν μὲν κούρους, λαιοῖσι δὲ κούρας....

actually links two pairs found in the Pythagorean Table; but this, in the absence of further evidence, cannot safely be regarded as more than a coincidence. It is also of interest, however, as showing that Parmenides, despite his emphatic theoretical negation of the world of sense, was yet prepared to go into considerable detail in his explanation of it (cf. also DK 28 A 50–4, especially 52). Presumably any account of the sensible world had at this period, perhaps owing to the influence of Alcmaeon, to take some account of physiological and embryological questions.

---

360 *On the right boys, on the left girls....*

CHAPTER XI

ZENO OF ELEA

DATE AND LIFE

The most reliable evidence for Zeno's date is the same passage of Plato's *Parmenides* as was used (p. 263) to determine the date of Parmenides. On the basis of that evidence, Zeno seems to have been born about 490–485 B.C. Once again the date given by Apollodorus for Zeno's *floruit*, namely 464–461,[1] conflicts with this; but we have already seen that his dating of the Eleatics depends solely on the date of the foundation of Elea. As with Parmenides, so with Zeno, Plato's testimony is obviously preferable.

[1] Diog. L. IX, 29 (DK 29 A 1) is unfortunately incomplete, but the date to be restored there is approximately indicated by **361** Suda s.v. Ζήνων (DK 29 A 2) ...ἦν γὰρ ἐπὶ τῆς οη ὀλυμπιάδος (468–465), μαθητὴς Ξενοφάνους ἢ Παρμενίδου. The verdict of Eusebius (DK 29 A 3) that Zeno's *floruit* was in 456–454 B.C., though nearer the mark, is shown to be equally unreliable by the fact that he makes Heraclitus and Zeno contemporaries.

Of Zeno's life, likewise, we know little more than we have already learnt in connexion with Parmenides. Like Parmenides he came from Elea; like Parmenides he is said to have been originally a Pythagorean (**340**); and like Parmenides he is credited, also by Strabo in **340**, with political activity. As a pupil of Parmenides his name is in fact constantly coupled with that of his master. In the one context in which his name repeatedly occurs by itself—the story of his part in a plot against a tyrant and of his courage under torture (see DK 29 A 1, 2, 6, 7, 8 and 9)—the details vary so much that the facts are impossible to reconstruct.

NATURE OF HIS WORK

362 Plato *Parmenides* 128 C (DK 29 A 12) ...ἔστι δὲ τό γε ἀληθὲς βοήθειά τις ταῦτα [τὰ γράμματα] τῷ Παρμενίδου λόγῳ πρὸς τοὺς ἐπιχειροῦντας αὐτὸν κωμῳδεῖν ὡς, εἰ ἕν ἐστι, πολλὰ καὶ γελοῖα

---

361 *He lived in the seventy-eighth Olympiad, being a pupil of Xenophanes or Parmenides.*

362 ...*In reality the book is a sort of defence of Parmenides' argument against those who try to make fun of it by showing that, if there is a One, many absurd and contradictory*

συμβαίνει πάσχειν τῷ λόγῳ καὶ ἐναντία αὑτῷ. ἀντιλέγει δὴ οὖν τοῦτο τὸ γράμμα πρὸς τοὺς τὰ πολλὰ λέγοντας, καὶ ἀνταποδίδωσι ταὐτὰ καὶ πλείω, τοῦτο βουλόμενον δηλοῦν, ὡς ἔτι γελοιότερα πάσχοι ἂν αὐτῶν ἡ ὑπόθεσις, εἰ πολλά ἐστιν, ἢ ἡ τοῦ ἓν εἶναι, εἴ τις ἱκανῶς ἐπεξίοι. διὰ τοιαύτην δὴ φιλονικίαν ὑπὸ νέου ὄντος ἐμοῦ ἐγράφη....

363 Plato *Phaedrus* 261 D τὸν οὖν Ἐλεατικὸν Παλαμήδην λέγοντα οὐκ ἴσμεν τέχνῃ ὥστε φαίνεσθαι τοῖς ἀκούουσι τὰ αὐτὰ ὅμοια καὶ ἀνόμοια, καὶ ἓν καὶ πολλά, μένοντά τε αὖ καὶ φερόμενα;

364 Diogenes Laertius VIII, 57 Ἀριστοτέλης δ' ἐν τῷ Σοφιστῇ φησι πρῶτον Ἐμπεδοκλέα ῥητορικὴν εὑρεῖν, Ζήνωνα δὲ διαλεκτικήν.

Such passages as **362** cannot be taken as historical unless they are supported by other evidence. But we shall see that there are reasons for accepting the suggestion that the opponents of Parmenides had attempted, in return for his criticisms, to make fun of his One, and we shall see also (pp. 299 ff.) what form these attempts could have taken. Thereupon, according to Plato, Zeno set about 'repaying them in the same coin with something to spare'. There is anyhow no doubt of the controversial nature of Zeno's work: he fully earns the remarks made about him in **363** and **364**. His characteristic method was, as **362** and **363** both suggest, to reduce his opponents' hypotheses to absurdity by deducing from them contradictory consequences. [The hypotheses to which he especially turned his destructive talents were two, namely plurality and motion, which were unquestioningly accepted by all except the Eleatics themselves; but for all that, his arguments may well have been aimed particularly at the Pythagoreans.] His primary object must indeed be exactly as Plato represents it in **362**; he is rallying to the rescue of the Parmenidean One against its pluralist assailants.

---

consequences follow for his argument. This book is a retort against those who believe in plurality; it pays them back in their own coin, and with something to spare, by seeking to show that, if anyone examines the matter thoroughly, yet more absurd consequences follow from their hypothesis of plurality than from that of the One. In such a spirit of contention I wrote it while I was a young man....

363 *Do we not then know that this Eleatic Palamedes argues with such skill that the same things appear to his listeners to be both like and unlike, both one and many, both at rest and in motion?*

364 *Aristotle in the* Sophist *says that Empedocles was the first to discover rhetoric and Zeno dialectic.*

ARGUMENTS AGAINST PLURALITY

365 Fr. 1, Simplicius *Phys.* 141, 1 and Fr. 2, *ibid.* 139, 8 εἰ πολλά ἐστι, καὶ μεγάλα ἐστὶ καὶ μικρά· μεγάλα μὲν ὥστε ἄπειρα τὸ μέγεθος εἶναι, μικρὰ δ' οὕτως ὥστε μηθὲν ἔχειν μέγεθος.

εἰ μὴ ἔχοι μέγεθος τὸ ὄν, οὐδ' ἂν εἴη. εἰ γὰρ ἄλλῳ ὄντι προσγένοιτο, οὐδὲν ἂν μεῖζον ποιήσειεν· μεγέθους γὰρ μηδενὸς ὄντος, προσγενομένου δέ, οὐδὲν οἷόν τε εἰς μέγεθος ἐπιδοῦναι. καὶ οὕτως ἂν ἤδη τὸ προσγινόμενον οὐδὲν εἴη. εἰ δὲ ἀπογινομένου τὸ ἕτερον μηδὲν ἔλαττον ἔσται μηδὲ αὖ προσγινομένου αὐξήσεται, δῆλον ὅτι τὸ προσγενόμενον οὐδὲν ἦν οὐδὲ τὸ ἀπογενόμενον.

εἰ δὲ ἔστιν, ἀνάγκη ἕκαστον μέγεθός τι ἔχειν καὶ πάχος καὶ ἀπέχειν αὐτοῦ τὸ ἕτερον ἀπὸ τοῦ ἑτέρου. καὶ περὶ τοῦ προύχοντος ὁ αὐτὸς λόγος. καὶ γὰρ ἐκεῖνο ἕξει μέγεθος καὶ προέξει αὐτοῦ τι. ὅμοιον δὴ τοῦτο ἅπαξ τε εἰπεῖν καὶ ἀεὶ λέγειν· οὐδὲν γὰρ αὐτοῦ τοιοῦτον ἔσχατον ἔσται οὔτε ἕτερον πρὸς ἕτερον οὐκ ἔσται.

οὕτως εἰ πολλά ἐστιν, ἀνάγκη αὐτὰ μικρά τε εἶναι καὶ μεγάλα· μικρὰ μὲν ὥστε μὴ ἔχειν μέγεθος, μεγάλα δὲ ὥστε ἄπειρα εἶναι.

366 Fr. 3, Simplicius *Phys.* 140, 29 εἰ πολλά ἐστιν, ἀνάγκη τοσαῦτα εἶναι ὅσα ἐστὶ καὶ οὔτε πλείονα αὐτῶν οὔτε ἐλάττονα. εἰ δὲ τοσαῦτά ἐστιν ὅσα ἐστί, πεπερασμένα ἂν εἴη.

εἰ πολλά ἐστιν, ἄπειρα τὰ ὄντα ἐστίν· ἀεὶ γὰρ ἕτερα μεταξὺ τῶν ὄντων ἐστί, καὶ πάλιν ἐκείνων ἕτερα μεταξύ. καὶ οὕτως ἄπειρα τὰ ὄντα ἐστί.

---

365 *If there is a plurality, things will be both great and small; so great as to be infinite in size, so small as to have no size at all.*

If what is had no size, it would not even be. For if it were added to something else that is, it would make it no larger; for being no size at all, it could not, on being added, cause any increase in size. And so what was added would clearly be nothing. Again if, when it is taken away, the other thing is no smaller, just as when it is added it is not increased, obviously what was added or taken away was nothing.

But if it is, each thing must have a certain size and bulk, and one part of it must be at a certain distance from another part; and the same argument holds about the part in front of it —it too will have some size, and some part of it will be in front. And it is the same thing to say this once and to go on saying it indefinitely; for no such part of it will be the last, nor will one part ever be unrelated to another.

So if there is a plurality, things must be both small and great; so small as to have no size at all, so great as to be infinite.

366 *If there is a plurality, things must be just as many as they are, no more and no less. And if they are just as many as they are, they must be limited.*

If there is a plurality, the things that are are infinite; for there will always be other things between the things that are, and yet others between those others. And so the things that are are infinite.

These two arguments against plurality are all that survive of a set of, according to Proclus (*in Parm.* 694, 23, DK 29 A 15), no less than forty. The first of the two is actually reconstructed from four separate quotations in Simplicius, *Phys.* pp. 139–41 (DK 29 B 1 and 2); but, as Zeller suggested, the four pieces together seem to make up a single argument. Simplicius (*ibid.* 139, 18–19) tells us, moreover, that the second paragraph in the passage as it is here printed followed on from Zeno's previous demonstration ὅτι οὐδὲν ἔχει μέγεθος ἐκ τοῦ ἕκαστον τῶν πολλῶν ἑαυτῷ ταὐτὸν εἶναι καὶ ἕν, 'that nothing has size because each of the many is self-identical and one'. This addition, as H. Fraenkel pointed out (*AJP* 63 (1942) 14 ff.), greatly enhances the neatness of the pattern. The whole argument can in fact be briefly summarised, as it is by G. E. L. Owen (*Proc. Ar. Soc.*, 1958, 201), as follows: 'The paradox had two arms. The first began by arguing that the units in a collection can have no size at all: else they would have parts and be not units but collections of units. The second began by arguing that, on the contrary, there cannot be anything that has no size at all; for there cannot be a thing which if it were added to or subtracted from something else would not affect the size of that thing.' The purport of the second argument, though not its precise motive, is comparatively plain.

A significant feature of these two arguments (but not necessarily, of course, of all the others that are now lost) is that both alike admit of at least two interpretations. Zeller, for instance, who is followed by Ross (*Aristotle, Physics* 479, note on 187 a 1), paraphrased the latter as follows: 'The many must be both limited and unlimited in *number*. Limited, because it is as many as it is; no more nor less. Unlimited, because two things are two only when they are separated; in order that they may be separated, there must be something between them; and so too between this intermediate and each of the two, and so *ad infinitum*.' H. D. P. Lee, on the other hand, writes of this same dilemma (*Zeno of Elea* 31): 'The *second* part must again make nonsense unless it is understood that the "things" in question are supposed to have the properties of points on a line. And the argument is simply that between any two points a and a_1 it is possible to take further points a_2 and a_3 and so on.' This same divergence of interpretation is found also in their respective comments on the argument in **365**: while Lee's interpretation is again geometrical, Zeller's is again arithmetical.

The reason for this difference of interpretation rests ultimately in the ambiguity of the hypothesis εἰ πολλά ἐστιν. In his discussion of the Pythagoreans whom he believed that Zeno was attacking, Cornford (*Plato and Parmenides* 58) wrote as follows: 'The assertion that "things are many" probably covered the following propositions. (1) There is a plurality of concrete things, bodies capable of motion, such as our senses show us.... (2) Each of these concrete bodies is a number, or plurality of units.' The first of these propositions, on which Zeller bases his interpretation, is self-evident; the second, on which Lee relies, calls for further comment.

367 Simplicius *Phys.* 99, 13 (DK 29 A 21), quoting Alexander ὡς γὰρ ἱστορεῖ...Εὔδημος, Ζήνων...ἐπειρᾶτο δεικνύναι ὅτι μὴ οἷόν τε τὰ ὄντα πολλὰ εἶναι τῷ μηδὲν εἶναι ἐν τοῖς οὖσιν ἕν, τὰ δὲ πολλὰ πλῆθος εἶναι ἑνάδων. (Cf. Philoponus *Phys.* 42, 9; DK 29 A 21.)

368 Eudemus *ap.* Simplicium *Phys.* 97, 12 καὶ Ζήνωνά φασι λέγειν, εἴ τις αὐτῷ τὸ ἓν ἀποδοίη τί ποτέ ἐστιν, ἕξειν τὰ ὄντα λέγειν.

These two passages, both based on Eudemus, make it clear that in his opinion the plurality that Zeno was especially attacking was 'a plurality of units', πλῆθος ἑνάδων. By exposing the contradictions involved in the notion of the unit Zeno sought to demolish the hypothesis of plurality. Accordingly, by one view at least, it is only when, in the arguments preserved in **365** and **366**, we substitute for the single word πολλά, 'plurality', the phrase πλῆθος ἑνάδων, 'a plurality of units', that Zeno's purpose is fully apparent. For not only had Zeno's principal opponents, the Pythagoreans, maintained that everything in the universe—sun and moon, man and horse, justice and opportunity—was a sum of spatially extended units (see pp. 248ff.); they had also, if only tacitly, confused these spatially extended units with the points of geometry. It is against this confusion in particular that, according to Tannery, Cornford, Lee and others, Zeno's arguments against both plurality and motion are alike directed.

To suppose that this special anti-Pythagorean significance is merely accidental seems unjust to Zeno; it might indeed have been

---

367 *As Eudemus...records, Zeno...used to try to prove that it is impossible that existing things should be a plurality by arguing that there is no unit in existing things and that plurality is a sum of units.*

368 *They say that Zeno used to argue that, if anyone would explain to him whatever the one was, he would then be able to account for existing things.*

the prime motive of his arguments. It may be true, as some scholars have lately objected, that there are no traces in extant fifth-century literature of an explicit equation of numbers with atoms; and it has also been maintained against Tannery and his followers that, in W. A. Heidel's words (*AJP* 61 (1940) 21), 'there is not, so far as I know, a single hint in our sources that the Greeks themselves were aware of the purpose of Zeno to criticize the fundamental doctrines of the Pythagoreans'. Neither of these objections seems, however, at all conclusive. If the confusion between units, points and atoms was, as was suggested in Chapter IX, a tacit confusion arising from the inability to imagine incorporeal entities, then it is not only not surprising that there is as yet no explicit equation, it would be very surprising indeed if there were. And as for the failure of our sources to point out the special anti-Pythagorean purport of Zeno's arguments, that could well come about because our sources, especially Aristotle himself, were concerned with the validity of the arguments in their own day rather than with the *ad hominem* motive that inspired them. At the same time, to suppose that this was their only motive is no doubt an over-simplification; that the clause εἰ πολλά ἐστιν was not intended to bear, at least among others, its superficially obvious sense of 'if there is a plurality of concrete things' seems very hard to believe.

A great deal has been written lately about the paradoxes of Zeno and much of the most recent literature has been sternly critical of Tannery's view. If we possessed only the surviving arguments against plurality, which have of course the great advantage of being preserved in Zeno's own words, the case for seeing a special anti-Pythagorean purpose in Zeno's work would be greatly weakened. But we have also Aristotle's version of the four arguments against motion, to the fourth of which Tannery gave at last a real and a sharp point. It is upon them that Tannery's followers must principally base their case, and meanwhile the wisest course may well be to regard the question as still an open one.

ARGUMENTS AGAINST MOTION

369 Aristotle *Phys.* Z9, 239b9 (DK 29A25) τέτταρες δ' εἰσὶν οἱ λόγοι περὶ κινήσεως Ζήνωνος οἱ παρέχοντες τὰς δυσκολίας τοῖς λύουσιν.

---

369 *Zeno's arguments about motion, which cause such trouble to those who try to solve the problems that they present, are four in number.* (After Gaye)

Zeno's arguments against motion, unlike those against plurality, were originally only four in number, of which Aristotle discusses each in turn (though in a somewhat garbled version) in *Physics* Z9. It will be best to discuss each separately; but since the four were undoubtedly intended to stand together, the full purpose of each being dependent on the other three, we must first consider the combined object of the four together.

Theories of motion depend inevitably on theories of the nature of space and time; and two opposed views of space and time were held in antiquity. Either space and time are infinitely divisible, in which case motion is continuous and smooth-flowing; or else they are made up of indivisible minima—ἄτομα μεγέθη—in which case motion is what Lee aptly calls 'cinematographic', consisting of a succession of minute jerks. We shall find that Zeno's arguments are directed against both theories—the first two arguments against the former view, the last two against the latter. The four arguments are really, in fact, two pairs; and further, to complete the neatness of the pattern, the first member of each pair aims to prove that motion is impossible for a single body—that is to say, is impossible absolutely—while the second aims to prove that it is impossible for more than one body—that is to say, relatively. Finally, it was presumably against the Pythagoreans in particular that these four arguments together were most valid and damaging; for it was the Pythagoreans alone who, by their confusion of spatially extended and indivisible units with the points of geometry, would be logically compelled to admit, under cross-examination, that they held simultaneously the two contradictory theories of space and motion.

(i) *The Stadium*

370 Aristotle *Phys.* Z9, 239b11 (continuing **369**) . . . πρῶτος μὲν ὁ περὶ τοῦ μὴ κινεῖσθαι διὰ τὸ πρότερον εἰς τὸ ἥμισυ δεῖν ἀφικέσθαι τὸ φερόμενον ἢ πρὸς τὸ τέλος. . . .

371 Aristotle *Topics* Θ8, 160b7 πολλοὺς γὰρ λόγους ἔχομεν ἐναντίους ταῖς δόξαις, καθάπερ Ζήνωνος, ὅτι οὐκ ἐνδέχεται κινεῖσθαι οὐδὲ τὸ στάδιον διελθεῖν.

---

370 . . . *The first asserts the non-existence of motion on the ground that that which is in locomotion must arrive at the half-way stage before it arrives at the goal*. . . . (Trans. Gaye)

371 *For we have many arguments contrary to accepted opinion, such as Zeno's that motion is impossible and that you cannot traverse the stadium.*

372 Aristotle *Phys.* Z2, 233a21 διὸ καὶ ὁ Ζήνωνος λόγος ψεῦδος λαμβάνει τὸ μὴ ἐνδέχεσθαι τὰ ἄπειρα διελθεῖν ἢ ἅψασθαι τῶν ἀπείρων καθ' ἕκαστον ἐν πεπερασμένῳ χρόνῳ. διχῶς γὰρ λέγεται καὶ τὸ μῆκος καὶ ὁ χρόνος ἄπειρον, καὶ ὅλως πᾶν τὸ συνεχές, ἤτοι κατὰ διαίρεσιν ἢ τοῖς ἐσχάτοις. τῶν μὲν οὖν κατὰ ποσὸν ἀπείρων οὐκ ἐνδέχεται ἅψασθαι ἐν πεπερασμένῳ χρόνῳ, τῶν δὲ κατὰ διαίρεσιν ἐνδέχεται· καὶ γὰρ αὐτὸς ὁ χρόνος οὕτως ἄπειρος. ὥστε ἐν τῷ ἀπείρῳ καὶ οὐκ ἐν τῷ πεπερασμένῳ συμβαίνει διιέναι τὸ ἄπειρον, καὶ ἅπτεσθαι τῶν ἀπείρων τοῖς ἀπείροις, οὐ τοῖς πεπερασμένοις.

Zeno's first argument amounts simply to this: 'It is impossible to traverse the stadium; because before you reach the far end you must first reach the half-way point; before you reach the half-way point you must reach the point half way to it; and so on *ad infinitum*.' In other words, on the assumption that space is infinitely divisible and that therefore any finite distance contains an infinite number of points, it is impossible to reach the end of an infinite series in a finite time. Aristotle's answer to this conundrum in **372**, even if philosophically unsatisfactory,[1] shows that in this case he has rightly understood the problem.

[1] On the philosophical aspect of this and the other arguments against motion see Ross, *Aristotle, Physics* 71–85. Ross himself concludes about this first argument: (i) that since Aristotle himself, from whom almost the whole of our knowledge of all four arguments derives, evidently regards the solution he gives in **372** as 'an adequate *argumentum ad hominem* as against Zeno', Zeno must therefore have 'made the paradox turn on a contrast between the infinite number of divisions of space to be covered in covering a finite space, and the finitude of a particular portion of time' (p. 73); (ii) that none the less 'the fact apparently remains that, before it gets to the end of the line, the moving body will have had to get to the end of an infinite series, i.e. to have got to the end of something that has no end' (p. 74), and that so understood 'Zeno's first paradox still awaits its final answer' (p. 75). See also the controversy in *Analysis* vols. 11 (1951) to 15 (1954), which however is hardly relevant to Zeno's intentions.

---

372 *Hence Zeno's argument makes a false assumption in asserting that it is impossible for a thing to pass over or severally come in contact with infinite things in a finite time. For there are two senses in which length and time and generally anything continuous are called 'infinite': they are called so either in respect of divisibility or in respect of their extremities. So while a thing in a finite time cannot come in contact with things quantitatively infinite, it can come in contact with things infinite in respect of divisibility: for in this sense the time itself is also infinite: and so we find that the time occupied by the passage over the infinite is not a finite but an infinite time, and the contact with the infinites is made by means of moments not finite but infinite in number.* (Trans. Gaye)

(ii) *Achilles and the tortoise*

373 Aristotle *Phys.* Z9, 239b14 δεύτερος δ' ὁ καλούμενος 'Αχιλλεύς. ἔστι δ' οὗτος ὅτι τὸ βραδύτατον οὐδέποτε καταληφθήσεται θέον ὑπὸ τοῦ ταχίστου· ἔμπροσθεν γὰρ ἀναγκαῖον ἐλθεῖν τὸ διῶκον ὅθεν ὥρμησε τὸ φεῦγον, ὥστ' ἀεί τι προέχειν ἀναγκαῖον τὸ βραδύτερον. ἔστι δὲ καὶ οὗτος ὁ αὐτὸς λόγος τῷ διχοτομεῖν, διαφέρει δ' ἐν τῷ διαιρεῖν μὴ δίχα τὸ προσλαμβανόμενον μέγεθος.

Having in 'the Stadium' dealt with a single moving body, Zeno proceeds in 'Achilles' to deal with the relative motion of two bodies. The argument this time is as follows: 'Achilles can never overtake a tortoise; because by the time he reaches the point from which the tortoise started, it will have moved on to another point; by the time he reaches that second point it will have moved on again; and so *ad infinitum*.' Aristotle's comment on this conundrum is again sensible as far as it goes: the underlying theory of space is indeed the same as in 'the Stadium'—namely that it is infinitely divisible—but this time the series is not, as it was in 'the Stadium', the simple geometrical progression $\frac{1}{2}, \frac{1}{4}, \frac{1}{8}, \frac{1}{16}$ ..., but somewhat more complicated.

That concludes Zeno's attempt to disprove 'continuous' motion, and he now proceeds to 'cinematographic' motion.

(iii) *The flying arrow*

374 Aristotle *Phys.* Z9, 239b30 τρίτος δ' ὁ νῦν ῥηθείς, ὅτι ἡ ὀιστὸς φερομένη ἕστηκεν. συμβαίνει δὲ παρὰ τὸ λαμβάνειν τὸν χρόνον συγκεῖσθαι ἐκ τῶν νῦν· μὴ διδομένου γὰρ τούτου οὐκ ἔσται ὁ συλλογισμός. (Cf. *ibid.* 239b5, where, however, the text is corrupt.)

This third argument can be confidently reconstructed as follows: 'An object is at rest when it occupies a space equal to its own dimensions. An arrow in flight occupies, at any given moment, a

---

373 *The second is the so-called Achilles, and it amounts to this, that in a race the quickest runner can never overtake the slowest, since the pursuer must first reach the point whence the pursued started, so that the slower must always hold a lead. This argument is the same in principle as that which depends on bisection, though it differs from it in that the spaces with which we successively have to deal are not divided into halves.* (Trans. Gaye)

374 *The third is that already given above, to the effect that the flying arrow is at rest, which result follows from the assumption that time is composed of moments: if this assumption is not granted, the conclusion will not follow.* (Trans. Gaye)

space equal to its own dimensions. Therefore an arrow in flight is at rest.' It is easy to see that this argument, unlike the two that precede it, treats time and space alike as composed of indivisible minima; as Aristotle puts it, it assumes τὸν χρόνον συγκεῖσθαι ἐκ τῶν νῦν.

(iv) *The moving rows*

375 Aristotle *Phys.* Z9, 239b33 τέταρτος δ' ὁ περὶ τῶν ἐν σταδίῳ κινουμένων ἐξ ἐναντίας ἴσων ὄγκων παρ' ἴσους, τῶν μὲν ἀπὸ τέλους τοῦ σταδίου τῶν δ' ἀπὸ μέσου, ἴσῳ τάχει, ἐν ᾧ συμβαίνειν οἴεται ἴσον εἶναι χρόνον τῷ διπλασίῳ τὸν ἥμισυν. ἔστι δ' ὁ παραλογισμὸς ἐν τῷ τὸ μὲν παρὰ κινούμενον τὸ δὲ παρ' ἠρεμοῦν τὸ ἴσον μέγεθος ἀξιοῦν τῷ ἴσῳ τάχει τὸν ἴσον φέρεσθαι χρόνον. τοῦτο δ' ἐστὶ ψεῦδος. οἷον ἔστωσαν οἱ ἑστῶτες ἴσοι ὄγκοι ἐφ' ὧν τὰ ΑΑ, οἱ δ' ἐφ' ὧν τὰ ΒΒ ἀρχόμενοι ἀπὸ τοῦ μέσου τῶν Α, ἴσοι τὸν ἀριθμὸν τούτοις ὄντες καὶ τὸ μέγεθος, οἱ δ' ἐφ' ὧν τὰ ΓΓ ἀπὸ τοῦ ἐσχάτου, ἴσοι τὸν ἀριθμὸν ὄντες τούτοις καὶ τὸ μέγεθος, καὶ ἰσοταχεῖς τοῖς Β. συμβαίνει δὴ τὸ πρῶτον Β ἅμα ἐπὶ τῷ ἐσχάτῳ εἶναι καὶ τὸ πρῶτον Γ, παρ' ἄλληλα κινουμένων. συμβαίνει δὲ καὶ τὸ Γ παρὰ πάντα τὰ Β διεξεληλυθέναι, τὸ δὲ Β παρὰ τὰ ⟨Α⟩ ἡμίση· ὥστε ἥμισυν εἶναι τὸν χρόνον· ἴσον γὰρ ἑκάτερόν ἐστιν παρ' ἕκαστον. ἅμα δὲ συμβαίνει τὰ Β παρὰ πάντα τὰ Γ παρεληλυθέναι· ἅμα γὰρ ἔσται τὸ πρῶτον Γ καὶ τὸ πρῶτον Β ἐπὶ τοῖς ἐναντίοις ἐσχάτοις,

---

375 *The fourth argument is that concerning the two rows of bodies, each row being composed of an equal number of bodies of equal size, passing each other on a race-course as they proceed with equal velocity in opposite directions, the one row originally occupying the space between the goal and the middle point of the course and the other that between the middle point and the starting-post. This, he thinks, involves the conclusion that half a given time is equal to double that time. The fallacy of the reasoning lies in the assumption that a body takes an equal time in moving with equal velocity past a body that is in motion and a body of equal size that is at rest; which is false. For instance (so runs the argument), let* Α, Α ... *be the stationary bodies of equal size,* Β, Β ... *the bodies, equal in number and in size to* Α, Α, ..., *originally occupying the half of the course from the starting-post to the middle of the* Α*'s, and* Γ, Γ ... *those originally occupying the other half from the goal to the middle of the* Α*'s, equal in number, size, and velocity to* Β, Β .... *Then three consequences follow:*

First, as the Β*'s and the* Γ*'s pass one another, the first* Β *reaches the last* Γ *at the same moment as the first* Γ *reaches the last* Β. *Secondly, at this moment the first* Γ *has passed all the* Β*'s, whereas the first* Β *has passed only half ⟨the* Α*'s⟩, and has consequently occupied only half the time occupied by the first* Γ, *since each of the two occupies an equal time in passing each body. Thirdly, at the same moment all the* Β*'s have passed all the* Γ*'s: for the first* Γ *and the first* Β *will simultaneously reach the opposite ends of the course, since (so says Zeno) the time occupied by the first* Γ *in passing each of*

ἴσον χρόνον παρ' ἕκαστον γινόμενον τῶν Β ὅσον περ τῶν Α, ὥς φησι, διὰ τὸ ἀμφότερα ἴσον χρόνον παρὰ τὰ Α γίγνεσθαι.

376 Diagram of Alexander *ap.* Simplicium *Phys.* 1016, 14

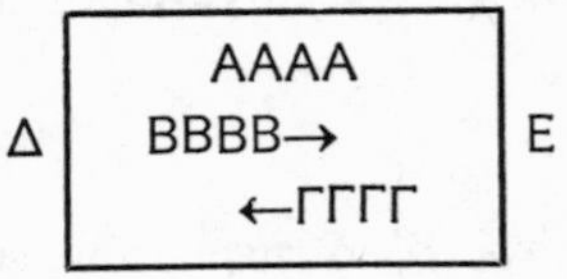

Δ	AAAA BBBB→ ←ΓΓΓΓ	Ε

Α ὄγκοι ἑστῶτες
Β ὄγκοι κινούμενοι ἀπὸ τοῦ Δ ἐπὶ τὸ Ε
Γ ὄγκοι κινούμενοι ἀπὸ τοῦ Ε ἐπὶ τὸ Δ
Δ ἀρχὴ τοῦ σταδίου
Ε τέλος τοῦ σταδίου

This final argument is much the most complicated of the four and it is virtually certain that Aristotle himself has misunderstood it; Zeno was far too shrewd to have been guilty of the paralogism of which Aristotle accuses him. The clue to the true significance of the argument lies in its relation to the other three: as 'Achilles' stands to 'the Stadium', so will this conundrum stand to the 'Flying Arrow'. In other words, this argument too will be based on the assumption that space and time are composed of indivisible minima.

Indeed the only way in which any sense can be made of the argument is to suppose—and by so supposing it becomes perhaps the most telling of the whole set—that each of Zeno's ὄγκοι (a deliberately vague word meaning 'solid bodies' or 'masses') represents one such indivisible minimum of space, and that those in the rows Β and Γ are alike moving at such a speed as to pass one Α in one indivisible minimum of time. Zeno is of course fully justified in asking his opponents—or those of them at least who believed in indivisible minima—to visualize such a situation. If space does indeed consist of indivisible minima, then it is clearly legitimate to draw a diagram to represent, on however magnified a scale, a number of such minima; and if the same is true of time, then the rest of the data is equally legitimate. But once so much is granted, then the rest of the argument is valid. For while each Β has passed two Α's—which, by the data, means in two indivisible

---

the Β*'s is equal to that occupied by it in passing each of the* Α*'s, because an equal time is occupied by both the first* Β *and the first* Γ *in passing all the* Α*'s.* (After Gaye)

376 Α = *stationary bodies.*
Β = *bodies moving from* Δ *towards* Ε.
Γ = *bodies moving from* Ε *towards* Δ.
Δ = *starting-post.*
Ε = *goal.*

minima of time—each Γ has passed four B's—which again by the data must have taken four indivisible minima. It is true, of course, that unless the argument is concerned with indivisible minima it is, as Aristotle says, totally invalid. But as soon as it is seen to be concerned with indivisible minima, both of space and time, then it does most ingeniously demonstrate that these so-called indivisible minima are divisible after all. And upon the unfortunate Pythagoreans, who had hitherto confused the indivisible units of arithmetic with the points in infinitely divisible geometrical magnitudes, this last argument must finally have impressed the urgent need for revision of their suppositions.[1]

[1] For a full and lucid exposition of this last argument see H. D. P. Lee, *Zeno of Elea* 83–102.

SPACE

377 Aristotle *Phys.* Δ3, 210b22 (DK29A24) ὃ δὲ Ζήνων ἠπόρει, ὅτι 'εἰ ἔστι τι ὁ τόπος, ἔν τινι ἔσται', λύειν οὐ χαλεπόν.

378 Aristotle *Phys.* Δ1, 209a23 ἡ γὰρ Ζήνωνος ἀπορία ζητεῖ τινα λόγον· εἰ γὰρ πᾶν τὸ ὂν ἐν τόπῳ, δῆλον ὅτι καὶ τοῦ τόπου τόπος ἔσται, καὶ τοῦτο εἰς ἄπειρον πρόεισιν.

This apparently isolated argument calls for little comment, being cited chiefly because reference will be made to it in the next chapter (p. 302). It is, however, worth noting that the premise εἰ πᾶν τὸ ὂν ἐν τόπῳ, 'if everything real is in space', confirms the point made several times already (see especially pp. 188 f. and 246 ff.) that the Presocratics could imagine no form of existence other than spatial.

---

377 *Zeno's problem—that 'if Place is something, it must be in something'—is not difficult to solve.* (Trans. Hardie)

378 *Zeno's difficulty demands an explanation: for if everything that exists has a place, place too will have a place, and so on* ad infinitum. (Trans. Hardie)

CHAPTER XII

MELISSUS OF SAMOS

DATE AND LIFE

379 Diogenes Laertius IX, 24 (DK 30 A 1) Μέλισσος Ἰθαγένους Σάμιος. οὗτος ἤκουσε Παρμενίδου.... γέγονε δὲ καὶ πολιτικὸς ἀνὴρ καὶ ἀποδοχῆς παρὰ τοῖς πολίταις ἠξιωμένος· ὅθεν ναύαρχος αἱρεθεὶς ἔτι καὶ μᾶλλον ἐθαυμάσθη διὰ τὴν οἰκείαν ἀρετήν...φησὶ δ' Ἀπολλόδωρος ἠκμακέναι αὐτὸν κατὰ τὴν τετάρτην καὶ ὀγδοηκοστὴν ὀλυμπιάδα.

380 Plutarch *Pericles* 26 (DK 30 A 3) πλεύσαντος γὰρ αὐτοῦ (*sc.* Pericles) Μέλισσος ὁ Ἰθαγένους, ἀνὴρ φιλόσοφος στρατηγῶν τότε τῆς Σάμου, καταφρονήσας τῆς ὀλιγότητος τῶν νεῶν ἢ τῆς ἀπειρίας τῶν στρατηγῶν, ἔπεισε τοὺς πολίτας ἐπιθέσθαι τοῖς Ἀθηναίοις. καὶ γενομένης μάχης νικήσαντες οἱ Σάμιοι καὶ πολλοὺς μὲν αὐτῶν ἄνδρας ἑλόντες πολλὰς δὲ ναῦς διαφθείραντες ἐχρῶντο τῇ θαλάσσῃ καὶ παρετίθεντο τῶν ἀναγκαίων πρὸς τὸν πόλεμον ὅσα μὴ πρότερον εἶχον. ὑπὸ δὲ τοῦ Μελίσσου καὶ Περικλέα φησὶν αὐτὸν Ἀριστοτέλης[1] ἡττηθῆναι ναυμαχοῦντα πρότερον.

[1] I.e. in the lost Πολιτεία Σαμίων.

These two passages tell us virtually all we know of the life of Melissus. The battle in which he defeated the Athenian fleet was fought in 441/40 B.C., and it is probably for that reason that Apollodorus fixed his *floruit* at 444–441. Whether or not he was, as Diogenes tells us, a pupil of Parmenides, he certainly followed

---

379 *Melissus son of Ithagenes, a Samian. He was a pupil of Parmenides....He was a statesman, and was held in great honour by the citizens; and later, when he was elected admiral, he won even greater fame for his personal courage....Apollodorus says that he flourished in the eighty-fourth Olympiad.*

380 *For when Pericles had set sail, Melissus, son of Ithagenes, a philosopher who was then in command of Samos, was so contemptuous of the small number of the Athenian ships or of their commanders' inexperience that he persuaded the Samians to attack. A battle took place which the Samians won. They took so many prisoners and destroyed so many ships that they had command of the sea, and they devoted to the prosecution of the war certain supplies which they did not till then possess. Pericles himself, according to Aristotle, had also been defeated by Melissus in an earlier naval battle.*

him very closely. We shall see reason to suppose that he was also acquainted with contemporary Pythagoreanism.

Melissus' book is said by Simplicius (*Phys.* 70, 16, DK 30 A 4), to whom we owe the preservation of the ten surviving fragments, to have been entitled Περὶ φύσεως ἢ περὶ τοῦ ὄντος, 'About nature or reality'—a version of the title given by later commentators to books by the Presocratics (see p. 102 n. 1). Its date is impossible to determine; but if we are to trust Plato that Zeno wrote his treatise as a young man (see **362**), then it is at least highly probable that Melissus' book is considerably the later of the two. We shall find that there is internal evidence also to the same effect.

REALITY IS INFINITE

381 Fr. 2, Simplicius *Physics* 29, 22 and 109, 20 ὅτε τοίνυν οὐκ ἐγένετο, ἔστι τε καὶ ἀεὶ ἦν καὶ ἀεὶ ἔσται καὶ ἀρχὴν οὐκ ἔχει οὐδὲ τελευτήν, ἀλλ' ἄπειρόν ἐστιν. εἰ μὲν γὰρ ἐγένετο, ἀρχὴν ἂν εἶχεν (ἤρξατο γὰρ ἄν ποτε γινόμενον) καὶ τελευτήν (ἐτελεύτησε γὰρ ἄν ποτε γινόμενον)· ὅτε δὲ μήτε ἤρξατο μήτε ἐτελεύτησεν, ἀεί τε ἦν καὶ ἀεὶ ἔσται ⟨καὶ⟩ οὐκ ἔχει ἀρχὴν οὐδὲ τελευτήν· οὐ γὰρ ἀεὶ εἶναι ἄνυστόν, ὅ τι μὴ πᾶν ἔστι.

382 Fr. 3, *ibid.* 109, 31 ἀλλ' ὥσπερ ἔστιν ἀεί, οὕτω καὶ τὸ μέγεθος ἄπειρον ἀεὶ χρὴ εἶναι.

383 Fr. 4, *ibid.* 110, 3 ἀρχήν τε καὶ τέλος ἔχον οὐδὲν οὔτε ἀίδιον οὔτε ἄπειρόν ἐστιν.

384 Fr. 5, *ibid.* 110, 5 εἰ μὴ ἓν εἴη, περανεῖ πρὸς ἄλλο.

385 Fr. 6, Simplicius *de caelo* 557, 16 εἰ γὰρ ⟨ἄπειρον⟩ εἴη, ἓν εἴη ἄν· εἰ γὰρ δύο εἴη, οὐκ ἂν δύναιτο ἄπειρα εἶναι, ἀλλ' ἔχοι ἂν πείρατα πρὸς ἄλληλα.

---

381 *Since, then, it did not come into being, it is now, always was and always will be, without either beginning or end, but infinite. For if it had come into being, it would have a beginning (for it would at some time have begun coming into being) and an end (for it would at some time have stopped coming into being); but since it neither began nor ended, it always was and always shall be, without either beginning or end; for it is not possible for anything to exist for ever unless it all exists.*

382 *But just as it exists for ever, so too it must for ever be infinite in magnitude.*

383 *Nothing that has a beginning and an end is either eternal or infinite.*

384 *If it were not one, it would be bounded by something else.*

385 *For if it were ⟨infinite⟩, it would be one; for if it were two, the two could not be infinite, but would be limited by one another.*

Faithfully as he followed Parmenides in other respects, Melissus yet broke away from him, as these fragments amply show, on one very important point. Whereas the One of Parmenides was finite and spherical (see **350** and **351**), the One of Melissus is unequivocally declared, to the irritation of Aristotle,[1] to be infinite in extent[2] as well as in time. For this remarkable change there seem to have been two main reasons, of which we will consider the simpler first. Melissus himself tells us, in **384** and **385**, that if there were more than one Being, they would be bounded by one another. He argues for the unity of the One, in other words, from its infinity. But that his real object was rather to prove its infinity from its unity is obvious enough even in these fragments, and is even more apparent from the following summary description of the Eleatics:

386 Aristotle *de gen. et corr.* A8, 325a14 (DK30A8) ἓν καὶ ἀκίνητον τὸ πᾶν εἶναί φασι καὶ ἄπειρον ἔνιοι· τὸ γὰρ πέρας περαίνειν ἂν πρὸς τὸ κενόν.

Melissus is in fact countering the possible objection to the Sphere of Parmenides that, if it is indeed 'limited on every side', then something must surely lie outside its limits, and that something can only be the void.

[1] Aristotle had a profound but unjust contempt for Melissus whom he dismisses with such words as φορτικός 'crude' (*Phys.* A3, 185a10, DK30A7) or μικρὸν ἀγροικότερος 'a little too naïve' (*Met.* A5, 986b26, DK *ibid.*).

[2] This has lately been denied by G. Vlastos (*Gnomon* 25 (1953) 34), who, having argued on the strength of fr. 9 (**391** below) that the One of Melissus is incorporeal, writes: 'How then could Melissus affirm that Being is incorporeal while infinite in magnitude? Because, I suggest, the infinity in question is that of beginningless and endless duration, not that of unlimited spatial extension.' I find it incredible that, if this was what Melissus wished to say, he should have included the words τὸ μέγεθος in **382** or written οὔτε ἀίδιον οὔτε ἄπειρον in **383**. The only answer to Vlastos' question seems to me to be to suppose that Melissus still thought that the only kind of existence was existence in space; see below, pp. 303 f.

His second motive for the change is also discernible in the fragments, this time in **381** and **383**. The One must have neither beginning nor end. There has been a prolonged discussion concerning **381** as to whether it signifies a temporal or a spatial

---

386 *They say that the universe is one and motionless, and some add that it is infinite; for its limit would limit it against the void.*

beginning and end; but since the next two fragments make it clear that Melissus denied both, the question is relatively unimportant. There can in any case be no doubt that Melissus is once again improving upon Parmenides' description of his Sphere as 'limited on every side' and 'equally poised from the centre in every direction'. The objection that he is this time countering seems, therefore, to be this: if, as Parmenides' own language suggests, the One has a beginning, a middle and an end, then surely it is no longer one but three.

There is some ground for the conjecture that these two possible objections to the One of Parmenides had actually been raised. Besides Plato's reference in the *Parmenides* to 'those who try to make fun of Parmenides' One by showing its many absurd and contradictory consequences' (see **362**)—words which themselves suggest destructive arguments of exactly this type—there are two passages from Aristotle which point in the same direction:

387 Aristotle *Phys.* Δ9, 216b22 εἰσὶ δέ τινες οἳ διὰ τοῦ μανοῦ καὶ πυκνοῦ οἴονται φανερὸν εἶναι ὅτι ἔστι κενόν. εἰ μὲν γὰρ μὴ ἔστι μανὸν καὶ πυκνόν, οὐδὲ συνιέναι καὶ πιλεῖσθαι οἷόν τε. εἰ δὲ τοῦτο μὴ εἴη, ἢ ὅλως κίνησις οὐκ ἔσται ἢ κυμανεῖ τὸ ὅλον, ὥσπερ ἔφη Ξοῦθος.

388 Aristotle *de caelo* A1, 268a10 καθάπερ γάρ φασι καὶ οἱ Πυραγόρειοι, τὸ πᾶν καὶ τὰ πάντα τοῖς τρισὶν ὥρισται· τελευτὴ γὰρ καὶ μέσον καὶ ἀρχὴ τὸν ἀριθμὸν ἔχει τὸν τοῦ παντός, ταῦτα δὲ τὸν τῆς τριάδος.

It is not, unfortunately, clear from **387** just how much Aristotle intends to ascribe to Xuthus; but even if it is only the fantastic view that when there is motion 'the universe bulges', it still seems likely enough that the motive underlying the suggestion was nothing but the desire to make fun of Parmenides' Sphere. We are told by Simplicius, in his comment on this passage (683, 24, DK33), that Xuthus was, as we should hope, a Pythagorean. It

---

387 *There are some who think that the existence of rarity and density shows that there is a void. If rarity and density do not exist, they say, neither can things contract and be compressed. But if this were not to take place, either there would be no movement at all, or the universe would bulge, as Xuthus said.* (Trans. Hardie)

388 *For, as the Pythagoreans say, the world and all that is in it is determined by the number three, since beginning and middle and end give the number of the world, and the number they give is the triad.* (After Stocks)

may possibly have been in answer to Xuthus, or at any rate to the argument that outside Parmenides' One must be the void, that Zeno, following his usual practice of reducing his opponents' hypotheses to absurdity, included among his arguments one that was directed against the notion of τόπος, 'space' (see p. 297).[1] When, finally, we learn that the theory in **388** was held by, among others,[2] Ion of Chios, whose first tragedy is said in the Suda (s.v. Ἴων Χῖος, DK 36 A 3) to have been produced in 452–449 B.C., and who, according to Harpocration (s.v. Ἴων, DK 36 A 1), was υἱὸς Ὀρθομένους, ἐπίκλησιν δὲ Ξούθου, 'son of Orthomenes, who was known as Xuthus',[3] we have perhaps enough evidence to justify a tentative conclusion. Melissus' solitary departure from the guidance of Parmenides may well have been forced upon him by the criticisms of the Pythagoreans.

[1] Space and the void are very closely associated in Greek thought. The precise relation between the two is actually defined in **389** Aristotle *Phys.* Δ 1, 208 b 25 ἔτι οἱ τὸ κενὸν φάσκοντες εἶναι τόπον λέγουσιν· τὸ γὰρ κενὸν τόπος ἂν εἴη ἐστερημένος σώματος. Elsewhere, however, the two are often treated as entirely synonymous; e.g. **390** Hippolytus *Ref.* 1, 11, 2 (DK 28 A 23, about Parmenides) ἀίδιον εἶναι τὸ πᾶν...καὶ ὅμοιον, οὐκ ἔχον δὲ τόπον ἐν ἑαυτῷ.

[2] The same view was evidently held also by the Pythagorean Occelus (DK 48, 8), who seems, however, so far as we can judge from our very unreliable information, to have belonged to a later generation of the school.

[3] It may well be true, as Kranz suggests in his note at DK 1, 377, that the father of Ion was nicknamed Xuthus in allusion to the myth that provided Euripides with the plot for his tragedy. But that does not alter the fact that Xuthus is mentioned under that name by Aristotle himself.

THE ONE IS INCORPOREAL

391 Simplicius *Phys.* 109, 34 ὅτι γὰρ ἀσώματον εἶναι βούλεται τὸ ὄν, ἐδήλωσεν εἰπών· (Fr. 9) εἰ μὲν οὖν [ὂν D, οὖν EF, Diels, DK] εἴη, δεῖ αὐτὸ ἓν εἶναι· ἓν δ' ἐὸν δεῖ αὐτὸ σῶμα μὴ ἔχειν. εἰ δὲ ἔχοι πάχος, ἔχοι ἂν μόρια, καὶ οὐκέτι ἓν εἴη.

---

389 *Again, the theory that the void exists involves the existence of place: for one would define void as space bereft of body.* (After Hardie)

390 (*He said that*) *the whole is eternal...and homogeneous, and has no space within it.*

391 *For he made it clear that he means that what exists is incorporeal when he wrote: 'If it is, it must be one; and being one, it must have no body. If it were to have bulk, it would have parts and be no longer one.'*

Simplicius, who was no fool and who evidently had the book of Melissus before him as he wrote, actually quotes this fragment in two pieces on two separate occasions (the other being *Phys.* 87, 6), with the object on each occasion of showing that the Eleatic One was incorporeal. Yet in spite of this fact, which alone would seem decisive enough, Burnet (*EGP* 327), following the second thoughts of Zeller, regards the statement that the One of Melissus was incorporeal as 'incredible', and argues instead that the fragment must have been 'directed against the Pythagorean assumption of ultimate units'. None of the arguments by which he supports his contention carry, however, the slightest weight, not even the alleged similarity between this fragment of Melissus and fragment 1 of Zeno (**365**). For whereas there is no mention in any of Zeno's fragments of the Eleatic but only of the Pythagorean (or at any rate the pluralists') One, the exact reverse is true of Melissus. This is in no way surprising. It was Zeno's characteristic method (see pp. 287 f.) to base his essentially destructive arguments upon the suppositions of his opponents. Melissus by contrast was essentially constructive and only incidentally critical. Moreover—and this is a very important point—the constructive and destructive approaches are, as this very fragment reveals, by no means easy to reconcile. If, indeed, the argument of the fragment is interpreted as an attack upon the Pythagorean unit-atoms, it succeeds in demolishing the Pythagorean 'plurality of ones' (πλῆθος ἑνάδων, cf. **367**) only at the expense of the Eleatic One. The same is, of course, true also of Zeno's arguments against plurality; but since Zeno's purpose was primarily to demolish the system of his opponents, it is open to doubt whether, even if he was aware of this fact, he would have allowed it to deter him. With Melissus, whose object was to vindicate the Eleatic One, the case is altogether different. If anything that possesses σῶμα and πάχος, 'body' and 'bulk', must thereby possess also μόρια, 'parts', and so sacrifice its unity, then the only way to preserve the unity of the Eleatic One is obviously to deny it these attributes. This fact is so evident that Melissus, with his constructive intent and the consequent desire to anticipate objections, can hardly have failed to observe it. It has already been suggested (pp. 300 f.) that it was partly to avoid a form of this argument that Melissus explicitly stated that his One was infinite, without spatial beginning or end. The further suggestion seems to follow that, on this question of the corporeality of the One, Melissus marks another parallel advance from the position of Parmenides. Parmenides, though he described his One as indivisible and homogeneous, had yet conveyed the distinct impression, in so describing it, that it possessed parts. The Pythagoreans pounced upon this oversight and based upon it one of their 'attempts to make fun of the One' (**362**). Zeno in turn answered the Pythagoreans, using their own type of argument to refute them. Here, as elsewhere, it seems to have been left to Melissus to adapt the positive aspect of Eleaticism in the light of the purely negative disputes of his immediate predecessors. The obvious, if not indeed the inevitable, adaptation would seem to be embodied in this fragment. Another step has been taken towards the apprehension of the abstract; but it is still only a step in that direction, not the eventual arrival at the goal. It is admittedly difficult for us to imagine anything except empty space which is at once infinite in extent and yet has no 'body' or 'bulk'; and even empty space can be imagined to have, what Melissus' One did not have, 'parts'. But Melissus' own words allow no escape from the conclusion that that was the way his mind was working. If he had been capable of imagining something that was not only incorporeal but non-spatial as well, the outcome of his thought would have been different; but the only safe deduction to be drawn from the surviving fragments of his book, which must always remain the best guide to his meaning,[1] is that he was not capable. And since neither of his approximate contemporaries, Empedocles and Anaxagoras, was any more successful in this respect than he was, that conclusion is perhaps less startling than it might otherwise be.

[1] The pseudo-Aristotelian treatise *de Melisso Xenophane Gorgia* (*MXG*), written about the time of Christ, tells us virtually nothing about Melissus' doctrine that we do not learn direct from the fragments. Its author's purpose, moreover, is so critical that its reliability is doubtful.

MELISSUS FORESHADOWS ATOMISM

392 Fr. 8, Simplicius *de caelo* 558, 21 μέγιστον μὲν οὖν σημεῖον οὗτος ὁ λόγος, ὅτι ἓν μόνον ἐστιν· ἀτὰρ καὶ τάδε σημεῖα. εἰ γὰρ ἦν πολλά, τοιαῦτα χρὴ αὐτὰ εἶναι οἷόν περ ἐγώ φημι τὸ ἓν εἶναι. εἰ γὰρ ἔστι γῆ καὶ ὕδωρ καὶ ἀὴρ καὶ πῦρ καὶ σίδηρος καὶ χρυσός,

---

392 *This argument, then, is the greatest proof that it is one alone; but the following are proofs of it also. If there were a plurality, things would have to be of the same kind as I say that the one is. For if there is earth and water, and air and fire, and iron and gold, and*

καὶ τὸ μὲν ζῶον τὸ δὲ τεθνηκός, καὶ μέλαν καὶ λευκὸν καὶ τὰ ἄλλα ὅσα φασὶν οἱ ἄνθρωποι εἶναι ἀληθῆ, εἰ δὴ ταῦτα ἔστι, καὶ ἡμεῖς ὀρθῶς ὁρῶμεν καὶ ἀκούομεν, εἶναι χρὴ ἕκαστον τοιοῦτον οἷόν περ τὸ πρῶτον ἔδοξεν ἡμῖν, καὶ μὴ μεταπίπτειν μηδὲ γίνεσθαι ἑτεροῖον, ἀλλὰ ἀεὶ εἶναι ἕκαστον οἷόν πέρ ἐστιν. νῦν δέ φαμεν ὀρθῶς ὁρᾶν καὶ ἀκούειν καὶ συνιέναι· δοκεῖ δὲ ἡμῖν τό τε θερμὸν ψυχρὸν γίνεσθαι καὶ τὸ ψυχρὸν θερμὸν καὶ τὸ σκληρὸν μαλθακὸν καὶ τὸ μαλθακὸν σκληρὸν καὶ τὸ ζῶον ἀποθνῄσκειν καὶ ἐκ μὴ ζῶντος γίνεσθαι, καὶ ταῦτα πάντα ἑτεροιοῦσθαι, καὶ ὅ τι ἦν τε καὶ ὃ νῦν οὐδὲν ὁμοῖον εἶναι, ἀλλ' ὅ τε σίδηρος σκληρὸς ἐὼν τῷ δακτύλῳ κατατρίβεσθαι ὁμουρέων [Bergk Diels; ὁμοῦ ῥέων mss.], καὶ χρυσὸς καὶ λίθος καὶ ἄλλο ὅ τι ἰσχυρὸν δοκεῖ εἶναι πᾶν, ἐξ ὕδατός τε γῆ καὶ λίθος γίνεσθαι· ὥστε συμβαίνει μήτε ὁρᾶν μήτε τὰ ὄντα γινώσκειν. οὐ τοίνυν ταῦτα ἀλλήλοις ὁμολογεῖ. φαμένοις γὰρ εἶναι πολλὰ καὶ ἀίδια καὶ εἴδη τε καὶ ἰσχὺν ἔχοντα, πάντα ἑτεροιοῦσθαι ἡμῖν δοκεῖ καὶ μεταπίπτειν ἐκ τοῦ ἑκάστοτε ὁρωμένου. δῆλον τοίνυν, ὅτι οὐκ ὀρθῶς ἑωρῶμεν οὐδὲ ἐκεῖνα πολλὰ ὀρθῶς δοκεῖ εἶναι· οὐ γὰρ ἂν μετέπιπτεν, εἰ ἀληθῆ ἦν· ἀλλ' ἦν οἷόν περ ἐδόκει ἕκαστον τοιοῦτον. τοῦ γὰρ ἐόντος ἀληθινοῦ κρεῖσσον οὐδέν. ἢν δὲ μεταπέσῃ, τὸ μὲν ἐὸν ἀπώλετο, τὸ δὲ οὐκ ἐὸν γέγονεν. οὕτως οὖν, εἰ πολλὰ εἴη, τοιαῦτα χρὴ εἶναι οἷόν περ τὸ ἕν.

This skilful attack upon the validity of the senses may well be, as Burnet suggests (*EGP* 328), directed especially against Anaxagoras; in which case, of course, it too, as well as the possible

---

if one thing is living and another dead, and if things are black and white and all that men say they really are—if that is so, and if we see and hear aright, each one of these must be such as we first decided, and they cannot be changed or altered, but each must be always just as it is. But, as it is, we say that we see and hear and understand aright, and yet we believe that what is warm becomes cold, and what is cold warm; that what is hard turns soft, and what is soft hard; that what is living dies, and that things are born from what lives not; and that all those things are changed, and that what they were and what they are now are in no way alike. We think that iron, which is hard, is rubbed away by contact with the finger; and so with gold and stone and everything which we fancy to be strong, and that earth and stone are made out of water; so that it turns out that we neither see nor know realities. Now these things do not agree with one another. We said that there were many things that were eternal and had forms and strength of their own, and yet we fancy that they all suffer alteration, and that they change from what we see each time. It is clear, then, that we did not see aright after all, nor are we right in believing that all these things are many. They would not change if they were real, but each thing would be just what we believed it to be; for nothing is stronger than true reality. But if it has changed, what is has passed away and what is not has come into being. So then, if there were a plurality, things would have to be of just the same nature as the one. (After Burnet)

rejoinder to Ion of Chios in **381** and **383**, is evidence for dating the work of Melissus relatively late. Its prime importance lies, however, at the beginning and the end. There can be little question, as we shall see when we come to Leucippus (pp. 404 ff.), that Melissus' reiterated assertion, 'if there were a plurality, each one of the many would have to be just such as I say the One is'—an assertion that was intended, of course, as a *reductio ad absurdum* of plurality—provided the atomists with the basis of their entire system. Greek atomism is precisely a plurality in which each one of the many is, in almost every essential respect, just such as Melissus said that the One was.[1]

[1] There is another respect in which Melissus may have unconsciously helped the Atomists to answer Parmenides. In section 7 of the long fr. 7 he amplifies Parmenides' argument in **350** and **351** by first explicitly equating not-being with the void and then deducing the impossibility of motion from the non-existence of the void: since there is no empty space there is nowhere for the real to move to. This may perhaps be another of Melissus' replies to the Pythagorean critics of Parmenides. But be that as it may, there can be little doubt that when Melissus wrote, in the middle of this argument, οὐκ ἂν οὖν εἴη τό γε μηδέν, 'for what is nothing could not exist', he made it easier for Leucippus to arrive at the solution summarised by Aristotle in **552** and **554**, and put most succinctly in the paradox in **554**, οὐθὲν μᾶλλον τὸ ὂν τοῦ μὴ ὄντος εἶναι, 'not-being exists no less than being'.

CHAPTER XIII

PHILOLAUS OF CROTON AND EURYTUS OF CROTON

DATE

393 Plato *Phaedo* 61 E (Cebes speaking) καὶ Φιλολάου ἤκουσα, ὅτε παρ' ἡμῖν διητᾶτο.

394 Diogenes Laertius IX, 38 φησὶ δὲ καὶ Ἀπολλόδωρος ὁ Κυζικηνὸς Φιλολάῳ αὐτὸν (*sc.* Democritus) συγγεγονέναι.

395 Diogenes Laertius VIII, 46 τελευταῖοι γὰρ ἐγένοντο τῶν Πυθαγορείων, οὓς καὶ Ἀριστόξενος εἶδε, Ξενόφιλός τε ὁ Χαλκιδεὺς ἀπὸ Θρᾴκης καὶ Φάντων ὁ Φλιάσιος καὶ Ἐχεκράτης καὶ Διοκλῆς καὶ Πολύμναστος Φλιάσιοι καὶ αὐτοί. ἦσαν δὲ ἀκροαταὶ Φιλολάου καὶ Εὐρύτου τῶν Ταραντίνων.

These three passages, being consistent one with another, provide the best evidence available for dating Philolaus.[1] If we accept the further statement of Apollodorus (*ap.* Diog. L. IX, 41, **549**) that Democritus was born about 460–457 B.C., then we can take it that Philolaus too was born somewhere around the middle of the fifth century, and was about fifty years of age when he was lecturing in Thebes. His name is repeatedly linked, as it is in **395**, with that of Eurytus. In dealing with these two at this point we are, therefore, deserting a strictly chronological order; there is no question that they were both considerably later than either Empedocles or Anaxagoras. There is, however, one fact of considerable importance about each which it will be more convenient to discuss before we leave the subject of the interaction between Pythagoreans and Eleatics and proceed to the post-Parmenidean pluralists.

[1] The statement of Iamblichus (*V.P.* 104) that Philolaus and Eurytus were pupils of Pythagoras in his old age is obviously absurd. Both are usually associated with Croton, but sometimes with Tarentum (as in **395**) or Metapontium.

---

393 *I heard Philolaus lecture when he lived in our town* [i.e. Thebes].

394 *Apollodorus of Cyzicus, too, says that Democritus and Philolaus were contemporaries.*

395 *For the last of the Pythagoreans, whom Aristoxenus saw, were Xenophilus the Chalcidian from Thrace, and Phanton, Echecrates, Diocles and Polymnastos, all of Phleious. They were pupils of Philolaus and Eurytus, the Tarentines.*

(I) PHILOLAUS

Story of Plato's plagiarism

396 Diogenes Laertius VIII, 84 (DK44A1) Φιλόλαος Κροτωνιάτης Πυθαγορικός. παρὰ τούτου Πλάτων ὠνήσασθαι τὰ βιβλία τὰ Πυθαγορικὰ Δίωνι γράφει....γέγραφε δὲ βιβλίον ἕν. (ὅ φησιν Ἕρμιππος λέγειν τινὰ τῶν συγγραφέων Πλάτωνα τὸν φιλόσοφον παραγενόμενον εἰς Σικελίαν πρὸς Διονύσιον ὠνήσασθαι παρὰ τῶν συγγενῶν τοῦ Φιλολάου ἀργυρίου Ἀλεξανδρινῶν μνῶν τετταράκοντα καὶ ἐντεῦθεν μεταγεγραφέναι τὸν Τίμαιον. ἕτεροι δὲ λέγουσι τὸν Πλάτωνα λαβεῖν αὐτά, παρὰ Διονυσίου παραιτησάμενον ἐκ τῆς φυλακῆς νεανίσκον ἀπηγμένον τῶν τοῦ Φιλολάου μαθητῶν.)

This curious story, of which this passage shows that there were several variant versions (cf. **266**), seems likely to have originated with Aristoxenus. It was certainly Aristoxenus who, in his desire to detract from Plato's originality, asserted that the *Republic* was largely based on a work of Protagoras; and this is clearly a story of the same malicious order. Its historical importance is of course negligible, but it serves to raise the important question of the authenticity of the fragments still preserved in Philolaus' name.

The fragments of 'Philolaus'

More than twenty fragments are attributed to Philolaus, some of considerable length. If they are genuine, they undoubtedly constitute much the best evidence that we possess concerning the Pythagoreanism of the fifth century. Unfortunately, opinion seems still to be divided on the question of their authenticity. Though much has been written both for and against them, all the more important arguments are conveniently to be found in the works of three scholars only. Ingram Bywater (*J. Philol.* I, 21–53), who played a large part in originally subjecting the fragments to suspicion, and Erich Frank (*Plato und die sogenannten Pythagoreer* 263–335) between them set out the whole case against the frag-

---

396 *Philolaus of Croton, a Pythagorean. It was from him that Plato, in a letter, told Dion to buy the Pythagorean books....He wrote one book. (Hermippus says that according to one writer the philosopher Plato went to Sicily, to the court of Dionysius, bought this book from Philolaus' relatives for 40 Alexandrian*(!) minae, *and from it copied out the* Timaeus. *Others say that Plato acquired the books by securing from Dionysius the release from prison of a young man who had been one of Philolaus' pupils.)*

ments, while R. Mondolfo (Zeller–Mondolfo I, 2, 367–82) is the chief advocate for the defence. On the whole the argument must be pronounced so far to have gone in favour of the prosecution: Mondolfo, even if he has succeeded in producing an explanation or a precedent for every single suspicious feature, has hardly succeeded in explaining away what might be thought the strongest of all arguments against the fragments, the unduly large number of such suspicious or unusual features. It is impossible in the present context to recapitulate all the detailed arguments already adduced by either party. One general argument must suffice.

A careful reading of the fragments reveals in them a notable resemblance to Aristotle's extant accounts of Pythagoreanism. The most striking example is probably that afforded by the following comparison:

397 Fr. 5, Stobaeus *Anth.* I, 21, 7*c* ὅ γα μὰν ἀριθμὸς ἔχει δύο μὲν ἴδια εἴδη, περισσὸν καὶ ἄρτιον, τρίτον δὲ ἀπ' ἀμφοτέρων μειχθέντων ἀρτιοπέριττον· ἑκατέρω δὲ τῶ εἴδεος πολλαὶ μορφαί, ἃς ἕκαστον αὐταυτὸ σημαίνει.[1]

398 Aristotle *Met.* A 5, 986 a 17 (cf. **289**) τοῦ δ' ἀριθμοῦ στοιχεῖα τό τε ἄρτιον καὶ τὸ περιττόν...τὸ δ' ἓν ἐξ ἀμφοτέρων εἶναι τούτων (καὶ γὰρ ἄρτιον εἶναι καὶ περιττόν)....ἕτεροι δὲ τῶν αὐτῶν τούτων τὰς ἀρχὰς δέκα λέγουσιν εἶναι τὰς κατὰ συστοιχίαν λεγομένας·

πέρας καὶ ἄπειρον
περιττὸν καὶ ἄρτιον....

[1] The fact that the fragments are in Doric has been used as an argument both for and against them.

There are several other such resemblances,[1] sufficient to establish at least a strong probability that Aristotle's account of Pythagoreanism and that given by the author of the fragments are interdependent. If, therefore, it can be shown that the author of the fragments was dependent upon Aristotle rather than *vice versa*, then the case against the fragments is virtually conclusive.

---

397 *Number has two special forms, odd and even, and a third derived from the mixture of these two, even-odd. Each form has many manifestations, which every individual thing reveals in its own nature.*

398 *The elements of number (they say) are the even and the odd...the 1 proceeds from both of these (for it is both even and odd).... Other members of this same school say there are ten principles, which they arrange in two columns of cognates—limit and unlimited, odd and even....*

[1] Compare especially fr. 10 with Ar. *de an.* A4, 407b31; also fr. 1 with *Met.* A5, 987a13–19 (DK58B8); fr. 2 with *de caelo* A7, 274a30–3 and *Phys.* Γ4, 203a10–15 (DK58B28); and fr. 7 with *Met.* N3, 1091a15 (DK58B26) and *de caelo* B13, 293a21 (DK58B37).

There are three considerations that point firmly in that direction:

(1) It is to be noted that Aristotle mentions Philolaus by name only once in his extant writings (at *Eth. Eud.* B8, 1225a33, DK44B16), and he there tells us nothing of the slightest importance. That, if Aristotle actually derived much of his information about Pythagorean doctrine from Philolaus' book, is an almost inconceivable state of affairs.

(2) One of the minor resemblances between the two authors' phraseology is of a very suspicious nature. In the middle of fragment 6 occurs the following sentence:

399 Fr. 6, Stobaeus *Anth.* 1, 21, 7*d* ...ἐπεὶ δὲ ταὶ ἀρχαὶ ὑπᾶρχον οὐχ ὁμοῖαι οὐδ' ὁμόφυλοι ἔσσαι, ἤδη ἀδύνατον ἦς κα αὐταῖς κοσμηθῆναι, εἰ μὴ ἁρμονία ἐπεγένετο ᾧτινιῶν ἅδε τρόπῳ ἐγένετο.

It is surprising enough in itself to find the author of the fragments expressing, in the last four words, perplexity about what seems to have been the most important constituent in his whole cosmology. It becomes more surprising still when we find Aristotle, in **313**, voicing an almost identical doubt. For even if Aristotle is here faithfully reproducing an obscurity or omission in the early Pythagorean cosmogony, it would be difficult to maintain that once that vital omission had been consciously acknowledged, as it evidently was by the author of these fragments, it would have been left unrepaired.

(3) If, finally, we look at fragments 3, 4, 6 and especially 11, we find that they are all concerned with a theory of knowledge. It will suffice to quote one only:

400 Fr. 4, Stobaeus *Anth.* 1, 21, 7*b* καὶ πάντα γα μὰν τὰ γιγνωσκόμενα ἀριθμὸν ἔχοντι· οὐ γὰρ οἷόν τε οὐδὲν οὔτε νοηθῆμεν οὔτε γνωσθῆμεν ἄνευ τούτου.

---

399 *...But since the first principles were not by nature alike or akin, it would be impossible for them ever to have been arranged, had not harmony supervened, in whatever way it came into being.*

400 *And all things that can be known contain number; without this nothing could be thought or known.*

This theory is in itself regarded by both Bywater and Frank—though their contention is disputed by Mondolfo—as a palpable anachronism. 'We are required', wrote Bywater (*loc. cit.* p. 35), 'to believe it to have been propounded in a pre-Socratic school of thought, and at a time when the critical enquiry "How is knowledge possible?" had barely been started, much less settled. But after Plato's time the unknowableness of matter without form (ὕλη ἄγνωστος καθ' αὑτήν, says Aristotle) became with various modifications a received formula wherever his influence extended.' It is, however, only when this argument is combined with that other of the resemblance between Aristotle and the author of the fragments that it acquires its full force. For in Aristotle's accounts of Pythagoreanism, though there is abundant evidence of the cosmological significance of numbers, there is nowhere the faintest suggestion that among their other functions they are the only cause of knowledge. This once again, seeing that Aristotle often discusses Pythagoreanism for the express purpose of enquiring what early traces he can find of his own doctrines, seems an almost inconceivable omission. Moreover he consistently represents the Pythagoreans as concerned only with physical phenomena, with never a mention of such an epistemology as that of the fragments. Finally, the argument that the existence of knowledge implies the existence of stable realities is always represented by Aristotle (e.g. at *Met.* A9, 990b11) as peculiarly Platonic, resulting from the blending of Pythagoreanism with Heracliteanism (cf. *ibid.* A6, 987a29); yet it may fairly be claimed that fragments 4, 5 and especially 6 reveal a familiarity with that argument. Irrespective, therefore, of Bywater's contention that the epistemology of the fragments is anachronistic (which, even if not by itself conclusive, can hardly be dismissed as entirely groundless), it seems virtually certain, from Aristotle's complete silence on the subject, that that epistemology was not in fact part of the pre-Platonic Pythagoreanism.

For these and other reasons the fragments attributed to Philolaus can be dismissed, with regret but little hesitation, as part of a post-Aristotelian forgery, based, not without skill, on Aristotle's own accounts of the Pythagorean system.

Other evidence concerning Philolaus

Whereas there is abundant information concerning Philolaus in the works of several late writers, there is scarcely so much as a mention of him in any early and reliable author. Plato and Aristotle each mention him once only, in the passages already cited (see **393** and p. 310), and from neither of these passages do we learn anything of importance about his doctrine. Otherwise there are only two sources of information that are at all reliable: namely, first, a quotation in the *Theologumena Arithmeticae* (p. 82, 10 de Falco; DK44A13) from a lost work by Speusippus *On Pythagorean Numbers*, which was largely based, we are told, on the writings of Philolaus; and second, a passage from Meno's *Iatrica* in the so-called Anonymus Londinensis. The former tells us something of the properties of the Decad, and so suggests that in regard to numbers Philolaus was faithful to the Pythagorean tradition. The latter, which describes the fundamental principles of his medical and physiological theories, is so interesting that a considerable part of it is worth quoting.

401 Meno *ap.* Anon. Londinensem XVIII, 8 (DK44A27) Φιλόλαος δὲ Κροτωνιάτης συνεστάναι φησὶν τὰ ἡμέτερα σώματα ἐκ θερμοῦ. ἀμέτοχα γὰρ αὐτὰ εἶναι ψυχροῦ, ὑπομιμνήσκων ἀπό τινων τοιούτων· τὸ σπέρμα εἶναι θερμόν, κατασκευαστικὸν δὲ τοῦτο τοῦ ȝῴου· καὶ ὁ τόπος δέ, εἰς ὃν ἡ καταβολή (μήτρα δὲ αὕτη), ἐστὶν θερμοτέρα καὶ ἐοικυῖα ἐκείνῳ· τὸ δὲ ἐοικός τινι ταὐτὸ δύναται ᾧ ἔοικεν· ἐπεὶ δὲ τὸ κατασκευάȝον ἀμέτοχόν ἐστιν ψυχροῦ, καὶ ὁ τόπος δέ, ἐν ᾧ ἡ καταβολή, ἀμέτοχός ἐστιν ψυχροῦ, δῆλον ὅτι καὶ τὸ κατασκευαȝόμενον ȝῷον τοιοῦτον γίνεται. εἰς δὲ τούτου τὴν κατασκευὴν ὑπομνήσει προσχρῆται τοιαύτῃ· μετὰ γὰρ τὴν ἔκτεξιν εὐθέως τὸ ȝῷον ἐπισπᾶται τὸ ἐκτὸς πνεῦμα ψυχρὸν ὄν· εἶτα πάλιν καθαπερεὶ χρέος ἐκπέμπει αὐτό. διὰ τοῦτο δὴ καὶ ὄρεξις τοῦ ἐκτὸς

---

401 *Philolaus of Croton holds that our bodies are composed of the hot; for they have no share in the cold, as he reasons from considerations such as the following: the sperm is warm, and it is the sperm that produces the living thing; and the place in which it is deposited (i.e. the womb) is, like it, warm; and what is like something has the same power as that which it resembles. Since, then, the productive factor has no share in the cold, and also the place in which it is deposited has no share in the cold, clearly the living thing produced will also be of the same nature. With regard to its production, he makes use of the following reasoning: immediately after its birth the living thing draws in the breath outside, which is cold; and then, as if of necessity, it expels it again. This desire for the breath outside arises*

πνεύματος, ἵνα τῇ ἐπεισάκτῳ τοῦ πνεύματος ὁλκῇ θερμότερα ὑπάρχοντα τὰ ἡμέτερα σώματα πρὸς αὐτοῦ καταψύχηται.

Then follow a number of detailed doctrines which, in the present context, are of importance only as showing that Philolaus had something more than a merely conventional interest in medical and physiological matters.

The significance of the passage quoted is that it shows a remarkable similarity, both in the general picture it draws and also, in the last three sentences, in vocabulary, to the passages quoted in chapter IX which describe the beginning of the Pythagorean cosmogony, **312**, **315**, and **316**. Just as the sperm, which is warm, is deposited in the womb, so also, in cosmogony, the first unit, which represents the principle of Limit, is somehow implanted in the midst of the surrounding Unlimited; and just as the child, immediately after birth, inhales the breath outside, so also the first unit, immediately after it is generated, proceeds to draw in the void from the surrounding Unlimited. There are of course discrepancies between the cosmogonical and the biological processes: whereas, for instance, Philolaus insists that the womb itself, like the sperm deposited in it, is warm, the Unlimited in which the first unit is implanted represents darkness, while Limit, and the first unit likewise, stand for light. But the general similarity between the two pictures is perhaps sufficient to suggest that Philolaus is at this point maintaining an analogy between the macrocosm and the microcosm; and in that case, whichever of the two was originally the model for the other, his embryological theories may perhaps provide some support for a particularly conjectural stage in the reconstruction of the Pythagorean cosmology in chapter IX.

(2) EURYTUS AND HIS PEBBLES

Slight as is our reliable information about Philolaus, about his associate Eurytus we know even less. We have, however, one solitary piece of information about him which is at once unusually well attested and, despite its superficial triviality, probably of considerable importance.

---

in order that, as the result of the inhalation of the breath, our bodies, which are by nature too warm, may be cooled by it.

402 Aristotle *Met.* N5, 1092b8 οὐθὲν δὲ διώρισται οὐδὲ ὁποτέρως οἱ ἀριθμοὶ αἴτιοι τῶν οὐσιῶν καὶ τοῦ εἶναι, πότερον ὡς ὅροι, οἷον αἱ στιγμαὶ τῶν μεγεθῶν, καὶ ὡς Εὔρυτος ἔταττε τίς ἀριθμὸς τίνος, οἷον ὁδὶ μὲν ἀνθρώπου ὁδὶ δὲ ἵππου, ὥσπερ οἱ τοὺς ἀριθμοὺς ἄγοντες εἰς τὰ σχήματα τρίγωνον καὶ τετράγωνον, οὕτως ἀφομοιῶν ταῖς ψήφοις τὰς μορφὰς τῶν φυτῶν, ἢ ὅτι [ὁ] λόγος ἡ συμφωνία ἀριθμῶν....

403 Alexander *Met.* 827, 9, commenting on **402** κείσθω λόγου χάριν ὅρος τοῦ ἀνθρώπου ὁ $\overline{\sigma\nu}$ ἀριθμός, ὁ δὲ $\overline{\tau\xi}$ τοῦ φυτοῦ· τοῦτο θεὶς ἐλάμβανε ψηφῖδας διακοσίας πεντήκοντα τὰς μὲν πρασίνας τὰς δὲ μελαίνας ἄλλας ⟨δὲ⟩ ἐρυθρὰς καὶ ὅλως παντοδαποῖς χρώμασι κεχρωσμένας. εἶτα περιχρίων τὸν τοῖχον ἀσβέστῳ καὶ σκιαγραφῶν ἄνθρωπον καὶ φυτὸν οὕτως ἐπήγνυ τάσδε μὲν τὰς ψηφῖδας ἐν τῇ τοῦ προσώπου σκιαγραφίᾳ, τὰς δὲ ἐν τῇ τῶν χειρῶν, ἄλλας δὲ ἐν ἄλλοις, καὶ ἀπετέλει τὴν τοῦ μιμουμένου ἀνθρώπου διὰ ψηφίδων ἰσαρίθμων ταῖς μονάσιν, ἃς ὁρίζειν ἔφασκε τὸν ἄνθρωπον.

404 Theophrastus *Met.* 11, 6a19 (p. 12 Ross-Fobes; DK45, 2) τοῦτο γὰρ (*sc.* μὴ μέχρι του προελθόντα παύεσθαι) τελέου καὶ φρονοῦντος, ὅπερ Ἀρχύτας ποτ' ἔφη ποιεῖν Εὔρυτον διατιθέντα τινὰς ψήφους· λέγειν γὰρ ὡς ὅδε μὲν ἀνθρώπου ὁ ἀριθμός, ὅδε δ' ἵππου, ὅδε δ' ἄλλου τινὸς τυγχάνει.

The statement in **404** that the information concerning this curious practice of Eurytus comes from Archytas is a strong indication of its accuracy: no more trustworthy witness could be found on this generation of Pythagoreans. The only question, therefore, is what Eurytus was attempting to prove with his pebbles.

---

402 *Once more, it has in no sense been determined in which way numbers are the causes of substances and of being—whether (1) as limits (as points are of spatial magnitudes): this is how Eurytus decided what was the number of what (e.g. of man, or of horse), viz. by imitating the figures of living things with pebbles, as some people bring numbers into the forms of triangle and square; or (2) is it because harmony is a ratio of numbers...?* (Trans. Ross)

403 *For the sake of argument let the definition of man be the number 250 and that of plant 360. Having settled that, he used to take 250 pebbles, some green, some black, others red and, in short, of a variety of colours. Then he would smear the wall with unslaked lime and make a shaded drawing of a man or a plant; some pebbles he fixed in the drawing of the face, others in the hands, and others elsewhere, until he had completed the drawing of a man in the number of pebbles equal to the number of units which he claimed to define man.*

404 *For this* (sc. *not stopping half-way*) *is the mark of the really sensible man; just as, for instance, Archytas once said that Eurytus used to do when he distributed his pebbles; for he apparently used to claim that such and such was the number of man, such and such that of horse, and such and such that of anything else.*

It is usually assumed that, retaining the early Pythagoreans' confusion between units and atoms, he claimed, by drawing these pictures with pebbles, to determine the number of unit-atoms that constituted the objects, such as man and horse, which he represented. But for a variety of reasons that seems a very improbable explanation of his procedure. Eurytus, being one of the foremost Pythagoreans of his generation, is surely unlikely to have altogether ignored Zeno's devastating exposure of the earlier Pythagoreans' confusion. Again, it seems scarcely credible that he should have believed in unit-atoms of such a magnitude that their number in such an object as man or horse could be so easily determined, especially by means of a drawing in only two dimensions. And finally, as we learn from **403**, he had in any case already decided upon the appropriate number before he began to delineate the object in question. There is every reason to suppose that his purpose was somewhat less ingenuous than this explanation suggests.

A more plausible explanation would seem to be as follows. Eurytus might well have held that it was possible with his pebbles so to delineate the external form of a man or a horse that the resulting figure could represent nothing but a man or a horse. That is to say, he would mark off the surfaces that were peculiarly those of a man or a horse, and the points that bounded those surfaces, and then, by counting the number of points needed to represent a man so that it could be nothing but a man, consider that he had corroborated the equation of man with a particular number. This is exactly the method that **403** suggests. He started, according to that account of his procedure, with a σκιαγραφία—that is to say, probably (though the word is occasionally used to mean only an outline drawing), a drawing shaded to give the illusion of solidity. He was probably in fact thinking in three dimensions, not two only. The boundary points of a three-dimensional object could hardly be represented by a three-dimensional arrangement of pebbles, simply because of the mechanical difficulties involved; but by means of a shaded drawing they could be represented by an arrangement of pebbles on a two-dimensional surface. Further, if the pebbles used were of different colours, as **403** again tells us that they were, the arrangement of pebbles would appear no longer a merely arbitrary scattering but an intelligible representation.

In strong support of this suggestion is the reason for which Aristotle tells us in **402** that Eurytus developed this practice. The doctrine that lies behind the words οἷον αἱ στιγμαὶ τῶν μεγεθῶν, 'as points define magnitudes', is referred to in several other passages of Aristotle, and even if not explicitly, at least by a process of elimination, attributed to the Pythagoreans. One such passage has already been quoted, **320**; this time we will select others:

405 Aristotle *Met.* Z2, 1028b15 (DK58B23) δοκεῖ δέ τισι τὰ τοῦ σώματος πέρατα, οἷον ἐπιφάνεια καὶ γραμμὴ καὶ στιγμὴ καὶ μονάς, εἶναι οὐσίαι, καὶ μᾶλλον ἢ τὸ σῶμα καὶ τὸ στερεόν.

406 Aristotle *Met.* Z11, 1036b8 ἀποροῦσί τινες ἤδη καὶ ἐπὶ τοῦ κύκλου καὶ τοῦ τριγώνου, ὡς οὐ προσῆκον γραμμαῖς ὁρίζεσθαι καὶ τῷ συνεχεῖ, ἀλλὰ πάντα ταῦτα ὁμοίως λέγεσθαι ὡσανεὶ σάρκες ἢ ὀστᾶ τοῦ ἀνθρώπου καὶ χαλκὸς καὶ λίθος τοῦ ἀνδριάντος. καὶ ἀνάγουσι πάντα εἰς τοὺς ἀριθμούς, καὶ γραμμῆς τὸν λόγον τὸν τῶν δύο εἶναί φασιν.

If, as is generally supposed, Alexander is right in telling us that the anonymous thinkers in **406** were Pythagoreans, then it would appear that, besides the earlier doctrine that the line equals 2 because two extended points placed side by side constitute a line, there was also another and subtler Pythagorean view by which a line was a stretch of continuous magnitude bounded by two points. It seems likely that this is a post-Zenonian revision of the traditional view, in which case it may reasonably be ascribed to the generation of Philolaus and Eurytus. And in that case again the procedure of Eurytus begins to look less absurd. Just as a tetrahedron, for instance, could be represented by the number 4, *qua* the number of points required to bound its surfaces, so also, Eurytus may well have thought, could a physical body such as man or horse be represented by however many pebbles were found necessary to bound the visible and tangible surfaces peculiar to that particular body. Expressed in its most general terms, in fact, the οὐσία or essence of an object would be held, as in **405**, to consist in its

---

405 *Some think the limits of body, i.e. surface, line, point and unit, are substances, and more so than body or the solid.* (Trans. Ross)

406 *Some are in doubt even in the case of the circle and the triangle, thinking that it is not right to define these by lines and by continuous space, but that all these are to the circle or the triangle as flesh or bones are to man, and bronze or stone to the statue; and they reduce all things to numbers, and they say the formula of 'line' is that of 'two'.* (Trans. Ross)

surfaces, or more precisely, since a surface is derived from points, in the points that bounded those surfaces. Physical matter and geometrical magnitude alike are bounded by surfaces, lines and points; and the number of points required to bound any object, whether mathematical figure or physical body, is the number with which that object is equated. Finally, as the inclusion of the word πέρατα in **405** (and also in the passage quoted earlier, **320**) clearly suggests, both types of equation are applications, revised in the light of Eleatic criticism, of the traditional Pythagorean doctrine of the imposition of Limit upon the Unlimited.

THE UNIT AS EVEN-ODD

One last Pythagorean doctrine remains to be discussed, that mentioned in a passage from Aristotle's *Metaphysics* already cited in this chapter (**398**), by which the unit is neither odd nor even but both even and odd. We saw earlier (p. 241) that in the pre-Parmenidean Pythagoreanism the unit was unquestionably regarded as a manifestation of the principle of Limit only. It seems likely, therefore, that the present view represents once again a later modification of Pythagorean doctrine in the light of Eleatic criticism. Unfortunately Aristotle himself here, as usual, refuses to distinguish between an earlier and a later Pythagoreanism, but simply groups all Pythagorean doctrines together in his general survey. The following passage, however, seems to preserve for us a genuine Pythagorean tradition.

407 Theo Smyrnaeus p. 21, 20 Hiller τῶν δὲ ἀριθμῶν ποιοῦνται τὴν πρώτην τομὴν εἰς δύο· τοὺς μὲν γὰρ αὐτῶν ἀρτίους, τοὺς δὲ περιττούς φασι. καὶ ἄρτιοι μέν εἰσιν οἱ ἐπιδεχόμενοι τὴν εἰς ἴσα διαίρεσιν, ὡς ἡ δυάς, ἡ τετράς· περισσοὶ δὲ οἱ εἰς ἄνισα διαιρούμενοι, οἷον ὁ ε̄, ὁ ζ̄. πρώτην δὲ τῶν περισσῶν ἔνιοι ἔφασαν τὴν μονάδα. τὸ γὰρ ἄρτιον τῷ περισσῷ ἐναντίον· ἡ δὲ μονὰς ἤτοι περιττόν ἐστιν ἢ ἄρτιον· καὶ ἄρτιον μὲν οὐκ ἂν εἴη· οὐ γὰρ ὅπως εἰς ἴσα, ἀλλ' οὐδὲ ὅλως διαιρεῖται· περιττὴ ἄρα ἡ μονάς. κἂν ἀρτίῳ δὲ ἄρτιον προσθῇς, τὸ πᾶν γίνεται ἄρτιον· μονὰς δὲ ἀρτίῳ προστιθεμένη τὸ

---

407 *The first division of numbers that they make is into two classes, calling some even, some odd. Even numbers are those which can be divided into equal parts (e.g. 2 or 4), odd those which can be divided only into unequal parts (e.g. 5 or 7). Some held that the first of the odd numbers is 1. For even is the contrary of odd; 1 is either odd or even; it cannot be even; for so far from being divisible into equal parts, it cannot be divided at all; whence it follows that 1 is odd. Again, if you add even to even, the whole is even; but*

πᾶν περιττὸν ποιεῖ· οὐκ ἄρα ἄρτιον ἡ μονὰς ἀλλὰ περιττόν. Ἀριστοτέλης δὲ ἐν τῷ Πυθαγορικῷ τὸ ἓν φησιν ἀμφοτέρων μετέχειν τῆς φύσεως· ἀρτίῳ μὲν γὰρ προστεθὲν περιττὸν ποιεῖ, περιττῷ δὲ ἄρτιον, ὃ οὐκ ἂν ἠδύνατο εἰ μὴ ἀμφοῖν τοῖν φυσέοιν μετεῖχε· διὸ καὶ ἀρτιοπέριττον καλεῖσθαι τὸ ἕν. συμφέρεται δὲ τούτοις καὶ Ἀρχύτας.

It is hard to resist the conclusion that this passage represents two distinct stages in the development of Pythagoreanism. In the original view there are only two classes of number, even and odd, of which the former comprises those numbers which are divisible into halves, the latter those which are divisible only into unequal parts.[1] The unit itself, though it will not fit into either class, is asserted to be odd because it cannot be even, and its equation with Limit is thereby justified. But sooner or later the fact must be acknowledged that according to these definitions the unit cannot be odd any more than it can be even. So, while the traditional definitions are retained essentially unaltered, the third category is introduced to contain the unit and the unit only. Arithmetically, of course, the consequence of the change is of no great significance. The first odd number is no longer 1 but 3; but the unit can presumably remain the principle of numbers and their mode of generation need not necessarily be altered. Metaphysically, however, since odd is Limit and even Unlimited, the consequences seem to be of the utmost significance. No longer is the first unit, the starting-point of Pythagorean cosmogony, regarded as the embodiment of Limit in the Unlimited, it is instead the first product of the blending of the two principles; and by that simple change another of the Eleatic criticisms, that directed against the 'inhalation' of the one principle by the other (cf. pp. 253 and 274), is duly acknowledged and countered.

[1] This early definition of odd and even numbers is also preserved, in very similar words, both by Aristoxenus *ap.* Stob. *Anth.* 1, 1, 6 (DK 58 B 2) and by Nicomachus *I.A.* 1, 7 (p. 13, 15 Hoche). The twofold classification of number in Theo's first sentence is to be contrasted with what may well have been (despite the probable spuriousness of the actual fragment) the genuine view of Philolaus in **397** above.

---

add 1 to an even number and it makes the whole odd; whence it follows that 1 is not even but odd. Aristotle, however, in his work on the Pythagoreans, says that 1 partakes of the nature of both; for when added to an even number it makes it odd, when added to an odd, even—which would be impossible if it did not partake of the nature of both; and so, he says, it is called even-odd. Archytas too agrees with Aristotle on this point.

THE POST-PARMENIDEAN SYSTEMS

The last stage of Presocratic philosophy consists primarily of the pluralist systems of Empedocles and Anaxagoras, of the combination of pluralism and monism represented by the atomism of Leucippus and Democritus, and finally of the re-adapted Ionian monism of Diogenes of Apollonia. Each of these systems is, in its own way, a deliberate reply to Parmenides. Parmenides seemed, to his contemporaries and immediate successors, to have established once and for all certain canons with which, until Plato himself exposed the fallacies on which they were based, all future cosmologists must somehow comply. Being, in the first place, must not be allowed to spring from Not-being: anything that was claimed as real must also be ultimate. Again, the void, being sheer non-existence, can find no place in any account of reality. Third, plurality cannot come from an original unity: if there is to be a plurality, it too, like reality, must be ultimate. And finally, motion must no longer be simply taken for granted, an explanation must be given of its existence—which involved also an explanation and justification of sense-perception. Any future system that ignored any one of these canons would, for the time being at least, have been considered from the outset untenable.

This estimate of the strength of Parmenides' influence is no mere conjecture. Both Empedocles and Anaxagoras repeatedly and clearly reveal, not only by their thought but also by the language in which it is expressed, an almost servile observance of the Parmenidean demands; atomism, although its method of complying with the Parmenidean canons shows a courageous refusal to be intimidated, is nevertheless in a very special sense the outcome of the Eleatic paradox; and Diogenes, even though he reverts to the single specific substance of Anaximenes, incorporates much from Anaxagoras and Leucippus in order to protect himself against Elea. Since one of the most interesting and important aspects of the history of early Greek philosophy—and it is an aspect that can easily be lost from sight—is its peculiar continuity, a part of each of the main chapters that follow will be devoted to showing, where possible in the philosophers' own words, how these post-Parmenidean systems are deliberately designed to take account of the findings of the Way of Truth.

CHAPTER XIV

EMPEDOCLES OF ACRAGAS

DATE

408 Diogenes Laertius VIII, 74 (DK31A1) ἤκμαζε δὲ κατὰ τὴν τετάρτην καὶ ὀγδοηκοστὴν ὀλυμπιάδα.

409 Diogenes Laertius VIII, 51 (DK31A1) Ἐμπεδοκλῆς, ὥς φησιν Ἱππόβοτος, Μέτωνος ἦν υἱὸς τοῦ Ἐμπεδοκλέους Ἀκραγαντῖνος...λέγει δὲ καὶ Ἐρατοσθένης ἐν τοῖς Ὀλυμπιονίκαις τὴν πρώτην καὶ ἑβδομηκοστὴν ὀλυμπιάδα νενικηκέναι τὸν τοῦ Μέτωνος πατέρα, μάρτυρι χρώμενος Ἀριστοτέλει. Ἀπολλόδωρος δ' ὁ γραμματικὸς ἐν τοῖς Χρονικοῖς φησιν ὡς

ἦν μὲν Μέτωνος υἱός, εἰς δὲ Θουρίους
αὐτὸν νεωστὶ παντελῶς ἐκτισμένους
⟨ὁ⟩ Γλαῦκος ἐλθεῖν φησιν.

...Ἀριστοτέλης γὰρ αὐτόν, ἔτι τε Ἡρακλείδης, ἑξήκοντα ἐτῶν φησι τετελευτηκέναι.

410 Aristotle *Met.* A3, 984a11 (DK31A6) Ἀναξαγόρας δὲ ὁ Κλαζομένιος τῇ μὲν ἡλικίᾳ πρότερος ὢν τούτου (*sc.* Empedocles), τοῖς δ' ἔργοις ὕστερος....

411 Simplicius *Phys.* 25, 19, quoting Theophrastus Ἐμπεδοκλῆς ὁ Ἀκραγαντῖνος οὐ πολὺ κατόπιν τοῦ Ἀναξαγόρου γεγονώς, Παρμενίδου δὲ ζηλωτὴς καὶ πλησιαστὴς καὶ ἔτι μᾶλλον τῶν Πυθαγορείων....

Empedocles' precise dates are impossible to determine. Apollodorus, whom Diogenes is doubtless following in **408**, is, as usual,

---

408 *He flourished in the eighty-fourth Olympiad.*

409 *Empedocles, according to Hippobotus, was the son of Meton, himself son of Empedocles, and came from Acragas....Eratosthenes, in his* Olympic victors, *says that the father of Meton won a victory in the seventy-first Olympiad, and he cites Aristotle as evidence. But Apollodorus the grammarian writes in his* Chronicles *that 'he was the son of Meton, and Glaucus says that he came to Thurii very soon after its foundation'.... According to Aristotle, and also Heraclides, he died at the age of sixty.*

410 *Anaxagoras of Clazomenae, who, though older than Empedocles, was later in his philosophical activity....* (Trans. Ross)

411 *Empedocles of Acragas was born not long after Anaxagoras, and was an admirer and associate of Parmenides, and even more of the Pythagoreans....*

definite enough; but it seems most likely that he has arrived at his answer by simply assuming that Empedocles was forty years old when Thurii was founded (i.e. in Ol. 84, 444–441 B.C.). Accordingly it has often been suggested that the date given by Apollodorus is considerably too late.[1] In the absence of any reliable and decisive evidence, there is no ground for more than the very tentative conclusion that Empedocles' *floruit* must have been somewhere around the middle of the century. That, at any rate, as we shall see (pp. 380 f.), tallies with what we are told in **410** and **411** about the relative dates of Empedocles and Anaxagoras.

[1] See Diels, 'Gorgias und Empedokles', *SB Ber.* (1884) 343 ff.

LIFE

Empedocles, like Pythagoras and Heraclitus, was a favourite subject (cf. p. 183) for apocryphal biographical tales. A considerable number of them, drawn from numerous sources, are preserved by Diogenes. For the most part they are concerned either with his political activities or with his death, and it is the former group alone which may perhaps contain a germ of truth. He is said to have been an ardent democrat, to have broken up some otherwise unknown organization called the Thousand, and to have refused the kingship of his city (see Diogenes Laertius VIII, 66 and 63, DK 31 A 1). Here at least we do seem to have something other than a misguided embellishment of his own words in his poems; indeed we might almost conclude from his poems that his views were aristocratic rather than democratic. It would be unwise, however, to accept even these stories at their face value; they do no more than testify to a probably genuine tradition that as a democrat he took a leading part in the politics of his city. He was evidently also an accomplished orator: Aristotle, in his lost dialogue *Sophist*, apparently called him the inventor of rhetoric (Diog. L. VIII 57, DK 31 A 1), and Gorgias is said to have been his pupil. Finally, his fame as a doctor, which is suggested by his own words in fragment 112,[1] is proved by the numerous references to him in later medical writings.

[1] For whole fr. (and refs.) see **478**, but cf. especially **412** ll. 10–12

οἱ μὲν μαντοσυνέων κεχρημένοι, οἱ δ' ἐπὶ νούσων
παντοίων ἐπύθοντο κλύειν εὐηκέα βάξιν,
δηρὸν δὴ χαλεπῇσι πεπαρμένοι ⟨ἀμφ' ὀδύνῃσιν⟩.

---

412 *...some seeking prophecies, while others, for many a day stabbed by grievous pains, beg to hear the word that heals all manner of illness.*

WRITINGS

The two poems from which the surviving fragments come were called respectively Περὶ φύσεως, *On Nature*, and Καθαρμοί, *Purifications*. According to Diogenes Laertius (VIII, 77) these two poems together ran to five thousand lines,[1] while the Suda (s.v. Empedocles, DK 31 A 2) tells us that *On Nature* was in two books, together comprising some two thousand lines. The extant verses even of the poem *On Nature* represent, therefore, less than a fifth of the original whole, while those of the *Purifications*, if the figure given by Diogenes is correct, are even more fragmentary.

In addition to these two poems Diogenes (*l.c.*) says that there was also a work of six hundred lines on medicine, which the Suda (*l.c.*) however tells us was in prose. Several other works are also ascribed by later authorities to Empedocles, including no less than forty-three tragedies, but it seems very unlikely that they are in fact his.

[1] **413** Diog. L. VIII, 77 (DK 31 A 1) τὰ μὲν οὖν Περὶ φύσεως αὐτῷ καὶ οἱ Καθαρμοὶ εἰς ἔπη τείνουσι πεντακισχίλια. Diels, however, on the ground that the Καθαρμοί is unlikely to have extended to 3000 lines, suggested reading πάντα τρισχίλια instead.

THE PROBLEM

Though the precise order of the fragments cannot be certainly determined, and though in a few cases it is even doubtful from which poem a fragment comes, the arrangement of Diels is now generally accepted. On the basis of the fragments alone it is possible to reconstruct the system of Empedocles with greater confidence than most of the Presocratic philosophers allow. The chief difficulty in his case is of quite a different order. Whereas the poem *On Nature* is primarily concerned to give a physical explanation of the universe and its contents, and in the process seems to leave no room for an immortal soul, the *Purifications* is based upon the Pythagorean belief in transmigration. The resulting conflict between the two poems has been resolved, in modern times, in a variety of ways. While some scholars, including both Zeller and Burnet, are content to conclude that Empedocles held simultaneously beliefs that are not only incompatible but actually

---

413 *His* On nature *and* Purifications *together comprise as much as 5000 lines.*

contradictory, others have argued that the two poems must belong to separate stages of Empedocles' life. The following exposition, which partly stems from notes taken at Cornford's lectures in 1936, will attempt to show that, while the former of these two views is far preferable to the latter, it still lays undue stress upon the alleged incompatibility of the two poems. It will always remain a difficult question what view Empedocles really did take of the soul; but unless one poem is used to throw light upon the obscurities of the other, even more difficult problems will remain to be solved.

THE INFLUENCE OF PARMENIDES AND ITS EFFECTS

414 Fr. 11, Plutarch *adv. Colot.* 12, 1113C and Fr. 12, [Aristotle] *MXG* 2, 975b1

νήπιοι· οὐ γάρ σφιν δολιχόφρονές εἰσι μέριμναι,
οἳ δὴ γίγνεσθαι πάρος οὐκ ἐὸν ἐλπίζουσιν
ἤ τι καταθνῄσκειν τε καὶ ἐξόλλυσθαι ἁπάντῃ.
(Fr. 12) ἔκ τε γὰρ οὐδάμ' ἐόντος ἀμήχανόν ἐστι γενέσθαι
καί τ' ἐὸν ἐξαπολέσθαι ἀνήνυστον καὶ ἄπυστον·
αἰεὶ γὰρ τῇ γ' ἔσται, ὅπῃ κέ τις αἰὲν ἐρείδῃ.

415 Fr. 13, Aetius 1, 18, 2

οὐδέ τι τοῦ παντὸς κενεὸν πέλει οὐδὲ περισσόν.

416 Fr. 14, [Aristotle] *MXG* 2, 976b24

τοῦ παντὸς δ' οὐδὲν κενεόν· πόθεν οὖν τί κ' ἐπέλθοι;

417 Fr. 6, Aetius 1, 3, 20

τέσσαρα γὰρ πάντων ῥιζώματα πρῶτον ἄκουε·
Ζεὺς ἀργὴς Ἥρη τε φερέσβιος ἠδ' Ἀιδωνεὺς
Νῆστίς θ' ἣ δακρύοις τέγγει κρούνωμα βρότειον.

---

414 *Fools—for they have no far-reaching thoughts—who fancy that that which formerly was not can come into being or that anything can perish and be utterly destroyed. For coming into being from that which in no way is is inconceivable, and it is impossible and unheard-of that that which is should be destroyed. For it will ever be there wherever one may keep pushing it.*

415 *Nor is any part of the whole either empty or over-full.*

416 *And no part of the whole is empty; whence then could anything enter into it?*

417 *Hear first the four roots of all things: shining Zeus, life-bringing Hera, Aidoneus and Nestis who with her tears fills the springs of mortal men with water.*

418 Fr. 17, l. 6, Simplicius *Phys.* 158, 6

καὶ ταῦτ' ἀλλάσσοντα διαμπερὲς οὐδαμὰ λήγει,
ἄλλοτε μὲν Φιλότητι συνερχόμεν' εἰς ἓν ἅπαντα,
ἄλλοτε δ' αὖ δίχ' ἕκαστα φορεύμενα Νείκεος ἔχθει.

These fragments amply suffice to show the strength of the influence exercised by Parmenides on Empedocles. A comparison of **414** with fragment 8 of Parmenides (especially ll. 16–21, **347**), or of **415** and **416** with lines 22–25 of the same fragment (**348**), reveals that Empedocles was not only complying with the Parmenidean canons but doing so consciously and deliberately. It might even be maintained that this compliance is the basis of Empedocles' system; for these few fragments, besides affording an eloquent indication of Empedocles' dependence on Parmenides, can be made to serve also as an introduction to his cosmology.

Parmenides had maintained that reality cannot come from unreality nor plurality from an original unity. Empedocles meets both demands simultaneously. There never was, he replies, an original unity; there were rather four eternally distinct substances, Zeus, Hera, Aidoneus and Nestis, or Fire, Air, Earth and Water.[1] These between them fill the whole of space, leaving no place in the universe for the non-existent void. All things consist of these elements, or irreducible forms of matter, in various proportions. When a thing is said to come into existence or to perish, all that has really happened is that one temporary combination of these indestructible elements has been dissolved and another been established. Change in fact is nothing but a re-arrangement; and to account for the motion in space which alone could effect such a reshuffling, two motive forces, Love and Strife, take their place along with the elements as the only ultimate realities. So all four of the Parmenidean demands (see p. 319) are duly met, and already, in meeting them, Empedocles has evolved the essentials of his system. In following his cosmology through the peculiar cycle which he imposed upon it, we shall be merely filling in the details of an outline that has already emerged.

[1] It is characteristic of Empedocles that he should present the 'four roots' at their first appearance in mythological guise. Nestis is certainly Water,

---

418 *And these things never cease from continual shifting, at one time all coming together, through Love, into one, at another each borne apart from the others through Strife.*

but even in antiquity there was a difference of opinion concerning the other three. Fire, which is here probably represented by Zeus, is in frs. 96 and 98 called Hephaestus. For Empedocles' belief in the corporeality of air see **453**.

EMPEDOCLES' DEFENCE OF THE SENSES

419 Fr. 3, l. 9, Sextus *adv. math.* VII, 125

ἀλλ' ἄγ' ἄθρει πάσῃ παλάμῃ, πῇ δῆλον ἕκαστον,
μήτε τιν' ὄψιν ἔχων πίστει πλέον ἢ κατ' ἀκουὴν
ἢ ἀκοὴν ἐρίδουπον ὑπὲρ τρανώματα γλώσσης,
μήτε τι τῶν ἄλλων, ὁπόσῃ πόρος ἐστὶ νοῆσαι,
γυίων πίστιν ἔρυκε, νόει δ' ᾗ δῆλον ἕκαστον.

One of the first questions Empedocles had to tackle was whether or not the senses are a reliable guide to the truth. In these important verses, which are shown by the rest of the fragment to come from the introduction to the poem, he is as deliberately contradicting Parmenides as he is elsewhere obeying him. Clearly the sort of cosmology on which he is about to embark demands, as indeed any cosmology must, faith in the validity of sense-perception. So far, therefore, from following Parmenides in his condemnation of the senses, he instructs his readers to make full but discriminating use of them, taking care to employ each sense for the appropriate purpose.[1]

[1] Line 10 may contain also an implied criticism of Heraclitus: **420** fr. 101 *a*, Polybius XII, 27 ὀφθαλμοὶ [τῶν] ὤτων ἀκριβέστεροι μάρτυρες. Perhaps, however, Heraclitus only meant that seeing something for oneself is better than hearing second-hand reports; but cf. pp. 207 ff.

THE SPHERE

421 Frr. 27 and 28[1]

ἔνθ' οὔτ' ἠελίοιο διείδεται ὠκέα γυῖα
οὐδὲ μὲν οὐδ' αἴης λάσιον μένος οὐδὲ θάλασσα·
ἀλλ' ὅ γε πάντοθεν ἶσος ⟨ἑοῖ⟩ καὶ πάμπαν ἀπείρων

---

419 *But come, consider with all thy powers how each thing is manifest, neither holding sight in greater trust as compared with hearing, nor loud-sounding hearing above the clear evidence of thy tongue, nor withhold thy trust from any of the other limbs, wheresoever there is a path for understanding, but think on each thing in the way by which it is manifest.*

420 *Eyes are more accurate witnesses than ears.*

421 *Here are distinguished neither the swift limbs of the sun nor the shaggy might of the earth nor the sea; but rather, equal ⟨to himself⟩ from every side and quite without end, he*

οὕτως Ἁρμονίης πυκινῷ κρύφῳ ἐστήρικται
σφαῖρος κυκλοτερὴς μονίῃ περιηγέι γαίων.

422 Fr. 29, Hippolytus *Ref.* VII, 29

οὐ γὰρ ἀπὸ νώτοιο δύο κλάδοι ἀίσσονται,
οὐ πόδες, οὐ θοὰ γοῦν', οὐ μήδεα γεννήεντα,
ἀλλὰ σφαῖρος ἔην καὶ ⟨πάντοθεν⟩ ἶσος ἑαυτῷ.

[1] This is probably a single fr., of which Plut. (*de fac. lun.* 12, 926 E) quotes ll. 1–2 (though he refers them to the rule of Strife and reads ἀγλαὸν εἶδος for ὠκέα γυῖα), Simpl. (*Phys.* 1183, 30) ll. 1, 4 and 5, and Stob. (*Anth.* I, 15, 2*a*, *b*) ll. 3 and 5. Diels prints ll. 1, 2, 4 and 5 as fr. 27 and ll. 3 and 5 as fr. 28 (a solution which does not, however, evade the principal problem, that posed by Plut.'s citation of ll. 1–2).

In these fragments Empedocles' debt to Parmenides is again obvious: though **422** doubtless reflects also the influence of Xenophanes' attack upon anthropomorphic gods (see pp. 168 f.), Empedocles' Sphere is indisputably modelled on that of Parmenides. What Empedocles has done in fact is to take the sphere of Parmenides and fill it from the outset with the four eternally distinct elements. But this single change from an original unity to an original plurality makes the whole difference to the sequel. Whereas with Parmenides the sphere, being a unity, can never undergo the slightest change, with Empedocles it proves to be but one phase in a never-ending cosmic cycle.

THE COSMIC CYCLE

423 Fr. 17, 1–13, Simplicius *Phys.* 158, 1

δίπλ' ἐρέω· τοτὲ μὲν γὰρ ἓν ηὐξήθη μόνον εἶναι
ἐκ πλεόνων, τοτὲ δ' αὖ διέφυ πλέον' ἐξ ἑνὸς εἶναι.
δοιὴ δὲ θνητῶν γένεσις, δοιὴ δ' ἀπόλειψις·
τὴν μὲν γὰρ πάντων σύνοδος τίκτει τ' ὀλέκει τε,
ἡ δὲ πάλιν διαφυομένων θρεφθεῖσα διέπτη.

---

stays fast in the close covering of Harmony, a rounded sphere rejoicing in his circular solitude.

422 *Two branches spring not from his back, he has no feet, no swift knees, no fertile parts; rather was he a sphere, equal to himself from every side.*

423 *A double tale will I tell: at one time it grew to be one only from many, at another it divided again to be many from one. There is a double coming into being of mortal things and a double passing away. One is brought about, and again destroyed, by the coming together of all things, the other grows up and is scattered as things are again divided. And*

καὶ ταῦτ' ἀλλάσσοντα διαμπερὲς οὐδαμὰ λήγει,
ἄλλοτε μὲν Φιλότητι συνερχόμεν' εἰς ἓν ἅπαντα,
ἄλλοτε δ' αὖ δίχ' ἕκαστα φορεύμενα Νείκεος ἔχθει.
⟨οὕτως ᾗ μὲν ἓν ἐκ πλεόνων μεμάθηκε φύεσθαι⟩
ἠδὲ πάλιν διαφύντος ἑνὸς πλέον' ἐκτελέθουσι,
τῇ μὲν γίγνονταί τε καὶ οὔ σφισιν ἔμπεδος αἰών·
ᾗ δὲ διαλλάσσοντα διαμπερὲς οὐδαμὰ λήγει,
ταύτῃ δ' αἰὲν ἔασιν ἀκίνητοι κατὰ κύκλον.[1]

[1] Lines 7–8 and 10–13 are almost identical with ll. 5–6 and 9–12 of fr. 26, which is also preserved by Simpl. at *Phys.* 33, 19. Line 9 above, which is needed to complete the sense, is l. 8 of fr. 26 interpolated here by Diels.

The cosmic cycle which Empedocles is here describing is the most peculiar feature in his whole system. This never-ending cycle would seem (though this has been disputed) to have four stages, two polar stages represented by the rule of Love and the rule of Strife, and two transitional stages, one from the rule of Love towards the rule of Strife, and the other back again from the rule of Strife towards the rule of Love. The rule of Love itself, in which 'all things unite in one through Love' (l. 7), is of course the Sphere described in the fragments in the last section. It is a uniform mixture of the four elements—so uniform that nothing whatever can be discerned in it. Before we proceed to follow the cosmic cycle through the other three stages, it will be as well to pause at this first stage (for though the cycle is never-ending and has therefore no chronologically first stage, the rule of Love is still the logical starting-point of the process), and consider in more detail the various ingredients in the mixture.

THE FOUR ROOTS AND LOVE AND STRIFE

424 Fr. 17, l. 14, Simplicius *Phys.* 158, 13 (continuing **423**)

ἀλλ' ἄγε μύθων κλῦθι· μάθη γάρ τοι φρένας αὔξει·
ὡς γὰρ καὶ πρὶν ἔειπα πιφαύσκων πείρατα μύθων,

---

these things never cease from continual shifting, at one time all coming together, through Love, into one, at another each borne apart from the others through Strife. ⟨So, in so far as they have learnt to grow into one from many,⟩ and again, when the one is sundered, are once more many, thus far they come into being and they have no lasting life; but in so far as they never cease from continual interchange of places, thus far are they ever changeless in the cycle.

424 *But come, hearken to my words; for learning increaseth wisdom. As I said before when I declared the limits of my words, a double tale will I tell: at one time it grew to be*

δίπλ' ἐρέω· τοτὲ μὲν γὰρ ἓν ηὐξήθη μόνον εἶναι
ἐκ πλεόνων, τοτὲ δ' αὖ διέφυ πλέον' ἐξ ἑνὸς εἶναι,
πῦρ καὶ ὕδωρ καὶ γαῖα καὶ ἠέρος ἄπλετον ὕψος,
Νεῖκός τ' οὐλόμενον δίχα τῶν, ἀτάλαντον ἁπάντῃ,
καὶ Φιλότης ἐν τοῖσιν, ἴση μῆκός τε πλάτος τε·
τὴν σὺ νόῳ δέρκευ, μηδ' ὄμμασιν ἧσο τεθηπώς·
ἥτις καὶ θνητοῖσι νομίζεται ἔμφυτος ἄρθροις,
τῇ τε φίλα φρονέουσι καὶ ἄρθμια ἔργα τελοῦσι,
Γηθοσύνην καλέοντες ἐπώνυμον ἠδ' Ἀφροδίτην·
τὴν οὔ τις μετὰ τοῖσιν ἑλισσομένην δεδάηκε
θνητὸς ἀνήρ· σὺ δ' ἄκουε λόγου στόλον οὐκ ἀπατηλόν.
ταῦτα γὰρ ἶσά τε πάντα καὶ ἥλικα γένναν ἔασι,
τιμῆς δ' ἄλλης ἄλλο μέδει, πάρα δ' ἦθος ἑκάστῳ,
ἐν δὲ μέρει κρατέουσι περιπλομένοιο χρόνοιο.
καὶ πρὸς τοῖς οὔτ' ἄρ τι ἐπιγίγνεται οὐδ' ἀπολήγει·
εἴτε γὰρ ἐφθείροντο διαμπερές, οὐκέτ' ἂν ἦσαν·[1]
τοῦτο δ' ἐπαυξήσειε τὸ πᾶν τί κε; καὶ πόθεν ἐλθόν;
πῇ δέ κε κἠξαπόλοιτο, ἐπεὶ τῶνδ' οὐδὲν ἔρημον;
ἀλλ' αὔτ' ἔστιν ταῦτα, δι' ἀλλήλων δὲ θέοντα
γίγνεται ἄλλοτε ἄλλα καὶ ἠνεκὲς αἰὲν ὁμοῖα.

425 Fr. 21, l. 9, Simplicius *Phys.* 159, 21

ἐκ τούτων γὰρ πάνθ' ὅσα τ' ἦν ὅσα τ' ἔστι καὶ ἔσται,
δένδρεά τ' ἐβλάστησε καὶ ἀνέρες ἠδὲ γυναῖκες,
θῆρές τ' οἰωνοί τε καὶ ὑδατοθρέμμονες ἰχθῦς,
καί τε θεοὶ δολιχαίωνες τιμῇσι φέριστοι.

---

one only from many, at another it divided again to be many from one, fire and water and earth and the vast height of air, dread Strife too, apart from these, everywhere equally balanced, and Love in their midst, equal in length and breadth. On her do thou gaze with thy mind, and sit not with dazed eyes; for she is recognized as inborn in mortal limbs; by her they think kind thoughts and do the works of concord, calling her Joy by name and Aphrodite. Her does no mortal man know as she whirls around amid the others; but do thou pay heed to the undeceitful ordering of my discourse. For all these are equal, and of like age, but each has a different prerogative and its own character, and in turn they prevail as time comes round. And besides these nothing else comes into being nor ceases to be; for if they were continually being destroyed, they would no longer be; and what could increase this whole, and whence could it come? And how could these things perish too, since nothing is empty of them? Nay, there are these things alone, and running through one another they become now this and now that and yet remain ever as they are.

425 *From these things sprang all things that were and are and shall be, trees and men and women, beasts and birds and water-bred fishes, and the long-lived gods too, most mighty*

αὐτὰ γὰρ ἔστιν ταῦτα, δι᾽ ἀλλήλων δὲ θέοντα
γίγνεται ἀλλοιωπά· τόσον διὰ κρῆσις ἀμείβει.

[1] It looks as if a line had fallen out here, balancing the εἴτε clause and completing what in its present form appears an incomplete argument.

In these passages the influence of Parmenides is once again obvious enough: certain lines in **424** could well have come from Parmenides himself. Empedocles is in fact playing his usual part of mediator. Taking, presumably, those opposite substances which had been most conspicuous in earlier cosmologies, the hot, the cold, the wet and the dry (the first pair of which were definitely used by Anaximander, while both pairs were mentioned in Heraclitus fr. 126), and explicitly asserting that they are eternally distinct, he places them in the Parmenidean sphere and, by merely mixing and reshuffling them, accounts for birth, death, change and all physical phenomena. As he is at pains to point out, his elements do not, either in nature or behaviour, break any of the Parmenidean canons. He has already effectively restored, by a mere revision of pre-Parmenidean ideas, plurality and diversity; he is about to restore, by the introduction of his two motive forces, motion, change and time. In fact the only Parmenidean tenet that he has sacrificed is that which Parmenides himself had valued most of all, his monism. That gone, the rest follows without further infringement.

The elements, Empedocles says in both **424** and **425**, comprise the whole of material reality: 'there are these alone.' Simplicius would seem therefore to be fully justified in the following comment on Empedocles:

426 Simplicius *Phys.* 25, 21 (DK31A28) οὗτος δὲ τὰ μὲν σωματικὰ στοιχεῖα ποιεῖ τέτταρα, πῦρ καὶ ἀέρα καὶ ὕδωρ καὶ γῆν, ἀίδια μὲν ὄντα, πλήθει δὲ καὶ ὀλιγότητι μεταβάλλοντα κατὰ τὴν σύγκρισιν καὶ διάκρισιν, τὰς δὲ κυρίως ἀρχάς, ὑφ᾽ ὧν κινεῖται ταῦτα, Φιλίαν καὶ Νεῖκος. δεῖ γὰρ διατελεῖν ἐναλλὰξ κινούμενα τὰ στοιχεῖα,

---

in their prerogatives. For there are these things alone, and running through one another they assume many a shape: so much change does mixing effect.

426 *He makes the material elements four in number, fire, air, water and earth, all eternal, but changing in bulk and scarcity through mixture and separation; but his real first principles, which impart motion to these, are Love and Strife. The elements are*

ποτὲ μὲν ὑπὸ τῆς Φιλίας συγκρινόμενα, ποτὲ δὲ ὑπὸ τοῦ Νείκους διακρινόμενα· ὥστε καὶ ἓξ εἶναι κατ' αὐτὸν τὰς ἀρχάς.

Empedocles was certainly feeling his way towards the distinction here drawn between the material and the efficient cause. Love, he explicitly says, is the same as Aphrodite, which we recognize in ourselves but not in the universe. He is in fact drawing, and literally believing in, the analogy between the universe as a whole and man. Love and Strife are not, therefore, mere mechanical forces disguised under mythical or allegorical names. Empedocles believes, as the analogy shows, that sexual love and cosmic Love are one and the same self-existent external force which acts upon the person or the thing that loves.[1] At the same time he is still unable to imagine any form of existence other than spatial extension, and in consequence his Love and Strife are still represented (in **424**, ll. 19–20) as if they too were material.[2] We have seen earlier (pp. 302 ff.) how gradual was the advance towards the apprehension of the abstract. Empedocles here takes another step in that direction. We shall see, on pp. 374 f., how Anaxagoras takes yet another. But it was not until Plato elaborated his theory of Ideas that the goal was eventually reached.

[1] Aristotle in his comments on Empedocles goes further than this and says that Love and Strife have a moral character. Cf. **427** Aristotle *Met.* A4, 985a4 (DK 31 A 39) εἰ γάρ τις ἀκολουθοίη καὶ λαμβάνοι πρὸς τὴν διάνοιαν καὶ μὴ πρὸς ἃ ψελλίζεται λέγων Ἐμπεδοκλῆς, εὑρήσει τὴν μὲν Φιλίαν αἰτίαν οὖσαν τῶν ἀγαθῶν, τὸ δὲ Νεῖκος τῶν κακῶν· ὥστ' εἴ τις φαίη τρόπον τινὰ καὶ λέγειν καὶ πρῶτον λέγειν τὸ κακὸν καὶ τὸ ἀγαθὸν ἀρχὰς Ἐμπεδοκλέα, τάχ' ἂν λέγοι καλῶς.... Aristotle may be right: there is little doubt that Empedocles was to some extent influenced by the moral dualism of the Pythagoreans.

[2] Cf. **428** Aristotle *Met.* Λ9, 1075b1 ἀτόπως δὲ καὶ Ἐμπεδοκλῆς· τὴν γὰρ Φιλίαν ποιεῖ τὸ ἀγαθόν, αὕτη δ' ἀρχὴ καὶ ὡς κινοῦσα (συνάγει γάρ) καὶ

---

continually subject to an alternate change, at one time mixed together by Love, at another separated by Strife; so that the first principles are, by his account, six in number.

427 *For if we were to follow out the view of Empedocles, and interpret it according to its meaning and not to its lisping expression, we should find that Love is the cause of good things, and Strife of bad. Therefore, if we said that Empedocles in a sense both mentions, and is the first to mention, the bad and the good as principles, we should perhaps be right....* (After Ross)

428 *Empedocles also has a paradoxical view; for he identifies the good with Love. But this is a principle both as mover (for it brings things together) and as matter (for it is part of the mixture).* (Trans. Ross)

ὡς ὕλη· μόριον γὰρ τοῦ μίγματος. Note that in this passage also, as in **427**, Love is credited with a moral character—though in both cases this may be only Aristotle's own interpretation.

DISRUPTION OF THE SPHERE

429 Aristotle *Met.* B4, 1000b12 καὶ ἅμα δὲ αὐτῆς τῆς μεταβολῆς αἴτιον οὐθὲν λέγει ἀλλ' ἢ ὅτι οὕτως πέφυκεν·

(Fr. 30) ἀλλ' ὅτε δὴ μέγα Νεῖκος ἐνὶ μελέεσσιν ἐθρέφθη,
εἰς τιμάς τ' ἀνόρουσε τελειομένοιο χρόνοιο
ὅς σφιν ἀμοιβαῖος πλατέος παρ' ἐλήλαται ὅρκου·

ὡς ἀναγκαῖον μὲν ὂν μεταβάλλειν.

430 Simplicius *Phys.* 1184, 2 ἀρξαμένου δὲ πάλιν τοῦ Νείκους ἐπικρατεῖν τότε πάλιν κίνησις ἐν τῷ Σφαίρῳ γίνεται·

(Fr. 31) πάντα γὰρ ἑξείης πελεμίζετο γυῖα θεοῖο.

These two brief fragments are all that survive of Empedocles' description of the disruption of the Sphere. At that stage in the cosmic cycle when the rule of Love was complete, Strife was evidently altogether excluded from the Sphere. Indeed one short fragment may well, in its context, have said exactly that:

431 Fr. 27*a*, Plutarch *Maxime cum princ.* 2, 777C

οὐ στάσις οὐδέ τε δῆρις ἀναίσιμος ἐν μελέεσσιν.

When we come to the opposite polar stage in the cycle, we shall find Empedocles, in his description of the disruption of the rule of Strife, saying that 'a soft, immortal stream of blameless Love kept running in' (see **464**). Presumably, therefore, the reverse process has been taking place in the Sphere: Strife, at one stage completely excluded, has been flowing back into the Sphere until it attains a sufficient proportion to assert itself. When that happens, motion begins, and cosmogony, in the normal sense, is initiated. But, as Aristotle complains in **429**, what higher power it is that determines 'by a mighty oath' the timing of the alternations in the cosmic

---

429 *And at the same time Empedocles mentions no cause of the change itself, except that things are so by nature. 'But when Strife waxed great in the limbs, and sprang to his prerogatives as the time was fulfilled which is fixed for them in turn by a broad oath'—this implies that change was necessary.* (After Ross)

430 *But when Strife began once more to prevail, then there is again motion in the Sphere; 'for all the god's limbs in turn began to quake.'*

431 *There is no discord nor unseemly rivalry in his limbs.*

cycle is very far from clear. It might conceivably be maintained that Love and Strife had themselves sworn the oath; but it seems much more likely that Empedocles is here guilty of an undetected confusion, at one moment asserting that the four elements and Love and Strife are alone ultimate, at another suggesting that even for them there are laws laid down which they cannot infringe.

COSMOGONY

(i) *The first stages*

432 Fr. 38, Clement *Strom.* v, 48, 3

εἰ δ' ἄγε τοι λέξω πρῶθ' †ἥλιον ἀρχήν†,
ἐξ ὧν δῆλ' ἐγένοντο τὰ νῦν ἐσορῶμεν ἅπαντα,
γαῖά τε καὶ πόντος πολυκύμων ἠδ' ὑγρὸς ἀὴρ
Τιτὰν ἠδ' αἰθὴρ σφίγγων περὶ κύκλον ἅπαντα.

433 Aetius ii, 6, 3 Ἐμπεδοκλῆς τὸν μὲν αἰθέρα πρῶτον διακριθῆναι, δεύτερον δὲ τὸ πῦρ, ἐφ' ᾧ τὴν γῆν, ἐξ ἧς ἄγαν περισφιγγομένης τῇ ῥύμῃ τῆς περιφορᾶς ἀναβλύσαι τὸ ὕδωρ· ἐξ οὗ θυμιαθῆναι τὸν ἀέρα, καὶ γενέσθαι τὸν μὲν οὐρανὸν ἐκ τοῦ αἰθέρος, τὸν δὲ ἥλιον ἐκ τοῦ πυρός, πιληθῆναι δὲ ἐκ τῶν ἄλλων τὰ περίγεια.

434 [Plutarch] *Strom. ap.* Eusebium *P.E.* i, 8, 10 (DK 31 A 30) Ἐμπεδοκλῆς ὁ Ἀκραγαντῖνος...ἐκ πρώτης φησὶ τῆς τῶν στοιχείων κράσεως ἀποκριθέντα τὸν ἀέρα περιχυθῆναι κύκλῳ· μετὰ δὲ τὸν ἀέρα τὸ πῦρ ἐκδραμὸν καὶ οὐκ ἔχον ἑτέραν χώραν ἄνω ἐκτρέχειν ὑπὸ τοῦ περὶ τὸν ἀέρα πάγου. εἶναι δὲ κύκλῳ περὶ τὴν γῆν φερόμενα δύο ἡμισφαίρια τὸ μὲν καθόλου πυρός, τὸ δὲ μικτὸν ἐξ ἀέρος καὶ ὀλίγου πυρός, ὅπερ οἴεται τὴν νύκτα εἶναι. τὴν δὲ ἀρχὴν τῆς κινήσεως συμβῆναι ἀπὸ τοῦ τετυχηκέναι κατά ⟨τι⟩ τὸν ἀθροισμὸν ἐπιβρίσαντος τοῦ πυρός.

---

432 *Come, I shall tell thee first of the sun†, and whence became manifest all the things we now behold, the earth and the billowing sea, the damp air and the Titan aither who fastens his circle around all things.*

433 *Empedocles holds that aither was the first to be separated off, next fire, and after that earth. From the earth, as it was excessively constricted by the force of the rotation, sprang water. From water air came by evaporation. The heavens arose from the aither, the sun from the fire, while terrestrial things were compressed from the other elements.*

434 *Empedocles of Acragas...holds that the air that was separated off from the original mixture of the elements flowed around in a circle; and after the air fire ran outwards and, having nowhere else to go, ran upwards under the solidified periphery around the air. There are, he says, two hemispheres revolving round the earth, one consisting entirely of fire, the other of a mixture of air with a little fire; this latter he supposes to be night. Their motion arises from the fact that the accumulation of fire in one region gives it preponderance there.*

In these passages we see the earliest stages of cosmogony. Air,[1] being the first of the elements to be separated out of the sphere, took up a position surrounding the world, and evidently (to judge from **434**) its outermost margin solidified to form the firmament. When, however, fire followed air upwards, it seems to have displaced the air enclosed in the upper half of this solid firmament, and the air thereupon sank, taking a little fire with it, into the lower half. Two hemispheres are thus formed inside the firmament, the diurnal and the nocturnal, and when the concentration of fire in the upper hemisphere somehow[2] so upsets the balance of the sphere as to start a circular motion, the result is the alternation of day and night.

[1] **433** is one of several passages which suggest that Empedocles sometimes called air 'aither', though the two were normally regarded as distinct. Admittedly in **432** 'aither' must stand for fire; but equally clearly in **453** (ll. 5, 7, 18 and 24) it represents air.

[2] Why a concentration of a *light* element, Fire, in the *upper* hemisphere should start a circular motion is altogether obscure; but the evidence strongly suggests that Empedocles thought it did.

(ii) *The heavenly bodies*

435 [Plutarch] *Strom. ap.* Eusebium *P.E.* I, 8, 10 (DK31A30) (continuing **434**) ὁ δὲ ἥλιος τὴν φύσιν οὐκ ἔστι πῦρ, ἀλλὰ τοῦ πυρὸς ἀντανάκλασις ὁμοία τῇ ἀφ' ὕδατος γινομένῃ. σελήνην δέ φησιν συστῆναι καθ' ἑαυτὴν ἐκ τοῦ ἀποληφθέντος ἀέρος ὑπὸ τοῦ πυρός. τοῦτον γὰρ παγῆναι καθάπερ καὶ τὴν χάλαζαν. τὸ δὲ φῶς αὐτὴν ἔχειν ἀπὸ τοῦ ἡλίου. Cf. Aetius II, 20, 13 (DK31A56).

436 Aetius II, 13, 2 Ἐμπεδοκλῆς πύρινα (*sc.* εἶναι τὰ ἄστρα) ἐκ τοῦ πυρώδους, ὅπερ ὁ ἀὴρ ἐν ἑαυτῷ περιέχων ἐξανέθλιψε κατὰ τὴν πρώτην διάκρισιν.

437 Aetius II, 13, 11 Ἐμπεδοκλῆς τοὺς μὲν ἀπλανεῖς ἀστέρας συνδεδέσθαι τῷ κρυστάλλῳ, τοὺς δὲ πλανήτας ἀνεῖσθαι.

---

435 *The sun is not in its nature fire, but rather a reflexion of fire like that which comes from water. The moon, he says, was composed of air that had been shut in by fire; this air was solidified, like hail. The moon gets its light from the sun.*

436 *Empedocles says that the stars are made of fire, composed of the fiery element which the air originally contained but squeezed out at the first separation.*

437 *Empedocles says that the fixed stars were attached to the ice* (i.e. *the frozen periphery*), *while the planets were unattached.*

438 Fr. 42, Plutarch *de fac. in orbe lun.* 16, 929C

ἀπεστέγασεν δέ οἱ αὐγάς,
ἔστ' ἂν ἴῃ καθύπερθεν,[1] ἀπεσκνίφωσε δὲ γαίης
τόσσον ὅσον τ' εὖρος γλαυκώπιδος ἔπλετο μήνης.

439 Aristotle *de caelo* B13, 295a13 διὸ δὴ καὶ τὴν γῆν πάντες ὅσοι τὸν οὐρανὸν γεννῶσιν ἐπὶ τὸ μέσον συνελθεῖν φασιν. ὅτι δὲ μένει, ζητοῦσι τὴν αἰτίαν καὶ λέγουσιν οἱ μὲν τοῦτον τὸν τρόπον, ὅτι τὸ πλάτος καὶ τὸ μέγεθος αὐτῆς αἴτιον, οἱ δ' ὥσπερ Ἐμπεδοκλῆς τὴν τοῦ οὐρανοῦ φορὰν κύκλῳ περιθέουσαν καὶ θᾶττον φερομένην τὴν τῆς γῆς φορὰν κωλύειν καθάπερ τὸ ἐν τοῖς κυάθοις ὕδωρ· καὶ γὰρ τοῦτο κύκλῳ τοῦ κυάθου φερομένου πολλάκις κάτω τοῦ χαλκοῦ γινόμενον ὅμως οὐ φέρεται κάτω πεφυκὸς φέρεσθαι διὰ τὴν αὐτὴν αἰτίαν.

[1] The text of this fr. is corrupt. The above version is Diels' conjecture for the ms. ἀπεσκεύασε...ἔστε αἶαν καθύπερθεν.

These passages contain the most notable of Empedocles' astronomical theories. The statement in **435** that the sun is not itself fire but a reflexion of fire involves a difficulty. Aetius tells us (II, 20, 13, DK31A56) that the fire reflected by the sun is that which, according to **434**, is concentrated in the diurnal hemisphere; but in that case its reflexion cannot be in the opposite hemisphere, because that is the nocturnal. A possible solution seems to be that suggested by Burnet (*EGP* 238) that 'the light of the fiery hemisphere is reflected by the earth on to the fiery hemisphere itself in one concentrated flash'.[1] Empedocles knew, as **435** goes on to tell us, that the moon shines by reflected light. His complicated view of the nature of the sun looks like a curious application of the same theory.

[1] Cf. Plut. *de Pyth. or.* 12,400B (DK31B44), which supports this interpretation. Against it, however, is the suggestion in the same passage of Aetius (II, 20, 13) that the sun is a solid object (κρυσταλλοειδής, 'crystalline') in the fiery hemisphere which carries it round (but cf. n. 1 on p. 156).

---

438 *But she kept off the sun's rays, so long as it was passing over above her, and cast a shadow over as much of the earth as was the breadth of the pale-faced moon.*

439 *All those who generate the heavens hold that it was for this reason that the earth came together to the centre. They then seek a reason for its staying there; and some say, in the manner explained, that the reason is its size and flatness, others, like Empedocles, that the motion of the heavens, moving about it at a higher speed, prevents movement of the earth, as the water in a cup, when the cup is given a circular motion, though it is often underneath the bronze, is for this same reason prevented from moving with the downward movement which is natural to it.* (After Stocks)

For the rest these passages are straightforward enough. **438** shows that Empedocles knew also the true cause of eclipses, while **439** is one of the few reliable passages affording evidence of simple argument from observation on the part of the Presocratic physicists (cf. p. 149 n., and p. 341, **453** and comment).

(iii) *Organic compounds*

440 Fr. 96, Simplicius *Phys.* 300, 21

ἡ δὲ χθὼν ἐπίηρος ἐν εὐστέρνοις χοάνοισι
τὼ δύο τῶν ὀκτὼ μερέων λάχε Νήστιδος αἴγλης,
τέσσαρα δ' Ἡφαίστοιο· τὰ δ' ὀστέα λευκὰ γένοντο
Ἁρμονίης κόλλῃσιν ἀρηρότα θεσπεσίῃσιν.

441 Fr. 98, Simplicius *Phys.* 32, 6

ἡ δὲ χθὼν τούτοισιν ἴση συνέκυρσε μάλιστα,
Ἡφαίστῳ τ' ὄμβρῳ τε καὶ αἰθέρι παμφανόωντι,
Κύπριδος ὁρμισθεῖσα τελείοις ἐν λιμένεσσιν,
εἴτ' ὀλίγον μείζων εἴτε πλεόνεσσιν ἐλάσσων·
ἐκ τῶν αἷμά τε γέντο καὶ ἄλλης εἴδεα σαρκός.

These two fragments show that Empedocles was concerned (as indeed he had to be, in order to explain how composite organisms could come into existence from a mixture of the four elements) not only with the elements themselves and the complete objects which they ultimately formed, but also with such intermediate substances (the proximate materials of the complete objects) as bone and flesh. He seems to have been the first of the Presocratic philosophers to pay much attention to such compounds; but, essential as they are in his cosmogony, they still did not apparently figure so prominently in Empedocles as they did in Anaxagoras (see pp. 378 ff.). The exact proportions in which these substances are compounded reveal the influence of Pythagoreanism on Empedocles. We shall see later (pp. 351 ff.) that this is by no means the only manifestation of that influence.

---

440 *The kindly earth received in its broad funnels two parts of gleaming Nestis out of the eight, and four of Hephaestus; and there arose white bones fitted together by the divine bonds of Harmony.*

441 *And the earth came together with these in almost equal proportions, with Hephaestus, with moisture and with brilliant aither, and so it anchored in the perfect harbours of Kupris, either a little more of it or less of it with more of the others. From these did blood arise, and the forms of flesh besides.*

FOUR STAGES OF EVOLUTION

At this point we meet a further complication in Empedocles' physical system. Not only is there, as we have already seen (pp. 326 f.), a cosmic cycle of two polar and two transitional stages, but also, in each of the latter, there are evidently two distinct stages in the evolution of living things. The four stages together seem to be accurately summarized in the following passage:

442 Aetius v, 19, 5 (DK 31 A 72) Ἐμπεδοκλῆς τὰς πρώτας γενέσεις τῶν ζῴων καὶ φυτῶν μηδαμῶς ὁλοκλήρους γενέσθαι, ἀσυμφυέσι δὲ τοῖς μορίοις διεζευγμένας, τὰς δὲ δευτέρας συμφυομένων τῶν μερῶν εἰδωλοφανεῖς, τὰς δὲ τρίτας τῶν ὁλοφυῶν, τὰς δὲ τετάρτας οὐκέτι ἐκ τῶν ὁμοιομερῶν [Diels, ὁμοίων mss.] οἷον ἐκ γῆς καὶ ὕδατος, ἀλλὰ δι' ἀλλήλων ἤδη, τοῖς μὲν πυκνωθείσης [τοῖς δὲ καὶ τοῖς ζῴοις] τῆς τροφῆς, τοῖς δὲ καὶ τῆς εὐμορφίας τῶν γυναικῶν ἐπερεθισμὸν τοῦ σπερματικοῦ κινήματος ἐμποιησάσης· τῶν δὲ ζῴων πάντων τὰ γένη διακριθῆναι διὰ τὰς ποιὰς κράσεις....

With the aid of this passage it is possible to allocate to the appropriate stage of evolution most of the fragments of Empedocles that are concerned with the generation of living things. It will be best to describe the first three of the four stages before considering which two belong to the phase in the cosmic cycle now under discussion and which to the transition from the rule of Strife back to the rule of Love.

Stage 1: disunited limbs

443 Fr. 57, Aristotle *de caelo* Γ 2, 300 b 30 (l. 1) and Simplicius *de caelo* 587, 1 (ll. 2–3)

ᾗ πολλαὶ μὲν κόρσαι ἀναύχενες ἐβλάστησαν,
γυμνοὶ δ' ἐπλάζοντο βραχίονες εὔνιδες ὤμων,
ὄμματά τ' οἷ' ἐπλανᾶτο πενητεύοντα μετώπων.

---

442 *Empedocles held that the first generations of animals and plants were not complete but consisted of separate limbs not joined together; the second, arising from the joining of these limbs, were like creatures in dreams; the third was the generation of whole-natured forms; and the fourth arose no longer from the homoeomerous substances such as earth or water, but by generation, in some cases as the result of the condensation of their nourishment, in others because feminine beauty excited the sexual urge; and the various species of animals were distinguished by the quality of the mixture in them....*

443 *Here sprang up many faces without necks, arms wandered without shoulders, unattached, and eyes strayed alone, in need of foreheads.*

This fragment clearly describes the first of the four stages described by Aetius in **442**. At this stage, according to the brief and incomplete fr. 58, 'solitary limbs wandered about seeking for union'. The next stage therefore shows them having achieved, if at random, the union they were seeking.

Stage 2: monsters and deformities

444 Fr. 59, Simplicius *de caelo* 587, 20

αὐτὰρ ἐπεὶ κατὰ μεῖζον ἐμίσγετο δαίμονι δαίμων
ταῦτά τε συμπίπτεσκον, ὅπῃ συνέκυρσεν ἕκαστα,
ἄλλα τε πρὸς τοῖς πολλὰ διηνεκῆ ἐξεγένοντο.

445 Fr. 60, Plutarch *adv. Colot.* 28, 1123B

...εἱλίποδ' ἀκριτόχειρα....

446 Fr. 61, Aelian *Nat. anim.* XVI, 29

πολλὰ μὲν ἀμφιπρόσωπα καὶ ἀμφίστερνα φύεσθαι,
βουγενῆ ἀνδρόπρῳρα, τὰ δ' ἔμπαλιν ἐξανατέλλειν
ἀνδροφυῆ βούκρανα, μεμειγμένα τῇ μὲν ἀπ' ἀνδρῶν
τῇ δὲ γυναικοφυῆ σκιεροῖς [στείροις Diels] ἠσκημένα γυίοις.

These fragments describe vividly enough Aetius' second stage, a period of monsters and deformities. We learn also from the following passage that at this stage in evolution, as presumably at each of the others too, those creatures that were accidentally fitted to survive did so, while the rest perished:

447 Aristotle *Phys.* B8, 198b29 ὅπου μὲν οὖν ἅπαντα συνέβη ὥσπερ κἂν εἰ ἕνεκά του ἐγίνετο, ταῦτα μὲν ἐσώθη ἀπὸ τοῦ αὐτομάτου συστάντα ἐπιτηδείως· ὅσα δὲ μὴ οὕτως, ἀπώλετο καὶ ἀπόλλυται, καθάπερ Ἐμπεδοκλῆς λέγει τὰ 'βουγενῆ ἀνδρόπρῳρα'.

---

444 *But as one divine element mingled further with another, these things fell together as each chanced to meet other, and many other things besides these were constantly resulting.*

445 *...with rolling gait and countless hands....*

446 *Many creatures were born with faces and breasts on both sides, man-faced ox-progeny, while others again sprang forth as ox-headed offspring of man, creatures compounded partly of male, partly of the nature of female, and fitted with shadowy* [or *sterile* Diels] *parts.*

447 *Wherever, then, everything turned out as it would have if it were happening for a purpose, there the creatures survived, being accidentally compounded in a suitable way; but where this did not happen, the creatures perished and are perishing still, as Empedocles says of his 'man-faced ox-progeny'.*

On the ground that he combined belief in evolution with this theory of the survival of the fittest, Empedocles has sometimes been extravagantly claimed to have anticipated Darwin (cf. also on Anaximander, p. 142).

Stage 3: 'whole-natured forms'

448 Fr. 62, Simplicius *Phys.* 381, 31

νῦν δ' ἄγ', ὅπως ἀνδρῶν τε πολυκλαύτων τε γυναικῶν
ἐννυχίους ὅρπηκας ἀνήγαγε κρινόμενον πῦρ,
τῶνδε κλύ'· οὐ γὰρ μῦθος ἀπόσκοπος οὐδ' ἀδαήμων.
οὐλοφυεῖς μὲν πρῶτα τύποι χθονὸς ἐξανέτελλον,
ἀμφοτέρων ὕδατός τε καὶ εἴδεος αἶσαν ἔχοντες·
τοὺς μὲν πῦρ ἀνέπεμπε θέλον πρὸς ὁμοῖον ἱκέσθαι,
οὔτε τί πω μελέων ἐρατὸν δέμας ἐμφαίνοντας
οὔτ' ἐνοπὴν οἷόν τ' ἐπιχώριον ἀνδράσι γυῖον.

This third stage, the stage of 'whole-natured forms' without distinction of sex, may possibly have been the origin of the theory put into the mouth of Aristophanes in Plato's *Symposium.*[1] These 'whole-natured forms' are the outcome of the tendency of fire 'to join its like'; and that tendency in turn is the outcome of the influence of Strife, the function of which, as we shall see, is to break up the uniform mixture of the elements, the work of Love, into four separate masses. As the process of separation continues, the sexes are eventually distinguished and we reach the last of Aetius' four stages.

[1] Widely different interpretations are, however, possible. Simplicius, for instance, thinks that a 'whole-natured form' has no distinct parts at all, while Aristotle regards it as merely a form of seed.

Where Stages 1–3 belong

449 Aristotle *de caelo* Γ2, 300b25 ἔτι δὲ τοσοῦτον ἐπανέροιτ' ἄν τις, πότερον δυνατὸν ἢ οὐχ οἷόν τ' ἦν κινούμενα ἀτάκτως καὶ μείγνυσθαι τοιαύτας μίξεις ἔνια ἐξ ὧν συνίσταται τὰ κατὰ φύσιν

---

448 *Come now, hear how the fire, as it was separated, caused to spring up the night-born scions of men and of tearful women; for this is a tale that is neither irrelevant nor uninformed. First sprang up from the earth whole-natured forms, having a share of both water and fire; these the fire sent forth, desiring to reach its like, showing forth as yet neither the lovely form of the limbs, nor the voice nor the organ proper to men.*

449 *There is a further question, too, which might be asked. Is it possible or impossible that bodies in unordered movement should combine in some cases into combinations like*

συνιστάμενα σώματα. λέγω δ' οἷον ὀστᾶ καὶ σάρκας, καθάπερ Ἐμπεδοκλῆς φησι γίνεσθαι ἐπὶ τῆς Φιλότητος· λέγει γάρ (cf. **443**) 'πολλαὶ μὲν κόρσαι ἀναύχενες ἐβλάστησαν'.

450 Aristotle *de anima* Γ6, 430a28 ...καθάπερ Ἐμπεδοκλῆς ἔφη 'ᾗ πολλῶν μὲν κόρσαι ἀναύχενες ἐβλάστησαν', ἔπειτα συντίθεσθαι τῇ Φιλίᾳ....

451 Aristotle *de gen. et corr.* B7, 334a5 ἅμα δὲ καὶ τὸν κόσμον ὁμοίως ἔχειν φησὶν ἐπί τε τοῦ Νείκους νῦν καὶ πρότερον ἐπὶ τῆς Φιλίας.

The question of which evolutionary stages belong to which phase in the cosmic cycle has been much debated. But these passages leave little room for doubt. It is clear from **449** that the first stage belongs to the period when Love is gaining ascendancy;[1] and since the second stage follows immediately upon the first, that too must obviously belong there. On the other hand **451**, and especially the word νῦν, 'now', shows that the present state of the world belongs to the other transitional phase, when Strife is gaining upon Love. That leaves only the third stage; and as that third stage is, as we have just seen, only the prelude to the present, the pattern is complete. The third and fourth stages belong, in that order, to the phase of the cycle that we are now considering, the progressive disruption of the Sphere by Strife; and the fourth stage is that which the actual world has now reached. The first and second stages, on the other hand, belong to the last phase in the cosmic cycle, which is yet to be discussed (pp. 346ff.).

[1] That Aristotle's phrase ἐπὶ τῆς Φιλότητος (or Φιλίας) refers, not to the rule of Love, but to the period when Love is again gaining ascendancy is clear from (among other considerations) the following passage: **452** Simplicius *de caelo* 587, 24 (DK31B59) ἐπὶ τῆς Φιλότητος...οὐχ ὡς ἐπικρατούσης ἤδη τῆς Φιλότητος, ἀλλ' ὡς μελλούσης ἐπικρατεῖν.

---

those of which bodies of nature's composing are composed, such, I mean, as bones and flesh? Yet this is what Empedocles asserts to have occurred under Love. 'Many a head', says he, 'came to birth without a neck.'

450 *...as Empedocles said that 'where heads of many creatures came to birth without necks', they are then put together by Love....*

451 *At the same time he asserts that the world is in the same state now in the period of Strife as it was earlier in that of Love.*

452 *By 'in the period of Love' he means, not when Love was already in control, but when it was going to be.*

Stage 4: the present world

Since the world as we know it belongs to the fourth and last of the evolutionary stages of **442**, it is here that the relatively numerous fragments belong that are concerned with such specialized sciences as botany, embryology and physiology. In each of these Empedocles made important contributions to Greek thought. A number of brief fragments (77–81) concerned with botany—a subject to which Empedocles seems to have been the first Greek to pay much attention—are supplemented by a fairly detailed summary by Aetius (v, 26, 4, DK 31 A 70). Plants, Empedocles maintained, were the first living things to appear, being, like the 'whole-natured forms' of **448**, temporary combinations of fire moving upwards from beneath the earth to join its like in the firmament, and earth moving downwards under the same impulse. Again like the 'whole-natured forms', plants are not yet sexually differentiated, but, combining the two sexes in one, reproduce themselves by bearing 'eggs' (fr. 79). The fragments concerned with embryology (63–70) are likewise very brief, but are again supplemented by Aetius (v, 7, 1; 8, 1; 10, 1; 11, 1; 12, 2; all in DK 31 A 81). Male children are conceived in the warmer part of the womb (fr. 67) and contain a greater proportion of the hot than do female. 'The substance of the child's limbs is divided' between the parents (fr. 63), or in other words is derived from both—a view that was by no means universal in the ancient world, the Pythagoreans, for instance, believing that it derived entirely from the father—but the child will resemble whichever of the parents has contributed most. As for physiology, Empedocles here again attached great importance to the principle of the attraction of like to like; not only does it account for nutrition and growth (Aetius v, 27, 1, DK 31 A 77), but also for pleasure and pain (Aetius IV, 9, 15, DK 31 A 95). It is not possible to describe in detail all Empedocles' biological and physiological theories that have been preserved; from the point of view of the historian of philosophy his chief importance lies elsewhere. But there are a few special topics falling under this general heading that are sufficiently notable to merit inclusion.

(*a*) *Respiration*

453 Fr. 100, Aristotle *de respiratione* 7, 473b9

ὧδε δ' ἀναπνεῖ πάντα καὶ ἐκπνεῖ· πᾶσι λίφαιμοι
σαρκῶν σύριγγες πύματον κατὰ σῶμα τέτανται,
καί σφιν ἐπὶ στομίοις πυκιναῖς τέτρηνται ἄλοξιν
ῥινῶν ἔσχατα τέρθρα διαμπερές, ὥστε φόνον μὲν
κεύθειν, αἰθέρι δ' εὐπορίην διόδοισι τετμῆσθαι.
ἔνθεν ἔπειθ' ὁπόταν μὲν ἀπαΐξῃ τέρεν αἷμα,
αἰθὴρ παφλάζων καταΐσσεται οἴδματι μάργῳ,
εὖτε δ' ἀναθρῴσκῃ, πάλιν ἐκπνέει, ὥσπερ ὅταν παῖς
κλεψύδρῃ παίζουσα διειπετέος χαλκοῖο—
εὖτε μὲν αὐλοῦ πορθμὸν ἐπ' εὐειδεῖ χερὶ θεῖσα
εἰς ὕδατος βάπτῃσι τέρεν δέμας ἀργυφέοιο,
οὐδεὶς ἄγγοσδ' ὄμβρος ἐσέρχεται, ἀλλά μιν εἴργει
ἀέρος ὄγκος ἔσωθε πεσὼν ἐπὶ τρήματα πυκνά,
εἰσόκ' ἀποστεγάσῃ πυκινὸν ῥόον· αὐτὰρ ἔπειτα
πνεύματος ἐλλείποντος ἐσέρχεται αἴσιμον ὕδωρ.
ὣς δ' αὔτως, ὅθ' ὕδωρ μὲν ἔχῃ κατὰ βένθεα χαλκοῦ
πορθμοῦ χωσθέντος βροτέῳ χροῒ ἠδὲ πόροιο,
αἰθὴρ δ' ἐκτὸς ἔσω λελιημένος ὄμβρον ἐρύκει,
ἀμφὶ πύλας ἠθμοῖο δυσηχέος ἄκρα κρατύνων,
εἰσόκε χειρὶ μεθῇ, τότε δ' αὖ πάλιν, ἔμπαλιν ἢ πρίν,
πνεύματος ἐμπίπτοντος ὑπεκθέει αἴσιμον ὕδωρ.
ὣς δ' αὔτως τέρεν αἷμα κλαδασσόμενον διὰ γυίων
ὁππότε μὲν παλίνορσον ἀπαΐξειε μυχόνδε,

---

453 *So do all things inhale and exhale: there are bloodless channels in the flesh of them all, stretched over their bodies' surface, and at the mouths of these channels the outermost surface of skin is pierced right through with many a pore, so that the blood is kept in but an easy path is cut for the air to pass through. Then, when the fluid blood rushes away thence, the bubbling air rushes in with violent surge; and when the blood leaps up, the air is breathed out again, just as when a girl plays with a* klepsydra *of gleaming brass. When she puts the mouth of the pipe against her shapely hand and dips it into the fluid mass of shining water, no liquid enters the vessel, but the bulk of the air within, pressing upon the frequent perforations, holds it back until she uncovers the dense stream; but then, as the air yields, an equal bulk of water enters. In just the same way, when water occupies the depths of the brazen vessel and the passage of its mouth is blocked by human hand, the air outside, striving inwards, holds the water back, holding its surface firm at the gates of the ill-sounding neck until she lets go with her hand; and then again (the reverse of what happened before), as the breath rushes in, an equal bulk of water runs out before it. And in just the same way, when the fluid blood surging through the limbs rushes backwards and*

αἰθέρος εὐθὺς ῥεῦμα κατέρχεται οἴδματι θῦον,
εὖτε δ᾽ ἀναθρῴσκῃ πάλιν ἐκπνέει ἶσον ὀπίσσω.

This celebrated passage, with its implicit proof of the corporeality of air, is often cited, along with **439**, as evidence that the Presocratics in general, and Empedocles in particular, were familiar with the experimental method of modern science. 'The rise of the experimental method' writes Burnet (*EGP* 27) 'dates from the time when the medical schools began to influence the development of philosophy, and accordingly we find that the first recorded experiment of a modern type is that of Empedokles with the *klepsydra*.[1] We have his own account of this (fr. 100), and we can see how it brought him to the verge of anticipating Harvey and Torricelli.' This is of course an exaggerated view. That Empedocles made occasional use, if not of experiment, at least of simple observation, cannot be disputed. It might easily be maintained, however, that all he is here doing is using an isolated observation to illustrate a theory already reached by methods far removed from the experimental technique of modern science. And even if the opposite view be taken, that his observation of the *klepsydra* was the result of deliberate research (which it quite patently was not), this same fragment proves conclusively that his experiments were scarcely, as Burnet claimed, modern in character. For, as Cornford replied (*Principium Sapientiae* 6), 'this theory could have been tested by anyone who would sit in a bath up to his neck and observe whether any air bubbles passed through the water into, or out of, his chest as he breathed'.[2]

[1] The κλεψύδρα, usually translated 'water-clock', was a metal vessel with a narrow neck and with its base perforated, like a modern coffee-strainer, with numerous small holes. For further details of experiments with it see [Aristotle] *Probl.* XVI, 8, 914b9 (DK 59A69), which, however, is concerned with Anaxagoras rather than Empedocles. Cf. also **498**.

[2] Vlastos (*Gnomon* 27 (1955) 73), having quoted this sentence, continues: 'But what is there in Empedocles' theory to imply that minute quantities of air passing through water out of (or into!) one's chest would cause bubbles? Nothing at all; bubbles or no bubbles, the theory would survive the bath experiment.' Even that criticism, however, whether or not it is valid against Cornford, seems to support the present point, that Empedocles knew nothing of the experimental method as it is now understood.

---

inwards, straightway a stream of air comes in with swift surge; but when the blood leaps up again, an equal quantity of air is again breathed back.

(*b*) *Sense-perception*

454 Fr. 109, Aristotle *Met.* B4, 1000b6

γαίῃ μὲν γὰρ γαῖαν ὀπώπαμεν, ὕδατι δ' ὕδωρ,
αἰθέρι δ' αἰθέρα δῖον, ἀτὰρ πυρὶ πῦρ ἀίδηλον,
στοργὴν δὲ στοργῇ, νεῖκος δέ τε νείκεϊ λυγρῷ.

455 Theophrastus *de sensu* 7 (DK31A86) Ἐμπεδοκλῆς δὲ περὶ ἁπασῶν (*sc.* αἰσθήσεων) ὁμοίως λέγει καί φησι τῷ ἐναρμόττειν εἰς τοὺς πόρους τοὺς ἑκάστης αἰσθάνεσθαι· διὸ καὶ οὐ δύνασθαι τὰ ἀλλήλων κρίνειν, ὅτι τῶν μὲν εὐρύτεροί πως, τῶν δὲ στενώτεροι τυγχάνουσιν οἱ πόροι πρὸς τὸ αἰσθητόν, ὡς τὰ μὲν οὐχ ἁπτόμενα διευτονεῖν τὰ δ' ὅλως εἰσελθεῖν οὐ δύνασθαι.

Theophrastus goes on to describe in some detail, and to criticize, Empedocles' explanation of the various senses, especially sight and hearing. But these two passages give the essentials that apply to all the senses alike. Perception is due to an element (here including Love and Strife) in the body of the perceiver meeting with the same element outside. 'All things that have come into existence', according to fragment 89,[1] are continually giving off effluences; and when these effluences are of the right size to fit into the pores of the sense organ, then the required meeting takes place and perception arises.[2] (On sense-perception see also **419** and comment.)

[1] See **456** Plutarch *Quaest. nat.* 19, 916D σκόπει δὴ κατ' Ἐμπεδοκλέα (Fr. 89)

γνούς, ὅτι πάντων εἰσὶν ἀπορροαί, ὅσσ' ἐγένοντο·

οὐ γὰρ ζῴων μόνον οὐδὲ φυτῶν οὐδὲ γῆς καὶ θαλάττης, ἀλλὰ καὶ λίθων ἄπεισιν ἐνδελεχῶς πολλὰ ῥεύματα καὶ χαλκοῦ καὶ σιδήρου· καὶ γὰρ φθείρεται πάντα καὶ ὄλωλε τῷ ῥεῖν ἀεί τι καὶ φέρεσθαι συνεχῶς.

---

454 *For with earth do we see earth, with water water, with air bright air, with fire consuming fire; with Love do we see Love, Strife with dread Strife.*

455 *Empedocles has the same theory about all the senses, maintaining that perception arises when something fits into the passages of any of the senses. So one sense cannot judge the objects of another, since the passages of some are too wide, of others too narrow, for the object perceived, so that some things pass straight through without making contact while others cannot enter at all.*

456 *Consider the matter in Empedocles' words, 'knowing that there are effluences of all things that came into being'. Not only animals and plants and earth and sea, but also stones and brass and iron continuously give off many a stream; for everything is worn away and perishes from the continual motion of a ceaseless flux.*

[2] It is perhaps worth remarking that this explanation of sense-perception (as also the account of respiration in **453**) would appear to involve the admission of void. It looks as if Empedocles, when he came to details, was not always faithful to his fundamental principles.

(*c*) *Consciousness*

457 Fr. 103, Simplicius *Phys.* 331, 12

τῇδε μὲν οὖν ἰότητι Τύχης πεφρόνηκεν ἅπαντα.

458 Fr. 105, Porphyry *ap.* Stobaeum *Anth.* I, 49, 53

αἵματος ἐν πελάγεσσι τεθραμμένη (*sc.* ἡ καρδία) ἀντιθορόντος,
τῇ τε νόημα μάλιστα κικλήσκεται ἀνθρώποισιν·
αἷμα γὰρ ἀνθρώποις περικάρδιόν ἐστι νόημα.

459 Theophrastus *de sensu* 9 (DK31A86) ὡσαύτως δὲ λέγει καὶ περὶ φρονήσεως καὶ ἀγνοίας. (10) τὸ μὲν γὰρ φρονεῖν εἶναι τοῖς ὁμοίοις, τὸ δ' ἀγνοεῖν τοῖς ἀνομοίοις, ὡς ἢ ταὐτὸν ἢ παραπλήσιον ὂν τῇ αἰσθήσει τὴν φρόνησιν. διαριθμησάμενος γὰρ ὡς ἕκαστον ἑκάστῳ γνωρίζομεν, ἐπὶ τέλει προσέθηκεν ὡς

(Fr. 107) ἐκ τούτων ⟨γὰρ⟩ πάντα πεπήγασιν ἁρμοσθέντα
καὶ τούτοις φρονέουσι καὶ ἥδοντ' ἠδ' ἀνιῶνται.

διὸ καὶ τῷ αἵματι μάλιστα φρονεῖν· ἐν τούτῳ γὰρ μάλιστα κεκρᾶσθαι [ἐστὶ] τὰ στοιχεῖα τῶν μερῶν.

These passages, which follow naturally upon Empedocles' theory of sense-perception, are of central importance for the interpretation of his system as a whole. Everything, according to **457** (which is expanded by Aetius IV, 5, 12, DK31A96), has a share of thought, which in man, according to **458**, resides chiefly in the blood around the heart. But blood, as we saw in **441**, is, like all the other constituents of the body, a merely temporary combination of the four elements; indeed it is just because the four elements are most evenly proportioned in the blood, and blood is therefore

---

457 *So by the will of Fortune all things possess thought.*

458 ...(*The heart*) *dwelling in the sea of blood which surges back and forth, where especially is what is called thought by men; for the blood around men's hearts is their thought.*

459 *And he has the same theory about wisdom and ignorance. Wisdom is of like by like, ignorance of unlike by unlike, wisdom being either identical with or closely akin to perception. For having enumerated how we know each thing by its equivalent, he added at the end that 'out of these things are all things fitted together and constructed, and by these do they think and feel pleasure or pain'. So it is especially with the blood that they think; for in the blood above all other parts the elements are blended.*

equally perceptive of all four elements outside, that it is the chief seat of perception. It seems inevitably to follow that both perception and thought (which, if not identical, are at any rate, as **459** says, very closely related) are as temporary as the physical compound on which they depend. Where, then, is there room in Empedocles' physical poem for the immortal soul that is the very basis of the *Purifications*? That is a question that must eventually be discussed (pp. 357 ff.). Meanwhile, however, the last two phases in the cosmic cycle, the rule of Strife and the reverse cosmogony, remain to be described.

THE RULE OF STRIFE

460 Fr. 26, ll. 3–7, Simplicius *Phys.* 33, 21 (cf. **418**)

αὐτὰ γὰρ ἔστιν ταῦτα, δι' ἀλλήλων δὲ θέοντα
γίγνοντ' ἄνθρωποί τε καὶ ἄλλων ἔθνεα θηρῶν
ἄλλοτε μὲν Φιλότητι συνερχόμεν' εἰς ἕνα κόσμον,
ἄλλοτε δ' αὖ δίχ' ἕκαστα φορούμενα Νείκεος ἔχθει,
εἰσόκεν ἓν συμφύντα τὸ πᾶν ὑπένερθε γένηται.

461 Aristotle *Met.* A4, 985a23 (DK31A37) πολλαχοῦ γοῦν αὐτῷ (*sc.* Empedocles) ἡ μὲν Φιλία διακρίνει τὸ δὲ Νεῖκος συγκρίνει. ὅταν μὲν γὰρ εἰς τὰ στοιχεῖα διίστηται τὸ πᾶν ὑπὸ τοῦ Νείκους, τότε τὸ πῦρ εἰς ἓν συγκρίνεται καὶ τῶν ἄλλων στοιχείων ἕκαστον· ὅταν δὲ πάλιν ὑπὸ τῆς Φιλίας συνίωσιν εἰς τὸ ἕν, ἀναγκαῖον ἐξ ἑκάστου τὰ μόρια διακρίνεσθαι πάλιν.

If Empedocles ever described the rule of Strife in detail, the description has not survived; the only references to it in extant fragments are those in **418** and **460**. The omission, however, is sufficiently repaired by **461**. Whereas during the rule of Love the four elements were so evenly mixed that the whole sphere presented no perceptible qualities whatever, during the rule of Strife they are completely separated one from the other into four homogeneous masses. Even if Empedocles himself gave no detailed

---

460 *There are these alone, but running through one another they become men and the tribes of beasts, at one time coming together through Love into one order, at another each borne apart from the others by the enmity of Strife, till they have grown into one and are utterly subdued.*

461 *At least on many occasions he makes Love segregate things and Strife aggregate them. For when the universe is dissolved into its elements by Strife, fire is aggregated into one, and so is each of the other elements; but when again under the influence of Love they come together into one, the parts must again be segregated out of each element.* (After Ross)

description of the rule of Strife, it is perhaps legitimate to imagine four concentric spheres, with (to judge from two isolated hints from Aristotle[1]) the lighter elements, fire and air, outside, and the heavier, earth and water, nearer to the centre. And in that case (to judge this time from the opposite polar stage, the rule of Love, in which Strife is altogether excluded from the Sphere) Love would now be excluded, while Strife presumably pervaded each of the four separated elements (but see the next section).

[1] (1) **462** Ar. *de gen. et corr.* B6, 334a1 (DK31B53) διέκρινε μὲν γὰρ τὸ Νεῖκος, ἠνέχθη δ' ἄνω ὁ αἰθὴρ οὐχ ὑπὸ τοῦ Νείκους, ἀλλ' ὁτὲ μέν φησιν ὥσπερ ἀπὸ τύχης—

(fr. 53) οὕτω γὰρ συνέκυρσε θέων τοτέ, πολλάκι δ' ἄλλως—
ὁτὲ δέ φησι πεφυκέναι τὸ πῦρ ἄνω φέρεσθαι.

(2) **463** Ar. *Phys.* B4, 196a20 (DK31B53) ...'Εμπεδοκλῆς οὐκ ἀεὶ τὸν ἀέρα ἀνωτάτω ἀποκρίνεσθαί φησιν, ἀλλ' ὅπως ἂν τύχῃ.

TRANSITION BACK TO RULE OF LOVE

464 Fr. 35, Simpl. *de caelo* 529, 1 and *Physics* 32, 13, and Fr. 36, Stobaeus *Anth.* 1, 10, 11

αὐτὰρ ἐγὼ παλίνορσος ἐλεύσομαι ἐς πόρον ὕμνων,
τὸν πρότερον κατέλεξα, λόγου λόγον ἐξοχετεύων,
κεῖνον· ἐπεὶ Νεῖκος μὲν ἐνέρτατον ἵκετο βένθος
δίνης, ἐν δὲ μέσῃ Φιλότης στροφάλιγγι γένηται,
ἐν τῇ δὴ τάδε πάντα συνέρχεται ἓν μόνον εἶναι,
οὐκ ἄφαρ, ἀλλὰ θελημὰ συνιστάμεν' ἄλλοθεν ἄλλα.
τῶν δὲ συνερχομένων ἐξ ἔσχατον ἵστατο Νεῖκος.[1]
πολλὰ δ' ἄμεικτ' ἔστηκε κεραιομένοισιν ἐναλλάξ,
ὅσσ' ἔτι Νεῖκος ἔρυκε μετάρσιον· οὐ γὰρ ἀμεμφέως
τῶν πᾶν ἐξέστηκεν ἐπ' ἔσχατα τέρματα κύκλου,

---

462 *For though Strife was segregating the elements, it was not by Strife that aither was borne upwards; on the contrary, he sometimes speaks as if it happened by mere chance—'for so, at the time, it chanced to be running, though often otherwise'—while sometimes he says it is the nature of fire to be borne upwards.*

463 *...Empedocles says that the air is not always separated into the highest region, but as it may chance.*

464 *But now I shall turn back again to the channel of song that I proclaimed before, drawing off from my discourse another discourse. When Strife had reached to the lowest depth of the whirl, and Love was in the middle of the eddy, under her do all these things come together so as to be one, not all at once, but congregating each from different directions at their will. And as they came together Strife began to move outwards to the circumference. Yet alternating with the things that were being mixed many other things remained unmixed, all that Strife, still aloft, retained; for not yet had it altogether retired from them, blame-*

ἀλλὰ τὰ μέν τ' ἐνέμιμνε μελέων τὰ δέ τ' ἐξεβεβήκει.
ὅσσον δ' αἰὲν ὑπεκπροθέοι, τόσον αἰὲν ἐπῄει
ἠπιόφρων Φιλότητος ἀμεμφέος ἄμβροτος ὁρμή·
αἶψα δὲ θνήτ' ἐφύοντο, τὰ πρὶν μάθον ἀθάνατ' εἶναι.
ζωρά τε τὰ πρὶν ἄκρητα διαλλάξαντα κελεύθους.
τῶν δέ τε μισγομένων χεῖτ' ἔθνεα μυρία θνητῶν,
παντοίαις ἰδέῃσιν ἀρηρότα, θαῦμα ἰδέσθαι.

465 Aristotle *de caelo* Γ 2, 301 a 14 ἐκ διεστώτων δὲ καὶ κινουμένων οὐκ εὔλογον ποιεῖν τὴν γένεσιν. διὸ καὶ Ἐμπεδοκλῆς παραλείπει τὴν ἐπὶ τῆς Φιλότητος· οὐ γὰρ ἂν ἠδύνατο συστῆσαι τὸν οὐρανὸν ἐκ κεχωρισμένων μὲν κατασκευάζων, σύγκρισιν δὲ ποιῶν διὰ τὴν Φιλότητα· ἐκ διακεκριμένων γὰρ συνέστηκεν ὁ κόσμος τῶν στοιχείων, ὥστ' ἀναγκαῖον γίνεσθαι ἐξ ἑνὸς καὶ συγκεκριμένου.

[1] L. 7 of fr. 35 is, in the text of Simplicius, identical with l. 16. Since fr. 36, consisting of the solitary line that is printed above as l. 7, fits so naturally into the context, it seems most probable that Simplicius himself is responsible for an error in transcription and that the fr. ran as here printed.

Aristotle's remark in **465**, that Empedocles passes over the cosmogony of the transition to the rule of Love, is not perhaps strictly true; not only **464** but also, as we saw, **443** to **446** are all concerned with this phase in the cosmic cycle. But there is no denying that **464** is both vague in outline and obscure in detail. What, for instance, is the δίνη, 'whirl', of l. 4, and how did it arise? (The δίνη described on p. 333 is clearly not the same as this one.) And is its 'lowest depth', to which Strife is said in l. 3 to have fallen, the same as 'the outermost boundaries of the circle' in l. 10? It would seem that it must be so, but it is far from clear

---

lessly, to the outermost boundaries of the circle, but while some parts of it had gone forth, some still remained within. And in proportion as it was ever running forth outwards, so a gentle immortal stream of blameless Love was ever coming in. And straightway what before had attained to immortality became mortal, what had been unmixed before was now mixed, each exchanging its path. And as these things mingled, countless tribes of mortal things were spread abroad, endowed with shapes of every kind, a wonder to behold.

465 *But there is no sense in starting generation from an original state in which bodies are separated and in movement. Hence Empedocles omits the period when Love was gaining ascendancy; for he could not have constructed the heavens by building them up out of bodies in separation, making them combine by the power of Love; since our world has its constituent elements in separation, and therefore presupposes a previous state of unity and combination.* (After Stocks)

from Empedocles' own words. The reason for this obscurity is not hard to guess. Empedocles, by his introduction of the cosmic cycle, has set himself a task which might well overtax even the most fertile imagination: he has imposed upon himself the necessity of describing a cosmogony and a world that are the exact reverse of the world we know and of the cosmogony that brought it into being. It cannot even be said that the cosmic cycle was unavoidable: it would surely have been a simpler undertaking to describe the emergence from the Sphere of a world in which the two motive forces, Love and Strife, instead of prevailing alternately, reached a stable equilibrium. Why then—and this is another question of central importance for our understanding of Empedocles' system—did he introduce the cosmic cycle at all? The answer is to be found, if at all, in the *Purifications*. Between the physical poem and the *Purifications* there are certain remarkable parallels of detail, on which comment will be made on pp. 349ff. But the most remarkable parallel of all is that between the cosmic cycle in the physical poem and the cycle through which the soul passes in the *Purifications*. It is, at the least, very probable that it is the analogy, already encountered in Empedocles (p. 330), between microcosm and macrocosm, man and the world, that induced him so to complicate his cosmology with the otherwise arbitrary cycle.

THE 'PURIFICATIONS'

The *Purifications* is concerned with the fall of man and with the practices necessary for his restoration. The scheme is found elsewhere in Pindar's 'Orphic' odes, and especially in the second *Olympian*, written in 476 B.C. for Theron of Acragas, Empedocles' own city. The cycle in this scheme starts from unity and peace, falls into disorder and strife, recovers, and so begins again. It was probably this cycle of the soul that suggested to Empedocles his cosmic cycle. At any rate we find not only that the cosmic cycle runs as parallel as possible to it but also that, whenever he can, Empedocles marks the parallel with parallel phrases. The best course will be to follow the pattern already adopted in discussing the physical poem, and look in turn at what little evidence survives about each phase of the soul's cycle.

THE STATE OF PRIMAL INNOCENCE

466 Fr. 128, Porphyrius *de abstinentia* II, 21

οὐδέ τις ἦν κείνοισιν Ἄρης θεὸς οὐδὲ Κυδοιμὸς
οὐδὲ Ζεὺς βασιλεὺς οὐδὲ Κρόνος οὐδὲ Ποσειδῶν,
ἀλλὰ Κύπρις βασίλεια.
τὴν οἵ γ' εὐσεβέεσσιν ἀγάλμασιν ἱλάσκοντο
γραπτοῖς τε ζῴοισι μύροισί τε δαιδαλεόδμοις
σμύρνης τ' ἀκρήτου θυσίαις λιβάνου τε θυώδους,
ξανθῶν τε σπονδὰς μελίτων ῥίπτοντες ἐς οὖδας·
ταύρων τ' ἀκρήτοισι φόνοις οὐ δεύετο βωμός,
ἀλλὰ μύσος τοῦτ' ἔσκεν ἐν ἀνθρώποισι μέγιστον,
θυμὸν ἀπορραίσαντας ἐνέδμεναι ἠέα γυῖα.

According to Hesiod (*Works and Days* 109), whose word on such subjects carried great weight, the rule of Kronos belongs to the Golden Age at the beginning of the world. Irrespective, therefore, of the reigns of Zeus and Poseidon (the latter of which has been confidently but quite conjecturally (cf. chapter I, pp. 37 ff.) said to be borrowed by Empedocles from the 'traditional' Orphic mythology), the important point in **466** is that, even before the reign of Kronos, Kupris reigned alone and there was no god Ares. Now Kupris is plainly identical with Aphrodite, with whom, in **424**, the cosmic force of Love is expressly equated, while Ares equally plainly represents Strife. The primal state of man's innocence exactly corresponds, therefore, to the cosmic rule of Love, when Strife is wholly excluded. Moreover, if it be true, as most modern scholars except Bignone agree, that fr. 134 comes from the *Purifications*, then the parallel between the two poems calls for no further proof:

467 Fr. 134, Ammonius *de interpretatione* 249, 6 Busse

οὐδὲ γὰρ ἀνδρομέῃ κεφαλῇ κατὰ γυῖα κέκασται,
οὐ μὲν ἀπαὶ νώτοιο δύο κλάδοι ἀΐσσονται,

---

466 *They had no god Ares nor Kudoimos, nor king Zeus nor Kronos nor Poseidon, but Kupris as queen. Her did they propitiate with holy images, with paintings of living creatures, with perfumes of varied fragrance and with sacrifice of pure myrrh and sweet-scented frankincense, casting to the ground libations of golden honey. Their altar was not steeped in the pure blood of bulls, but rather was this the greatest abomination among men, to tear out the life from the goodly limbs and eat them.*

467 *He boasts not a human head upon his body, two branches spring not from his*

οὐ πόδες, οὐ θοὰ γοῦν', οὐ μήδεα λαχνήεντα,
ἀλλὰ φρὴν ἱερὴ καὶ ἀθέσφατος ἔπλετο μοῦνον,
φροντίσι κόσμον ἅπαντα καταΐσσουσα θοῇσιν.

The close parallelism between this and the description of the Sphere in **422** is obvious.[1] But even if Bignone is right and this fragment actually comes, like **422**, from the physical poem, it is still perhaps worth noting that, while cosmogony is evidently a sort of dismemberment of the Sphere by the forces of Strife, dismemberment of living things is described at the end of **466** as 'the greatest abomination among men'.[2] To emphasize the analogy between the cosmic rule of Love and the reign of Kupris in man's primal innocence is not, of course, to say that they are one and the same; the point is rather that the latter may serve to explain the obscurities of the former.

[1] On such verbal parallels it is admittedly arguable that, of two unconnected poems, passages from one (including this passage, which has been said to be concerned with Apollo) were subsequently adapted to the other. That argument, however, seems to be considerably weakened, if not invalidated, by the parallelism of content between the two poems.

[2] A further indication of the parallelism is to be found in Aristotle's description of the cosmic Sphere (at *Met.* B4, 1000b3) as εὐδαιμονέστατον, 'happiest' or 'most blessed'. It could perhaps be argued that this is merely another trace of the Pythagorean moral dualism; but the survival of that dualism in Empedocles supports the view that the cosmic state and man's state are parallel.

THE PRIMAL SIN AND FALL OF MAN

468 Fr. 136, Sextus *adv. math.* IX, 129

οὐ παύσεσθε φόνοιο δυσηχέος; οὐκ ἐσορᾶτε
ἀλλήλους δάπτοντες ἀκηδείῃσι νόοιο;

469 Fr. 137, Sextus *adv. math.* IX, 129

μορφὴν δ' ἀλλάξαντα πατὴρ φίλον υἱὸν ἀείρας
σφάζει ἐπευχόμενος μέγα νήπιος· οἱ δ' ἀπορεῦνται
λισσόμενον θύοντες· ὁ δ' αὖ νήκουστος ὁμοκλέων

---

shoulders, no feet has he, no swift knees, no shaggy parts; rather is he only a holy, unspeakable mind, darting with swift thoughts over the whole world.

468 *Will ye not cease from ill-sounding bloodshed? See ye not that in careless folly ye are consuming one another?*

469 *Father lifts up his own dear son, his form changed, and, praying, slays him—witless fool; and the people are distracted as they sacrifice the imploring victim; and he,*

σφάξας ἐν μεγάροισι κακὴν ἀλεγύνατο δαῖτα.
ὡς δ' αὔτως πατέρ' υἱὸς ἑλὼν καὶ μητέρα παῖδες
θυμὸν ἀπορραίσαντε φίλας κατὰ σάρκας ἔδουσιν.

470 Fr. 139, Porphyrius *de abstinentia* II, 31

οἴμοι ὅτι οὐ πρόσθεν με διώλεσε νηλεὲς ἦμαρ,
πρὶν σχέτλι' ἔργα βορᾶς περὶ χείλεσι μητίσασθαι.

The second stage in the religious poem is the primal sin and the consequent fall of man. In 'Orphic' myth this primal sin was committed by the Titans, who dismembered and ate the child Dionysus; in the *Purifications* of Empedocles, before man's fall 'the altar did not reek with pure bull's blood' (**466**, l. 8). But with Empedocles, as **468** and **469** suggest,[1] the primal sin seems to have been rather bloodshed and meat-eating in general. This primal sin evidently led to the general fall of man: the fall is conceived as collective, and leads to the end of the rule of Kupris. But at the same time, apparently, this did not preclude also the particular fall of the individual soul. **470** shows in fact that the individual soul falls through exactly the same crime as led to the collective fall; and once the individual soul has fallen we pass to the next stage in its cycle.

[1] Although **468** and **469** do not describe the primal sin but contemporary sin, there can be little doubt that this contemporary sin is a repetition of the primal sin.

INCARNATION AND TRANSMIGRATION

471 Fr. 115, Hippolytus *Ref.* VII, 29 and Plutarch *de exilio* 17, 607 C

ἔστιν Ἀνάγκης χρῆμα, θεῶν ψήφισμα παλαιόν,
ἀίδιον, πλατέεσσι κατεσφρηγισμένον ὅρκοις·
εὖτέ τις ἀμπλακίῃσι φόνῳ φίλα γυῖα μιήνῃ,
⟨νείκεΐ θ'⟩ ὅς κ' ἐπίορκον ὁμαρτήσας ἐπομόσσῃ,
δαίμονες οἵτε μακραίωνος λελάχασι βίοιο,

---

deaf to its cries, slays it and makes ready in his halls an evil feast. And likewise son seizes father, and children their mother, and, tearing out the life, eat the flesh of their dear ones.

470 *Alas that the pitiless day of death did not first destroy me before I contrived the wretched deed of eating flesh with my lips.*

471 *There is an oracle of Necessity, ancient decree of the gods, eternal and sealed with broad oaths: whenever one of those demi-gods, whose lot is long-lasting life, has sinfully defiled his dear limbs with bloodshed, or following strife has sworn a false oath, thrice ten*

τρίς μιν μυρίας ὥρας ἀπὸ μακάρων ἀλάλησθαι,
φυομένους παντοῖα διὰ χρόνου εἴδεα θνητῶν
ἀργαλέας βιότοιο μεταλλάσσοντα κελεύθους.
αἰθέριον μὲν γάρ σφε μένος πόντονδε διώκει,
πόντος δ' ἐς χθονὸς οὖδας ἀπέπτυσε, γαῖα δ' ἐς αὐγὰς
ἠελίου φαέθοντος, ὁ δ' αἰθέρος ἔμβαλε δίναις·
ἄλλος δ' ἐξ ἄλλου δέχεται, στυγέουσι δὲ πάντες.
τῶν καὶ ἐγὼ νῦν εἰμι, φυγὰς θεόθεν καὶ ἀλήτης,
νείκεϊ μαινομένῳ πίσυνος.

472 Fr. 118, Clement *Strom.* III, 14, 2

κλαῦσά τε καὶ κώκυσα ἰδὼν ἀσυνήθεα χῶρον.

473 Fr. 121, Hierocles *ad carmina aurea* 24 and Proclus *in Cratylum* p. 97 Pasquali

...ἀτερπέα χῶρον,
ἔνθα Φόνος τε Κότος τε καὶ ἄλλων ἔθνεα Κηρῶν
αὐχμηραί τε Νόσοι καὶ Σήψιες ἔργα τε ῥευστὰ
Ἄτης ἀν λειμῶνα κατὰ σκότος ἠλάσκουσιν.

The fallen soul, as is clear from **471**, goes the round of the elements, banished from its proper abode. We may compare the so-called *apeniautism* of Hesiod's *Theogony* 793 ff.—banishment, that is, for a 'great year', a period the length of which varies in different sources but in Empedocles is 30,000 seasons. It may perhaps be that this period is, in Empedocles, the same as that of the cosmic cycle, but there is unfortunately no evidence to substantiate the conjecture. Empedocles, it should be noted, has no equivalent of Hell: on the contrary, the soul, as **472** and **473** show, pays the penalty for its sin in this world—a world, as other fragments prove, of opposites;[1] and its objective throughout its successive incarnations is, as we shall see in the next section, to

thousand seasons does he wander far from the blessed, being born throughout that time in the forms of all manner of mortal things and changing one baleful path of life for another. The might of the air pursues him into the sea, the sea spews him forth on to the dry land, the earth casts him into the rays of the burning sun, and the sun into the eddies of air. One takes him from the other, but all alike abhor him. Of these I too am now one, a fugitive from the gods and a wanderer, who put my trust in raving strife.

472 *I wept and wailed when I saw the unfamiliar place.*

473 *...a joyless place, where Bloodshed and Wrath, and tribes of Fates too, withering Plagues and Corruptions and Deluges roam in the darkness over the field of Doom.*

escape again from the wheel of birth back to the state of bliss from which it has fallen.[2]

[1] Cf. e.g. **474** Fr. 122, Plutarch *de tranq. an.* 15, 474B (which, as Burnet says (*EGP* 223 n. 2), 'is closely modelled on the Catalogue of Nymphs in *Iliad* XVIII, 39 sqq.')

ἔνθ' ἦσαν Χθονίη τε καὶ Ἡλιόπη ταναῶπις,
Δῆρίς θ' αἱματόεσσα καὶ Ἁρμονίη θεμερῶπις,
Καλλιστώ τ' Αἰσχρή τε, Θόωσά τε Δηναίη τε,
Νημερτής τ' ἐρόεσσα μελάγκουρός τ' Ἀσάφεια.

This list, which is continued in fr. 123, is clearly a catalogue, in mythical garb, of the opposites that characterize this Ἄτης λειμών or 'vale of tears' (**473**, l. 4).

[2] It is difficult at this stage to avoid language which may mistakenly suggest that the soul which has sinned *falls into* this world. Actually of course, by the interpretation here offered, it has been in this world throughout. Just as the four stages of the cosmic cycle all take place within the Sphere, so the soul too goes through all the stages in its cycle inside this world. Since, however, (1) the world is at present reverting to the rule of Strife (see p. 339), (2) Empedocles is yet convinced that he himself is about to escape from the wheel of birth back to the primal state of bliss (see the next section), it seems that the cycle of the individual soul and the cosmic cycle, though parallel, are not synchronized.

Such, so far as the extant fragments permit a reconstruction, was the nature of man's primal sin and fall. But at this stage we must turn back to the physical poem, and especially to fr. 30 (**429**): 'But when Strife waxed great in the limbs, and sprang to his prerogatives as the time was fulfilled which is fixed for them in turn by a broad oath...'. Few as are the lines that survive about the first disruption of the cosmic rule of Love, it is surely not pure accident that they contain so many echoes of man's fall. Strife is the cause of the disruption of the cosmic Sphere: strife is the cause of man's fall (**471**, ll. 13–14). In the cosmic cycle there is the fulness of time set for the alternation of Love and Strife: the duration of the fall of man from the rule of Kupris to the world of opposites is fixed at 30,000 seasons (**471**, l. 6). The pact between Love and Strife in the physical world is confirmed 'by a broad oath': the oracle of Necessity that fixed the period of the soul's banishment is 'sealed by broad oaths'. Once again in fact these echoes in a mere three lines are sufficient to establish that the cosmic disrup-

474 *There were Chthonie and far-seeing Heliope, bloody Rivalry and kindly-faced Harmony, Beauty and Ugliness, Swiftness and Tardiness, lovely Truthfulness and black-haired Obscurity.*

tion of the original Sphere is parallel to, and probably therefore suggested by, the fall of man through the dismemberment of living things.

ESCAPE FROM WHEEL OF BIRTH

475 Fr. 127, Aelian *Nat. anim.* XII, 7

ἐν θήρεσσι λέοντες ὀρειλεχέες χαμαιεῦναι
γίγνονται, δάφναι δ' ἐνὶ δένδρεσιν ἠυκόμοισιν.

476 Fr. 117, Diogenes Laertius VIII, 77

ἤδη γάρ ποτ' ἐγὼ γενόμην κοῦρός τε κόρη τε
θάμνος τ' οἰωνός τε καὶ ἔξαλος ἔλλοπος ἰχθύς.

477 Frr. 146 and 147, Clement *Strom.* IV, 150, 1 and V, 122, 3

εἰς δὲ τέλος μάντεις τε καὶ ὑμνοπόλοι καὶ ἰητροὶ
καὶ πρόμοι ἀνθρώποισιν ἐπιχθονίοισι πέλονται,
ἔνθεν ἀναβλαστοῦσι θεοὶ τιμῇσι φέριστοι,
ἀθανάτοις ἄλλοισιν ὁμέστιοι, αὐτοτράπεζοι
†ἐόντες†, ἀνδρείων ἀχέων ἀπόκληροι, ἀτειρεῖς.

478 Fr. 112, Diogenes Laertius VIII, 62 and Clement *Strom.* VI, 30

ὦ φίλοι, οἳ μέγα ἄστυ κατὰ ξανθοῦ Ἀκράγαντος
ναίετ' ἀν' ἄκρα πόλεος, ἀγαθῶν μελεδήμονες ἔργων,
ξείνων αἰδοῖοι λιμένες, κακότητος ἄπειροι,
χαίρετ'· ἐγὼ δ' ὑμῖν θεὸς ἄμβροτος, οὐκέτι θνητὸς
πωλεῦμαι μετὰ πᾶσι τετιμένος, ὥσπερ ἔοικα,
ταινίαις τε περίστεπτος στέφεσίν τε θαλείοις.
τοῖσιν ἅμ' ⟨εὖτ'⟩ ἂν ἵκωμαι ἐς ἄστεα τηλεθάοντα,
ἀνδράσιν ἠδὲ γυναιξί, σεβίζομαι· οἱ δ' ἅμ' ἕπονται
μυρίοι ἐξερέοντες, ὅπῃ πρὸς κέρδος ἀταρπός,

---

475 *Among beasts they are born as lions that lurk in their mountain lairs, and among fair-tressed trees as laurels.*

476 *For already have I once been a boy and a girl, a bush and a bird and a dumb sea fish.*

477 *But at the end they come among men on earth as prophets, bards, doctors and princes; and thence they arise as gods mighty in honour, sharing with the other immortals their hearth and their table, without part in human sorrows or weariness.*

478 *Friends who dwell throughout the great town of golden Acragas, up by the citadel, men mindful of good deeds, unversed in wickedness, havens of respect for strangers, all hail. I go about among you all an immortal god, mortal no more, honoured as is my due and crowned with garlands and verdant wreaths. Whenever I enter the prosperous townships with these my followers, men and women both, I am revered; they follow me in countless*

οἱ μὲν μαντοσυνέων κεχρημένοι, οἱ δ' ἐπὶ νούσων
παντοίων ἐπύθοντο κλύειν εὐηκέα βάξιν,
δηρὸν δὴ χαλεπῇσι πεπαρμένοι ⟨ἀμφ' ὀδύνῃσιν⟩.

It is only when we come to this fourth and last stage in the soul's cycle that the parallel between it and the cosmic cycle becomes really illuminating; for it was the fourth and last stage in the cosmic cycle that appeared so arbitrary and unnatural. The fourth stage in the soul's cycle consists, as we should expect, in the return to primal innocence and bliss; it is obviously in fact, from the point of view of fallen man, the most vital stage of all. The return is accomplished by the gradual ascent, with which these passages are concerned, up the scale of lives. **475**, according to Aelian who preserves it, is concerned with the highest incarnations —next, that is, to man—in the animal and vegetable kingdoms; while **476** tells us that Empedocles himself had once sunk so low in the scale as to become a bush. The top rung of the scale is found in **477**, namely 'prophets, bards, doctors and princes'—and Empedocles himself was all of these. Having climbed so far, he is at last on the eve of escape from the cycle and will be reincarnated no more. As he says in **478**, which is the introduction to the *Purifications*, and as he virtually repeats in fr. 113, 'I go about among you an immortal god, no mortal now.' No wonder therefore that, with bliss just ahead, he regards this stage as all-important; and no wonder that, regarding the otherwise inexplicable cosmic cycle as parallel to the cycle of the soul, he felt compelled to describe that most obscure stage in the cosmic cycle, the return from the rule of Strife to the rule of Love. The motive was sufficient to stimulate him even to so difficult a task.

ARE THE TWO POEMS REALLY INCOMPATIBLE?

Though the parallelism between the two poems tells strongly against the view that they are quite separate and independent and must therefore belong to different periods in Empedocles' life, there is still no denying that they seem to take two widely different views of the nature of the soul. The last question to be considered, then, is whether the two poems are, as they are usually thought to be, fundamentally incompatible, or whether, in view of the marked

---

numbers, asking where lies the path to gain, some seeking prophecies, while others, for many a day stabbed by grievous pains, beg to hear the word that heals all manner of illness.

similarities between them, some escape cannot be found from this conclusion. It will be best to approach the question from two opposite angles, and consider, first, whether the religious poem does indeed reveal belief in the survival of the individual soul, as opposed to mere reabsorption into a sort of common reservoir of consciousness, and second, whether the physical poem does indeed preclude the possibility of any part of the soul, as opposed to the whole of it, surviving death.

INDIVIDUAL SURVIVAL

479 Fr. 142, *Volumina Herculanensia* no. 1012, col. 18

τὸν δ' οὔτ' ἄρ τε Διὸς τέγεοι δόμοι αἰγ⟨ιόχοιο
οὔ⟩τε ποτ' Ἀΐδεω δέ⟨χετ'. . . .

(Cf. **477** l. 4

ἀθανάτοις ἄλλοισιν ὁμέστιοι, αὐτοτράπεζοι. . . .)

480 Fr. 133, Clement *Strom.* v, 81, 2

οὐκ ἔστιν πελάσασθαι (*sc.* τὸ θεῖον) ἐν ὀφθαλμοῖσιν ἐφικτὸν
ἡμετέροις ἢ χερσὶ λαβεῖν, ᾗπέρ τε μεγίστη
πειθοῦς ἀνθρώποισιν ἁμαξιτὸς εἰς φρένα πίπτει.

(Cf. **467** ll. 4–5

ἀλλὰ φρὴν ἱερὴ καὶ ἀθέσφατος ἔπλετο μοῦνον,
φροντίσι κόσμον ἅπαντα καταΐσσουσα θοῇσιν.)

481 Hippolytus *Ref.* VII, 29 (DK31B115) καὶ τοῦτό ἐστιν ὃ λέγει περὶ τῆς ἑαυτοῦ γεννήσεως ὁ Ἐμπεδοκλῆς·

τῶν καὶ ἐγὼ νῦν εἰμι, φυγὰς θεόθεν καὶ ἀλήτης (= **471** l. 13),

τουτέστι θεὸν καλῶν τὸ ἓν καὶ τὴν ἐκείνου ἑνότητα, ἐν ᾧ ἦν πρὶν ὑπὸ τοῦ Νείκους ἀποσπασθῆναι καὶ γενέσθαι ἐν τοῖς πολλοῖς τούτοις τοῖς κατὰ τὴν τοῦ Νείκους διακόσμησιν.

Of these passages **479** (the reference of which is perhaps, however, too obscure to support argument) and the line from **477** are

---

479 *Him will neither the vaulted halls of aegis-bearing Zeus nor the house of Hades ever welcome. . . .*

480 *It is not possible to reach to god and set him before our eyes, nor to grasp him with our hands—and that is the broadest way of persuasion leading to the minds of men.*

481 *This is just what Empedocles says about his own birth—'Of these I too am now one, a fugitive from the gods and a wanderer.' He calls by the name of god, that is to say, the One and its unity, in which he himself dwelt before he was snatched thence by Strife and born into this world of plurality which Strife has organized.*

couched in language so material that, unless they are more figurative than is generally supposed, they seem strongly to suggest individual survival. On the other hand **480** and the two lines from **467**, passages which reflect the influence of Xenophanes, might be thought to tell equally strongly against it. If God is of this intangible nature, then it is certainly a tenable view that the individual soul, after escape from the cycle of birth, is merely reabsorbed into the 'sacred mind'.[1] Such is certainly the interpretation of Hippolytus in **481**; but a bishop is perhaps hardly a reliable authority on such a topic. Though the evidence on this question is far from conclusive, it seems safest on the whole to trust to those of Empedocles' own phrases that tell against any such abstract conception of immortality.

[1] Apart from the alleged reference to Apollo in **467**, other Olympian deities appear in the fragments of the Καθαρμοί, notably in **466** and **479**. It seems unlikely that they are only different aspects of a single divine mind.

THE PHYSICAL BASIS OF CONSCIOUSNESS

482 (=**458** l. 3) αἷμα γὰρ ἀνθρώποις περικάρδιόν ἐστι νόημα.

483 (=**441** l. 5) ἐκ τῶν (*sc.* the four elements) αἷμά τε γέντο....

484 (=**454**) γαίῃ μὲν γὰρ γαῖαν ὀπώπαμεν, ὕδατι δ' ὕδωρ,
αἰθέρι δ' αἰθέρα δῖον, ἀτὰρ πυρὶ πῦρ ἀίδηλον,
στοργὴν δὲ στοργῇ, νεῖκος δέ τε νείκεϊ λυγρῷ.

485 Aristotle *de anima* A4, 408a13 ὁμοίως δὲ ἄτοπον καὶ ⟨τὸ⟩ τὸν λόγον τῆς μίξεως εἶναι τὴν ψυχήν· οὐ γὰρ τὸν αὐτὸν ἔχει λόγον ἡ μίξις τῶν στοιχείων καθ' ἣν σάρξ καὶ καθ' ἣν ὀστοῦν· συμβήσεται οὖν πολλάς τε ψυχὰς ἔχειν καὶ κατὰ πᾶν τὸ σῶμα, εἴπερ πάντα μὲν ἐκ τῶν στοιχείων μεμειγμένων, ὁ δὲ τῆς μίξεως λόγος ἁρμονία καὶ ψυχή. ἀπαιτήσειε δ' ἄν τις τοῦτό γε καὶ παρ' Ἐμπεδοκλέους·

---

482 *For the blood around men's hearts is their thought.*

483 *From these* (sc. *the four elements*) *did blood arise....*

484 *For with earth do we see earth, with water water, with air bright air, with fire consuming fire; with Love do we see Love, Strife with dread Strife.*

485 *In the same way it is absurd to identify the soul with the formula of the mixture; for the mixture of the elements that produces flesh has not the same formula as that which produces bone, and so, if everything does indeed consist of a mixture of the elements and if the formula of the mixture is indeed the harmony that is the soul, the same thing will prove to have many souls distributed throughout its body. This is indeed a question that one might*

ἕκαστον γὰρ αὐτῶν λόγῳ τινί φησιν εἶναι· πότερον οὖν ὁ λόγος ἐστὶν ἡ ψυχή, ἢ μᾶλλον ἕτερόν τι οὖσα ἐγγίγνεται τοῖς μέλεσι; ἔτι δὲ πότερον ἡ Φιλία τῆς τυχούσης αἰτία μίξεως ἢ τῆς κατὰ τὸν λόγον; καὶ αὕτη πότερον ὁ λόγος ἐστὶν ἢ παρὰ τὸν λόγον ἕτερόν τι;

These passages, taken together, not only present the second aspect of the problem but also suggest a possible solution. It is clear from **483** and **484** that Empedocles himself describes the blood in two different ways according to the point of view that is uppermost in his mind at the moment. Viewed simply as a physical compound it is described as a mixture, in nearly equal proportions, of the four elements and nothing else. But viewed as the seat of consciousness—and this is the point of view that concerns us—it was evidently assumed to contain also Love and Strife. Aristotle actually inferred from **484** that, since soul consists of all six factors, each of them must therefore be a seat of consciousness, recognizing its like outside (see, e.g., *de an.* A 2, 404 b 8, DK 31 B 109); but this is generally admitted to be a false inference. It is only when all six ingredients are combined in appropriate proportions that the whole mixture acquires consciousness; and though it is still with the earth in the eye that we see earth, we should not be conscious of seeing it if there were not the other ingredients of consciousness present as well, including Love and Strife.

Is there then any part of this composite consciousness, the product of all six factors, that can remain conscious in separation from the body? Modern scholars unanimously, and perhaps rightly, say no; but not so Aristotle. Aristotle was obviously puzzled over this question of the relation of the migrating soul to the consciousness of the blood, but he never asserts, as moderns do, that the latter precludes the former. It appears from **485**, where he is actually puzzling over the problem, that he concluded that Empedocles must have held a ψυχὴ ἁρμονία doctrine ('the soul is an attunement'), the soul which is an attunement being the proportion of the mixture. But he evidently could not make out how in that case the migrating soul came in at all. Was it perhaps a

---

put to Empedocles, who maintains that everything owes its existence to the formula of its constituents. Is then this formula itself the soul, or is the soul rather something of a different nature that arises in the limbs? And again, is Love the cause of any chance mixture, or of the mixture in accordance with the formula? And is Love itself the actual formula, or something different over and above the formula?

portion of Love that maintained the proportion? 'Is Love', he asks in the last sentence, 'the proportion itself or something over and above it?' And with that question he does suggest a possible answer to the present problem.

Love is itself, of course, indestructible and immutable; but there must be a portion of it in every living, changing and perishable thing. It is therefore inevitably contaminated, in all composite things, with Strife; and so, even though essentially immutable, and preserving its identity even when contaminated, it is not, as the result of this contamination, reabsorbed at the dissolution of the body into the mass of Love, but enters, its identity preserved, into another body. Eventually, however, it can become so purified as to rid itself of the contamination of Strife; and then, at its next release, it will either be reabsorbed and return to the unity—the rule of Kupris—from which it had fallen, or else, possibly, remain as a separate bundle of Love until all Love is reabsorbed in the Sphere.[1] It seems possible (but no more than that) that Aristotle's vague suggestion is right and that Empedocles himself did think like this. Such an interpretation has at any rate the great advantage over any other yet offered that, by providing the migrating soul with a physical basis, it resolves the monstrous incompatibility between the two poems, and so allows us to attach due importance to the obvious parallels between them.

[1] Cf. the adjectives δολιχαίων in **425** and μακραίων in **471**.

There is one last passage which lends support to this reconciliation:

486 Plutarch *de exilio* 17, 607D οὐ γὰρ αἷμα, φησίν (*sc.* Empedocles), ἡμῖν οὐδὲ πνεῦμα συγκραθέν, ὦ ἄνθρωποι, ψυχῆς οὐσίαν καὶ ἀρχὴν παρέσχεν· ἀλλ' ἐκ τούτων τὸ σῶμα συμπέπλασται γηγενὲς καὶ θνητόν. τῆς δὲ ψυχῆς ἀλλαχόθεν ἡκούσης δεῦρο, τὴν γένεσιν ἀποδημίαν ὑποκορίζεται, τῷ πρᾳοτάτῳ τῶν ὀνομάτων· τὸ δὲ ἀληθέστατον φεύγει καὶ πλανᾶται θείοις ἐλαυνομένη δόγμασι καὶ νόμοις.

---

486 *For it is not our blood, he says, nor the blending of our breath that produced the essential principle of soul; rather from these ingredients the body is moulded, which is earth-born and mortal. Since the soul has come hither from elsewhere, he euphemistically calls birth a sojourn abroad—the most comforting of all names; but in truth the soul is a fugitive and a wanderer, banished by the decrees and laws of the gods.*

It seems likely enough that in this passage, which follows close upon the quotation of five lines of fr. 115 (**471**), Plutarch is paraphrasing a lost passage of the *Purifications*; and in that case it provides just the corroboration required. For by the implication that Empedocles regarded the migrating soul and physical consciousness as quite distinct, Plutarch would seem to have proved, what it is most desirable to prove in order to account for the parallelism between them, the connexion and compatibility between the two compartments of Empedocles' thought.

CONCLUSION

If this necessarily tentative interpretation of Empedocles' view of the soul is correct, then it places him in a direct current of thought flowing from Homer down to Plato, Aristotle and beyond. For Homer, no doubt reflecting a popular view, distinguishes between θυμός, the conscious soul, and ψυχή, the life-soul, the former perishing with the body, the latter surviving. True that, when separated from the body, the surviving soul in Homer is a mere shadow, which can only be restored to conscious life by drinking blood; to Empedocles, on the other hand, it is of divine race and has fallen for the very reason that it has tasted blood. But that contrast might well be deliberate—in which case, of course, it would prove that Empedocles is consciously following Homer in distinguishing the two souls. Again, looking forward, the same twofold distinction is clear enough in Plato. In the *Timaeus*, for instance, he contrasts the immortal part of the soul, which is created by the Demiurge himself, with the mortal, including perception, which is added by the created deities at the moment of union with the body. Most striking of all, we find the same distinction in the 'active reason' of Aristotle, which, whatever its nature, alone has no bodily organ and therefore alone survives death. For the reasons suggested it seems not unlikely that Empedocles is, in this respect, the connecting link between Homer on the one side and Plato on the other. More than any other of the Presocratics Empedocles is demonstrably influenced by his predecessors; Anaximander, Xenophanes, the Pythagoreans, Parmenides, all left their mark upon him, and even his view of the soul may possibly have owed something to the view of Heraclitus (see pp. 205 ff.). The fact that, as we saw, Homer himself provided the model for the catalogue of opposites in frr. 122 (**474**) and 123 is of course of no significance: the stylistic influence of Homer on Greek hexameter and elegiac verse was so strong that it would be more surprising if Empedocles did *not* reflect it. But it is at least a tenable view that in Empedocles the influence of Homer (or of the popular semi-philosophical views which Homer reflects) went deeper than that.

CHAPTER XV

ANAXAGORAS OF CLAZOMENAE

DATE AND LIFE

487 Diogenes Laertius II, 7 (DK59A1) λέγεται δὲ κατὰ τὴν Ξέρξου διάβασιν εἴκοσιν ἐτῶν εἶναι, βεβιωκέναι δὲ ἑβδομήκοντα δύο. φησὶ δ' Ἀπολλόδωρος ἐν τοῖς Χρονικοῖς γεγενῆσθαι αὐτὸν τῇ ἑβδομηκοστῇ ὀλυμπιάδι (i.e. 500–497 B.C.), τεθνηκέναι δὲ τῷ πρώτῳ ἔτει τῆς ἑβδομηκοστῆς ὀγδοῆς (i.e. 468/7; ὀγδοηκοστῆς ὀγδοῆς Scaliger, i.e. 428/7). ἤρξατο δὲ φιλοσοφεῖν Ἀθήνησιν ἐπὶ Καλλίου (i.e. 456/5) ἐτῶν εἴκοσιν ὤν, ὥς φησι Δημήτριος ὁ Φαληρεὺς ἐν τῇ τῶν Ἀρχόντων ἀναγραφῇ, ἔνθα καί φασιν αὐτὸν ἐτῶν διατρῖψαι τριάκοντα...(12)...περὶ δὲ τῆς δίκης αὐτοῦ διάφορα λέγεται. Σωτίων μὲν γάρ φησιν ἐν τῇ Διαδοχῇ τῶν φιλοσόφων ὑπὸ Κλέωνος αὐτὸν ἀσεβείας κριθῆναι, διότι τὸν ἥλιον μύδρον ἔλεγε διάπυρον· ἀπολογησαμένου δὲ ὑπὲρ αὐτοῦ Περικλέους τοῦ μαθητοῦ, πέντε ταλάντοις ȝημιωθῆναι καὶ φυγαδευθῆναι. Σάτυρος δ' ἐν τοῖς Βίοις ὑπὸ Θουκυδίδου φησὶν εἰσαχθῆναι τὴν δίκην ἀντιπολιτευομένου τῷ Περικλεῖ· καὶ οὐ μόνον ἀσεβείας, ἀλλὰ καὶ μηδισμοῦ· καὶ ἀπόντα καταδικασθῆναι θανάτῳ...(14)...καὶ τέλος ἀποχωρήσας εἰς Λάμψακον αὐτόθι κατέστρεψεν. ὅτε καὶ τῶν ἀρχόντων τῆς πόλεως ἀξιούντων τί βούλεται αὐτῷ γενέσθαι, φάναι, τοὺς παῖδας ἐν ᾧ ἂν ἀποθάνῃ μηνὶ κατ' ἔτος παίȝειν συγχωρεῖν. καὶ φυλάττεται τὸ ἔθος καὶ νῦν. (15) τελευτήσαντα δὴ αὐτὸν ἔθαψαν ἐντίμως οἱ Λαμψακηνοί....

---

487 *He is said to have been twenty years old at the time of Xerxes' crossing, and to have lived to seventy-two. Apollodorus says in his* Chronicles *that he was born in the seventieth Olympiad and died in the first year of the eighty-eighth. He began to be a philosopher at Athens in the archonship of Callias, at the age of twenty, as Demetrius Phalereus tells us in his* Register of archons, *and they say he spent thirty years there.... There are different accounts given of his trial. Sotion, in his* Succession of philosophers, *says that he was prosecuted by Cleon for impiety, because he maintained that the sun was a red-hot mass of metal, and that after Pericles, his pupil, had made a speech in his defence, he was fined five talents and exiled. Satyrus in his* Lives, *on the other hand, says that the charge was brought by Thucydides in his political campaign against Pericles; and he adds that the charge was not only for impiety but for Medism as well; and he was condemned to death in absence....Finally he withdrew to Lampsacus, and there died. It is said that when the rulers of the city asked him what privilege he wished to be granted, he replied that the children should be given a holiday every year in the month in which he died. The custom is preserved to the present day. When he died the Lampsacenes buried him with full honours.*

488 Aristotle *Met.* A3, 984a11 (=**410**) Ἀναξαγόρας δὲ ὁ Κλαζομένιος τῇ μὲν ἡλικίᾳ πρότερος ὢν τούτου (*sc.* Empedocles), τοῖς δ' ἔργοις ὕστερος....

489 Plato *Phaedrus* 270A (DK59A15) ὃ (*sc.* τὸ ὑψηλόνουν) καὶ Περικλῆς πρὸς τῷ εὐφυὴς εἶναι ἐκτήσατο· προσπεσὼν γὰρ οἶμαι τοιούτῳ ὄντι Ἀναξαγόρᾳ, μετεωρολογίας ἐμπλησθεὶς καὶ ἐπὶ φύσιν νοῦ τε καὶ ἀνοίας ἀφικόμενος, ὧν δὴ πέρι τὸν πολὺν λόγον ἐποιεῖτο Ἀναξαγόρας, ἐντεῦθεν εἵλκυσεν ἐπὶ τὴν τῶν λόγων τέχνην τὸ πρόσφορον αὐτῇ.

These passages suffice to show the difficulty of determining the dates of Anaxagoras' life. The first section of **487**, most of which probably represents mere conjecture by Apollodorus based on a statement of Demetrius Phalereus which it is impossible to reconstruct, immediately presents acute problems of chronology; for even if we accept, as we apparently must, the emendation of Scaliger and conclude that Anaxagoras lived from *ca.* 500 to 428 B.C., it is still necessary, in order to make the passage consistent, to suppose that the words ἐπὶ Καλλίου, 'in the archonship of Callias', should rather read ἐπὶ Καλλιάδου, 'in the archonship of Calliades', i.e. 480 B.C. That would give the following outline:

Born	500/499 B.C.
Came to Athens and began his philosophical activities	480/79 B.C.
Died at Lampsacus	428/7 B.C.

All that can be said is that these dates may well be approximately right; for **488**, which might have thrown some light on the problem, is robbed of most of its value, not only by our ignorance of the exact dates of Empedocles (see pp. 320f.), but also by the ambiguity of its last phrase, which may mean either that Anaxagoras wrote his book after Empedocles (the more probable interpretation), or that he was more up-to-date (or even, by Alexander's interpretation, inferior) in his views.

---

488 *Anaxagoras of Clazomenae, who, though older than Empedocles, was later in his philosophical activity....* (Trans. Ross)

489 *Pericles acquired high-mindedness in addition to his natural talents; for he fell in, I believe, with Anaxagoras, who already possessed this quality, and steeping himself in natural speculation, and grasping the true nature of mind and folly (which were the subjects of much of Anaxagoras' discussion), he drew from that source anything that could contribute towards the art of debate.*

The problem of the date of his trial is even more difficult. A. E. Taylor (*CQ* 11 (1917) 81–7) held that (1) Plato consistently conveys the impression that Anaxagoras was an important figure in Athens before Pericles' rise to fame but not after Socrates grew up; (2) Anaxagoras could not have attained the position at Lampsacus that the last sentences of **487** suggest unless he had spent a considerable time there. He therefore concludes that 'the account given by Satyrus was right in placing his prosecution at the beginning and not at the close of Pericles' political career', i.e. *ca.* 450 B.C. On the other hand J. A. Davison (*CQ* N.S. 3 (1953) 33–45), arguing in favour of accepting both Satyrus' and Sotion's accounts, surmises that there must have been an amnesty (otherwise unattested) in *ca.* 445/4 B.C. by which Anaxagoras was permitted to return to Athens, and estimates the relevant dates as follows:

Prosecuted by Thucydides	*ca.* 456/5 B.C.
Conjectured amnesty after Thirty Years' Peace	*ca.* 445/4 B.C.
Prosecuted by Cleon	*ca.* 433–430 B.C.
Died at Lampsacus	428/7 B.C.

Fortunately, from the point of view of the historian of philosophy, the exact date of the trial (or trials) is of relatively little importance. There is ample evidence in the fragments of Anaxagoras' own book that he wrote later than either Parmenides or Zeno (see pp. 368 ff.); and it seems likely, though it is incapable of proof, that while Anaxagoras (in accordance with the more probable interpretation of **488**) includes implicit criticism of Empedocles, Melissus (see p. 305) aims one of his arguments primarily, if not exclusively, at Anaxagoras. Fortunately too, the most important facts of his life are not in dispute. There can be no question that he spent a large part of his active life in Athens,[1] that he was fairly intimately associated with Pericles,[2] that he was prosecuted on a charge (at least among others) of impiety, and that he thereupon withdrew to Lampsacus.[3]

[1] Anaxagoras is said to have taught both Archelaus (see ch. XVI) and Euripides. Cf. **490** Strabo 14, p. 645 Cas. Κλαζομένιος δ' ἦν ἀνὴρ ἐπιφανὴς 'Αναξαγόρας ὁ φυσικός, 'Αναξιμένους ὁμιλητὴς τοῦ Μιλησίου· διήκουσαν δὲ τούτου 'Αρχέλαος ὁ φυσικὸς καὶ Εὐριπίδης ὁ ποιητής. Since

490 *Anaxagoras the natural philosopher was a distinguished Clazomenian, an associate of Anaximenes of Miletus; and his own pupils included Archelaus the natural philosopher and Euripides the poet.*

the statement that Anaxagoras was an associate of Anaximenes can mean no more than that he reproduced elements of Anaximenes' cosmology, it could be argued that the tradition of Anaxagoras' own influence on Archelaus and Euripides need imply no more. But even by 450 B.C. Euripides was at least thirty years old, and it seems almost certain that, in a society as small as the intellectual circle at Athens, he would already have made the acquaintance of Anaxagoras. For passages in Euripides in which the influence of Anaxagoras is said to be manifest see DK 59 A 20 *a–c*, 30, 33, 48 and 112, the last of which seems on the whole to be a good deal the most convincing.

[2] Cf. Plutarch *Pericles* 4 (DK 59 A 15), 5, 8 etc.; also **491** Plutarch *Nicias* 23 (DK 59 A 18) ...καὶ Ἀναξαγόραν εἱρχθέντα μόλις περιεποιήσατο Περικλῆς.

[3] Cf. **492** Alcidamas *ap.* Aristotle *Rhet.* B 23, 1398b 15 καὶ Λαμψακηνοὶ Ἀναξαγόραν ξένον ὄντα ἔθαψαν καὶ τιμῶσιν ἔτι καὶ νῦν.

WRITINGS

493 Plato *Apology* 26 D Μὰ Δί', ὦ ἄνδρες δικασταί, ἐπεὶ τὸν μὲν ἥλιον λίθον φησὶν εἶναι, τὴν δὲ σελήνην γῆν. Ἀναξαγόρου οἴει κατηγορεῖν, ὦ φίλε Μέλητε, καὶ οὕτω καταφρονεῖς τῶνδε καὶ οἴει αὐτοὺς ἀπείρους γραμμάτων εἶναι, ὥστε οὐκ εἰδέναι ὅτι τὰ Ἀναξαγόρου βιβλία τοῦ Κλαζομενίου γέμει τούτων τῶν λόγων; καὶ δὴ καὶ οἱ νέοι ταῦτα παρ' ἐμοῦ μανθάνουσιν ἃ ἔξεστιν ἐνίοτε, εἰ πάνυ πολλοῦ, δραχμῆς ἐκ τῆς ὀρχήστρας πριαμένους Σωκράτους καταγελᾶν, ἐὰν προσποιῆται ἑαυτοῦ εἶναι, ἄλλως τε καὶ οὕτως ἄτοπα ὄντα.

494 Diogenes Laertius I, 16 οἱ δὲ ἀνὰ ἓν σύγγραμμα Μέλισσος, Παρμενίδης, Ἀναξαγόρας.

Very probably Anaxagoras did indeed write only the one book; various other writings attributed to him by late and unreliable authorities—a treatise on perspective, another on the squaring of the circle and a book of problems—if they ever existed at all, are most unlikely to be the genuine work of Anaxagoras. His one

---

491 *...Pericles had difficulty in rescuing Anaxagoras from imprisonment.*

492 *The inhabitants of Lampsacus buried Anaxagoras although he was a foreigner and even to this day still honour him.*

493 *'By Zeus, gentlemen of the jury, it is because he says that the sun is a stone, the moon earth.' Do you imagine, friend Meletus, that you are accusing Anaxagoras, and do you despise the jury, and think them so illiterate that they do not know that the rolls of Anaxagoras of Clazomenae are packed with such theories? The young, I suppose, learn these things from me—things which you can sometimes buy for a drachma, dear as that may be, in the* orchestra, *and then mock Socrates if he claims them as his own, particularly when they are so absurd.*

494 *Those who wrote only one book include Melissus, Parmenides and Anaxagoras.*

book, moreover, though it is said by Burnet (apparently on the strength of the plural βιβλία in **493**, which 'perhaps implies that it filled more than one roll'[1]) to have been 'of some length', would seem more probably to have been quite short. Not only do the fragments preserved by Simplicius seem to give us, with considerable repetitions, the whole basis of his system; but also the statement in **493** that the book could be bought for a drachma is a strong indication that it ran to no great length. The economics of Athens in 399 B.C. are by no means easy to reconstruct, but what evidence there is shows that the purchasing power of a drachma was by then quite small. No doubt in the latter part of his book Anaxagoras pursued his general principles into such detailed topics as astronomy, meteorology, physiology and sense-perception —subjects on which there is plenty of second-hand evidence but very few and scanty fragments. But he must in that case have dealt with them with the same summary brevity that characterizes some of the fragments surviving from the earlier part. The extant fragments, which together comprise about a thousand words, can hardly represent less than an eighth of the original whole and may well represent a considerably larger fraction.[2]

[1] Simplicius also implies that in his day Anaxagoras' work was divided into more than one part: at, e.g., *Phys.* 34, 29 (DK 59 B 4) and 155, 26 (DK 59 B 1) he speaks of 'the first part' (or 'book') of the work *On Nature*. This certainly seems to tell in favour of Burnet's view. But there is nothing in Socrates' words in **493** to suggest that the book was a long one except the plural βιβλία, 'books'; and the word βιβλίον, even in the plural, carries (at this date at least) no definite implication of length. It seems more likely, for the reasons given in this section, that if the work was originally divided, as it was in Simplicius' time, into more than one part, they were very short parts.

[2] Prof. A. H. M. Jones has very kindly corroborated this calculation with the following note: 'The simplest calculation is on the assumption that the copyist would be a slave χωρὶς οἰκῶν. His owner would expect an ἀποφορά from a skilled slave of at least 2 obols a day; Timarchus' σκυτοτόμοι (Aeschines I, 97) paid him 2 obols and their foreman 3 obols; Nicias and others in the fifth century got 1 obol a day for unskilled mine slaves, but this included amortization (the hirer had to replace those who died) (Xenophon *Poroi* IV, 14–15). Food is reckoned at 2 obols a day by Dem. IV, 28, but this is probably an underestimate, as Dem. is trying to prove that his scheme could be run quite cheaply. The Eleusinian accounts (*I.G.*² II and III 1672–3, of 329–327 B.C.) allow 3 obols a day for public slaves for τροφή. One must also allow for clothes and other extras, and for the slave's own profit (he would have to allow for slack times when he had no work, and he also expected to put by to pay for his freedom); also for the cost of

papyrus (I fear this cannot be calculated as we do not know in what units it was bought). However, a man's time alone would amount to at least a drachma a day; skilled men (carpenters, stonemasons etc.) are paid 2 to 2½ drachmae a day in the Eleusinian accounts.

A book sold for a drachma would, therefore, be such as could be copied in well under a day.'

THE PROBLEM

No Presocratic philosopher has given rise to more dispute, or been more variously interpreted, than has Anaxagoras. Among recent attempts to reconstruct his system the most notable are those of Tannery (*Pour l'histoire de la science hellène*, 2nd edition), Bailey (*Greek Atomists and Epicurus*, App. I), Cornford (*CQ* 24 (1930) 14ff. and 83ff.), Peck (*CQ* 25 (1931) 27ff. and 112ff.), and Vlastos (*Philos. Rev.* 59 (1950) 31ff.). At the beginning of Cornford's reconstruction the problem, as it is usually understood, is succinctly stated as follows: 'Anaxagoras' theory of matter...rests on two propositions which seem flatly to contradict one another. One is the principle of Homoeomereity: A natural substance, such as a piece of gold, consists solely of parts which are like the whole and like one another—every one of them gold and nothing else. The other is: "There is a portion of everything in everything", understood to mean that a piece of gold (or any other substance), so far from containing nothing but gold, contains portions of every other substance in the world. Unless Anaxagoras was extremely muddleheaded, he cannot have propounded a theory which simply *consists* of this contradiction. One or the other proposition must be reinterpreted so as to bring them into harmony. Some critics attack one, some the other; some try to modify both.' The following reconstruction, though it owes something to each of those listed above, has probably rather more in common with some of the ancient interpretations than it has with any of the modern. It is actually very doubtful whether any critic, ancient or modern, has ever fully understood Anaxagoras, and there are some points on which certainty is now unattainable. There are, however, two principles which every reconstruction should observe: first that the only entirely reliable guide to the opinions of Anaxagoras is his own words; and second (a principle often overlooked in modern times) that he is much more likely to have meant what he said than what, though he could easily have said it, he did not in fact say. If the result of observing these two principles is unpalatable, then it must be remembered that what is unpalatable to us, and even what was unpalatable to Aristotle and his successors, need not necessarily have been so to Anaxagoras himself.

The system of Anaxagoras, like that of Empedocles before him and that of the atomists after, is to a large extent a conscious reaction to the theories of his predecessors. It will be easiest, therefore, to base our reconstruction of it on his reaction to Parmenides, Zeno and other Presocratics.

ANAXAGORAS' REACTION TO PARMENIDES AND THE EARLIER PLURALISTS

495 Fr. 1, Simplicius *Phys.* 155, 26 ὁμοῦ πάντα χρήματα ἦν, ἄπειρα καὶ πλῆθος καὶ σμικρότητα· καὶ γὰρ τὸ σμικρὸν ἄπειρον ἦν. καὶ πάντων ὁμοῦ ἐόντων οὐδὲν ἔνδηλον ἦν ὑπὸ σμικρότητος· πάντα γὰρ ἀήρ τε καὶ αἰθὴρ κατεῖχεν, ἀμφότερα ἄπειρα ἐόντα· ταῦτα γὰρ μέγιστα ἔνεστιν ἐν τοῖς σύμπασι καὶ πλήθει καὶ μεγέθει.

496 Fr. 4 (latter half), *ibid.* 34, 21 (for rest of fr. 4 see **510** and **525**) πρὶν δὲ ἀποκριθῆναι ταῦτα πάντων ὁμοῦ ἐόντων οὐδὲ χροιὴ ἔνδηλος ἦν οὐδεμία· ἀπεκώλυε γὰρ ἡ σύμμιξις ἁπάντων χρημάτων, τοῦ τε διεροῦ καὶ τοῦ ξηροῦ καὶ τοῦ θερμοῦ καὶ τοῦ ψυχροῦ καὶ τοῦ λαμπροῦ καὶ τοῦ ζοφεροῦ, καὶ γῆς πολλῆς ἐνεούσης καὶ σπερμάτων ἀπείρων πλῆθος οὐδὲν ἐοικότων ἀλλήλοις. οὐδὲ γὰρ τῶν ἄλλων οὐδὲν ἔοικε τὸ ἕτερον τῷ ἑτέρῳ. τούτων δὲ οὕτως ἐχόντων ἐν τῷ σύμπαντι χρὴ δοκεῖν ἐνεῖναι πάντα χρήματα.

Simplicius, to whom we owe the preservation of almost all the fragments, tells us that **495** was the opening of Anaxagoras' book. It shows at the outset how extreme was the reaction of Anaxagoras against the Eleatic monism. Whereas Parmenides had written (in **347**):

οὐδέ ποτ' ἦν οὐδ' ἔσται, ἐπεὶ νῦν ἔστιν ὁμοῦ πᾶν,
ἕν, συνεχές,

---

495 *All things were together, infinite in respect of both number and smallness; for the small too was infinite. And while all things were together, none of them were plain because of their smallness; for air and aither covered all things, both of them being infinite; for these are the greatest ingredients in the mixture of all things, both in number and in size.*

496 *But before these things were separated off, while all things were together, there was not even any colour plain; for the mixture of all things prevented it, of the moist and the dry, the hot and the cold, the bright and the dark, and of much earth in the mixture and of seeds countless in number and in no respect like one another. For none of the other things either are like one to the other. And since this is so, we must suppose that all things are in the whole.*

('nor was it at some time past, nor shall it be, since it *is* now all at once, one, continuous'), Anaxagoras in his very first sentence starts by substituting ὁμοῦ πάντα χρήματα for ὁμοῦ πᾶν, ἕν; next admits the forbidden ἦν; and finally, in the words ἄπειρα σμικρότητα, denies also the implication of indivisibility in Parmenides' συνεχές. The world, according to Anaxagoras, arose from a universal mixture of every single thing that was ultimately to emerge; only by putting 'all things together' into this original mixture could coming into being and perishing be effectually eliminated. This is put very clearly in the following passage:

497 Fr. 17, Simplicius *Phys.* 163, 20 τὸ δὲ γίνεσθαι καὶ ἀπόλλυσθαι οὐκ ὀρθῶς νομίζουσιν οἱ Ἕλληνες· οὐδὲν γὰρ χρῆμα γίνεται οὐδὲ ἀπόλλυται, ἀλλ' ἀπὸ ἐόντων χρημάτων συμμίσγεταί τε καὶ διακρίνεται. καὶ οὕτως ἂν ὀρθῶς καλοῖεν τό τε γίνεσθαι συμμίσγεσθαι καὶ τὸ ἀπόλλυσθαι διακρίνεσθαι.

Here it cannot be doubted that Anaxagoras is explicitly accepting one of the Parmenidean demands. There can be little doubt either that the rejection of the other demands, in **495**, is equally deliberate.

The original mixture, as Anaxagoras says in both **495** and **496**, was so uniform a mixture of so many diverse ingredients that nothing would have been perceptible to an imaginary observer except perhaps 'air[1] and aither' (see pp. 382ff.). The list of ingredients in the long sentence in **496**, which has been a source of difficulty to modern commentators, is probably not intended to be exhaustive. Apart from the 'numberless seeds', of which more will be said later, the other ingredients listed can be reasonably explained by reference to the views of others of Anaxagoras' predecessors. There had in the past been two main types of pluralism. There had been those who, like Anaximander, the Pythagoreans and Heraclitus, had in one way or another regarded the world as a battlefield of the opposites; and there had been Empedocles, who had solidified the warring opposites into the four eternal and immutable elements. Neither type of pluralism, to Anaxagoras' mind, went far enough. His own original mixture must contain, not only the traditional opposites (of which the hot and the cold

497 *The Greeks are wrong to recognize coming into being and perishing; for nothing comes into being nor perishes, but is rather compounded or dissolved from things that are. So they would be right to call coming into being composition and perishing dissolution.*

are Anaximander's, the wet and the dry are also possibly his or possibly added from Heraclitus, while the bright and the dark are presumably the Pythagorean φῶς and σκότος (see **289**)), nor only the Empedoclean elements (here probably exemplified by earth, because two of the others, air and aither (or fire), have already been mentioned as ingredients in **495**); it must contain also 'innumerable seeds in no way like each other'.

[1] Anaxagoras evidently followed Empedocles in accepting also the Parmenidean equation of the void with Not-being. Cf. **498** Aristotle *Phys.* Δ6, 213a22 οἱ μὲν οὖν δεικνύναι πειρώμενοι ὅτι οὐκ ἔστιν (*sc.* τὸ κενόν), οὐχ ὃ βούλονται λέγειν οἱ ἄνθρωποι κενόν, τοῦτ' ἐξελέγχουσιν, ἀλλ' ἁμαρτάνοντες λέγουσιν, ὥσπερ Ἀναξαγόρας καὶ οἱ τοῦτον τὸν τρόπον ἐλέγχοντες. ἐπιδεικνύουσι γὰρ ὅτι ἔστι τι ὁ ἀήρ, στρεβλοῦντες τοὺς ἀσκοὺς καὶ δεικνύντες ὡς ἰσχυρὸς ὁ ἀήρ, καὶ ἐναπολαμβάνοντες ἐν ταῖς κλεψύδραις (see **453**). In Anaxagoras, therefore, as in Empedocles, air, being corporeal, is clearly distinguished from the non-existent void. Cf. also Aristotle *de caelo* Δ2, 309a19 (DK59B68), where Aristotle groups Empedocles and Anaxagoras together as (1) denying the existence of the void, (2) giving no explanation of differences of weight.

ANAXAGORAS' REACTION TO ZENO

499 Fr. 3, Simplicius *Phys.* 164, 17 οὔτε γὰρ τοῦ σμικροῦ ἔστι τό γε ἐλάχιστον, ἀλλ' ἔλασσον ἀεί (τὸ γὰρ ἐὸν οὐκ ἔστι τὸ μὴ οὐκ εἶναι)—ἀλλὰ καὶ τοῦ μεγάλου ἀεὶ ἔστι μεῖζον. καὶ ἴσον ἐστὶ τῷ σμικρῷ πλῆθος, πρὸς ἑαυτὸ δὲ ἕκαστόν ἐστι καὶ μέγα καὶ σμικρόν.

500 Fr. 5, *ibid.* 156, 10 τούτων δὲ οὕτω διακεκριμένων γινώσκειν χρὴ ὅτι πάντα οὐδὲν ἐλάσσω ἐστὶν οὐδὲ πλείω (οὐ γὰρ ἀνυστὸν πάντων πλείω εἶναι), ἀλλὰ πάντα ἴσα ἀεί.

There is good reason to suppose that in these two brief fragments Anaxagoras is explicitly replying to Zeno. It is at any rate a striking coincidence that, of the only two of Zeno's arguments

---

498 *Those who try to show that the void does not exist do not disprove what people really mean by it, but argue erroneously; this is true of Anaxagoras and of those who refute the existence of the void in this way. They merely give an ingenious demonstration that air is something—by straining wine-skins and showing the resistance of the air, and by cutting it off in* klepsydras. (After Hardie)

499 *Neither is there a smallest part of what is small, but there is always a smaller (for it is impossible that what is should cease to be). Likewise there is always something larger than what is large. And it is equal in respect of number to what is small, each thing, in relation to itself, being both large and small.*

500 *And when these things have been thus separated, we must know that all things are neither more nor less (for it is not possible that there should be more than all), but all things are always equal.*

against plurality which have survived in his own words, one should end as follows: **501** Zeno Fr. 1, Simplicius *Phys.* 141, 6 (=**365**) οὕτως εἰ πολλά ἐστιν, ἀνάγκη αὐτὰ μικρά τε εἶναι καὶ μεγάλα· μικρὰ μὲν ὥστε μὴ ἔχειν μέγεθος, μεγάλα δὲ ὥστε ἄπειρα εἶναι, and the other should begin thus: **502** Zeno Fr. 3, Simplicius *Phys.* 140, 29 (=**366**) εἰ πολλά ἐστιν, ἀνάγκη τοσαῦτα εἶναι ὅσα ἐστὶ καὶ οὔτε πλείονα αὐτῶν οὔτε ἐλάττονα. Since both these statements are of a somewhat unusual character, it seems most likely that, when Anaxagoras echoes them both so exactly as he does, he is doing so quite deliberately.

500 is of comparatively little importance. Zeno's argument had been directed against the Pythagorean confusion between the units of arithmetic, the points of geometry and the atoms of physics. Any physical body, according to the Pythagoreans, consisted of a number of units; and, since units are by definition indivisible, the number attaching to any finite body is itself necessarily finite. But if units are also geometrical points, then, since geometrical space is by definition infinitely divisible, the number is at the same time infinite. Anaxagoras' reply is a direct contradiction: even though, as he has said in **495**, things are ἄπειρα καὶ πλῆθος καὶ σμικρότητα, they are still 'no more and no less than they are'.

It is **499** which contains the important part of Anaxagoras' reply to Zeno. Zeno's argument in **501** had again been aimed primarily at the Pythagorean confusion of units, points and atoms: since every physical body consists of an infinite number of points, it must, if those points have magnitude, be infinitely large, and, if they have no magnitude, have none itself either. The consequences of Zeno's arguments were, as Cornford pointed out (*Plato and Parmenides* 60–1), twofold: 'the first was reflected in the separation of arithmetic from geometry; . . . the second . . . was the distinction between the geometrical solid and the sensible body, which the Pythagoreans had confused. . . . The atomists, Leucippus and Democritus, saw that, if physical bodies need not have all the properties of geometrical solids, they could elude Zeno's dilemmas. They could reply: "We grant that all geometrical magnitudes are infinitely divisible and that a geometrical point has no parts or

501 *So if there is a plurality, things must be both small and great; so small as to have no magnitude at all, so great as to be infinite.*

502 *If there is a plurality, things must be just as many as they are, neither more nor less.*

magnitude; but our atoms are not either the points or the solids of geometry, but compact bodies, which, if they were large enough, you could see and touch...." ...The atom thus ceased to be confused with the unit of number and the point of geometry, and became a purely physical body whose essential property was impenetrability.' The answer of Leucippus and Democritus was not, however, the only possible answer to Zeno: it could equally easily have been granted that physical matter, like geometrical magnitude, was infinitely divisible. This, as is evident from **499**, is the answer that Anaxagoras chose to give. 'I grant', he means, 'that physical matter, like geometrical magnitude, is infinitely divisible; but physical matter composes sensible bodies, and since sensible bodies exist and have magnitude, the same must be true of physical matter. However far you subdivide matter [Zeller's reading τομῇ for τὸ μὴ is attractive], you can never reduce it to sheer nothingness; even the smallest imaginable particle must still possess some magnitude. In consequence each thing is indeed both great and small: great because it contains an infinite number of parts, and small because those parts are themselves of an infinitesimal smallness.' Anaxagoras' theory of matter is in fact deliberately adopted, like that of the atomists, as an answer to Zeno; and when that answer is added to his answer to Parmenides, one half of the basis of his system is now complete. He is enabled, by his belief in the infinite divisibility of matter, to devise a cosmogony and to give an account of change which does indeed eliminate the forbidden coming-into-being of what was not.

MIND

503 Fr. 12, Simplicius *Phys.* 164, 24 and 156, 13 τὰ μὲν ἄλλα παντὸς μοῖραν μετέχει, νοῦς δέ ἐστιν ἄπειρον καὶ αὐτοκρατὲς καὶ μέμεικται οὐδενὶ χρήματι, ἀλλὰ μόνος αὐτὸς ἐφ' ἑαυτοῦ ἐστιν. εἰ μὴ γὰρ ἐφ' ἑαυτοῦ ἦν, ἀλλά τεῳ ἐμέμεικτο ἄλλῳ, μετεῖχεν ἂν ἁπάντων χρημάτων, εἰ ἐμέμεικτό τεῳ· ἐν παντὶ γὰρ παντὸς μοῖρα ἔνεστιν, ὥσπερ ἐν τοῖς πρόσθεν μοι λέλεκται· καὶ ἂν ἐκώλυεν αὐτὸν τὰ συμμεμειγμένα, ὥστε μηδενὸς χρήματος κρατεῖν ὁμοίως ὡς καὶ

---

503 *All other things have a portion of everything, but Mind is infinite and self-ruled, and is mixed with nothing but is all alone by itself. For if it was not by itself, but was mixed with anything else, it would have a share of all things if it were mixed with any; for in everything there is a portion of everything, as I said earlier; and the things that were mingled with it would hinder it so that it could control nothing in the same way as it does*

μόνον ἐόντα ἐφ' ἑαυτοῦ. ἔστι γὰρ λεπτότατόν τε πάντων χρημάτων καὶ καθαρώτατον, καὶ γνώμην γε περὶ παντὸς πᾶσαν ἴσχει καὶ ἰσχύει μέγιστον· καὶ ὅσα γε ψυχὴν ἔχει, καὶ τὰ μείζω καὶ τὰ ἐλάσσω, πάντων νοῦς κρατεῖ. καὶ τῆς περιχωρήσιος τῆς συμπάσης νοῦς ἐκράτησεν, ὥστε περιχωρῆσαι τὴν ἀρχήν. καὶ πρῶτον ἀπό του σμικροῦ ἤρξατο περιχωρεῖν, ἐπὶ δὲ πλέον περιχωρεῖ, καὶ περιχωρήσει ἐπὶ πλέον. καὶ τὰ συμμισγόμενά τε καὶ ἀποκρινόμενα καὶ διακρινόμενα πάντα ἔγνω νοῦς. καὶ ὁποῖα ἔμελλεν ἔσεσθαι καὶ ὁποῖα ἦν, ἅσσα νῦν μὴ ἔστι, καὶ ὅσα νῦν ἔστι καὶ ὁποῖα ἔσται, πάντα διεκόσμησε νοῦς, καὶ τὴν περιχώρησιν ταύτην ἣν νῦν περιχωρεῖ τά τε ἄστρα καὶ ὁ ἥλιος καὶ ἡ σελήνη καὶ ὁ ἀὴρ καὶ ὁ αἰθὴρ οἱ ἀποκρινόμενοι. ἡ δὲ περιχώρησις αὕτη ἐποίησεν ἀποκρίνεσθαι. καὶ ἀποκρίνεται ἀπό τε τοῦ ἀραιοῦ τὸ πυκνὸν καὶ ἀπὸ τοῦ ψυχροῦ τὸ θερμὸν καὶ ἀπὸ τοῦ ζοφεροῦ τὸ λαμπρὸν καὶ ἀπὸ τοῦ διεροῦ τὸ ξηρόν. μοῖραι δὲ πολλαὶ πολλῶν εἰσι. παντάπασι δὲ οὐδὲν ἀποκρίνεται οὐδὲ διακρίνεται ἕτερον ἀπὸ τοῦ ἑτέρου πλὴν νοῦ. νοῦς δὲ πᾶς ὅμοιός ἐστι καὶ ὁ μείζων καὶ ὁ ἐλάττων. ἕτερον δὲ οὐδέν ἐστιν ὅμοιον οὐδενί, ἀλλ' ὅτων πλεῖστα ἔνι, ταῦτα ἐνδηλότατα ἓν ἕκαστόν ἐστι καὶ ἦν.

504 Fr. 13, Simplicius *Phys.* 300, 31 καὶ ἐπεὶ ἤρξατο ὁ νοῦς κινεῖν, ἀπὸ τοῦ κινουμένου παντὸς ἀπεκρίνετο, καὶ ὅσον ἐκίνησεν ὁ νοῦς πᾶν τοῦτο διεκρίθη· κινουμένων δὲ καὶ διακρινομένων ἡ περιχώρησις πολλῷ μᾶλλον ἐποίει διακρίνεσθαι.

505 Fr. 9, *ibid.* 35, 14 ...οὕτω τούτων περιχωρούντων τε καὶ

---

now being alone by itself. For it is the finest of all things and the purest, it has all knowledge about everything and the greatest power; and mind controls all things, both the greater and the smaller, that have life. Mind controlled also the whole rotation, so that it began to rotate in the beginning. And it began to rotate first from a small area, but it now rotates over a wider and will rotate over a wider area still. And the things that are mingled and separated and divided off, all are known by Mind. And all things that were to be, all things that were but are not now, all things that are now or that shall be, Mind arranged them all, including this rotation in which are now rotating the stars, the sun and moon, the air and the aither that are being separated off. And this rotation caused the separating off. And the dense is separated off from the rare, the hot from the cold, the bright from the dark and the dry from the moist. But there are many portions of many things, and nothing is altogether separated off nor divided one from the other except Mind. Mind is all alike, both the greater and the smaller quantities of it, while nothing else is like anything else, but each single body is and was most plainly those things of which it contains most.

504 *And when Mind initiated motion, from all that was moved Mind was separated, and as much as Mind moved was all divided off; and as things moved and were divided off, the rotation greatly increased the process of dividing.*

505 *...as these things rotated thus and were separated off by the force and speed (of*

ἀποκρινομένων ὑπὸ βίης τε καὶ ταχυτῆτος. βίην δὲ ἡ ταχυτὴς ποιεῖ. ἡ δὲ ταχυτὴς αὐτῶν οὐδενὶ ἔοικε χρήματι τὴν ταχυτῆτα τῶν νῦν ἐόντων χρημάτων ἐν ἀνθρώποις, ἀλλὰ πάντως πολλαπλασίως ταχύ ἐστι.

506 Fr. 14, *ibid.* 157, 7 ὁ δὲ νοῦς, ὃς ἀεί ἐστι, τὸ κάρτα [so Diels: ὅσα ἐστί τε κάρτα Simplic. mss.] καὶ νῦν ἐστιν ἵνα καὶ τὰ ἄλλα πάντα, ἐν τῷ πολλῷ περιέχοντι καὶ ἐν τοῖς προσκριθεῖσι καὶ ἐν τοῖς ἀποκεκριμένοις.

Another Parmenidean demand with which Anaxagoras had to comply was that motion should not be simply taken for granted but explained. In place of Empedocles' Love and Strife (moral and psychological forces expressed in corporeal terms, see **424**) Anaxagoras substitutes the single intellectual motive force of Mind. It too, like Love and Strife, has many of the qualities of an abstract principle. 'It has all knowledge about everything, and the greatest strength; it controls all things that have life'; and 'it set in order all things that were to be', including, of course, the cosmic revolution. Yet at the same time it is 'the finest of all things and the purest'; it is 'all alike, both the larger and the smaller quantities'; and though it is 'mixed with nothing', it is none the less present 'there, where everything else is, in the surrounding mass, and in what has been united and separated off'. Anaxagoras in fact is striving, as had several of his predecessors, to imagine and describe a truly incorporeal entity. But as with them, so still with him, the only ultimate criterion of reality is extension in space. Mind, like everything else, is corporeal, and owes its power partly to its fineness, partly to the fact that it alone, though present in the mixture, yet remains unmixed.

How Mind imparted the first rotatory movement is by no means obvious; it may be that even Anaxagoras himself had no clear mental picture of the process. It appears, however, that the area affected was at first small but is still steadily increasing. The speed of the revolution is immense, and therefore its effect on the original mixture is very powerful (**505**). The immediate consequence is progressive separation: the moment the rotation takes in a new

---

their rotation). And the speed creates the force. Their speed is like the speed of nothing that now exists among men, but it is altogether many times as fast.

506 *But Mind, which ever is, is assuredly even now where everything else is too, in the surrounding mass and in the things that have been either aggregated or separated.*

area, as it is doing all the time, the ingredients of that area begin at once to separate off (**504**). It is in fact the rotation which is directly responsible for the separation, which leads in turn to cosmogony. Mind, having initiated the rotation, remains alone ultimately responsible; but at the same time, as is evident from the statement at the end of **504**, once the original motion has been imparted, purely mechanical factors begin to operate and the agency of Mind itself becomes less direct. This is a feature of Anaxagoras' system which, to the irritation of Plato and Aristotle (see **522** and note), becomes more pronounced as his cosmogony proceeds.

With the introduction of Mind the basis of the system is complete. Anaxagoras is, like Empedocles, in a sense a dualist; and his dualism is, for the first time, in a sense a dualism of Mind and matter.[1] But both members of this dualism are peculiar. Mind, like matter, is corporeal and owes its power over matter to its fineness and purity. Matter itself, so far from being pure, is originally at least an infinitely divisible mixture of every form of substance that the world is ultimately to contain.

[1] Cf. **507** Theophrastus *Phys. Op.* fr. 4 *ap.* Simplicium *Phys.* 27, 17 (DK 59 A 41) καὶ οὕτω μὲν λαμβανόντων δόξειεν ἂν ὁ Ἀναξαγόρας τὰς μὲν ὑλικὰς ἀρχὰς ἀπείρους ποιεῖν, τὴν δὲ τῆς κινήσεως καὶ τῆς γενέσεως αἰτίαν μίαν τὸν νοῦν· εἰ δέ τις τὴν μίξιν τῶν ἁπάντων ὑπολάβοι μίαν εἶναι φύσιν ἀόριστον καὶ κατ' εἶδος καὶ κατὰ μέγεθος, συμβαίνει δύο τὰς ἀρχὰς αὐτὸν λέγειν τήν τε τοῦ ἀπείρου φύσιν καὶ τὸν νοῦν.

IN EVERYTHING A PORTION OF EVERYTHING

508 Fr. 6, Simplicius *Phys.* 164, 26 καὶ ὅτε δὲ ἴσαι μοῖραί εἰσι τοῦ τε μεγάλου καὶ τοῦ σμικροῦ πλῆθος, καὶ οὕτως ἂν εἴη ἐν παντὶ πάντα· οὐδὲ χωρὶς ἔστιν εἶναι, ἀλλὰ πάντα παντὸς μοῖραν μετέχει. ὅτε τοὐλάχιστον μὴ ἔστιν εἶναι, οὐκ ἂν δύναιτο χωρισθῆναι, οὐδ'

---

507 *Such being their theory, Anaxagoras would appear to make his material principles infinite, but the cause of motion and coming into being one only, namely Mind. But if we were to suppose that the mixture of all things was a single substance, indefinite both in form and in extent, then it follows that he is really affirming two first principles only, namely the substance of the infinite and Mind.*

508 *And since the portions of the great and of the small are equal in number, so too all things would be in everything. Nor is it possible that they should exist apart, but all things have a portion of everything. Since it is not possible that there should be a smallest part, nothing can be put apart nor come-to-be all by itself, but as things were originally, so they*

ἂν ἐφ' ἑαυτοῦ γενέσθαι, ἀλλ' ὅπωσπερ ἀρχὴν εἶναι καὶ νῦν πάντα ὁμοῦ. ἐν πᾶσι δὲ πολλὰ ἔνεστι καὶ τῶν ἀποκρινομένων ἴσα πλῆθος ἐν τοῖς μείζοσί τε καὶ ἐλάσσοσι.

509 Fr. 11, *ibid.* 164, 23 ἐν παντὶ παντὸς μοῖρα ἔνεστι πλὴν νοῦ, ἔστιν οἷσι δὲ καὶ νοῦς ἔνι.

These two fragments say what they want to say briefly, emphatically and, one might have thought, clearly. **508** tells us that, as in the original mixture, so now in everything, of whatever size, that is being separated off, *all things* are together; while **509**, by its addition of the words πλὴν νοῦ, drives home the point that, just as the original mixture contained not only the traditional opposites and the Empedoclean elements but 'countless seeds' as well, so now everything contains a portion of *everything except Mind*. That is unquestionably what Anaxagoras himself says; and he repeats it more than once in a later fragment which has already been quoted, **503**. Those who maintain, as the majority of recent commentators do, that when Anaxagoras said: 'in everything there is a portion of everything' he can only have meant that in everything there is a portion of all the opposites, can only do so at the expense of accusing Anaxagoras of saying what he did not mean. It is surely inconceivable that any Greek, let alone a practised thinker like Anaxagoras, should have written ἐν παντὶ παντὸς μοῖρα ἔνεστι if by παντός he really meant to signify something quite different from παντί. Whatever παντί and παντός are or are not intended to include, it must in fairness to Anaxagoras be assumed that they include the same things. And that those things comprise other things than the opposites seems to follow inevitably from a comparison of fr. 6, **508**, with fr. 4, **496**.

When Anaxagoras adds at the end of **509** that there are some things also in which Mind is present, the statement is to be compared with that other sentence in **503** which tells us that Mind controls everything that has life. If there are some things in which Mind is present, there are obviously other things in which it is not. Mind is presumably therefore to be imagined as discontinuously distributed throughout the world in living things;

---

must be now too, all together. In all things there are many ingredients, equal in number in the greater and in the smaller of the things that are being separated off.

509 *In everything there is a portion of everything except Mind; and there are some things in which there is Mind as well.*

which would explain how Anaxagoras could speak, as he does near the end of **503**, of 'both the greater and the smaller quantities' of it.

'SEEDS' AND 'PORTIONS'

The chief problem in any reconstruction which assumes that Anaxagoras meant what he said is to determine the relation of the σπέρματα of **496** to the μοῖραι of **503**, **508** and **509**. If Anaxagoras really believed (and this at least is never disputed) in the infinite divisibility of matter, how is it that there are already 'seeds' present in the original mixture? To answer this crucial question, it will be easiest first to consider what precisely Anaxagoras means by the word μοῖρα and only then to consider why the 'seeds' need be introduced at all.

μοῖρα is not, of course, in the way in which σπέρμα is, employed by Anaxagoras as a semi-technical term; but for all that, he seems to have used the word in a sense that requires careful consideration. An Anaxagorean μοῖρα is a 'portion' in the sense of a 'share' rather than of a 'piece' or 'particle'. The essential characteristic of such a 'portion' seems to be that it is something which neither in theory nor in practice can ever be actually reached and separated out from that which contains it. However far you may subdivide matter, and however infinitesimal a piece of it you may thereby reach, Anaxagoras will always reply, exactly as Zeno would have replied of a geometrical line, that so far from being irreducible, it still contains an infinite number of 'portions'. This indeed is precisely the nature of Anaxagoras' reaction to Zeno; and it is probably what he means when he says in **508** that 'the portions of the great and of the small are equal in number'. Both the infinitely great and the infinitesimally small alike contain an infinite number of 'portions'. In effect, of course, such a theory is indistinguishable from a theory of fusion such as Bailey (*Greek Atomists and Epicurus*, App. I) attributes to Anaxagoras; but it remains, as a theory, widely different. Neither of the illustrations that are usually cited, the analogy of the mixture of liquids such as water and wine and that of the mixture of grains such as those of sugar and sand, is at all adequate to the theory. The only satisfactory analogy is that suggested by the influence of Zeno, the analogy of the infinite number of points in even the shortest line. By that analogy alone can we see how Anaxagoras, despite the infinite divisibility of matter, could still maintain that even the infinitesimally small contained a 'portion' of everything.

Unfortunately, the objection can be brought against such a theory—and indeed it has been brought by both ancient and modern critics—that in that case Anaxagoras' cosmogony is based upon a vicious regress. It is not, as a matter of fact, by any means certain that Anaxagoras himself would have regarded such a regress as undesirable. The very notion of an infinite regress was a new one, dating only from the time of Zeno, and it seems in no way improbable that Anaxagoras should have seen in it a welcome escape from Parmenides' denial of coming-into-being. But in any case Anaxagoras has an answer to his critics. As is evident from the fact that there is already an infinite number of 'seeds' in the original mixture, matter naturally tends, however infinitely divisible it may be, to coagulate into 'seeds', and there is therefore a natural unit of matter from which cosmogony can begin. So, it seems, Anaxagoras evaded the dilemma. On the one hand, certainly, the infinite regress must be retained: it is the only way in which there can be a 'portion' of everything in everything, and so both coming-into-being and change can be effectually eliminated. On the other hand, equally certainly, this same infinite regress must be somehow at least momentarily halted so that Anaxagoras can start moving in the opposite direction towards the building up of the sensible world. It is at this point that the 'seeds' (an appropriate word, since a seed is that from which larger things develop) have an essential part to play in the system.

'SEEDS' AND OPPOSITES

510 Fr. 4 (first sentence), Simplicius *Phys.* 34, 29 τούτων δὲ οὕτως ἐχόντων χρὴ δοκεῖν ἐνεῖναι πολλά τε καὶ παντοῖα ἐν πᾶσι τοῖς συγκρινομένοις καὶ σπέρματα πάντων χρημάτων καὶ ἰδέας παντοίας ἔχοντα καὶ χροιὰς καὶ ἡδονάς.... (Continues at **525**.)

511 Fr. 10, Σ *in* Gregor. Naz. XXXVI, 911 Migne πῶς γὰρ ἂν ἐκ μὴ τριχὸς γένοιτο θρὶξ καὶ σὰρξ ἐκ μὴ σαρκός;

512 Aristotle *Phys.* A4, 187a23 διαφέρουσι δὲ ἀλλήλων τῷ τὸν

510 *And since these things are so, we must suppose that there are many things of all sorts in everything that is being aggregated, seeds of all things with all sorts of shapes and colours and tastes....*

511 *How could hair come from what is not hair or flesh from what is not flesh?*

512 *These two, however, differ from each other in that Empedocles imagines a cycle of*

μὲν (*sc.* Empedocles) περίοδον ποιεῖν τούτων, τὸν δ' (*sc.* Anaxagoras) ἅπαξ, καὶ τὸν μὲν (*sc.* Anaxagoras) ἄπειρα, τά τε ὁμοιομερῆ καὶ τἀναντία, τὸν δὲ τὰ καλούμενα στοιχεῖα μόνον. ἔοικε δὲ 'Αναξαγόρας ἄπειρα οὕτως οἰηθῆναι διὰ τὸ ὑπολαμβάνειν τὴν κοινὴν δόξαν τῶν φυσικῶν εἶναι ἀληθῆ, ὡς οὐ γιγνομένου οὐδενὸς ἐκ τοῦ μὴ ὄντος (διὰ τοῦτο γὰρ οὕτω λέγουσιν, ἦν ὁμοῦ πάντα, καὶ τὸ γίγνεσθαι τοιόνδε καθέστηκεν ἀλλοιοῦσθαι, οἱ δὲ σύγκρισιν καὶ διάκρισιν)· ἔτι δ' ἐκ τοῦ γίγνεσθαι ἐξ ἀλλήλων τἀναντία· ἐνυπῆρχεν ἄρα· εἰ γὰρ πᾶν μὲν τὸ γιγνόμενον ἀνάγκη γίγνεσθαι ἢ ἐξ ὄντων ἢ ἐκ μὴ ὄντων, τούτων δὲ τὸ μὲν ἐκ μὴ ὄντων γίγνεσθαι ἀδύνατον (περὶ γὰρ ταύτης ὁμογνωμονοῦσι τῆς δόξης ἅπαντες οἱ περὶ φύσεως), τὸ λοιπὸν ἤδη συμβαίνειν ἐξ ἀνάγκης ἐνόμισαν, ἐξ ὄντων μὲν καὶ ἐνυπαρχόντων γίγνεσθαι, διὰ μικρότητα δὲ τῶν ὄγκων ἐξ ἀναισθήτων ἡμῖν. διό φασι πᾶν ἐν παντὶ μεμῖχθαι, διότι πᾶν ἐκ παντὸς ἑώρων γιγνόμενον· φαίνεσθαι δὲ διαφέροντα καὶ προσαγορεύεσθαι ἕτερα ἀλλήλων ἐκ τοῦ μάλισθ' ὑπερέχοντος διὰ πλῆθος ἐν τῇ μίξει τῶν ἀπείρων· εἰλικρινῶς μὲν γὰρ ὅλον λευκὸν ἢ μέλαν ἢ γλυκὺ ἢ σάρκα ἢ ὀστοῦν οὐκ εἶναι, ὅτου δὲ πλεῖστον ἕκαστον ἔχει, τοῦτο δοκεῖν εἶναι τὴν φύσιν τοῦ πράγματος.

Unfortunately the only two surviving sentences of Anaxagoras himself that give us any clue concerning the composition of the 'seeds' are those in **510** and **511**; and of these the latter may well represent, not Anaxagoras' own exact words, but a paraphrase by

---

such changes, Anaxagoras a single series. Anaxagoras again posited an infinity of principles, namely the homoeomerous substances and the opposites together, while Empedocles posits only the so-called 'elements'. The theory of Anaxagoras that the principles are infinite in number was probably due to his acceptance of the common opinion of the physicists that nothing comes into being from not-being. For this is the reason why they use the phrase 'all things were together', and the coming into being of such and such a kind of thing is reduced to change of quality, while others speak of combination and separation. Moreover, the fact that the opposites proceed from each other led them to the same conclusion. The one, they reasoned, must have already existed in the other; for since everything that comes into being must arise either from what is or from what is not, and it is impossible for it to arise from what is not (on this point all the physicists agree), they thought that the truth of the alternative necessarily followed, namely that things come into being out of existent things, i.e. out of things already present, but imperceptible to our senses because of the smallness of their bulk. So they assert that everything is mixed in everything, because they saw everything arising out of everything. But things, as they say, appear different from one another and receive different names according to the nature of the thing that is numerically predominant among the innumerable constituents of the mixture. For nothing, they say, is purely and entirely white or black or sweet or flesh or bone, but the nature of a thing is held to be that of which it contains the most. (After Hardie)

the scholiast on Gregorius Nazianzenus who preserves the argument. At this point, therefore, we are compelled to invoke secondary sources. But at least our secondary authorities (one of whom, Simplicius, certainly had Anaxagoras' book before him) are unanimous in attributing to Anaxagoras the views voiced by Aristotle in **512**.

It is fairly evident from **510**, where the 'seeds' are said to have diverse colours and tastes, that some at least of the opposites, such as bright and dark or sweet and bitter, were actually ingredients in the 'seeds'; and there can be little doubt that Aristotle is therefore right when he attributes to Anaxagoras the general argument that, since opposites 'come out of one another'—since, in other words, a thing becomes hotter from having been cooler and *vice versa*—they must have been present in one another all the time. But that does not seem to be, as it is sometimes taken to be, the end of the matter. **511** equally suggests, if somewhat less directly, that natural substances are on an equal footing with the opposites. For if hair cannot come from what is not hair nor flesh from what is not flesh, hair and flesh too, just like the opposites, must have been there all the time. Again, moreover, this inference is supported by Aristotle; for in the last sentence of **512**, in the list of examples of the things the predominance of which determines the apparent character of a whole body, there appear, besides the opposites, white, black and sweet, the natural substances, flesh and bone. The 'seeds' in fact contain, like the original mixture in which they were present, not only the opposites, nor only natural substances, but both together.

It is significant that Aristotle should so often, as he does in **512**, compare and contrast Empedocles and Anaxagoras. Anaxagoras seems to have felt, as has already become evident from the list of the ingredients of the original mixture in **496**, that Empedocles had not gone far enough. If everything consisted solely of the four elements, then in putting together the four elements in different proportions to form, say, flesh or bone, Empedocles had not, to Anaxagoras' mind, succeeded in eliminating the coming-into-being of something new. The only way to do that was to posit in everything the presence *ab initio* of everything which might emerge from it. Since there was no end to the apparent changes that might take place in the world, there must be, not only in the original mixture as a whole but in every constituent 'seed', a 'portion' not only of all the opposites but of every natural substance as well. In that way alone can hair and flesh come from the wheat which nourishes them without the coming-into-being of something new.

THE OPPOSITES

513 Fr. 8, Simplicius *Phys.* 175, 12 and 176, 29 οὐ κεχώρισται ἀλλήλων τὰ ἐν τῷ ἑνὶ κόσμῳ οὐδὲ ἀποκέκοπται πελέκει οὔτε τὸ θερμὸν ἀπὸ τοῦ ψυχροῦ οὔτε τὸ ψυχρὸν ἀπὸ τοῦ θερμοῦ.

This fragment should be compared with the last few sentences of **503** (beginning καὶ ἀποκρίνεται), where, incidentally, it is to be noted that Anaximenes' pair of opposites, the rare and the dense, are added to those of Anaximander and the Pythagoreans. The two passages together are often taken, along with those in the next section, as indicating that Anaxagoras did indeed regard the opposites as primary elements of superior status to natural substances. It seems more likely, however, in view of the evidence to the contrary, that he merely regarded the opposites as providing the best illustration of his general theory that 'in everything there is a portion of everything'. Heraclitus had already shown that one of a pair of opposites cannot exist without the other; while the very fact that they are opposites means that the existence of a close relation between them, whatever it may be, is more obvious than in the case of such substances as, say, gold and flesh. Indeed a particular argument which Anaxagoras is said to have used, the paradox that snow must really be black,[1] may well be no more than a later distortion of a statement to the effect that there is a 'portion' of 'the black' in snow. But even though the opposites do unquestionably, for this reason, figure very prominently in the fragments, the evidence still seems to suggest that, just as the hot and the cold cannot be cut off from one another with a hatchet, so are flesh, hair, gold, and every other natural substance equally inseparable one from another.

[1] **514** Sextus *Pyrrh.* I, 33 νοούμενα δὲ φαινομένοις (*sc.* ἀντιτίθεμεν), ὡς ὁ Ἀναξαγόρας τῷ λευκὴν εἶναι τὴν χιόνα ἀντετίθει ὅτι ἡ χιὼν ὕδωρ ἐστὶ πεπηγός, τὸ δὲ ὕδωρ ἐστὶ μέλαν, καὶ ἡ χιὼν ἄρα μέλαινά ἐστιν.

---

513 *The things in the one world-order are not separated one from the other nor cut off with an axe, neither the hot from the cold nor the cold from the hot.*

514 *We oppose the objects of thought to those of the senses, as Anaxagoras used to oppose to the view that snow is white the argument that snow is frozen water, and water is black, whence it follows that snow is black.*

THE BEGINNINGS OF COSMOGONY

515 Fr. 2, Simplicius *Phys.* 155, 31 καὶ γὰρ ἀήρ τε καὶ αἰθὴρ ἀποκρίνονται ἀπὸ τοῦ πολλοῦ τοῦ περιέχοντος, καὶ τό γε περιέχον ἄπειρόν ἐστι τὸ πλῆθος.

516 Fr. 15, *ibid.* 179, 3 τὸ μὲν πυκνὸν καὶ διερὸν καὶ ψυχρὸν καὶ τὸ ζοφερὸν ἐνθάδε συνεχώρησεν, ἔνθα νῦν ⟨ἡ γῆ⟩,[1] τὸ δὲ ἀραιὸν καὶ τὸ θερμὸν καὶ τὸ ξηρὸν ἐξεχώρησεν εἰς τὸ πρόσω τοῦ αἰθέρος.

517 Fr. 16, *ibid.* 179, 8 and 155, 21 ἀπὸ τουτέων ἀποκρινομένων συμπήγνυται γῆ· ἐκ μὲν γὰρ τῶν νεφελῶν ὕδωρ ἀποκρίνεται, ἐκ δὲ τοῦ ὕδατος γῆ, ἐκ δὲ τῆς γῆς λίθοι συμπήγνυνται ὑπὸ τοῦ ψυχροῦ, οὗτοι δὲ ἐκχωρέουσι μᾶλλον τοῦ ὕδατος.

[1] The supplement (which is not essential) is derived from the paraphrase of this fr. in Hippolytus *Ref.* 1, 8, 2.

515 suggests that in the progressive separation caused by the rotation the first things to emerge were air and aither (or fire).[1] There is, however, a difficulty here. We have already been told, in the opening sentences of the book, **495**, that in the original mixture 'nothing was visible because of its smallness; for air and aither, both being infinite, held all things in subjection'. Why, then, if air and aither are already distinguished in the original mixture, do they need to be separated off when the rotation begins? There seems to be only one satisfactory answer to that question, which, however, will only emerge from an examination of **516**.

[1] Cf. **518** Aristotle *de caelo* A3, 270b24 'Αναξαγόρας δὲ κατακέχρηται τῷ ὀνόματι τούτῳ (*sc.* αἰθήρ) οὐ καλῶς. ὀνομάζει γὰρ αἰθέρα ἀντὶ πυρός. Cf. e.g. Ar. *Meteor.* B9, 369b14 (DK59A84) and **521**.

The opposites, as we have already seen, exist in the form of 'portions' in the 'seeds', each 'seed' being characterized by that

---

515 *For air and aither are being separated off from the surrounding mass, which is infinite in number.*

516 *The dense and the moist and the cold and the dark came together here, where the earth now is, while the rare and the hot and the dry went outwards to the further part of the aither.*

517 *From these things, as they are separated off, the earth is solidified; for water is separated off from the clouds, earth from water, and from earth stones are solidified by the cold; and stones tend to move outwards more than water.*

518 *Anaxagoras employs this name* (i.e. *aither*) *incorrectly. For he speaks of aither in place of fire.*

of which it has most in it. When, therefore, **516** tells us that 'the dense, the moist, the cold and the dark came together where the earth now is', it means that the 'seeds' in which there was a preponderance of the dense, the moist, the cold and the dark over their respective opposites tended towards the centre of the rotation. They obeyed, in other words, two laws which Anaxagoras seems to have regarded as virtually axiomatic, the attraction of like to like and the tendency of the heavy to the centre, of the light to the circumference of a whirl.[1] The Empedoclean elements were not to Anaxagoras primary substances, but rather mixtures of 'seeds' of all sorts.[2] At this stage in cosmogony at least, earth is earth rather than anything else simply because of the predominance in its constituent 'seeds' of the dense and the rest over their opposites. Aither, on the other hand, consists of 'seeds' that are characterized by the rare, the hot and the dry. All that is happening, therefore, at this very early stage in the world's evolution is that the 'seeds' that are characterized by the same combination of opposites are tending together towards their appropriate place in the universe.

[1] **519** Simplicius *Phys.* 27, 11 (DK 59 A 41) καὶ ταῦτά φησιν ὁ Θεόφραστος παραπλησίως τῷ 'Αναξιμάνδρῳ λέγειν τὸν 'Αναξαγόραν· ἐκεῖνος (*sc.* Anaxagoras) γάρ φησιν ἐν τῇ διακρίσει τοῦ ἀπείρου τὰ συγγενῆ φέρεσθαι πρὸς ἄλληλα, καὶ ὅτι μὲν ἐν τῷ παντὶ χρυσὸς ἦν, γίνεσθαι χρυσόν, ὅτι δὲ γῆ, γῆν.

520 Diog. L. II, 8 (DK 59 A 1) καὶ νοῦν μὲν ἀρχὴν κινήσεως· τῶν δὲ σωμάτων τὰ μὲν βαρέα τὸν κάτω τόπον, τὰ δὲ κοῦφα τὸν ἄνω ἐπισχεῖν.... Cf. **119**.

[2] **521** Aristotle *de caelo* Γ 3, 302 a 28 'Αναξαγόρας δὲ 'Εμπεδοκλεῖ ἐναντίως λέγει περὶ τῶν στοιχείων. ὁ μὲν γὰρ πῦρ καὶ τὰ σύστοιχα τούτοις στοιχεῖά φησιν εἶναι τῶν σωμάτων καὶ συγκεῖσθαι πάντ' ἐκ τούτων, 'Αναξαγόρας δὲ τοὐναντίον· τὰ γὰρ ὁμοιομερῆ στοιχεῖα, λέγω δ' οἷον σάρκα καὶ ὀστοῦν καὶ τῶν τοιούτων ἕκαστον· ἀέρα δὲ καὶ πῦρ μείγματα τούτων καὶ τῶν ἄλλων σπερμάτων πάντων· εἶναι γὰρ ἑκάτερον αὐτῶν ἐξ ἀοράτων ὁμοιομερῶν

---

519 *Theophrastus says that the theory of Anaxagoras resembles that of Anaximander; for Anaxagoras says that, in the dividing up of the infinite, things of a like kind tend together, and what was gold or earth in the original whole becomes gold and earth respectively.*

520 *Mind, he says, initiates motion, and heavy bodies occupy the lower position, light bodies the upper....*

521 *Anaxagoras and Empedocles hold opposite views on the elements. Empedocles holds that fire and the rest of the list are the elements of bodies and that everything is made up of these; but Anaxagoras opposes this. He maintains that the homoeomerous substances (e.g. flesh, bone and so on) are the elements, while air or fire are mixtures of these and all other seeds; each of them is an aggregation of all the homoeomerous substances, which,*

πάντων ἠθροισμένον. διὸ καὶ γίγνεσθαι πάντ' ἐκ τούτων· τὸ γὰρ πῦρ καὶ τὸν αἰθέρα προσαγορεύει ταὐτό.

But if that is so, then the problem raised by the comparison of fr. 1, **495**, with fr. 2, **515**, is easily solved. All that the crucial sentence in fr. 1 is intended to tell us is that, in Cornford's words (*CQ* 24 (1930) 25), 'Aether and Air are merely collective names for the sets of hotter and colder (etc.) Seeds respectively. Both sets exist in the Mixture, and indeed together make up the whole Mixture; but originally they were completely jumbled together and coextensive.' Fr. 2, on the other hand, describes how these sets of 'seeds', originally completely intermingled, began to be separated one from the other to form two distinctive masses. Anaxagoras, true to his Ionian upbringing, has in fact allowed the traditional opposites, even though they are now reduced to the status of 'portions' in 'seeds' and are therefore on an equal footing with natural substances, to retain their traditional part in cosmogony; and at the same time he has found a place in his system for the Empedoclean elements.[1]

[1] This is another illustration of the way in which the responsibility of Mind becomes less direct as cosmogony proceeds. It is clearly the ground for Socrates' famous criticism of Anaxagoras' use of Mind in *Phaedo* 97B ff. Cf. especially **522** Plato *Phaedo* 98B7 (DK59A47) ἀπὸ δὴ θαυμαστῆς ἐλπίδος, ὦ ἑταῖρε, ᾠχόμην φερόμενος, ἐπειδὴ προϊὼν καὶ ἀναγιγνώσκων ὁρῶ ἄνδρα τῷ μὲν νῷ οὐδὲν χρώμενον οὐδέ τινας αἰτίας ἐπαιτιώμενον εἰς τὸ διακοσμεῖν τὰ πράγματα, ἀέρας δὲ καὶ αἰθέρας καὶ ὕδατα αἰτιώμενον καὶ ἄλλα πολλὰ καὶ ἄτοπα. This criticism is echoed by Aristotle *Met.* A4, 985a18 and Eudemus *ap.* Simpl. *Phys.* 327, 26 (both DK59A47).

So Anaxagoras' cosmogony is launched; and the process begun in **515** and **516** is continued in **517**. First air, which is at this stage the opposite of aither, is solidified into clouds; from clouds comes water; from water comes earth; and finally from earth are solidified stones. Not only is like continuing to be attracted by like, but also, evidently, the pressure at the centre of the rotation (cf. the βίη of **505**) is compressing the 'seeds' into ever more solid bodies. Of the ingredients in the 'seeds' it is still apparently the opposites that

---

however, are invisible. For this reason everything comes into being from these two (fire and aither being in Anaxagoras synonymous).

522 *From this wonderful hope, my friend, I was at once cast down: as I went ahead and read the book I found a man who made no use at all of Mind, nor invoked any other real causes to arrange the world, but explained things by airs and aithers and waters and many other absurdities.*

are the operative factor: stones are solidified from earth under the agency of the cold. But by now the opposites have fulfilled their main function; from now onwards their place will be largely taken by the substances with which they are mixed in the 'seeds'.

NOURISHMENT AND GROWTH

523 Aetius I, 3, 5 (DK59A46) Ἀναξαγόρας Ἡγησιβούλου ὁ Κλαζομένιος ἀρχὰς τῶν ὄντων τὰς ὁμοιομερείας ἀπεφήνατο. ἐδόκει γὰρ αὐτῷ ἀπορώτατον εἶναι, πῶς ἐκ τοῦ μὴ ὄντος δύναταί τι γίνεσθαι ἢ φθείρεσθαι εἰς τὸ μὴ ὄν. τροφὴν γοῦν προσφερόμεθα ἁπλῆν καὶ μονοειδῆ, ἄρτον καὶ ὕδωρ, καὶ ἐκ ταύτης τρέφεται θρὶξ φλὲψ ἀρτηρία σὰρξ νεῦρα ὀστᾶ καὶ τὰ λοιπὰ μόρια. τούτων οὖν γιγνομένων ὁμολογητέον ὅτι ἐν τῇ τροφῇ τῇ προσφερομένῃ πάντα ἐστὶ τὰ ὄντα, καὶ ἐκ τῶν ὄντων πάντα αὔξεται. καὶ ἐν ἐκείνῃ ἐστὶ τῇ τροφῇ μόρια αἵματος γεννητικὰ καὶ νεύρων καὶ ὀστέων καὶ τῶν ἄλλων· ἃ ἦν λόγῳ θεωρητὰ μόρια. οὐ γὰρ δεῖ πάντα ἐπὶ τὴν αἴσθησιν ἀνάγειν, ὅτι ἄρτος καὶ τὸ ὕδωρ ταῦτα κατασκευάζει, ἀλλ' ἐν τούτοις ἐστὶ λόγῳ θεωρητὰ μόρια. Cf. Simplicius *Phys.* 460, 12 (DK59A45).

This passage and others like it, along with fr. 10 (**511**), suggest that Anaxagoras was particularly interested in the problem of nutrition. His general principles, 'a portion of everything in everything' and the attraction of like to like, provide him with a simple solution—so simple, indeed, that he may well have arrived at those general principles from consideration of this very problem. For though there are certain inevitable differences of detail, the analogy between macrocosm—the world in which we live—and microcosm—the individual living thing—is in Anaxagoras especially plain.

---

523 *Anaxagoras of Clazomenae, son of Hegesiboulos, held that the first principles of things were the homoeomeries. For it seemed to him quite impossible that anything should come into being from the non-existent or be dissolved into it. Anyhow we take in nourishment that is simple and homogeneous, such as bread or water, and by this are nourished hair, veins, arteries, flesh, sinews, bones and all the other parts of the body. Which being so, we must agree that everything that exists is in the nourishment we take in, and that everything derives its growth from things that exist. There must be in that nourishment some parts that are productive of blood, some of sinews, some of bones, and so on—parts which reason alone can apprehend. For there is no need to refer the fact that bread and water produce all these things to sense-perception; rather, there are in bread and water parts which only reason can apprehend.*

Bread and water, like all other substances, consist of 'seeds'; and each of those 'seeds' contains a 'portion' of everything. (It is true, of course, that bread is not a natural substance, while water, as we have already seen, is a collection of 'seeds' of every sort; but if we substitute wheat, which is a natural substance, for the bread which both Aetius and Simplicius actually cite, it makes no difference to the argument.) When the bread (or wheat) is eaten, it is presumably broken up into its constituent 'seeds'; and since these are themselves infinitely divisible, some of them at least will probably be broken down, by the processes of mastication and digestion, into still smaller seeds. Thereupon those seeds in which flesh predominates proceed, by the attraction of like to like, to join the flesh of the body, hair joins hair, and so on. But since no such thing as a particle of pure substance can ever exist, the flesh from the bread that goes to join the flesh of the body must always carry with it a 'portion' of everything else, and so ensures that the flesh, like the loaf, will continue to contain a 'portion' of everything. Meanwhile, of course, those ingredients in the loaf that are irrelevant to nutrition, copper, for instance, or cork,[1] are for the most part—that is, all except the few 'portions' which are carried to join the flesh or hair of the body—eliminated by the digestive processes.

[1] The examples are Cornford's. Commenting on this passage from Aetius, he writes (*CQ* 24 (1930) 20): 'Corn feeds flesh and bones; therefore it contains particles of flesh and bone. It does not nourish silver or rubies; so why should it contain particles of these?...There is no motive here for asserting "a portion of *every substance*" in bread or corn or any other food as such. The assertion would be gratuitous as well as absurd.' But the argument that the contention 'a portion of everything in everything' is absurdly uneconomical, true as it may be in one way, overlooks the fact, on which comment has already been made above (pp. 380f.), that it is at least economical of effort. It would have been an unending task for Anaxagoras to determine what could and what could not come from what; and it is perhaps characteristic of Presocratic dogmatism that, rather than face that unending task, he should simply have asserted, as we have seen he several times did, 'a portion of everything in everything'.

HOMOEOMERIES

Three of the passages already quoted have used one or other of the words ὁμοιομερῆ or ὁμοιομέρειαι ('homoeomeries' or 'things with like parts'). None of these passages comes from Anaxagoras himself; two, **512** and **521**, come from Aristotle; one, **523**, to which many parallels could be found in Simplicius and others, comes from Aetius. It is actually very unlikely that Anaxagoras himself ever used either word; what the later commentators called ὁμοιομέρειαι, he himself seems to have called 'seeds'. Aristotle, who was probably the first to apply the phrase τὰ ὁμοιομερῆ to the theories of Anaxagoras, seems at least to have used it consistently. But in the later writers the precise meaning of either term is open to question.

Perhaps the most significant of the passages in Aristotle is that at the beginning of **512** in which he tells us that Anaxagoras regarded as primary elements both the opposites and τὰ ὁμοιομερῆ, 'the things with like parts'. Now Aristotle frequently uses the phrase τὰ ὁμοιομερῆ for his own purposes: τὰ ὁμοιομερῆ in his own system were natural substances, such as flesh or bone, metals, or the four elements, every part of which, in his own view, was exactly like the whole. It seems hardly likely that, when he used the phrase in connexion with the theories of Anaxagoras, he should have used it in a different sense. What **512** therefore tells us is that Anaxagoras regarded both the opposites and natural substances as primary elements. It is true that elsewhere in Aristotle, as in **521**, the homoeomerous substances appear alone as the primary elements of Anaxagoras; but that after all does not contradict the fuller statement in **512**. Our own reconstruction of Anaxagoras' system suggests that the fuller statement is correct. For in that system as reconstructed the opposites and the natural substances do indeed together comprise the 'everything' of which everything contains a 'portion'. Even if, therefore, the strictest possible interpretation is placed upon the phrase τὰ ὁμοιομερῆ in Aristotle, that still does not in the slightest degree undermine any arguments adduced in earlier sections of this chapter. It may be that Aristotle uses the phrase in a sense which Anaxagoras himself would not have allowed; whatever the natural substances were or were not in Anaxagoras' system, they were certainly not, as they were in Aristotle's own, homogeneous. But that does not invalidate the truth of the statement that in the system of Anaxagoras the primary elements were the opposites and the natural substances together.

Only in the later writers, when the term ὁμοιομέρεια creeps in alongside τὰ ὁμοιομερῆ, does the problem become more complicated. It is evident from, for instance, Lucretius I, 830 (DK 59 A 44) that the word ὁμοιομέρεια had by now become a catchword that was almost automatically applied to Anaxagoras' physical theories; and it seems very probable that many of those who used it did so without understanding its exact significance.[1] Simplicius, thanks to his familiarity with Anaxagoras' book, is probably our safest guide as to its correct usage. In the passages of Simplicius where either τὰ ὁμοιομερῆ or ὁμοιομέρειαι figure, the former can always be understood in the sense in which Aristotle used it, whereas the latter can usually, if not always, be taken to mean the 'seeds'. The fact is, of course, that the problem is somewhat academic. Not only did Anaxagoras himself apparently never use the words, but also, whatever interpretation be put upon them (except only the impossible interpretation of homogeneity), there is no difficulty in fitting them into the system as reconstructed. But if we have to speculate on why Anaxagoras' 'seeds' came to be called ὁμοιομέρειαι, then the most likely explanation is that, since every 'seed' contains a 'portion' of everything, not only every individual 'seed' but also everything composed of 'seeds' will, in a very real sense, contain similar 'portions'.

[1] Aetius, e.g., is clearly uncertain of the exact implications of the word ὁμοιομέρεια. **523** continues thus: **524** Aetius I, 3, 5 (DK 59 A 46) ἀπὸ τοῦ οὖν ὅμοια τὰ μέρη εἶναι ἐν τῇ τροφῇ τοῖς γεννωμένοις ὁμοιομερείας αὐτὰς ἐκάλεσε καὶ ἀρχὰς τῶν ὄντων ἀπεφήνατο....

SUMMARY OF THE PHYSICAL SYSTEM

Before proceeding to certain special doctrines, it will be as well to add a few last observations on the above reconstruction of the basis of Anaxagoras' system.

The problem which faced Anaxagoras was, of course, exactly the same as faced the atomists. He had to give an account of the origin of the world without either deriving a plurality from an original unity, or allowing the coming-into-being or change of anything real, or, finally, confusing geometrical space with physical matter. Given the same problem, the two solutions could hardly have been more different. Whereas Anaxagoras made matter, like magnitude, infinitely divisible, the atomists main-

---

524 *Since, therefore, the nourishment contains parts that are like the things which it produces, he called them homoeomeries and said that they were the first principles of existing things....*

tained that it was composed of indivisible minima; and whereas Anaxagoras eliminated both coming-into-being and the derivation of plurality from unity by postulating *ab initio* an infinite variety of substances, the atomists regarded all substance as absolutely homogeneous and accounted for the apparent variety of phenomena by mere differences of shape, size, position and arrangement. Both solutions are full of ingenuity, in outline and in detail. But for all their ingenuity, and for all the difference between them, they are each the outcome as much of the Eleatic paradox as of the inventiveness of their respective authors.

SPECIAL DOCTRINES

(i) *Innumerable worlds?*

525 Fr. 4, Simplicius *Phys.* 35, 3 (continuing **510**) ...καὶ ἀνθρώπους τε συμπαγῆναι καὶ τὰ ἄλλα ȝῷα ὅσα ψυχὴν ἔχει. καὶ τοῖς γε ἀνθρώποισιν εἶναι καὶ πόλεις συνῳκημένας καὶ ἔργα κατεσκευασμένα, ὥσπερ παρ' ἡμῖν, καὶ ἠέλιόν τε αὐτοῖσιν εἶναι καὶ σελήνην καὶ τὰ ἄλλα, ὥσπερ παρ' ἡμῖν, καὶ τὴν γῆν αὐτοῖσι φύειν πολλά τε καὶ παντοῖα, ὧν ἐκεῖνοι τὰ ὀνήιστα συνενεγκάμενοι εἰς τὴν οἴκησιν χρῶνται. ταῦτα μὲν οὖν μοι λέλεκται περὶ τῆς ἀποκρίσιος, ὅτι οὐκ ἂν παρ' ἡμῖν μόνον ἀποκριθείη, ἀλλὰ καὶ ἄλλῃ. (**496** follows.)

526 Simplicius *Phys.* 157, 9 καὶ μέντοι εἰπὼν 'ἐνεῖναι πολλά... ἡδονάς' (from **510**), καὶ 'ἀνθρώπους γε συμπαγῆναι...ψυχὴν ἔχει', ἐπάγει 'καὶ τοῖς γε ἀνθρώποισιν...χρῶνται' (from **525**). καὶ ὅτι μὲν ἑτέραν τινὰ διακόσμησιν παρὰ τὴν παρ' ἡμῖν αἰνίττεται, δηλοῖ τὸ 'ὥσπερ παρ' ἡμῖν' οὐχ ἅπαξ μόνον εἰρημένον. ὅτι δὲ οὐδὲ αἰσθητὴν μὲν ἐκείνην οἴεται, τῷ χρόνῳ δὲ ταύτης προηγησαμένην, δηλοῖ τὸ 'ὧν ἐκεῖνοι τὰ ὀνήιστα συνενεγκάμενοι εἰς τὴν οἴκησιν χρῶνται'. οὐ γὰρ 'ἐχρῶντο' εἶπεν, ἀλλὰ 'χρῶνται'.

---

525 (*We must suppose that*) *men have been formed and the other animals that have life; and that the men have inhabited cities and cultivated fields, just as we have here; and sun and moon and so on, just as we have; and that the earth brings forth for them all manner of produce, of which they garner the best into their houses and use it. So much, then, have I said about the process of separating off—that separation would have taken place not only here with us but elsewhere too.*

526 *Having said, however, 'there are many things...and tastes'* [from **510**] *and 'men have been formed...have life', he adds 'the men have...and use it'* [from **525**]. *That he is hinting at another world in addition to our own is clear from the phrase, which he uses more than once, 'just as we have'. And that he does not regard this other world as a perceptible world which preceded this world in time is clear from the words 'of which they garner the best into their houses and use it'. For he did not say 'used' but 'use'. Nor does*

ἀλλ' οὐδὲ ὡς νῦν κατ' ἄλλας τινὰς οἰκήσεις ὁμοίας οὔσης καταστάσεως τῇ παρ' ἡμῖν. οὐ γὰρ εἶπε 'τὸν ἥλιον καὶ τὴν σελήνην εἶναι παρ' ἐκείνοις ὥσπερ καὶ παρ' ἡμῖν', ἀλλ' 'ἥλιον καὶ σελήνην, ὥσπερ παρ' ἡμῖν', ὡς δὴ περὶ ἄλλων λέγων. ἀλλὰ ταῦτα μὲν εἴτε οὕτως εἴτε ἄλλως ἔχει, ζητεῖν ἄξιον.

Many scholars have maintained, on the strength of **525**, that Anaxagoras must have believed in a plurality of contemporary worlds. Yet some of the ancient evidence seems to suggest that he believed in one world only. Admittedly Aetius at one point (II, 4, 6, DK 59 A 65) lists Anaxagoras among those who held that the world was perishable, thereby suggesting that he believed in a succession of worlds; but Aetius, as was shown in the case of Anaximander (p. 124), was confused on this issue, and elsewhere (II, 1, 2, DK 59 A 63) lists Anaxagoras instead among those who believed in one world only. Simplicius is probably our most reliable witness, since he certainly had the relevant part of Anaxagoras' book before him; and though elsewhere in his commentary on the *Physics* (e.g. 154, 29, DK 59 A 64) he speaks of Anaxagoras' world in the singular, that need mean no more than that he was there concerned only with the world we know.[1] **526** gives us his considered view, and clearly acknowledges his uncertainty on the point. It is perhaps just possible that, as Cornford maintained, Anaxagoras is referring in **525**, not to other worlds, but to distant and unknown parts of this earth's surface, comparable with the 'hollows in the earth' in the myth in Plato's *Phaedo* (109 A ff.). But since the question was anyhow not for Anaxagoras (as it was for the atomists, see p. 412) one which arose inevitably from his first principles and consequently demanded a definite answer, it seems wisest to follow the guidance of Simplicius in **526** and leave the question open.

[1] Aristotle's remarks about Anaxagoras at, e.g., *Phys.* A 4, 187 a 23 ff., Θ 1, 250 b 18 ff., though they have been used as evidence that Anaxagoras believed in only one world, are either so generalized that they are of little value as evidence on this particular question, or else suggest only that in Aristotle's opinion Anaxagoras regarded this world (irrespective of the existence of others) as imperishable.

---

he mean that they are now inhabiting other regions of the same world as our own. For he did not say 'they have the sun and the moon just as we too have' but 'sun and moon, as we have'—as if he were talking of a different sun and moon. But it is debatable whether or not these considerations are valid.

(ii) *Astronomy and meteorology*

527 Fr. 18, Plutarch *de fac. in orb. lun.* 16, 929B ἥλιος ἐντίθησι τῇ σελήνῃ τὸ λαμπρόν.

528 Fr. 19, Σ BT *in Iliadem* 17, 547 Ἶριν δὲ καλέομεν τὸ ἐν τῇσι νεφέλῃσιν ἀντιλάμπον τῷ ἡλίῳ. χειμῶνος οὖν ἐστι σύμβολον· τὸ γὰρ περιχεόμενον ὕδωρ τῷ νέφει ἄνεμον ἐποίησεν ἢ ἐξέχεεν ὄμβρον.

529 Hippolytus *Ref.* I, 8, 3–10 (DK59A42) τὴν δὲ γῆν τῷ σχήματι πλατεῖαν εἶναι καὶ μένειν μετέωρον διὰ τὸ μέγεθος καὶ διὰ τὸ μὴ εἶναι κενὸν καὶ διὰ τὸ τὸν ἀέρα ἰσχυρότατον ὄντα φέρειν ἐποχουμένην τὴν γῆν. (4) τῶν δ' ἐπὶ γῆς ὑγρῶν τὴν μὲν θάλασσαν ὑπάρξαι ⟨ἔκ⟩ τε τῶν ἐν αὐτῇ ὑδάτων, ⟨ὧν⟩ ἐξατμισθέν⟨των⟩ τὰ ὑποστάντα οὕτως γεγονέναι, καὶ ἀπὸ τῶν καταρρευσάντων ποταμῶν. (5) τοὺς δὲ ποταμοὺς καὶ ἀπὸ τῶν ὄμβρων λαμβάνειν τὴν ὑπόστασιν καὶ ἐξ ὑδάτων τῶν ἐν τῇ γῇ. εἶναι γὰρ αὐτὴν κοίλην καὶ ἔχειν ὕδωρ ἐν τοῖς κοιλώμασιν.... (6) ἥλιον δὲ καὶ σελήνην καὶ πάντα τὰ ἄστρα λίθους εἶναι ἐμπύρους συμπεριληφθέντας ὑπὸ τῆς αἰθέρος περιφορᾶς. εἶναι δ' ὑποκάτω τῶν ἄστρων ἡλίῳ καὶ σελήνῃ σώματά τινα συμπεριφερόμενα ἡμῖν ἀόρατα. (7) τῆς δὲ θερμότητος μὴ αἰσθάνεσθαι τῶν ἄστρων διὰ τὸ μακρὰν εἶναι [καὶ διὰ] τὴν ἀπόστασιν τῆς γῆς· ἔτι δὲ οὐχ ὁμοίως θερμὰ τῷ ἡλίῳ διὰ τὸ χώραν ἔχειν ψυχροτέραν. εἶναι δὲ τὴν σελήνην κατωτέρω τοῦ ἡλίου πλησιώτερον ἡμῶν. (8) ὑπερέχειν δὲ τὸν ἥλιον μεγέθει τὴν Πελοπόννησον. τὸ δὲ φῶς τὴν σελήνην μὴ ἴδιον ἔχειν, ἀλλὰ ἀπὸ τοῦ ἡλίου. τὴν δὲ τῶν ἄστρων περιφορὰν ὑπὸ γῆν γίνεσθαι.

---

527 *The sun indues the moon with brightness.*

528 *We call the reflexion of the sun in the clouds a rainbow. So it is a sign of storm; for the moisture that suffuses the cloud either creates a wind or spills forth rain.*

529 *The earth (he thinks) is flat in shape, and stays suspended where it is because of its size, because there is no void and because the air, which is very strong, keeps the earth afloat on it.* (4) *Of the moisture on the earth, the sea came from the waters in the earth, the evaporation of which gave rise to all that has emerged, and from the rivers that flow into it.* (5) *Rivers owe their origin partly to rain, partly to the waters in the earth; for the earth is hollow, and in its hollows contains water....* (6) *The sun, the moon and all the stars are red-hot stones which the rotation of the aither carries round with it. Beneath the stars are certain bodies, invisible to us, that are carried round with the sun and moon.* (7) *We do not feel the heat of the stars because they are so far from the earth; moreover, they are not as hot as the sun because they occupy a colder region. The moon is beneath the sun and nearer to us.* (8) *The sun exceeds the Peloponnese in size. The moon has not any light of its own but derives it from the sun. The stars in their revolution pass beneath the earth.*

(9) ἐκλείπειν δὲ τὴν σελήνην γῆς ἀντιφραττούσης, ἐνίοτε δὲ καὶ τῶν ὑποκάτω τῆς σελήνης, τὸν δὲ ἥλιον ταῖς νουμηνίαις σελήνης ἀντιφραττούσης.... (10)...ἔφη δὲ γηίνην εἶναι τὴν σελήνην ἔχειν τε ἐν αὐτῇ πεδία καὶ φάραγγας. Cf. Diog. L. II, 8–9 (DK59A1).

527 and **528** are included mainly to show that Anaxagoras did indeed concern himself with the usual astronomical and meteorological questions. It is from the long passage of which **529** is a part that we get most of our information on the subject; and **529** for the most part speaks for itself. Clearly Anaxagoras' astronomy is much more rational than most of his predecessors', especially perhaps the view that the sun, moon and stars are huge incandescent stones. There is a story preserved by Diogenes Laertius[1] and Pliny that Anaxagoras predicted the fall of the large meteorite which fell at Aegospotami in 467 B.C. (cf. p. 439). Certainly this event caused a considerable stir; and though the suggestion that Anaxagoras predicted it is absurd, it may well have contributed towards his belief that the heavenly bodies were made of stone. It is because of their solidity, as **517** has already suggested, that they were originally thrown off from the earth at the centre of the cosmic revolution to take up their positions nearer the periphery. Presumably meteorites are heavenly bodies which, despite the speed of the revolution which normally keeps them aloft, have been drawn back to the earth by the familiar tendency of the heavy to move towards the centre of the revolution.

[1] **530** Diog. L. II, 10 (DK59A1) φασὶ δ' αὐτὸν προειπεῖν τὴν περὶ Αἰγὸς ποταμοὺς γενομένην τοῦ λίθου πτῶσιν, ὃν εἶπεν ἐκ τοῦ ἡλίου πεσεῖσθαι. Cf. Marmor Parium 57 and Pliny *N.H.* II, 149 (both DK59A11).

(iii) *Biology*

531 Fr. 22, Athenaeus II, 57D τὸ καλούμενον ὄρνιθος γάλα τὸ ἐν τοῖς ᾠοῖς λευκόν.

532 Hippolytus *Ref.* I, 8, 12 (DK59A42) ζῷα δὲ τὴν μὲν ἀρχὴν

---

(9) *Eclipses of the moon are due to its being screened by the earth, or, sometimes, by the bodies beneath the moon; those of the sun to screening by the moon when it is new.... (10) ...He held that the moon was made of earth, and had plains and ravines on it.*

530 *They say that he foretold the fall of the stone at Aegospotami, saying that it would fall from the sun.*

531 *What is called 'birds' milk' is the white of the egg.*

ἐν ὑγρῷ γενέσθαι, μετὰ ταῦτα δὲ ἐξ ἀλλήλων. Cf. Diog. L. II, 9 *ad fin.* (DK 59 A 1).

533 Theophrastus *Hist. plant.* III, 1, 4 Ἀναξαγόρας μὲν τὸν ἀέρα πάντων φάσκων ἔχειν σπέρματα καὶ ταῦτα συγκαταφερόμενα τῷ ὕδατι γεννᾶν τὰ φυτά....

531 is again quoted merely to show that Anaxagoras did include detailed doctrines in his book: its point presumably is that the white of an egg is the embryo's food. Several equally detailed theories are attributed to him by the ancient authorities, including Aristotle; but they are of no great importance for present purposes. The two most important of his biological theories are those in **532** and **533**. In his belief that life originated in 'the moist' he followed Anaximander (see pp. 141 f.), but the notion that it was brought down to the earth with the rain is curious.[1] All living things, of course, from plants at the bottom of the scale to man at the top,[2] have a portion of Mind (see **503** and **509**). Before living things came into existence Mind was presumably dispersed evenly throughout the mixture; but from the time when life originated it evidently began to localize itself in living things, so that there are now, according to **509**, only '*some* things in which there is Mind also'.

[1] This may be a development of the popular idea, exemplified in Aeschylus (see **26**), that rain is the semen of Ouranos, by which Gaia is fertilized.

[2] **534** Plutarch *Quaest. phys.* 1, 911 D ȝῷον γὰρ ἔγγειον τὸ φυτὸν εἶναι οἱ περὶ Πλάτωνα καὶ Ἀναξαγόραν καὶ Δημόκριτον οἴονται. Also **535** Ar. *de part. an.* Δ 10, 687 a 7 (DK 59 A 102) Ἀναξαγόρας μὲν οὖν φησι διὰ τὸ χεῖρας ἔχειν φρονιμώτατον εἶναι τῶν ȝῴων ἄνθρωπον.

(iv) *Sensation*

536 Fr. 21, Sextus *adv. math.* VII, 90 ὑπ' ἀφαυρότητος αὐτῶν (*sc.* τῶν αἰσθήσεων) οὐ δυνατοί ἐσμεν κρίνειν τἀληθές.

---

532 *Animals (he says) originally arose in the moisture, but later from one another.*

533 *Anaxagoras, when he says that the air contains the seeds of all things and that it is these seeds which, when carried down with the rain, give rise to plants....*

534 *The followers of Plato, Anaxagoras and Democritus regard a plant as an animal fixed in the earth.*

535 *Anaxagoras says, then, that it is his possession of hands that makes man the wisest of living things.*

536 *From the weakness of our senses we cannot judge the truth.*

537 Fr. 21*a*, *ibid.* VII, 140 ὄψις γὰρ τῶν ἀδήλων τὰ φαινόμενα.

538 Theophrastus *de sensu* 27ff. (DK59A92) Ἀναξαγόρας δὲ γίνεσθαι μὲν (*sc.* τὰ αἰσθητὰ) τοῖς ἐναντίοις· τὸ γὰρ ὅμοιον ἀπαθὲς ὑπὸ τοῦ ὁμοίου..., τὸ γὰρ ὁμοίως θερμὸν καὶ ψυχρὸν οὔτε θερμαίνειν οὔτε ψύχειν πλησιάζον οὐδὲ δὴ τὸ γλυκὺ καὶ τὸ ὀξὺ δι' αὐτῶν γνωρίζειν, ἀλλὰ τῷ μὲν θερμῷ τὸ ψυχρόν, τῷ δ' ἁλμυρῷ τὸ πότιμον, τῷ δ' ὀξεῖ τὸ γλυκὺ κατὰ τὴν ἔλλειψιν τὴν ἑκάστου· πάντα γὰρ ἐνυπάρχειν φησὶν ἐν ἡμῖν....ἅπασαν δ' αἴσθησιν μετὰ λύπης, ὅπερ ἂν δόξειεν ἀκόλουθον εἶναι τῇ ὑποθέσει· πᾶν γὰρ τὸ ἀνόμοιον ἁπτόμενον πόνον παρέχει. φανερὸν δὲ τοῦτο τῷ τε τοῦ χρόνου πλήθει καὶ τῇ τῶν αἰσθητῶν ὑπερβολῇ.

Like the other post-Parmenidean pluralists, Anaxagoras had to give an account of perception that would re-establish its validity. These three passages are all concerned with the senses, but otherwise they have little in common. **536**, as we are told by Sextus who preserved it, was concerned with imperceptible gradations of colour, and its general point seems to have been that though our senses show us what 'portions' predominate in a thing they are not adequate to reveal all the other 'portions' which that thing must contain. **537**, on the other hand (which may perhaps come from a discussion of epistemology rather than of perception), suggests that from what we can see we are enabled to imagine also what we cannot see. **538** contains only the most important excerpts from a detailed account of Anaxagoras' theories of perception. These few sentences suffice to show that in this field too Anaxagoras marks an advance upon most of his predecessors. His theory may have been developed in conscious opposition to that of Empedocles, who believed in perception of like by like (see **454**); but the notion that the perception of unlike by unlike is, as it were, an imperceptible pain is original and subtle.

---

537 *Appearances are a glimpse of the obscure.*

538 *Anaxagoras thinks that perception is by opposites, for like is not affected by like.... A thing that is as warm or as cold as we are does not either warm us or cool us by its approach, nor can we recognize sweetness or bitterness by their like; rather we know cold by warm, fresh by salt and sweet by bitter in proportion to our deficiency in each. For everything, he says, is in us already....Every perception is accompanied by pain, a consequence that would seem to follow from his hypothesis; for everything unlike produces pain by its contact; and the presence of this pain becomes clear either from too long a duration or from an excess of sensation.*

CHAPTER XVI

ARCHELAUS OF ATHENS

DATE AND LIFE

539 Diogenes Laertius II, 16 (DK 60 A 1) Ἀρχέλαος Ἀθηναῖος ἢ Μιλήσιος, πατρὸς Ἀπολλοδώρου, ὡς δέ τινες, Μίδωνος, μαθητὴς Ἀναξαγόρου, διδάσκαλος Σωκράτους· οὗτος πρῶτος ἐκ τῆς Ἰωνίας τὴν φυσικὴν φιλοσοφίαν μετήγαγεν Ἀθήναζε, καὶ ἐκλήθη φυσικός, παρὸ καὶ ἔληξεν ἐν αὐτῷ ἡ φυσικὴ φιλοσοφία, Σωκράτους τὴν ἠθικὴν εἰσαγαγόντος. ἔοικεν δὲ καὶ οὗτος ἅψασθαι τῆς ἠθικῆς. καὶ γὰρ περὶ νόμων πεφιλοσόφηκε καὶ καλῶν καὶ δικαίων.

The precise date of Archelaus is uncertain. Diogenes is almost certainly wrong in saying that Archelaus first brought physical speculation to Athens; that distinction probably belongs to Anaxagoras. Likewise the statement that physical philosophy ended with him is very dubious;[1] even Leucippus, let alone Democritus, was probably later than Archelaus. But the tradition that Archelaus was a pupil of Anaxagoras and teacher of Socrates is too well attested to be doubted,[2] and it gives us at least an approximate date. His importance lies chiefly in these distinguished associations; in comparison with either his master or his pupil his direct contribution to philosophy is very small. But he is of a certain interest as indicating the straits to which all but the very greatest of the later physicists were driven in their search for an original cosmology.

[1] This is doubtless merely an instance of the passion for organizing history into 'Ages'. Socrates introduces the 'Age of Ethics', so the 'Age of Physical Philosophy' must stop abruptly.

[2] See **541**, and also **540** Diog. L. II, 23 Ἴων δὲ ὁ Χῖος (see p. 302) καὶ νέον ὄντα (*sc.* Socrates) εἰς Σάμον σὺν Ἀρχελάῳ ἀποδημῆσαι. Cf. also Porphyry *Hist. phil.* fr. 11 Nauck (DK 60 A 3).

---

539 *Archelaus, of Athens or else Miletus, son of Apollodorus or, according to some accounts, of Midon, was a pupil of Anaxagoras and teacher of Socrates; it was he who first transferred physical philosophy from Ionia to Athens, and he was called a physicist. Moreover, physical philosophy came to an end with him, owing to Socrates' introduction of ethics. Archelaus too seems to have touched upon ethical questions, for he speculated as well about law, goodness and justice.*

540 *Ion of Chios says that in his youth Socrates went away with Archelaus to Samos.*

COSMOLOGY AND ZOOGONY

541 Simplicius *Phys.* 27, 23 καὶ Ἀρχέλαος ὁ Ἀθηναῖος, ᾧ καὶ Σωκράτη συγγεγονέναι φασὶν Ἀναξαγόρου γενομένῳ μαθητῇ, ἐν μὲν τῇ γενέσει τοῦ κόσμου καὶ τοῖς ἄλλοις πειρᾶταί τι φέρειν ἴδιον, τὰς ἀρχὰς δὲ τὰς αὐτὰς ἀποδίδωσιν ὥσπερ Ἀναξαγόρας. οὗτοι μὲν οὖν ἀπείρους τῷ πλήθει καὶ ἀνομογενεῖς τὰς ἀρχὰς λέγουσι, τὰς ὁμοιομερείας τιθέντες ἀρχάς....

542 Hippolytus *Ref.* 1, 9, 1 Ἀρχέλαος τὸ μὲν γένος Ἀθηναῖος, υἱὸς δὲ Ἀπολλοδώρου. οὗτος ἔφη τὴν μίξιν τῆς ὕλης ὁμοίως Ἀναξαγόρᾳ τάς τε ἀρχὰς ὡσαύτως. οὗτος δὲ τῷ νῷ ἐνυπάρχειν τι εὐθέως μῖγμα. (2) εἶναι ⟨δ'⟩ ἀρχὴν τῆς κινήσεως ⟨τὸ⟩ ἀποκρίνεσθαι ἀπ' ἀλλήλων τὸ θερμὸν καὶ τὸ ψυχρόν, καὶ τὸ μὲν θερμὸν κινεῖσθαι, τὸ δὲ ψυχρὸν ἠρεμεῖν.[1] τηκόμενον δὲ τὸ ὕδωρ εἰς μέσον ῥεῖν, ἐν ᾧ καὶ κατακαιόμενον ἀέρα γίνεσθαι καὶ γῆν, ὧν τὸ μὲν ἄνω φέρεσθαι, τὸ δὲ ὑφίστασθαι κάτω. (3) τὴν μὲν οὖν γῆν ἠρεμεῖν καὶ γενέσθαι διὰ ταῦτα, κεῖσθαι δ' ἐν μέσῳ οὐδὲν μέρος οὖσαν, ὡς εἰπεῖν, τοῦ παντός. ⟨τὸν δ' ἀέρα κρατεῖν τοῦ παντὸς⟩ [Roeper, Diels] ἐκδεδομένον ἐκ τῆς πυρώσεως, ἀφ' οὗ πρῶτον ἀποκαιομένου τὴν τῶν ἀστέρων εἶναι φύσιν, ὧν μέγιστον μὲν ἥλιον, δεύτερον δὲ σελήνην, τῶν δὲ ἄλλων τὰ μὲν ἐλάττω τὰ δὲ μείζω. (4) ἐπικλιθῆναι δὲ τὸν οὐρανόν φησι καὶ οὕτως τὸν ἥλιον ἐπὶ τῆς γῆς ποιῆσαι φῶς καὶ τόν τε ἀέρα ποιῆσαι διαφανῆ καὶ τὴν γῆν ξηράν. λίμνην γὰρ εἶναι τὸ πρῶτον, ἅτε κύκλῳ μὲν οὖσαν ὑψηλήν, μέσον δὲ κοίλην. σημεῖον δὲ φέρει τῆς

---

541 *Archelaus of Athens, the pupil of Anaxagoras with whom Socrates is said to have associated, tries to introduce something original of his own into cosmogony and other subjects, but still gives the same first principles as Anaxagoras had. Both hold that the first principles are infinite in number and different in kind, and they posit the homoeomeries as principles....*

542 (*1*) *Archelaus was by birth an Athenian, the son of Apollodorus. He believed in a material mixture like that of Anaxagoras and his first principles were the same; but he maintained that from the outset there was a certain mixture immanent in Mind.* (*2*) *The origin of motion was the separation one from the other of the hot and the cold, of which the former moves, the latter stays still. When water is liquefied it flows to the centre, and there it is burnt up to become air and earth, the former of which is borne upwards, while the latter takes up a position below.* (*3*) *For these reasons, then, the earth came into being, and lies at rest in the centre, forming no appreciable fraction of the whole universe. ⟨The air⟩ produced by the conflagration ⟨controls the universe⟩, and from its original combustion comes the substance of the heavenly bodies. Of these the sun is the biggest, the moon the second, and of the rest some are smaller, some larger.* (*4*) *He says that the heavens are inclined, with the result that the sun gave light on the earth, made the air transparent, and the earth dry. For it was originally a marsh, being lofty around the edge and hollow in the*

κοιλότητος ὅτι ὁ ἥλιος οὐχ ἅμα ἀνατέλλει τε καὶ δύεται πᾶσιν, ὅπερ ἔδει συμβαίνειν εἴπερ ἦν ὁμαλή. (5) περὶ δὲ ζῴων φησίν, ὅτι θερμαινομένης τῆς γῆς τὸ πρῶτον ἐν τῷ κάτω μέρει, ὅπου τὸ θερμὸν καὶ τὸ ψυχρὸν ἐμίσγετο ἀνεφαίνετο τά τε ἄλλα ζῷα πολλὰ καὶ οἱ ἄνθρωποι, ἅπαντα τὴν αὐτὴν δίαιταν ἔχοντα ἐκ τῆς ἰλύος τρεφόμενα (ἦν δὲ ὀλιγοχρόνια), ὕστερον δὲ αὐτοῖς ἡ ἐξ ἀλλήλων γένεσις συνέστη. (6) καὶ διεκρίθησαν ἄνθρωποι ἀπὸ τῶν ἄλλων καὶ ἡγεμόνας καὶ νόμους καὶ τέχνας καὶ πόλεις καὶ τὰ ἄλλα συνέστησαν. νοῦν δὲ λέγει πᾶσιν ἐμφύεσθαι ζῴοις ὁμοίως. χρῆσθαι γὰρ ἕκαστον καὶ τῶν ζῴων τῷ νῷ, τὸ μὲν βραδυτέρως, τὸ δὲ ταχυτέρως.

[1] Cf. the only surviving fragment of Archelaus, *ap.* Plut. *de primo frig.* 21 954F: ἡ ψυχρότης δεσμός ἐστιν ('coldness is the bond').

It would appear from these passages, which of course derive ultimately from Theophrastus,[1] that Archelaus took over the system of Anaxagoras but at numerous points, some fundamental, some superficial, made his own modifications or corrections. The following are the most interesting features of the revised cosmology:

(1) *Mind.* Whereas Mind in the system of Anaxagoras had been 'mixed with nothing' and had derived its power from its purity (see **503**), in Archelaus it seems to be deprived of its purity (**542**, § 1)[2] and therewith, perhaps, of its creative power.

(2) *Primary substance.* Though some of the ancient authorities suggest that Archelaus made air the primary substance (and one, Epiphanius, even that he chose earth), there can be little doubt that **541** and **542** preserve the most reliable tradition and that he started, like Anaxagoras, with 'seeds' or 'homoeomeries'. Whereas, however, Anaxagoras had made Mind initiate motion and so cause the separating off of 'the dense, the moist, the cold and the dark' from 'the rare, the hot and the dry' (see **516**), Archelaus seems (though the evidence is conflicting: cf. DK 60 A 10 and 18) to make the apparently automatic separation of the hot from the

---

middle. He adduces as a proof of this hollowness the fact that the sun does not rise and set at the same time for all men, as would inevitably happen if the earth were flat. (5) *On the subject of animals, he holds that when the earth was originally getting warm in the lower region, where the hot and the cold were mingled, many animals began to appear, including men, all with the same manner of life and all deriving their nourishment from the slime. These were short-lived; but later they began to be born from one another.* (6) *Men were distinguished from animals, and established rulers, laws, crafts, cities and so on. Mind, he says, is inborn in all animals alike; for each of the animals, as well as man, makes use of Mind, though some more rapidly than others.*

cold the cause of movement (**542**, §2). Thereby he exaggerates the tendency in Anaxagoras, to which Plato so strongly objected (see p. 384 n.), to delegate the responsibility of Mind to the opposites.

(3) *The four world-masses.* The method by which Archelaus brought the four world-masses into being from the opposites is somewhat obscure and very peculiar. Water seems to have been 'melted' or 'liquefied' from 'the cold' in its interaction with 'the hot' (which suggests, perhaps, that 'the cold' was conceived of as ice), and when it thereupon flowed to the centre, it was 'burnt up', again in its interaction with 'the hot', to form earth and air. The mobility of 'the hot' (i.e. fire), and the immobility of 'the cold' (i.e. perhaps ice, producing first water, and thence not only the stationary earth but also fluid air[3]), and the reaction between them, seem to constitute an essential and, so far as we can judge, an original feature of Archelaus' cosmogony.[4] There is no obvious motive for this revision of Anaxagoras except perhaps the desire to bring the Empedoclean 'elements' into greater prominence.

(4) *Zoogony.* The zoogony of Archelaus seems to represent a reversion from that of Anaxagoras, in which seeds were carried down to earth with the rain (see **533**), to that of Anaximander, in which 'living things arose from the moist element as it was evaporated by the sun' (see **139**).

[1] Diog. L. v, 42 lists among the writings of Theophrastus Περὶ τῶν Ἀρχελάου ᾱ ('1 book on the theories of Archelaus'); cf. pp. 3f.

[2] The relevant sentence of **542**, §1 is, however, so curiously expressed if this is really what it means that Zeller suggested reading τῷ νῷ συνυπάρχειν.

[3] Cf. **543** Diog. L. ii, 17 (DK 60 A 1) τηκόμενόν φησι τὸ ὕδωρ ὑπὸ τοῦ θερμοῦ, καθὸ μὲν εἰς τὸ ⟨κάτω διὰ τὸ⟩ πυρῶδες συνίσταται, ποιεῖν γῆν· καθὸ δὲ περιρρεῖ, ἀέρα γεννᾶν. The supplement by Diels, or something very like it, seems essential.

[4] This theory is extended in the Hippocratic *de victu*, an eclectic and very superficial quasi-philosophical treatise written, probably, toward the end of the fourth century B.C.

CONCLUSION

In general, it is hard to resist the conclusion that Archelaus was a second-rate thinker, motivated by the desire to revise the system

---

543 *He holds that water is liquefied by the hot; and in so far as it comes together to the lower region owing to the fiery element, it forms earth; in so far as it flows around, it creates air.*

of Anaxagoras by the inclusion of as many as possible of the doctrines of his most eminent predecessors. From Anaximander he borrowed, besides his biological theories, the primacy of the hot and the cold; from Anaximenes he apparently borrowed the doctrine of the condensation and rarefaction of air (see **143**);[1] from Empedocles he seems to have taken the four 'elements'; and from Anaxagoras he inherited, with a number of modifications of detail such as that concerning the shape of the earth (**542**, §4), almost everything else. It is hardly surprising that the resulting synthesis is lacking in great interest or importance.[2]

[1] Cf. **544** Aetius I, 3, 6 (DK 60 A 7) Ἀρχέλαος... ἀέρα ἄπειρον (*sc.* ἀρχὴν ἔφη εἶναι), καὶ τὴν περὶ αὐτὸν πυκνότητα καὶ μάνωσιν. τούτων δὲ τὸ μὲν εἶναι πῦρ τὸ δ' ὕδωρ.

[2] If more were known of Archelaus' ethical doctrines, this evaluation might possibly have to be revised. Almost all we are told about them is summarized in the following sentence, which comes very soon after **539**: **545** Diog. L. II, 16 (DK 60 A 1) καὶ τὸ δίκαιον εἶναι καὶ τὸ αἰσχρὸν οὐ φύσει, ἀλλὰ νόμῳ. This is of course the well-known Sophistic view, which may well have been read into Archelaus (perhaps, as Zeller suggested, because he had said something to the effect that men were at first without laws or morals and had only attained to them in course of time (cf. **542**, §6)) in a misguided attempt to credit the teacher of Socrates with a decent minimum of ethical teaching.

---

544 *Archelaus... (held that the first principle was) infinite air, with its condensation and rarefaction, the former of which was water, the latter fire.*

545 *(He maintained that) right and wrong exist only by convention, not by nature.*

CHAPTER XVII

THE ATOMISTS: LEUCIPPUS OF MILETUS AND DEMOCRITUS OF ABDERA

INDIVIDUAL CONTRIBUTIONS, AND DATES

546 Simplicius *Phys.* 28, 4 (=Theophrastus *Phys. Op.* fr. 8) Λεύκιππος δὲ ὁ Ἐλεάτης ἢ Μιλήσιος (ἀμφοτέρως γὰρ λέγεται περὶ αὐτοῦ), κοινωνήσας Παρμενίδῃ τῆς φιλοσοφίας, οὐ τὴν αὐτὴν ἐβάδισε Παρμενίδῃ καὶ Ξενοφάνει περὶ τῶν ὄντων ὁδόν, ἀλλ' ὡς δοκεῖ τὴν ἐναντίαν. ἐκείνων γὰρ ἓν καὶ ἀκίνητον καὶ ἀγένητον καὶ πεπερασμένον ποιούντων τὸ πᾶν καὶ τὸ μὴ ὂν μηδὲ ζητεῖν συγχωρούντων, οὗτος ἄπειρα καὶ ἀεὶ κινούμενα ὑπέθετο στοιχεῖα τὰς ἀτόμους καὶ τῶν ἐν αὐτοῖς σχημάτων ἄπειρον τὸ πλῆθος διὰ τὸ μηδὲν μᾶλλον τοιοῦτον ἢ τοιοῦτον εἶναι, καὶ γένεσιν καὶ μεταβολὴν ἀδιάλειπτον ἐν τοῖς οὖσι θεωρῶν. ἔτι δὲ οὐδὲν μᾶλλον τὸ ὂν ἢ τὸ μὴ ὂν ὑπάρχειν, καὶ αἴτια ὁμοίως εἶναι τοῖς γινομένοις ἄμφω. τὴν γὰρ τῶν ἀτόμων οὐσίαν ναστὴν καὶ πλήρη ὑποτιθέμενος ὂν ἔλεγεν εἶναι καὶ ἐν τῷ κενῷ φέρεσθαι, ὅπερ μὴ ὂν ἐκάλει καὶ οὐκ ἔλαττον τοῦ ὄντος εἶναί φησι. παραπλησίως δὲ καὶ ὁ ἑταῖρος αὐτοῦ Δημόκριτος ὁ Ἀβδηρίτης ἀρχὰς ἔθετο τὸ πλῆρες καὶ τὸ κενόν....

547 Diogenes Laertius x, 13 τοῦτον (*sc.* Epicurus) Ἀπολλόδωρος ἐν Χρονικοῖς Ναυσιφάνους ἀκοῦσαί φησι καὶ Πραξιφάνους· αὐτὸς δὲ οὔ φησιν, ἀλλ' ἑαυτοῦ ἐν τῇ πρὸς Εὐρύλοχον ἐπιστολῇ.

---

546 *Leucippus of Elea or Miletus (both accounts are current) had associated with Parmenides in philosophy, but in his view of reality he did not tread the same path as Parmenides and Xenophanes, but rather, it seems, the opposite path. For while they regarded the whole as one, motionless, uncreated and limited and forbade even the search for what is not, he posited innumerable elements in perpetual motion—namely the atoms—and held that the number of their shapes was infinite, on the ground that there was no reason why any atom should be of one shape rather than another; for he observed too that coming-into-being and change are incessant in the world. Further he held that not-being exists as well as being, and the two are equally the causes of things coming-into-being. The nature of atoms he supposed to be compact and full; that, he said, was being, and it moved in the void, which he called not-being and held to exist no less than being. In the same way his associate Democritus of Abdera posited as principles the full and the void....*

547 *Apollodorus in the* Chronicles *says that Epicurus was instructed by Nausiphanes and Praxiphanes; but Epicurus himself denies this, saying in the letter to Eurylochus that*

ἀλλ' οὐδὲ Λεύκιππόν τινα γεγενῆσθαί φησι φιλόσοφον οὔτε αὐτὸς οὔτε Ἕρμαρχος, ὃν ἔνιοί φασι (καὶ Ἀπολλόδωρος ὁ Ἐπικούρειος) διδάσκαλον Δημοκρίτου γεγενῆσθαι.

548 Cicero *Academica pr.* II, 37, 118 Leucippus plenum et inane; Democritus huic in hoc similis, uberior in ceteris.

549 Diogenes Laertius IX, 34 Δημόκριτος Ἡγησιστράτου, οἱ δὲ Ἀθηνοκρίτου, τινὲς Δαμασίππου, Ἀβδηρίτης ἤ, ὡς ἔνιοι, Μιλήσιος. . . . ὕστερον δὲ Λευκίππῳ παρέβαλε καὶ Ἀναξαγόρᾳ κατά τινας, ἔτεσιν ὢν αὐτοῦ νεώτερος τετταράκοντα. . . . (41) γέγονε δὲ τοῖς χρόνοις, ὡς αὐτός φησιν ἐν τῷ Μικρῷ διακόσμῳ, νέος κατὰ πρεσβύτην Ἀναξαγόραν, ἔτεσιν αὐτοῦ νεώτερος τετταράκοντα. συντετάχθαι δέ φησι τὸν Μικρὸν διάκοσμον ἔτεσιν ὕστερον τῆς Ἰλίου ἁλώσεως τριάκοντα καὶ ἑπτακοσίοις. γεγόνοι δ' ἄν, ὡς μὲν Ἀπολλόδωρος ἐν Χρονικοῖς, κατὰ τὴν ὀγδοηκοστὴν ὀλυμπιάδα (460–457 B.C.), ὡς δὲ Θρασύλος, ἐν τῷ ἐπιγραφομένῳ Τὰ πρὸ τῆς ἀναγνώσεως τῶν Δημοκρίτου βιβλίων, κατὰ τὸ τρίτον ἔτος τῆς ἑβδόμης καὶ ἑβδομηκοστῆς ὀλυμπιάδος (470/69), ἐνιαυτῷ, φησί, πρεσβύτερος ὢν Σωκράτους.

Leucippus was generally agreed to have evolved his theory of atoms in answer to the Eleatic elenchus: so Aristotle in **552** below. He was even assumed by late sources to have been an Eleatic; according to Diogenes Laertius IX, 30 (DK67A1) he was a pupil of Zeno. This we need not believe: it is not suggested by Aristotle, and is the kind of thing which might easily be asserted by Sotion and the other succession-writers. Miletus is given as his alternative birth-place; the *a priori* reasons for this are not so strong,

---

he instructed himself. He and Hermarchus both maintain that there never was a philosopher Leucippus, who some (including Apollodorus the Epicurean) say was the teacher of Democritus.

548 *Leucippus postulated atoms and void, and in this respect Democritus resembled him, though in other respects he was more productive.*

549 *Democritus, son of Hegesistratus (or by other accounts of Athenocritus or Damasippus), a citizen of Abdera or, as some say, of Miletus.... Later he met Leucippus and, according to some, Anaxagoras also, whose junior he was by forty years.... (41) As he himself says in the* Little World-system, *he was a young man in the old age of Anaxagoras, being forty years younger. He says that the* Little World-system *was composed 730 years after the capture of Troy. He would have been born, according to Apollodorus in the* Chronicles, *in the eightieth Olympiad; according to Thrasylus, in his book entitled* Preparation for reading the works of Democritus, *in the third year of the seventy-seventh, being one year (as he says) older than Socrates.*

though he obviously revived some Milesian astronomical theories; it might therefore be true. He may of course have visited Elea, but the Eleatic doctrines were known in Athens, and Melissus, against whom Leucippus perhaps chiefly reacted, was an Ionian. Singularly little was known about Leucippus, in any case, and in **547** his very existence seems to be denied by Epicurus and Hermarchus. But Epicurus is intent on proving his own originality; Burnet (*EGP* 330 n. 2) suggested that all Epicurus said was something like Λεύκιππον οὐδ' εἰ γέγονεν οἶδα, meaning 'I don't consider Leucippus worth discussing'. Alternatively, the emphasis might have been on the word φιλόσοφον: there was no *philosopher* Leucippus (i.e. Leucippus was no philosopher). It is clear from **552** that Aristotle considered Leucippus to be the inventor of atomism, and this is accepted also by Theophrastus in **546**. Normally they write simply of 'Leucippus and Democritus', though certain elaborations, e.g. of the theory of perception, are distinguished as Democritean. On the whole we might accept the assessment of Cicero in **548**; all our other evidence seems to show that the main theory was originated by Leucippus and accepted by Democritus, who worked out the details and introduced a few minor refinements. It would be very difficult here satisfactorily to distinguish the two, especially since many post-Theophrastean sources ignore Leucippus; where distinctions are traceable they will be pointed out. The doxographical passages mentioning Leucippus are collected in DK chapter 67: see also C. Bailey, *The Greek Atomists and Epicurus*, for a valiant attempt to distinguish the views of the two thinkers.

The date of Leucippus is not known independently, except from such guesses as that he was a pupil of Zeno. Democritus, however, evidently gave a clue to his own age in his work 'The Little World-system': he was about forty years younger than Anaxagoras. This fits Apollodorus' date in **549** (born 460–457 B.C.) better than Thrasylus', of some ten years earlier. In any case, if Democritus accepted 1184 B.C. as the year of the capture of Troy (and this, the Eratosthenic epoch-year, was merely the commonest of several dates), then the composition of the 'Little World-system' (on which see the next section) would be placed too early, in 454. The probability is that it was written after 430. Leucippus, presumably, was somewhat older, and his *floruit* (i.e. the composition of the 'Great World-system') might be put

around 440–435. A possible *terminus ante quem* is provided by Theophrastus' statement (**601**) that Diogenes of Apollonia derived some of his ideas from Leucippus; for Diogenes was already parodied in the *Clouds* of 423 B.C. (**617**).

WRITINGS

550 Diogenes Laertius IX, 45 (DK 68 A 33) τὰ δὲ βιβλία αὐτοῦ (*sc.* Democritus) καὶ Θρασύλος ἀναγέγραφε κατὰ τάξιν οὕτως ὡσπερεὶ καὶ τὰ Πλάτωνος κατὰ τετραλογίαν. (46) ἔστι δὲ ἠθικὰ μὲν τάδε·...φυσικὰ δὲ τάδε· [tetralogy III] Μέγας διάκοσμος (ὃν οἱ περὶ Θεόφραστον Λευκίππου φασὶν εἶναι), Μικρὸς διάκοσμος, Κοσμογραφίη, Περὶ τῶν πλανητῶν....

It is true that the 'Great World-system' is usually assigned to Democritus, since he was the elaborator of atomism and, apart from Epicurus, its chief exponent. Epicurus himself would presumably have credited it to Democritus. But Theophrastus' opinion in **550** counts for much: Aristotle came from a city in Thrace, and both he and his pupil Theophrastus devoted special works to Democritus. They were evidently aware of the distinction between Leucippus and Democritus, whereas it is natural that when the distinction became forgotten all early atomistic works should be attributed to Democritus. We may therefore provisionally accept Theophrastus' view that Leucippus wrote the Μέγας διάκοσμος, Democritus the Μικρὸς διάκοσμος;[1] with the possible modification that the former may have been a compendium of Leucippus' cosmological work with other, later, atomistic additions. One other work is attributed to Leucippus, namely *On Mind*: the quotation from him by Aetius (**568**) is assigned to this work, which may, of course, have been a section of the 'Great World-system'. The content of this fragment would certainly not be foreign to that work, and might have formed part of an attack on the concept of Mind in Anaxagoras.

[1] It seems probable that this work contained a description of the origin of civilization and culture, and that part of the description in Diodorus I, 7–8 (DK 68 B 5, 1) goes back to Democritus by way of Hecataeus of Abdera

---

550 *Thrasylus listed his books in order by tetralogies, just as he did Plato's books.* (*46*) *His ethical works comprised the following.... The physical books were these: The* Great World-system (*which Theophrastus' followers say was by Leucippus*), *the* Little World-system, *the* Cosmography *and* On the planets....

(see G. Vlastos, *AJP* 67 (1946) 51 ff.). However, Diodorus certainly used more than one Ionian source for this section, and it can be conceded that the account of cosmogony in I, 7 is not primarily atomistic.

Democritus, on the other hand, must have been one of the most prolific of all ancient authors. Thrasylus (or Thrasyllus), who arranged Plato's dialogues in tetralogies, did the same for Democritus according to **550**: there were thirteen tetralogies (comprising fifty-two separate works, some no doubt quite short) divided between the following general headings: Ethics (2 tetralogies), Physics (4), Mathematics (3), Music, including literature and language (2), Technical subjects (2). There were additional works which were probably not genuine.[1] It is a tantalizing misfortune, and a reflexion of later taste, that the considerable number of fragments that have survived (not all of which are certainly genuine) are nearly all taken from the ethical works.

[1] Among the works classed as Ὑπομνήματα and not included by Thrasylus (Diog. L. IX, 49, DK 68 A 33) are five concerned with foreign travel, for example a Chaldaean and a Phrygian dissertation. The attribution is perhaps related to the many stories in our ancient biographical sources that Democritus travelled extensively: for example **551** Diog. L. IX, 35 φησὶ δὲ Δημήτριος ἐν Ὁμωνύμοις καὶ Ἀντισθένης ἐν Διαδοχαῖς ἀποδημῆσαι αὐτὸν καὶ εἰς Αἴγυπτον πρὸς τοὺς ἱερέας γεωμετρίαν μαθησόμενον καὶ πρὸς Χαλδαίους εἰς τὴν Περσίδα, καὶ εἰς τὴν Ἐρυθρὰν θάλασσαν γενέσθαι. τοῖς τε Γυμνοσοφισταῖς φασί τινες συμμῖξαι αὐτὸν ἐν Ἰνδίᾳ καὶ εἰς Αἰθιοπίαν ἐλθεῖν. Another story is that Xerxes left Chaldaean overseers in Democritus' father's household, from whom Democritus learned much. There may have been some basis in fact for these stories of foreign contact. According to another anecdote Democritus said that he visited Athens, but that no one recognized him.

ORIGINS OF THE ATOMIC THEORY

552 Aristotle *de gen. et corr.* A8, 325 a 2 ἐνίοις γὰρ τῶν ἀρχαίων ἔδοξε τὸ ὂν ἐξ ἀνάγκης ἓν εἶναι καὶ ἀκίνητον· τὸ μὲν γὰρ κενὸν οὐκ ὄν, κινηθῆναι δ' οὐκ ἂν δύνασθαι μὴ ὄντος κενοῦ κεχωρισμένου, οὐδ' αὖ πολλὰ εἶναι μὴ ὄντος τοῦ διείργοντος.... (a 23) Λεύκιππος δ'

---

551 *Demetrius in his* Homonyms *and Antisthenes in his* Successions *say that he travelled to Egypt to visit the priests and learn geometry, and that he went also to Persia, to visit the Chaldaeans, and to the Red Sea. Some say that he associated with the 'naked philosophers' in India; also that he went to Aethiopia.*

552 *For some of the early philosophers thought that that which is must of necessity be one and immovable; for the void is not-being; motion would be impossible without a void apart from matter; nor could there be a plurality of things without something to separate*

ἔχειν ᾠήθη λόγους οἵτινες πρὸς τὴν αἴσθησιν ὁμολογούμενα λέγοντες οὐκ ἀναιρήσουσιν οὔτε γένεσιν οὔτε φθορὰν οὔτε κίνησιν καὶ τὸ πλῆθος τῶν ὄντων. ὁμολογήσας δὲ ταῦτα μὲν τοῖς φαινομένοις, τοῖς δὲ τὸ ἓν κατασκευάζουσιν ὡς οὐκ ἂν κίνησιν οὖσαν ἄνευ κενοῦ, τό τε κενὸν μὴ ὂν καὶ τοῦ ὄντος οὐθὲν μὴ ὄν φησιν εἶναι· τὸ γὰρ κυρίως ὂν παμπλῆρες ὄν. ἀλλ' εἶναι τὸ τοιοῦτον οὐχ ἕν, ἀλλ' ἄπειρα τὸ πλῆθος καὶ ἀόρατα διὰ σμικρότητα τῶν ὄγκων. ταῦτα δ' ἐν τῷ κενῷ φέρεσθαι (κενὸν γὰρ εἶναι), καὶ συνιστάμενα μὲν γένεσιν ποιεῖν, διαλυόμενα δὲ φθοράν.

553 Melissus Fr. 8 *fin.*, Simplicius *de caelo* 559, 11 (from **392**) ...ἢν δὲ μεταπέσῃ, τὸ μὲν ἐὸν ἀπώλετο, τὸ δὲ οὐκ ἐὸν γέγονεν. οὕτως οὖν, εἰ πολλὰ εἴη, τοιαῦτα χρὴ εἶναι οἷόν περ τὸ ἕν.

Aristotle plausibly regarded Leucippus' theory of indivisible particles moving in the void as an attempt to answer the Eleatic dilemma. This had implied among other things that anything which *is* could not alter, since that would involve its becoming what-is-not. Leucippus, it was held, agreed that such alterations of being were out of the question; but whereas the Eleatics had rejected void as patently not-being, and had thus made motion (of which void was held by Melissus to be a pre-condition) impossible, Leucippus boldly accepted the existence of void, and so was able to explain variety and change by the accretion and separation of distinct particles of real, fully existing stuff, which itself did not alter, but preserved the properties of Eleatic ἐόν. The idea that apparent alteration consists, in fact, of the rearrangement of indestructible matter had already been reached by Empedocles, and, in a particularly clear form, by Anaxagoras. The latter stated in fr. 17 (**497**) that 'no object comes-to-be or passes away, but is mixed or separated from existing objects'. But Empedocles and

---

them.... But Leucippus thought he had a theory which, being consistent with sense-perception, would not do away with coming-into-being or perishing or motion or the multiplicity of things. So much he conceded to appearances, while to those who uphold the one he granted that motion is impossible without void, that the void is not-being and that no part of being is not-being. For being, in the proper sense, is an absolute plenum. *But such a* plenum *is not one, but there is an infinite number of them, and they are invisible owing to the smallness of their bulk. They move in the void (for the void exists), and by their coming together they effect coming-into-being, by their separation perishing.*

553 *...But if it has changed, what is has passed away and what is not has come into being. So then, if there were a plurality, things would have to be of just the same nature as the one.*

Anaxagoras had continued to accept the Eleatic arguments about the impossibility of void; though it is not clear that their ideas about motion were entirely consistent with this position.[1] Further, an Eleatic could have objected, as Melissus did implicitly object in **384** and fr. 7, that different root-forms of matter did not meet the arguments about τὸ ἐόν being uniform; for if water, or a portion of flesh, for example, exists, then it might be argued that earth or bone, being different in some way at least, cannot exist. Leucippus, then, postulated a truly uniform type of material being. In this he may well have been following out the consequence evolved by Melissus in **392** as an absurdity, from an argument about the fallacy of the senses, that if there *are* many things, and not the uniform Eleatic One, then the many must each possess the properties of that One—homogeneity, permanence, lack of internal change, and indivisibility.

[1] Empedocles' theory of pores in the body actually presupposed the existence of the void which he formally denied, according to Aristotle *de gen. et corr.* A8, 325b1. See also n. 2 on p. 344.

The later accounts which make atomism a development of Eleaticism, and Leucippus, for example, a pupil of Zeno, were probably derived from the Aristotelian assessment; cf. Theophrastus in **546**. But this assessment is so plausible in itself that, even while admitting the tendency in Aristotle to over-schematize the relations of his philosophical forebears, we may yet accept it. Empedocles and Anaxagoras were unquestionably striving to overcome the Eleatic dilemma; it is *a priori* probable that Leucippus too, since he indubitably dealt with the same kind of problems, devoted careful attention to the Eleatics. Melissus had suggested a possible solution so clearly that it is difficult to believe that Leucippus' support of this very solution was independent. At the same time Leucippus remained faithful to the principles of his probably Ionian background, since he was now enabled to revert to a single material basis for phenomena. In the acceptance of void he was consciously correcting an Eleatic axiom.

ATOMS AND THE VOID

554 Aristotle *Met.* A4, 985b4 Λεύκιππος δὲ καὶ ὁ ἑταῖρος αὐτοῦ Δημόκριτος στοιχεῖα μὲν τὸ πλῆρες καὶ τὸ κενὸν εἶναί φασι,

---

554 *Leucippus and his associate Democritus hold that the elements are the full and the*

λέγοντες τὸ μὲν ὂν τὸ δὲ μὴ ὄν, τούτων δὲ τὸ μὲν πλῆρες καὶ στερεόν, τὸ ὄν, τὸ δὲ κενὸν καὶ μανόν, τὸ μὴ ὄν· διὸ καὶ οὐθὲν μᾶλλον τὸ ὂν τοῦ μὴ ὄντος εἶναί φασιν, ὅτι οὐδὲ τὸ κενὸν ⟨ἔλαττον⟩ τοῦ σώματος· αἴτια δὲ τῶν ὄντων ταῦτα ὡς ὕλην. καὶ καθάπερ οἱ ἓν ποιοῦντες τὴν ὑποκειμένην οὐσίαν τἆλλα τοῖς πάθεσιν αὐτῆς γεννῶσι, τὸ μανὸν καὶ τὸ πυκνὸν ἀρχὰς τιθέμενοι τῶν παθημάτων, τὸν αὐτὸν τρόπον καὶ οὗτοι τὰς διαφορὰς αἰτίας τῶν ἄλλων εἶναί φασιν. ταύτας μέντοι τρεῖς εἶναι λέγουσι, σχῆμά τε καὶ τάξιν καὶ θέσιν· διαφέρειν γάρ φασι τὸ ὂν ῥυσμῷ καὶ διαθιγῇ καὶ τροπῇ μόνον. τούτων δὲ ὁ μὲν ῥυσμὸς σχῆμά ἐστιν, ἡ δὲ διαθιγὴ τάξις, ἡ δὲ τροπὴ θέσις· διαφέρει γὰρ τὸ μὲν A τοῦ N σχήματι, τὸ δὲ AN τοῦ NA τάξει, τὸ δὲ Z τοῦ N θέσει.

555 Aristotle *On Democritus ap.* Simplicium *de caelo* 295, 1 (DK 68 A 37) Δημόκριτος...προσαγορεύει δὲ τὸν μὲν τόπον τοῖσδε τοῖς ὀνόμασι, τῷ τε κενῷ καὶ τῷ οὐδενὶ καὶ τῷ ἀπείρῳ, τῶν δὲ οὐσιῶν ἑκάστην τῷ τε δενὶ καὶ τῷ ναστῷ καὶ τῷ ὄντι. νομίζει δὲ εἶναι οὕτω μικρὰς τὰς οὐσίας ὥστε ἐκφυγεῖν τὰς ἡμετέρας αἰσθήσεις· ὑπάρχειν δὲ αὐταῖς παντοίας μορφὰς καὶ σχήματα παντοῖα καὶ κατὰ μέγεθος διαφοράς. ἐκ τούτων οὖν ἤδη καθάπερ ἐκ στοιχείων γεννᾷ καὶ συγκρίνει τοὺς ὀφθαλμοφανεῖς καὶ τοὺς αἰσθητοὺς ὄγκους. [δὲ A, δενὶ Diels, cf. DK 68 B 156.]

556 Simplicius *de caelo* 242, 18 (DK 67 A 14) οὗτοι γὰρ (*sc.* Leucippus, Democritus, Epicurus) ἔλεγον ἀπείρους εἶναι τῷ πλήθει τὰς ἀρχάς, ἃς καὶ ἀτόμους καὶ ἀδιαιρέτους ἐνόμιζον καὶ

---

void; they call them being and not-being respectively. Being is full and solid, not-being is void and rare. Since the void exists no less than body, it follows that not-being exists no less than being. The two together are the material causes of existing things. And just as those who make the underlying substance one generate other things by its modifications, and postulate rarefaction and condensation as the origin of such modifications, in the same way these men too say that the differences in atoms are the causes of other things. They hold that these differences are three—shape, arrangement and position; being, they say, differs only in 'rhythm, touching and turning', of which 'rhythm' is shape, 'touching' is arrangement and 'turning' is position; for A *differs from* N *in shape,* AN *from* NA *in arrangement, and* Z *from* N *in position.*

555 *Democritus...calls space by these names—'the void', 'nothing', and 'the infinite', while each individual atom he calls 'hing'* [i.e. '*nothing*' without '*not*'], *the 'compact' and 'being'. He thinks that they are so small as to elude our senses, but they have all sorts of forms and shapes and differences in size. So he is already enabled from them, as from elements, to create by aggregation bulks that are perceptible to sight and the other senses.*

556 *They* (sc. *Leucippus, Democritus, Epicurus*) *said that the first principles were infinite in number, and thought they were indivisible atoms and impassible owing to their*

ἀπαθεῖς διὰ τὸ ναστὰς εἶναι, καὶ ἀμοίρους τοῦ κενοῦ· τὴν γὰρ διαίρεσιν κατὰ τὸ κενὸν τὸ ἐν τοῖς σώμασι ἔλεγον γίνεσθαι....

These passages (to which **546** should be added; there are several other similar but less concise descriptions in Aristotle and the doxographers) state clearly enough the basis of the atomists' theory of matter. Full reality is assigned, as in the Milesian tradition, to the corporeal; but the corporeal is fully corporeal and homogeneous, like the Eleatic 'sphere' of Being—it contains no void and no interstices, so cannot be divided (**556**).[1] The atoms were so small as to be invisible (**555**); though Democritus might have allowed exceptions here (**560**). They were indivisible in fact, though not (since they had extension in space) in thought: in this way the old Eleatic argument against Pythagorean monads was circumvented. The solid atoms, infinite in number and shape,[2] are scattered throughout infinite void, which is declared to exist: it is called 'that which is not', in Eleatic phraseology, but is asserted nevertheless to have existence of a sort (it must have, *a priori*, to allow movement and coalescence of the atoms; the same preconception had been unconsciously adopted by Empedocles, see n. on p. 406).[3] The existence of the void is distinct, however, from the full corporeal existence of atoms. Aristotle in **555** is misleading when he calls the void 'space'; the atomists had no conception of bodies *occupying space*, and for them the void only exists where atoms are not, that is, it forms the gaps between them. The atoms differ from each other, not in matter, but only in arrangement and shape: all 'qualitative' differences in objects (which are conglomerates of atoms), therefore, are dependent on quantitative and local differences alone.

[1] This is probably Democritus' reason. Leucippus, according to a late doxographical source, held that the atoms were indivisible because of their smallness: **557** Galen *de elem. sec. Hippocr.* I, 2 (DK 68 A 49) ἀπαθῆ δ' ὑποτίθενται τὰ σώματα εἶναι τὰ πρῶτα (τινὲς μὲν αὐτῶν ὑπὸ σκληρότητος ἄθραυστα, καθάπερ οἱ περὶ Ἐπίκουρον, ἔνιοι δὲ ὑπὸ σμικρότητος ἀδιαίρετα, καθάπερ οἱ περὶ τὸν Λεύκιππον)....

---

compactness, and without any void in them; divisibility comes about because of the void in compound bodies....

557 *They suppose their primary bodies to be impassible (some of them, e.g. Epicurus' school, regarding them as unbreakable because of their hardness, others, e.g. the school of Leucippus, as indivisible because of their smallness)....*

[2] According to Aristotle, both Leucippus and Democritus made the number of shapes of atoms infinite: **558** Aristotle *de gen. et corr.* A2, 315b6 ἐπεὶ δ' ᾤοντο τἀληθὲς ἐν τῷ φαίνεσθαι, ἐναντία δὲ καὶ ἄπειρα τὰ φαινόμενα, τὰ σχήματα ἄπειρα ἐποίησαν.... It is unnecessary to postulate infinite shapes in order to account for the different objects of the phenomenal world, even if these are supposed to be infinite, for variety is provided by changes of position and order also. But a different motive for infinite shapes is suggested in **559** Theophrastus *Phys. Op.* fr. 8 *ap.* Simplic. *Phys.* 28, 9 (from **546**) ...καὶ τῶν ἐν αὐτοῖς (*sc.* ταῖς ἀτόμοις) σχημάτων ἄπειρον τὸ πλῆθος διὰ τὸ μηδὲν μᾶλλον τοιοῦτον ἢ τοιοῦτον εἶναι...(repeated at *Phys.* 28, 25). Bailey, *Greek Atomists* 81, suggests that this relatively sophisticated type of argument (which is, of course, fallacious) is probably the product of Democritus rather than Leucippus. Epicurus maintained that *infinite* shapes will eventually demand infinite sizes, and indeed Democritus may have suggested that some atoms are comparatively large: **560** Dionysius *ap.* Eusebium *P.E.* XIV, 23, 3 τοσοῦτον δὲ διεφώνησαν (*sc.* Epicurus and Democritus) ὅσον ὁ μὲν ἐλαχίστας πάσας καὶ διὰ τοῦτο ἀνεπαισθήτους, ὁ δὲ καὶ μεγίστας εἶναί τινας ἀτόμους, ὁ Δημόκριτος, ὑπέλαβεν. Aristotle in **552** asserted that Leucippus, and in **555** that Democritus, supposed all atoms to be invisible: possibly the latter passage is misleading. In any case Democritus is unlikely to have thought of anything larger than the specks of dust in a sunbeam; even those would be 'very large' in comparison with the vast majority.

[3] Cf. **561** Aristotle *Phys.* Δ6, 213a31 οὔκουν τοῦτο δεῖ δεικνύναι (*sc.* τοὺς πειρωμένους δεικνύναι ὅτι οὐκ ἔστι κενόν), ὅτι ἐστί τι ὁ ἀήρ, ἀλλ' ὅτι οὐκ ἔστι διάστημα ἕτερον τῶν σωμάτων, οὔτε χωριστὸν οὔτε ἐνεργείᾳ ὄν, ὃ διαλαμβάνει τὸ πᾶν σῶμα ὥστε εἶναι μὴ συνεχές, καθάπερ λέγουσι Δημόκριτος καὶ Λεύκιππος.... Empedocles' demonstration of the corporeal nature of air (**453**) is rightly dismissed as evidence for the non-existence of void.

THE FORMATION OF WORLDS

562 Diogenes Laertius IX, 31 (DK 67 A 1) τὸ μὲν πᾶν ἄπειρόν φησιν (*sc.* Leucippus)...τούτου δὲ τὸ μὲν πλῆρες εἶναι, τὸ δὲ

---

558 *Since they thought that truth lies in appearances, and appearances are contradictory and infinitely variable, they made the number of shapes infinite....*

559 *...he held that the number of shapes in the atoms was infinite on the ground that there was no reason why any atom should be of one shape rather than another....*

560 *To this extent they* (sc. *Epicurus and Democritus*) *differed, that one supposed that all atoms were very small, and on that account imperceptible; the other, Democritus, that there are some atoms that are very large.*

561 (*Those who try to prove that there is no void*) *should not prove that air is something but rather that there is not, either by abstraction or actually existing, any interval* (*as distinct from bodies*) *which so separates body as a whole as to make it discontinuous, as Democritus and Leucippus say it is....*

562 *Leucippus holds that the whole is infinite...part of it is full and part void....*

κενόν...κόσμους τε ἐκ τούτου ἀπείρους εἶναι καὶ διαλύεσθαι εἰς ταῦτα. γίνεσθαι δὲ τοὺς κόσμους οὕτω· φέρεσθαι 'κατὰ ἀποτομὴν ἐκ τῆς ἀπείρου' πολλὰ σώματα παντοῖα τοῖς σχήμασιν εἰς μέγα κενόν, ἅπερ ἀθροισθέντα δίνην ἀπεργάζεσθαι μίαν, καθ' ἣν προσκρούοντα καὶ παντοδαπῶς κυκλούμενα διακρίνεσθαι χωρὶς τὰ ὅμοια πρὸς τὰ ὅμοια. ἰσορρόπων δὲ διὰ τὸ πλῆθος μηκέτι δυναμένων περιφέρεσθαι, τὰ μὲν λεπτὰ χωρεῖν εἰς τὸ ἔξω κενόν, ὥσπερ διαττώμενα· τὰ δὲ λοιπὰ 'συμμένειν' καὶ περιπλεκόμενα συγκατατρέχειν ἀλλήλοις καὶ ποιεῖν πρῶτόν τι σύστημα σφαιροειδές. (32) τοῦτο δ' οἷον 'ὑμένα' ἀφίστασθαι περιέχοντα ἐν ἑαυτῷ παντοῖα σώματα· ὧν κατὰ τὴν τοῦ μέσου ἀντέρεισιν περιδινουμένων λεπτὸν γενέσθαι τὸν πέριξ ὑμένα, συρρεόντων ἀεὶ τῶν συνεχῶν κατ' ἐπίψαυσιν τῆς δίνης. καὶ οὕτω γενέσθαι τὴν γῆν, συμμενόντων τῶν ἐνεχθέντων ἐπὶ τὸ μέσον. αὐτόν τε πάλιν τὸν περιέχοντα οἷον ὑμένα αὔξεσθαι κατὰ τὴν ἐπέκκρισιν [Heidel, ἐπέκρυσιν mss.] τῶν ἔξωθεν σωμάτων· δίνῃ τε φερόμενον αὐτόν, ὧν ἂν ἐπιψαύσῃ, ταῦτα ἐπικτᾶσθαι. τούτων δέ τινα συμπλεκόμενα ποιεῖν σύστημα, τὸ μὲν πρῶτον κάθυγρον καὶ πηλῶδες, ξηρανθέντα δὲ καὶ περιφερόμενα σὺν τῇ τοῦ ὅλου δίνῃ εἶτ' ἐκπυρωθέντα τὴν τῶν ἀστέρων ἀποτελέσαι φύσιν. (Cf. also Aetius I, 4, 1–4, DK 67 A 24.)[1]

563 Aetius II, 7, 2 Λεύκιππος καὶ Δημόκριτος 'χιτῶνα' κύκλῳ καὶ 'ὑμένα' περιτείνουσι τῷ κόσμῳ διὰ τῶν ἀγκιστροειδῶν ἀτόμων συμπεπλεγμένον.

Hence arise innumerable worlds, and are resolved again into these elements. The worlds come into being as follows: many bodies of all sorts of shapes move 'by abscission from the infinite' into a great void; they come together there and produce a single whirl, in which, colliding with one another and revolving in all manner of ways, they begin to separate apart, like to like. But when their multitude prevents them from rotating any longer in equilibrium, those that are fine go out towards the surrounding void as if sifted, while the rest 'abide together' and, becoming entangled, unite their motions and make a first spherical structure. (32) This structure stands apart like a 'membrane' which contains in itself all kinds of bodies; and as they whirl around owing to the resistance of the middle, the surrounding membrane becomes thin, while contiguous atoms keep flowing together owing to contact with the whirl. So the earth came into being, the atoms that had been borne to the middle abiding together there. Again, the containing membrane is itself increased, owing to the attraction of bodies outside; as it moves around in the whirl it takes in anything it touches. Some of these bodies that get entangled form a structure that is at first moist and muddy, but as they revolve with the whirl of the whole they dry out and then ignite to form the substance of the heavenly bodies.

563 *Leucippus and Democritus envelop the world in a circular 'cloak' or 'membrane', which was formed by the hooked atoms becoming entangled.*

564 Hippolytus *Ref.* I, 13, 2 (DK 68 A 40) λέγει δὲ ὁμοίως Λευκίππῳ (*sc.* Δημόκριτος) περὶ στοιχείων, πλήρους καὶ κενοῦ... ἔλεγε δὲ ὡς ἀεὶ κινουμένων τῶν ὄντων ἐν τῷ κενῷ· ἀπείρους δ' εἶναι κόσμους καὶ μεγέθει διαφέροντας. ἐν τισὶ δὲ μὴ εἶναι ἥλιον μηδὲ σελήνην, ἐν τισὶ δὲ μείζω τῶν παρ' ἡμῖν καὶ ἐν τισὶ πλείω. (3) εἶναι δὲ τῶν κόσμων ἄνισα τὰ διαστήματα καὶ τῇ μὲν πλείους, τῇ δὲ ἐλάττους, καὶ τοὺς μὲν αὔξεσθαι, τοὺς δὲ ἀκμάζειν, τοὺς δὲ φθίνειν, καὶ τῇ μὲν γίνεσθαι, τῇ δ' ⟨ἐκ⟩λείπειν. φθείρεσθαι δὲ αὐτοὺς ὑπ' ἀλλήλων προσπίπτοντας. εἶναι δὲ ἐνίους κόσμους ἐρήμους ζῴων καὶ φυτῶν καὶ παντὸς ὑγροῦ.

[1] It looks as though συμμένειν, ὑμήν, and (in **563**) χιτών were actually derived from atomist contexts. The phrase κατὰ ἀποτομὴν ἐκ τῆς ἀπείρου (*sc.* χώρας) is closely paralleled in the Epicurean letter to Pythocles (*Ep.* II, 88; DK 67 A 24). Diogenes might have derived it from Democritus; but it is also possible that συμμένειν, ὑμήν, χιτών, as well as κατὰ ἀποτομήν, are merely Epicurean.—After προσκρούοντα supply Diels' ⟨ἀλλήλοις⟩.

The account in **562** of the formation of worlds (formally attributed to Leucippus, but no doubt representing the general views of Democritus also) is fairly detailed, but full of difficulties. The first stage is when a large collection of atoms becomes isolated, as it were, in a large patch of void. The second stage is when they form a whirl or vortex. How this occurs we cannot tell; it must happen 'by necessity',[1] as the result of a particular combination of their separate atomic movements, and a vortex would presumably not necessarily or commonly arise out of the circumstances of the first stage alone. The vortex-action causes like atoms to tend towards like.[2] (There is a good deal of reminiscence of Anaxagoras in all this: in him *Nous* started a vortex and similar particles came together to form bodies, **503** and pp. 382 f.)[3] The larger atoms congregate towards the middle, the smaller ones are squeezed out (**575**). A kind of membrane or garment (**563**) encloses the whole: whether this is formed by the smaller and extruded atoms (as

---

564 *Democritus holds the same view as Leucippus about the elements, full and void... he spoke as if the things that are were in constant motion in the void; and there are innumerable worlds, which differ in size. In some worlds there is no sun and moon, in others they are larger than in our world, and in others more numerous. (3) The intervals between the worlds are unequal; in some parts there are more worlds, in others fewer; some are increasing, some at their height, some decreasing; in some parts they are arising, in others failing. They are destroyed by collision one with another. There are some worlds devoid of living creatures or plants or any moisture.*

suggested by Aetius, DK67A24), or whether these are thrust right out of the σύστημα into the void (as suggested in **562**), is uncertain. Other atoms come into contact with the extremity of the revolving mass and are drawn within the membrane. Certain of these atoms become ignited by the speed of the revolution (**562** *ad fin.*) and so form the heavenly bodies; the bulkier ones at the centre 'stay together' (συμμένειν) to form the earth. Diogenes Laertius continues, after the end of **562**, with a description of cosmological details which are not particularly enlightening, but show us that here Leucippus tended to accept, not very critically, the old Ionian theories. One important and highly conservative idea of Leucippus is that the earth is flat, shaped like a tambourine (τυμπανοειδής, Aetius III, 10, 4); Democritus slightly emended this (*id.* III, 10, 5), but retained the overall flatness. Both appear to have held that the earth was tilted downward towards the south.[4] Since there are innumerable atoms and an infinite void, there is no reason why only one such world should be formed; Leucippus and Democritus therefore postulated innumerable worlds, coming-to-be and passing away throughout the void (**562** *init.*, **564**). They are the first to whom we can with absolute certainty attribute the odd concept of innumerable worlds (as opposed to successive states of a continuing organism), one which is reached entirely on the *a priori* grounds described above.[5] The doxographers, however, certainly attributed the idea of plural worlds (whether coexistent or successive) to some Ionians, conceivably by an error initiated by Theophrastus (see pp. 123ff., also p. 390). Democritus, according to **564**, seems to have embellished the idea by observing that there is no need for each world to have a sun and moon, and so on, or to have waters and give rise to life: the random nature of the cosmogonical process **562** would not always produce the same result. For example, if there were no further atoms to be attracted close to the outer membrane of a world, that world would presumably have no heavenly bodies.[6]

[1] So **565** Diog. L. IX, 45 (on Democritus) πάντα τε κατ' ἀνάγκην γίνεσθαι, τῆς δίνης αἰτίας οὔσης τῆς γενέσεως πάντων, ἣν ἀνάγκην λέγει. The whirl or vortex is called necessity because it produces the necessary (mechanical and *theoretically* determinable) collisions and unions of atoms:

---

565 *Everything happens according to necessity; for the cause of the coming-into-being of all things is the whirl, which he calls necessity.*

so **566** Aetius I, 26, 2 (Π. οὐσίας ἀνάγκης) Δημόκριτος τὴν ἀντιτυπίαν καὶ φορὰν καὶ πληγὴν τῆς ὕλης. In Aristotelian terms, combinations can be said to take place by *chance*: **567** Aristotle *Phys.* B4, 196a24 εἰσὶ δέ τινες οἳ καὶ τοὐρανοῦ τοῦδε καὶ τῶν κόσμων πάντων αἰτιῶνται τὸ αὐτόματον· ἀπὸ ταὐτομάτου γὰρ γενέσθαι τὴν δίνην καὶ τὴν κίνησιν τὴν διακρίνασαν καὶ καταστήσασαν εἰς ταύτην τὴν τάξιν τὸ πᾶν. For Aristotle they are chance events because they do not fulfil any final cause; but the atomists emphasized the other aspect of non-planned mechanical sequences, i.e. as necessity. So in the only extant saying of Leucippus himself: **568** Fr. 2, Aetius I, 25, 4 οὐδὲν χρῆμα μάτην γίνεται, ἀλλὰ πάντα ἐκ λόγου τε καὶ ὑπ' ἀνάγκης. Every object, every event, is the result of a chain of collisions and reactions, each according to the shape and particular motion of the atoms concerned.

[2] Democritus illustrates this traditional rule of the behaviour of things, both animate and inanimate, in **569** Fr. 164, Sextus *adv. math.* VII, 117 καὶ γὰρ ζῷα, φησίν, ὁμογενέσι ζῴοις συναγελάζεται ὡς περιστεραὶ περιστεραῖς καὶ γέρανοι γεράνοις καὶ ἐπὶ τῶν ἄλλων ὡσαύτως. ⟨ὣς⟩ δὲ καὶ ἐπὶ τῶν ἀψύχων, καθάπερ ὁρᾶν πάρεστιν ἐπί τε τῶν κοσκινευομένων σπερμάτων καὶ ἐπὶ τῶν παρὰ ταῖς κυματωγαῖς ψηφίδων... (similar grains, he continues, and pebbles of the same shape, congregate under the action of sieve or waves). The mechanical tendency of objects of similar shape and size to sort together under the influence of motion is especially relevant to atomism, of course, and goes beyond the naïve view of Homer, *Od.* 17, 218, that 'god always leads like to like'.

[3] According to Simplicius, Democritus held that the vortex was 'separated off': **570** Fr. 167, Simplic. *Phys.* 327, 24 ἀλλὰ καὶ Δημόκριτος, ἐν οἷς φησι 'δῖνον ἀπὸ τοῦ παντὸς ἀποκριθῆναι παντοίων ἰδεῶν' (πῶς δὲ καὶ ὑπὸ τίνος αἰτίας μὴ λέγει), ἔοικεν ἀπὸ ταὐτομάτου καὶ τύχης γεννᾶν αὐτόν. The idea of the initiator of the cosmogonical process being 'separated off' may go back to Anaximander (see **123** and pp. 132f.).

[4] So **571** Diog. L. IX, 33 (on Leucippus) ἐκλείπειν δ' ἥλιον καὶ σελήνην τῷ κεκλίσθαι τὴν γῆν πρὸς μεσημβρίαν· τὰ δὲ πρὸς ἄρκτῳ ἀεί τε νίφεσθαι καὶ κατάψυχρα εἶναι καὶ πήγνυσθαι. Most scholars have assumed a gap

---

566 *(On the nature of necessity) Democritus means by it the resistance and movement and blows of matter.*

567 *There are some who make chance the cause both of these heavens and of all the worlds: for from chance arose the whirl and the movement which, by separation, brought the universe into its present order.*

568 *Nothing occurs at random, but everything for a reason and by necessity.*

569 *For creatures (he says) flock together with their kind, doves with doves, cranes with cranes and so on. And the same happens even with inanimate things, as can be seen with seeds in a sieve and pebbles on the sea-shore....*

570 *When Democritus says that 'a whirl was separated off from the whole, of all sorts of shapes' (and he does not say how or through what cause), he seems to generate it by accident or chance.*

571 *Eclipses of sun and moon are due to the tilting of the earth towards the south; the regions towards the north are always under snow and are very cold and hard-frozen.*

after σελήνην, so that some other phenomenon than eclipse is explained by the tilting of the earth. The order of subjects in Diogenes is against a gap; but the tilting of the earth would be so utterly unsuitable as an explanation of eclipses that it seems reasonable to postulate either a textual displacement or a total misunderstanding by Diogenes or his sources. The tilting of the earth remains; it explains both the slant of the zodiac and the differences of climate, and is conceivably related to, though very different from, Anaximenes' theory that the sun is hidden behind high northern parts at night. Eclipses had already been correctly explained by Empedocles and Anaxagoras. Cf. also Aetius III, 12, 1–2 (DK 67 A 27 and 68 A 96).

5 Compare the well-known saying of Democritus' pupil Metrodorus of Chios, that it is strange for one ear of corn to be produced in a great plain, and for one world in the boundless.

6 It looks as though there is a reference here to Anaxagoras fr. 4 (**525**; the recurrence of the phrase παρ' ἡμῖν may be accidental). It is not at all certain, however, that that fragment described entirely separate worlds with separate suns and moons; *if* it did, then the fact that every world had the same structure justifies G. Vlastos' reference (*Philos. Rev.* 55 (1946) 53 f.) to 'the teleological streak in Anaxagorean physics', and his suggestion that Democritus' theory may be a 'conscious refutation' of it.

THE BEHAVIOUR OF ATOMS

(*a*) *Weight*

572 Aristotle *de gen. et corr.* A8, 326a9 καίτοι βαρύτερόν γε κατὰ τὴν ὑπεροχήν φησιν εἶναι Δημόκριτος ἕκαστον τῶν ἀδιαιρέτων.

573 Theophrastus *de sensu* 61 (DK 68 A 135) βαρὺ μὲν οὖν καὶ κοῦφον τῷ μεγέθει διαιρεῖ Δημόκριτος.... οὐ μὴν ἀλλ' ἔν γε τοῖς μεικτοῖς κουφότερον μὲν εἶναι τὸ πλέον ἔχον κενόν, βαρύτερον δὲ τὸ ἔλαττον. ἐν ἐνίοις μὲν οὕτως εἴρηκεν· (62) ἐν ἄλλοις δὲ κοῦφον εἶναί φησιν ἁπλῶς τὸ λεπτόν.

574 Aetius I, 3, 18 (DK 68 A 47) Δημόκριτος μὲν γὰρ ἔλεγε δύο (*sc.* ταῖς ἀτόμοις συμβεβηκέναι), μέγεθός τε καὶ σχῆμα, ὁ δὲ Ἐπίκουρος τούτοις καὶ τρίτον βάρος προσέθηκεν....I, 12, 6 Δημόκριτος τὰ πρῶτά φησι σώματα (ταῦτα δ' ἦν τὰ ναστά) βάρος μὲν οὐκ ἔχειν, κινεῖσθαι δὲ κατ' ἀλληλοτυπίαν ἐν τῷ ἀπείρῳ.

---

572 *Yet Democritus says that each of the indivisible bodies is heavier in proportion to its excess* (sc. *of bulk*).

573 *Democritus distinguishes heavy and light by size.... Nevertheless in compound bodies the lighter is that which contains more void, the heavier that which contains less. Sometimes he expressed it thus, but elsewhere he says simply that the fine is light.*

574 *Democritus named two* (sc. *properties of atoms*), *size and shape; but Epicurus added a third to these, namely weight....—Democritus says that the primary bodies* (i.e. *the solid atoms*) *do not possess weight but move in the infinite as the result of striking one another.*

575 Simplicius *de caelo* 712, 27 (DK 68 A 61) ...οἱ περὶ Δημόκριτον οἴονται πάντα μὲν ἔχειν βάρος, τῷ δὲ ἔλαττον ἔχειν βάρος τὸ πῦρ ἐκθλιβόμενον ὑπὸ τῶν προλαμβανόντων ἄνω φέρεσθαι καὶ διὰ τοῦτο κοῦφον δοκεῖν.

These passages present apparently contradictory opinions on the question whether the atoms, for Democritus, possessed weight, and if so, of what kind. Leucippus is not mentioned, and presumably did not think that the subject demanded special treatment. Aristotle in **572** is quite clear that for Democritus the atoms *had* weight, but that the weight depended on their size. We may here pause to consider what weight means: it means a tendency to move consistently in a certain direction, what we call 'downwards', and a resistance to 'upward' movement. This tendency might be explained by the operation of outside forces; there is no need to think of it as essential to all body, no matter what its environment, and in fact (as Burnet *EGP* 342f. argues) it appears that the concept of absolute weight as an essential attribute of body did not occur to the early physicists. Now bodies in our world do as a matter of experience seem to have weight; Democritus would obviously not deny this. Composite bodies are composed of atoms and void; void cannot have weight; therefore weight, *in our world*, must belong to atoms. But the atoms are solid, and of the same substance; therefore their weight varies directly with their size (**572**). Compound objects of the same size can differ in weight because of differences in the amount of void they contain (**573**, of which the last sentence does not indicate a real inconsistency). In our world all objects have weight of some kind and there is no such thing as absolute lightness, as there was for Aristotle: things which apparently tend upwards, such as fire, are actually being squeezed up by the compression of bulkier bodies (**575**). At this point it must be remembered that the atoms as such, and before being associated into bodies, differ from each other only in *size* and in *shape* (see e.g. **555**). These are their 'primary qualities'. The interaction of atoms is due to their collisions with and rebounds from each other, which are continuing effects of the original random motion (see p. 417); there is no mention of weight, or a

575 *...Democritus' school thinks that everything possesses weight, but that because it possesses less weight fire is squeezed out by things that possess more, moves upwards and consequently appears light.*

tendency to fall in one direction, as a cause of collision. (It is explicitly stated, in fact, most clearly by Aetius in **574**, that Epicurus *added* weight as an original property, and source of the behaviour, of atoms; he made their original motion a fall through space due to their weight.) 'Weight' only operates in a vortex, in a developed world, and is an expression of the tendency of bulky objects towards the centre of a whirl. Before becoming involved in a vortex an atom is not activated by weight at all.[1]

[1] This explanation has been worked out chiefly by Dyroff and Burnet, and is accepted by Bailey: it does seem adequately to account for some confusion in the ancient authorities.

(*b*) '*Original*' *and* '*derived*' *motion*

576 Aristotle *de caelo* Γ2, 300b8 διὸ καὶ Λευκίππῳ καὶ Δημοκρίτῳ, τοῖς λέγουσιν ἀεὶ κινεῖσθαι τὰ πρῶτα σώματα ἐν τῷ κενῷ καὶ τῷ ἀπείρῳ, λεκτέον τίνα κίνησιν καὶ τίς ἡ κατὰ φύσιν αὐτῶν κίνησις.

577 Aristotle *On Democritus ap.* Simplicium *de caelo* 295, 9 (continuing **555**) στασιάζειν δὲ καὶ φέρεσθαι ἐν τῷ κενῷ διά τε τὴν ἀνομοιότητα καὶ τὰς ἄλλας εἰρημένας διαφοράς, φερομένας δὲ ἐμπίπτειν καὶ περιπλέκεσθαι....

578 Aristotle *de caelo* Γ4, 303a5 φασὶ γὰρ (*sc.* Leucippus and Democritus) εἶναι τὰ πρῶτα μεγέθη πλήθει μὲν ἄπειρα, μεγέθει δὲ ἀδιαίρετα, καὶ οὔτ' ἐξ ἑνὸς πολλὰ γίγνεσθαι οὔτε ἐκ πολλῶν ἕν, ἀλλὰ τῇ τούτων συμπλοκῇ καὶ περιπαλάξει πάντα γεννᾶσθαι.

579 Alexander *Met.* 36, 21 οὗτοι γὰρ (*sc.* Leucippus and Democritus) λέγουσιν ἀλληλοτυπούσας καὶ κρουομένας πρὸς ἀλλήλας κινεῖσθαι τὰς ἀτόμους.

---

576 *So Leucippus and Democritus, who say that their primary bodies are always in motion in the infinite void, ought to specify what kind of motion—that is, what is the motion natural to them.*

577 *They struggle and move in the void because of the dissimilarities between them and the other differences already mentioned; and as they move they collide and become entangled....*

578 *For they* (sc. *Leucippus and Democritus*) *say that their primary magnitudes are infinite in number and indivisible in magnitude; the many does not come from one nor one from many, but rather all things are generated by the intertwining and scattering around of these primary magnitudes.*

579 *For they* (sc. *Leucippus and Democritus*) *say that the atoms move by mutual collisions and blows.*

580 Aetius I, 23, 3 Δημόκριτος ἓν γένος κινήσεως τὸ κατὰ παλμὸν ἀπεφαίνετο.

It is evident from **576** and other similar complaints by Aristotle, as well as from the lack of positive information on this point, that neither Leucippus nor Democritus gave any full account of an *original* motion of atoms—the motion, that is, which causes collisions, not that which is caused by collisions. Indeed, since atoms and the void have always existed, it is clear that there must always have been motion (whose eternity had to be postulated in order to avoid Eleatic arguments against a *beginning* of motion), and consequent collisions. To enquire, therefore, as Aristotle does, what was the 'natural' motion of atoms is less pertinent than at first appears. The real problem, philosophically speaking, is whether atoms and void have always existed; if this is accepted, one can also accept that they have always interacted with each other. However, if the atomists were forced to define an 'original' motion they could presumably say that it was a random motion, with no tendency in any atom to move in one direction rather than another. It is clear that collisions would very soon take place, and that the original motion would progressively be supplanted by the secondary motions which result from collision and rebound.

It is just possible, however, that Democritus, at any rate, did point to some kind of 'original' motion. Aristotle (*de an.* A2, 403b31 ff.) tells us that he held soul-atoms to be self-moving, like motes in a sunbeam; and it has been suggested that this image more aptly illustrates a random motion of atoms in general. In **577** it is suggested that motion in the void is originally caused by dissimilarities between the atoms. Democritus could not, of course, have meant that unlike exercised a force of repulsion on unlike, operating at a distance and not by contact. More probably the suggestion is that irregular atoms are in a state of disequilibrium in the void, and so undergo movement.[1]

[1] Simplicius may have misrepresented Aristotle here. When giving his own views the former is unreliable on this point; for at *Phys.* 1318, 35 (DK 68A58) he claims that the original motion of atoms is due to their *weight*, an Epicurean idea; and that it is through this, and because the void does not resist, that they are 'scattered around', περιπαλάσσεσθαι (περιπαλαίσεσθαι mss., em. Diels)—on which see the next note.

---

580 *Democritus said there was only one kind of motion, that due to vibration.*

The regular motion of atoms, and perhaps the only one which Leucippus and Democritus fully envisaged, is due to rebounds of atoms after collision. This is frequently called a 'derived' motion; in most of the doxographical accounts (e.g. **574**) it is the only one known. Collisions of atoms result either in 'intertwining' (συμπλοκή), if the atoms are of congruent shape, or in 'being scattered around' (περιπάλαξις), if not—that is, in rebounding in one direction or another. This is what is meant by Aristotle in **578**. Aetius in **580** assigns a special type of motion to Democritus, namely παλμός or 'vibration' (the verbal root of which is the same as that of περιπάλαξις; Bailey actually interpreted περιπάλαξις in **578** in the sense of παλμός, though not very plausibly). There is little doubt that Aetius is here reading an Epicurean idea into Democritus; Epicurus used this word to describe the invisible oscillation which, as he conceived, atoms underwent when confined in a complex body (Epicurus *Ep.* I, 43; cf. Bailey p. 332).[1]

[1] LSJ gives the meaning of περιπάλαξις as 'collision, combination' of atoms, though that of περιπαλάσσεσθαι is given as 'to be hurled around'. Both translations are imperfect. The meaning of παλάσσεσθαι is 'to be shaken about, or sprinkled', and that of its simpler form πάλλειν is 'to shake'. A transitional stage to the Epicurean παλμός-interpretation is perhaps seen at Theophrastus *de sensu* 66 *fin.* (DK 68 A 135). In **578** Aristotle simply means that things are produced by the entanglement and rebound of atoms; the latter does not of itself produce γένεσις, but is necessary for its continuity.

(*c*) *The formation of bodies*

581 Aristotle *On Democritus ap.* Simplicium *de caelo* 295, 11 (continuing **577**) ...φερομένας δὲ (*sc.* τὰς ἀτόμους) ἐμπίπτειν καὶ περιπλέκεσθαι περιπλοκὴν τοιαύτην ἣ συμψαύειν μὲν αὐτὰ καὶ πλησίον ἀλλήλων εἶναι ποιεῖ, φύσιν μέντοι μίαν ἐξ ἐκείνων κατ' ἀλήθειαν οὐδ' ἡντιναοῦν γεννᾷ· κομιδῇ γὰρ εὔηθες εἶναι τὸ δύο ἢ τὰ πλείονα γενέσθαι ἄν ποτε ἕν. τοῦ δὲ συμμένειν τὰς οὐσίας μετ' ἀλλήλων μέχρι τινὸς αἰτιᾶται τὰς ἐπαλλαγὰς καὶ τὰς ἀντιλήψεις τῶν σωμάτων· τὰ μὲν γὰρ αὐτῶν εἶναι σκαληνά, τὰ δὲ ἀγκιστρώδη, τὰ

---

581 ...*As they* (sc. *the atoms*) *move they collide and become entangled in such a way as to cling in close contact to one another, but not so as to form one substance of them in reality of any kind whatever; for it is very simple-minded to suppose that two or more could ever become one. The reason he gives for atoms staying together for a while is the intertwining and mutual hold of the primary bodies; for some of them are angular, some hooked, some*

δὲ κοῖλα, τὰ δὲ κυρτά, τὰ δὲ ἄλλας ἀναρίθμους ἔχοντα διαφοράς· ἐπὶ τοσοῦτον οὖν χρόνον σφῶν αὐτῶν ἀντέχεσθαι νομίζει καὶ συμμένειν ἕως ἰσχυροτέρα τις ἐκ τοῦ περιέχοντος ἀνάγκη παραγενομένη διασείσῃ καὶ χωρὶς αὐτὰς διασπείρῃ.

582 Simplicius *de caelo* 242, 21 (continuing **556**) ...ταύτας δὲ τὰς ἀτόμους ἐν ἀπείρῳ τῷ κενῷ κεχωρισμένας ἀλλήλων καὶ διαφερούσας σχήμασί τε καὶ μεγέθεσι καὶ θέσει καὶ τάξει φέρεσθαι ἐν τῷ κενῷ καὶ ἐπικαταλαμβανούσας ἀλλήλας συγκρούεσθαι, καὶ τὰς μὲν ἀποπάλλεσθαι, ὅπῃ ἂν τύχωσιν, τὰς δὲ περιπλέκεσθαι ἀλλήλαις κατὰ τὴν τῶν σχημάτων καὶ μεγεθῶν καὶ θέσεων καὶ τάξεων συμμετρίαν καὶ συμμένειν [Diels, συμβαίνειν mss.] καὶ οὕτως τὴν τῶν συνθέτων γένεσιν ἀποτελεῖσθαι.

These passages state more precisely what has been outlined in earlier extracts, e.g. **546** and **562**, namely how atoms make up the visible complex bodies of our experience. As a result of collision between atoms those which are of congruous shape do not rebound but remain temporarily attached to one another: for example a hook-shaped atom may become involved with an atom into whose shape the hook fits. Other congruous atoms colliding with this two-atom complex then become attached, until a visible body of a certain character is formed. It is emphasized that no real coalescence of atoms takes place: they simply come into contact with each other, and always retain their own shape and individuality. When a complex of atoms collides with another complex it may be broken up into smaller complexes or into its constituent atoms, which then resume their motion through the void until they collide with a congruous atom, or complex, once again.

There are considerable difficulties in this account. What part does the principle of like-to-like play? This principle, illustrated by Democritus in **569**, is used in the description of world-formation; for in **562** atoms of all shapes come together in a great void, and like tends to like when the smaller atoms go to the periphery, the

---

concave, some convex, and indeed with countless other differences; so he thinks they cling to each other and stay together until such time as some stronger necessity comes from the surrounding and shakes and scatters them apart.

582 *...these atoms move in the infinite void, separate one from the other and differing in shapes, sizes, position and arrangement; overtaking each other they collide, and some are shaken away in any chance direction, while others, becoming intertwined one with another according to the congruity of their shapes, sizes, positions and arrangements, stay together and so effect the coming into being of compound bodies.*

bulkier ones to the centre. It is likeness of size rather than shape that seems to be primarily in question here; and it is only in a vortex that the sorting of sizes takes place. In the collisions of atoms *not* primarily subject to a vortex, i.e. either outside the scattered areas of world-formation, or within a formed world where the vortex-action may be modified, coalescence is due to congruence (which implies difference, so far as συμπλοκή is concerned, and not similarity) rather than to the principle of like-to-like. **582** tells us that this congruence must operate in respect of shape, size, position, and order. But this is not a complete solution, since we are told of one particular shape of atom that cannot be subject to any obvious type of congruence with others of its shape, but which does nevertheless combine to make up a single type of complex (or rather two different but connected types). This is the spherical atom, of which both soul and fire were evidently held to be composed.[1] Soul, it might be argued, is regarded (as elsewhere in the fifth century) as scattered throughout the whole body; but even so some conjunction of soul-atoms seems necessary. Fire is a clearer case, for it is distinctly visible, and must be composed of spherical atoms and no (or very few) atoms of another shape. How did these atoms come together? They cannot have become implicated with or hooked on to one another, as a result of collision; rather they must have become conjoined by the operation of the principle of like-to-like. It seems, therefore, that Aristotle in **581** is misleading in implying that all examples of συμμένειν, i.e. of the formation of apparently stable complex bodies, are due to *implication* of atoms: there are occasions when other types of συμμετρία (see **582**), especially *similarity* of shape and size, are more relevant.

[1] Aristotle asserts in several passages that for the atomists soul- and fire-atoms were spherical, because they had to be mobile and penetrative: e.g. **583** *de an.* A 2, 405 a 11 τῶν δὲ σχημάτων εὐκινητότατον τὸ σφαιροειδὲς λέγει (*sc.* Δημόκριτος)· τοιοῦτον δ' εἶναι τόν τε νοῦν καὶ τὸ πῦρ. Compare *ibid.* 404 a 5 (DK 67 A 28), where soul is said to be recruited by the inhalation of spherical atoms from the atmosphere—an idea analogous, perhaps, to that of Heraclitus in **237**. Aristotle occasionally implies that the soul *is* fire, because of this community of shape; but the truth is that a spherical atom is neither soul nor fire, it is just a spherical atom. It takes on secondary properties only in association with other atoms; in the context

---

583 *Democritus says that the spherical is the most mobile of shapes; and such is mind and fire.*

of an animal body it is soul, in other contexts it is fire (cf. Cherniss, *Aristotle's Criticism of Presocratic Philosophy*, 290 n.). Nevertheless, the similarity of shape explains how soul can be nurtured from the atmosphere (which is not besouled, but contains some fire). Apart from soul (equivalent to mind according to Aristotle's account of atomism) and fire, no details have survived about which shape of atom gave rise to which secondary characteristics, except in the case of sensation—sharp atoms produce salty tastes, etc. (see **591** below). Aristotle understood that air and water (and earth, probably) were conglomerations of all shapes of atoms, πανσπερμίαι:

584 *de caelo* Γ4, 303a12 ποῖον δὲ καὶ τί ἑκάστου τὸ σχῆμα τῶν στοιχείων οὐθὲν ἐπιδιώρισαν (*sc.* Λεύκιππος καὶ Δημόκριτος), ἀλλὰ μόνον τῷ πυρὶ τὴν σφαῖραν ἀπέδωκαν· ἀέρα δὲ καὶ ὕδωρ καὶ τἆλλα μεγέθει καὶ μικρότητι διεῖλον, ὡς οὖσαν αὐτῶν τὴν φύσιν οἷον πανσπερμίαν πάντων τῶν στοιχείων. If this is accurate, then the atomists took over the idea from Anaxagoras (see p. 383).

SENSATION, THOUGHT AND KNOWLEDGE

585 Aristotle *de sensu* 4, 442a29 Δημόκριτος δὲ καὶ οἱ πλεῖστοι τῶν φυσιολόγων ὅσοι λέγουσι περὶ αἰσθήσεως ἀτοπώτατόν τι ποιοῦσιν· πάντα γὰρ τὰ αἰσθητὰ ἁπτὰ ποιοῦσιν.

586 Aetius IV, 8, 10 Λεύκιππος Δημόκριτος Ἐπίκουρος τὴν αἴσθησιν καὶ τὴν νόησιν γίνεσθαι εἰδώλων ἔξωθεν προσιόντων· μηδενὶ γὰρ ἐπιβάλλειν μηδετέραν χωρὶς τοῦ προσπίπτοντος εἰδώλου.

587 Theophrastus *de sensu* 50 (DK68A135) ὁρᾶν μὲν οὖν ποιεῖ (*sc.* Δημόκριτος) τῇ ἐμφάσει· ταύτην δὲ ἰδίως λέγει· τὴν γὰρ ἔμφασιν οὐκ εὐθὺς ἐν τῇ κόρῃ γίνεσθαι, ἀλλὰ τὸν ἀέρα τὸν μεταξὺ τῆς ὄψεως καὶ τοῦ ὁρωμένου τυποῦσθαι συστελλόμενον ὑπὸ τοῦ ὁρωμένου καὶ τοῦ ὁρῶντος· ἅπαντος γὰρ ἀεὶ γίνεσθαί τινα ἀπορροήν. ἔπειτα τοῦτον στερεὸν ὄντα καὶ ἀλλόχρων ἐμφαίνεσθαι τοῖς ὄμμασιν †ὑγροῖς†· καὶ τὸ μὲν πυκνὸν οὐ δέχεσθαι τὸ δὲ ὑγρὸν διιέναι....

---

584 *They* (sc. *Leucippus and Democritus*) *did not further define what particular shape belonged to each of the elements but merely attributed the sphere to fire; air, water and the rest they distinguished by magnitude and smallness, as if their substance was a sort of mixture of seeds of all the elements.*

585 *Democritus and the majority of natural philosophers who discuss perception are guilty of a great absurdity; for they represent all perception as being by touch.*

586 *Leucippus, Democritus and Epicurus say that perception and thought arise when images enter from outside; neither occurs to anybody without an image impinging.*

587 *Democritus explains sight by the visual image, which he describes in a peculiar way; the visual image does not arise directly in the pupil, but the air between the eye and the object of sight is contracted and stamped by the object seen and the seer; for from everything there is always a sort of effluence proceeding. So this air, which is solid and variously coloured, appears in the eye, which is moist(?); the eye does not admit the dense part, but the moist passes through....*

588 Alexander *de sensu* 56, 12 εἴδωλα γάρ τινα ὁμοιόμορφα ἀπὸ τῶν ὁρωμένων συνεχῶς ἀπορρέοντα καὶ ἐμπίπτοντα τῇ ὄψει τοῦ ὁρᾶν ᾐτιῶντο. τοιοῦτοι δὲ ἦσαν οἱ περὶ Λεύκιππον καὶ Δημόκριτον....

589 Democritus Fr. 9, Sextus *adv. math.* VII, 135 νόμῳ γλυκύ, νόμῳ πικρόν, νόμῳ θερμόν, νόμῳ ψυχρόν, νόμῳ χροιή, ἐτεῇ δὲ ἄτομα καὶ κενόν.... (136) ἡμεῖς δὲ τῷ μὲν ἐόντι οὐδὲν ἀτρεκὲς συνίεμεν, μεταπῖπτον δὲ κατά τε σώματος διαθήκην καὶ τῶν ἐπεισιόντων καὶ τῶν ἀντιστηριζόντων.

590 Democritus Fr. 11, Sextus *adv. math.* VII, 139 (DK68B11) γνώμης δὲ δύο εἰσὶν ἰδέαι, ἡ μὲν γνησίη, ἡ δὲ σκοτίη· καὶ σκοτίης μὲν τάδε σύμπαντα, ὄψις ἀκοὴ ὀδμὴ γεῦσις ψαῦσις. ἡ δὲ γνησίη, ἀποκεκριμένη δὲ ταύτης....ὅταν ἡ σκοτίη μηκέτι δύνηται μήτε ὁρῆν ἐπ' ἔλαττον μήτε ἀκούειν μήτε ὀδμᾶσθαι μήτε γεύεσθαι μήτε ἐν τῇ ψαύσει αἰσθάνεσθαι, ἀλλ' ἐπὶ λεπτότερον***.

It is a necessary consequence of the atomist doctrine, that everything consists of atoms and void, that all sensation should be explained as a form of contact or touch (**585**). The soul consists of spherical atoms (**583**) spread through the body, and the mind was presumably regarded as a concentration of soul-atoms. Thus thought is a process analogous to sensation, and takes place when the soul- or mind-atoms are set in motion by the impingement of congruent atoms from outside. This is implied in **586**; in the case of thought one might suppose that self-motion by the kinetic spherical atoms is also possible, to account for apparently spontaneous thoughts. A full account of Democritus' detailed explanation of the different senses is given by Theophrastus in his *de sensu*, §§49–83 (DK68A135); this account may contain some Peripatetic distortion and elaboration, but shows that Democritus, on this and on other subjects, went to great pains to work out the

---

588 *They attributed sight to certain images, of the same shape as the object, which were continually streaming off from the objects of sight and impinging on the eye. This was the view of the school of Leucippus and Democritus....*

589 *By convention are sweet and bitter, hot and cold, by convention is colour; in truth are atoms and the void.... In reality we apprehend nothing exactly, but only as it changes according to the condition of our body and of the things that impinge on or offer resistance to it.*

590 *There are two forms of knowledge, one genuine, one obscure. To the obscure belong all the following: sight, hearing, smell, taste, touch. The other is genuine, and is quite distinct from this....When the obscure form can no longer see more minutely nor hear nor smell nor taste nor perceive through touch, but finer ***.*

detailed mechanism of the atomic theory. The fullest, and least satisfactory, description is of vision. Leucippus had evidently (**588**) taken over the Empedoclean theory (p. 343) that effluences, now described as images, εἴδωλα, are given off by objects and affect the sense-organs. Democritus then held (**587**) that the visual image (ἔμφασις) in the pupil is the result of effluences (ἀπορροαί) both from the seen object and from the observer; these meet and form a solid impression (ἐντύπωσις) in the air, which then enters the pupil of the eye. The other senses are explained more simply, and with emphasis on the different effects of different sizes and shapes of atom;[1] none of the explanations stands close examination, and Aristotle and Theophrastus were able to make some very pertinent criticisms. We do not know, for example, how Democritus explained the sense of touch: as all senses depend ultimately on this sense, it is obviously a problem how sight or taste, for example, differ from it.

[1] E.g. of *taste*, **591** Theophrastus *de sensu* 66 (DK68A135) τὸν δὲ πικρὸν (*sc.* χυλὸν) ἐκ μικρῶν καὶ λείων καὶ περιφερῶν, τὴν περιφέρειαν εἰληχότων [-α mss., Diels; -ων scripsi] καὶ καμπὰς ἔχουσαν· διὸ καὶ γλίσχρον εἶναι καὶ κολλώδη. ἁλμυρὸν δὲ τὸν ἐκ μεγάλων καὶ οὐ περιφερῶν, ἀλλ' ἐπ' ἐνίων μὲν σκαληνῶν....*Sound* is transferred when the particles of voice or noise mingle with similar particles in the air (and thus, presumably, form εἴδωλα): **592** Aetius IV, 19, 3 (DK68A128; probably from Poseidonius, according to Diels) Δημόκριτος καὶ τὸν ἀέρα φησὶν εἰς ὁμοιοσχήμονα θρύπτεσθαι σώματα καὶ συγκαλινδεῖσθαι τοῖς ἐκ τῆς φωνῆς θραύσμασι.

It follows that there can be no unchanging knowledge, the same for all, of the secondary appearances (which are primary, however, for our experience) or 'qualities' of things. Hot and cold, and so on, are conventional: in reality there are simply atoms and void (**589**). We can *know* nothing of the former kind, for our perception of the secondary qualities is distorted by resistance in the medium, air, or by the special dispositions of our own soul-atoms. Democritus made other pronouncements of a sceptical nature (cf. also frr. 6, 7, 8); but in **590** it is clearly stated that there is a genuine kind of opinion apart from sensation; it operates on objects too fine

---

591 *Bitter taste is caused by small, smooth, rounded atoms, whose circumference is actually sinuous; therefore it is both sticky and viscous. Salt taste is caused by large, not rounded atoms, but in some cases jagged ones....*

592 *Democritus says that the air is broken up into bodies of like shape and is rolled along together with the fragments of the voice.*

for sensation to apprehend. The fragment itself breaks off at the crucial point, but Sextus' introductory comments (not quoted here) indicate that 'genuine' opinion is intellectual. Obviously, its objects are atoms and the void—it penetrates beyond the 'conventional' secondary characteristics to the ultimate reality. Leucippus and Democritus themselves had been employing this kind of judgement. Yet the mind, like the soul as a whole, operates through the mechanical motions and collisions of atoms, and its impressions must be subject to the same sort of distortions as those of sensation (for which cf. **589**, second part). It is clear, then, that Democritus should not have claimed, and perhaps did not claim, more than approximate truth for his 'genuine' opinions—the truth still lay 'in the depths' (fr. 117).[1]

[1] The difficulty of proving a conviction about atoms and the void, if we can only infer these from our possibly fallacious corporeal impressions, is implied in a rejoinder by the senses to the first part of **589** ('by convention...in reality atoms and void'), ascribed to Democritus by Galen: **593** Democritus Fr. 125, Galen *de medic. empir.* 1259, 8 Schoene (DK 68 B 125) ...τάλαινά φρήν, παρ' ἡμέων λαβοῦσα τὰς πίστεις ἡμέας καταβάλλεις; πτῶμα τοι τὸ κατάβλημα. This neat criticism is normally accepted as Democritean, but the possibility must not be overlooked that it is framed by a later critic as an intentional epilogue to, and corrective of, **589**. It is odd that Sextus did not quote it.

ETHICS

594 Fr. 174, Stobaeus *Anth.* II, 9, 3 ὁ μὲν εὔθυμος εἰς ἔργα ἐπιφερόμενος δίκαια καὶ νόμιμα καὶ ὕπαρ καὶ ὄναρ χαίρει τε καὶ ἔρρωται καὶ ἀνακηδής ἐστιν· ὃς δ' ἂν καὶ δίκης ἀλογῇ καὶ τὰ χρὴ ἐόντα μὴ ἔρδῃ, τούτῳ πάντα τὰ τοιαῦτα ἀτερπείη, ὅταν τευ ἀναμνησθῇ, καὶ δέδοικε καὶ ἑωυτὸν κακίζει.

595 Fr. 171, Stobaeus *Anth.* II, 7, 3*i* εὐδαιμονίη οὐκ ἐν βοσκήμασιν οἰκεῖ οὐδὲ ἐν χρυσῷ· ψυχὴ οἰκητήριον δαίμονος.

---

593 *...Wretched mind, do you, who get your evidence from us, yet try to overthrow us? Our overthrow will be your downfall.*

594 *The cheerful man, who is eager for just and lawful deeds, rejoices whether waking or sleeping and is strong and free from care; but he that cares nought for justice and does not the things that are right finds all such things joyless, when he remembers them, and is afraid and reproaches himself.*

595 *Happiness does not reside in cattle or gold; the soul is the dwelling-place of one's good or evil genius.*

596 Fr. 246, Stobaeus *Anth.* III, 40, 6 ξενιτείη βίου αὐτάρκειαν διδάσκει· μᾶζα γὰρ καὶ στιβὰς λιμοῦ καὶ κόπου γλυκύτατα ἰάματα.

597 Fr. 277, Stobaeus *Anth.* IV, 24, 32 (DK68B277) ὅτεῳ χρήμη τεά ἐστι παῖδα ποιήσασθαι, ἐκ τῶν φίλων τεύ μοι δοκεῖ ἄμεινον εἶναι, καὶ τῷ μὲν παῖς ἔσται τοιοῦτος οἷον ἂν βούληται· ἔστι γὰρ ἐκλέξασθαι οἷον ἐθέλει...ἢν δέ τις ποιῆται ἀπὸ ἑωυτοῦ, πολλοὶ ἔνεισι κίνδυνοι· ἀνάγκη γάρ, ὃς ἂν γένηται, τούτῳ χρῆσθαι.

We know of no ethical doctrines held specifically by Leucippus, but Democritus devoted a part, though evidently not a particularly large part, of his considerable output to this subject. It happens that nearly all of the 290 or so *verbatim* fragments that have come down to us are from the ethical writings. Many are preserved because John Stobaeus, the 5th-century-A.D. anthologist, incorporated them in his collection. Over a quarter of the total are ascribed to 'Democrates'; most critics now follow Diels and accept the majority of these as genuine fragments of Democritus. Democritus' ethics are not explicitly based upon atomist physical preconceptions, and atoms are not mentioned.[1] The ethical fragments express, in a graphic and highly developed gnomic form, the Hellenic sentiments of restraint, common sense, and sanity. Yet no irrational sanctions of behaviour are introduced, no Justice or Nature that could not be resolved into the interplay of atoms and void. Vlastos may well be right in calling Democritean ethics 'the first rigorously naturalistic ethics in Greek thought'. At the same time there is no pandering to sophistic amoralism: the ethical ideal is εὐθυμίη (otherwise termed εὐεστώ, ἀθαμβίη)—contentment founded on moral well-being. **594** and **595** show this clearly enough; the latter may contain a reference to Heraclitus fr. 119 (**250**). There are other, clearer references to Heraclitus; and Democritus also repeated Anaxagoras' famous pronouncement 'the things that appear are a vision of the unseen' (**537**), which has an obvious relevance to the atomic theory. **596** shows the non-hedonistic and indeed ascetic nature of much of his ethics,

---

596 *Service abroad teaches self-sufficiency; barley-bread and a straw mattress are the pleasantest medicines for hunger and fatigue.*

597 *He who feels any desire to beget a child seems to me better advised to take it from one of his friends; he will then have a child such as he wishes, for he can choose the kind he wants.... But if a man begets his own child, many are the dangers there; for he must make the best of him whatever his nature.*

a trend which was followed by Epicurus; while **597** is an amusing example of philosophical rationalism, which in a Mediterranean way rejects as secondary the emotional and psychological overtones which some would consider of first importance. It is not surprising, then, that Democritus seems to have influenced the earlier Cynics. His combination of urbanity, austerity and wit must have won for him an immediate public; though as it happens the new direction in logic and ethics taken by Socrates and Plato meant that his fame as an ethical teacher survived mainly through Epicurus.

[1] C. Bailey, *The Greek Atomists and Epicurus* 522, stated that 'there is no effort to set the picture of the "cheerful" man on a firm philosophical basis or to link it up in any way with the physical system'. This is probably too extreme a view: the ethical doctrines are certainly not incompatible with the physical, and connexions may have been established in parts of Democritus that have not survived. G. Vlastos, *Philos. Rev.* 54 (1945) 578ff. and 55 (1946) 53ff., describes some possible but relatively slight points of contact between Democritean ethics and physics.

CONCLUSION

Atomism is in many ways the crown of Greek philosophical achievement before Plato. It fulfilled the ultimate aim of Ionian material monism by cutting the Gordian knot of the Eleatic elenchus. Much as it owed not only to Parmenides and Melissus, but also to the pluralist systems of Empedocles and Anaxagoras, atomism was not, however, an eclectic philosophy like that of Diogenes of Apollonia. It was in essence a new conception, one which was widely and skilfully applied by Democritus, and which through Epicurus and Lucretius was to play an important part in Greek thought even after Plato and Aristotle. It also, of course, eventually gave a stimulus to the development of modern atomic theory—the real nature and motives of which, however, are utterly distinct.

CHAPTER XVIII

DIOGENES OF APOLLONIA

LIFE AND DATE

598 Diogenes Laertius IX, 57 Διογένης Ἀπολλοθέμιδος Ἀπολλωνιάτης, ἀνὴρ φυσικὸς καὶ ἄγαν ἐλλόγιμος. ἤκουσε δέ, φησὶν Ἀντισθένης, Ἀναξιμένους. ἦν δὲ τοῖς χρόνοις κατ' Ἀναξαγόραν.

The Apollonia of which Diogenes was a citizen was probably the Milesian foundation on the Pontus, rather than the Cretan city.[1] The statement that he was roughly contemporary with Anaxagoras must be taken together with Theophrastus' judgement in **601** that he was 'almost the youngest' of the physical philosophers, and with Aristophanes' parody in the *Clouds* (**617**), produced in 423 B.C. All this is consonant with a *floruit* around 440–430. The statement that the succession-writer Antisthenes made Diogenes a *pupil* of Anaximenes may be due to a misunderstanding by Laertius rather than by Antisthenes: Diogenes would naturally be placed in the Milesian tradition and associated with Anaximenes because of his material principle, but his relative lateness in date does not seem to have been in doubt.

[1] So Aelian, *V.H.* II, 31 (DK 64 A 3), who mentioned 'Diogenes the Phrygian' in a list of 'atheists'. Stephanus of Byzantium, on the other hand, associates 'Diogenes the physicist' with the Cretan city, the former Eleutherna (DK *ibid.*).

WRITINGS

599 Diogenes Laertius IX, 57 ἀρχὴ δὲ αὐτῷ τοῦ συγγράμματος ἥδε· (Fr. 1) λόγου παντὸς ἀρχόμενον δοκεῖ μοι χρεὼν εἶναι τὴν ἀρχὴν ἀναμφισβήτητον παρέχεσθαι, τὴν δὲ ἑρμηνείαν ἁπλῆν καὶ σεμνήν.

---

598 *Diogenes son of Apollothemis, an Apolloniate, a physicist and a man of exceptional repute. He was a pupil of Anaximenes, as Antisthenes says. His period was that of Anaxagoras.*

599 *This is the beginning of his book: 'It is my opinion that the author, at the beginning of any account, should make his principle or starting-point indisputable, and his explanation simple and dignified.'*

600 Simplicius *Phys.* 151, 20 ἐπειδὴ δὲ ἡ μὲν τῶν πλειόνων ἱστορία Διογένην τὸν Ἀπολλωνιάτην ὁμοίως Ἀναξιμένει τὸν ἀέρα τίθεσθαι τὸ πρῶτον στοιχεῖόν φησι, Νικόλαος δὲ ἐν τῇ περὶ θεῶν πραγματείᾳ τοῦτον ἱστορεῖ τὸ μεταξὺ πυρὸς καὶ ἀέρος τὴν ἀρχὴν ἀποφήνασθαι...,[1] ἱστέον ὡς γέγραπται μὲν πλείονα τῷ Διογένει τούτῳ συγγράμματα (ὡς αὐτὸς ἐν τῷ Περὶ φύσεως ἐμνήσθη καὶ πρὸς φυσιολόγους ἀντειρηκέναι λέγων, οὓς καλεῖ καὶ αὐτὸς σοφιστάς, καὶ Μετεωρολογίαν γεγραφέναι, ἐν ᾗ καὶ λέγει περὶ τῆς ἀρχῆς εἰρηκέναι, καὶ μέντοι καὶ Περὶ ἀνθρώπου φύσεως), ἐν δέ γε τῷ Περὶ φύσεως, ὃ τῶν αὐτοῦ μόνον εἰς ἐμὲ ἦλθε, προτίθεται μὲν διὰ πολλῶν δεῖξαι ὅτι ἐν τῇ ὑπ' αὐτοῦ τεθείσῃ ἀρχῇ ἐστι νόησις πολλή.

[1] According to Simplicius (*Phys.* 149, 18) the references by Aristotle in **106** to an 'intermediate' substance were interpreted by Nicolaus of Damascus and by Porphyry as referring to Diogenes of Apollonia. Clearly this was an inference from passages like **606**, where warm air (which might be taken as intermediate between fire and air) forms the all-important noetic substance.

There has been much debate about whether Diogenes wrote a single book which, like Anaxagoras' work, for example, covered different but nevertheless interrelated subjects, or whether, as Simplicius thought (**600**), he wrote at least four books: 'Against the Sophists', 'Meteorologia' (a highly dubious form of book-title), and 'On the nature of man', as well as the 'On nature' which Simplicius himself saw and from which he quoted nearly all our extant fragments. Diels held the former view, which is supported by **599**, and thought that a subdivision of the book in the Hellenistic period (suggested by a reference by Rufus in Galen, DK64B9, to the *second* book of Diogenes' 'On nature') could have misled Simplicius. Burnet (*EGP* 353) and W. Theiler, on the other hand, argued that Simplicius is unlikely to be wrong on this point. Yet Simplicius' argument in **600**, that what he took to be a divergence in the ancient interpretation of Diogenes' primary

---

600 *Since the generality of enquirers say that Diogenes of Apollonia made air the primary element, similarly to Anaximenes, while Nicolaus in his theological investigation relates that Diogenes declared the material principle to be between fire and air..., it must be realized that several books were written by this Diogenes* (*as he himself mentioned in* On nature, *where he says that he had spoken also against the physicists—whom he calls 'sophists'—and written a* Meteorology, *in which he also says he spoke about the material principle, as well as* On the nature of man)*; in the* On nature, *at least, which alone of his works came into my hands, he proposes a manifold demonstration that in the material principle posited by him is much intelligence.*

substance must have arisen from the existence of different and not entirely consistent accounts by Diogenes, is rendered invalid because Nicolaus could have derived his interpretation from the book available to Simplicius himself (see p. 428 n.). Further, that same book certainly included a great deal on the 'nature of man'; for the long and detailed fr. 6 (extracts in **619**), quoted by Aristotle, seems to give precisely what Simplicius claims (*Phys.* 153, 13, DK64B6) to have found in 'On nature', namely 'an accurate anatomy of the veins', and not to have come from a separate work on the nature of man. Similarly the subjects of the other separate books postulated by Simplicius could have been comprehended in one original work, and Simplicius might easily have mistaken references to other parts of this work for references to separate books; modern scholars are sometimes confronted by a similar ambiguity in Aristotle's references to his treatment of particular subjects elsewhere. Yet perhaps Diogenes *did* write at least one book other than Simplicius' 'On nature': for it is stated by Galen, *On medical experience* XXII, 3 (in R. Walzer's translation from the Arabic), that 'Diogenes, writing more briefly and compendiously than you (*sc.* Asclepiades), has collected the diseases and their causes and remedies in one treatise'. This Diogenes (mentioned also *ibid.* XIII, 4) may well be the Apolloniate, whom we know from Theophrastus (*de sensu* 43, DK64A19) and from another medical author ([Galen] *de humor.* XIX, 495 Kühn, DK64A29*a*) to have held views about diagnosis by the tongue and colour of the patient. He was, therefore, perhaps a professional doctor, who may have published a technical medical treatise as well as a general exposition of his cosmic theory.

The opening sentence of the latter, quoted in **599**, reminds one of the methodological claims made at the beginning of some of the older and more philosophically-inclined works of the Hippocratic corpus, notably *Ancient medicine*, *Airs waters places*, and *The nature of man*. It must be admitted to Diogenes' credit that his exposition and argumentation is, for his period, clear, simple and dignified.

THE ECLECTIC, BUT NOT VALUELESS, NATURE OF DIOGENES' THOUGHT

601 Theophrastus *Phys. op.* fr. 2 *ap.* Simplicium *Phys.* 25, 1 (DK64A5) καὶ Διογένης δὲ ὁ Ἀπολλωνιάτης, σχεδὸν νεώτατος

---

601 *Diogenes the Apolloniate, almost the youngest of those who occupied themselves with*

γεγονὼς τῶν περὶ ταῦτα σχολασάντων, τὰ μὲν πλεῖστα συμπεφορημένως γέγραφε, τὰ μὲν κατὰ Ἀναξαγόραν, τὰ δὲ κατὰ Λεύκιππον λέγων· τὴν δὲ τοῦ παντὸς φύσιν ἀέρα καὶ οὗτός φησιν ἄπειρον εἶναι καὶ ἀίδιον, ἐξ οὗ πυκνουμένου καὶ μανουμένου καὶ μεταβάλλοντος τοῖς πάθεσι τὴν τῶν ἄλλων γίνεσθαι μορφήν. καὶ ταῦτα μὲν Θεόφραστος ἱστορεῖ περὶ τοῦ Διογένους, καὶ τὸ εἰς ἐμὲ ἐλθὸν αὐτοῦ σύγγραμμα Περὶ φύσεως ἐπιγεγραμμένον ἀέρα σαφῶς λέγει τὸ ἐξ οὗ πάντα γίνεται τὰ ἄλλα.

Simplicius here obligingly distinguishes Theophrastus' judgement on Diogenes from his own appended comments. According to Theophrastus, then, most of Diogenes' theories were eclectic, being derived from Anaxagoras, from Leucippus, or, in the important matter of the material principle, from Anaximenes. This seems to be true so far as it goes; but it seems probable that Heraclitus should be added to the list of important influences (pp. 433f., 436ff., 442).[1] Although an eclectic, Diogenes seems to have been far more effective than Hippon of Samos, for example, or even Archelaus; he used elements from earlier systems as material for a unitary theory of the world which was more self-consistent, less complicated, more explicit and more widely applicable than its monistic forebears. He adapted Anaxagoras' 'Mind' to his own monistic conception, and thereby showed, perhaps more clearly than his predecessors, how the basic substance (which is itself, in certain forms, νόησις or intelligence) could control the operation of natural change; and in the explicitly teleological fragment (**604**, which must have been further expanded in other parts of Diogenes' work) he fully worked out an idea which seems to have been foreshadowed in Heraclitus and left uncompleted in Anaxagoras.

[1] H. Diller, *Hermes* 76 (1941) 359ff., argued that the Leucippean elements are negligible; and that *Melissus* was criticizing both Diogenes and Leucippus (the normal view being, of course, that Leucippus reacted to suggestions in Melissus, see pp. 405f.). The chronology of these three thinkers is admittedly loose enough to allow that they were all active, as Diller suggests, in the decade 440–430 B.C.; and we cannot be absolutely certain

---

these matters (i.e. *physical studies*), *wrote for the most part in an eclectic fashion, following Anaxagoras in some things and Leucippus in others. He, too, says that the substance of the universe is infinite and eternal air, from which, when it is condensed and rarefied and changed in its dispositions, the form of other things comes into being. This is what Theophrastus relates about Diogenes; and the book of Diogenes which has reached me, entitled* On nature, *clearly says that air is that from which all the rest come into being.*

about their relationship. Yet Diller bases his theory of the priority of Diogenes to Melissus largely on similarities of diction and vocabulary, and overlooks the fact that words like μετακοσμεῖσθαι were liable to be used in any philosophical writing of the latter half of the fifth century B.C. There *are* verbal similarities between Melissus fr. 7 and Diogenes fr. 2 (**602** below); but it seems clear, not that Melissus is rebuffing Diogenes, or even *vice versa*, but that both are reacting in different ways to pluralist explanations of the world.

ALL THINGS MUST BE MODIFICATIONS OF ONE BASIC SUBSTANCE

602 Fr. 2, Simplicius *Phys.* 151, 31 ἐμοὶ δὲ δοκεῖ τὸ μὲν ξύμπαν εἰπεῖν πάντα τὰ ὄντα ἀπὸ τοῦ αὐτοῦ ἑτεροιοῦσθαι καὶ τὸ αὐτὸ εἶναι. καὶ τοῦτο εὔδηλον· εἰ γὰρ τὰ ἐν τῷδε τῷ κόσμῳ ἐόντα νῦν, γῆ καὶ ὕδωρ καὶ ἀὴρ καὶ πῦρ καὶ τὰ ἄλλα ὅσα φαίνεται ἐν τῷδε τῷ κόσμῳ ἐόντα, εἰ τούτων τι ἦν ἕτερον τοῦ ἑτέρου, ἕτερον ὂν τῇ ἰδίᾳ φύσει, καὶ μὴ τὸ αὐτὸ ἐὸν μετέπιπτε πολλαχῶς καὶ ἑτεροιοῦτο, οὐδαμῇ οὔτε μίσγεσθαι ἀλλήλοις ἠδύνατο, οὔτε ὠφέλησις τῷ ἑτέρῳ οὔτε βλάβη, οὐδ' ἂν οὔτε φυτὸν ἐκ τῆς γῆς φῦναι οὔτε ζῷον οὔτε ἄλλο γενέσθαι οὐδέν, εἰ μὴ οὕτω συνίστατο ὥστε ταὐτὸ εἶναι. ἀλλὰ πάντα ταῦτα ἐκ τοῦ αὐτοῦ ἑτεροιούμενα ἄλλοτε ἀλλοῖα γίνεται καὶ εἰς τὸ αὐτὸ ἀναχωρεῖ.

This statement, which according to Simplicius' introductory remark (DK 64 B 2) came 'immediately after the proem'—that is, immediately or shortly after **599**—is a re-affirmation of monism in face, presumably, of the pluralist systems of Empedocles and Anaxagoras. It is based on a new argument: not that it is *simpler* to have a single originative and basic substance (which may have been the chief Milesian motive, partly consciously, but partly unconsciously through the influence of the mythical-genealogical tradition), but that interaction of any kind between absolutely and essentially distinct substances would be impossible. Of the

---

602 *My opinion, in sum, is that all existing things are differentiated from the same thing, and* are *the same thing. And this is manifest: for if the things that exist at present in this world-order—earth and water and air and fire and all the other things apparent in this world-order—if any of these were different from the other (different, that is, in its own proper nature), and did not retain an essential identity while undergoing many changes and differentiations, it would be in no way possible for them to mix with each other, or for one to help or harm the other, or for a growing plant to grow out of the earth or for a living creature or anything else to come into being, unless they were so composed as to be the same thing. But all these things, being differentiated from the same thing, become of different kinds at different times and return into the same thing.*

interactions named, 'helping' and 'harming' (probably), and plant and animal growth, are taken from the animate sphere; which suggests that Diogenes' view of the world is influenced by his physiological interests, much as Anaxagoras' theory seems to have been intimately connected with his reflexions on nutrition. Biological change cannot arise from the mere juxtaposition of totally different substances, as for example in Empedocles' 'recipes' for bone and flesh (**440** and **441**). This principle is extended by Diogenes to the inanimate world, too, which is analysed in terms of the four now recognized world-masses and the other natural substances, thus showing the effect of Anaxagoras' extension of natural substance beyond Empedocles' four 'roots' (**496**). **602** concludes with the earliest certain enunciation (cf. pp. 118f.) of a principle assigned by Aristotle to the Presocratics in general, that things are destroyed into that from which they came.[1]

[1] Simplicius, in his connecting comment (DK 64B2) between **602** and **604**, found it odd that air, which is to be identified as the single underlying substance, is mentioned in **602** as one of several world-constituents. But this suggests that atmospheric air is not the basic form of air, but a close derivative. The basic form of air is presumably the warm air that is intelligence, cf. **606**—if, that is, Diogenes distinguished any such 'basic' or true form.

602 may also be taken as a limitation of the principle expressed in Anaxagoras fr. 17 (**497**), that all coming-to-be is mixture, all passing-away is separation. Diogenes accepted this, but only if the elements of the mixture were of one kind and not, as Anaxagoras thought, of many different kinds. In this respect Diogenes may have been following Leucippus. The direct evidence for dependence on Leucippus, however, apart from Theophrastus' bare assertion in **601**, is slight.[1]

[1] Cf. **603** Diogenes Laertius IX, 57 (after **598**) ἐδόκει δὲ αὐτῷ τάδε· στοιχεῖον εἶναι τὸν ἀέρα, κόσμους ἀπείρους καὶ κενὸν ἄπειρον· τόν τε ἀέρα πυκνούμενον καὶ ἀραιούμενον γεννητικὸν εἶναι τῶν κόσμων· οὐδὲν ἐκ τοῦ μὴ ὄντος γίνεσθαι οὐδὲ εἰς τὸ μὴ ὂν φθείρεσθαι· τὴν γῆν στρογγύλην, ἠρεισμένην ἐν τῷ μέσῳ, τὴν σύστασιν εἰληφυῖαν κατὰ τὴν ἐκ τοῦ θερμοῦ περιφορὰν καὶ πῆξιν ὑπὸ τοῦ ψυχροῦ. (Cf. **610**.) This brief summary is

603 *His opinions were as follows. Air is the element, and there are innumerable worlds and infinite void. Air is generative of the worlds through being condensed and rarefied. Nothing comes to be from that which is not, nor is anything destroyed into that which is not. The earth is circular, supported in the centre* (sc. *of the world*), *having received its formation in accordance with the revolution proceeding from the hot and coagulation produced by the cold.*

indirectly derived from Theophrastus, but through a third-rate biographical source. There is only one other mention of the void in connexion with Diogenes (DK64A31). It might appear that its presence here is due to doxographical conjecture. Yet Theophrastus evidently credited Diogenes with innumerable worlds of atomistic type (see **610**, as well as the present passage), and Diogenes could certainly have taken this theory from Leucippus. If so, then he might also have followed Leucippus in postulating the void—a postulate intimately connected, for the atomists, with that of innumerable worlds.

THE BASIC SUBSTANCE CONTAINS DIVINE INTELLIGENCE, WHICH DIRECTS ALL THINGS FOR THE BEST

604 Fr. 3, Simplicius *Phys.* 152, 13 οὐ γὰρ ἄν, φησίν, οἷόν τε ἦν οὕτω δεδάσθαι ἄνευ νοήσιος ὥστε πάντων μέτρα ἔχειν,[1] χειμῶνός τε καὶ θέρους καὶ νυκτὸς καὶ ἡμέρας καὶ ὑετῶν καὶ ἀνέμων καὶ εὐδιῶν· καὶ τὰ ἄλλα, εἴ τις βούλεται ἐννοεῖσθαι, εὑρίσκοι ἂν οὕτω διακείμενα ὡς ἀνυστὸν κάλλιστα.

[1] Were it not for the difficulty of providing a subject for πάντων μέτρα ἔχειν, it would be natural to understand πάντα as the subject of δεδάσθαι. As it is, it seems preferable to understand something like the underlying substance referred to in **602** *fin.* as the subject both of δεδάσθαι and of ἔχειν.

According to Simplicius, **604** followed very closely upon **602**, and was itself followed by **605**. Diogenes set out his teleological belief in a prominent position, therefore, before the basic substance had been fully identified as air. According to that belief the world and its parts are arranged by a divine intelligence in the best possible way. This intelligence, according to Simplicius and to fr. 5 (**606**), is implicit in the basic substance. It is postulated because otherwise it would have been impossible for things to be divided up, and to be measured, as they patently are, into winter and summer, night and day, rain and wind and fair weather. It is the regularity of natural events, therefore, of year- and day-cycles and of the weather, which impressed Diogenes;[1] here he was surely to some extent dependent on Heraclitus, who stressed that the *measures* (**220–222**) of all natural change were preserved by the Logos, itself an expression or aspect of the archetypal substance, fire.

---

604 *For, he says, it would not be possible without intelligence for it* (sc. *the underlying substance*) *so to be divided up that it has measures of all things—of winter and summer and night and day and rains and winds and fair weather. The other things, too, if one wishes to consider them, one would find disposed in the best possible way.*

Heraclitus had instanced these same natural oppositions and cycles (cf. **205**, **207** and fr. 57) as evincing a basic unity because of the regularity of their measures. Diogenes' concept of the conscious purposefulness of nature, however, goes beyond Heraclitus; the latter, although he considered all things to be 'steered' by fire (**223**), held that this was in accordance with an objective natural rule (which could be regarded materially as Logos or fire itself) implicit in the constitution of things—a development, perhaps, of Anaximander's idea that natural interchanges were governed by a natural law of justice. Thus for Heraclitus pure fire was intelligent, but the regularity of natural events was achieved not so much by the deliberate exercise of this intelligence on every occasion as by the incorporation of the Logos (fire in a systematically metric function) in each separate thing, leading it to behave in a regular or measured way. For Diogenes, on the other hand, every natural event was evidently due directly to the intelligence of the pure form of the basic substance; and thus occasional local anomalies, which were permitted in the systems of Anaximander and Heraclitus, providing they were eventually corrected and counterbalanced, should not really take place. The difference in Diogenes' view is undoubtedly due to the influence of Anaxagoras' Mind, νοῦς (**503** ff.); the effect of which, however, as Socrates complained in **522**, was only too often merely mechanical.

[1] No doubt he was also impressed by the significant functions of the organs of living creatures. We know that he gave considerable attention to methods of sensation (see **616**) and breathing in different species—for example in fish (DK 64A31); and that such differences were explained by differences in natural structure, which might thus appear to be purpose-serving.

INTELLIGENCE AND LIFE ARE DUE TO AIR, WHICH IS THEREFORE THE BASIC FORM OF MATTER. AIR IS DIVINE AND CONTROLS ALL THINGS; IT TAKES DIFFERENT FORMS ACCORDING TO ITS DIFFERENCES IN HEAT, MOTION AND SO ON

605 Fr. 4, Simplicius *Phys.* 152, 18 ἔτι δὲ πρὸς τούτοις καὶ τάδε μεγάλα σημεῖα. ἄνθρωποι γὰρ καὶ τὰ ἄλλα ζῷα ἀναπνέοντα ζώει τῷ ἀέρι. καὶ τοῦτο αὐτοῖς καὶ ψυχή ἐστι καὶ νόησις, ὡς δεδηλώσεται

---

605 *Further, in addition to those, these too are important indications. Men and the other living creatures live by means of air, through breathing it. And this is for them both soul*

ἐν τῇδε τῇ συγγραφῇ ἐμφανῶς, καὶ ἐὰν τοῦτο ἀπαλλαχθῇ ἀποθνῄσκει καὶ ἡ νόησις ἐπιλείπει.

606 Fr. 5, Simplicius *Phys.* 152, 22 καί μοι δοκεῖ τὸ τὴν νόησιν ἔχον εἶναι ὁ ἀὴρ καλούμενος ὑπὸ τῶν ἀνθρώπων, καὶ ὑπὸ τούτου πάντας καὶ κυβερνᾶσθαι καὶ πάντων κρατεῖν· αὐτὸ γάρ μοι τοῦτο θεὸς δοκεῖ εἶναι καὶ ἐπὶ πᾶν ἀφῖχθαι καὶ πάντα διατιθέναι καὶ ἐν παντὶ ἐνεῖναι. καὶ ἔστιν οὐδὲ ἓν ὅ τι μὴ μετέχει τούτου· μετέχει δὲ οὐδὲ ἓν ὁμοίως τὸ ἕτερον τῷ ἑτέρῳ, ἀλλὰ πολλοὶ τρόποι καὶ αὐτοῦ τοῦ ἀέρος καὶ τῆς νοήσιός εἰσιν· ἔστι γὰρ πολύτροπος, καὶ θερμότερος καὶ ψυχρότερος καὶ ξηρότερος καὶ ὑγρότερος καὶ στασιμώτερος καὶ ὀξυτέρην κίνησιν ἔχων, καὶ ἄλλαι πολλαὶ ἑτεροιώσιες ἔνεισι καὶ ἡδονῆς καὶ χροιῆς ἄπειροι. καὶ πάντων τῶν ζῴων δὲ ἡ ψυχὴ τὸ αὐτό ἐστιν, ἀὴρ θερμότερος μὲν τοῦ ἔξω ἐν ᾧ ἐσμεν, τοῦ μέντοι παρὰ τῷ ἡλίῳ πολλὸν ψυχρότερος. ὅμοιον δὲ τοῦτο τὸ θερμὸν οὐδενὸς τῶν ζῴων ἐστίν (ἐπεὶ οὐδὲ τῶν ἀνθρώπων ἀλλήλοις), ἀλλὰ διαφέρει μέγα μὲν οὔ, ἀλλ' ὥστε παραπλήσια εἶναι. οὐ μέντοι ἀτρεκέως γε ὅμοιον οὐδὲν οἷόν τε γενέσθαι τῶν ἑτεροιουμένων ἕτερον τῷ ἑτέρῳ, πρὶν τὸ αὐτὸ γένηται. ἅτε οὖν πολυτρόπου ἐούσης τῆς ἑτεροιώσιος πολύτροπα καὶ τὰ ζῷα καὶ πολλὰ καὶ οὔτε ἰδέαν ἀλλήλοις ἐοικότα οὔτε δίαιταν οὔτε νόησιν ὑπὸ τοῦ πλήθεος τῶν ἑτεροιώσεων. ὅμως δὲ πάντα τῷ αὐτῷ καὶ ζῇ καὶ ὁρᾷ καὶ ἀκούει, καὶ τὴν ἄλλην νόησιν ἔχει ἀπὸ τοῦ αὐτοῦ πάντα.

(i.e. *life-principle) and intelligence, as will be clearly shown in this work; and if this is removed, then they die and intelligence fails.*

606 *And it seems to me that that which has intelligence is what men call air, and that all men are steered by this and that it has power over all things. For this very thing seems to me to be a god and to have reached everywhere and to dispose all things and to be in everything. And there is no single thing that does not have a share of this; but nothing has an equal share of it, one with another, but there are many fashions both of air itself and of intelligence. For it is many-fashioned, being hotter and colder and drier and moister and more stationary and more swiftly mobile, and many other differentiations are in it both of taste and of colour, unlimited in number. And yet of all living creatures the soul is the same, air that is warmer than that outside, in which we exist, but much cooler than that near the sun. But in none of living creatures is this warmth alike (since it is not even so in individual men); the difference is not great, but as much as still allows them to be similar. Yet it is not possible for anything to become truly alike, one to the other, of the things undergoing differentiation, without becoming the same. Because, then, the differentiation is many-fashioned, living creatures are many-fashioned and many in number, resembling each other neither in form nor in way of life nor in intelligence, because of the number of differentiations. Nevertheless they all live and see and hear by the same thing, and have the rest of their intelligence from the same thing.*

607 Fr. 7, Simplicius *Phys.* 153, 19 καὶ αὐτὸ μὲν τοῦτο καὶ ἀίδιον καὶ ἀθάνατον σῶμα, τῶν δὲ τὰ μὲν γίνεται, τὰ δὲ ἀπολείπει.[1]

608 Fr. 8, Simplicius *Phys.* 153, 20 ἀλλὰ τοῦτό μοι δῆλον δοκεῖ εἶναι, ὅτι καὶ μέγα καὶ ἰσχυρὸν καὶ ἀίδιόν τε καὶ ἀθάνατον καὶ πολλὰ εἰδός ἐστι.

[1] This is the old contrast between god and man, or god and the world: the perfect and the imperfect (cf. p. 180). Simplicius noted (DK 64 B 7) that both the divine and the world are made of the same thing, air, for Diogenes. It is nevertheless legitimate to contrast the pure, divine form of air with its derivative, corporeal forms; the severity of this contrast is due to its traditional formulation.

Simplicius obviously omitted something that came between **604** and **605** in Diogenes' book, so that we do not know the 'signs' (cf. Melissus fr. 8 *init.*, **392**) mentioned in **605**: presumably they too were signs that the basic substance was air. Perhaps the gradual diminution of decaying bodies, 'into thin air', might have been one such indication, the nature of semen (see p. 444 and **619**) another. The sign that is mentioned, that all creatures live by breathing air, which is both soul (life-principle) and intelligence, is obviously the most important of all; it was probably stated in Anaximenes, indeed (cf. pp. 161 f.), but would occur naturally to anyone of pronounced physiological interests like Diogenes. That breath is the life-substance is deduced in **605** from the fact that life leaves the body with the breath, and was implicit in some Homeric uses of θυμός and ψυχή. The connexion of πνεῦμα, breath, with πνεῦμα, wind, was perhaps first made by Anaximenes. That air is also intelligence is, on the one hand, an inference from its *divinity* as the life-principle; on the other it may be a reasonable development of a view like Heraclitus', that the intelligent substance (in his case Logos or fire) is inhaled by breathing.[1] But even in Homer the distinction between life (ψυχή) and intelligence or feeling (θυμός) was blurred.

[1] Diogenes succeeded in accounting for the dual function of air (as life, and as intelligence and perception) in his detailed physiological theory; for air as sensation see p. 442 below, for air as life cf. **609** Aetius v, 24, 3

---

607 *And this very thing is both eternal and immortal body, but of the rest some come into being, some pass away.*

608 *But this seems to me to be plain, that it is both great and strong and eternal and immortal and much-knowing.*

(DK 64 A 29) Διογένης (*sc.* φησὶ) ἐὰν ἐπὶ πᾶν τὸ αἷμα διαχεόμενον πληρώσῃ μὲν τὰς φλέβας, τὸν δὲ ἐν αὐταῖς περιεχόμενον ἀέρα ὤσῃ εἰς τὰ στέρνα καὶ τὴν ὑποκειμένην γαστέρα, ὕπνον γεγενῆσθαι καὶ θερμότερον ὑπάρχειν τὸν θώρακα· ἐὰν δὲ ἅπαν τὸ ἀερῶδες ἐκ τῶν φλεβῶν ἐκλίπῃ, θάνατον συντυγχάνειν. This is analogous to Heraclitus' theory of waking, sleeping and death as descending stages of consciousness, due to the diminution of soul-fire.

Air is god; it steers, has power over, inheres in, and disposes all things (**606** *init.*); it is eternal and immortal (**607**, **608**). In these descriptions, whose hieratic quality (particularly **606** with its repetition of πάντας, πάντων, πᾶν etc.) has been rightly remarked, Diogenes seems to collect together all the phraseology of his predecessors—of Anaximander (**110**), Heraclitus (**223**) and Anaxagoras (**503**) in particular. His emphasis in **606** that all things absolutely participate in air may be intended as a correction of Anaxagoras, for whom Mind only existed in animate things. For Diogenes all things are made of air, but the inanimate is divided from the animate world by the fact that only in some things is warm air found. In **606** the animate is chiefly in question; differences are explained by air changing in accordance with its warmth, dryness, motion, and other characteristics, which give it different 'tastes and colours'. It may be noted here that, in spite of Theophrastus' assessment in **601**, Diogenes does not appear to be interested in explaining all changes of air as being due solely to rarefaction and condensation; at least he describes some alteration in terms of what should be derivative and secondary changes, like those of temperature. In fact, the distinguishing mark of the divine is its temperature, not its density; Diogenes has clearly overlooked, or at least failed to stress, the elegant consistency of Anaximenes.

Intelligence is *warm* air, warmer than the atmosphere (which is presumably air verging towards water), but cooler than the air round the sun (which is verging towards fire). There are indefinite slight variations in the temperature-range of intelligence-producing air, thus accounting for countless variations in perception, intelligence, and way of life. Moderate warmth is the *differentia* of

---

609 *Diogenes says that if the blood, pouring into every part, fills the veins and pushes the air enclosed in them into the chest and the stomach below, then sleep occurs and the middle part of the body is warmer; but if all the airy part goes away from the veins, death occurs simultaneously.*

soul-air; thus Diogenes achieves a rational distinction between the animate and the inanimate world, while retaining (unlike Anaxagoras) a common substance for both, and thus keeping his monistic conception intact. Neatness, rather than originality, is his contribution here. Anaximenes had already assumed that both soul and the world were made of air, and that they were nevertheless distinguished, presumably by degree of concentration—though this is not explicitly stated; and for Heraclitus, too, the archetypal form of matter, fire, was also, in certain forms, soul-substance—which acted not only within animate creatures but also, as noetic and directive, on the world as a whole.

DETAILED PHYSICAL DOCTRINES

(i) *Cosmogony and cosmology*

610 [Plutarch] *Strom.* 12 Διογένης ὁ Ἀπολλωνιάτης ἀέρα ὑφίσταται στοιχεῖον· κινεῖσθαι δὲ τὰ πάντα ἀπείρους τε εἶναι τοὺς κόσμους. κοσμοποιεῖ δὲ οὕτως· ὅτι τοῦ παντὸς κινουμένου, καὶ ᾗ μὲν ἀραιοῦ ᾗ δὲ πυκνοῦ γινομένου, ὅπου συνεκύρησεν τὸ πυκνὸν συστροφῇ ⟨τὴν γῆν⟩ ποιῆσαι καὶ οὕτως τὰ λοιπὰ κατὰ τὸν αὐτὸν λόγον, τὰ ⟨δὲ⟩ κουφότατα τὴν ἄνω τάξιν λαβόντα τὸν ἥλιον ἀποτελέσαι. [συστροφὴν ποιῆσαι mss., em. Kranz, cf. **603**. ⟨δὲ⟩ Diels.]

611 Aetius II, 13, 5+9 Διογένης κισηροειδῆ τὰ ἄστρα, διαπνοὰς δὲ αὐτὰ νομίζει τοῦ κόσμου· εἶναι δὲ διάπυρα. συμπεριφέρεσθαι δὲ τοῖς φανεροῖς ἄστροις ἀφανεῖς λίθους καὶ παρ' αὐτὸ τοῦτ' ἀνωνύμους· πίπτοντας δὲ πολλάκις ἐπὶ τῆς γῆς σβέννυσθαι καθάπερ τὸν ἐν Αἰγὸς ποταμοῖς πυροειδῶς κατενεχθέντα ἀστέρα πέτρινον.

Diogenes' cosmogony is unoriginal, and is dependent on Anaxagoras (for the idea of the noetic substance starting a vortex) and on the Milesian tradition (the dense coalescing at the centre to form earth, the rarer material going to the extremity, by like-to-

---

610 *Diogenes the Apolloniate premises that air is the element, and that all things are in motion and the worlds innumerable. He gives this account of cosmogony: the whole was in motion, and became rare in some places and dense in others; where the dense ran together centripetally it made the earth, and so the rest by the same method, while the lightest parts took the upper position and produced the sun.*

611 *Diogenes says that the heavenly bodies are like pumice-stone, and he considers them as the breathing-holes of the world; and they are fiery. With the visible heavenly bodies are carried round invisible stones, which for this reason have no name: they often fall on the earth and are extinguished, like the stone star that made its fiery descent at Aegospotami.*

like and differentiation). Both **610** and **603** assign innumerable worlds to Diogenes (see n. on pp. 432f.); these were of atomistic type, presumably after Leucippus—coming-to-be, that is, and passing away throughout the boundless void (cf. also Aetius II, 1, 3, DK 64 A 10). Aristotle's comment (**134**) that according to some natural philosophers the world was drying up was referred by Alexander (**135**) to Diogenes as well as to Anaximander; Alexander adds (DK 64 A 17) that Diogenes explained the saltness of the sea by the sun's evaporating the sweet water, which may suggest that this drying of the sea was a simple meteorological comment not necessarily concerned with cosmic cycles or innumerable worlds.[1] The heavenly bodies (of which the sun is probably farther away than the stars, cf. **610** *fin.*) are like pumice-stone, and glowing; doubtless their pumice-like consistency is postulated so that they can be very light, and interpenetrated by fire. The great Aegospotami meteorite of 467 B.C. had evidently impressed Diogenes (as it had Anaxagoras, cf. p. 392), who inferred that there must be other such bodies revolving unseen in the sky. This may be Diogenes' own idea (cf. p. 156). Other astronomical details are derivative: that the sun is a concentration of rays from the aither (Aetius II, 20, 10, DK 64 A 13) is from Empedocles (p. 334); that the earth, which is a circle, presumably a round disc, is tilted toward the south (Aetius II, 8, 1, DK 59 A 67) is ascribed also to Anaxagoras and Leucippus; whether or not it is derived from Anaximenes is questionable (see pp. 156f.).

[1] It is probable that Diogenes is referred to (though perhaps not exclusively; for this kind of detail he was classed with Anaximenes) in **612** Aristotle *Meteor.* B 2, 355 a 21 τὸ δ' αὐτὸ συμβαίνει καὶ τούτοις ἄλογον καὶ τοῖς φάσκουσι τὸ πρῶτον ὑγρᾶς οὔσης καὶ τῆς γῆς, καὶ τοῦ κόσμου τοῦ περὶ τὴν γῆν ὑπὸ τοῦ ἡλίου θερμαινομένου, ἀέρα γενέσθαι καὶ τὸν ὅλον οὐρανὸν αὐξηθῆναι, καὶ τοῦτον πνεύματά τε παρέχεσθαι καὶ τὰς τροπὰς αὐτοῦ ποιεῖν. That the drawing up of vapour by the sun was mentioned by Diogenes is proved by his solution of that popular natural problem, the cause of the flooding of the Nile: **613** Σ *in* Apollonium Rhod. IV, 269 Διογένης δὲ ὁ 'Απολλωνιάτης ὑπὸ ἡλίου ἁρπάζεσθαι τὸ ὕδωρ τῆς θαλάσσης,

---

612 *The same illogicality results both for these and for those who say that when the earth, too, was at first moist, and the part of the world round the earth was being heated by the sun, air was produced and the whole heaven was increased, and that air causes winds and makes the turnings of the sun.*

613 *Diogenes the Apolloniate says that the water of the sea is snatched up by the sun,*

ὃ τότε εἰς τὸν Νεῖλον καταφέρεσθαι· οἴεται γὰρ πληροῦσθαι τὸν Νεῖλον ἐν τῷ θέρει διὰ τὸ τὸν ἥλιον εἰς τοῦτον τὰς ἀπὸ γῆς ἰκμάδας τρέπειν. Diogenes used ἰκμάδες, moist secretions or emanations, to explain another popular natural problem too, that of magnetism: **614** Alexander *Quaest.* II, 23 (DK 64 A 33) (περὶ τῆς 'Ηρακλείας λίθου, διὰ τί ἕλκει τὸν σίδηρον.) Διογένης δὲ ὁ 'Απολλωνιάτης πάντα τὰ ἐλατά φησιν καὶ ἀφιέναι τινὰ ἰκμάδα ἀφ' αὑτῶν πεφυκέναι καὶ ἕλκειν ἔξωθεν τὰ μὲν πλείω τὰ δὲ ἐλάττω, πλείστην δὲ ἀφιέναι χαλκόν τε καὶ σίδηρον.... (The magnet, on the contrary, absorbs more emanations than it discharges, and therefore draws in the superfluous emanations of iron and bronze, which are 'akin' to it—and so also attracts the metals themselves.) Similarly Empedocles, DK 31 A 89.

(ii) *Physiology:* (*a*) *Cognition*

615 Theophrastus *de sensu* 39 ff. (DK 64 A 19) Διογένης δ' ὥσπερ τὸ ζῆν καὶ τὸ φρονεῖν τῷ ἀέρι καὶ τὰς αἰσθήσεις ἀνάπτει· διὸ καὶ δόξειεν ἂν τῷ ὁμοίῳ ποιεῖν (οὐδὲ γὰρ τὸ ποιεῖν εἶναι καὶ πάσχειν, εἰ μὴ πάντα ἦν ἐξ ἑνός)· τὴν μὲν ὄσφρησιν τῷ περὶ τὸν ἐγκέφαλον ἀέρι·...(40) τὴν δ' ἀκοήν, ὅταν ὁ ἐν τοῖς ὠσὶν ἀὴρ κινηθεὶς ὑπὸ τοῦ ἔξω διαδῷ πρὸς τὸν ἐγκέφαλον. τὴν δὲ ὄψιν [ὁρᾶν] ἐμφαινομένων εἰς τὴν κόρην, ταύτην δὲ μειγνυμένην τῷ ἐντὸς ἀέρι ποιεῖν αἴσθησιν· σημεῖον δέ· ἐὰν γὰρ φλεγμασία γένηται τῶν φλεβῶν, οὐ μείγνυσθαι τῷ ἐντὸς οὐδ' ὁρᾶν ὁμοίως τῆς ἐμφάσεως οὔσης. τὴν δὲ γεῦσιν τῇ γλώττῃ διὰ τὸ μανὸν καὶ ἁπαλόν. περὶ δὲ ἁφῆς οὐδὲν ἀφώρισεν οὔτε πῶς οὔτε τίνων ἐστίν. ἀλλὰ μετὰ ταῦτα πειρᾶται λέγειν διὰ τί συμβαίνει τὰς αἰσθήσεις ἀκριβεστέρας εἶναι καὶ τῶν ποίων. (41) ὄσφρησιν μὲν οὖν ὀξυτάτην οἷς ἐλάχιστος ἀὴρ ἐν τῇ κεφαλῇ·

---

and then comes down into the Nile; for he thinks that the Nile floods in summer through the sun turning into it the emanations from earth.

614 (*On why the Heraclean stone* (i.e. *the magnet*) *attracts iron.*) *Diogenes the Apolloniate says that all ductile metals naturally discharge from themselves, and draw in from outside, a kind of emanation, some more and others less; but that bronze and iron discharge it in the greatest quantity....*

615 *Diogenes attributes thinking and the senses, as also life, to air. Therefore he would seem to do so by the action of similars* (*for he says that there would be no action or being acted upon, unless all things were from one*). *The sense of smell is produced by the air round the brain....* (*40*) *Hearing is produced whenever the air within the ears, being moved by the air outside, spreads toward the brain. Vision occurs when things are reflected on the pupil, and it, being mixed with the air within, produces a sensation. A proof of this is that, if there is an inflammation of the veins* (i.e. *those in the eye*), *there is no mixture with the air within, nor vision, although the reflexion exists exactly as before. Taste occurs to the tongue by what is rare and gentle. About touch he gave no definition, either about its nature or its objects. But after this he attempts to say what is the cause of more accurate sensations, and what sort of objects they have.* (*41*) *Smell is keenest for those who*

τάχιστα γὰρ μείγνυσθαι· καὶ πρὸς τούτοις ἐὰν ἕλκῃ διὰ μακροτέρου καὶ στενωτέρου· θᾶττον γὰρ οὕτω κρίνεσθαι· διόπερ ἔνια τῶν ζῴων ὀσφραντικώτερα τῶν ἀνθρώπων εἶναι· οὐ μὴν ἀλλὰ συμμέτρου γε οὔσης τῆς ὀσμῆς τῷ ἀέρι πρὸς τὴν κρᾶσιν μάλιστα ἂν αἰσθάνεσθαι τὸν ἄνθρωπον. . . . ὅτι δὲ ὁ ἐντὸς ἀὴρ αἰσθάνεται μικρὸν ὢν μόριον τοῦ θεοῦ, σημεῖον εἶναι, διότι πολλάκις πρὸς ἄλλα τὸν νοῦν ἔχοντες οὔθ' ὁρῶμεν οὔτ' ἀκούομεν. (43) ἡδονὴν δὲ καὶ λύπην γίνεσθαι τόνδε τὸν τρόπον· ὅταν μὲν πολὺς ὁ ἀὴρ μίσγηται τῷ αἵματι καὶ κουφίζῃ κατὰ φύσιν ὢν καὶ κατὰ πᾶν τὸ σῶμα διεξιών, ἡδονήν· ὅταν δὲ παρὰ φύσιν καὶ μὴ μίσγηται συνιζάνοντος τοῦ αἵματος καὶ ἀσθενεστέρου καὶ πυκνοτέρου γινομένου, λύπην. ὁμοίως καὶ θάρσος καὶ ὑγίειαν καὶ τἀναντία. . . . (44) φρονεῖν δ', ὥσπερ ἐλέχθη, τῷ ἀέρι καθαρῷ καὶ ξηρῷ· κωλύειν γὰρ τὴν ἰκμάδα τὸν νοῦν· διὸ καὶ ἐν τοῖς ὕπνοις καὶ ἐν ταῖς μέθαις καὶ ἐν ταῖς πλησμοναῖς ἧττον φρονεῖν· ὅτι δὲ ἡ ὑγρότης ἀφαιρεῖται τὸν νοῦν, σημεῖον, διότι τὰ ἄλλα ζῷα χείρω τὴν διάνοιαν· ἀναπνεῖν τε γὰρ τὸν ἀπὸ τῆς γῆς ἀέρα καὶ τροφὴν ὑγροτέραν προσφέρεσθαι. τοὺς δὲ ὄρνιθας ἀναπνεῖν μὲν καθαρόν, φύσιν δὲ ὁμοίαν ἔχειν τοῖς ἰχθύσι· καὶ γὰρ τὴν σάρκα στιφράν, καὶ τὸ πνεῦμα οὐ διιέναι διὰ παντός, ἀλλὰ ἱστάναι περὶ τὴν κοιλίαν. . . . τὰ δὲ φυτὰ διὰ τὸ μὴ εἶναι κοῖλα μηδὲ ἀναδέχεσθαι τὸν ἀέρα παντελῶς ἀφῃρῆσθαι τὸ φρονεῖν.

Slightly over half of Theophrastus' description is given in **615**; for the remainder see DK. Some of Theophrastus' explanations show his own interpretation, notably like-to-like as a principle of sensation, and 'symmetry', which has apparently been super-

---

have least air in their heads, for it is mixed most quickly; and, in addition, if a man draws it in through a longer and narrower channel; for in this way it is more swiftly assessed. Therefore some living creatures are more perceptive of smell than are men; yet nevertheless, if the smell were symmetrical with the air, with regard to mixture, man would smell perfectly. . . . That the air within perceives, being a small portion of the god, is indicated by the fact that often, when we have our mind on other things, we neither see nor hear. (43) *Pleasure and pain come about in this way: whenever air mixes in quantity with the blood and lightens it, being in accordance with nature, and penetrates through the whole body, pleasure is produced; but whenever the air is present contrary to nature and does not mix, then the blood coagulates and becomes weaker and thicker, and pain is produced. Similarly confidence and health and their opposites. . . .* (44) *Thought, as has been said, is caused by pure and dry air; for a moist emanation inhibits the intelligence; for this reason thought is diminished in sleep, drunkenness and surfeit. That moisture removes intelligence is indicated by the fact that other living creatures are inferior in intellect, for they breathe the air from the earth and take to themselves moister sustenance. Birds breathe pure air, but have a constitution similar to that of fishes; for their flesh is solid, and the breath does not penetrate all through but stays around the abdomen. . . . Plants, through not being hollow and not receiving air within them, are completely devoid of intelligence.*

imposed on Diogenes' idea of κρᾶσις, correct mixture. All sensation is caused by air, air from the outside meeting and mixing with, or simply agitating, air in the sense-organ itself or in the brain, whither it is led by blood-channels from the sense-organ. Clarity of perception depends on the fineness of the air in the body and the fineness and directness of the blood-channel by which the air is conveyed. Apparently the air is mixed with blood on its journeys through the head; when air naturally permeates the blood throughout the whole body, pleasure is produced. Thinking (φρονεῖν) depends on pure, dry air; it is not clear from **615** exactly where or how this functions,[1] but Simplicius tells us in **619** that air mixed with blood and pervading the body through the blood-channels produces thought (being distinguished from pleasure, presumably, by its purity, dryness and warmth). One may compare Anaxagoras' Mind, which was 'purest and finest of all substances' (**503**), and Heraclitus' soul-fire; in Diogenes, as in Heraclitus, moisture (ἰκμάς again) quenches or inhibits intelligence. Differences of intelligence and of animation are explained partly by differences of surrounding air (that near the ground is moist and heavy, therefore plants have a very low degree of life),[2] partly by differences of bodily structure (birds cannot properly assimilate their pure surrounding air).

[1] However, a theory is advanced, in one of the earlier Hippocratic treatises, which seems probably to be derived from Diogenes: **616** [Hippocrates] *de morbo sacro* 16 (DK64C3*a*) κατὰ ταῦτα νομίζω τὸν ἐγκέφαλον δύναμιν ἔχειν πλείστην ἐν τῷ ἀνθρώπῳ. οὗτος γὰρ ἡμῖν ἐστι τῶν ἀπὸ τοῦ ἠέρος γινομένων ἑρμηνεὺς ἢν ὑγιαίνων τυγχάνῃ· τὴν δὲ φρόνησιν ὁ ἀὴρ παρέχεται. οἱ δ' ὀφθαλμοὶ καὶ τὰ ὦτα καὶ ἡ γλῶσσα καὶ αἱ χεῖρες καὶ οἱ πόδες, οἷα ἂν ὁ ἐγκέφαλος γινώσκῃ, τοιαῦτα πρήσσουσι· γίνεται γὰρ ἐν ἅπαντι τῷ σώματι τῆς φρονήσιός τι, ὡς ἂν μετέχῃ τοῦ ἠέρος, ἐς δὲ τὴν ξύνεσιν ὁ ἐγκέφαλός ἐστιν ὁ διαγγέλλων. ὅταν γὰρ σπάσῃ τὸ πνεῦμα ὥνθρωπος ἐς ἑωυτόν, ἐς τὸν ἐγκέφαλον πρῶτον ἀφικνεῖται καὶ οὕτως ἐς τὸ λοιπὸν σῶμα σκίδναται ὁ ἀὴρ καταλελοιπὼς ἐν τῷ ἐγκεφάλῳ ἑωυτοῦ τὴν ἀκμὴν καὶ ὅ τι ἂν ᾖ φρόνιμόν τε καὶ γνώμην ἔχον. This writer attaches particular importance to the brain.

---

616 *Accordingly I consider that the brain has the most power in man. For, if it is in sound condition, it is our interpreter of the things that come into being through air; and air provides intelligence. The eyes and ears and tongue and hands and feet do whatsoever the brain determines; for there is an element of intelligence in the whole body, according as each part partakes of air, but it is the brain that is the messenger to the understanding. For whenever man draws breath into himself it arrives first at the brain, and thus the air spreads into the rest of the body after leaving behind its choicest part in the brain, and whatever of it is intelligent and possesses judgement.*

[2] Diogenes is undoubtedly the source of Socrates' remarks in the *Clouds*:

617 Aristophanes *Clouds* 227

οὐ γὰρ ἄν ποτε
ἐξηῦρον ὀρθῶς τὰ μετέωρα πράγματα,
εἰ μὴ κρεμάσας τὸ νόημα καὶ τὴν φροντίδα
λεπτὴν καταμείξας ἐς τὸν ὅμοιον ἀέρα·
εἰ δ' ὢν χαμαὶ τἄνω κάτωθεν ἐσκόπουν,
οὐκ ἄν ποθ' ηὗρον· οὐ γὰρ ἀλλ' ἡ γῆ βίᾳ
ἕλκει πρὸς αὑτὴν τὴν ἰκμάδα τῆς φροντίδος.

—Aristotle (*de respir.* 2, 471a2, DK64A31) criticized Diogenes for his theory that fish breathed a small amount of air in water, but that fresh air was too much for them.

(*b*) *Anatomy and reproduction*

618 Fr. 6, Aristotle *Hist. animalium* Γ2, 511b31 (DK64B6) αἱ δὲ φλέβες ἐν τῷ ἀνθρώπῳ ὧδ' ἔχουσιν· εἰσὶ δύο μέγισται· αὗται τείνουσι διὰ τῆς κοιλίας παρὰ τὴν νωτιαίαν ἄκανθαν, ἡ μὲν ἐπὶ δεξιά, ἡ δ' ἐπ' ἀριστερά, εἰς τὰ σκέλη ἑκατέρα τὰ παρ' ἑαυτῇ καὶ ἄνω εἰς τὴν κεφαλὴν παρὰ τὰς κλεῖδας διὰ τῶν σφαγῶν. ἀπὸ δὲ τούτων καθ' ἅπαν τὸ σῶμα φλέβες διατείνουσιν, ἀπὸ μὲν τῆς δεξιᾶς εἰς τὰ δεξιά, ἀπὸ δὲ τῆς ἀριστερᾶς εἰς τὰ ἀριστερά, μέγισται μὲν δύο εἰς τὴν καρδίαν περὶ αὐτὴν τὴν νωτιαίαν ἄκανθαν, ἕτεραι δ' ὀλίγον ἀνωτέρω διὰ τῶν στηθῶν ὑπὸ τὴν μασχάλην εἰς ἑκατέραν τὴν χεῖρα τὴν παρ' ἑαυτῇ· καὶ καλεῖται ἡ μὲν σπληνῖτις, ἡ δὲ ἡπατῖτις.... (512b1) ἕτεραι δ' εἰσὶν αἱ ἀπὸ ἑκατέρας τείνουσαι διὰ τοῦ νωτιαίου μυελοῦ εἰς τοὺς ὄρχεις λεπταί· ἕτεραι δ' ὑπὸ τὸ δέρμα καὶ διὰ τῆς σαρκὸς τείνουσιν εἰς τοὺς νεφροὺς καὶ τελευτῶσιν εἰς τοὺς ὄρχεις τοῖς ἀνδράσι, ταῖς δὲ γυναιξὶν εἰς τὰς ὑστέρας. (αἱ δὲ φλέβες αἱ μὲν

---

617 *For never would I have correctly discovered the affairs on high, except by hanging up my thought and mingling my rarefied intelligence with air of like kind. If I had stayed on the ground and considered from beneath the things above, never would I have discovered them; for the truth is that the earth draws to itself by force the emanation of intelligence.*

618 *The veins in man are as follows. There are two veins pre-eminent in magnitude. These extend through the belly along the backbone, one to right, one to left; either one to the leg on its own side, and upwards to the head, past the collar-bones, through the throat. From these, veins extend all over the body, from that on the right hand to the right side and from that on the left hand to the left side; the most important ones, two in number, to the heart in the region of the backbone; other two a little higher up through the chest in underneath the armpit, each to the hand on its own side: of these two, one being termed the spleen-vein, and the other the liver-vein.... There is also another pair, running from each of these through the spinal marrow to the testicles, thin and delicate. There is, further, a pair running a little underneath the cuticle through the flesh to the kidneys, and these with men terminate at the testicle, and with women at the womb. (The veins that*

πρῶται ἐκ τῆς κοιλίας εὐρύτεραί εἰσιν, ἔπειτα λεπτότεραι γίγνονται, ἕως ἂν μεταβάλωσιν ἐκ τῶν δεξιῶν εἰς τὰ ἀριστερὰ καὶ ἐκ τούτων εἰς τὰ δεξιά.) αὗται δὲ σπερματίτιδες καλοῦνται. τὸ δ' αἷμα τὸ μὲν παχύτατον ὑπὸ τῶν σαρκωδῶν ἐκπίνεται· ὑπερβάλλον δὲ εἰς τοὺς τόπους τούτους λεπτὸν καὶ θερμὸν καὶ ἀφρῶδες γίνεται.

619 Simplicius *Phys.* 153, 13 καὶ ἐφεξῆς (after **606**) δείκνυσιν ὅτι καὶ τὸ σπέρμα τῶν ȝῴων πνευματῶδές ἐστι, καὶ νοήσεις γίνονται τοῦ ἀέρος σὺν τῷ αἵματι τὸ ὅλον σῶμα καταλαμβάνοντος διὰ τῶν φλεβῶν, ἐν οἷς καὶ ἀνατομὴν ἀκριβῆ τῶν φλεβῶν παραδίδωσιν. ἐν δὴ τούτοις σαφῶς φαίνεται λέγων ὅτι ὃν ἄνθρωποι λέγουσιν ἀέρα, τοῦτό ἐστιν ἡ ἀρχή.

619 seems to show that the long fragment on the blood-channels, **618**, actually came in the book called by Simplicius *On nature*. That the semen is aerated is stated in both **618** and **619**; this is important, since semen produces new life, and its aerated nature (conceivably noted by Pherecydes, though see p. 57) is an important indication that air is the vital substance. Semen, for Diogenes and for other early theorists on the anatomy of the body, was a product of the blood, which was also, of course, aerated (though not so conspicuously), and thus conveyed sensation and thought. The great detail of the account of the blood-channels (the central part of which is omitted here) shows that Diogenes' physiological interests,[1] which connected with and perhaps partly motivated the general theory, were of no merely incidental importance to him; in this we may compare Empedocles (also a doctor of some kind, cf. p. 321) and Anaxagoras (p. 393). There is no doubt that from Alcmaeon and Empedocles onwards the more easily determinable structure of the human body was used as a clue to that of the whole world. The assumption of a parallelism between the two seems to have been held in some form by Anaximenes, probably as a

---

leave the stomach are comparatively broad just as they leave; but they become gradually thinner, until they change over from right to left and from left to right.) These veins are termed the spermatic veins. The blood is thickest when it is imbibed by the fleshy parts; when it is transmitted to these regions it becomes thin, warm, and frothy. (After D'Arcy Thompson)

619 *And in the continuation he shows that also the sperm of living creatures is aerated, and acts of intelligence take place when the air, with the blood, gains possession of the whole body through the veins; in the course of which he gives an accurate anatomy of the veins. Now in this he clearly says that what men call air is the material principle.*

development of the entirely unscientific tendency to treat the outside world as a person, to animate it and regard it as a living organism. This assumption was grounded in reason as a result of integrations like that of Heraclitus, who had emphasized very strongly that the Logos or arrangement of *all* things, of men and of the world as a whole, was essentially the same.

[1] Diogenes, like Empedocles and Anaxagoras, also paid attention to embryology (cf. DK 64 A 25–8); treating, for example, the old problem of whether the embryo is produced from the male contribution only, or from both male and female (cf. p. 340).

CONCLUSION

With Diogenes and Democritus, who were little if at all older than Socrates, the Presocratic period is legitimately held to end. During the second half of the fifth century B.C., particularly during the Peloponnesian War and under the influence of the mature Socrates and the Sophists, the old cosmological approach—by which the primary aim was to explain the outside world as a whole, man being considered only incidentally—was gradually replaced by a humanistic approach to philosophy, by which the study of man became no longer subsidiary but the starting-point of all enquiry. This re-orientation was a natural development: in part it was determined by social factors, but in part, as will have become apparent, it was the product of tendencies in the Presocratic movement itself.

SELECTIVE BIBLIOGRAPHY

For full bibliography of recent work on the Presocratics see D. Tarrant, *The Year's Work in Classical Studies* 1939–45 and 1945–7; D. J. Allan, *Philosophical Quarterly* 1 (1950–1) 61 ff.; E. L. Minar Jr., *Classical Weeekly* 47 (1954) 161 ff. and 177 ff.

BURNET, J., *Early Greek Philosophy*, 4th ed. (London, 1930).
CHERNISS, H., *Aristotle's Criticism of Presocratic Philosophy* (Baltimore, 1935).
—— 'The characteristics and effects of Presocratic philosophy', *Journal of the History of Ideas* 12 (1951), 319–45.
CORNFORD, F. M., 'Mystery religions and Pre-Socratic philosophy', *Cambridge Ancient History*, IV (Cambridge, 1939), ch. 15.
—— *Principium Sapientiae* (Cambridge, 1952).
FRÄNKEL, H., *Dichtung und Philosophie des frühen Griechentums* (New York, 1951) (American Philological Assoc. Philological Monographs 13).
GUTHRIE, W. K. C., *A History of Greek Philosophy*, I (Cambridge, 1962).
JAEGER, W., *The Theology of the Early Greek Philosophers* (Oxford, 1947).
ROBIN, L., *Greek Thought*, English trans. (London, 1928) 1–147.
TANNERY, P., *Pour l'Histoire de la Science Hellène*, 2nd ed. (Paris, 1930).
ZELLER, E., *Die Philosophie der Griechen*, I, i and I, ii, respectively 7th and 6th eds. (Leipzig, 1923 and 1920), edited and enlarged by W. Nestle.
—— *La Filosofia dei Greci*, I, i and I, ii, edited and enlarged by R. Mondolfo (Florence, 1932 and 1938).

Text

DIELS, H., *Die Fragmente der Vorsokratiker*, 5th, 6th and 7th eds., edited with additions by W. Kranz (Berlin, 1934–54).

Assessment of Sources

CHERNISS, H., *Aristotle's Criticism of Presocratic Philosophy* (Baltimore, 1935).
DIELS, H., *Doxographi Graeci* (Berlin, 1879).
JACOBY, F., *Apollodors Chronik* (Berlin, 1903).
MCDIARMID, J., 'Theophrastus on the Presocratic causes', *Harvard Studies in Classical Philology* 61 (1953), 85–156.
SNELL, B., 'Die Nachrichten über die Lehren des Thales', *Philologus* 96 (1944) 170–82.
(See also the works listed under Burnet, Robin, Kahn, Kerschensteiner.)

Mythical cosmogony and cosmology

DODDS, E. R., *The Greeks and the Irrational* (Berkeley, 1951) 147–9 with notes (On Orphism.)

GUTHRIE, W. K. C., *The Greeks and their Gods* (London, 1950).
HÖLSCHER, U., 'Anaximander und die Anfänge der Philosophie', *Hermes* 81 (1953) 257 ff. and 385 ff.
LINFORTH, I. M., *The Arts of Orpheus* (Berkeley, 1941).
NILSSON, M. P., *Geschichte der griechischen Religion*, I, 2nd ed. (Munich, 1955). (See Index II, s.v. 'Kosmogonie', 'Kosmogonische Mythen'.)
SCHWABL, H., s.v. 'Weltschöpfung' in Pauly–Wissowa, *Realencyclopädie*.

Thales
HÖLSCHER, U., *op. cit.* 385 ff.
SNELL, B., *op. cit.*

Anaximander
HÖLSCHER, U., *op. cit.* esp. 257–77, 415–18.
KAHN, C. H., *Anaximander and the Origins of Greek Cosmology* (New York, 1960).
KIRK, G. S., 'Some problems in Anaximander', *Classical Quarterly* N.S. 5 (1955) 21–38.
KRAUS, W., 'Das Wesen des Unendlichen bei Anaximander', *Rheinisches Museum* 93 (1949–50) 364–79.
MATSON, W. I., 'The naturalism of Anaximander', *Review of Metaphysics* 6 (1952–3) 387–95.
VLASTOS, G., 'Equality and justice in early Greek cosmologies', *Classical Philology* 42 (1957) 156–78.

Xenophanes
DEICHGRÄBER, K., 'Xenophanes περὶ φύσεως', *Rheinisches Museum* 87 (1938) 1–31.
KERFERD, G. B., *Gnomon* 29 (1957), 127–31.

Heraclitus
GIGON, O., *Untersuchungen zu Heraklit* (Leipzig, 1935).
KERSCHENSTEINER, JULA, 'Der Bericht des Theophrast über Heraklit', *Hermes* 83 (1955) 385–411.
KIRK, G. S., 'Heraclitus and death in battle (fr. 24 D)', *American Journal of Philology* 70 (1949) 384–93.
—— *Heraclitus, the Cosmic Fragments* (Cambridge, 1954).
—— 'Men and opposites in Heraclitus', *Museum Helveticum* 14 (1957) 155–63.
MONDOLFO, R., in Mondolfo–Zeller, *La Filosofia dei Greci*, I, iv (Florence, 1961) *passim*.
REINHARDT, K., 'Heraklits Lehre vom Feuer', *Hermes* 77 (1942) 1–27.
VLASTOS, G., 'On Heraclitus', *American Journal of Philology* 76 (1955) 337–68.

Pythagoras and the early Pythagoreans
CORNFORD, F. M., *Plato and Parmenides* (London, 1939), ch. I.

FESTUGIÈRE, A. J., 'Les "Mémoires Pythagoriques" cités par Alexandre Polyhistor', *Revue des Études Grecques* 58 (1945) 1–65.

HEIDEL, W. A., 'The Pythagoreans and Greek Mathematics', *American Journal of Philology* 51 (1940) 1–33.

RAVEN, J. E., *Pythagoreans and Eleatics* (Cambridge, 1948), chs. 1 and 4.

Alcmaeon

VLASTOS, G., 'Isonomia', *American Journal of Philology* 74 (1953) 337–66.

Parmenides

CALOGERO, G., *Studi sull'Eleatismo* (Rome, 1932).

CORNFORD, F. M., *Plato and Parmenides* (London, 1939), ch. 2.

COXON, A. H., 'The Philosophy of Parmenides', *Classical Quarterly* 28 (1934) 134–44.

MORRISON, J. S., 'Parmenides and Er', *Journal of Hellenic Studies* 75 (1955) 59–68.

REINHARDT, K., *Parmenides und die Geschichte der griechischen Philosophie* (Bonn, 1916).

Zeno

FRÄNKEL, H., 'Zeno of Elea's Attacks on Plurality', *American Journal of Philology* 63 (1942) 1–25 and 193–206.

LEE, H. D. P., *Zeno of Elea* (Cambridge, 1936).

OWEN, G. E. L., 'Zeno and the Mathematicians', *Proceedings of the Aristotelian Society* (1958) 199–222.

ROSS, W. D., *Aristotle's Physics* (Oxford, 1936) 71–85.

THOMSON, J. F., 'Tasks and Super-Tasks', *Analysis* 15 (1954) 1–13.

Philolaus and Eurytus

BYWATER, I., 'On the fragments attributed to Philolaus the Pythagorean', *Journal of Philology* 1 (1868) 21–53.

FRANK, E., *Plato und die sogenannten Pythagoreer* (Halle, 1923) 263–335.

MONDOLFO, R., 'Sui frammenti di Filolao', *Rivista di Filologia* N.S. (1937) 225–45.

RAVEN, J. E., *op. cit.* chs. 7–11.

—— 'Polyclitus and Pythagoreanism', *Classical Quarterly* N.S. 1 (1951) 147–52.

Empedocles

BIGNONE, E., *Empedocle, Studio critico* (Turin, 1916).

CALOGERO, G., 'L'Eleatismo di Empedocle', *Studi in Onore di L. Castiglioni*, 1 (Florence, 1960) 129–67.

FURLEY, D. J., 'Empedocles and the Clepsydra', *Journal of Hellenic Studies* 77 (1957) 31–4.

Anaxagoras

CORNFORD, F. M., 'Anaxagoras' theory of matter', *Classical Quarterly* 24 (1930) 14–30 and 83–95.

Peck, A. L., 'Anaxagoras: predication as a problem in physics', *Classical Quarterly* 25 (1931) 27–37 and 112–20.

Vlastos, G., 'The physical theory of Anaxagoras', *Philosophical Review* 59 (1950) 31–57.

Leucippus and Democritus

Bailey, C., *The Greek Atomists and Epicurus* (Oxford, 1928).

Schmid, W., 'Der Ausgang der altionischen Naturphilosophie: die Atomistik', Schmid–Stählin, *Geschichte der griechischen Literatur*, 1. 5 (Munich, 1948) 224–349.

Vlastos, G., 'Ethics and physics in Democritus', *Philosophical Review* 54 (1945) 578 ff. and 55 (1946) 53 ff.

Diogenes of Apollonia

Diller, H., 'Die philosophiegeschichtliche Stellung des Diogenes von Apollonia', *Hermes* 76 (1941) 359 ff.

Studies of special subjects or concepts

Beare, W., *Greek Theories of Elementary Cognition* (Oxford, 1906).

Fritz, K. von, 'Νοῦς, νοεῖν and their derivatives in Presocratic philosophy', *Classical Philology* 40 (1945) 223–42 and 41 (1946) 12–34.

Heath, T. L., *A History of Greek Mathematics*, 1 (Oxford, 1921).

—— *Aristarchus of Samos* (Oxford, 1933) (pp. 1–133 on pre-Platonic astronomy).

Neugebauer, O., *The Exact Sciences in Antiquity* (2nd ed., Providence, R.I., 1957).

Rohde, E., *Psyche*, English trans. (London, 1925).

Sambursky, S., *The Physical World of the Greeks*, English trans. (London, 1956).

Snell, B., *The Discovery of the Mind*, English trans. (Oxford (Blackwell), 1953), chs. 7, 9, 10.

INDEX OF PASSAGES

A page-number in bold type indicates that the passage in question is quoted in full, with translation, on that page. Other, ordinary-type, page-references to such a passage will normally be to citations of the *passage*-number, which should be found by turning to the bold-type page-reference first.

E.g. Aetius I, 3, I is quoted on p. **76**, where its passage-number is seen to be **68**; and the reference on p. 77 is simply to this passage-number, **68**.

Usually, only the first line is specified in the references to passages quoted.

GENERAL INDEX

For ancient authors see also the Index of Passages (pp. 451 ff.). Reference is not normally made in this General Index to the content of passages quoted or cited, unless this is the subject of further comment.